TREASURES OF THE MEDICI

TREASURES OF THE MEDICI

ANNA MARIA MASSINELLI · FILIPPO TUENA

Photographs by
ALFREDO DAGLI ORTI

With 215 illustrations in color

THE VENDOME PRESS

Opposite frontispiece: Detail of the cover of a rock-crystal and enameled gold cup made by Gasparo Miseroni, a Milanese who set up a workshop in Florence and dealt with Cosimo I's court. The cover in gold openwork was made in France and dates to the time when the vase belonged to Catherine de Médicis. The piece also is traditionally associated with Diane de Poitiers due to controversy surrounding the interpretation of the engraved monogram. It is illustrated in its entirety on page 108.

The authors wish to thank the directors and staff of the Museo degli Argenti and the Museo del Bargello for their constant assistance. Special thanks also go to Kirsten Aschengreen Piacenti for her contributions and to Elisabetta Nardinocchi Paolini, Michael Bohr, and Rodolfo Bargelli for their suggestions.

The captions for chapters 1 and 4 are by Filippo Tuena, those for chapters 2 and 3 are by Anna Maria Massinelli, who also prepared the collection of documents (pages 230–33) and the bibliography.

Photographs by Alfredo Dagli Orti. The portraits of the Medici on pages 12–15, 150, and 182 and the photographs on pages 189, 208, and 209 are from the Archivio De Agostini.

Created by Fenice 2000

Published in the USA in 1992
by The Vendome Press
515 Madison Avenue
New York, NY 10022

Distributed in the USA and Canada by
Rizzoli International Publications
300 Park Avenue South, New York, NY 10010

First published in 1992 by Istituto Geografico De Agostini, Novara

Library of Congress Cataloging-in-Publication Data

Massinelli, Anna Maria.
Treasures of the Medici/by Anna Maria Massinelli and Filippo Tuena; photographs by Alfredo Dagli Orti
p. cm.
Includes bibliographical references and index.
ISBN 0-86565-135-3 : $45.00
1. Art objects—Catalogs. 2. Medici, House of—Art collections—Catalogs. 3. Art objects—Private collections—Italy—Florence—Catalogs. 4. Art objects—Private collections—Italy—Naples—Catalogs. I. Tuena, Filippo M. II. Title.
NK550.I82M426 1992 92-12965
730 ' .074'4551—dc20 CIP

Typesetting by Christopher Hyams Hart
Printed in Italy by Rotolito Lombarda s.p.a., Pioltello (Milan)

Contents

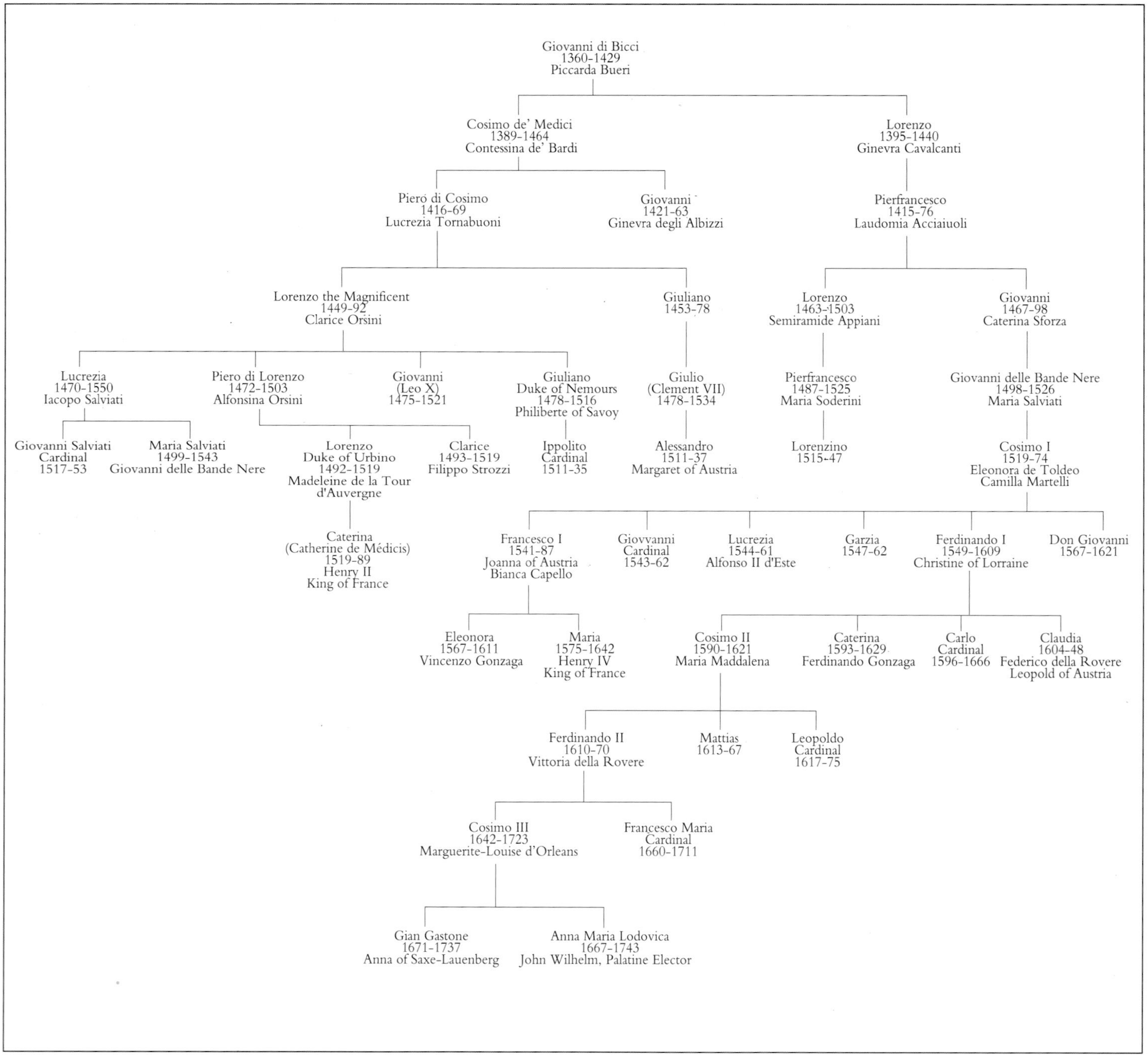
Giovanni di Bicci 1360-1429 Piccarda Bueri
Cosimo de' Medici 1389-1464 Contessina de' Bardi
Lorenzo 1395-1440 Ginevra Cavalcanti
Piero di Cosimo 1416-69 Lucrezia Tornabuoni
Giovanni 1421-63 Ginevra degli Albizzi
Pierfrancesco 1415-76 Laudomia Acciaiuoli
Lorenzo the Magnificent 1449-92 Clarice Orsini
Giuliano 1453-78
Lorenzo 1463-1503 Semiramide Appiani
Giovanni 1467-98 Caterina Sforza
Lucrezia 1470-1550 Iacopo Salviati
Piero di Lorenzo 1472-1503 Alfonsina Orsini
Giovanni (Leo X) 1475-1521
Giuliano Duke of Nemours 1478-1516 Philiberte of Savoy
Giulio (Clement VII) 1478-1534
Pierfrancesco 1487-1525 Maria Soderini
Giovanni delle Bande Nere 1498-1526 Maria Salviati
Giovanni Salviati Cardinal 1517-53
Maria Salviati 1499-1543 Giovanni delle Bande Nere
Lorenzo Duke of Urbino 1492-1519 Madeleine de la Tour d'Auvergne
Clarice 1493-1519 Filippo Strozzi
Ippolito Cardinal 1511-35
Alessandro 1511-37 Margaret of Austria
Lorenzino 1515-47
Cosimo I 1519-74 Eleonora de Toldeo Camilla Martelli
Caterina (Catherine de Médicis) 1519-89 Henry II King of France
Francesco I 1541-87 Joanna of Austria Bianca Capello
Giovvanni Cardinal 1543-62
Lucrezia 1544-61 Alfonso II d'Este
Garzia 1547-62
Ferdinando I 1549-1609 Christine of Lorraine
Don Giovanni 1567-1621
Eleonora 1567-1611 Vincenzo Gonzaga
Maria 1575-1642 Henry IV King of France
Cosimo II 1590-1621 Maria Maddalena
Caterina 1593-1629 Ferdinando Gonzaga
Carlo Cardinal 1596-1666
Claudia 1604-48 Federico della Rovere Leopold of Austria
Ferdinando II 1610-70 Vittoria della Rovere
Mattias 1613-67
Leopoldo Cardinal 1617-75
Cosimo III 1642-1723 Marguerite-Louise d'Orleans
Francesco Maria Cardinal 1660-1711
Gian Gastone 1671-1737 Anna of Saxe-Lauenberg
Anna Maria Lodovica 1667-1743 John Wilhelm, Palatine Elector

Preface

The appearance of a new book on the Medici treasures, prepared by two specialists in the field, will be widely welcomed. The importance of the subject is tied to that of the Medici themselves, who were recognized as noble patrons of the arts as early as the 15th century, when the fame of individual members of the family was so great that it assured them a leading role in international politics. As grand dukes, they enjoyed diminished political importance, but were linked by marriage to Europe's most powerful families, and as patrons and collectors their star shone until the end.

The Medici boasted of their fame in the world of art, and every family member contributed in some way to increasing it. Cosimo Pater Patriae, his son Piero, and then his son Lorenzo the Magnificent are luminous names whose fame the cadet branch of the family sought to emulate. In 1635, for the celebration of the marriage of Ferdinando II to Vittoria della Rovere, the theme chosen for the wall decoration of the waiting room of the grand ducal apartment in the Pitti Palace was Lorenzo the Magnificent as protector of the arts and the Muses banished from Parnassus: the Medici grand dukes considered themselves direct successors to Lorenzo, whom they wanted remembered as a great patron.

When he came to power, Cosimo I sought to reacquire those parts of the collection that had been dispersed when the Medici were exiled from the city, and he personally undertook a program of artistic embellishment designed to increase the glory of his court. His eldest son, Francesco, began the workshops that Ferdinando I moved into the Uffizi while setting up, on the top floor, the Gallery with the splendid Tribuna at its center. The first inventory is dated 1589, and many of the precious objects listed then still exist.

The hall was filled with paintings, cabinets, sculpture, and marbles that embellished the walls; bronzes and busts stood on shelves and mantels, and vases of semiprecious stones with their splendid mounts were enclosed in cupboards that were opened only on special occasions. In the Sala di Madama was the collection of Catherine de Médicis—including vases in semiprecious stone from circa 1550—associated with her granddaughter Christine of Lorraine, who had brought them with her to Florence when she married Grand Duke Ferdinando in 1589. Other rooms, filled with weapons, scientific instruments, ivories, and amber pieces, were opened upon the request of privileged "tourists" of the period, who commented on them with wonder.

The Pitti Palace, aside from its valuable furnishings, housed the private collection of the grand duke until it was combined with that of the Uffizi in 1770. The Wardrobe stayed in the Palazzo Vecchio after the grand dukes moved their residence to the Pitti Palace.

In 1719 Anna Maria Lodovica, the last of the Medici, returned, a widow, to the Pitti. Her father died in 1728, her brother, Gian Gastone, in 1737. The dynasty was at an end. Gian Gastone was succeeded by Francis Stephen of Lorraine, husband of Maria Theresa and, as Francis I, Holy Roman emperor from 1745. Anna Maria sensed that the family's inheritance was threatened by the greed of its successors and tried to take measures to protect it. She instituted the "Crown Jewels" (1739), a collection of the oldest and most valuable of the Medici jewels, which were left in perpetuity to the grand dukes but tied to the land of Tuscany. She organized and modernized her own jewels, and in her will of 1741 left the entire artistic inheritance of her family to the city of Florence. She was farsighted, and on the basis of the will it was even possible to retrieve paintings stolen by the Nazis during World War II. But even she could not escape destiny: as soon as she died, Francis Stephen had everything sold—the Crown Jewels, the private jewel collection, the knickknacks and wonderful antique jeweled objects—except for the few pieces that are today the pride of the Museo degli Argenti. They were taken to Vienna and placed in the Hofburg until returned to Florence in 1923.

The part of the collection not specifically tied to Florence was immediately sold: the stupendous Wardrobe, the weapons, the collection of celadon and blue-and-white porcelain, mostly Chinese.

This book presents a detailed account of the collection. The choice of the objects illustrated reflects today's distribution of the treasure among Florentine museums, most of the pieces being in the Museo degli Argenti. The many close-up views in the plates reveal the magical world of the jeweler's art at the Florentine court. This book recounts in an exemplary way the history of the treasures and, together with its rich illustrative documentation, fills a void that has been long lamented. On the one hand it renders due homage to illustrious collectors, and on the other it furnishes an implicit invitation to visit the Museo degli Argenti, a princely treasure-house unique in Italy and among the greatest in all of Europe.

Kirsten Aschengreen Piacenti
Director, Museo degli Argenti, Florence

A collection and its history

The 15th-century collections of the Medici family were based on ancient Imperial models and on those followed by other reigning families in Europe. Cosimo de' Medici does not seem to have sought personal aggrandizement, but in his heart he certainly longed to see his descendants enjoy the highest princely honors. He understood that there were certain advantages, some of them political, in being seen as a patron of the arts and a collector, for doing so led to comparison with the powerful of all ages and brought general admiration.

An exceptional quantity of masterpieces in carved stone, many of them antique—gems, cameos, vases in *pietre dure* (semiprecious stone), as well as vases in gold and silver embellished with jewels—made up the 15th-century nucleus of the Medici treasure, begun by Giovanni di Bicci and Cosimo and followed by Cosimo's sons Giovanni and Piero and then expanded most of all by Lorenzo the Magnificent, who in many cases had his pieces engraved with the monogram LAV.R.MED.

Tables set with gold and silverware were one of the most obvious signs of a family's wealth, and vases carved in semiprecious stones aroused an intellectual fascination with antiquity and the Orient, as well as the memory of the Roman Empire, which had known great collections of carved stone. Indeed, the Roman passion for such stones reached morbid extremes in the case of Nero, who is said to have smashed his splendid rock-crystal Homeric cups, bearing scenes from Homer's poems, to make sure that no one after him might enjoy them.

The treasures of the early Medici, without doubt among the richest and choicest of the time, did not escape the effects of the eclecticism of Renaissance collecting, following the fashion which can be traced back to Jean, duc de Berry. During the second half of the 14th century, in his castle at Mehun-sur-Yèvre, the duke accumulated an astonishing quantity of cameos, vases, gold and silver medals, illuminated manuscripts, and curios both mechanical and natural. The splendors of his collections were still well known in Florence in the middle of the 15th century, when Filarete remembered how the duke paid no attention to expense, and on hearing of an object that would fit his collection did all he could to obtain it. In the same way the interests of the Medici, with a strong predilection for the antique, were extremely varied, and when Charles VIII and his invading army arrived in 1494 and the Medici palace in the Via Larga was sacked, among the many precious objects carted off by the French were a large and complete unicorn horn and two fragments of another (actually narwhal tusks).

Medici power was reestablished in Florence under Cosimo I, and the reassembled Medici treasure was then placed in the Palazzo Vecchio, between the clerical offices and the Wardrobe and then in the Wardrobe of the Pitti Palace.

The Wardrobe served as a large depository in which were stored and classified all the objects used at court, from the most ordinary to the most precious, including wearing apparel, jewelry, and silverware. The Uffizi was used to store those pieces that, due to artistic or scientific interest, had value as museum exhibits or made up the inheritance of various family members. By the end of the 16th century the Uffizi's Gallery had become a sort of enormous *Wunderkammer* where, along with sculpture and paintings, the preferences of the Medici were reflected in precious materials, unusual objects, and those of a didactic character. Visitors, who could be taken from one end of the Gallery to the other in practical wooden wheelchairs, could inspect masterpieces carved in stone, small sculptures in bronze, marble, alabaster, and precious stones, silver and ivory, gems, cameos, gold medallions, antiquities of various sorts, as well as amber, exotic rarities, priceless weapons, natural curiosities of every kind, and mathematical instruments. All these objects reflected the taste of various family members and their collecting habits and had been added over time to the original treasure that had been preserved in the Tribuna and inventoried in detail in 1589. In the midst of the astonishing variety of objects that made up the treasury of the Tribuna of the Uffizi, works in precious and semiprecious stones stood out for their variety and value.

Precious stones occupy a special place in the history of the Medici treasures. Beginning in the reign of Cosimo I, who became duke in 1539, careful searches were made both to obtain rough stones from mines and works of ancient and modern manufacture. Emulating the Imperial Roman practice, the first grand duke of Florence opened marble quarries and metal mines in Tuscany. His sons Francesco and Ferdinando commissioned objects for the court and invited highly skilled Milanese stone engravers to Florence, who arrived along with goldsmiths and cabinetmakers from beyond the Alps.

Throughout the 17th century, in the Florentine court foreign artisans and artists could harness local skills to reach new heights in goldsmithing and cabinetwork. For as long as the duchy lasted, the creation of lapidary mosaics—drawing on Florentine skills and the inheritance of ancient Rome—was the boast of the Medici court and a skill that the powerful rulers of Europe sought to emulate. In the course of the 17th century the production of carved vases declined, and lapidaries seem to have concentrated on perfecting mosaics. The nucleus of vases collected at the end of the preceding century, together with the specimens brought as dowry by Christine of Lorraine, remained among the most precious relics of the Medici treasure and were one of its principal attractions. Originally divided between the Tribuna and the Sala di Madama, these were brought together in the Sala delle Gemme—the gem room—at the end of the 18th century, along with the vases of Lorenzo the Magnificent and his gems and cameos.

The treasures of the Medici that can still be seen in Florentine museums and the Museo Nazionale in Naples are works of the greatest importance in the realm of the decorative arts. More than a little nostalgia, however, is aroused by the thought of how much more of the Medici treasure we might delight in had much of it not been carried off at various points in history, even though the last family member did all in her power to prevent the complete dispersal of her valuable inheritance.

In 1737, when Anna Maria Lodovica, the Electress Palatine, was forced to surrender to Francis Stephen, duke of Lorraine, the inheritance of the family that ended with her, she added with uncommon farsightedness the famous clause that nothing was to be "transported or taken out of the capital of the state of the grand duchy." She may have been led to this decision by a conviction that the great treasures of art accumulated over nearly two centuries by her predecessors was inseparable from their city and the sites they selected to house it. Or perhaps she was following a desire to keep alive the memory of the Medici princes by means of this collection of objects, which, more than any biographical or historic account, reflected the temperament, taste, and peculiarities of each of them. The Gallery, the homes in the city, and the villas as she left them formed a visual history of the family and constituted an intricate web of events, purchases, gifts, and heredity.

Had she ever been shown the Raphael-inspired tapestry in the Vatican of the sack of the Via Larga palace in 1494, in which Cardinal Giovanni, Giuliano, and Piero flee while looking back one last time at the sad image of Florence and the Marzocco as a French soldier drags away a cart full of antique sculpture and others carry off paintings, chests, and vases, the scene might have been a cruel premonition for her. As it happened, all the pieces not protected by the famous clause concerning "cabinets, furniture, silverware, and objects of personal use" ended up being sold within a few decades. Francis Stephen's son Leopold, grand duke of Tuscany from 1765 to 1790, set about reorganizing the Tuscan state. In his *Florentine History from the Earliest Authentic Records*, the English historian Henry Edward Napier records, "Not even the ancient Medici Wardrobe, which had long rested in splendid idleness, was saved the frugality of Leopold . . . almost all the Medici homes, in all of Tuscany, had their special Wardrobes, independent of the great warehouse of Medici splendor in Florence, and all of these were put on public sale. Velvets, damask, golden embroideries, chairs, frames and mirrors of weighty silver, golden bracelets, the finest laces, fringes and valuable silk materials, all were sold to the public or condemned to be burnt. Gian Gastone's bed, embroidered with a profusion of pearls and other gems, was taken apart, and many objects of exquisite workmanship of jewelry and precious metals, symbols of the good taste and magnificence of the Medici, were either broken up or sold to earn half a million crowns."

There were attempts at theft at the Gallery during the 17th century. The treatment that Cosimo III had meted out to the servants of the Marchese Giovan Lorenzo Malaspina, found guilty of having taken golden medals and precious stones from the cabinets of the Tribuna (although some were recovered), was used as an example: when they confessed, they were hanged. A century later, when the custodian Giuseppe Bianchi could not resist the temptation of appropriating some of the splendid 16th-century gold settings, semiprecious-stone vases, and other jewels, he was condemned to death. With characteristic generosity, Leopold commuted the sentence to life exile.

Of course, the new grand duke might have felt greater resentment had the goods belonged to him personally, and he could well appreciate Bianchi's greed. In 1743, the "State Jewels," those "precious little things" of the Medici family so dear to Anna Maria, were secretly sent off to Vienna and were only partly returned to Italy in 1923. The large so-called Florentine Diamond bought by Ferdinando I in Rome in 1601, which Cosimo II had cut and which mesmerized travelers visiting the Tribuna, adorned the crown of Francis as Holy Roman emperor at his coronation in Frankfurt in 1745.

Giuseppe Pelli Bencivenni, powerless and embittered witness to these events, noted in his diary on November 27, 1785: "H.R.H., stripping the Royal Wardrobe and distributing the best items as suits him, has taken apart many pieces, many decorations, many mountings for vases, even of the reliquaries of San Lorenzo, various coverings of codices, etc., and has melted down the metal, sending it to the mint. This does not mean he is avaricious. In all conscience I could neither believe nor assert that." In 1789, however, Leopold directed his attention to the very crown of the grand duchy, and Pelli then became freer with his opinions: "And thus it is that the treasure has been taken apart, consumed, dispersed, broken, destroyed. Of the riches of the Medici only the name will remain. The jewels are in Vienna with Francis I. Most of the antiquities have been melted down."

The precious metals ended in a melting pot, but the documented fate of other Medici relics was no less cruel. Between 1773 and 1780, the sumptuous Medici armory was dispersed. Even the cabinets designed for the Tribuna of the Uffizi by Bernardo Buontalenti at the end of the 16th century suffered a sad fate. The enormous piece of furniture built for Ferdinando I was relegated to the Royal Museum of Physics. By then, the symmetrical arrangement of semiprecious stones that decorated its ebony frame seemed more suitable to a museum of natural sciences: the cabinet was considered nothing more than a specimen case for stones. Special care was taken to remove a large pearl, the size of a head of garlic, mounted in a sort of vase of flowers, as well as other gems: sapphires, rubies, topazes, aquamarines, amethysts. The director of the new museum took the cabinet apart himself. Judging barbarous the precious work of antique stone inlay, he arranged the panels of semiprecious stones in "methodical" series in the Royal Museum of Physics. The gold lunettes with their jasper backgrounds, made after a model by Giambologna, were deemed unsuitable for the museum and sold. They passed through various hands until 1821, at which time the director of the Gallery bought them back from a certain Gaetano Tartini Salvatici, who offered them for sale at 600 scudi as the work of Benvenuto Cellini.

During the reign of Leopold, the Wardrobe provided a loophole in Anna Maria's will. After 1797 the Labors of Hercules, made in silver by Giambologna, were dispersed, thus becoming one of the most lamentable losses of 16th-century decorative sculpture. Somewhat suspicious is the annotation of the director of the Gallery, who consigned them to the Office of Revisions and Audits with "suitable orders," though we do not now know what those orders were.

Little was left for the melting pot of the French when they entered Florence in 1799. What precious objects still remained in the Gallery were hidden, but that inexhaustible source, the Wardrobe, still remained to provide material to be plundered. It was then that the large silver plates that Cosimo III received as gifts every year on St. John's day, according to the will of Cardinal Lazzaro Pallavicini, were lost. These exquisite masterpieces of baroque Roman silver can today be recognized in the Museo degli Argenti, without their metallic glow, in a series of fifty-eight drawings made in 1746 for the Doccia factory.

Thefts from the Medici treasure have continued until recently. In 1860, when the jewels of the Uffizi had been together in the Sala delle Gemme for nearly eighty years, nine vases in semiprecious stone and one in crystal were stolen but later recovered. Sixty-nine rings in gold and two hundred seventy-four carved stones were also taken but then only partly recovered, without their precious mounts.

Notwithstanding the series of thefts and depredations, of which we have noted only the most glaring examples, what remains of the Medici treasure is still remarkable, and the definition "treasure" could be expanded from the artifacts in precious materials to include palaces and historical documents. Such documents, in fact, are an invaluable heritage since they recount and describe the lost treasures, which, precisely because of the existence of these documents, are not completely lost. Everything was written down at court. The same attention was devoted to recording the coming and going of the simplest object of everyday use as to the rarest jewel. Thus the existence, in great part, of the palaces, the masterpieces of art they contained, and the files that connect the contents to their respective houses all permit a partial reweaving of the history of the Medici treasures based on fact rather than merely on memory.

Portraits of the Medici:

Rulers for three centuries

Below left: Portrait of Cosimo de' Medici (1389–1464), founder of Medici power in Florence, by Pontormo (1518); Uffizi, Florence. Having inherited the wealth, philanthropic habits, and popularity of the family from Giovanni di Bicci, Cosimo ruled Florence with a close circle of friends. Below right: One of the best known of the many portraits of Lorenzo the Magnificent (1449–92), today in the Museo degli Argenti, made in the 16th century by the Florentine Girolamo Macchietti.

Two portraits in the Uffizi by Agnolo di Cosimo, known as Il Bronzino, a student of Pontormo who was on close terms with the Medici court from 1539. Far left: Lorenzo de' Medici (1395–1440), brother of Cosimo. Left: Alessandro de' Medici (1511–37), duke of Florence. Lorenzo lived in the shadow of his more famous brother; Alessandro, natural son of Giulio de' Medici (Pope Clement VII), returned to Florence in 1530 with the army of Charles V and seven years later was murdered by Lorenzino, a cousin of the other branch of the family from Cafaggiolo.

Below left and right: Two contemporary portraits of Cosimo I (1519–74), the first family member to assume the grand ducal crown, in 1569. On the left is a marble bust by Baccio Bandinelli, the bronze bust on the right is a masterpiece by Benvenuto Cellini; both are in the Bargello, Florence. Cellini made several pieces in gold and intaglio for Eleonora de Toledo, Cosimo's refined consort. Below far right: Portrait by an anonymous 16th-century artist of Catherine de Médicis, queen of France (Uffizi, Florence). At 14 Catherine (1519–89) married the duke of Orléans, the future Henry II, and played a leading role in French history during the tormented years of the Wars of Religion. Bottom left: Eleonora de' Medici with her children, painted by Frans Pourbus the Younger (Palazzo Ducale, Mantua). Eleonora (1567–1611), eldest daughter of Francesco I and Joanna of Austria, married Vincenzo Gonzaga, duke of Mantua, in 1584; her entry into the city for the marriage took place in an atmosphere of princely pomp. Bottom right: Portrait by Bronzino of Francesco I de' Medici (1541–87), grand duke of Tuscany (Uffizi, Florence).

Below left: Oval relief portraits in porphyry and serpentine by Francesco Ferruccio Del Tadda (both in the Bargello, Florence) showing Christine of Lorraine (1565–1637) and her husband, Ferdinando de' Medici (1549–1609). At 15, Ferdinando assumed his red cardinal's hat and became the Medici ambassador to Rome in 1563. Grand duke from 1587, he changed his cardinal's robes for those of a papal delegate when he married Christine of Lorraine in 1589. He organized the grand ducal workshops in the Casino di San Marco in a systematic way and claimed, perhaps not without justification, to have invented inlay work. In addition to dynastic continuity, Christine of Lorraine brought to the grand duke a considerable dowry of objects in semiprecious stones, part of which she inherited from Catherine de Médicis, who died the year Christine married. Below right: Cosimo II de' Medici with his wife, Maria Maddalena of Austria, and his son Ferdinando in an anonymous 18th-century portrait (Uffizi, Corridoio Vasariano). Cosimo II, son and heir of Ferdinando I, was always in poor health and died in 1621 aged 31.

Below left: Portrait of Ferdinando II de' Medici. Below right: Portrait of Cosimo III de' Medici. Both are by the Flemish artist Justus Sustermans (1597–1681) and are in the Pitti Palace. Sustermans worked in a courtly and idealistic style and became an official painter of the Medici court in Florence, where he died. Ferdinando II (1610–70), grand duke of Tuscany from 1621, surrounded himself with priests and learned monks, was a friend of Galileo and Evangelista Torricelli, and founded the celebrated Accademia del Cimento, the first academy of natural sciences in Europe. Bottom left: Bust in semiprecious stone of Vittoria della Rovere, Ferdinando II's consort, by Giuseppe Antonio Torricelli, ca. 1697 (Florence, formerly in the Conservatorio La Quiete, now in the Museo degli Argenti). Cosimo III (1642–1723) became grand duke in 1670 and was the penultimate ruler of the dynasty: his son Gian Gastone died in 1737 without issue, and as stipulated in a treaty signed by the European powers in Vienna two years earlier, the succession passed to Francis Stephen, duke of Lorraine, husband of Maria Theresa, and Holy Roman emperor as Francis I.

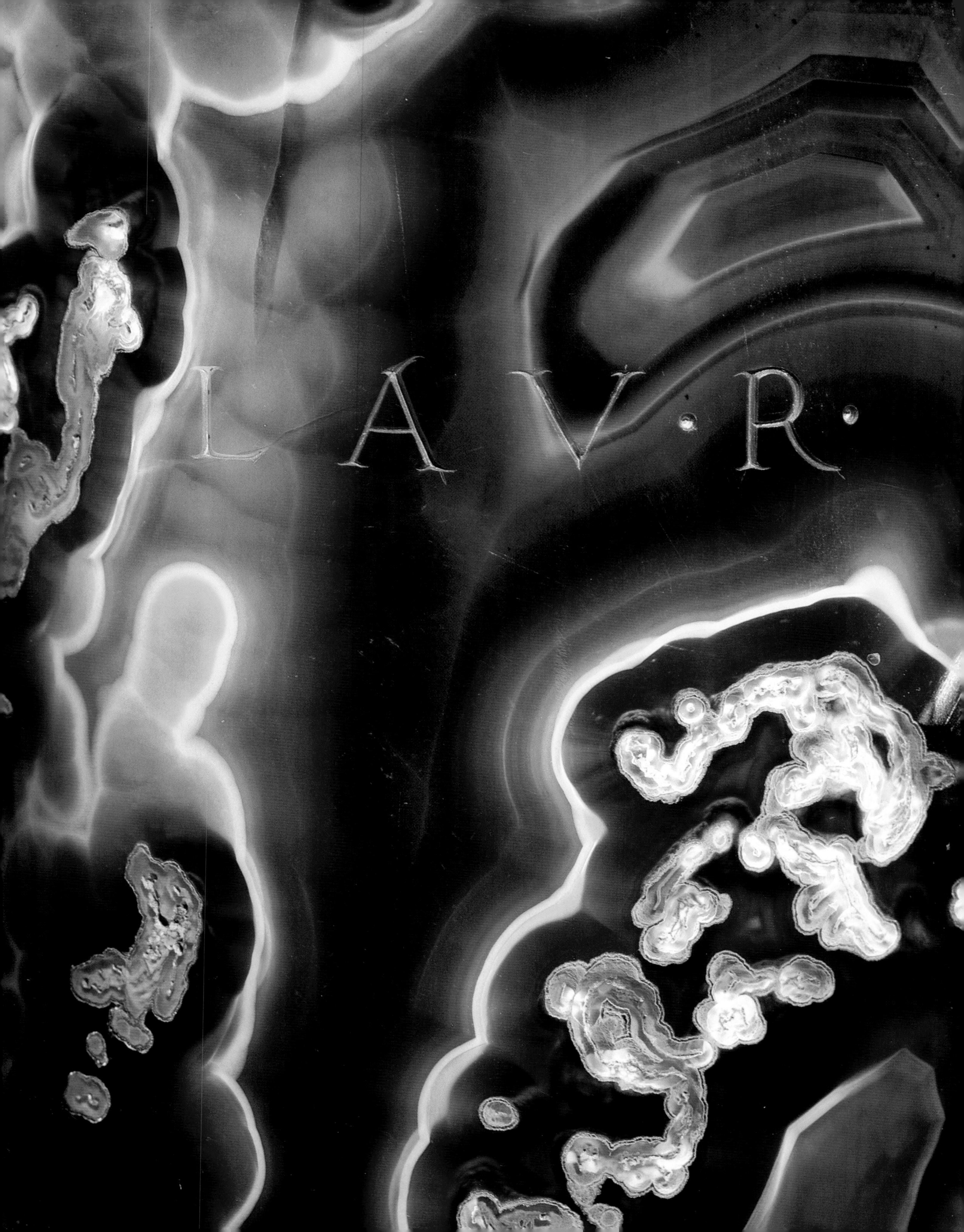
L A V·R·

The first Medici: humanist collecting

Detail of an antique sardonyx vase inscribed LAV.R.MED. The entire piece is illustrated on page 39.

From the earliest Medici collections—those dating back to before the reign of Cosimo—a moderate number of objects remain, above all in semiprecious stone. These are jewels, cameos, and vases—collected by Cosimo, Piero, known as Il Gottoso ("the Gouty"), and Lorenzo—which, after many adventures, have come down to us substantially intact. They bring with them the notion of a collection as a mirror of taste. Throughout the history of the early Medici passion for collecting we see the rise of this typically Renaissance concept: the patron, the collector, as "one who possesses." The collector shows his virtue through the objects he chooses to collect; these are not simply the tangible manifestation of his magnificence, but rather the ennoblement of riches and their moral justification.

The nucleus of the Medici collection is composed of works in *pietre dure* (semiprecious stones). Over the years, studies have shown that these belong both to antiquity and to their own times, were made both in the Far East and Europe, and have as a sole common denominator the material from which they are fashioned.

Collecting works in semiprecious stone is a tradition dating back to ancient Rome. During the Imperial age, such pieces were made for the extremely rich. Such sophisticated rulers as Hadrian and the Byzantine emperors collected vases and cameos in semiprecious stone, using them for both ceremonial purposes and private use. Originally a court art, glyptics—the carving of precious and semiprecious stones—reached Europe above all after the sack of Constantinople in 1204, when the Imperial collections were broken up to make their way into the treasuries of European cathedrals or courts. Such monarchs as Roger II and Frederick II collected them to carry on a classical tradition, whereas the great European cathedrals usually used them as reliquaries, inventing for some of the rarer pieces miraculous origins or qualities.

These collectors were well aware of the almost voluble essence of things made from semiprecious stone. The difficulties involved in working such materials, the quirks of nature that were enhanced and displayed in specific detail, all harked back to a classical tradition that is ever-present in Mediterranean culture. A large portion of Pliny's works is dedicated to explaining the mysteries of lithology, the study of the origins of stones, their magic, divinatory, and therapeutic powers, which should make evident that works in semiprecious stone purportedly hid mysterious virtues that could not help but fascinate the people of the late Middle Ages.

The precious mounts that embellished vases and cameos served the purpose of framing works of nature bent to the will of man, but it would be an error to pay undue attention to the skill of goldsmiths in making settings for carved stones. Even if such work was not always marginal, its function was primarily that of embellishing the stones.

The principal glyptic collections and the most important engravers' workshops flourished above all in Venice, Burgundy, and Sicily, which is to say in Europe's major commercial centers. Thus, when Florence became a major center of European commerce, it was natural for the Medici to begin collecting such works. They did so in emulation of their cultural models, the great bankers of the north and, above all, the emperors of ancient Rome. This sense of reviving a classical tradition—an important element in Renaissance humanism—must be kept clearly in mind when examining the history of collecting in Florence during the flowering of the Renaissance. It must not be underrated, and collecting must not be considered only from the viewpoint of the history of aesthetics or taste, since it was an attempt to recall the classical era and make comparisons with Roman and Greek traditions.

Nothing remains of the sacred and secular gold and silverware that the Medici possessed, for these were the first objects to attract the attention of thieves, since they were eminently portable and made of materials that could easily be disposed of for ready cash. The jewels and the vases of semiprecious stones might well have gone the same way had not fate decreed a different future for them. These objects were always treated with great care and attention, almost as an inalienable asset, and they were preserved with an effort that matched their value, as they held a particular place in the family's affections.

In 1502 Leonardo da Vinci examined some of the vases on behalf of Isabella d'Este, who had heard they might be for sale, and he spoke of them in most enthusiastic terms, admiring the quality of the stones as well as the integrity and originality of the pieces. "All this pleased Leonardo as being a new thing, and admirable in the diversity of the colors," duly reported Francesco Malatesta to Isabella d'Este.

The sophistication needed by collectors of such works was noted by Lorenzo Ghiberti, who suggested the most fitting method for viewing the subtleties and refinements of intaglio engraving: "The finely illustrated stones, being hollowed out, the strong light and the reflections therefrom do confound comprehension. This sculpture can be seen no better than by turning the hollowed part to a strong light, for then it can be seen perfectly. However, it should not be marveled at if that which is to be seen is very often hidden." Ending his description with a sibylline comment on the levity of works of art and on the difficulty with which they can be comprehended, the great Florentine artist seems almost to wish to pay homage to collectors of these works.

It is not known whether Averardo, considered the founder of the family, did any collecting, but a small amount of information exists concerning his son, Giovanni di Bicci (1360–1429). A man with a melancholy air but with a sagacious and pungent spirit and quick to jest, he is known to have had Dello paint "all the furnishings of one room." Since ostentatious painted furniture was a sign of wealth and distinction, and owning it or having it made required a special and extremely costly permit, we could speculate that Giovanni di Bicci enhanced this furniture with objects and paintings of equivalent value, or at least that he was not insensitive to luxury. Little more can be said of him as a collector, except that he was part of the group assembled to commission Florence's Baptistery doors. On that occasion he may have been called upon as a city notable, rather than as a critic or connoisseur. Then again, he was on good terms with Ghiberti, close to Filippo Brunelleschi, and made a large contribution toward the decoration of the Basilica of San Lorenzo, taking on himself most of the cost of the sacristy and apse.

As can be seen, Giovanni's interests, or what little we know of them, were more those of a sponsor than those of a collector. We know nothing of his collection of cabinet pieces, if it indeed existed.

The birth of a collection: Cosimo the Elder, Pater Patriae

Cosimo de' Medici (1389–1464), Giovanni's eldest son, sometimes known as Cosimo the Elder and, after his death, given the official title of "Pater Patriae" by the city of Florence, was the first of his family to collect precious objects systematically. Educated by such illustrious scholars as Nicolao di Pietro and Roberto de' Rossi, he began a dazzling political career that aroused such jealousy and rancor that he was forced to leave for Padua and Venice in 1433. He went accompanied by Michelozzo, who acted as a counselor in more than just artistic matters and later built the palace on the Via Larga. Exile did Cosimo little harm, and when he returned to Florence in 1434 he found his fame had grown and strengthened.

Cosimo numbered among his close friends such leading humanists as Niccolò Niccoli, Janos Argyropoulos, Cristoforo Landino, and Marsilio Ficino. Ficino considered Cosimo a second father, and Cosimo entrusted him with the translation of Plato's works. Cosimo also associated with first-rank artists, including Filippo Brunelleschi, who continued to work on the Basilica of San Lorenzo, Fra Filippo Lippi, Fra Angelico, and Donatello. Of these, Donatello was perhaps Cosimo's favorite. Vasari wrote that "Cosimo thought so highly of Donatello's talent that he kept him continually occupied; and in return Donatello loved Cosimo so well that he could understand all he wanted, from the slightest sign, and he never disappointed him." Among the most famous works Donatello made for Cosimo were a *David* and *Judith Slaying Holofernes*, which originally stood in the courtyard of the Medici palace on the Via Larga.

Cosimo was extremely intelligent and versatile. One of his contemporaries, the well-educated and reliable Florentine bookseller Vespasiano da Bisticci, recalled that "When giving audience to a scholar he discoursed concerning letters; in the company of theologians he showed his acquaintance with theology, a branch of learning always studied by him with delight. So also with regard to philosophy. Astrologers found him well versed in their science, for he had a certain faith in astrology and employed it to guide him on certain private occasions. Musicians in like manner perceived his mastery of music, wherein he took great pleasure. The same was true of sculpture and painting; both of these art forms he understood completely and showed much favor to all worthy craftsmen." Cosimo's greatest interest seems to have been architecture, and Vespasiano relates that "without his opinion and advice no public building of any importance was begun or carried to completion."

Except on rare occasions, this famous founder of the family fortune is not known to have collected jewelry or precious objects. On one occasion he was remembered to have taken interest in a jewel, but perhaps this was only to evaluate its value as security. Even so, it is well known that Cosimo possessed the horn of a unicorn—actually, the tusk of a narwhal—mounted in gold, and although this piece entered the collection as security for a loan, it indicates an interest in cabinets of curiosities that was by no means superficial.

Pinpointing exactly how and when the collection of gems, added to over the generations, originally began is extremely difficult, but further documentation indicates that Cosimo took an interest in such objects. In 1426 he made a journey to Rome, and on that occasion he would without doubt have been able to add to the collection. Ciriaco d'Ancona, himself a passionate collector of antiquities, mentioning this briefly, speaks of "*prectiosa multa suppellectilia*" among Cosimo's collections.

In any case, perhaps his son Giovanni, even though he could not have been more than eight years old at the time (1428), bought a masterpiece of ancient stone carving. Vasari tells us how "There fell into the hands of Giovanni de' Medici a large carnelian engraved in intaglio with a scene showing the flaying of Marsyas at Apollo's command. It was said that it had once served as the Emperor Nero's seal. Because of the stone's weight and size, and the marvelous engraving, it was a very rare object, and Giovanni gave it to Lorenzo [Ghiberti] with instructions to mount it in gold. After many months' work Lorenzo finally completed the setting, producing a work that was no less perfect than the beautiful intaglio of the stone itself."

We have, as a contemporary document regarding this episode, an extract from Ghiberti's *Commentario:* "In that time I did bind with gold a carnelian of the size of a nut, on the surface of which had been engraved three figures most exquisitely done by the hand of an excellent master of old. I made as a stem the figure of a dragon with wings slightly opened and head lowered, the neck rising in the middle, its wings held the seal; this dragon, or worm, as we call it, was among ivy leaves, which I cut by my own hand around those figures with ancient letters forming the name of Nero, all of which I made with great diligence. The following figures were in that carnelian: an old man sitting upon a rock with the skin of a lion and tied around a dead tree; at his feet kneels an infant who looks toward a youth holding in his right hand a sheet of paper and in his left a zither. It seemed that the infant asked the youth for instruction. These three figures were made to represent our ages. They were certainly from the hand of Pyrogotiles or Polycletus: they were as perfect as anything you might ever see engraved."

It must be said that Vasari was right and Ghiberti mistaken as to the identity of the figures engraved. They do not show the Three Ages of Man, but the prelude to the drama of Marsyas being flayed alive by Apollo as the consequence of a musical competition. The theme is extremely macabre, but its humanistic significance enjoyed a certain success during the Renaissance, perhaps also due to this carnelian, the iconographic fate of which is documented by a number of works of art that drew their inspiration from it.

Marsyas, the satyr son of Iagnides, was recognized as the inventor of the flute, even though an Attic version of the legend diminishes his importance and treats him merely as a cunning fellow, saying that he picked the flute up from the ground after Athena had invented it and then abandoned it when she realized that in order to play it she had to puff out her cheeks and thus distort her face. Marsyas, in any case, became so adept at playing the instrument that he challenged Apollo, inventor of the lyre, to a contest to determine the supremacy of their respective instruments. Apollo accepted the challenge on condition that the victor might do as he wished with the vanquished. The Muses acted as judges. The lyre won, and the indignant god had Marsyas undergo the horrible and excessive punishment of being flayed alive. He then nailed his skin to a tree.

The carnelian depicts the moment immediately following the competition. Marsyas is tied to the tree awaiting his fate, the flute lies on the ground, its empty case hanging from a branch of the tree. Olympus intercedes without success with Apollo, who deigns him no more than a glance.

Today, it is supposed that the carnelian was the work of Dioscorides, an engraver favored by Augustus, and that it was part of the emperor's collection. In any case its fame was such that it inspired artists such as Gerard David, Sandro Botticelli, and even Raphael, who used a variation on the theme for the decoration of the Vatican rooms.

Another cameo in the Medici collections is said to have once been part of Cosimo's private collections. This is a portrait of Nero as a poet laureate with a thin beard, facing right. Nothing more is stated in the documents about Cosimo's collections, although it is most likely that the majority of the works of art he owned ended up among the collections of his son Piero.

Piero the Gouty, collector prince

Cosimo's second son, Giovanni (1421–63), though a great pleasure-seeking epicure, lover of literature and music, and collector of musical instruments, does not seem to have disdained rare and precious objects and is known to have taken an interest in the acquisition of ancient sculpture.

We have much more information regarding the collections of Cosimo's eldest son, Piero (1416–69), a figure who has perhaps been disregarded and certainly underestimated, being dwarfed by the family's most illustrious and best-known members, his father and his son Lorenzo. Piero was educated by his father to love the fine arts, and in spite of poor health—or perhaps because of it—he applied himself seriously to enjoying them. Although Piero is remembered most of all because of his great collection of ancient books, his interests were not limited to that field. In fact, Piero was among the foremost Medici collectors, and thanks to the inventory of 1456—the oldest to have survived—we know precisely the make-up of his possessions.

The first page reads as follows: "IHC MCCCCLVI.

Hereinafter is written the inventory of all those things which are the property of myself, Piero, son of Cosimo de' Medici, which I do find on this fifteenth day of September in the year given above." Although some of this personal property may have been donated by Cosimo, who was a still alive at that date, Piero was referring to what was his as heir. It is extremely important to pay attention to this confirmation of the effective owner of the property because it is a clear indication of Piero's interest in the family collections.

Let us then briefly analyze this inventory, noting that it is divided into categories, which makes identification of the pieces easier but gives us no indication of their place in the house, a factor that is far from negligible.

On page four are listed "Jewels and Similar Objects." Among these are seven vases, twenty-one jewels and rings in semiprecious stone, a number of diamonds, sapphires, pearls, and precious stones, both mounted and unmounted, and all the assortment of curios appertaining to a Renaissance prince. We note the narwhal tusk that once belonged to his father, 300 silver medals, fifty-three gold ones, thirty-seven in brass, a "bridle bit with hawk's claws in gold," "the loose tongue of a serpent," "a small box in unicorn and ebony," and then objects for personal use, such as a number of belts woven in gold and silver, "equipment for training birds, embellished with silver," "barber's equipment embellished with silver," and "a purse worked in gold containing razor, comb, and scissors." There follows a number of Oriental works, called Damascus ware, and porcelain and antique glassware. Nor are omitted "five chiming clocks," "a box containing scales, beans, and weights," and "a chessboard in jasper with chessmen" for the amusement of his lordship.

Several years later, in 1465, Piero had another inventory drawn up, which is of great interest because the brief descriptions are accompanied by an estimated value in florins; this informs us not only of the additions to the collection but also of the value given to each piece. A florin, or ducat, was a gold coin weighing approximately 3.50 grams; at the time, a house in the city might cost about 1,000, and a few hundred constituted a good yearly income for most Florentines. Let us consider only those articles to which the greatest value is given.

Among the jewelry stands out "a necklace of gold made in enameled plaits wherein are 234 pearls, twenty-seven diamond points, and twenty-seven almond-shaped rubies, with an enameled pendant hanging from it with twelve pearls, three rubies, and one diamond," valued at as much as 1,000 florins; a "shoulder pin of a pound of gold with a large, flat balas ruby and three large pearls and a diamond with many facets," having the notable value of 5,000 florins; and two other, more simple pins totaling 2,500 florins. There then follow countless pearls and other precious stones variously mounted and worked.

Now let us turn to the gems. To begin with, we see that the number of cameos and engraved stones has reached thirty and that the vases now number fifteen. This is already a small collection that includes several masterpieces, such as a cameo in sardonyx of "Icarus and Daedalus, Pasiphae and Artemis" valued at the large sum of 100 florins. This work from Anatolia can be dated to the 1st century B.C. Then there is "Aphrodite on a Lion Led by Eros," a cameo in agate onyx, the work of Protarchos, valued at 60 florins. Another of Piero's masterpieces is the extremely large "Poseidon and Athena Competing for the Dominion of Attica," valued at 180 florins. Among the engravings, perhaps the gem of greatest overall value is the "Triton and Nereids," although among the most highly valued pieces is a cameo showing "The Entry into the Ark," now in the British Museum, valued at 300 florins. This is, in fact, a miniature masterpiece, due to the unusual subject and the number of tiny figures cleverly engraved in the stone.

Passing on to the vases, we find, along with an object as spurious as "a porcelain cup set in gold, with stamped foot and cover" valued at 200 florins, a fine series of vases in semiprecious stone. An estimated value of the grand sum of 300 florins is given to "a crystal cup set in silver gilt with enameled decoration, having a cover bearing the arms of the duke of Milan"; the same value is given to "an apothecary jar in jasper with silver-gilt and enameled handles and cover," which is most probably one of the mounted jasper vases attributed in the past to Giusto da Firenze. The value of 500 florins each is given to "a jasper wash basin" and "an apothecary jar with handle in chalcedony set in fine gold." The highest value of the collection, 700 florins, goes to "a crystal cup with cover mounted in gold, with enameled figures and pearls and balas rubies, and sapphires and rubies," which is the rock-crystal cup with Burgundian mounting now in the Treasury of San Lorenzo. This is the most preciously decorated of all the pieces in the collection and, given its Burgundian origin, was unique even in Renaissance Florence.

As can be seen, Piero's collections are of immense importance, and their value is particularly high when compared with the few dozen florins given for paintings by such well-known artists as Sandro Botticelli and Piero di Cosimo, who worked for the Medici, or for bronzes by Donatello, which were considered of equivalent value. Analysis of the works owned by Piero does not exhaust our interest in his collecting. It must be remembered that to the father of Lorenzo the Magnificent we owe the creation of a studiolo in the palace on the Via Larga that was not only one of the first of such small rooms built for study in Italy, but also served as a model for similar rooms built during the following century by his descendants Cosimo I and Francesco.

The construction of the studiolo was justified by his collection of precious objects as well as by his wish to be able to admire them in a place—separate from the rest of the palace—built for that very purpose, a room where their intrinsic qualities would best be set off. This collection, which along with architecture was Piero's passion, is remembered by Filarete, who writes that Piero had "the effigies and images of all the Emperors and Worthies of the past, some made of gold, some of silver, some of bronze, of precious stones or of marble and other materials which are wonderful to behold. At other times he will look at his jewels and precious stones, of which he has a marvelous quantity of great value, some engraved, others not. He takes great pleasure and delight in looking at these and in discussing their various excellencies. Another day he will inspect his vases of gold and silver and other precious materials and praise their noble worth and the skill of the masters who wrought them. Then at other times he will look at various other praiseworthy objects from all parts of the world, and at various strange suits of armor . . . he has so many of these things that, giving one day to each one of them, article by article, there are so many as would take him a month before he again looked at the first one, which would give him renewed pleasure, considering that a month would have passed since last he saw it."

Should Piero's collection be looked at one piece at a time, a month would not suffice. What is more, the studiolo also housed Piero's library. Filarete remarked that with their precious bindings, these books looked like "a pile of gold."

Let us now attempt to reconstruct, from a closer point of view, this delightful place, which although tiny in size was capable of arousing profound feelings. The studiolo was probably a room without windows, approximately twelve by fifteen feet, with wooden paneling, trompe-l'oeil painting on the cabinets, and a glazed terracotta floor by Luca della Robbia. The ceiling, a barrel vault decorated with twelve glazed terracotta tondos representing the months of the year, is credited to the same artist. The vases and jewels were probably placed in the inlaid cabinets.

We can reconstruct the studiolo thanks to the contemporary descriptions of Filarete, of the poet Piero Parenti, who visited it in 1456 and 1457, and of Vasari, who saw it in the next century. This famous room disappeared during the various reconstructions of the palace on the Via Larga, and the Della Robbia terracottas are now in the Victoria and Albert Museum in London.

To conclude this brief analysis of Piero's collecting, we can say that his entire collection must have been quite conspicuous, as the 1465 inventory valued the jewels at 12,205 ducats, the rings at 1,972, the pearls at 3,512, the cameos and engravings at 2,579, 4,580 for the vases, 3,600 for the curios, and 6,702 for the silverware, giving a total of 35,150 ducats. In value, the semiprecious-stone objects thus amounted to 20 percent of the whole collection, which cannot but make us regret the dispersal of most of the pieces from this treasure, of which, sadly, we now have only a somewhat vague idea.

The treasure of Lorenzo

On his father's death in 1469, the twenty-year-old Lorenzo (1449–92) inherited the family property. He had also inherited the family passion for fine arts and antiquities. Piero's studiolo, along with the garden, remained the focal point of the Medici collections. It was there that important visitors, merchants and politicians, were met and duly impressed by the family's hidden riches. Like other ruling families, the Medici used their wealth to demonstrate their social importance.

Because they were so easily transportable, the jewels belonging to the Medici collection occupy an important place in the history of Renaissance politics, as they were used as presentation gifts, were exchanged for other treasures, served to cement alliances, and at times caused bitter quarrels. Such private family collections clearly gave their owners a cachet that made up for their lack of ancient lineage.

It was, in fact, during a political mission that young Lorenzo managed to acquire the most significant jewels in his family's collection, a group of carved stones, a large part of which were once in the possession of Pope Paul II, the Venetian Pietro Barbo, perhaps the greatest Renaissance collector of carved stones. Paul II's collection passed into the hands of the far less possessive Sixtus IV, who gave pieces from the collection not only to Lorenzo but probably to other illustrious political personalities, in order to improve his personal relationships and obtain support. Recalling the occasion, Lorenzo wrote, "In September 1471 I was elected Ambassador to Rome for the coronation of Pope Sixtus, where I was shown much honor, and thence did I bring back the two antique marble heads portraying Augustus and Agrippa, which were given me by the same Pope Sixtus, and furthermore I brought back our insignia in engraved chalcedony, along with many other cameos and medals, which were bought there, among others the chalcedony one."

In this extract from Lorenzo's memoirs the two best-known pieces of the collection are mentioned: the Farnese Cup ("our insignia"), and Diomedes and the Palladium ("the chalcedony one"). Although Diomedes and the Palladium was from the Barbo collection and was given to Lorenzo by Sixtus IV, it is less certain how he came by the Farnese Cup, for it did not belong to Paul II and therefore must have been acquired by Lorenzo from another source.

The Farnese Cup is, among ancient cameos, one of the richest in charm and history. It bears on one side a complex allegory of the fertility of the Nile, and on the other an image of the head of Medusa. Both the subject matter and the manufacture of the piece suggest that it was made somewhere in the Near East during the Imperial period.

The other gem mentioned by Lorenzo as having been among those bought in Rome was a chalcedony piece showing Diomedes' theft of the Palladium (the sacred image of Pallas Athena kept in the temple of Athena at Troy and stolen by the Greek warrior Diomedes—although other versions claim Aeneas took it when he fled Troy and brought it to Rome). This, sadly, is lost, although various copies as well as plaster and bronze casts survive as witness to its beauty. This carving has an interesting and well-documented history. It was first owned by Niccolò Niccoli, the great Florentine humanist (1363–1437), and Ghiberti gives us a contemporary account in his *Commentario:* "Among the most remarkable things that I ever saw is a piece of engraved chalcedony, which was in the hands of one of our fellow citizens, by name Niccolò Niccoli. He was a most diligent man and in our times an investigator and searcher after many remarkable ancient things, both inscriptions and volumes of Greek and Latin books [his collection of manuscripts was the beginning of the Laurentian Library]. Among other things he also had this chalcedony, which is more perfect than any other thing I have ever seen. It was oval in shape, and upon it was the figure of a youth holding a knife in his hand, he stood with one foot almost kneeling on an altar and with the right leg seated on the altar and his foot resting on the ground, which was so vividly described with such art and skill that it was marvelous to behold. In his left hand he bore a piece of cloth within which was held a small idol. It seemed that the youth threatened it with the knife: all those skilled and trained in sculpture and painting who saw this were of one accord in saying it was a marvelous thing, with all the proportions and measurements that any statue or sculpture must have, and by all talents was it praised most greatly."

Vespasiano da Bisticci, in his *Lives of Illustrious Men of the 15th Century*, recounts how Niccolò Niccoli, whom he calls Nicolao, came by this acquisition: "It so happened that one day, as Nicolao left his house, he saw a boy who carried a chalcedony stone around his neck, on which was a figure by the hand of Pilicretus, most worthy. He asked the boy whose son he was and, on hearing the name of the father, sent to ask if he would sell it. He was happy, for the man did not know what it was and did not value it. He sent him five florins. To the good man whose stone it was, it seemed that more than half was a gift. Then, Nicolao, having this chalcedony, showed it off as a most singular figure, which it was. There being in Florence a patriarch, in the time of Pope Eugenius, by the name of Master Luigi, and he, taking great pleasure in such things, sent word to Nicolao, praying him to let him see this chalcedony. He sent it, and it pleased him so much that he kept it and sent back to Nicolao two hundred golden ducats; and he did so in such a manner that Nicolao, not being very rich, had to be content to give it to him. It then went, after the death of the patriarch, into the hands of Master Pagolo; from whence Lorenzo de' Medici had it." In the inventory of 1492, the gem that had cost Niccoli just a few coins was valued by Lorenzo at as much as 1,500 florins, partly as a result of passing from one powerful owner to another.

Lorenzo was not content with just buying antique gems and worked to bring modern engravers to Florence. According to Vasari he invited Giovanni delle Corniole, portraitist of Gerolamo Savonarola, and as early as 1477, Pietro di Neri Razzanti, evidently an expert engraver, was given a ten-year permit on the condition that he respect the obligation to teach his art to the Florentines.

Lorenzo increased the collections by means of such important purchases as the estate of Cardinal Francesco Gonzaga in 1483, but did not disdain small purchases. He often made use of trusted advisers, many more expert than he, and in 1488 one of them, Luigi Andrea Lotti da Barberino, set him on guard against the purchase of a modern carnelian passed off as being antique. Then again, Lorenzo was a careful collector who did not allow himself to be carried away and evidently did not have an exaggerated interest in ancient works. His purchases never had that hint of folly one encounters elsewhere, and he kept himself within reasonable limits. More than once he refused to buy a work of art he considered too costly. In 1490, he wrote to Andrea da Foiano, regarding an antique bust that the latter had brought to his attention, "I would gladly buy it from him who owns it, should he wish to sell it at its proper value."

Lorenzo the Magnificent was also interested in such automata as mechanical clocks. On June 14, 1477, he received a letter from Ambrogio Spannocchi, advising him of the arrival of Dionisius of Viterbo, who had "built a clock with such art and so many figures working together at the same time that it is marvelous to behold." His passion for clocks is also witnessed in the inventory where seven are mentioned, among them one "to be placed in a niche with hearts and perforations in gilt copper, which runs without counterbalance, with arms and sprites enameled on the face where the hours are shown."

Thanks to the intervention of Lorenzo, on January 26, 1490, the papal tiara of Pope Innocent was ransomed back for the princely sum of 80,000 florins. The tiara had been given as a pledge to the cardinals.

Fortunately, just as we have an inventory of Piero's possessions, we have one for Lorenzo, dated 1492, which includes values for the pieces listed. The vases and cameos (twenty-seven vases, forty-six cameos, and over fifty rings) appear to have increased in number and value in an exponential progression indicative of even greater interest. One of the two Roman double-handled vases in sardonyx, now in the Museo degli Argenti, is valued at as much as 2,000 florins. However, not everything increased so significantly. The rock-crystal goblet with Burgundian mounts that Piero had valued at 700 florins is appraised at 800 in Lorenzo's inventory, in fact a decrease in value considering that thirty years separate the two estimates. This modest valuation might indicate lack of interest in the mount, the vase's most important feature, in relation to the rock crystal, a not particularly rare material. On the other hand, Lorenzo was well aware of the uniqueness of the Farnese Cup, which he estimated at 10,000 florins, a sum exceeding the value of all the other vases. This was an excessive amount, perhaps, but for Lorenzo the cup was the finest masterpiece in the collection, a unique and inimitable object that deserved this extremely high valuation in view of his affection for it.

There is also a notable increase in value for the jewels bought by Piero. Poseidon and Athena increases from 180 florins to 800; Noah's Ark reaches 2,000. The group of cameos and engravings bought in Rome, originally from the collection of Paul II, is given a high value. Dionysus Driven in a Chariot is valued at 1,000 florins; Hippolytus and Phaedra, 500; the Palladium, 1,500; Nero's Seal, which can be considered the family jewel, did not exceed 1,000 florins.

Particular mention should be given to two jewels preserved, in Piero's studiolo, making that room as much a dressing room as a study. These are "a pendant with a cut diamond set in a mount of gold, which is in the folds of a snake with a pear-shaped pearl, of approximately 38 carats, clear and perfect in both color and skin," worth 3,000 florins, and "a shoulder clasp with a pierced balas-ruby mount, set in four arms and with two large pearls set around it, each of approximately 20 carats, with a diamond in the said group set in a mount, in all four pieces," valued at 2,200 florins. Let us end this analysis of the 1492 inventory by mentioning a precious set of tableware comprising "one dagger, one small knife, one fork with a unicorn handle, all furnished with gold scabbards."

Political misfortunes and family riches: from Piero to Duke Alessandro

Immense wealth could not save Lorenzo from physical decline, and he died in April 1492. It was perhaps prior to his death that the Medici family jewels began to bear the engraved inscription LAV. R. MED, which can be interpreted both as "Lorenzo Medici" and, in a more aristocratic manner, as "Lorenzo Rex Medici." Not all the Medici jewels bear this inscription, and the practice ended without explanation, almost as though the patient task of engraving the jewels was suddenly interrupted, perhaps by Lorenzo's death. The inheritance passed into the hands of his son Piero (1472–1503), known as "the Unfortunate," since revolts soon forced the Medici family to flee from Florence. When be became head of the Medici family, Piero also became leader of the Florentine state, a role entrusted to him by the Republic itself. Unfortunately, he was not cut out to be a politician, enjoying instead his "good fortune, spending his time occupied in the pleasures of youth and too fond of the love of women and of ballgames." Innocent pleasures such as these distracted him from affairs of state. Yet Piero had an excellent education, having been taught mainly by the humanist and poet Politian (1454–94), and was a fair poet with a knowledge of books. We know that, on more than one occasion, the prudent Lorenzo, who sought advice regarding his purchases, took note of his son's opinion. Piero sometimes accompanied guests on visits to the family collections, and on one occasion he informed his father that the guest—in this case the humanist Ermolao Barbaro—had greatly appreciated "the house, the medallions, the vases and cameos, and in fact everything, even the garden."

Guilty perhaps of having taken on a task too great for his capabilities, the young Piero was forced to witness the entry of Charles VIII into Florence in 1494; Piero's flight marked the end of Medici rule for a time. In anticipation of this calamity, much of the family wealth was hidden with friends or in convents. The story of the sack of the Medici Palace during which many family works of art were stolen is not true, but still the collections were dispersed. Vasari recalls how Michelangelo di Viviano, the father of Baccio Bandinelli, took part in this job of preservation: "To this Michelagnolo, on their departure from Florence in the year 1494, did the Medici leave much silver and gold, which was all held by him in greatest secrecy and faithfully kept until their return: and they then praised him greatly for his faithfulness and gave him a reward."

Once he arrived in the palace, King Charles did, in fact, ask to be shown the Medici collections, by then well hidden. On abandoning the city in 1494, Piero took with him some of the most precious gems, including Nero's Seal, the Chariot of Phaeton, and the Palladium. In spite of this, once he took refuge in Venice, Piero complained of having lost pieces worth 100,000 ducats, doubtless an exaggeration but one that gives an idea of the overall value of his collection.

Some of the works that had been hidden during the sack were later returned to Piero in exile, many, including the Farnese Cup, went to Lorenzo Tornabuoni, and yet others were scattered. Some pieces, however, were lost, including Piero's silverware and almost all the property belonging to Giovanni de' Medici (Lorenzo's son, then a cardinal, later Pope Leo X), which was requisitioned to pay reparations for the damage caused by the French.

The engraver Cristoforo Foppa, writing to Ludovico Sforza, duke of Milan, on February 9, 1495, relates the destiny of the jewels after Piero's flight. The engraver had visited the collection and seen the insignia, but "the best is not to be found, which is to say Nero's Seal, the Chariot of Phaeton, the chalcedony; of gold medallions there are one thousand, of silver three thousand. They then showed me the vases, which are fifteen." From another inventory we learn that in 1496 Piero pledged his collection as security to the banker Agostino di Mariano Chigi. The cameos and engravings were preserved in "twenty silver boxes and in a mirrored box," amounting to a total of 167, plus "two other small cameos and a large chalcedony head of a bearded old man and six other engraved stones of various types."

In closing the subject of the collection's dispersal, we can surmise that most of the silverware was melted down, the vases and cameos given as security to Agostino Chigi ended up in Rome in the hands of Cardinal Giovanni de' Medici, and only a few vases remained in Florence. Upon the family's return to Florence in 1512 a considerable number of jewels was returned, as was the collection of antiquities from the garden, which had been dispersed in a sale in 1494; these became the possessions of Giuliano, Lorenzo's younger son. The sack that followed the second flight of the Medici from the city, in 1527, was not worse. On this occasion also treasures were hidden, and by a curious coincidence, perhaps as a family tradition, Baccio Bandinelli—whose father, Michelangelo di Viviano, had hidden treasures over thirty years earlier—was among those entrusted with valuables.

As mentioned, the collections belonging to Cardinal Giovanni de' Medici (1475–1521) were scattered, but no mention has been made of his merits, including having set in order Lorenzo's collection of books, which had been broken up after Piero's flight from the city. As Pope Leo X, he visited Florence, and during one of those visits, in 1515–16 or 1520, he donated four vases containing relics that he had acquired in the East. Perhaps among these were some of Lorenzo's vases, which had come into his hands in Rome. With this small nucleus, the collection of vases in semiprecious stone, although in a religious guise, returned to adorn Florence. Among works commissioned by him from goldsmiths was the crozier of San Lorenzo, an object of great sophistication, formed by a laurel branch ending in a scroll from which rises the bust of the saint holding a palm and the instruments of his martyrdom. From one of the knots on the branch appears the coat of arms of the Medici pope, almost as though the laurel branch were generating new life. It is easy to understand the message Leo X, son of Lorenzo, wanted to deliver.

The nucleus of the family moved, with Pope Leo, from Florence to a gilded but uncertain exile in Rome, where they longed to return home but still wished to dominate their new scene.

Leo died suddenly in 1521 and was succeeded by Adrian VI, who died after only twenty months as pope. Cardinal Giulio de' Medici was then raised to the papal throne as Clement VII. A natural son of Giuliano, Lorenzo's brother, he had been born only a few weeks before his father's death. Only after the Pazzi conspiracy did Antonio da Sangallo appear before Lorenzo to inform him that the child had been baptized in his presence and given the name Giulio; Lorenzo then took care of his education. Giulio moved to Rome to take up an ecclesiastical career. Because of his hostility to the Holy Roman Emperor Charles V, imperial troops under Charles de Bourbon attacked Rome in 1527, sacking the city and holding Clement prisoner for several months. In 1534, during Clement's last year as pope, an interesting event occurred concerning the Medici family, setting the pope and young Lorenzino, son of Pierfrancesco, against one another. According to the historian Benedetto Varchi, it seems that Lorenzino, under cover of darkness, stole several heads forming part of the bas-reliefs of the Arch of Constantine. Clement, enraged and unaware of the perpetrator's identity, called for equal punishment—beheading—for the guilty party. When he learned that this was his relative, Clement made a diplomatic retreat, and young Lorenzino, in his defense, ingeniously stated that he had done the deed because he was "desirous, according to the custom of our forefathers, of those curiosities."

Clement VII's collection included a plate bearing the papal coat of arms made by Valerio Belli, now in Munich's Residenz, and a chest made by the same Vicenza engraver. In 1533, the pope gave the chest to Francis I of France on the occasion of the marriage of Francis's son, the future Henry II, to Caterina de' Medici (Catherine de Médicis). In 1589, this same chest returned to Florence as part of the dowry of Christine of Lorraine, as will be seen later.

The pope never again visited Florence, although in a munificent gesture he donated to the city a large number of Lorenzo the Magnificent's vases, which, transformed into reliquaries, were used to decorate the Basilica of San Lorenzo. It seemed only right to Clement to send them back to the city in which the original collection had been formed. To make certain the donation would not become dispersed or broken up, the pope fixed extremely rigid rules. First of all, vases containing precious relics were to be exhibited in public only once a year and on other extremely rare occasions. Transgressors were promised excommunication and, above all, the "*indignationem Omnipotentis Dei*."

The donation, made in 1532, had been a long time in preparation and numbered forty-two vases, individually described, along with their relics. As early as 1525 Clement VII had the idea of making this donation and had prepared a rough plan for setting the reliquaries above the main altar of the basilica on a ciborium that was to be designed by Michelangelo. In the meantime, while the project moved ahead slowly, Rome was sacked, causing further dispersal of the collection. When it was once again recovered, the project was subjected to radical changes, and as time went on the ciborium was replaced by a stone tribune on the counterfacade of the church. The design, completed in 1532, seems to derive its harmonious proportions from contemporary works in the Laurentian Library. In the end, it was here that the vases stood with their respective relics until the 18th century, when Cosimo III requested certain relics be moved to the Palatine Chapel in the Pitti Palace.

In 1785, during the Hapsburg-Lorraine rule, the vases were transferred en masse to the Uffizi and were assembled in the Sala delle Gemme. In San Lorenzo they were replaced by baroque reliquaries, some manufactured by Florentine masters and others made in southern Germany. These works were of silver with applied precious stones or of ebony and silver.

That history, however, belongs to other centuries. During the 16th century, Duke Alessandro (1511–37), the natural son of Clement VII, brought the family back into a predominant position in Florence. He found more attraction in worldly than in spiritual pleasures, and the Medici historian Gaetano Pieraccini, author of a basic work on hereditary transmission of human characteristics, speaks of him as a "constitutional amoral delinquent: proud, overbearing, egoistic, sensual, he thought of nothing other than his own success and happiness." Little evidence of his art collections remains today. He commissioned a few small carvings from Domenico di Polo of Vetri, who worked in Florence until 1547, making a number of portraits of the first duke and supervising stone engraving. In 1532 he carved a figure of Hercules on the emerald that later served Cosimo as a seal. Benvenuto Cellini made several medallions for Duke Alessandro.

Generally hated, Alessandro met a bad end, many of the family's palaces were razed, and a large portion of the Medici family possessions was dispersed. Even the home of Lorenzino de' Medici—who, together with a hired assassin, stabbed Alessandro to death—was sacked, and all his property stolen. The damage was anything but slight, and his losses were estimated at 20,000 scudi.

The duke's collection met a better fate, most of it passing into the hands of his widow, Margaret of Austria, the natural daughter of Charles V. Her portion included, among other things, the chalcedony cup, Nero's Seal, and many cameos and carved pieces. When she moved to Rome and became the wife of Ottavio Farnese, she took this collection with her, and it became part of that family's hereditary property, which explains its presence today in the Museo Nazionale of Naples, where the Farnese collections of antiquities are also housed.

From a 1586 inventory we discern evidence of the number of carved stones in Margaret's possession. Even so many years after Alessandro's death, the Medici jewels still stand out. A small chest lined with "black calf" and provided with two locks held the Farnese Cup—which by then had a hole in the center—and a smaller damascened iron box containing, among other things, the cameo of Noah's Ark, the Centaur, and Nero's Seal.

Carnelian carving of Apollo, Olympus, and Marsyas known as Nero's Seal. 15¾ x 13¾ inches. Naples, Museo Nazionale.

Attributed to Dioscorides, one of the most important craftsmen of the classical age and lapidary at the court of Augustus, this stone, known as Nero's Seal, has a colorful history. An extremely precious object, it was once set in a mount designed and executed by Lorenzo Ghiberti, which gives an idea of its importance to the Medici. The very first object known to have been collected by the family, it passed into the Farnese collection after Margaret of Austria's marriage to Don Ottavio Farnese. There was almost a dispute as to the legality of the inheritance.

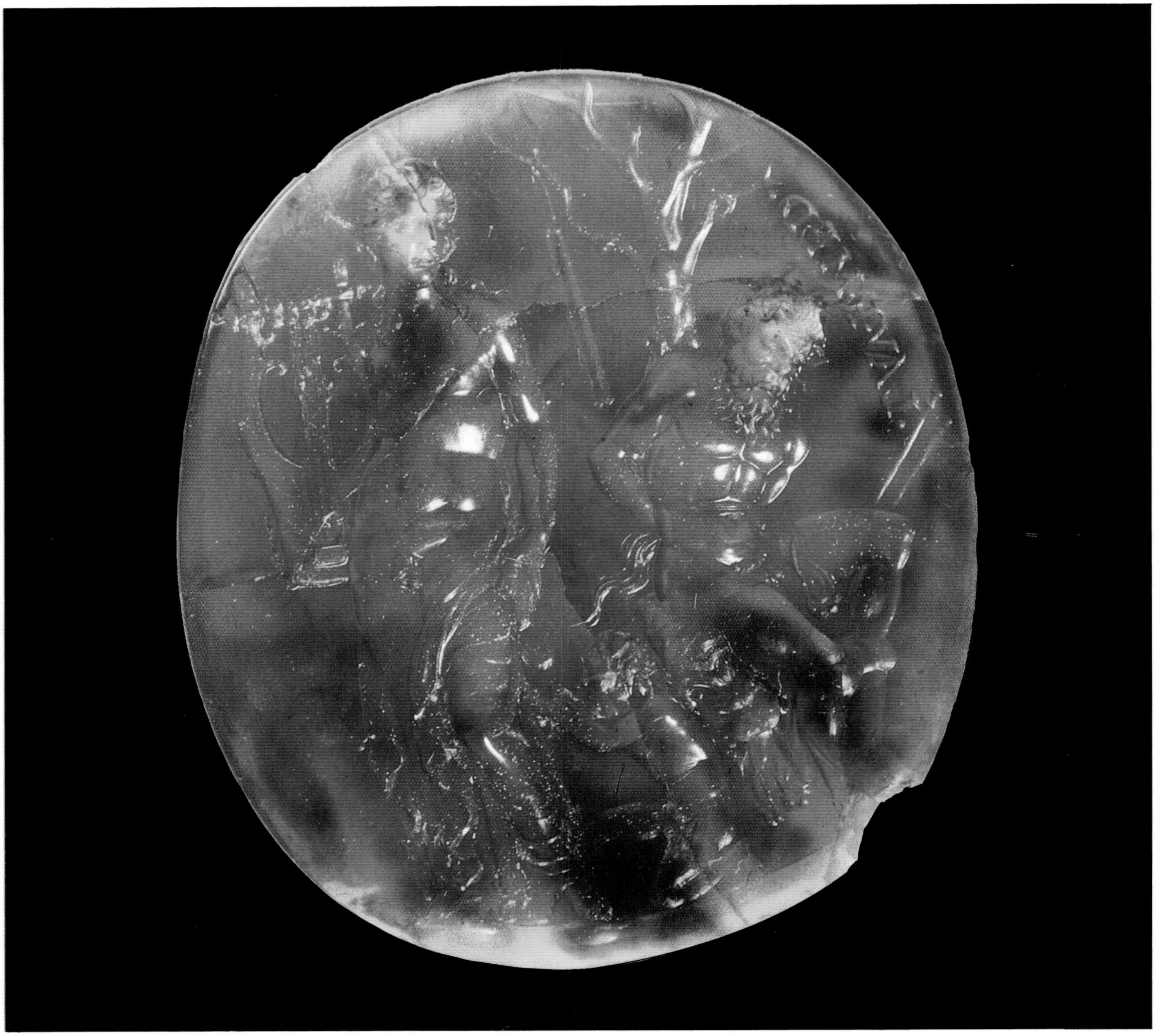

Cameo in sardonyx agate known as the Farnese Cup. Carved on both sides. Diameter 8 inches. Naples, Museo Nazionale.

This is perhaps one of the most impressive cameos of ancient times. On one side appears a perfect and striking representation of Medusa (overleaf), on the other (above and page 33) a complex allegory made up of a group of eight figures alludes in all probability to the Fertility of the Nile. The allegory cannot be compared in quality to the dramatic expression of the Medusa, which possibly is not only attributable to the hand of a different artist, but may even belong to a different time and place, albeit within the confines of classical and Middle Eastern antiquity. Furthermore, the engraving on both sides, a feature rarely seen in ancient times, leads to the conclusion that the work was executed in two or more periods. Purchased by Lorenzo in 1471 during a journey to Rome, the Farnese Cup was highly valued in all family inventories, higher, in fact, than any other cameo or vase in the collection.

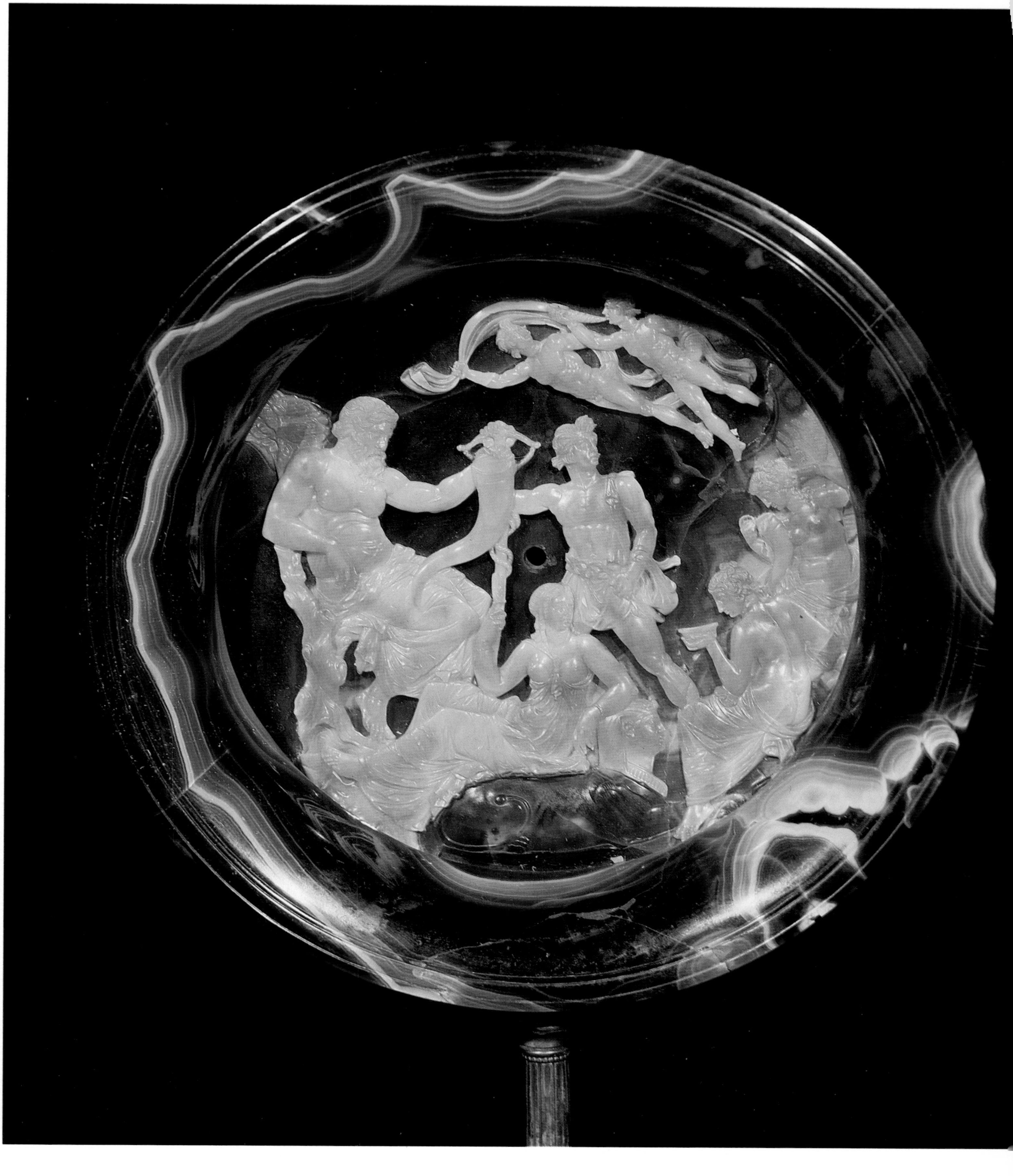

Below: Sardonyx cup, inscribed LAV.R.MED., with silver-gilt mounts. Height 9 inches. Florence, Museo degli Argenti.

Most probably this cup is a work from the Byzantine world, datable to the 7th or 8th centuries. It once had a silver cover bearing the arms of Lorenzo de' Medici and the emblem of the ostrich feather, personal symbol of Lorenzo the Magnificent. Thus both the piece's acquisition and its mount can be dated to between 1470 and 1492.

Opposite: Double cup in yellow jasper, inscribed LAV.R.MED., with silver-gilt mounts. Height 12 inches. Florence, Museo degli Argenti.

The stone carving and mount are certainly of the Renaissance; the mount may be from 15th-century Florence. The spherical cutting of the stone is, in fact, exceedingly simple and basic.

Cup in amethystine jasper, inscribed LAV.R.MED., with silver-gilt mounts. Height 5¼ inches. Florence, Museo degli Argenti.

This cup is characterized by the use of a rare and variegated stone: it was observed that in order to best exploit the qualities of such multicolor materials, a spherical form was more appropriate than a faceted one and also better suited to handling such transparent materials as rock crystal. The mount can be dated to the period of the formation of the Medici collection.

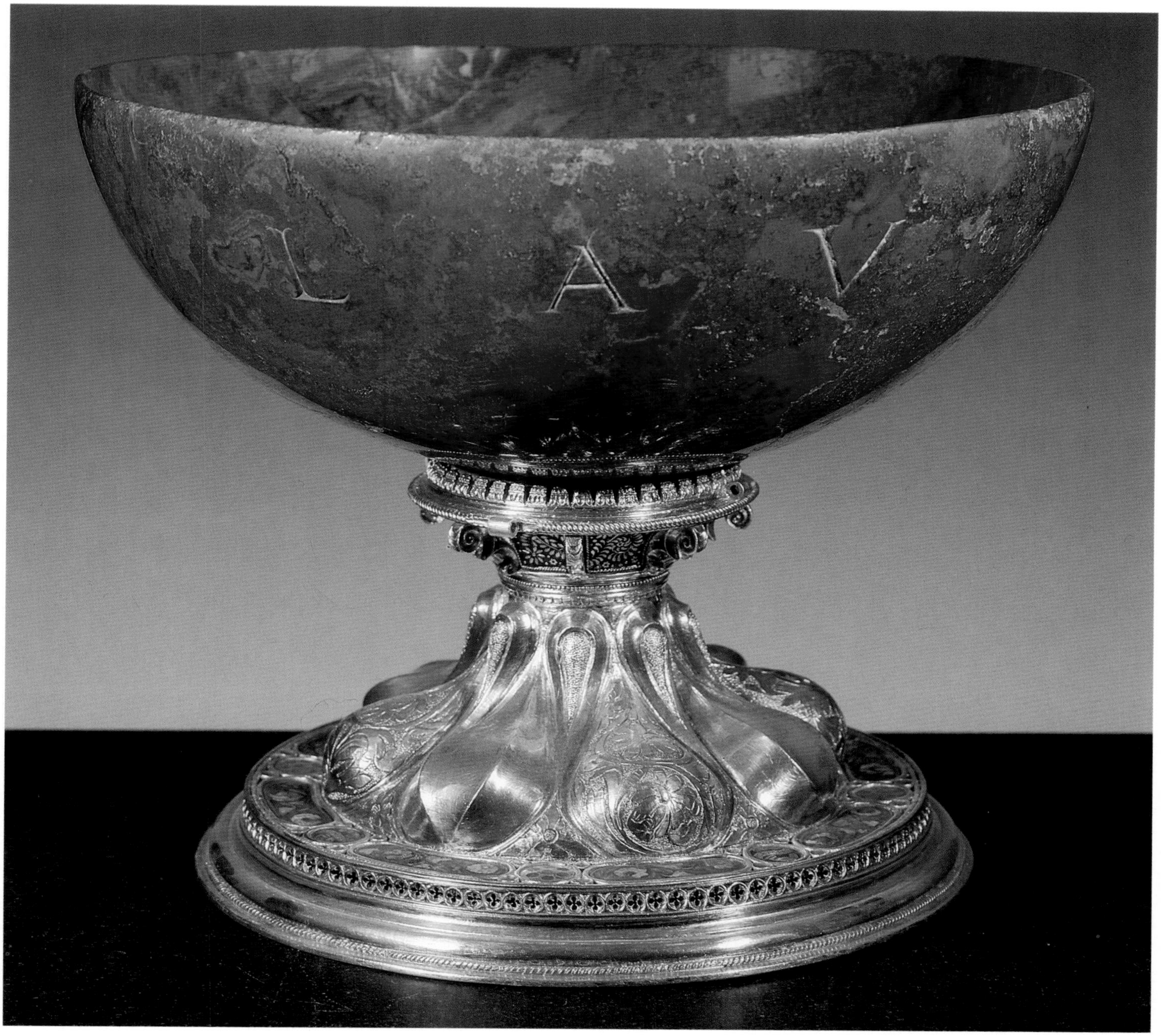

Cup in red jasper, inscribed LAV.R.MED., with silver-gilt mounts and enameled decoration. Height 8½ inches. Florence, Museo degli Argenti.

This is a late medieval work of European ambience; there are several similar pieces in the Medici collection. The simplicity of the workmanship and the finishing at the rim confirm such a hypothesis. The cup originally had a rim mount as well as a matching cover, as can be seen in a 16th-century drawing. The mounts were made in Florence for the Medici.

Above: Covered vase in sardonyx, inscribed LAV.R.MED., with silver-gilt mounts. Height 5 1/2 inches. Florence, Museo degli Argenti.

The opinion that the cover does not belong to the vase is probably correct, for this is probably a marriage of two pieces of different origin and time made perhaps when the mounts were created. The lower part of the vase is of ancient origin, perhaps from the Orient, while the cover may even date from the time of the Renaissance.

Opposite: Two-handled covered vase in sardonyx, inscribed LAV.R.MED., with silver-gilt mounts. Height 17 3/4 inches. Florence, Museo degli Argenti.

The stonecutting of this vase is antique, no later than the 4th century, perhaps executed during the early empire, and can be matched with a copious catalog of vases in sardonyx with handles very similar to this. The mounts probably date to the reign of Francesco I, and since the base bears the grand ducal crown they are certainly later than 1570.

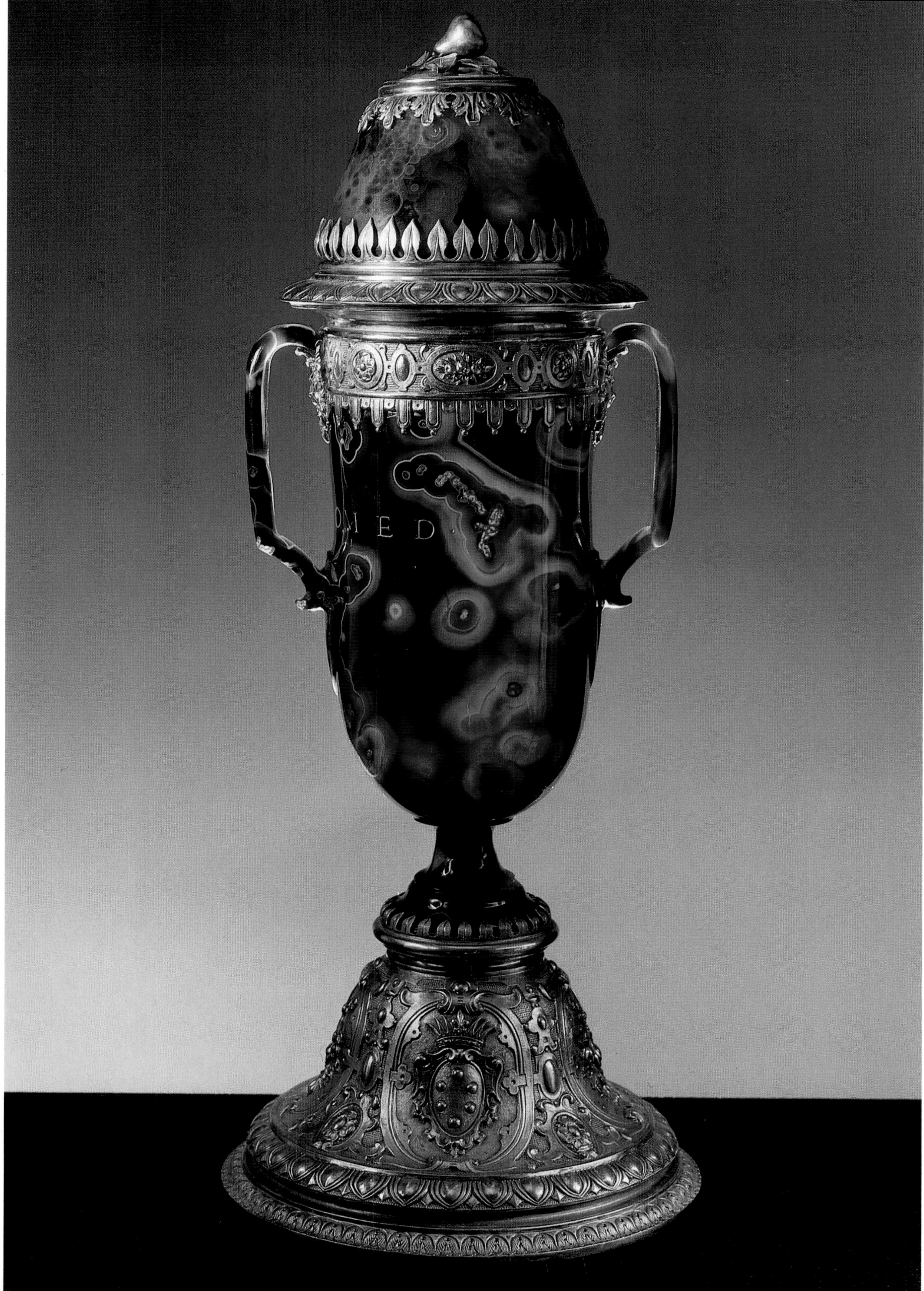

Red jasper vase, inscribed LAV.R.MED., with two handles and cover, with silver-gilt mounts and enameled decoration. Height 10½ inches. Florence, Museo degli Argenti.

This vase can be associated with a group of similar pieces in the Medici collections in its technique, materials, and mounts. Here the outline is linear rather than convex. The vase was among those donated to the Basilica of San Lorenzo by Clement VII and contained "the hand with skin of St. Sabina." It was given an estimated value of 130 florins in Piero's 1464 inventory. Below: Detail of the base.

M E D

***Below:* Two-handled jasper vase, inscribed LAV.R.MED., with cover and silver-gilt mounts and enameled decoration. Height 16 ½ inches. Florence, Museo degli Argenti.**

This vase was long believed to be a Fatimid work on the basis of studies by Ernst Kris, a noted authority on antique gems. More recently, and after convincing arguments, it has been given a later date, somewhere between the 14th and 15th century, and a Western origin, probably Venice. The vase bears a close relationship to the piece shown on the previous page. The likeness is not limited to similarity of stone or workmanship: both have the only original silver-gilt mounts in the nucleus of the Medici collection that can be attributed to the goldsmith Giusto da Firenze. Other Medici vases have mounts attributed to Giusto, leading to the assumption that this goldsmith's participation in the production of works for the Medici was anything but occasional. The mounts of this vase probably date to before 1465 and are among those that belonged to Piero de' Medici. Below right: Detail of the cover.

***Opposite:* Sardonyx jug, inscribed LAV.R.MED., with silver-gilt mounts. Height 16 ½ inches. Florence, Museo degli Argenti.**

One of the vases donated by Clement VII to the Basilica of San Lorenzo, this conserved the relics of St. Andrew the Apostle. The workmanship of the jug reveals Sassanid influence; it was probably made around the 8th century. The handle has the stylized form of a panther rampant, also found in other objects from that environment. Bottom right: Detail of the lid.

Amethyst double cup, inscribed LAV.R.MED., with silver-gilt mounts. Height 11 inches. Florence, Museo degli Argenti.

Unlike many similar works, the cover of this cup appears to be original. It is probable that the cup and mounts are contemporaneous, dating to the early 15th century, of Italian, possibly Florentine, origin (without necessarily claiming Tuscan workmanship for the stone carving). Other Medici vases have similar mounts.

Amethyst vase, inscribed LAV.R.MED., with silver-gilt mounts. Height 6 inches. Florence, Museo degli Argenti.

This vase is fairly similar to that on the opposite page, although the mounts are less rich and elaborate. Originally the upper half had a far richer mount, as can be seen in the illustrated catalog of vases. The amethyst was most probably worked at a more recent date than originally thought, not much earlier than the mounts.

Below left: Sardonyx vase, inscribed LAV.R.MED., with matching lid and silver-gilt mounts. Height 4 inches. Florence, Museo degli Argenti.

This vase of a beautifully uniform sardonyx cannot be identified in the inventories of the period although it bears the initials of Lorenzo. The first inventory to mention it is that relating to Clement VII's gift to the Basilica of San Lorenzo in 1532. This vase contained the relics of St. Nicholas of Bari and St. Marcellus Martyr, and its dating poses a number of problems.

Below right: Tiger's-eye jasper vessel, inscribed LAV.R.MED., with matching lid and gold mounts. Height 7⅓ inches. Florence, Museo degli Argenti.

One of the most elegant pieces in the collection, this cup is the culmination of European lapidary work. Both the cup and the mount are Burgundian works of the 15th century, and in comparison to other continental works they show a notable evolution, especially in the delicate modulation of the stone. The gold mounts are further evidence of the importance given to the vessel.

Opposite: Rock-crystal jug with handle. Height 16 inches. Florence, Museo degli Argenti.

This vessel, whose original mounts in gold are now reduced to that on the rim, is an interesting example of Fatimid production of the 10th century. The Arabic inscription carved on the shoulder of the vase can be translated "For the personal use of the Commander of the Commanders" and refers to Husein, to whom the Fatimids owed a great debt in the foundation of their Egyptian dynasty.

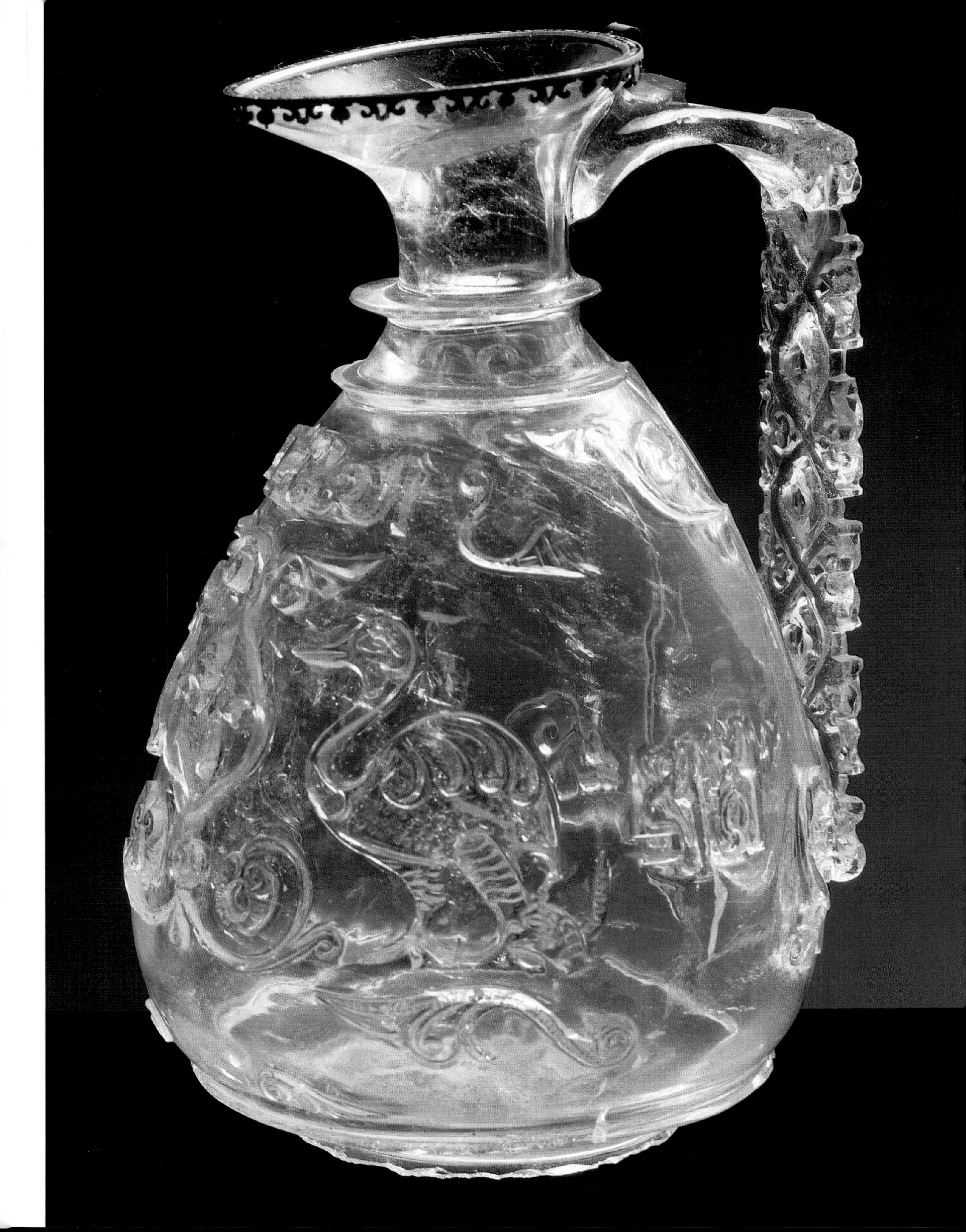

Rock-crystal cup with enameled gold mounts and supported by two silver angels. Height 12½ inches (vase alone 3¾ inches). Florence, Treasury of San Lorenzo.

This cup, to which the baroque support by Cosimo Merlini was added in the early 18th century, is a Burgundian work dating from the beginning of the 15th century. Probably purchased by Piero de' Medici—it is mentioned in the inventory of 1463—it has always been considered, because of its extremely ornate mounts, the most precious of the Medici vases. The elaborate mounts terminated in a now lost diamond tip, but the piece is still of particularly great value for its workmanship as well as six balas rubies, six sapphires, and twelve pearls. Merlini's support, an almost unique example of a baroque application to an early Medici vase, was perhaps intended to give value to the vase, but more probably emphasized the importance of the relic it contained—a thorn from the Crown of Christ—that replaced "the whole of one of St. Catherine's fingers," which the cup contained when it was donated by Clement VII. On the subject of the exchange of reliquaries in 1785, we should note that the reliquaries that remained in the Basilica of San Lorenzo were all made of rock crystal. The display of relics favored this choice, so the reliquaries that actually "showed" their contents were kept in the basilica, whereas the vases in colored, nontransparent stone were transferred to the Pitti Palace.

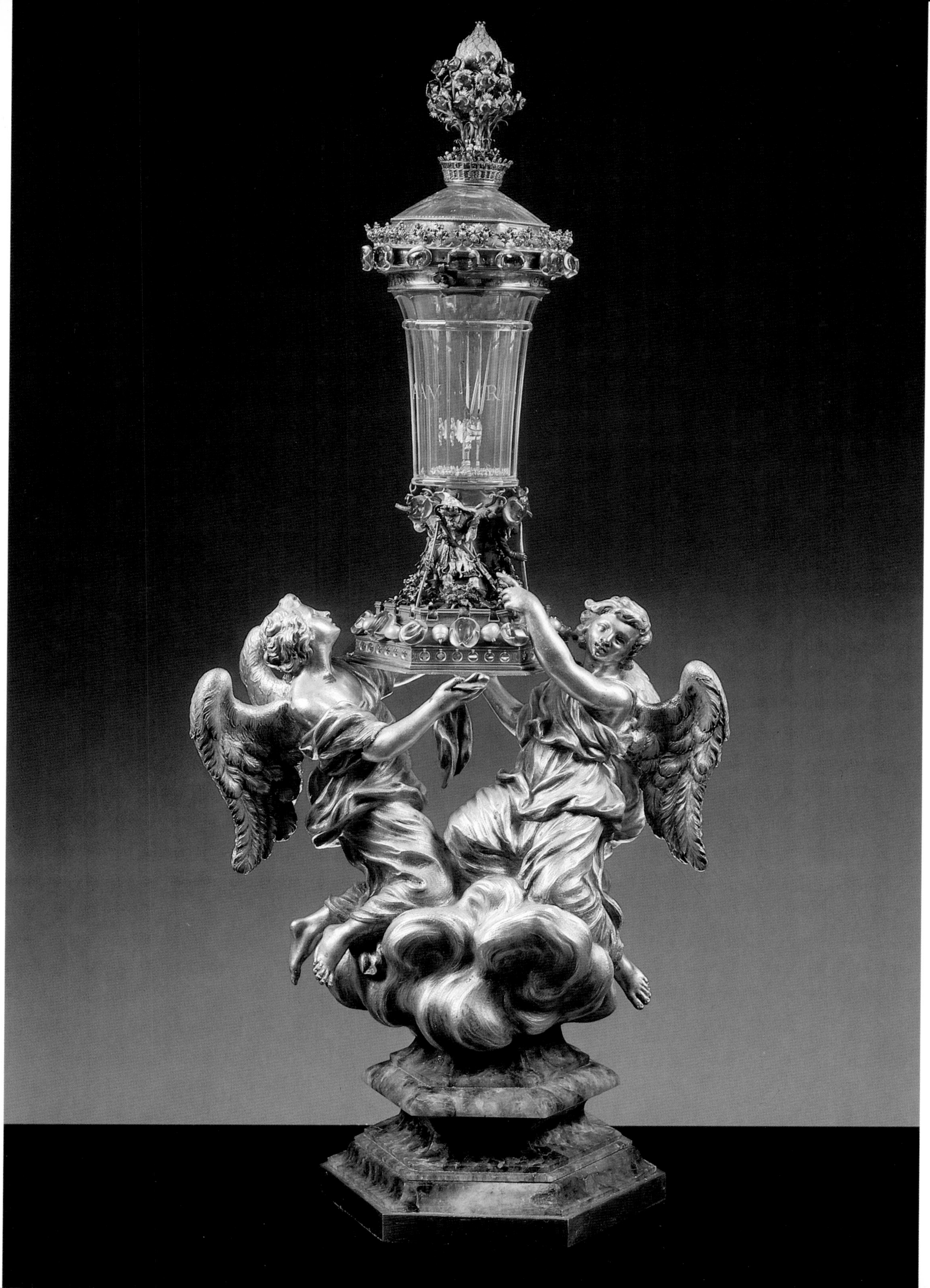

Left: Rock-crystal cup with matching lid and silver-gilt mounts and enameled decoration. Height 17¾ inches. Florence, Treasury of San Lorenzo.

The mounts of this unusually shaped cup are similar in type and workmanship to the double cup illustrated on page 52. Both the base and handles, formed by dragons rampant, are Venetian works of the mid-15th century. It is probable that the cup is of the same origin. The reliquary, donated by Clement VII, contained relics of St. Peter and St. Gregory, pope.

Opposite: Cylindrical two-handled rock-crystal vase with silver-gilt mounts and enameled decoration. Height 12¾ inches. Florence, Treasury of San Lorenzo.

The mounts dominate the vase without distorting its shape. Its creator was the goldsmith Francesco d'Antonio of Siena, who was active between 1440 and 1480, and to whose hand we owe the reliquary of the robe of St. Bernardino of Siena. The carving is probably Venetian, in any case European. It is probable that the Medici family first purchased the vase and then had it mounted by d'Antonio, who may also have worked in Florence. In fact, on the mount appear the initials M.L.M., interpreted as Magnus Laurentius Medices. This vase formed part of the nucleus of works donated by Clement VII.

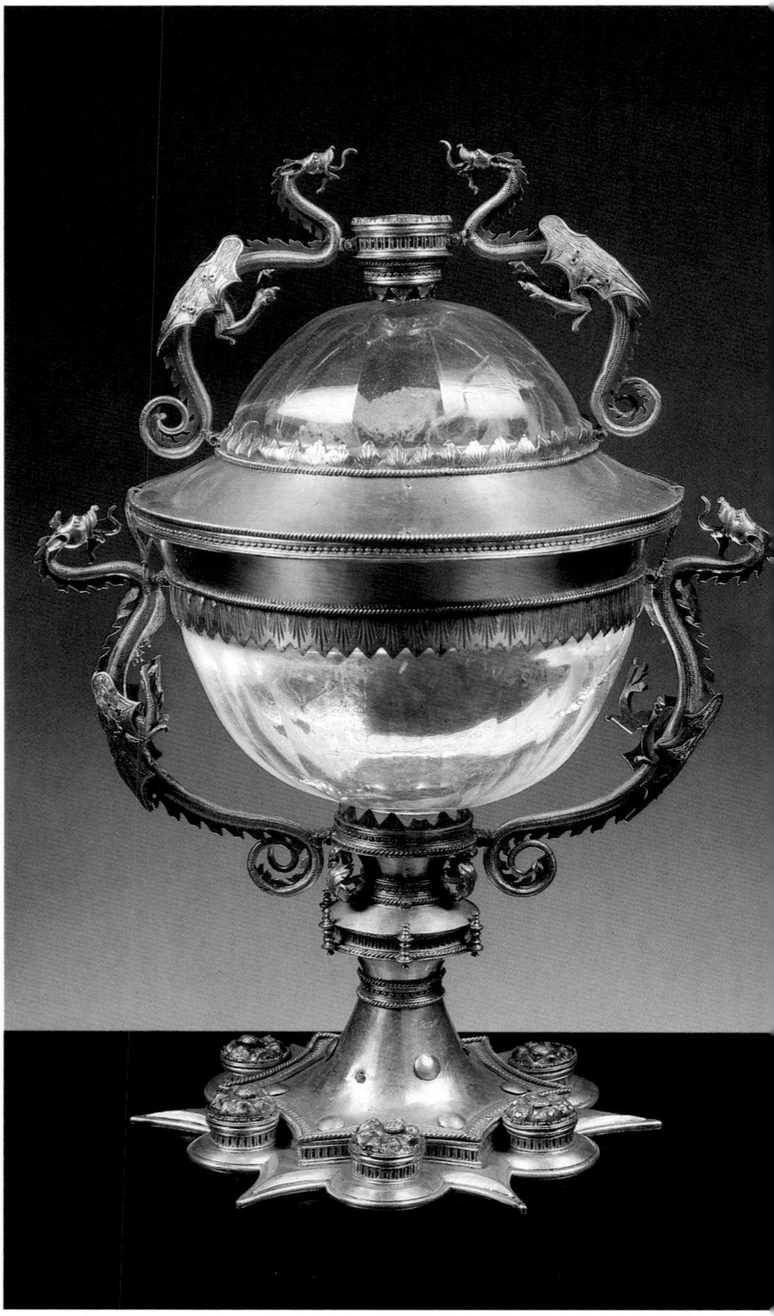

Rock-crystal jug, inscribed LAV.R.MED., with matching lid and silver-gilt mounts. Height 14¾. Florence, Treasury of San Lorenzo.

Although its handle is similar to others of Muslim manufacture, this jug's stiffness and symmetrical form tend to date it much later, around the 12th century, and suggest a European origin. Having once belonged to Lorenzo, the piece went to Rome and returned to Florence along with the donation made by Clement VII. It originally contained relics of Saints Cosmas and Damian.

Opposite right: Rock-crystal double cup with silver-gilt mounts and enameled decoration. Height 13 inches. Florence, Treasury of San Lorenzo.

In this double cup, probably made and mounted in Venice during the 15th century, the mounts have an extremely important function, providing handles that would otherwise be nonexistent. This method of using different materials, such as silver, which is more common and malleable, to avoid the difficulty of making the handles out of the same block as body of the vase is typical of amateur workmanship. The model of the double cup itself reveals workmanship that is not particularly sophisticated. Above: Detail of the cover.

***Left:* Rock-crystal bottle mounted in silver gilt with enameled decoration to form an ampulla. Height 7 3/4 inches. Florence, Treasury of San Lorenzo.**

The singular quality of this piece derives from the mounts, which radically change the form and function of the bottle, something rarely seen among the Medici vases. At times, antique mounts—which have for the most part been lost—included double handles, but these additions did not modify the nature of the vase itself. In this case, in addition to the handle a spout with a zoomorphic mask has been added, transforming the bottle into an ampulla, which presupposes liturgical use of the piece before it was transformed into a reliquary at the time of Clement VII's donation.

***Opposite:* Rock-crystal bottle with enameled gold mounts. Height 11 3/4 inches. Florence, Treasury of San Lorenzo.**

This Fatimid bottle has gold mounts with the Medici arms as well as the emblem of Cosimo I together with a scroll bearing the inscription COSMUS MED. FLOREN. ET SENARUM DVX II. D.D. In consequence, it can be dated to 1555, after Cosimo's conquest of Siena. It would thus appear not to be a work belonging to the collection of the early Medici; however, there is no guarantee that the mount was not added to a vase already in the collection. The intrinsic quality of the bottle, which is similar in style to the other illustrated here, is extremely high.

EX OSSIB

Cosimo I and his sons: the treasures of the grand dukes

Detail of the enameled gold cover of a cup made by French artists. The entire piece is illustrated on page 107.

Shortly after taking over the government of the city of Florence in 1537, young Cosimo expressed his grand aspirations in a series of commissions intended to enhance his reputation. During the years in which the court was transferred into the appropriately enlarged and embellished Palazzo della Signoria (1540), the organization of the Wardrobe was improved. A recording system kept by members of the duke's own staff accounted for the entrance and withdrawal of the pieces stored first at the Palazzo Vecchio and later also in the Pitti Palace in special rooms and cupboards. The Wardrobe thus served as a warehouse for both works of art and objects of daily life and remained in constant use until the end of the Medici grand duchy and then during the period of Lorraine rule.

The jewels of Cosimo I in the Wardrobe of the Palazzo Vecchio

Inventories of the Wardrobe were compiled scrupulously and regularly. Today these inventories provide interesting information on purchases or gifts of all the things that, taken together, form the immense inheritance that constituted the true treasure of the house of Medici, property destined for the personal enjoyment of the duke and his family.

Only a small part of what is listed and described remains in Florentine collections, but from these documents we gain information on much that was lost during the course of time, making it possible for us to sketch a clearer outline of the Medici art collections.

This selection of objects perfectly defines the concept of a treasure, which presupposes a nucleus of articles whose rarity or intrinsic worth gives them a high aesthetic and monetary value. In fact, included in the categories making up the collection of the Wardrobe were, for example, the so-called curiosities: antique fragments and statues that were much sought after in the more ordered climate of those years and that were brought from Rome and Venice at great expense. Other materials of great worth were all the objects forming the "earthenware" section, such as maiolica and porcelain, and including antique vases discovered within Tuscany, such as the so-called Arezzo vases mentioned by Vasari. Between 1544 and 1551 there are notes relating to purchases of hundreds of examples of Venetian maiolica, part of which was sent in 1545 by Duchess Eleanora to her father, the viceroy of Naples. Also worthy of notice were Chinese porcelains, which the court factories attempted to imitate starting in Cosimo's time.

Notable among the articles in metal are those in bronze: antique and contemporary statuettes, medals, objects of various sorts (mortars, bells, etc.); also the Islamic pieces, several examples of which had passed to Cosimo from Lorenzo the Magnificent, such as two spherical incense burners of 14th-century Syrian manufacture. The fascination of these articles lay above all in their ability to evoke distant and mysterious lands, in the strangeness of their ornamentation. The techniques used fed Duke Cosimo's strong quest for scientific knowledge and his interest in the variations among differing cultures.

The lists of jewels and precious rarities in the inventories made from 1560 until his death mention an enormous quantity of marvelous gold pieces. Objects not made from precious metals (with the exception of the most commonly used kitchen utensils) were extremely limited, but we find articles in semiprecious stone, antique colored marble, Oriental crystal, and Venetian glass, whose value was no less than that of precious metal, taking into consideration the difficulty involved in discovering them.

However, as often occurs in princely families, gold and silver pieces and those including precious stones are the ones most easily affected by changes in fashion, sold for ready cash, or stolen. In any case, to give an overall idea of the brilliance of Cosimo's treasure there are still the inventories, with rich information on artists, exchanges of gifts, and recurring forms and decoration. If we examine the inventory dating from 1560–68 we can extract from an infinity of precious pieces, objects that are described with an accuracy that allows us to fill in our knowledge of the models and quality of the art of Florentine goldsmiths of the period. For example, among the "Miscellaneous Goldsmiths' Works" are cups, one with a putto molded on the cover and another described as having a crystal cover mounted in gold, allowing an engraved star to be glimpsed on the bottom. The simplest are without a stem, but others are frequently found raised on high "segmented" supports, with elaborate handles ornamented with molded masks in the form of snails or snakes. One "vase of gold taken from the antique" had as its handle a figure of Hercules, and another, presented to the prince of Bavaria in 1565, had two lions' mouths as handles. Among the most decorative examples we find one "all enameled, with a body in the form of a shell, with a high foot with figures and on its cover a figure of Neptune and another little figure at the summit" and a "goblet with four mouthpieces and masks with four chains like a lamp," made by the goldsmith Niccolò Santini.

The vases are also accompanied by innumerable "goldworks." A "jewelcase in walnut with five drawers" held, for example, a "Ducal Marzocco in gold" (the Marzocco was the heraldic lion of Florence) decorated with various bezels. There were numerous necklaces and chains holding the "Golden Fleece," the highest award of the house of Burgundy, which Cosimo, like Europe's most important sovereigns, had the privilege of receiving. On one, Niccolò Santini had made "little gold hooks for the cords or ribbons" from which the duke's fleece was hung; generally speaking, clothing accessories had the connotation of precious jewels. Among the belts is one "of enameled gold with its tassel and button, with its buckle in the shape of a shield with a small head." There are "smooth" and "sculpted" buttons, ones rounded like a small melon, some small and others large like those in the so-called antique style made by the goldsmith Niccolò Santini to decorate two Genoese costumes. Then there was a fan made of twenty-four white feathers "with handle in gold." Even the natural curiosities so greatly prized in the Renaissance courts were a pretext for the display of precious materials. Perhaps the very "horn of a unicorn" that was once owned by Lorenzo the Magnificent lay in a case of "crimson velvet" and was embellished with "two ferrules at the top in enameled gold, in which were set nine small stones, that is three emeralds, three rubies, and three diamonds, and a smaller ferrule at the bottom in enameled gold, with diamond chips."

It is not rare to find in the documents information on objects received or sent as gifts, such as the "blessed rose," evidently made of gold, sent by Pope Pius IV to Cosimo I, or the "dagger bound in worked gold" donated by Cosimo to the prince of Bavaria on December 28, 1565.

Although the quantity of gold objects stored in the Wardrobe was remarkable, the amount of silverware appears to have been far greater. The inventories set down long lists of "loaves of solid silver for working," which were drawn on by the goldsmiths paid for making the wide variety of objects used in court life. Those included "silver steps for ladies when mounting a horse," "silver horse trappings made in seven pieces," "instruments in gilded silver for cleaning the tongues of sick persons," a "silver trombone in its case without key recovered after the death of Messir Lorenzo Trombone," six silver vases "in the shape of apothecary jars," a "bowl made for washing the feet of His Excellency by Niccolò Santini . . . with arms on the bottom and two bells," "two bedwarmers with covers worked with foliage and the arms of His Excellency and with a mask that takes the ferrule" made by the same goldsmith, a "silver bowl with spoon and handle for mixing medicines," and the "hunter's leash in drawn silver" that was to be found in the duke's writing desk.

One of the most recurrent forms was the silver "navicular" vases often gilded or encrusted with mother-of-pearl;

otherwise the silver is patterned with a "diamond-chipped" surface, or ornamented with classical festoons and molded masks. The documents describe one incompletely ornamented vase as being "commenced by Benvenuto," obviously Cellini.

Plates, cups, goblets, salt cellars, and pepper pots, jars for oil and vinegar can be counted by the thousand, and those broken were handed over to the goldsmiths to be melted down. Many have the typically Mannerist decoration that can be seen in drawings for vases and caskets by such Florentine painters of the period as Salviati. This is true of a navicular vase "with lip and ram's head and dolphin handles," or one made by the goldsmith Giorgio Corsi "for oil and vinegar worked in the shape of two ducks with their necks and heads for mouths." Among the wine coolers one had masks and "three little turtles for feet," with a vase in the middle with "three vine-tendrils for partitions," and another made by Niccolò Santini "large with figures and snakes for handles, inside a round vase to hold snow with four eagle's feet holding four balls on which it rests." This type of support using bird claws resting on a ball can be seen fairly frequently among the silver objects in the Wardrobe; another example is that of "two eagle's claws in silver with balls, for use as candlesticks." Certain mounts of nautilus shells in Florence's Museo degli Argenti also rest on birds' feet holding a shell and may have been from the hand of the same maker.

Going down the list of vases, we find one with gold garlands and a wolf on the lid, a bowl with a star on the handle and "a conch shell on one side and a head on the other." The cutlery ranges from simple, occasionally gilded forms bearing the Medici arms to such elaborate forms as a golden spoon with a crystal handle decorated with garnets, or a fork "with a little putto at its head, bearing as arms balls and the Salviati crest," which evidently belonged to Maria Salviati, the duke's mother. The collection of silverware was further increased in 1560 by the addition of a group of vases inherited from Don Francesco de Toledo, including a number of cups, basins, and jugs retrieved from Siena immediately after the death of Eleonora's brother.

There was a great amount of ecclesiastical jewelry, including a silver pax—a tablet decorated with a sacred image ceremonially kissed by participants at mass—made by Piero di Martino "in gold touch needle, with the Deposition of Christ," which had been delivered on May 5, 1562. Another pax with a Pietà "ornamented with fillet and a figurine on the top" was returned by Domenico Poggini after he "patched up" the heads of the figurines; it was donated to the church of Portoferraio in 1568. Much silver was used in the palace chapel, including chalices, candlesticks, crosses, thuribles, incense boats, some of which was by Matteo Castrucci. Among the works by Santini listed in 1566 was a "silver book, within which was portrayed Our Lord Jesus Christ and the Virgin Mother, with the four Evangelists and other figures in bas-relief, with a slender chain and small silver bell." Naturally, the statues for the altar of the palace chapel were also in silver, and documents mention six figures of Apostles, including a statue of St. Andrew attributed to Vincenzo Danti. Silver statues of a secular nature, such as the "silver satyr with a lamp in his hand," are also frequent, and at times we find indications of gilt-copper objects of worship, such as a large chalice brought from Milan and an "ancient" cross purchased in Pisa.

In 1569, a particularly precious gift was sent to Rome, to Duke Cosimo's second son, Ferdinando, who had recently become a cardinal; this was a casket in silver gilt "all worked, which opens out entirely with drawers that pull out on runners . . . containing inkpot, watch, and alarm and other useful odds and ends, and above the top compartment a Crucifix with St. George and at the foot, around the sides, the signs of the four Evangelists, with its body covered in purple velvet with a coat of arms in gold."

Other, less elaborate, caskets are mentioned, such as one in ebony with silver ornaments covered in gold leaf and ovals with figures in bas-relief, or all in silver, like the one with figures and trophies and five crystal medallions.

Many Oriental or rock crystals were made into religious objects, and some were reliquaries that had belonged to Duchess Eleonora de Toledo. Particularly precious was "a cross of Oriental crystal with gold crucifix, base in enameled gold, with four columns of crystal furnished with enameled gold and with its container of gold in a case covered with red velvet, delivered by the hand of the Lord Knight Thomaso de' Medici along with other possessions of the late Gracious Lady Duchess of Happy Memory."

Rock-crystal objects were highly prized by the duchess, and after her death in 1562 many are indicated as having belonged to her, some being of a secular character. Among these, the most elaborate might have been a cup of "Oriental crystal, on a golden base and having two gold bells in the form of snakes, with Neptune engraved in the bottom, with two small rubies on the upper border and handles." Eleonora owned a crystal drinking cup in the form of a shell with a gold bowl, base, and stem, and a gold rosette on the cover.

It appears that this sort of object was available in Pisa, where a "little jug of cracked Oriental crystal, with a gold circlet worked around its base" and two cups in black and red leather cases were purchased in 1562. In that year we are informed that a gift of a rock-crystal cross with crucifix and stand in silver gilt was sent to the duke from the same city by a "German baron."

On glancing at the objects in the possession of Eleonora, whom Cosimo married in 1539, we better understand some odd changes in her taste, which have generally passed unnoticed. Some quarrels that took place at court were mentioned by Benvenuto Cellini in his autobiography and give an idea of the duchess's determination when an object, such as a string of pearls, caught her fancy. Cellini had discussed their poor quality with Duke Cosimo, but the duchess implored: "My Lord, Your Excellency, by your grace buy me that necklace of pearls, for I have a great desire of it." He responded, "I do not intend to buy it . . . because I do not like to throw away money . . . as these pearls are neither round, nor equal, and there are among them many that are old." His wife's insistence, backed by the trusty goldsmith Bernardone, forced the duke to buy even those pearls considered by Cellini to be ugly. Baroque pearls, such as those so greatly desired by the duchess, did not as yet enjoy much favor, but a few decades later, unique jewels were produced by court goldsmiths using fascinating combinations of these pearls. Another indication of the duchess's rather extravagant taste is a small marble sculpture that is the most bizarre item in the ancient ducal collections. This squatting putto in Florence's Museo degli Argenti is holding a duck, and his face is contorted in a comical grimace because a large hand holding his right ear appears to be inflicting an unpleasant punishment on him. The duchess, who apparently appreciated such unusual themes as this Punishment of Eros, also showed a love of materials uncommon in Florence, such as coral, of which we find a number of examples listed in the collection. "A basin of coral, with its body painted / A stump of coral whose two branches are carved with a crucifix and a St. George / Four drawers full of corals, some petrified some not / Two stumps of coral in two walnut boxes that open with rolling shutters, in one of which there is the story of Orpheus and in the other figures. Found in the lower desk of the Wardrobe on June 13, 1561, with other things belonging to the late Illustrious Lady Duchess of Happy Memory / Two branches of coral, one more brightly colored than the other, consigned by master Sir Thomaso de' Medici along with other things belonging to the late Illustrious Lady Duchess of Happy Memory . . . Eight pieces of coral of the Mystery of the Passion of Our Lord consigned by Master Sir Thomaso de' Medici with other things belonging to the late Illustrious Lady Duchess of Happy Memory . . . Ten teaspoons, with handles in coral, bowl in silver / One small branch of coral somewhat blunted with its base in gold with a figurine and six tiny gold animals in said coral." Among objects using mother-of-pearl are many chess sets, also a walking stick with a mother-of-pearl handle and silver ferrule, three intarsia boxes that belonged to Eleonora, and several teaspoons. The lists of natural curios also indicate a number of nautilus shells, among which are "two shells in mother-of-pearl which serve to hold powder and shot for an arquebus, covered with little garnets and with mount of silver gilt"; four of them come from Eleonora's possessions.

Cosimo's great passion for semiprecious stones can be seen in the wide use of heliotrope jasper and lapis lazuli not only in the manufacture of vases, but for the most varied range of objects. These included dagger- and knife-handles, among which was a "silver rapier with a green and white jasper handle, with two knives with lapis handles, sharkskin sheath, and black leather belt worked with thread of drawn silver" and a red jasper riding whip with gilded silver. Salt cellars and cups in semiprecious stone sometimes had bizarre mounts, for example, an agate salt cellar "furnished with silver with four fish teeth." On occasion these were decorated with a simple gold border that was occasionally enameled and set with rubies or diamonds. Some vases, however, such as a heliotrope cup with satyr, appear to have been merely carved. Ivory pieces, on the contrary, are rare and include several ornaments for walking sticks. One ebony stick had "an ivory handle and gold ferrule, given to His Most Illustrious Excellency to lean on." Ivory pieces are seen in greater number, one "worked with figures without mount," among the others there was a piece that was "large, black, worked with foliage in bands of gilt copper with a black chain."

Clothes were richly embroidered in silver, gold, and pearls. Eleonora's dresses were taken apart after her death and the innumerable pearls removed from them reused for such other purposes as completing the canopy of a "rich bed" made by Antonio Bachiacca. Particularly magnificent thrones and pavilions are listed along with "jewels of various sorts," such as the "cloth cap for the top of a pavilion embroidered in a pattern of birds and roses with large and small pearls, gold pendants and turquoise silk tassels, with a golden pommel fixed on the stake, such pommel twenty-seven bezels of gold containing the following gems: six faceted and flat diamonds of various shapes, eight emerald chips, thirteen ruby chips, two hundred and forty-nine settings, one hundred and five both medium and small turquoises, thirty-six chrysolites, thirty-six not very fine sapphires, seventy-two balas rubies, among which there are some spinel-like sapphires." Even among the horses' harnesses there are some fine embroideries, including a "lady's saddle of crimson velvet, embroidered in gold with pearls."

One of the most important occasions for exhibiting the court treasures took place in 1562 when Prince Francesco, Duke Cosimo's eldest son, paid a visit to Spain. Preparations for this journey went on for months. A long list of gentlemen, together with pages, lackeys, stewards, cellarmen, cup-bearers, carvers, barbers, a butler, a master of ceremonies, and a "good doctor" was to follow in his train, all chosen from among his most trusted servants. The gentleman responsible for the preparations intended to make the best possible show: "two chambers in velvet and cloth of gold . . . two others in cloth alone with the hall and the two chambers in rich tapestry. . . . a pair of chambers of less rich tapestry and two camp beds." Above all, the silverware was considered extremely important. "The more Your Excellency gives, the better will it seem to me, but in any case a large set of flat undecorated silverware will be needed, and beyond this certain vases and a gilded set to decorate the sideboard." The lists of silverware prepared for this outing leave no doubt as to the desire to amaze the Spanish court. Also of interest are indications "for the dress of the Prince," to whom it was suggested that he "not load himself too heavily, considering the fashions, which here are not like those of the court. It would be money thrown away, as clothes can be made every day there, and it would be better to take lengths of cloth."

The seventh decade of the century was marked by a series of events that were to have profound changes at the Medici court. During Prince Francesco's trip to Spain, which lasted until 1563, the duke's two young sons, Cardinal Giovanni and Don Garzia, as well as Eleonora de Toledo fell sick and died of malaria. In 1564 Cosimo handed over the reins of government to his son Francesco, while Ferdinando was made cardinal, receiving his hat the following year. In 1565 there was the marriage of Francesco I with Joanna of Austria, although the illicit and therefore much deprecated relationship between Francesco and his Venetian mistress Bianca Capello had already begun, and they later married. The now elderly Duke Cosimo was also involved in a number of amorous intrigues and in 1567 fathered a son, Don Giovanni, with his mistress Eleonora degli Albizi, who was shortly replaced by her cousin Camilla Martelli, whom Cosimo secretly married in April 1570, just a few months prior to his much desired nomination as grand duke by Pope Pius V. This marriage did not receive the approval of his children who, on the contrary, were so disgusted by it that in an edict dated February 20, 1573, Francesco declared that he protested against any gifts made in the past, present, or future to Signora Martelli. On the grand duke's death, she retired to a convent, taking with her all the jewels and silverware that she was able to keep, part of which she gave to her daughter, Virginia Medici, on February 7, 1585 (see inventory on page 230).

Francesco I, the Dux Mechanicus

"He has found the manner of fusing rock crystal and making drinking cups and other things thereof, working them in the furnace in the same way as one works ordinary glass, and for this purpose he has paid certain of our Murano masters of great ability. These vases, most noble and fair in themselves and their material, are still more desirable in that they are made by the hands of the prince, and are also most beautiful in their working. He has also found the manner of making Indian porcelain, and all his attempts are successful in that they are of the same quality as those of the Indies, in lightness, subtlety, firing, and all the other conditions; His Excellency told me that it had taken him ten years before he had discovered it, and he was enlightened somewhat by one who had come from the Levant. . . . He often has jewels cut, and now, in addition to pictures, which he has made out of different colored stones, whose design is transmitted from one into the other, he also has had carved certain pieces of lapis. He enjoys making false jewels, which are so similar to real ones that at times the jewelers themselves are fooled, and he showed me a small vase made by himself of emerald which is truly most fair . . . He also has a not indifferent taste in painting, sculpture, miniatures, mounted cameos, medallions, and all sorts of curios, and he spends almost all his time among these things in a place known as the 'Casino,' wherein he doth enter in the morning and remains until the hour of luncheon, and after having taken his luncheon doth return there until the evening."

This profile of the scion of the Medici house, given by the Venetian ambassador Vincenzo Gussoni in 1576, is without doubt one of the best portraits of the alchemist prince. Francesco inherited from Cosimo an interest in rare and precious materials and gathered together in the Casino di San Marco a large group of men "skilled in all the arts," setting himself up as the interpreter and demiurge of extremely advanced experiments, from the purification and melting of crystal and glass to the manufacture of porcelain. He was interested in the melting of metals and the most amazing chemical transformations, "but above all," reported Gussoni, "he takes much pleasure in distilling, creating many liquids and sublimated oils for the treating of many infirmities, and he has cures for almost all of them. He doth make, among others, an oil of such excellent virtue that when anointing the wrists, the heart, and the stomach, and the throat, it doth cure all kinds of poison, restores those with the plague, and preserves the health. It is a most potent remedy for pestilences and all sorts of malign fevers, and he has told me that, desiring to experiment on persons condemned to die by drinking poison, they were completely cured by said oil, of which he desired me to partake of a small phial. He doth also greatly delight in fireworks, and I have heard him say, as well as many of his supporters, that he has a way of making a fireball of such great artifice that when it leaves the cannon it can be made to burst where any man desires. . . . He has also (so he tells me) found the manner of multiplying saltpeter, taking (as he says) 100 pounds of salt and 10 of saltpeter, and causing the whole to become saltpeter with certain of his arts." Absorbed in his experiments, at the same time, he "negotiates with secretaries regarding affairs of state." The interests he so passionately cultivated were to prove decisive for the future development of the arts in Florence, and the peculiar "locales" of his direct creation were to remain among the most fascinating. Although they were soon dismantled, recent scholarship allows us to appreciate the worth of such complexes as the studiolo in the Palazzo Vecchio, or the Tribuna of the Uffizi, or the spectacular inventions in the park of the Pratolino Villa.

The iconological orchestration of the studiolo was devised by Vincenzo Borghini in 1570, and the symbolism of the elements painted on the panels of the cabinets as well as the scenes on the ceiling must have alluded to the precious materials that the room was to contain: "The small room which is being remade is intended to serve as a storeroom for rare and precious things, both for value and for artistry, that is to say jewels, medallions, engraved stones, mounted crystals and vases, devices (locks and the like), and similar things not too large in size, placed each in its own cabinet according to type. The program seems equal to the value and quality of the objects, the figures in the paintings which are to be above and around the room and on the cabinets referring in a certain manner to the things contained therein."

Here were kept in an orderly manner these precious objects produced in the workshops of the Casino di San Marco by north Italian artisans, such as Milanese engravers, Murano glassworkers, and these from beyond the Alps, including the majority of the goldsmiths working at court during the second half of the century.

Whereas the studiolo was designed to function as a display room for pieces from the Wardrobe, a proper gallery was set up in Palazzo del Casino di San Marco in which small bronzes were featured. This exhibit was anything but casual, since those alchemical metamorphoses in which the prince was so interested took place during the very process of metal casting. In spite of Cosimo's predilection for gathering together antique and modern bronzes, the reaffirmation of sculpture in Florence must be attributed to Francesco and was largely due to the skill of a refined northern artist, the Fleming Jean Boulogne, known as Giambologna, or Giovanni Bologna. However, as one went through the Casino gallery several small marble, alabaster, or silver statues alternated with those in bronze and with natural and exotic curiosities. Of this nucleus are still preserved the splendid nautilus shells with mounts "in the German fashion," along with a notable group of small bronzes mounted on wooden bases decorated with gold fillets or covered with small stone panels. But Francesco was planning the design of a new, mystic site in which to collect together all the valuable productions of the grand duchy's workshops, the rarest pieces of the family collection, and anything else his agents managed to procure from time to time on the market.

The prince's jewelers and the first works in semiprecious stone *(pietra dura)*

Recent careful studies of the grand duke's archives paint an overall picture of the activity of the artisans employed at court. Cosimo I's interest in rare stones, which under Francesco became one of the principal activities of the Casino di San Marco workshops, presupposed a close cooperation between engravers and goldsmiths. The former had been called from Milan, where there were many lapidary workshops; certain of these, such as that of Gasparo Miseroni, had been in contact with Cosimo I. From 1572, the Florentine court had its own workshop of lapidary engravers after Francesco invited Ambrogio and Stefano Caroni, brothers who were joined, in 1575, by Giorgio di Cristofano Gaffurri. The contribution of goldsmiths was of vital importance in the final stage of the production of precious vases sculpted by engravers. They created the strange gold mounts with harpies, masks, or polychrome enamels, as well as the settings for precious stones. Along with Niccolò Santini, Cencio della Nera, the brothers Matteo, Salvestro, and Bartolomeo Castrucci (who had already worked for Cosimo), in 1574 we find the Fleming Hans Domes, who resided in the Pitti Palace, as well as artists with workshops on the Ponte Vecchio or in the Mercato Nuovo, such as Giovan Battista Cervi, who had furnished the court with jewels and mounts for vases.

The arrival in Florence, on September 24, 1573, of the Dutch goldsmith Jacques Bylivelt was an important event in view of the position he managed to obtain for himself at the Florentine court. This goldsmith, who had been apprenticed in Delft, immediately gained Francesco's esteem, and it is thanks to his cooperation with Gaffurri as well as the inventive genius of Bernardo Buontalenti that one of the most celebrated lapis-lazuli vases in the grand duke's collections was created. He appears to have been continually employed in the manufacture of the most important jewels produced during the reign of Francesco, among which was a large frontlet for Joanna of Austria, a diadem for Bianca Capello, and the new grand duke's crown, which remained intact until 1788.

Numerous examples of the elaborate mounts made during those years still remain in the Museo degli Argenti, despite the thefts and illegal tamperings that occurred in the Gallery, where the vases were preserved during the 17th and 18th centuries, including in some cases drastic alterations to the original mounts. However, what remains reveals the splendors of the grand ducal treasures.

With the prince concentrating on precious materials and experimenting with the most sophisticated contemporary techniques, mosaics in *pietra dura*—semiprecious stone—were also perfected. In 1568, Vasari described these with great admiration, tracing them back to the Florentine Bernardino di Porfirio da Leccio, who had been in the service of Duke Cosimo in 1560. A lost table by Porfirio, a cabinet, and another table made at the time of which Vasari writes must have marked the start of the so-called Florentine mosaic work, the manufacture of which was officially institutionalized by Ferdinando I on September 3, 1588. For stone inlay, which was to remain the most sophisticated art of the Florentine court, Francesco was indebted to numerous masters who brought the enchanting mosaic technique to Florence. It was in 1568 that Francesco wrote to Cardinal Giovanni Ricci requesting a skilled lapidary, and the choice fell on a certain "Franciosino," that is to say Giovanni "Mynardo," a restorer of antique sculpture and an expert painter, who was invited to France in 1579 by Catherine de Médicis and became famous throughout Europe.

Only rare examples—fragments really—remain of the first attempts to make these mosaics of semiprecious stone or "of gems," as Vasari describes them fittingly. There is, for example, a table, now in Florence's Museum of Mineralogy, that belonged to a large cabinet Bernardo Buontalenti intended for Ferdinando I. Thin sections of such semi-precious stones as jasper, lapis lazuli, heliotrope, carnelian, agate, and chalcedony were cut into rectangles, circles, almond shapes, or lozenges and inserted into geometrical grids enclosed by strips of silver or gilt copper on a background generally of ebony or, in the case of the lost table worked on by Bernardino di Porfirio, "Oriental alabaster." The influence of ancient Roman mosaics determined the arrangement of the inlays, which are distinguished by the direct matching of the stones, combined in fantastic geometrical figures or in enchanting, naturalistic compositions including flowers and animals.

The years of Cardinal Ferdinando

While Francesco was to be successor to the government of the grand duchy, Ferdinando was to receive his cardinal's hat in Rome in 1563. After having resided in Rome for several years at the Palazzo di Firenze, the Florentine embassy in the Campo di Marzo, in 1574 Ferdinando began discussing the purchase of the Villa at Trinità dei Monti with the heirs of Cardinal Ricci. In the following year he moved there, undertaking a series of modifications and structural changes that employed an army of artists, including Bartolomeo Ammannati, who extended the villa, and Jacopo Zucchi, who decorated its rooms. In a biography by Piero Usimbardi, more than one mention is made of Ferdinando's initiatives during his years in Rome and of his manner of life at court. "In Rome, he always kept a numerous household including men of every nation, even from beyond the Alps, and in particular from all the principal cities of Italy. At his table always sat men of notable worth and science, to whom he listened gladly. And for many years did he honorably treat and keep in his house Master Pietro Angeli Bargeo. . . . He treated with honesty and housed in comfortable conditions the patriarch of Antioch, who came to Rome to recognize the Holy See; from him he received fair books about Arabia and Chaldaea, in whose languages he prepared to print the Holy Scriptures, to be sent to those countries." Such accounts indicate that the young cardinal was a careful interpreter of literary and antiquarian culture, perfectly at ease in the contemporary atmosphere of Rome, surrounded by councilors and scholars of the caliber of Pietro Angeli from Barga, known as "il Bargeo," with whom he held learned discourses.

Judging from contemporary accounts, the founders and carpenters were kept extremely busy, and in a short time the villa and its park had taken on a new look, in part due to the ongoing purchase of ancient sculpture, which was set about the halls and garden. The inventory of the Wardrobe dating to those years allows us to document the work of artists the cardinal must have held in high esteem, among them the sculptor Pietro da Barga. His provenance, Barga, gives us reason to suppose that he arrived at the Villa Medici in Pietro Angeli's train, and the little information we have concerning him in documents regarding Ferdinando's court is concentrated in the years between 1576 and 1589.

We know of a series of bronzes in the Bargello, Florence's national museum of sculpture, that he is supposed to have made during his stay at the Villa Medici, and in these he shows his ability to satisfy, with an original understanding of ornamentation, the cardinal's decidedly antiquarian tastes. This series, homogeneous both in size and patina, depicts some of the most famous examples of antique statuary to be found in Roman collections. There are bronzes copies of a Daphnis, Bacchus, and Satyr from the Della Valle collection, later purchased in part by Cardinal Ferdinando; a Laocoön, Antinous, Hercules and Telephus from the courtyard of the Belvedere; and a

Hercules at rest from the Farnese Palace. The group includes a faun and an Andromeda, models for which have yet to be identified, and also Michelangelo's famous *Bacchus,* which stood for a long time in Jacopo Galli's garden in Rome and was purchased by the Medici in 1570–71: by then it had been elevated to the ranks of the most prized marvels of the city. This series is distinguished from other works by Barga in the Bargello by traces of gilding and a greenish patina, a quite original solution probably inspired by a desire to enhance the ornamental character of these small bronzes, which were presumably part of a decorative program. For example, the series of bronzes could have been placed along the front of one of those cabinets of scholarly intent that were extremely common during the second half of the 16th century and were used to house medallions or cameos. It was for a cabinet of this type, decorated by the painter Jacopo Zucchi, that Pietro da Barga made another series of small gilded bronzes that included reductions of two Michelangelo masterpieces, *Dawn* and *Dusk*, from the New Sacristy in the church of San Lorenzo in Florence. Sketchy notes about Cardinal Ferdinando's Wardrobe also show the sculptor engaged in making a crucifix "of ivory and alabaster," "ivory points for making two crucifixes," and, in 1576, he is mentioned as having contributed to the Wardrobe "a shining black stone of Spain." As of now, we cannot trace any works of this kind to his hand, and our information on this sculptor is extremely scanty. A register of payments kept by Ferdinando's administration and dating to 1587–88 allows us to reveal his name, Pietro Simoni, and in 1589 he was still among the "members of His Serene Highness' household."

With the exception of the cabinet bronzes, no other work by Simoni can be linked to the furnishing of the Villa Medici, and it is possible that all the bronzes that turned up at the Uffizi during the second half of the 18th century were sent to Florence immediately after they were made. The inventories, on the other hand, mention several works by Giambologna, such as "a crucifix in metal with ebony cross," or the "three bronze figurines on a base of wood, painted black . . . of which two female figures, one naked in the act of sleeping, and one kneeling with one knee on the ground, one hand to her head and the other at her left breast, with a cloth draped at her feet, and an upright Hercules."

Among the artists at the Roman court during the 1580s we find the goldsmith known as Leonardo Fiammingo (Leonard the Fleming), a refined artist from Antwerp who stayed in Rome for about a decade after having spent time in Augsburg. This goldsmith—whose real name was Leonard Zaerles—was employed above all in the manufacture of bizarre naturalistic jewels, with flowers, animals, precious stones, and baroque pearls, all greatly prized by the cardinal. Even after his departure for Frankfurt in 1588, Zaerles kept up a regular correspondence with the Florentine court, since Ferdinando I, now grand duke, seemed unable to manage without his help and advice concerning making his most precious jewels, such as a stupendous collar, known as the Ferdinando collar, with 5,000 diamonds, which Zaerles designed in Frankfurt. He returned to Florence in 1608 with the sole object of completing this work with his own hands.

The jewels of Eleonora and Maria de' Medici

In 1584 Eleonora, eldest daughter of Grand Duke Francesco I and Joanna of Austria, became the bride of Vincenzo Gonzaga, duke of Mantua. Events preceding the celebration of the wedding took on tones that were, to say the least, picturesque, as the groom, who had already been through one failed marriage with Margherita Farnese, was suspected of being "but little suited for marriage with a virgin maid." In the prenuptial agreement between the two families, the Medici required that the duke undergo a test of virility that would "precede the performance of all other things." The Gonzagas managed to rid themselves of the infamous accusation, although not without difficulty, and the wedding with Francesco's daughter was celebrated with the greatest possible pomp. The princess brought as dowry three hundred thousand scudi, part of which was in jewels. Apparently Cardinal Ferdinando himself chose and arranged for the manufacture of the precious dowry by his most trusted goldsmith, Leonard Zaerles.

The chest in which they were placed was of no less value. A detailed plan of the container remains along with a list of the jewels and their respective places in external drawers and in secret interior compartments (see inventory on page 233). The structure, primarily of ebony, had geometrical decorations in bamboo on its sides and back. The cover and interior facing, on which the little drawers opened, were decorated with engraved openwork silver appliqués, and in the central portion was a miniature painted on copper with the Judgment of Paris. A mirror was set on the inside of the top door. This rare surviving design for a piece of 16th-century furniture leads us to a further description of the cabinet in Cardinal Ferdinando's inventory, where it is attributed to Leonardo Fiammingo (Zaerles), here referred to as an engraver: "An ebony cabinet covered with flowers, outlined on four sides with silver thread, the bottom inside panel inlaid with leaves of silver and the top panel, which opens like a cover, inlaid with leaves of silver, and in the middle a sphere of rock crystal, and on the front of the drawers there are festoons and swags, and silver cartouches, and four harpies, and the central door is covered by a composition with small figures and ornamentation in silver, made by Master Leonardo Fiammingo, engraver."

The duchess arrived in Mantua in April 1584, accompanied by Cardinal Ferdinando, and was greeted by the noble ladies of the city. The Gonzaga family, too, tried their best not to seem wanting in jewels. Belisario Vinta, Francesco's secretary, wrote from Mantua on April 30, 1584: "The Serene bride, before entering the city, halted and rested at the Palazzo del Te, received there by the Marchesa del Vasto in the company of other ladies and gentlewomen. A large collation was prepared, and My Lord the Duke passed by the Palazzo del Te in his carriage to meet her, and having embraced her and kissed her tenderly, took up into his carriage the Lord Cardinal de' Medici, and conducted him to his palace in the city. . . . My Lord the Prince also visited her at the Palazzo del Te and presented her with a headdress of pearls, diamonds, and rubies to wear like a crown, and My Lord Duke sent her a necklace of pearls, diamonds, and rubies, with a pendant jewel and three very large pear-shaped pearls, striking in appearance, which they say is worth sixty-five thousand scudi."

Eleonora, it appears, had inherited the family passion for jewels, and it seems that shortly after her arrival in Mantua she enquired whether these gentlefolk had "fair pearls, and in what quantity." They replied that they had, but not as many as those in her possession, and that these were already all pledged to "Madama Serenissima." In 1600, Ferdinando arranged the marriage by proxy of Maria, Eleonora's sister, to Henry IV of France. Her dowry appeared immense in the eyes of the French court. In biographies the wedding is recorded as an exceptional spectacle, and the glittering ship on which the queen traveled with her entourage was filled with jewels. Among the precious possessions listed in the inventory of 1609–10 (F. L. Bruel, 1908) are a number of pieces stated to have come from Florence, a large enameled pendant, for example, with a showy diamond and numerous smaller stones, or a pair of gold bracelets decorated with many diamonds and pearls. The brilliant given her by Ferdinando is supposed to have been the one valued at 150,000 lire that "she wore upon her breast on the day her marriage to King Henry IV was ratified in Lyons."

The grand duke's treasure, from the Tribuna to the Sala di Madama

After the death of Francesco in October 1587, his brother Ferdinando resigned as cardinal and became the head of the grand duchy. The humanist Pietro Angeli was among the assistants from his Roman years who accompanied him to Florence. Emilio de' Cavalieri was also called to Florence from Rome, and in September 1588 became superintendent of all the workshops that had been united at the Uffizi since 1586, the so-called Gallery of Works that Ferdinando ran like a factory. Among the most important goldsmiths was Odoardo Vallet, the Frenchman mentioned as having been at court as early as 1588 and known to have made a splendid mount for a rock-crystal vase. Michele Mazzafirri, previously in Francesco's service, was mostly engaged during these years in minting coins. To him we owe a great many gold medallions that Ferdinando had made after his arrival in Florence bearing his portrait, his device depicting a swarm of bees, and the motto MAJESTATE TANTUM. Angeli and Emilio de' Cavalieri provided design motifs for the reverse of gold medallions, but we are not certain these were ever used.

As to works in semiprecious stone, interest seems to have been principally in mosaics, while sculpted vases became less and less frequent. The enormous quantity of vases that Francesco assembled had almost all been placed in the Tribuna, which represented the essence of his taste as a collector, and Ferdinando seems to have wished to impose his own ideas on this room too. The most immediate demonstration of this is seen in the creation of a "new cabinet" planned in 1588 by Bernardo Buontalenti for the Tribuna that appears as almost completed in the inventory made the following year. This was placed close to the octagonal cabinet that the same architect had designed for Francesco. The two sumptuous pieces of furniture, inlaid with semiprecious stones, held some true treasures: Francesco's a large quantity of gold and silver medallions, Ferdinando's cameos, unmounted precious gems, and curios of various kinds listed in detail in the later inventory of the Tribuna dated 1704. The relief panels in Florence's Museo degli Argenti bearing Francesco's "Acts," for which the models had been provided by Giambologna, were cast in gold by Cesare Targone and never placed, as planned, in his cabinet, which stood in the center of the Tribuna. It was Ferdinando who used the lunettes for his cabinet, so that the celebration of the most important public works performed by Francesco merged with Gaffurri's gold oval depicting Cosimo I's monument with the Piazza della Signoria in the background. The front of the new cabinet was a sort of dynastic apologia in which Ferdinando, carved in effigy on the top of the piece, appears above an arch of yellow jasper.

Ferdinando had placed things of his own among the nucleus of objects on the shelves and in the wardrobes: the greatly prized antique turquoise head of Tiberius, mounted in gold by Antonio Gentili da Faenza, and a famous uncut diamond purchased in Rome in 1601. However, it was Francesco's mark that remained indelible in the grand duke's *Wunderkammer* in the mystic atmosphere of the place that recalled the melancholy prince and the phantasmagorical collection of his objects, ranging from the precious to the bizarre.

During the 18th century the Tribuna still maintained the atmosphere and fascination of the late 16th century. It impressed travelers and remained a model for foreign collectors. It was, however, during those years that the progressive dismantling of one of the most exceptional exhibition complexes of all time was carried out. A strict system was put into effect, and the materials in the Uffizi were divided into categories and periods during the period of Lorraine rule, and whatever no longer matched contemporary taste was removed. In this reforming atmosphere the two cabinets from the Tribuna also suffered. Francesco's, which was in the Sala di Madama during the early 17th century, was moved to the Pitti Palace, while Ferdinando's went to the new Royal Museum of Physics. The value of the materials attracted attention to many pieces, various gold mounts were smuggled out, and innumerable objects were sold. Among the most serious losses was a group of sculptures in silver based on models by Giambologna, including a series showing the Labors of Hercules. The sculptor had, in fact, created a cycle of twelve pieces for Francesco I, of which only seven appear to have been cast in silver. All but one were placed in 1589 on the shelves of the Tribuna, and the remaining piece must have been left in the Wardrobe. During the 17th century the statues were removed, and at the start of the 18th century they were used to decorate three sumptuous display cases Cosimo III had built to contain his collection of ambers and ivories. In 1726 the custodian of the Gallery, Francesco Bianchi, was also given the piece that had not previously been placed in the Tribuna. The opulent decoration of the display cases included two other silver statuettes that had been removed from the Tribuna: a satyr holding a lantern and a silver version of another famous Giambologna work: the *Night Fisherman*.

At the close of the 18th century, the three display cases were described as follows: "One display case with a chestnut frame veneered in jacaranda . . . with six crystals and four bronze figures lying on top, coated with silver, all adorned with various carvings and gilded festoons, with ten small twigs of coral spreading apart at the top . . . above at the top of the frontispiece, a rough mined nugget of emerald, in which can be seen many small emeralds and one as large as a nut, hexagonal, embraced by a silver crab in relief, which is inside two shells also in silver, held by two tritons in full relief that appear to be in the sea, the whole thing in silver . . . two showcases with a chestnut frame veneered in jacaranda . . . above which showcases are distributed the following figures: one group of figures in cast silver by Giambologna, which depicts Hercules fighting the Centaur . . . a similar figure in cast silver made by the same, which depicts Hercules with the wild boar on his shoulders . . . a similarly cast group in silver depicting a kneeling satyr holding an antique lantern with both hands . . . a group of two figures in the same cast silver made by the aforementioned depicting the might of Hercules killing Cacus, with the club lying on the ground . . . a cast silver figure depicting a night hunter with birds tied at his belt, a cap on his head, and an iron club in his right hand and night light in his left, which can be raised and moved, similarly of silver, all worked with bas-reliefs and arabesques, with a silver stand with grass and birds in bas-relief . . . one as above cast in silver by Gio. Bologna [Giambologna] representing Hercules clothed in the lion's skin and upon his shoulders a globe representing the celestial sphere enameled in many colors . . . one silver figure cast by the same . . . representing naked Hercules killing the Hydra . . . A group of silver figures . . . of Hercules overcoming Antaeus . . . a cast silver figure . . . of Hercules in the act of killing the lion . . . one as above in silver-plated bronze representing the naked Hercules carrying the club on his shoulder." The Giambologna groups were sent to be polished in 1790, and on October 7, 1797, they appear to have been removed from the Uffizi and put back in the Wardrobe; from here they were handed over to the superintendent of the Office for Revisions and Audits, with "suitable orders in regard thereto," and from that moment all trace of them has been lost.

When the marriage of Ferdinando I to Christine of Lorraine was celebrated in 1589, the collections were further enriched by another extremely important group of precious objects, which the grand duchess had inherited from her grandmother, Catherine de Médicis. This consisted mostly of gold-mounted vases in semiprecious stones, of which some examples—such as the rock-crystal cup engraved with spirals and foliage—still survive. This has been linked to the activity of Gasparo Miseroni, a

Milanese lapidary, and has a lid of pierced gold plate bearing the monogram of Henry II of France ambiguously entwined with that of Catherine, or of Diane de Poitiers; it is usually designated the cup of Diane de Poitiers. Among the objects of greatest importance to arrive in Florence with Christine of Lorraine was a casket with engraved crystal inserts made by Valerio Belli between 1530 and 1532 for Clement VII and presented by him in 1533 to Francis I of France on the occasion of the marriage of Catherine to Henry II. Christine of Lorraine's taste in collecting seems perfectly in harmony with that of the Florentine court: the so-called Sala di Madama, or "Room of Idols," in the Uffizi, which contained her collection, appears to be closely comparable to the Tribuna. Here, numerous "idols," that is to say antique and modern bronzes, alternated with Catherine de Médicis' vases, miniatures, cameos, and such curios as the "tiny horse in mother-of-pearl trimmed with gold," "a gold pen with green enameled vine leaves and a white holder," "a round gold mirror, whose case, in which are five heads of French princes in miniature, opens like a box." The list of her jewels, drawn up in 1609 with values by Odoardo Vallet and Giovan Battista Sassi, also describes a large number of pieces that, in many cases, recall Zaerles's naturalistic creations. There are, in fact, eight pieces in the shape of an S, each with nine diamonds, made by him, but there is a prevalence of jewels of international taste produced by the grand duke's goldsmiths at the end of the 1500s. Among these are such curious objects as a "toothpick with falcon's claw trimmed in gold" and numerous gifts made by the grand duke, including a "jewel engraved on its inside on a ruby placed over a pearl" and a ring "with a flat ruby, the one with which the Grand Duke wed Madama." Certain jewels are noted to have originated in the French court; for example, a gold ring with a large diamond received from the king of France as a gift at Marseilles and a large gold flower, with 140 diamonds, sent by the queen of France.

Cast brass vessel engraved and damascened in gold and silver. Persia, late 15th–early 16th century. Height 5 inches. Florence, Museo Nazionale del Bargello.

This vessel has inscriptions in Arabic on its neck and in Persian on its body. It comes from the group of Islamic metal objects listed in the collections of the early grand dukes. Cosimo I kept objects of this kind in the Calliope Cabinet in the Palazzo Vecchio. From 1589 onward the vessel is listed in the Tribuna of the Uffizi.

Spherical perfume-burner. Syria, 14th century. Diameter 5 inches. Florence, Museo Nazionale del Bargello.

This perfume-burner, in pierced and engraved brass, damascened with silver and gold, belongs to a group of Islamic metal objects originating from the early Medici collections, probably even from that of Lorenzo the Magnificent, who owned about one hundred such pieces, half of Italian manufacture but inspired by Oriental models. This perfume-burner reappears in the Calliope Cabinet in the Palazzo Vecchio in the mid-16th century, together with a large selection of small bronzes and curios of various types that Cosimo I assembled there. In 1589, we find it among the objects brought back to the Tribuna of the Uffizi.

Below: Porphyry Venus and Cupid, by Pier Maria Serbaldi (ca. 1455–ca. 1520). Early 16th century. Height 10¼ inches. Florence, Museo degli Argenti.

Venus is shown holding Eros by one arm; he has set his quiver on the ground, and possibly he was originally shown holding an arrow in each hand. With her left hand the goddess holds a bird that rests on a pedestal on which the name of the sculptor is engraved in Greek. Known as Tagliacarne ("flesh-cutter"), the sculptor was noted by Vasari as having given a new impulse to the working porphyry.

Opposite: Onyx cameo showing Cosimo I de' Medici and his family, by Giovanni Antonio de' Rossi (Milan 1517–Rome after 1575). 7¼ x 6½ inches. Florence, Museo degli Argenti.

Vasari mentions this cameo as one of the most important works of the Milanese artist: "along with the fair engraving and relief works which he has done in certain engravings, he hath made for Duke Cosimo de' Medici an extremely large cameo, that is to say one third of an arm, and of equal width, in which he hath carved from the center upwards two figures; that is, His Excellency and the Most Illustrious Lady Duchess Leonora, his wife, who both hold with their hands a tondo, within which Florence. Around them, depicted in life, are Prince Don Francesco with Cardinal Don Giovanni, Don Grazia, and Don Arnando [Garzia and Ferdinando], and Don Pietro, together with Donna Isabella and Donna Lucrezia, all their children; a more marvelous work in cameo, or a larger one, is not to be seen." In its present state, the cameo seems incomplete, since the bottom edge is clearly broken.

Above: Onyx cameo with portrait of Philip II of Spain (1527–98), in a mount of enameled gold. 1½ x 1⅓ inches. Florence, Museo degli Argenti.

The reverse of this cameo shows a portrait of Don Carlos (1545–68). It was acquired from the Milanese lapidary Gasparo Miseroni, who may have been only an intermediary; the cameo may not be of his hand. As to the date at which it was made, various hypotheses range from 1550 to 1557. The cameo comes from the collection of Eleonora de Toledo.

Below: Lapis-lazuli vase. $6\frac{1}{2}$ x $14\frac{1}{3}$ x $9\frac{1}{2}$ inches. Florence, Museo degli Argenti.

This single-handled vase is made from a large block of lapis lazuli; sculptured gadrooning spreads out from the base, while the handle is in the form of a dolphin surmounted by a shell. The court goldsmith Hans Domes was commissioned to make a gold mount, but never completed it and returned the vase to the Wardrobe in 1599 with an incomplete, roughly sketched mask.

Bottom: Heliotrope cup, by Gasparo Miseroni. $3\frac{1}{3}$ x $10\frac{1}{4}$ x $4\frac{3}{4}$ inches. Florence, Museo degli Argenti.

This cup, carved from a block of heliotrope, is in the form of a shell wrapped in the tentacles of a monster, the head of which can be seen on the lip. It has been identified as a piece bought by Cosimo I in 1557 for 300 scudi from the Milanese lapidary Gasparo Miseroni, an expert in this type of work, in whose workshop shell-shaped vases with twining monsters formed a recurrent motif.

Right: Steel and gilt-copper parade helmet. Italy, ca. 1470–1570. 21 inches. Florence, Museo Nazionale del Bargello.

This helmet is mentioned in the inventories of the grand ducal armory from the beginning of the 17th century. The piece is interesting for its splendid 15th-century crest of an eagle's head applied to a simple helmet flanked by two gilt-copper wings of modest quality but great ornamental effect.

Overleaf: Lapis-lazuli flask with gold and gilt-copper mounts, inscribed FM on the foot with the crown of the grand duke and the date 1583, by Bernardo Buontalenti (1531–1608) and Jacques Bylivelt (1550–1603). Height 16 inches. Florence, Museo degli Argenti.

The form is based on an extant drawing by Buontalenti. The tapered flask's smooth surface is broken only by the presence of sculpted acanthus leaves at the base and by the bodies of two harpies, with necks and heads in enameled gold, that act as handles (detail on page 79). Other ornaments on the side of the vase, seen in Buontalenti's drawing, were omitted by the carver, who simply delineated the shoulder and the base of the neck with molded stripes for emphasis. This piece figures among those vases that were tampered with in the Gallery during the second half of the 18th century. Upon an inspection to calculate the extent of damage, the goldsmith Cosimo Siries stated that the original gold chain had been replaced by the present gilt-copper one.

Left: Rock-crystal vase in the shape of a bird, mounted in enameled gold, from the Sarachi workshop. Height 12½ inches. Florence, Museo degli Argenti.

The body of this bird-shaped vase is decorated with two engraved scenes showing wolf and boar hunts based on designs from engravings by Etienne Delaune. The gold mounts are decorated with naturalistic motifs in black enamel as frequently seen in the pieces originating from the Sarachi workshop, which produced a number of articles for the Florentine court for the marriage of Ferdinando I in 1589. Among these, it is certain, was the table basin known as the "Galley." It is possible that the vase illustrated here was made for the same occasion; it figures, along with the basin, in the Tribuna of the Uffizi from 1589.

Right: Lapis-lazuli cup with enameled gold mounts, by Giovanni Battista Cervi (1532–86). 3 x 6 inches. Florence, Museo degli Argenti.

This cup, carved in the shape of a snail, is embellished with a large enameled gold handle in the form of a snake that was completed by the goldsmith Giovanni Battista Cervi in 1576. It forms one of the rare surviving examples of early semiprecious-stone carving at the Florentine court. Comparison with the gold and silver vases kept in the Wardrobe dating from halfway through the century shows that shapes and decoration already experimented with in precious metals were also adopted for semiprecious-stone vessels. The shell or boat shape, decorated with gadrooning, masks, borders, and harpies, also forms a recurrent repertoire for lapidary works. From 1589 onward the cup is mentioned as being situated in the Tribuna of the Uffizi.

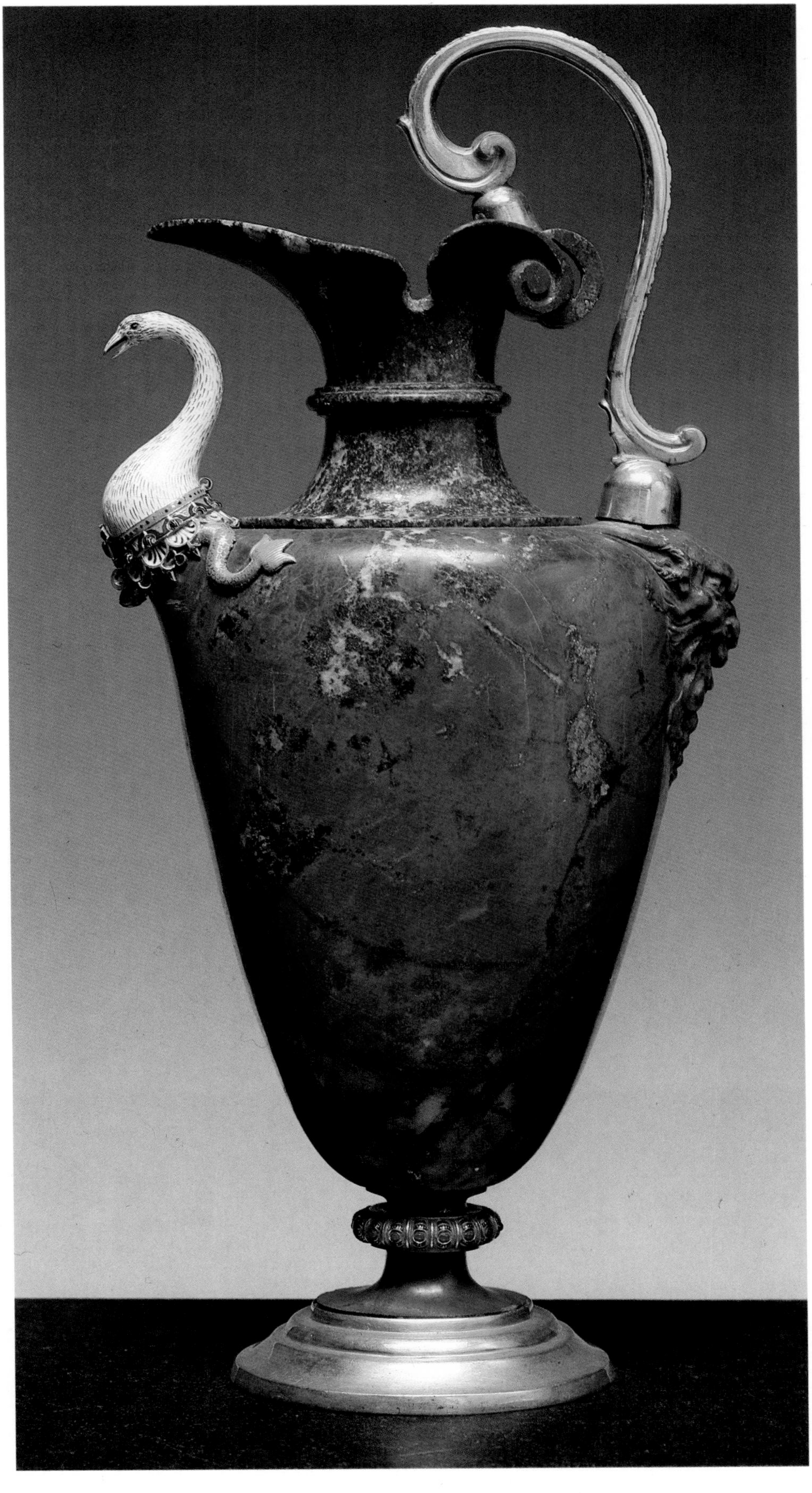

Lapis-lazuli pitcher mounted in enameled gold and gilt bronze, by Hans Domes (active 1563–1601). Height 10¾ inches. Florence, Museo degli Argenti.

The manufacture of this piece, made from three pieces of lapis lazuli of varying quality, can be traced back to the workshops in the Casino di San Marco. The mounts were completed by the court goldsmith Hans Domes in 1578. Along with the enameled gold shoulder ornament in the shape of a peacock, the mounts consisted of a large golden scroll handle with a dragon's head, and a golden foot. The latter, however, were removed when precious objects were dismantled in the Gallery during the second half of the 17th century, an act for which the custodian Giuseppe Bianchi was considered responsible. On this occasion the lip of the vase was broken in order to remove the handle, which was then replaced by the present one.

Jasper vase in the form of a hydra mounted in enameled gold set with pearls, diamonds, and rubies. Height 13⅓ inches. Florence, Museo degli Argenti.

This vase was assembled from twelve pieces of jasper. The heads of the hydra are fixed to its oblong body by means of an enameled gold mask (detail overleaf); the curled and scaly tail is fixed with a strip of gold. The rim of the vase is also edged with a band of gold with small cast heads in which diamonds are embedded. On the top of the lid stands a gold statuette of Hercules (opposite). The production of this vase has been traced to the workshop of Annibale Fontana, but the suggestion that Michele Mazzafirri was involved in the making of the mounts is erroneous, having been based on payments made to him for casting the Labors of Hercules. The documents in question refer to the casting of the Giambologna sculptures.

Above: Jasper vase in the form of a hydra mounted in enameled gold set with pearls, diamonds, and rubies. Height 13 1/3 inches. Florence, Museo degli Argenti.

Detail of the mask holding the heads of the hydra on the vase illustrated on the preceding page.

Overleaf, bottom left: Agate cup with enameled gold mounts and marble base. Height 3 1/3 inches. Florence, Museo degli Argenti.

This cup with lobed body was considered an object of antique manufacture. Its mounts were commissioned from the goldsmith Hans Domes in 1588 and included, along with the serpent-shaped enameled gold handles, a gold circle at its foot, which was replaced later by the present marble base.

***Overleaf, top left:* Lapis-lazuli cup with chased and enameled gold mount, by Hans Domes (active 1563–1601). 4 x 8¼ x 5 inches. Florence, Museo degli Argenti.**

This tazza in the shape of an incense-boat with gadrooning carved on its body shows one of the most frequently recurring forms in the grand ducal production of the second half of the 16th century. In 1589 the goldsmith Hans Domes was paid to make the splendid enameled gold mount, which was originally a large handle in the form of a serpent with the Medici arms in the middle. The handle was attached to the edge of the lip by means of a still visible enameled mask (above). A gold border decorates the pedestal.

***Overleaf, right:* Rock-crystal jug with enameled gold mounts. 7¾ x 7¾ inches. Florence, Museo degli Argenti.**

This jug, with two raised handles in the shape of volutes and two spouts, is decorated with engraved foliage and scrollwork and with gadrooning around the base. The original gold mount on the foot has been tampered with. The somewhat unusually shaped jug, which can be compared with another piece in the Louvre dating from the end of the 16th century, comes from the group of objects in the Tribuna of the Uffizi.

Opposite top: Rock-crystal vase in the shape of a dragon with enameled gold mounts, from the Sarachi workshop. Height 9 inches. Florence, Museo degli Argenti.

The body of this vase is engraved with plant motifs, the head and tail of the dragon act as handles; the back of the animal is formed by the cover, to which wings are fixed. The manufacture of crystal vases in the shape of animals, dragons, birds, and fish was characteristic of the workshops of Milanese lapidaries; examples of an extremely high quality come from the workshop of the Sarachi brothers, to whom this vase has been attributed, as well as from those of other Milanese artisans operating in Florence at the Casino di San Marco.

Right: Rock-crystal flask with gold mounts. Height 9¾ inches. Florence, Museo degli Argenti.

The scenes engraved on the body of this vase depict on one side Orpheus among the Muses (detail overleaf) and on the other the Judgment of Midas; at its neck two lion's heads in high relief hold gold rings to which a chain is attached. Both in decoration and shape this flask has certain similarities with works known to have come from the Sarachi workshop that are preserved in Munich and Dresden. From 1589 on it is recorded as being in the Tribuna of the Uffizi.

Opposite, bottom left: Incised rock-crystal vase in the form of a fish with enameled gold mounts. 8½ x 11¾ inches. Florence, Museo degli Argenti.

Fish, birds, dragons, and other imaginary animals were created in the workshops of the Milanese lapidaries, who were expert in working crystal, and various specimens of this genre show up in the cabinets of the Tribuna of the Uffizi in 1589.

Opposite, bottom right: Rock-crystal vase in the shape of a fish with cut and enameled gold mounts. Height 7¾ inches. Florence, Museo degli Argenti.

This fish-shaped vase, whose body is engraved with plant motifs, rests on a pedestal made up of two entwined dolphins. In 1589 it was in the Tribuna of the Uffizi along with another similar piece, now also in the Museo degli Argenti. During the second half of the 18th century, it was sent, along with other vases, to the Royal Museum of Physics.

Above: Rock-crystal flask with gold mounts. Height 9¾ inches. Florence, Museo degli Argenti.

Detail of the scene showing Orpheus among the Muses incised on the body of a flask illustrated in its entirety on the preceding page.

Opposite: Turquoise mask with diamonds and silver-gilt and enameled mounts. Height 14 inches. Florence, Museo degli Argenti.

This is a 17th-century imitation an of exotic mask. The mount, in the form of a tree, acts as a pedestal; two oak branches frame the mask. The symbolism of oak (rovere in Italian) leads to the conclusion that the piece belonged to the collections of Vittoria della Rovere.

Jade mask, Teotihuacán art, A.D. 250–600. 6 x 6¾ x 2 inches. Florence, Museo degli Argenti.

This mask, used for funeral or ritual purposes, is one of the most interesting examples from a group of pre-Columbian objects in the grand duke's collections. According to old photographs, the eyes were originally painted white with pupils made, in all probability, of discs of polished obsidian; the teeth still bear traces of paint. This piece can be identified as the "mask in green marble with painted eyes and teeth" in a list of the objects from the Casino di San Marco that were handed over to Francesco Bianchi, custodian of the Uffizi, in 1723.

Ivory hunting horn with gilt-metal mounts, southern Italy, 11th century. 17¾ inches. Florence, Museo Nazionale del Bargello.

This hunting horn, made from seven pieces of ivory, is divided by bands of stylized engraved animals. Similar examples had already been noted in the Wardrobe during the reign of Cosimo I, one of which, in ivory, was said to have been "worked with figures, but without trimming."

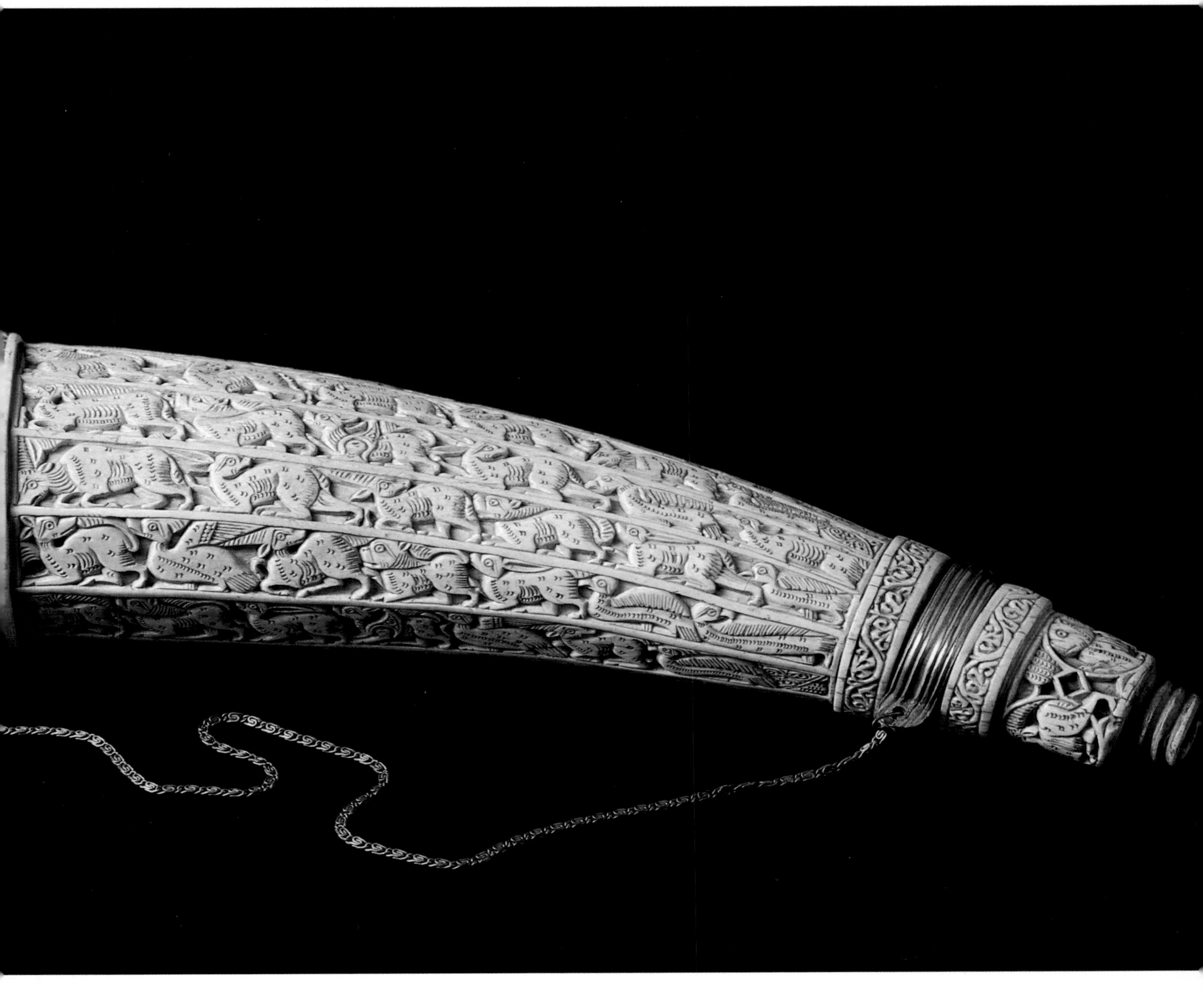

Rock-crystal table basin with mounts of enameled gold, cameos, emeralds, rubies, and gilt bronze, from the Sarachi workshop. 15 x 15¾ x 13 inches. Florence, Museo degli Argenti.

Several biblical scenes can be distinguished on the body of this vase, decorated with engraved vines: the gathering of the manna and Moses drawing water from the rock. A sea monster with raised arms is sculpted on the cover (opposite, detail seen from above), and a crenellated tower is fixed on the stern between two dolphins. The gold handles are shaped like harpies, and an enameled gold band with inset cameos and emeralds forms a border for the cover. The piece, the presence of which is recorded from 1589 in the Tribuna of the Uffizi, was made by the Sarachi brothers on the occasion of the marriage of Ferdinando I to Christine of Lorraine.

Above left: Rock-crystal cup with silver mounts, by Giovan Battista Metellino (active end 16th–early 17th century). Height 12 inches. Florence, Museo degli Argenti.

This cup, in the shape of a shell, rests on the head of a dolphin, the body of which forms the handle. The silver pedestal is decorated with palmettes engraved and chased. The piece can be associated with works produced in the workshop of the Milanese artist Giovan Battista Metellino, to whose hand are attributed several drawings. A similar example is in Dresden.

Above right: Rock-crystal vase with gold mounts. Height 8 inches. Florence, Museo degli Argenti.

By the strange shape of this vase, with the head and neck of a dragon acting as handle and engraving on the surface of the body of the animal, we can attribute this piece to the Milanese workshops of the mid-16th century. Previously the property of Catherine de Médicis, this vase arrived in Florence along with the other objects inherited by Christine of Lorraine.

Opposite: Rock-crystal cup. 13 1/3 x 7 1/4 inches. Florence, Museo degli Argenti.

This cup, in the shape of a lobed shell, shows the body of a monster partially in relief, on one portion of the rim, and partially engraved on the bottom. The remaining part of the cup is decorated with foliage and scrollwork. An object of Milanese manufacture, the vase shows many similarities with a table basin preserved in Munich and can be traced back to the workshop of Annibale Fontana.

Rock-crystal cup with enameled gold mounts. Height 7¼ inches. Florence, Museo degli Argenti.

This cup, with a scalloped rim, is decorated along its edge with a naturalistic motif that alternates with harpies. On the bottom (detail, opposite) are combats among marine deities alternating with sailing ships. The piece has lost some of its gold mounts, originally formed by a circlet on the base—with eight small baskets of fruit and flowers, of which five still remain—and by splendid handles in the shape of a two-faced winged terminus (detail overleaf). It can be ascribed to Milanese masters of the second half of the 16th century.

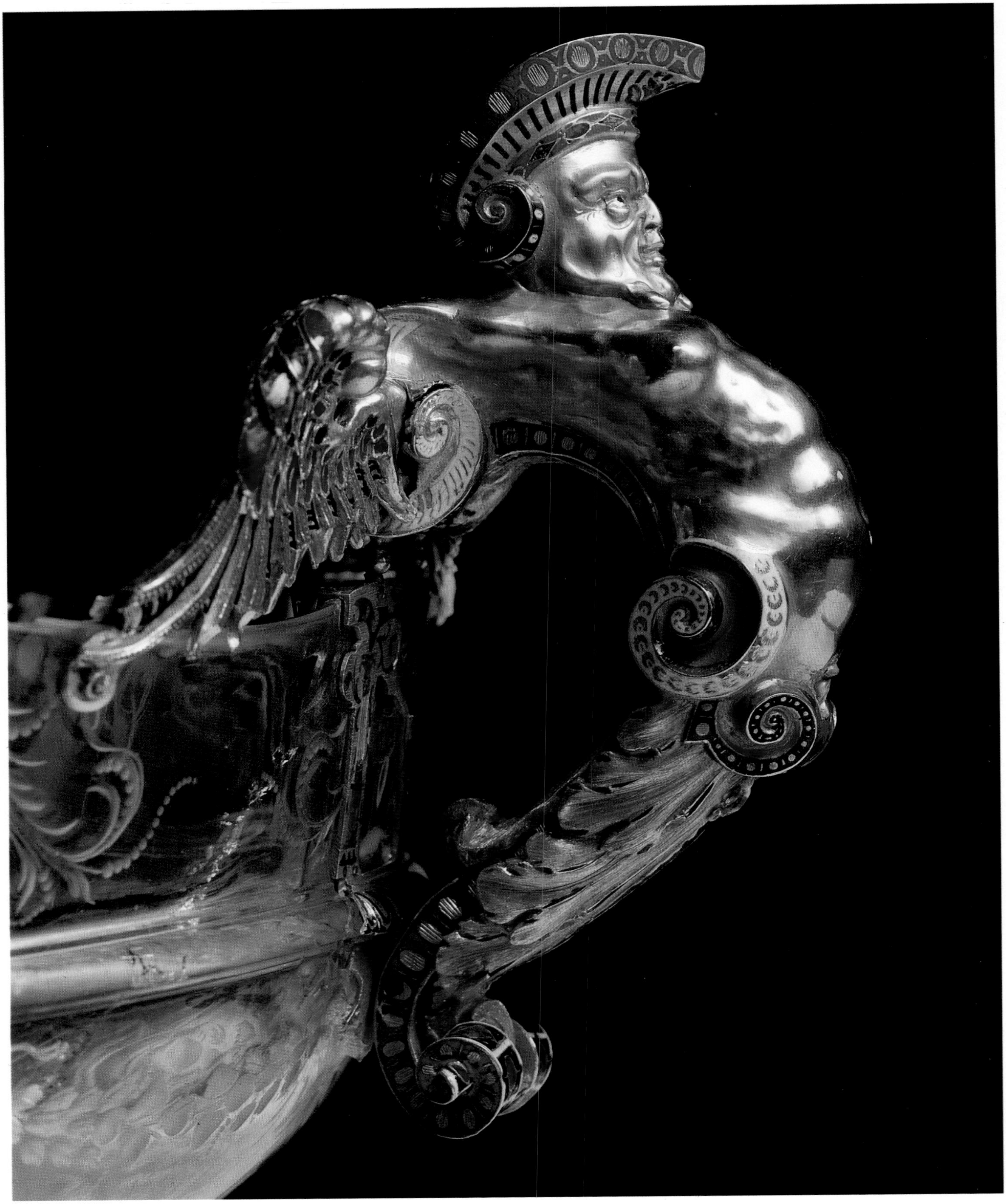

Lapis-lazuli salt cellar with silver-gilt mounts. Height 7 inches. Florence, Museo degli Argenti.

This piece, with a pyramidal top, is decorated with gadrooning and is one of the most original pieces invented by lapidaries working in the grand ducal workshops. Its original mounts were tampered with during the 18th century when it stood in a cabinet in the Tribuna of the Uffizi.

Rock-crystal flask with enameled gold and silver-gilt mounts. Height 10⅓ inches. Florence, Museo degli Argenti.

This hexagonal flask is decorated with foliage, grotesques, and festoons; in the lower band, figures of Bacchus, Pomona, and Minerva can be identified. It entered the grand duke's collections along with the inheritance of Catherine de Médicis and passed to her granddaughter Christine of Lorraine in 1589.

Above: Rock-crystal table basin with gold mounts and garnets, from the Sarachi workshop. Height 5 inches. Florence, Museo degli Argenti.

On the body of the piece are engraved foliage and scrollwork and the body of a dragon, whose head, in full relief, is fixed to the rim. The piece can be associated with the type of table basin known as "galley" basins, manufactured in the Milanese workshop of the Sarachi brothers (one of the most elegant examples is illustrated on page 94).

Opposite: Rock-crystal jug with silver mounts. Height 12¾ inches. Florence, Museo degli Argenti.

This jug with raised handle is decorated with garlands and festoons of fruit and flowers engraved on the shoulder and with acanthus leaves on the lower part of the body; a silver mask connects the handle to the body. The piece belongs to the group from the Tribuna of the Uffizi.

Rock-crystal plate engraved with Noah's Ark and mounted in silver gilt, by Giovanni dei Bernardi. Diameter 12 inches. Florence, Museo degli Argenti.

This plate, with an attached rim engraved with gadrooning, has in the center a scene depicting Noah's Ark (detail, opposite) and surrounding it figures of the Four Winds with various birds flying in toward the center. It comes from the inheritance of Catherine de Médicis and was bequeathed by her to her granddaughter Christine of Lorraine.

Above: Incised crystal cup with cover and foot in enameled gold and rubies. 3 x 3 x 4⅓ inches. Florence, Museo degli Argenti.

This cup with its volute-shaped handle is decorated with a frieze of incised vegetal motifs below the lip and by gadrooning around the lower part. Its splendid mounts, a strip at the base and a cover of enameled gold with naturalistic motifs, are still perfectly preserved.

Right: Emerald-paste cup with enameled gold mounts, attributed to Gasparo Miseroni (active ca. 1550–75). Height 3⅓ inches. Florence, Museo degli Argenti.

The head of a sea monster sculpted in full relief acts here as a handle, the tentacles being carved on the body. This piece can be associated with the Milanese workshop of Gasparo Miseroni.

Heliotrope cup with cover and base of enameled gold, French workmanship. Height 4¼ inches. Florence, Museo degli Argenti.

This simple cup with its smooth surface is made valuable by an elaborate cover in engraved and enameled gold set with rubies; its ring-handle is in the form of a snake. It belongs to the group of objects that came to Florence in the inheritance of Catherine de Médicis. *A detail of the cover can be seen on page 56.*

Rock-crystal cup with enameled gold mounts, by Gasparo Miseroni (active ca. 1550–75). Height 9 inches. Florence, Museo degli Argenti.

The body of this piece is decorated with engraved leaves and foliage, while on the lower part of the bowl acanthus leaves are carved in relief. The baluster pedestal is undecorated. The work, which can associated with the production of the Milanese artist Gasparo Miseroni, belonged to Catherine de Médicis, and it was in France that it was embellished with the cover in pierced gold openwork, bearing the monograms HC for Henry II of France and Catherine de Médicis. However, the monogram is sometimes interpreted as relating to Diane de Poitiers, with whom the piece is generally associated. (The cover is shown below, and a detail appears in the frontispiece.)

Jasper flask with pearls, rubies, onyx cameo, and mounts in enameled gold, attributed to the Sarachi workshop. Height 11 inches. Florence, Museo degli Argenti.

This jasper flask is sculpted in the shape of a double shell joined along the edge by a strip of gold that was originally set with pearls and emeralds. A cameo showing the head of a blackamoor is mounted at the center (detail, opposite), and there is evidence of another cameo having been set on the opposite side. The work arrived in Florence with the objects owned by Christine of Lorraine.

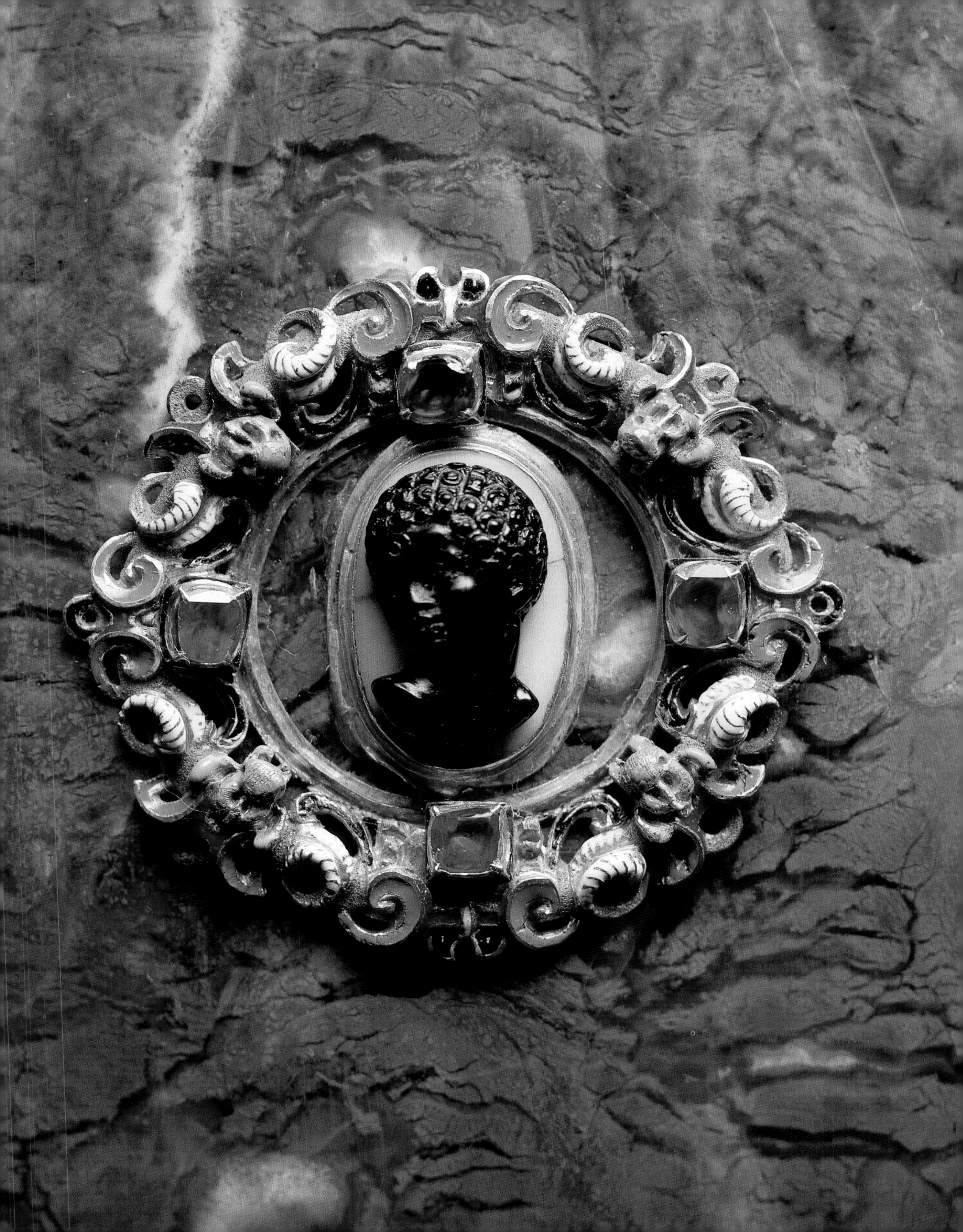

Opposite: Rock-crystal jug with enameled gold and gilt-metal mounts, by Annibale Fontana. 15½ x 7¼ inches. Florence, Museo degli Argenti.

The body of this jug is made from three pieces of engraved crystal: hunting scenes appear in the upper part; at the center, in rectangular frames, can be seen figures of Neptune, Juno, Ceres, and Vulcan; on the lower part are ovals with landscapes. The original crystal foot was tampered with during the 18th century.

Below: Dendritic lapis-lazuli cup with mounts in enameled gold and pearls, from the Miseroni workshop (Milan, second half 16th century). Height 6 inches. Florence, Museo degli Argenti.

The pure lines of this covered cup, without any sculpted decoration, accentuate the decorative effect of the stone, with its bold whitish markings. Forty-three pearls are set along the gold mounts on the edge of the lip and around the foot. The cup is from the inheritance of Catherine de Médicis.

Above: Oriental agate cup with enameled gold mounts. Height 3 1/3 inches, diameter 4 3/4 inches. Florence, Museo degli Argenti.

In view of an ever-increasing interest in the working of stone and in antiquities, even the simplest pieces received serious attention and evaluation. This cup, made of a material that is particularly fascinating due to its ever-changing and subtly honeyed tones, has been embellished with important mounts: an enameled gold rim and handles in the shape of dolphins.

Opposite: Bloodstone goblet with enameled gold mounts. Height 4 3/4 inches. Florence, Museo degli Argenti.

This goblet stands on a baluster pedestal and has on its body a sculptured mask and gadrooning; the enameled gold bands on the rim and foot can be associated with the work of Prague goldsmiths of the second half of the 16th century.

Opposite: Sardonyx vase with enameled gold mounts. Height 5 1/3 inches. Florence, Museo degli Argenti.

This vase has been judged to be an antique work of the 4th century. It has 16th-century, presumably French, mounts. The cover, in chased and enameled gold, set with rubies, lacks the original handle in the shape of a snake, evidence of which can be found in the documents. It joined the Medici collections as part of Christine of Lorraine's treasure.

Above: Bohemian jasper cup with enameled gold mounts. 3 1/4 x 4 1/2 x 3 inches. Florence, Museo degli Argenti.

The oval bowl rests on a baluster pedestal and still has its lively original enameled gold mounts. It comes from the treasury of the Tribuna of the Uffizi, where many small vases, such as this tiny example, were distributed among the cabinets or displayed on shelves.

Above: Jasper vase in the form of a dragon, with mounts of enameled gold, pearls, and rubies, from the Sarachi workshop. Height 8 1/4 inches. Florence, Museo degli Argenti.

This vase, which still has its original mounts, repeats, in jasper, the dragon shape and can be compared with a similar example preserved in Vienna bearing the arms of Archbishop Wolf Dietrich von Raitenau. From 1589, there is evidence of it being in the Tribuna of the Uffizi.

Reliquary of the Flagellation in silver, chalcedony, agate, and rock crystal, attributed to Giovanni Antonio Dosio (1533–post 1610). Height 21 inches. Florence, Treasury of San Lorenzo.

The reliquary, in the shape of a hexagonal temple in silver, rests on a pedestal containing six small drawers, in which three relics are kept, the most important of which is from the post of the Flagellation. Six columns in semiprecious stone rest on pedestals in which crystal tiles are inset. The cupola is adorned with rows of diamond-faceted crystals. At the center, on the raised platform, is represented the scene of the Flagellation (detail, opposite) with figures in silver gilt and Christ in carnelian. An anonymous drawing for the reliquary is in the Uffizi. The piece belonged to Christine of Lorraine; from 1621 on it figures in her chapel at the Pitti Palace, while from 1624 until the second half of the 18th century it was preserved in the Uffizi.

Right: ***Bust of Tiberius, the head in turquoise, with gold and Oriental agate base, by Antonio Gentili da Faenza (1519–1609). Height $8\frac{1}{4}$ inches. Florence, Museo degli Argenti.***

Cardinal Ferdinando commissioned this small portrait of Tiberius in 1580 from the goldsmith Antonio Gentili, who made the gold base decorated with a Medusa's head on the chest. From 1589 onward, the piece figures on the shelves of the Tribuna of the Uffizi, along with many other small precious-stone busts finished in gold and silver that had been put together during those years by the court goldsmiths.

Below: Chalcedony cameo depicting a triumphal procession, set in a gold mount engraved with the words DNICUS ROMANUS F., by Domenico Romano. 2 x 3 inches. Florence, Museo degli Argenti.

The triumphal procession illustrated on this cameo was interpreted at the end of the 17th century as showing the entry of Cosimo I into Siena. The known provenance contradicts this reading. The cameo belonged to the bishop of Viterbo, whose collection was offered for sale to Francesco in 1565 but was purchased only ten years later. The personage on the triumphal carriage has been identified as Philip II of Spain. The scene, carved on a number of planes within the white layer of the chalcedony, demonstrates the skill of Domenico Romano, whose career remains somewhat obscure.

Opposite: Bronze head of Julius Caesar with alabaster toga. Height $8\frac{1}{2}$ inches. Florence, Museo Nazionale del Bargello.

This small portrait in bronze is fixed to an alabaster bust carved from a single block, which also forms the base on which it rests. This work, which comes from the Tribuna of the Uffizi, shows the taste for combining different materials that Francesco I applied to the field of small sculptures.

Opposite: Bust in hyacinth (zircon) and Oriental alabaster with silver-gilt mount. Height 2 1/4 inches. Florence, Museo degli Argenti.

This small sculpture was formed by combining a zircon head and an alabaster bust; the mantle falling from the shoulder and the drapery on the breast are of gilt metal.

Below: Bust of a woman in chalcedony, quince-colored alabaster, and gilt brass. Height 5 inches. Florence, Museo degli Argenti.

This little bust, of ancient inspiration but late 16th-century manufacture, comes from a group of eight placed at the top of the octagonal cabinet designed by Buontalenti for Francesco I and located in the Tribuna of the Uffizi. It still preserves the original mount with the drapery held at the center by a mask.

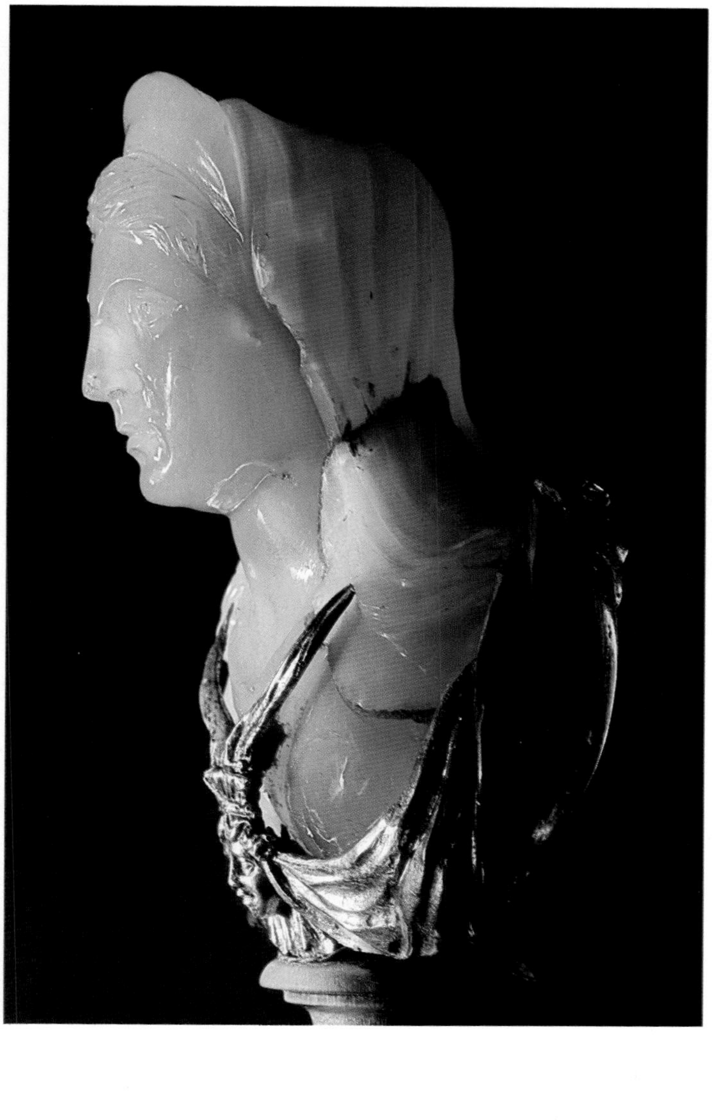

Above: Hyacinth (zircon) bust with gold coiffure, diamonds, and enameled gold mounts. Height 2 1/2 inches. Florence, Museo degli Argenti.

This head and half bust are made out of a single piece of hyacinth, the hair is reproduced in gold, with four small diamonds set in it. The drapery is enameled with white, turquoise, and yellow stripes and is held at the breast by a diamond; the stand is also in gold enameled with flowers. On the back of the bust is a small door made of gold enameled with flowers.

Agate vase with silver-gilt mounts. Height 4¾ inches. Florence, Museo degli Argenti.

The body of this vase is completely sculpted in the form of a spiral and is surmounted by a turned baluster cover. It is mounted in enameled silver-gilt, with handles terminating in dragons' heads.

Lapis-lazuli vase with gold mounts. Height 3¼ inches, diameter 1½ inches. Florence, Museo degli Argenti.

This small vase, decorated with gadrooning on the lower part of the body, is closed by a cover with a small knop and was originally a reliquary or unguent container. Many small vases of this type, carved in semiprecious stones and decorated with precious-metal mounts, show up in the Medici inventories among the display vases of the treasury of the Gallery and among the jewels. They could be used to hold perfumed essences or cosmetics; often encountered during the second half of the 17th century are the so-called perfume belts, composed of a sequence of small vases, in semiprecious stones, containing essences such as amber oil and musk.

Agate vase with enameled gold mounts. Height 2¼ inches. Florence, Museo degli Argenti.

This small, bulbous agate vase has mounts in enameled gold in the form of two dragons that act as handles; they still bear the rings to which a chain must originally have been attached.

Opposite: Agate cup with cover and enameled gold mounts. Height 4½ inches. Florence, Museo degli Argenti.

This covered cup has acanthus leaves carved on the lower part of the bowl, which rests on a spirally fluted pedestal. The mount is in pierced, enameled gold, and the handle of the cover is in the form of a cherub cast in full relief in gold and enameled en ronde bosse.

Jasper cup with mounts in enameled silver gilt. 8 x 8 x 6 inches. Florence, Museo degli Argenti.

This cup was carved from three pieces of jasper and is of an irregular form, rather like a shell embraced by a monster. This bizarre motif, dear to the Milanese lapidary Gasparo Miseroni, is here presented in a vase of German manufacture.

Heliotrope cup with enameled silver mounts. 5 x 3½ x 2¾ inches. Florence, Museo degli Argenti.

This cup, carved from three pieces of heliotrope, is of an irregular form and decorated by incised vegetal motifs and gadrooning. A bizarre detail is the presence of the small carved insect resting on its lip.

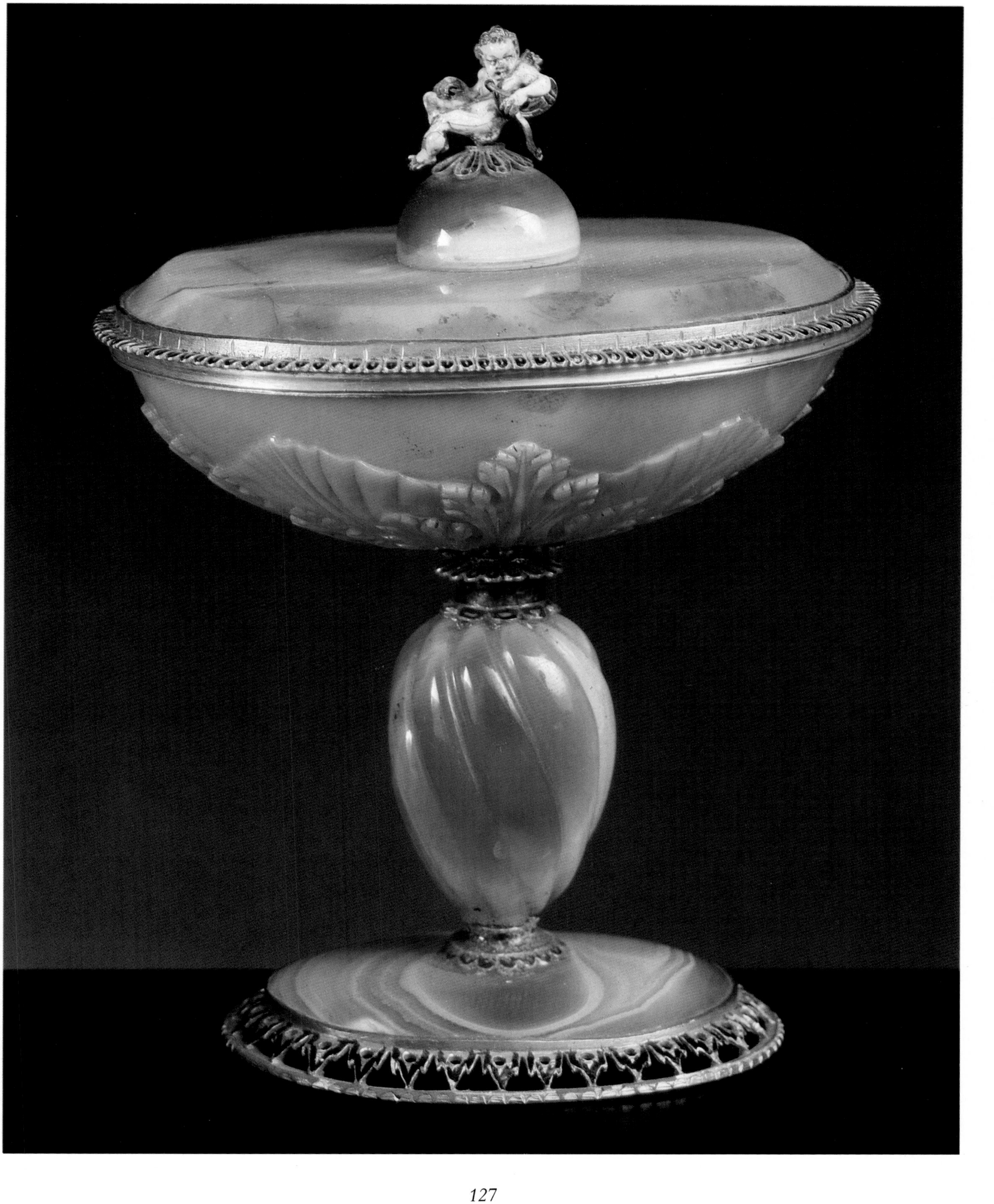

Opposite: Double-nautilus pitcher with mounts of silver gilt, rubies, and turquoises. Flemish, 16th century. Height 12 inches. Florence, Museo degli Argenti.

This piece, made up of two nautilus shells, has extremely elaborate mounts and is encrusted with rubies and turquoises. A snake curls around the dragon-shaped beak and extends up to a small horse's head; another snake acts as a handle to the cover of the spout; and a third is curled around the handle. This piece is recognizable in the inventories of Francesco I.

Below: Engraved double-nautilus cup with silver-gilt mounts. Flemish, 16th century. Height 10 inches. Florence, Museo degli Argenti.

The body is formed from two nautilus shells, the surfaces of which were first engraved with flowers and foliage and then gilded; the mounts are shaped from sheet silver. This piece entered the Uffizi in 1621 from the collection in the Gallery of the Casino di San Marco and is identifiable in the 1587 inventory made on the death of Grand Duke Francesco.

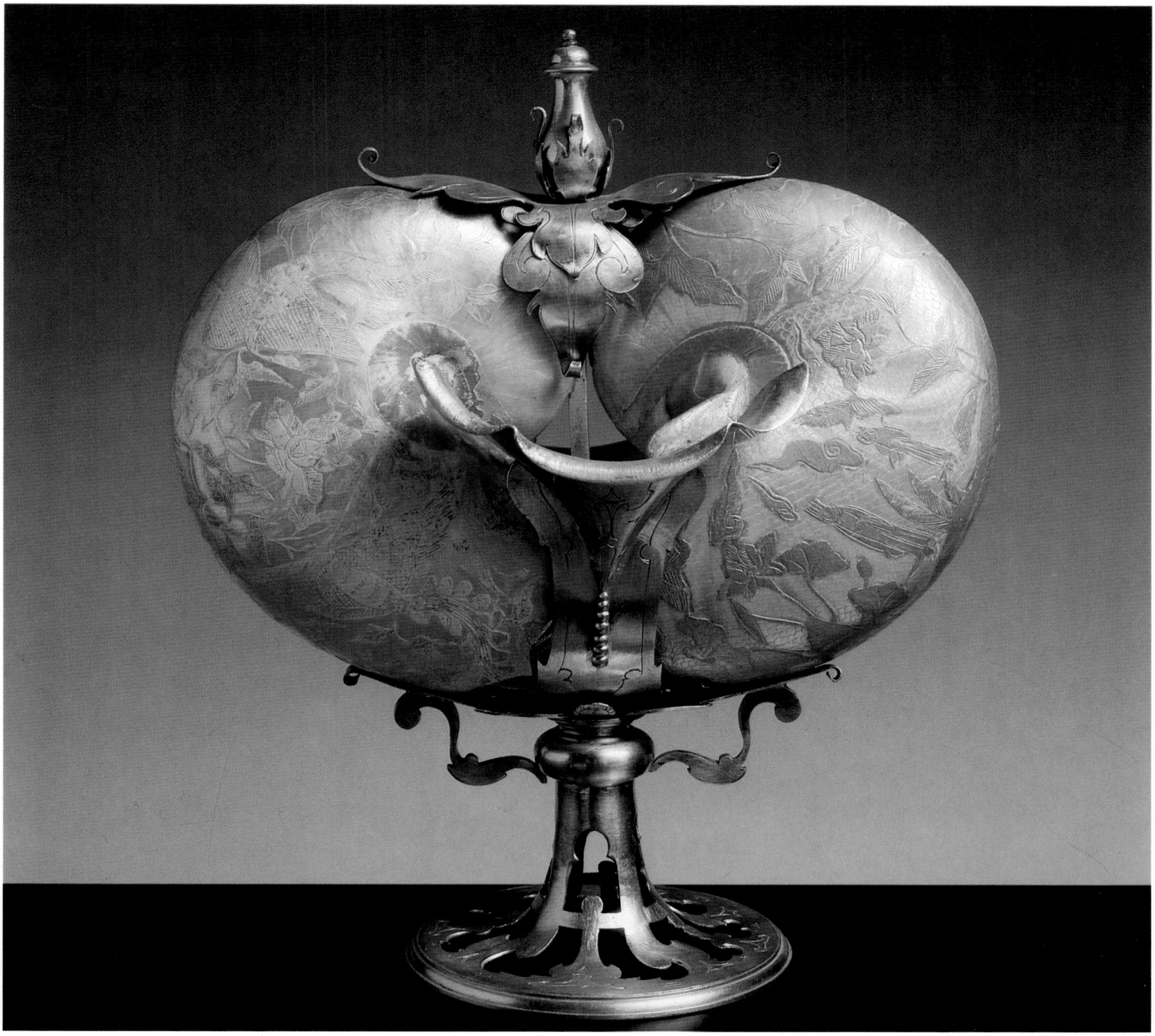

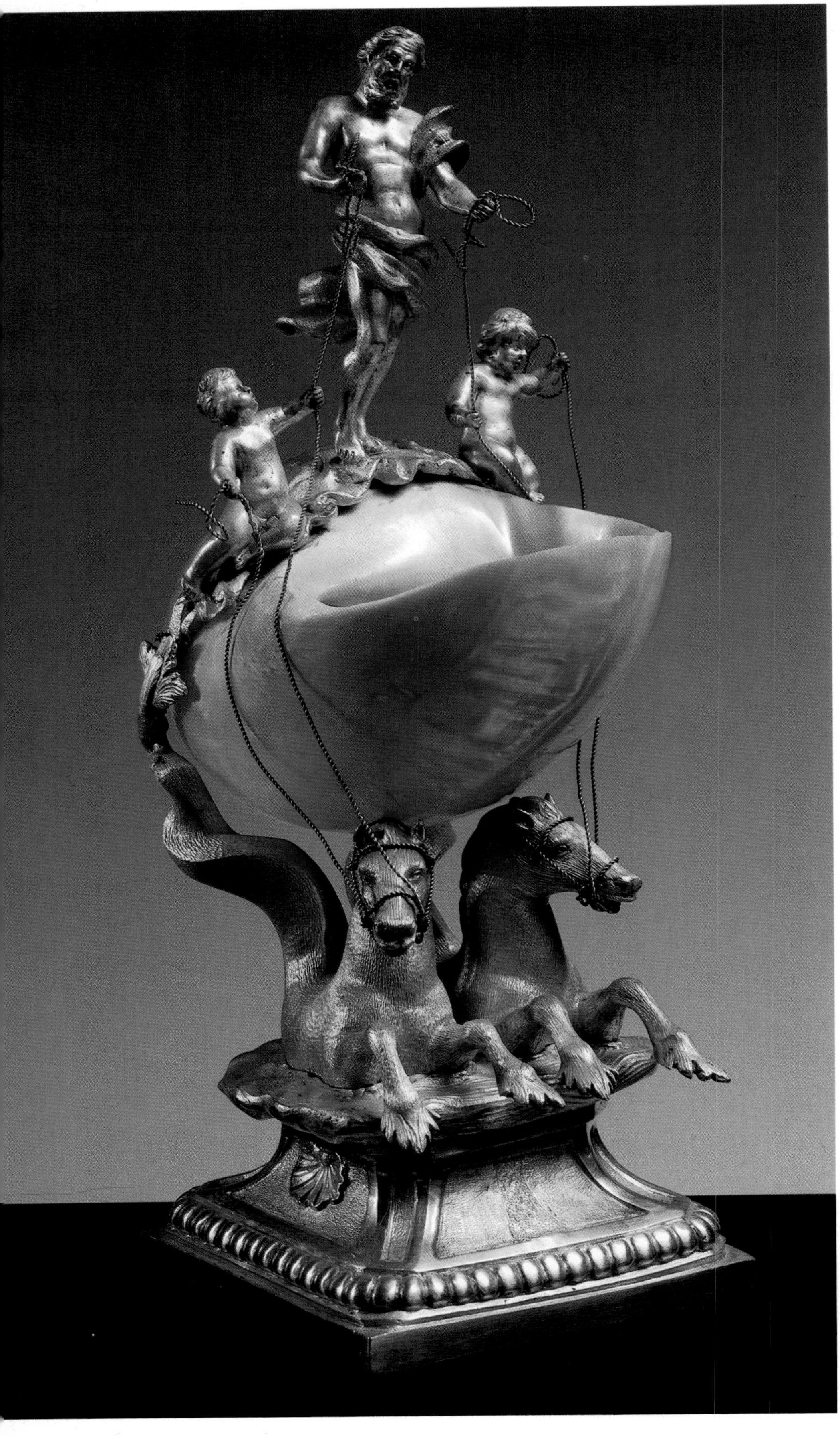

Nautilus salt cellar with gilt-bronze mounts. German, 17th century. Height 13 inches. Florence, Museo degli Argenti.

This salt, made from a nautilus shell, rests on two gilt-bronze seahorses and is surmounted by a small statue of Neptune flanked by two cherubs (detail, opposite). A similar object is mentioned in the Gallery of the Casino di San Marco, but its supporting mount is described as having the shape of a dragon.

Nautilus vase with mounts in silver gilt and gilt bronze. German, ca. 1600. Height 13 inches. Florence, Museo degli Argenti.

The mounts of this nautilus shell are extremely elaborate and unusual: silver seahorses are placed on the lip, and a figurine riding a snail surmounts the shell. The pedestal is in the form of an exotically dressed statuette holding on a leash a lion with a tail in the form of a snake (detail, right).

Bronze inkstand, by Niccolò Tribolo (1500–58). Height 11½ inches. Florence, Museo Nazionale del Bargello.

Bronze was one of the materials best loved by the first grand dukes. Among the many statuettes—often with subjects taken from antiquity—first placed in the Palazzo Vecchio, then in the Casino di San Marco, and finally in the Gallery, can be found bronze bells, mortars, and inkstands. This satyr, identified as a work by Niccolò Tribolo, is seated on a vase that may have served as an inkwell.

Hercules with the boar, bronze, by Giambologna (1529–1608). Height 17⅓ inches. Florence, Museo Nazionale del Bargello.

The lost series of the Labors of Hercules in silver that Giambologna made for Francesco I is known from a number of variations in bronze. Of the planned sequence of twelve groups, the sculptor must have completed only seven, of which six are recorded as having been placed in 1589 in the Tribuna of the Uffizi. The court goldsmith Michele Mazzafirri made the silver original from which this bronze was copied.

Opposite: Crouching Venus, bronze engraved with the initials I.B.F. on the bracelet, by Giambologna (1529–1608). Height 10 inches. Florence, Museo Nazionale del Bargello.

The subject of this bronze is taken from a famous antique marble, the Crouching Venus, repeated in Renaissance times in a number of variations. Giambologna made two bronzes with this subject, of which many copies were made. From April 7, 1584, one example was to be found in the Villa Medici, in Rome, together with other statuettes by the same sculptor.

62

Bronze goat on a walnut base with lapidary inlay work and gold filleting, by Andrea Briosco, known as "il Riccio" (ca. 1470–1532). Height 7¾ inches. Florence, Museo Nazionale del Bargello.

Among the many bronzes acquired by Francesco I are numerous examples by Venetian masters. The goat made by "il Riccio" is listed as being in the Gallery of the Casino di San Marco from 1587 and can be identified with the "bronze billy-goat on a base of walnut worked with gold and with mixed marble stones thereon."

The presence of the original base is noteworthy, as original supports were usually removed.

Opposite: Bagpipe player in gilt bronze, by Giambologna (1529–1608). Height 4¾ inches. Florence, Museo Nazionale del Bargello.

This bronze, inspired by a Dürer engraving of 1514, forms one of the popular subjects so dear to Giambologna, who also made a silver version of the Fowler for Francesco I de' Medici, which stood in the Tribuna of the Uffizi from 1589 on. A number of variations of the bagpipe player are known; that belonging to the Medici collection is one of the most refined examples.

Opposite: Gold cross decorated with enamel and inset rock crystals and topazes. Florence, Museo degli Argenti.

Crystals and topazes are mounted on the front of this gold cross enameled with flowers and foliage. This is one of the few jewels to have been found during the second half of the 19th century, when the tombs of the grand dukes were re-opened. Nearly all the jewels were found to have been removed, with the exception of one small ring and two medallions belonging to Grand Duke Ferdinando; this cross was found in the tomb of Cardinal Carlo.

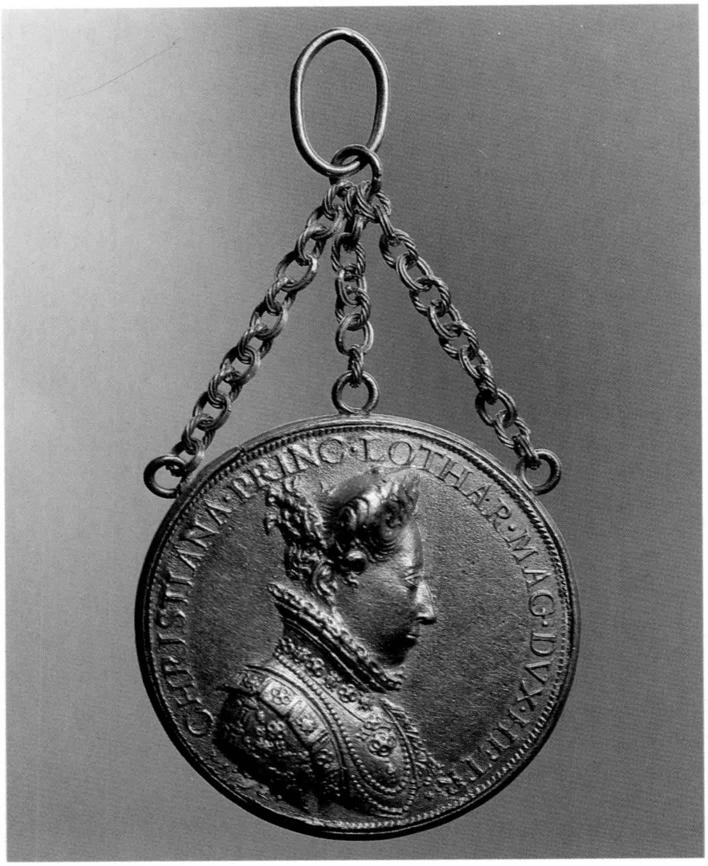

Gold medallions with portraits of Ferdinando I and Christine of Lorraine, by Michele Mazzafirri. Florence, Museo Nazionale del Bargello.

Mazzafirri, who was superintendent of the grand ducal mint for several years, made medallions for Ferdinando I, many of which bore the device of the swarm of bees and the motto MAIESTATE TANTUM, adopted by the grand duke. These examples feature on one side the portrait of Ferdinando and on the other that of his wife, Christine of Lorraine.

Bronze Laocoön with greenish patina and traces of gilding, by Pietro Simoni da Barga (known from 1571 to 1589). Height 12½ inches. Florence, Museo Nazionale del Bargello.

Pietro Simoni's repertoire of reproductions based on celebrated antique and contemporary statuary models inevitably included the celebrated Laocoön group, found in the garden of the Belvedere of the Vatican. The sculptor recreated the group with the father's arm reaching up, as was done in the restoration by Montorsoli.

Opposite: Bronze of Hercules and Telephus with greenish patina and traces of gilding, by Pietro Simoni da Barga (known from 1571 to 1589). Height 11 inches. Florence, Museo Nazionale del Bargello.

This small bronze was given by the sculptor to the Wardrobe of Cardinal Ferdinando in 1576; this is another example of a small-scale reproduction of a famous antique model, in this case the group of Hercules and Telephus that was part of the collection of ancient sculptures in the Belvedere garden in the Vatican.

Left: Bronze satyr with greenish patina and traces of gilding, by Pietro Simoni da Barga (known from 1571 to 1589). Height 12 inches. Florence, Museo Nazionale del Bargello.

This is a copy of one of the two marble fauns that stood in the courtyard of the Palazzo Della Valle in Rome during the 16th century; in comparison to the original, it has been simplified by the omission of the panther's skin on the shoulders. Due to the greenish patina and traces of gilding it can be traced to a group of small bronzes that Pietro Simoni made in Rome around 1576 during the period of his activity at the Villa Medici.

Opposite: Bronze Daphnis with greenish patina and traces of gilding, by Pietro Simoni da Barga (known from 1571 to 1589). Height 10 inches. Florence, Museo Nazionale del Bargello.

This bronze is taken from an antique model, in marble, belonging to the collection of the Roman Della Valle family and bought by Cardinal Ferdinando in 1584. Both during his years at the Villa Medici and immediately after his return to Florence, the sculptor Pietro Simoni made for Ferdinando a number of small copies after the most famous examples of antique and Renaissance statuary. Among other things, he is to be credited with a cycle of gilt bronzes that decorated the front of a cabinet, now lost, the presence of which is traceable at the Villa Medici until the 17th century.

Cosimo II and Ferdinando II: the taste of the 17th century

Detail of a silver plaque with an allegorical figure of Fortitude from a buckler made for Grand Duke Cosimo II by Gasparo Mola. *See also illustration on page 156.*

Cosimo II, eldest of the eight children of Ferdinando I, succeeded his father in 1609, after his marriage to Maria Maddalena of Austria, at the age of nineteen. During his brief reign the activity in the court workshops was extremely intense, and the Gallery of Works reached extraordinary heights in the execution of stone mosaics. The collaboration between stonecutters and such artists as Ligozzi defined the naturalistic treatment that, until the following century, characterized the splendid tabletops or panels for cabinets, chests, and clocks that were so greatly admired in all European courts.

The period of Cosimo II: the artists and style of the early 17th century

A progressive revival occurred among the goldsmiths active in this period. Of the older generation, Odoardo Vallet, the craftsman who, in 1619, had made one of the most refined objects ever produced by the Florentine court, the extremely fine mounts for a pure rock-crystal vase, was still active. Among foreign artists, the Swede Jonas Falck, who held a dominant position, and Cosimo Merlini, noted in the gallery since 1614, were associated with works of exceptional importance. In 1618 Merlini completed a large gold enameled reliquary cross featuring cherubs' heads and set with pearls, garnets, topazes, emeralds, carnelians, amethysts, and aquamarines; this cross appears to have been donated to the Institute of Santa Maria del Fiore "to contain the wood of the most Holy Cross" and is now in Florence's Museo dell'Opera del Duomo.

Sacred goldwork received encouragement in the religious atmosphere of Christine of Lorraine's court; her mysticism was shared by her son Cosimo and by Maria Maddalena of Austria. A huge silver-gilt reliquary of the Holy Cross stands out among the objects preserved in the Pitti Palace chapel. It is studded with precious and semiprecious stones, allegorical figures, cherubs, putti, and the Redeemer in half or full relief. This sumptuous object, which still belongs stylistically to the late 16th century, has many similarities in technique and ornament with the cross in the Museo dell'Opera del Duomo due to the rich setting of stones in sequence and alternation as well as the molded relief castings, which gives the piece its opulent, magnificent character. It is possible that the reliquary in the Museo degli Argenti also came from the workshop of Cosimo Merlini, maker of the cross in the Museo dell'Opera del Duomo. The frequent references to him in contemporary documents are not reflected in a large number of pieces that can be linked to him with certainty. However, we know that he and Falck worked together on a semiprecious-stone panel destined for a gold altar front commissioned as an ex-voto by Cosimo II for the church of San Carlo Borromeo in Milan. Unfortunately, the grand duke died before work was completed, so the gem-encrusted relief remained in the Florentine collections.

The Milanese Gasparo Mola figures among the artists working during the time of Cosimo II: he worked primarily as a minter, but sources also mention him in connection with the manufacture of ornamental suits of armor that were considered "works of great wonder."

In the meantime at the Medici court, a typically northern taste made such materials as ivory and amber increasingly fashionable, and the presence of Maria Maddalena of Austria without doubt must have been a determining factor. The inventory of her chapel in the Pitti Palace permits us to verify, as early as 1616, the presence of amber candlesticks, altarpieces, caskets, and sacred figurines. In 1632, a tabernacle dated 1618–19 and made by Georg Schreiber arrived. At the beginning of the 18th century, Grand Duke Cosimo III transported all these objects to the Gallery and put them away in enormous cabinets especially constructed for that purpose. Mattias, the younger son of Cosimo II, seems to have inherited a passion for northern artifacts from his mother. He served as a general during the Thirty Years' War and in 1633 brought from Germany a group of twenty-seven ivory vases that had come into the possession of the German Colonel Keller during the sack of Coburg. His brother, Cardinal Leopoldo (1617–75), shared this taste and owned a multitude of ivory statuettes, some procured in Rome by his agent Agostino Monanni. Among these figures is a large number of copies of famous antique and modern statuary made by Balthasar Stockamer of Nuremberg.

A refined collector, Cardinal Leopoldo was cultivated in many fields and even in antiques showed a fine intuition and faultless eye: his collections of bronzes, medals, marbles, inscriptions, and cameos were all carefully selected. He also collected paintings and drawings with great passion and had a predilection for miniatures, which might be considered the most precious of paintings. His agent Paolo del Sera appears to have paid no heed to expense when purchasing these tiny portraits, which the cardinal kept in his traveling gallery, an ebony cabinet with silver embellishments. This piece of furniture is now lost, but Giuseppe Bianchi made a drawing of it when the cardinal's cabinet, which became a museum piece, was exhibited in the Sala dell'Ermafrodita at the Uffizi. Until 1781, when it was sent to the storerooms of the Wardrobe and lost, inventories provide detailed descriptions of it. This traveling cabinet, made to measure for a collection from which the cardinal did not want to be parted even during his travels, was described as follows: "An ebony-veneered cabinet 1½ arms high and 2½ arms wide, within which are sixty drawers that pull open, with handles and silver rosettes, and a tassel for each of silk and silver to pull out said drawers, each bearing a little picture, covered with black velvet. . . . and above said drawers there are many pictures round and oval of varying sizes in copper and paper on which are painted the portraits of princes and other personages, with silver framing crystal. In all there are five hundred and eleven portraits, two doors are in the front of said ebony cabinet, with four worked and pierced silver hinges and two similar silver bolts with stirrups. The base is in carved pear wood stained black, partially turned, with a silver-plate lock and iron frame and key."

Jewels continued to turn up in large quantities in the Wardrobe: some were precious pieces of earlier origin that had remained as heirlooms, like those, housed in an iron chest, that once had been the property of Grand Duke Ferdinando I and were left in the custody of Jacques Bylivelt and listed in the inventory only in 1621. Another group had been returned in 1620, their previous appurtenance to Lady Eleonora "of happy memory" is specified, perhaps the daughter of Francesco I who became the bride of Vincenzo Gonzaga.

Inventories and the family wealth: the inheritance of Ferdinando II

A set of papers describing the precious objects that passed in 1621 into the hands of the youthful Ferdinando II, shortly after the death of Cosimo II, is a good indication of the quantity of treasure accumulated by the early grand dukes. The list starts with a detailed description of the royal crown, with the exact number of its precious stones, almost all rubies, diamonds, and emeralds. Among the four collars stands out the so-called Ferdinando collar, commissioned by Grand Duke Ferdinando I from the then elderly Leonard Zaerles after he had moved to Frankfurt. It is made up of eleven large rosettes, on each of which was centered a large diamond, surrounded by smaller ones, with pear-shaped pearl pendants. Among the "collars" that follow, one was composed of diamonds and rubies with a particularly large ruby serving as pendant, another had a diamond pendant "of a somewhat citrine hue," in the shape of a cross. A cross dotted with diamonds, rubies, and emeralds also belonged to the collar decorated with many colored stones and enamels, which was said to be made in Spanish style. In the list, we find typical naturalistic creations of the late 16th century, including characteristic small animals cleverly making use of the natural form of baroque pearls: "a jewel in the form of a bird, the body of which is pearl, and below it a branch with diamonds and a small gold chain . . . a jewel in the shape of a bull, enameled in white, encrusted with rubies and diamonds, with a pendant pearl in the center of its body . . . a jewel in the form of a camel enameled in white, with a cluster of rubies and small diamonds and a pendent pearl . . . a jewel made in the form of a lion in mother-of-pearl with rubies, diamonds, emeralds, and pearls, with a pear-shaped pearl pendant . . . a jewel with a horse enameled in white and set with a diamond and upon it an armed man with a small diamond hung below and a pearl above . . . a jewel in the form of a cupid shooting his arrow full of rubies and diamonds. . . a jeweled cupid enameled in white standing with his feet on four pearls, and the rest of the jewel set with diamonds, rubies, and emeralds, with four pendant pearls . . . a jewel in the shape of Cleopatra with the body in mother-of-pearl, with a large emerald in back with five rubies, or rather six, and one diamond on the head . . . a jewel in the shape of a sea monster with the body in mother-of-pearl and the rest in enameled gold with rubies . . . a jewel in the form of an elephant, enameled, with a figure on it . . . a jewel in the form of a crab, the upper part being of emerald and the rest of gold . . . a jewel in the form of a cat with its back in mother-of-pearl and a pearl pendant . . . a jewel in the form of a dog enameled in white with tiny little rubies and a diamond under its foot with three pearls below for a pendant . . . a jewel in the shape of a phoenix with an emerald, two rubies, and two little diamonds . . . a jewel in the shape of a mermaid with an emerald in the middle and three seed pearls . . . a jewel in the shape of a boat of mother-of-pearl, set with rubies and diamonds with three pendant pearls." Various such examples figure among the jewels that had been passed through inheritance to the Electress Palatine, some of which later returned to Florence.

The list also notes necklaces, among which one was made up of one hundred and thirty two "dice," each with four diamonds, and a watch pendant in the form of a cross. Perfumed pomanders were kept in velvet, leather, or lead containers: "a lead box, covered in red, which contains a pomander in the form of a pine cone with a green-enameled gold branch, and a perfume vase in gold and enameled in white." Then follow all those precious articles that served to decorate heads of hair, listed under "Plumes and Other Jewels to Wear on the Head." There is a large, faceted 14-carat Venetian diamond with a hole "to wear above on the head." The plumes were shaped like a rose or branch, with a snake or phoenix in the center, or else a wheel of rubies and diamonds. Diamonds and pearls predominate, and there was an all-diamond "plume with an initial picked out in diamonds, and a crown above with a lily." Another headdress was an enameled "dragon of turquoise set with diamonds." Among the pearls stands out a case with the arms of Grand Duchess Christine of Lorraine, which held a pear-shaped pearl from Venice of "most beautiful skin," weighing 16 carats.

No less elaborate were the "hair buckles," one of which bore the seven planets with diamonds mounted in steel. Hundreds of enameled gold buttons set with precious stones follow, and among the bracelets were some worked "in Milanese fashion"; others, placed in an Indian-style box, were set with turquoises and cameos, while those in the so-called Spanish fashion consisted of eight pieces decorated with cameos and pearls. Among the clothing accessories were brightly enameled studs and ferrules in gold or steel. Innumerable rings, kept by the dozen in little leather drawers, were in the shape of snakes or dragons. Occasionally, they have a crown or star, and in one is mounted an engraved turquoise tortoise and six little diamonds. Pearl pendants predominated among the earrings, but one pair was in the form of a vase with emeralds mounted in gold. Cases for timepieces take on an incredible variety of shapes and materials; one had a cameo with a bas-relief head and diamonds, another was in the form of a lily, one in topaz, another was shaped like a heart and completely covered with rubies. The list of jewels includes a number of small book covers in openwork enameled gold, and among the objects on a long list of "Miscellaneous Items" can be found the rarest and most curious objects: "a Turkish dagger with its jade sheath all covered with rubies and four small diamonds . . . a gold decorated emerald whistle with a round pearl and gold toothpicks within. . . a gold Turkish cup covered with rubies, turquoises, and emeralds . . . a box within which is the gold handle of a fan worked in the Spanish fashion, set with various table-cut diamonds, cabochon rubies, two large cabochon emeralds, and small round pearls . . . a large sapphire in the form of a little flask with a stopper of gold and six small rubies." The inventory was countersigned by Princess Maria Maddalena who, together with her mother-in-law Christine of Lorraine, was regent until 1628.

Vittoria della Rovere and the inheritance of Urbino

In the meantime, Claudia, the nineteen-year-old daughter of Ferdinando I who had recently been left a widow and whose child, Vittoria della Rovere, was the sole heir to the duchy of Urbino, returned to Florence from Urbino in 1623. Vittoria's betrothal to Ferdinando II was immediately ordained, and in 1634, when she reached the age of fourteen, after having lived for a long time in the monastery of La Crocetta, the wedding was celebrated. Thanks to her dowry, some of the most famous paintings now in the Uffizi became part of the grand ducal collections, along with a rare collection of maiolica from Urbino. As may be expected, the inventory of her possessions, dating back to 1663, lists a great amount of furniture, silverware, embroidery, and ivory, as well as paintings and sculpture. Among the silverware, there were numerous religious articles, such as chalices, candlesticks, and patens, a number of statuettes in full relief among which one of "St. Francis of Paola with a stick in his hand and a sack on his shoulder."

Her long stay in the monastery of La Crocetta had not caused Vittoria della Rovere to eschew objects of a more secular nature, and her inventory shows a strong tendency to follow those collecting preferences so clearly seen in the Medici family. For example, we find among her silverware a "wolf's jawbone covered with gilded silver," a "silver basin all gilded, decorated in chased bas-relief with scenes of the four quarters of the world, figures, animals, and garlands; a shield in the middle bears two figures in a ship," and a "large silver turtle, partly gilded inside and out, worked with fish of all waters, in the center a figure in bas-relief, and standing on its back a crab with two little snails."

Certain silver articles, such as a silver-gilt bell worked in bas-relief with leaves and figures and the coat of arms of Cardinal Della Rovere, were probably family objects; other pieces may possibly have been gifts, as for instance a "book-holder in silver plate with a base in the form of a cartouche and handle with the head of a figure in bas-relief, bearing the arms of the house of Farnese." Most of the food warmers and coolers bore the Della Rovere arms, but some bear those of the Farnese, and a V surmounted by a crown was engraved on certain polished silver "regal" plates.

In the lists of "Various Goldworks" figure "two large shells of solid gold, one with a crab on it, and two little snails on top," and also "a gold pen for drawing lines with an ebony shaft."

There are various antique marbles, among them "a marble figure with one foot resting on a little dog, with a cherub on the shoulder, approximately one arm's-length high," which can still be found in the Sala dell'Ermafrodita of the Uffizi. Furnishings showed off the most precious

Vittoria della Rovere, grand ducchess of Tuscany (1622–95), wife of Ferdinando II de' Medici, in a painting by Justis Sustermans (Museo degli Argenti, Florence).

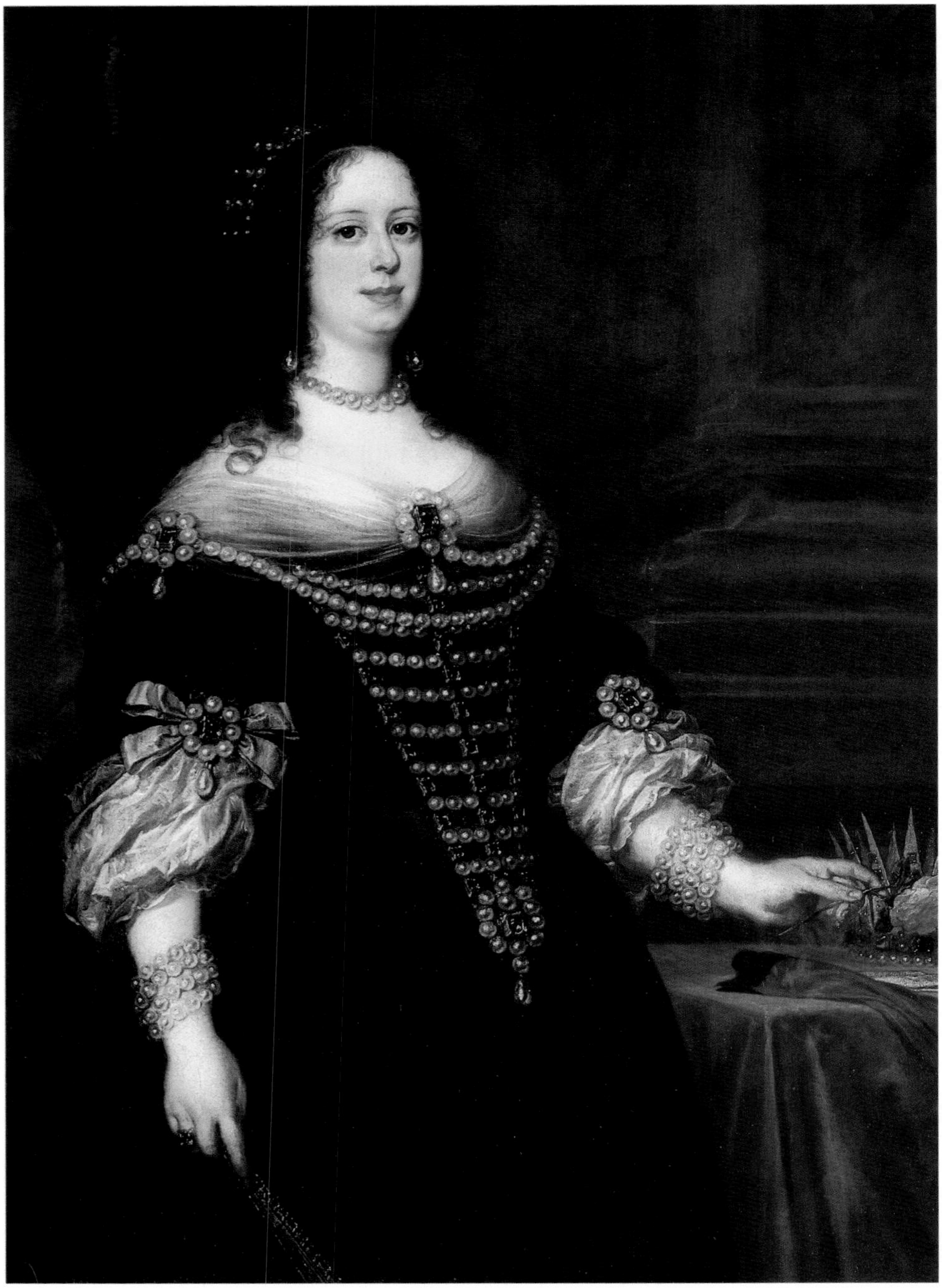

materials: tables were ebony inlaid with ivory, and there were cabinets, caskets, and comb cases in ivory or bone, sometimes painted in Indian fashion, as well as tortoiseshell clocks. But the list also describes articles in bronze and copper, miniatures, and a number of ivories. Among the latter are several crucifixes, of which two have crosses in ebony, two turned candlesticks in openwork, a round reliquary with baluster base, twenty-seven figurines "some standing and some mounted on horseback," a seal handle, two skulls, seventy-five combs of various types and sizes, a small ivory box containing an oval crystal engraved with figures on horseback, and a number of animals. Then there are a variety of objects such as "the head of a putto in cameo with gold fillet . . . a little oval of mother-of-pearl engraved in a tondo of jasper with a cover that bears in the middle a strip of silver . . . two India nuts, one with a spout and one without . . . the handle for a seal in jasper."

When the childless duke of Urbino abdicated, Ferdinando considered advancing a claim on that duchy in the name of Vittoria della Rovere, but in order to avoid offending the pope he did not pursue it and allowed Urbino to become part of the Papal States. Despite this disappointment, Vittoria della Rovere's treasures notably increased the Medici collections, and during the course of the 17th century, the property of other Medici princes, in accordance with the law regulating family inheritance, gradually returned to the main collection.

At the end of the century, therefore, the wonders in the Uffizi had become ever more varied, fully reflecting the tastes and collecting passions of the various family members. Stone engravers were extremely active in the Gallery during the long reign of Ferdinando II, and they created works of great value that the grand duke could either proudly exhibit or donate to other European potentates.

Emulating the early grand dukes, Ferdinando had an elaborate architectural cabinet in ebony and semiprecious stones made following designs by Matteo Nigetti, now in the Tribuna of the Uffizi. During these years gifts arrived from beyond the Alps that bear comparison with Florentine pieces, for example, a vase in semiprecious stone and a Chinese nephrite cup came from the elector of Saxony, and during his visit to Innsbruck in 1628 Grand Duke Ferdinando received from Claudia de' Medici's second husband, Ferdinand of Tyrol, the famous Stipo d'Alemagna (German Cabinet), made in Augsburg and now in the Museo degli Argenti. Until the period of Lorraine rule, its many compartments and drawers were used to store jewels, medallions, and stones. Covered with panels of painted semiprecious stones, this unique piece of furniture boasted such unexpected marvels as a small altar, an organ, and a clock with chimes. The latter was connected to silver automata (since lost) on the top of the cabinet that represented Christ striking down Lucifer; the mechanism of the clock caused these automata to move.

Ex-voto of semiprecious stones, gemstones, and gilded metal, made for Cosimo II by Michele Castrucci, Gualtiero Cecchi, and Jonas Falck, based on a drawing by Giulio Parigi. 21 1/2 x 25 1/3 inches. Florence, Museo degli Argenti.

In the bas-relief, Grand Duke Cosimo II, with clothing and mantle of chased and enameled gold, kneels on a cushion of lapis lazuli and gold, while he offers up a scepter and crown studded with diamonds on an altar of red jasper. In the background is a view of the cathedral of Florence (detail, opposite) in lapidary mosaic. The relief was designed to decorate a gold altar-front that Cosimo II wished to donate to the church of San Carlo Borromeo in Milan, should he be healed from sickness. The grand duke, however, died in 1621, and the projected gift was never sent. This precious ex-voto remained in Florence, where, during the second half of the 18th century, the gold was melted down and the relief reset in its present frame. Giuseppe Pelli Bencivenni, who was able to see the altar-front still intact in 1779, judged it the most beautiful work to have come from the grand duke's workshops and recalled that although it was kept in the Wardrobe, it was put on public view in the chapel of the Pitti Palace on Maundy Thursday.

Rock-crystal vase with mounts of enameled gold, rubies, and emeralds, by Odoardo Vallet, 1618–19. Height 15 inches. Florence, Museo degli Argenti.

The complete absence of engraved ornamentation on the body of this vase underlines to the maximum its extremely precise structure as well as the elaborate mounts, made by the goldsmith Odoardo Vallet between 1618 and 1619 (details, below right and opposite). Giulio Pignatta painted a view of the Tribuna in 1715 and depicted this very vase, standing among the many in the treasure on a table in the middle of the room. At that time the splendid mount was still intact, whereas a few decades later one of the two handles was removed.

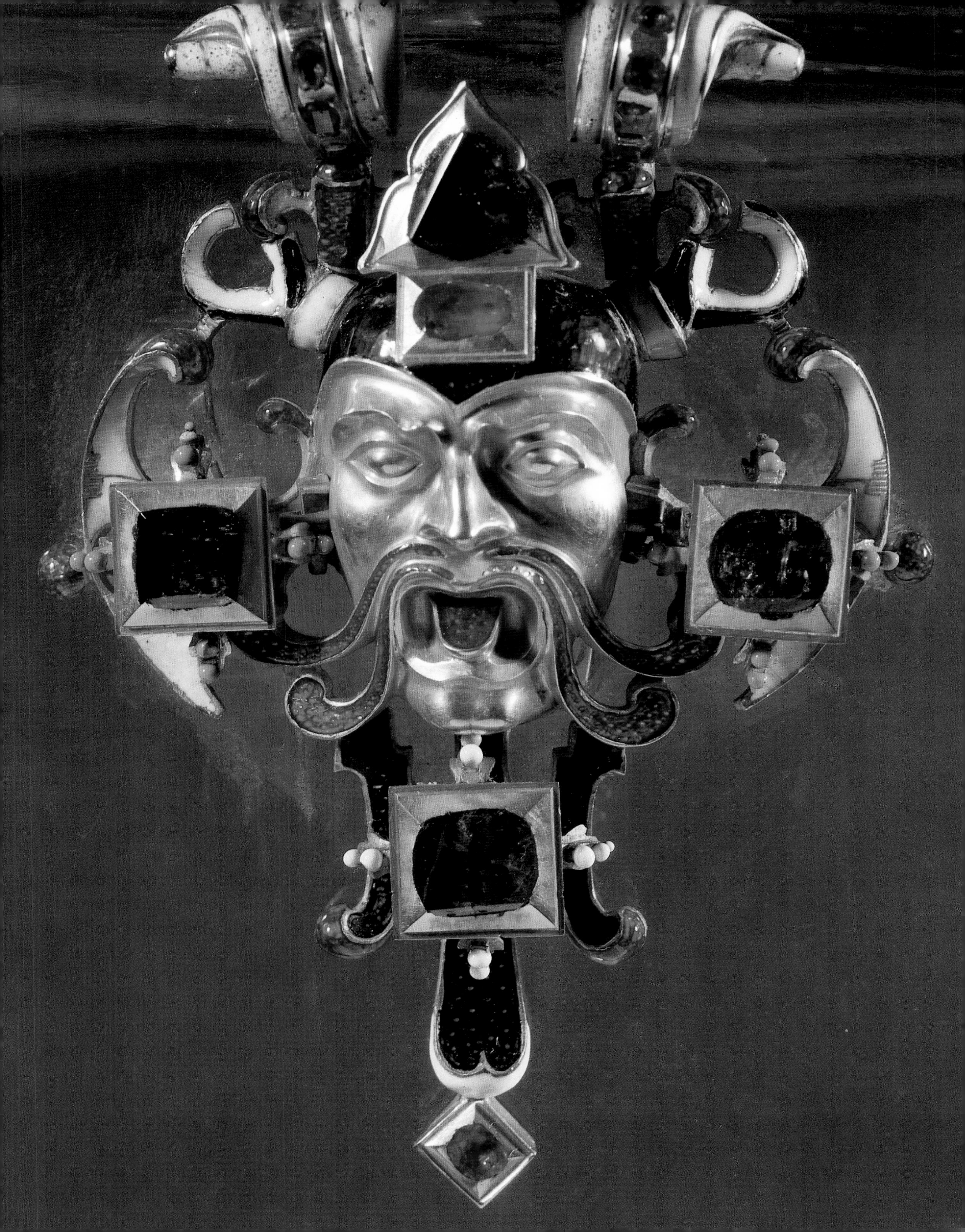

Buckler and helmet in burnished steel, gilt copper, and silver, by Gasparo Mola (1580–1640). Florence, Museo Nazionale del Bargello.

Gasparo Mola, superintendent of the Medici mint, also made arms for Grand Duke Cosimo II; sources refer to this buckler and helmet as being of exceptional beauty: the decoration in gilt copper on a background of burnished steel represents a true masterpiece of the art of chasing. Amid the thickly twined foliage on the outer border of the buckler are a series of imperial portraits, the signs of the zodiac, and six silver plaques with allegorical figures: Faith, Hope, Temperance, Fortitude, Prudence, Justice. The helmet has a dragon as crest and bears two other silver plaques showing Fame and Charity.

Round shield of damascened steel with gold, bamboo, silk, mother-of-pearl, leather, and velvet. Persia, early 17th century. Diameter 23⅓ inches. Florence, Museo Nazionale del Bargello.

This round shield appears among the arms kept in the Wardrobe beginning in 1631. The circumstances of its arrival in Florence probably date to 1613, when the Emir Fakr-ed-Din, proposing an alliance against the Turks, sent Grand Duke Cosimo II two such round shields as a gift. Above: Detail of the decoration.

Below left and opposite: Gold medallions with portraits of Cosimo II and Maria Maddalena of Austria, by Guillaume Dupré (1576–1643). Diameter $3\frac{3}{4}$ inches (without frame). Florence, Museo Nazionale del Bargello.

These medallions, which date to 1613, are in gold, but several bronze and gilt-bronze versions of them also exist. The French medallist's skill at portraying his subject and his attention to the details of clothing here achieve their highest levels.

Above right: Gilt-copper medallion with the portrait of Francesco, son of Ferdinando I de' Medici, by Guillaume Dupré (1576–1643). Diameter $3\frac{3}{4}$ inches (without frame). Florence, Museo Nazionale del Bargello.

This medallion, with a beaded edge, has a shaped frame set with precious stones, pommel, and ring from which it hung. The French artist here portrayed the fourth son of Ferdinando I and Christine of Lorraine, who died at the age of 20.

MAR·MAGDALENÆ·ARCH·AVSTR·MAG·D·ETR

Sculpture of St. Peter in semiprecious stones. Height 13 inches. Florence, Museo degli Argenti.

This statue belongs to a cycle of eight sculptures destined for the ciborium of the Princes' Chapel in San Lorenzo, which was never completed. The project was worked out in 1602 by Don Giovanni de' Medici, and a drawing by Matteo Nigetti interprets the wishes of this industrious son of Francesco I. The complex was to have consisted of a base decorated with relief panels, an architectural elevation on two levels divided by niches and columns and covered by a cupola. Four of the statues, which were intended for the niches on the facade, were completed ca. 1605 by the sculptor and lapidary Orazio Mochi. The others, including the St. Peter shown here, were completed shortly before mid-century based on models by the same artist.

Agate vase with silver-gilt mounts with enameled decoration and diamonds. Germany. Height 8 1/4 inches. Florence, Museo degli Argenti.

The circumstances of the arrival of this vase in Florence have been explained thanks to documents discovered by Kirsten Aschengreen Piacenti. It figures in a list of objects sent as gifts by the elector of Saxony to Grand Duke Ferdinando II that also included a Chinese nephrite cup, a box, and a small cabinet in ebony and ivory "for remedies." The vase has enameled silver-gilt mounts with vine-shoots engraved à jour *and an encrustation of diamonds. The figurine on the cover (detail, right) originally held a shield with the arms of Saxony; the same coat of arms also appears on the green velvet case, with a trimming of silver ribbon, in which the vase was kept.*

Opposite: Ivory reproductions of Michelangelo's Dawn and Dusk. Germany, second half of the 17th century. 8 inches. Florence, Museo degli Argenti.

These statuettes are from the group of ivories that belonged to Cardinal Leopoldo and are mentioned in the inventory of his collection made in 1675.

Right: Onyx cameo of the Pietà with enameled gold mount. 4 x 3¾ inches. Florence, Museo degli Argenti.

This hexagonal cameo has been attributed to a French-Burgundian source sometime during the first half of the 15th century. The enameled gold mount dates to the first half of the 17th century.

Below: Dying Gaul in bronze, stamped IO. FR. SUSINI FLOR. FE., by F. Susini. Height 8 inches. Florence, Museo Nazionale del Bargello.

Susini made refined bronzes, often based on antique models. Kept in the Villa della Petraia during the 17th century, this bronze entered the Uffizi in 1772.

Above: Ivory dog on an ebony box edged with ivory. Height 2 1/4 inches, length 7 inches, box 10 x 6 inches. Florence, Museo degli Argenti.

This box belonged to Maria Maddalena of Austria. The little dog carved in ivory and placed on the cover is a King Charles spaniel, a breed much loved by the Stuart king Charles II. The statuette, which honors a dog that belonged to Maria Maddalena, was a present from her husband; it passed into the collection of Ferdinando II and was later kept at the Uffizi, from where it was transferred to the Pitti Palace during the second half of the 18th century.

Opposite: Ivory caged horse on a black horn base, by Filippo Planzone. Height 6 1/4 inches. Florence, Museo degli Argenti.

This horse and cage are made from a single piece of ivory. The artist Filippo Planzone, a Sicilian working in Genoa, gave the horse to Grand Duke Ferdinando II in 1624.

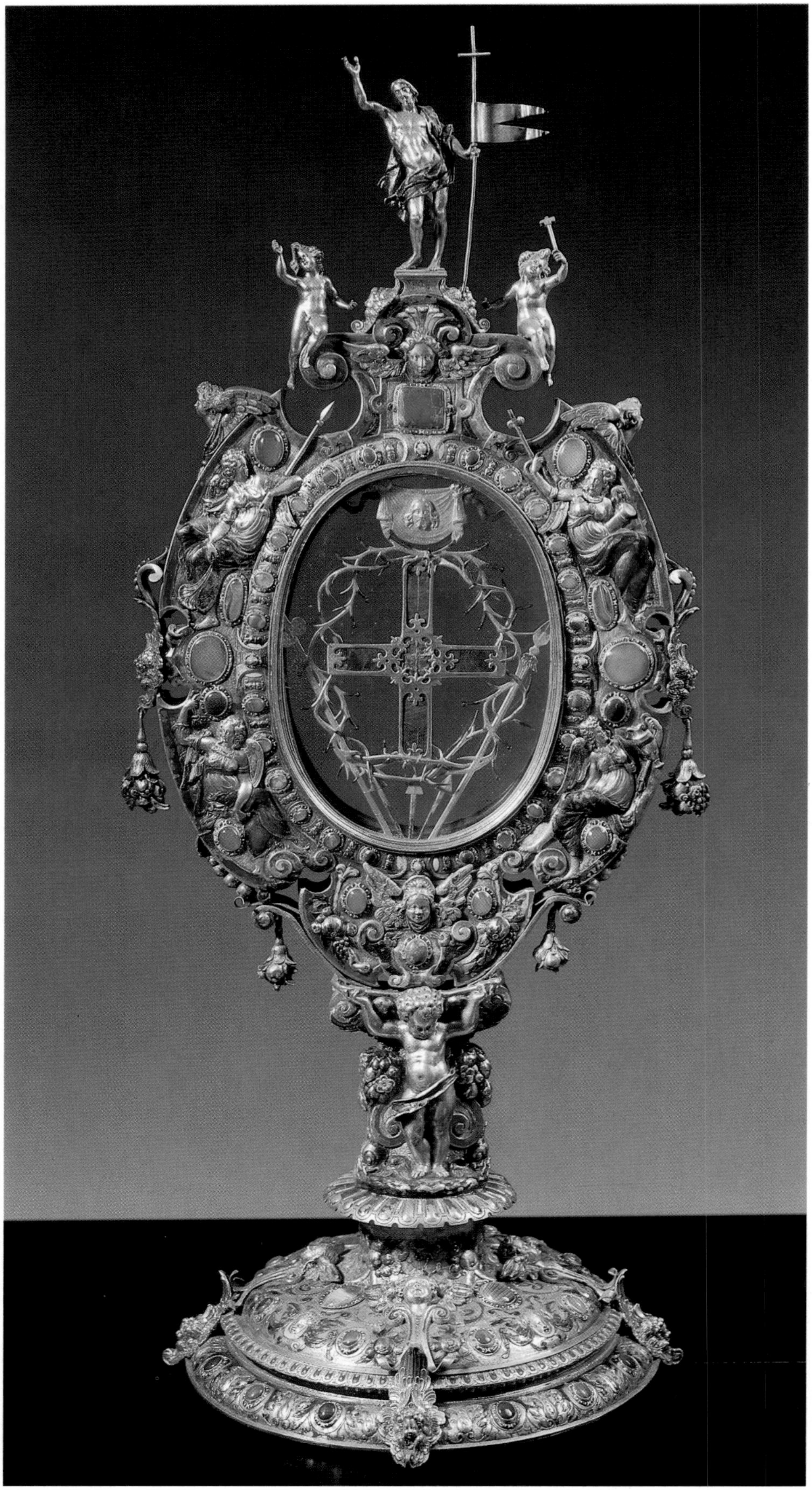

Reliquary of the Holy Cross in silver gilt encrusted with semiprecious stones, perhaps by Cosimo Merlini. Height 28¾ inches. Florence, Museo degli Argenti.

The striking appearance of this reliquary (details opposite and overleaf) is due to the thick ornamentation of semiprecious stones in varying sizes, which extends over its entire surface. On the silver-gilt support these stones alternate with numerous brightly enameled bas-relief representations of fruit, masks, and allegorical female figures. The silver-gilt figure of the Redeemer, in full relief, on the top of the reliquary is flanked by two cherubs. At the sides hang garlands of fruit, a motif repeated on the frame, beside the cherubs, and on the base. This precious reliquary was originally in the chapel of Grand Duchess Maria Maddalena in the Pitti Palace. The closest comparison with this work, which dates from the early decades of the 17th century, is a reliquary of the Passion made in 1620 by the court goldsmith Cosimo Merlini that was presented by the grand duchess to the Museo dell'Opera del Duomo. The slightly archaic taste in decoration, certain technical similarities, as well as the origin of both reliquaries among the possessions of Maria Maddalena give us reason to attribute this piece to Merlini.

***Right:* Female bust in bas-relief made of various stones, baroque pearls, and enameled gold. $21\frac{1}{2} \times 15\frac{3}{4}$ inches. Florence, Museo degli Argenti.**

This bas-relief, on a background of agate, shows a woman in profile, her turban and bosom in pearls with drapery in enameled gold. There is no evidence indicating when this object entered the grand ducal collections, but its originality and bizarre composition give a notion of the exceptional quality of the Medici cameos, one of the most prized genres at the Florentine court.

***Left:* Chalcedony cameo with gold mount. $15\frac{3}{4} \times 20\frac{1}{2}$ inches. Florence, Museo degli Argenti.**

This cameo depicts the recumbent Venus with two cupids holding a drape behind her and a satyr looking on; on the back is engraved a man's head in profile. The work has been associated with Alessandro Masnago, a craftsman working during the second half of the 16th century, but the only evidence we have of it in the Gallery dates from the second half of the 17th century.

DE OS
S MARIÆ

Cosimo III and Gian Gastone: the end of the dynasty

Detail of the reliquary of St. Mary of Egypt (early 18th century) illustrated in its entirety on page 200.

Cosimo III (1642–1723), who became grand duke in 1670, never enjoyed a good reputation in early Medici histories, and the worst aspects of the dynasty's end were usually attributed to him. As often happens, this was really the reflection of a state of affairs that was slowly proceeding toward a predetermined conclusion. However, it is now unanimously agreed that during his long reign the reduced commissioning of major works of art was paralleled by a flourishing of the decorative arts. Above all goldsmithing and glyptics took on new life, many masterpieces were produced, and the Uffizi collections were enlarged and reorganized.

Cosimo III, collecting and devotion

Cosimo III's less than pleasing physical appearance surely did not help him, but nobody now would attribute Florence's aesthetic decline to the penultimate Tuscan grand duke. On the contrary, as studies of his interminable reign proliferate, more is done to correct this pseudohistorical fiction. To Cosimo's close attention to courtly arts was added an interest in botany and many other sciences. Furthermore, to some of his contemporaries he appeared "a pleasant man, of exceeding jovial nature," a judgment that may have been near the truth.

During his youth, he was not averse to such refined profane pleasures as hunting, a sport in which he had participated with skill since the tender age of ten, and he was fascinated by women and on educational voyages to London met several to whom he sent, with uncommon gallantry, perfumes and fashion accessories upon his return home.

However, his happy nature gradually took a more sober turn, and an important visit to Rome in 1700 became a pilgrimage to the Holy City's churches, rather than a study of its fine arts. He became a canon of St. John Lateran in order to be permitted to see the relics of the tribune of St. Peter. He returned to Florence with a small collection of sacred objects, which he displayed to privileged visitors with great pride and reverence. In view of this, we can understand why most of the new works ordered by Cosimo from goldsmiths were religious in nature, for the most part reliquaries. The reliquaries were kept in the palace chapel, but other religious pieces were to be found in his private rooms. An English visitor was told that Cosimo had in his apartment "a machine . . . whereon were fixed little images in silver of every saint in the calendar. The machine was made to turn so as to present in front the saint of the day, before which he continually performed his offices."

An act that exemplifies Cosimo's religious mania is recorded in a letter to the duke of Parma, in 1721: "His Highness amuses himself with teaching Christian doctrine to three Cossack children, aged seven to twelve, who have been sent to him as a gift by the bishop of Krakow, and although they be most insolent and annoying, His Highness treats them with great patience and with the pious thought of the merit he acquires by setting those three souls on the road to God."

It is no wonder that the majority of scholars tend to overemphasize this side of Cosimo's nature, underlining a certain aggravated violence that made extremes meet. It is not rare to come across comments accentuating his cruel, intolerant character. Nor does marriage seem to have improved him. He married Marguerite-Louise, a cousin of Louis XIV of France, by proxy in April 1661. Being of a balanced and merry disposition, she could not long stand the atmosphere of the Florentine court. Unable to tolerate Cosimo's character, she quarreled with him and after giving him three children retired to Poggio a Caiano until 1674, when she fled Florence for the Convent of Montmartre in Paris. Upon the death of Cardinal Leopoldo in 1675, Cosimo and his mother, Vittoria, were left as the arbiters of Florentine taste.

Florence was not simply a nest of spies as biographers would lead us to think. During the reign of Cosimo the libraries of Francesco Marucelli and Antonio Magliabechi were formed, and after their deaths in 1703 and 1714 their collections were left to the city. The grand duke brought from Rome most of the family collection of ancient statues, and thus the Uffizi acquired such great antique masterpieces as the *Venus,* the *Wrestlers,* the *Knife-grinder,* and *Niobe*. Advised wisely by Francesco Redi, Cosimo continued the tradition of collecting gems and cameos and became a passionate naturalist collector. As a consequence, the already fine collection of such rare and precious materials as ivory and amber grew in importance and was kept in an opulently gilded and ornamented display case.

Cosimo's collection of coins and medals was enormous, and on one occasion in 1679 he bought nearly 13,000 pieces. This early passion was soon curtailed, however, and Cosimo had the collection of over 30,000 coins and medals neatly arranged in cupboards that he then sealed shut. Scholars who frequented the court complained of his selfishness, and Noris, as close as he was to Cosimo, found himself denied access to the collections and compared himself to Tantalus in classical mythology. In effect Cosimo considered these collections both useless and harmful as the time and energy they took distracted him from his religious devotions.

In spite of this, the family art collections grew under Cosimo. The collection of gems was increased by the legacy of the knowledgeable Cardinal Leopoldo, who died in 1675. The cardinal had been wisely advised by experts, particularly Pietro Andrea Andreini, who also helped Queen Christina of Sweden. Filippo Buonarroti, called from Rome in 1699, took an interest in the collection, dealing above all with administrative questions, and reorganizing the collections according to a new and more functional indexing system, although he did not forget his old passion for antiques. Toward the end of the grand duchy, Sebastiano Bianchi was added to these experts, and he suggested that the new grand duke, Gian Gastone, purchase the fine Andreini collection of over 300 antique gems.

A number of artists obtained privileges and favors at Cosimo's court, although their talents did not always merit such treatment. The grand duke honestly believed that artistic creations could be used to disguise faults and deficiencies, and he sacrificed much of the labors of the court workshops to this end. The gifts he regularly sent to European courts tended to be somewhat provincial when compared with those of the great continental power centers with which he wished to establish relations.

The grand duke's workshops were specifically organized to produce a court art totally subjected to the needs of the grand duke. The workshop directors, who lived at court, were in close contact with Cosimo, pandered to his slightest whim, and occupied positions that were partly artistic, partly political.

In 1683 the direction of the Gallery was assumed by Diacinto Maria Marmi, who made several pieces of sculptural furniture, such as the anthropomorphic wall tables in the Pitti Palace, and directed the creation of monumental architectural cabinets like the one owned by Vittoria della Rovere. Having become a "court gentleman," Marmi contributed to the new look of the Pitti Palace and was a capable artisan able to design in the moderate Florentine baroque taste. In his drawings, he at times seems to have difficulty balancing invention and technical ability, and we could surmise that Cosimo was not particularly satisfied.

In Giovanni Battista Foggini (1652–1725) the grand duke found someone better suited to his needs, and in 1695 Foggini was given responsibility for all the Gallery works. As early as 1687 he had been awarded the much sought-after position of "First Sculptor to the Most Serene House," a title that gave its possessor predominance over other court artists. What is more, when he became director of Gallery works, he kept his previous position, something that had never before occurred, and thus gained absolute and total control over the artistic affairs of the court.

This artist, carefully trained through the study of Florentine Mannerism and Roman baroque, dedicated himself fully to the Gallery, provided preparatory drawings for a large quantity of works, and followed up their production assiduously, often participating directly in the manufacture. Examples of this are semiprecious-stone caskets and gilt-bronze pieces that, although not belonging to the grand ducal treasury, give a good idea of his work as regards small objects.

A true masterpiece among these small objects is the bronze frame with semiprecious stones for Carlo Dolci's painting now in the Pitti Palace that served in 1697 as a wedding gift for Prince Gian Gastone. Foggini also worked for Cosimo's eldest son, Prince Ferdinando, designing clocks for his fine and large collection. Foggini was the source of innumerable works that he either made himself or inspired through lively and clever drawings. We shall comment later on some of the most significant.

Generally speaking, Foggini prepared a model or drawing and delegated production of the various parts to specialists; for gold he often used the gilder Pietro Motti, whose name appears on several bills along with that of the goldsmith Cosimo Merlini, to whom we owe many important pieces. For work in semiprecious stones, Foggini chose his alter ego, Giovanni Antonio Torricelli.

An artist highly esteemed at court was the Bavarian ivory-carver Philipp Sengher, also a "Gentleman of the Chamber" and in direct contact with Cosimo. Two medallions joined by a chain that bear the portrait of the grand duke and his monogram surmounted by a crown are a tour de force by this artist. Cut out of a single piece of ivory and skillfully decorated in bas-relief, they show Cosimo around 1675 at a fairly early age and perhaps were a presentation piece. This artist's skill can be seen in many works now in the Museo degli Argenti, such as two vases that, if this were possible, seem even more masterful than the medallions.

Continuing this rapid survey of court artists, we come upon Massimiliano Soldani Benzi (1656–1740), another extremely important artist, who obtained the prestigious job of "Master of Coins and Keeper of the Mint" and began the renaissance of that institution thanks to the issue of a series of over fifty beautiful coins celebrating the magnificence of the family. Cosimo III was enormously interested in this art and sent his sculptor to Paris so that he could practice the subtle technique of engraving coins, and Soldani was granted the patronage of Louis XIV, who patiently sat three times for one of the first medallion portraits made by the sculptor in Paris.

On his return to Florence, Soldani did not abandon this art, but continued to practice it along with his activity as a sculptor, specializing in small- and medium-sized bronzes. Foggini, director of the Gallery, often turned to him for sculptural pieces, and Soldani seems to have operated independently on such projects. He also had notable influence in goldwork and other decorative arts. His splendid series of small bronzes inspired by classical sculpture belonging to the Medici family takes us back to a similar series owned by Cosimo I and Ferdinando I. This was a rare concession to the secular and the classical in the court art of Cosimo III, and although a few of these pieces remained at the Florentine court, most of them ended up in great foreign collections. Soldani worked not only for Cosimo and foreign patrons but was among the favored artists of Prince Ferdinando, for whom he made a number of pieces.

We have examined the consequences of the long reign of Cosimo III on Florentine art, and his stubbornness, egocentricity, and absolute will also had a deleterious influence on court art. This was true throughout the fifty years of his reign. The basic purpose of court art was to glorify the grand duke, and this did little to stimulate artistic creativity. Cardinal Francesco Maria de' Medici (1660–1711), the grand duke's brother, could have changed the direction of taste but could in no way improve the situation.

The artistic history of Cosimo III's reign is recorded in

the small group of important pieces created by his artists as well as in the development of his workshops. These were workshops in the true sense, where work was executed by a team of craftsmen, and here the absolutist spirit reigning in Florence was reflected, especially under Foggini's supervision. Cosimo's mysticism propelled his artists to produce works of a religious character, sometimes with wonderful results.

The first pieces produced, such as the Soldani reliquaries, were bichromatic silver and black, and this was later slowly replaced by more complex techniques and the use of more varied materials. The reliquary for the crib of the Christ Child was first outlined by Merlini in February 1695 in a letter to the grand duke's secretary and was finished in record time on January 5, 1697, when the artist brought the elaborate finished work into the "Chamber of His Most Serene Highness." Much of this work was executed by a team of workshop artists, and today large parts are missing, including a pair of chalcedony angels on alabaster clouds and the silver heads of cherubs on a round cloud of the same stone. Merlini was responsible for the goldwork, Torricelli for engraving the semiprecious stones. From correspondence we know that some part of the reliquary was to have been made in Milan, where a complete colored-wax model was sent so that the layout of the entire work could be more clearly understood by the artists of the Lombard city.

During his pilgrimage to Rome for the Holy Year in 1700, the grand duke presented Pope Innocent XII with a bas-relief semiprecious-stone representation of the Annunciation with an extremely rich frame of gilt bronze, silver, and semiprecious stones, in the manner of Foggini. The pope was delighted with the elaborate work, which, in fact, enjoyed good fortune and was particularly appreciated by the grand duke, who ordered a number of variations for various purposes, such as a holy-water container made for the Electress Palatine Anna Maria Lodovica, which Cosimo presented to her in 1704. This devotional image was particularly dear to the city and to the grand duke, who constantly employed it for official gifts: a number of versions appear in different collections.

That same year, Torricelli created another religious work for the grand duke, perhaps his masterpiece, the door in semiprecious stones for the tabernacle of the Palatine Chapel in the Pitti Palace. These opulent religious works must have cost Cosimo a small fortune, particularly considering the large quantities of precious materials and the number of craftsmen needed for such undertakings. Even so, the workshops continued to produce masterpieces, and the grand duke's taste does not appear to have been satisfied by more modest productions. In 1709 Foggini completed the Elector's Cabinet, a large showpiece in ebony, gilt bronze, and semiprecious stones that Cosimo wanted to present to the Elector Palatine Johann Wilhelm, husband of his daughter, Anna Maria Lodovica.

In 1713 the workshops completed the reliquary of the Dominican Saints, another of the masterpieces ordered by Cosimo III for the Palatine Chapel. This was an architectural work in the form of a small hexagonal temple with decorations in gilt bronze and semiprecious stones. The prototype that inspired this work is probably the Temple of the Tribune built by Bernardo Buontalenti for Francesco I, and the reliquary reflects the religious interpretation willed by the reigning grand duke. The work's eclecticism and style would seem to come from Foggini, who personally oversaw and directly participated in the creation of the large reliquary of the Patron Saints of Tuscany, completed in 1718. Its structure was similar to that of the reliquary of the Dominican Saints, but on an octagonal instead of a hexagonal base and surmounted by a silver cloud. The whole concoction was embellished with garlands of semiprecious-stone fruit and gilt-bronze decorations. At various points on this structure were enthroned twenty-two silver statuettes of Tuscany's patron saints. The work, commissioned by the grand duke, was placed in the Chapel of Reliquaries and exhibited to the public on Maundy Thursday. The original was dismantled in 1769 and plundered by the French in 1799, and only seven statues of saints and five reliquary-bearing cherubs remain from this great devotional structure.

As had happened previously, the silver and gold of the later Medici suffered from the vandalism of French troops, who completed the job begun by the first of the Lorraine rulers who, forced by economic needs, had sold off a large quantity of antique goldwork. Almost nothing is left of these pieces, although we know who made them. Cosimo Merlini, a descendant of the original Merlini, and Bernardo Holzmann were court favorites whose masterpiece is perhaps the Impruneta altar-front. The grand duke wanted to decorate the altar of the Impruneta with a votive front recalling the cure of his son Ferdinando. The altar, started in 1695 and completed almost twenty years later, is made up mainly of a large silver plate divided into three panels, in the center of which appears the kneeling figure of the patron, modeled after Cosimo II's ex-voto. At the sides are two ovals with Jesus crowning the patron saints of Tuscany and the Madonna in Glory. The overall predominance of silver, which alternates with small semiprecious-stone inserts, with respect to other works of the 18th century makes this a sort of creation in negative, which possibly had as its precedent the altar of the Annunziata by Nigetti.

This rapid survey reveals Cosimo III as a refined patron of the arts, one who left his mark on the Florentine taste of his time.

Grand Prince Ferdinando

Cosimo III's son Ferdinando (1663–1713) was an extremely refined and discriminating collector as well as an able and much admired musician. It was in music that he excelled, performing with skill on the harpsichord and singing with obvious talent. He created a theater in the villa at Pratolino for the performance of music he commissioned, including operas by Alessandro Scarlatti. He supervised these productions meticulously, devoting great care to even the smallest detail as if he wished to produce, way ahead of his time, a synthesis of all the arts. These efforts seem pathetic today because Ferdinando was overshadowed by his father. Because he predeceased his father and was thus denied the opportunity to take any active role in affairs of state, more than a touch of melancholy is associated with this cultivated prince, a man dedicated to the arts, but without land, dominions, or power.

Ferdinando dedicated much of his passion for collecting to the Venetian lagoon and such painters as Giuseppe Maria Crespi and Sebastiano Ricci, both of whom worked for him in the Pitti Palace. In 1706 he arranged Florence's first exhibition of paintings, in the cloister of the Santissima Annunziata. The exhibition was even provided with a catalog, which Ferdinando prepared himself.

Ferdinando's future seemed assured. Among his many good teachers were Viviani, the doctor Francesco Redi, Noris, and the Lorenzini brothers. Leibniz met him in Florence and spoke of him as a man destined for success. Eager to see the dynasty provided with an heir, Cosimo selected a wife for Ferdinando, Violante Beatrice of Bavaria, and she arrived in Florence in November 1688 aboard a carriage encrusted with gems. This arranged marriage was not necessarily unhappy, but it was childless.

Philipp Sengher (died 1723), in Florence from 1675 to 1713, worked for Ferdinando and taught him the art of ivory turning. A small ivory vase made by Ferdinando demonstrates his family ties to the first grand dukes, Cosimo and Francesco, who also enjoyed such trifles.

Ferdinando had a decided preference for ivory and commissioned many works from the ivory carver Balthasar Permoser (1651–1732), in Florence between 1676 and

1690. This artist engraved the portrait of the grand prince's wife, Violante Beatrice, and presented it to Ferdinando on his wedding. It is an extremely conceptual work, and the fine lines of the engraving render the spirit of the princess with extreme care. In 1688 Permoser made a famous series of knife handles for Ferdinando, but they were probably never put to their intended use and were instead immediately transformed into small studio sculptures by the addition of ebony and ivory plinths. The series, consisting of Adam and Eve and two groups of putti, was probably meant to have been larger. Of the four handles the figure of Adam is the best, for the artist managed to free himself from the slightly curved shape characteristic of ivory engravings. Other such works by Permoser are mentioned in the Medici inventories along with occasional wood engravings commissioned by Ferdinando.

The grand prince was among Soldani's major patrons. Soldani's Faun Bearing a Kid, today in the Bargello, appears in the 1713 inventory, and Ferdinando commissioned the splendid series of bronze bas-reliefs of the Four Seasons, now in the Bayerisches Nationalmuseum, around 1708. Ferdinando was so enthusiastic about this work that he kept the terracotta models, now in the Museo degli Argenti, in his apartments, judging them well-suited "to his most exquisite taste."

When Ferdinando died in 1713, an inventory was made of his collections. These included forty-one clocks, some of extremely rich architectural form, decorated with silver cornices, rock-crystal knobs, gilt-copper, and silver filigree, some with tortoiseshell decorations or gilded and painted brass figures.

Gian Gastone, the last grand duke

When Cosimo III died in 1723, his youngest son, Gian Gastone (1671–1737), took the throne at the age of fifty-two. It was his destiny to be the last grand duke. As long as his mental state permitted, Gian Gastone was not particularly negligent in his running of public affairs and made use of extremely capable advisers, such as Filippo Buonarroti. He was not, however, a great collector. Bored by the precious objects he inherited, he exchanged pieces with art dealers who would later exchange the same objects back to him at increased prices. His curiosity was aroused by the gloomy, grotesque paintings of Alessandro Magnasco, by witchcraft, and by the prowess of acrobats. He showed an interest in medals by Lorenzo Maria Weber, who had taken over Soldani's post at the Florentine mint, and had a copy cast in gold of one showing himself and,. on the reverse, a view of the Apennines.

The creation of works in semiprecious stone continued until the death of Cosimo III, at which time Francesco Ghinghi (1689–1762), a student of Foggini's who had taken the place of Torricelli, moved to Naples and set up a workshop for the creation of these pieces. The collecting of gems continued under Gian Gastone, and the previously mentioned acquisition of the Andreini collection was his greatest addition to the collection. Since the beautiful antique cameo representing Antoninus Pius sacrificing to Hope, now in the Archeological Museum of Florence, first appears in the Medici collections in a 1736 inventory, it was probably purchased by Gian Gastone. Thanks to Bianchi, the reorganization of the collections that had begun at the end of the previous century continued, and in 1690 the grand duke's carpenters were ordered to build new cabinets for the gems. The culmination of these efforts was the publication in 1731–32 of the *Museum Florentinum I e II*, by Gori, in which the collection's masterpieces, 1,218 stones, are illustrated and described. Around 1736 Gian Gastone was in possession of over 1,800 cameos and carved stones.

Gian Gastone died in 1737, leaving his widowed sister, Anna Maria Lodovica (1667–1743), as the last member of

Anna Maria de' Medici (1667–1743) with her husband, the Elector Palatine Johann Wilhelm, in a painting by Gian Francesco Douren (Florence, Pitti Palace).

the Medici family. The gloomy Medici mausoleum of San Lorenzo was then under construction, and she often visited to check on its progress, well aware that when she entered the mausoleum she would end an era.

When she was twenty-three, Anna Maria had been married to the Elector Palatine Johann Wilhelm. For that wedding, Cosimo had used the grand duchy's workshops to create an exemplary trousseau of works of art. In 1709, Anna Maria took the Elector's Cabinet, a prie-dieu, and other art objects to Düsseldorf.

When she returned to Florence a childless widow, she brought back her private objects, including her collection of jewelry, now known as the "Electress' Jewels." She exhibited them with pride in two display cases that she had made in her apartments. Now reduced to a few dozen, the "jeweled trinkets" of the electress then amounted to 1,000. Many of the pieces were taken apart, the stones sold in Eastern markets and the gold melted down. Many were dispersed at auction in Germany, others followed the Lorraine grand dukes when they returned to Vienna as emperors. Those now in the Museo degli Argenti were returned thanks to the peace treaty between Italy and Austria after World War I.

Those that remain do not form a homogenous group. Some of the jewels belonged to the electress's dowry and therefore come from the ancient Medici collections; others are contemporary German, Flemish, and Dutch works. Although incomplete, the collection permits a valid study of late Renaissance and proto-baroque goldwork.

When her brother Gian Gastone died, Anna Maria knew the Medici family was on the brink of extinction and did her best to pass the dynasty on to the Lorraines. While she prepared for this passage, she made efforts to keep the family collections intact. The will she set down clearly specified that "The successive grand dukes, of that which is for the ornamentation of the State, for the use of the public, and to attract the curiosity of foreigners—all the furniture, effects and rarities . . . such as cabinets, paintings, statues, libraries, jewels, and other precious things—nothing shall be transported and removed from the Capital and the State of the Grand Duchy." In this way, the Medici collections were saved from the danger of complete dispersal.

Below: Turned-ivory cup. Height 12½ inches. Florence, Museo degli Argenti.

The story associated with this and other ivories from the grand duke's collections is extremely eventful. This piece is, in fact, one of 27 cups that formed part of the spoils of war plundered by one of Mattias de Medici's officers in 1632, during the siege of Coburg. All these works date to between 1618 and 1631.

Below right: Turned-ivory cup with chain, by Johann Eisenberg, 1626. Height 20 inches. Florence, Museo degli Argenti.

This cup also comes from the group taken as plunder in Coburg. Several of these pieces were made by the duke of Saxony himself, probably in collaboration with his engravers. Grand Prince Ferdinando also made certain objects for his own enjoyment in this exotic and rare material.

Opposite: Turned-ivory cup, by Marcus Heiden, 1628 (signed and dated). Height 12 inches. Florence, Museo degli Argenti.

Marcus Heiden was one of the ivory turners who worked for the duke of Saxe-Coburg. Like the other pieces illustrated here, this piece, with its anthropomorphic decoration, comes from the spoils of the siege of Coburg. The turned work that makes up the sphere stands on a carved base, creating a harmonious combination of the two most frequently used methods of working ivory.

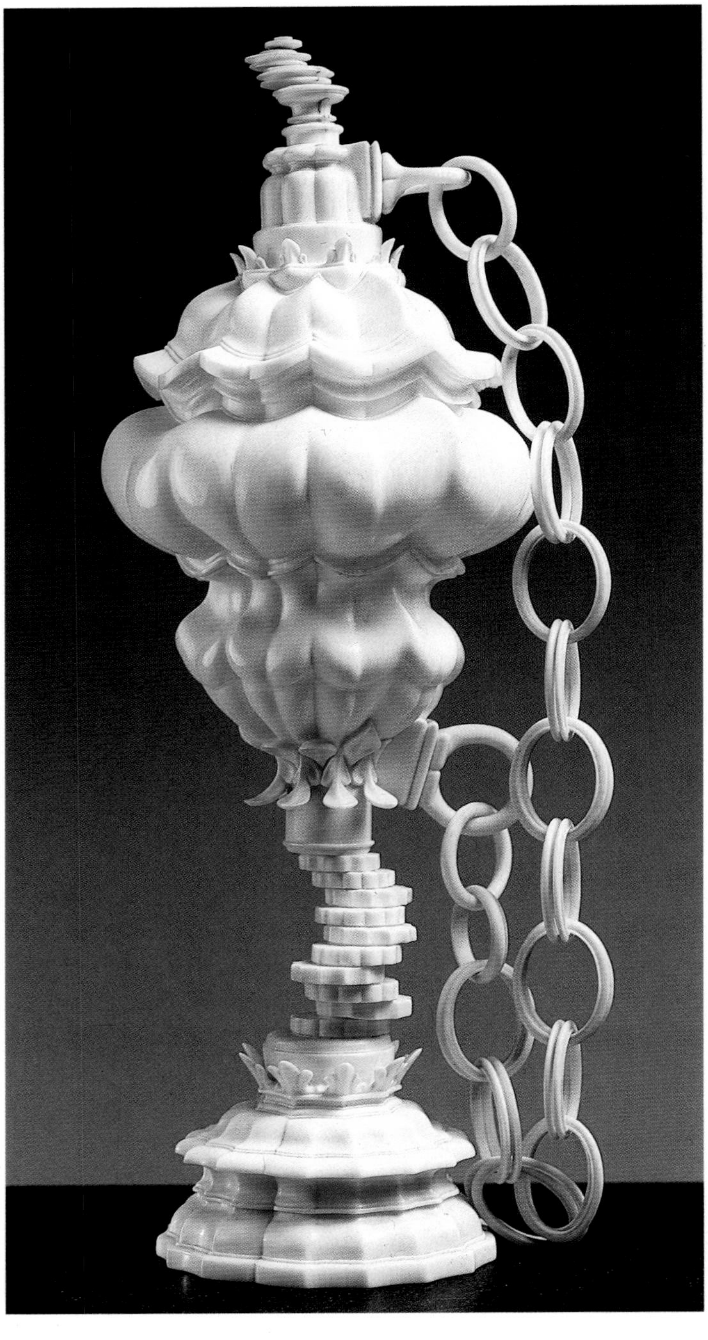

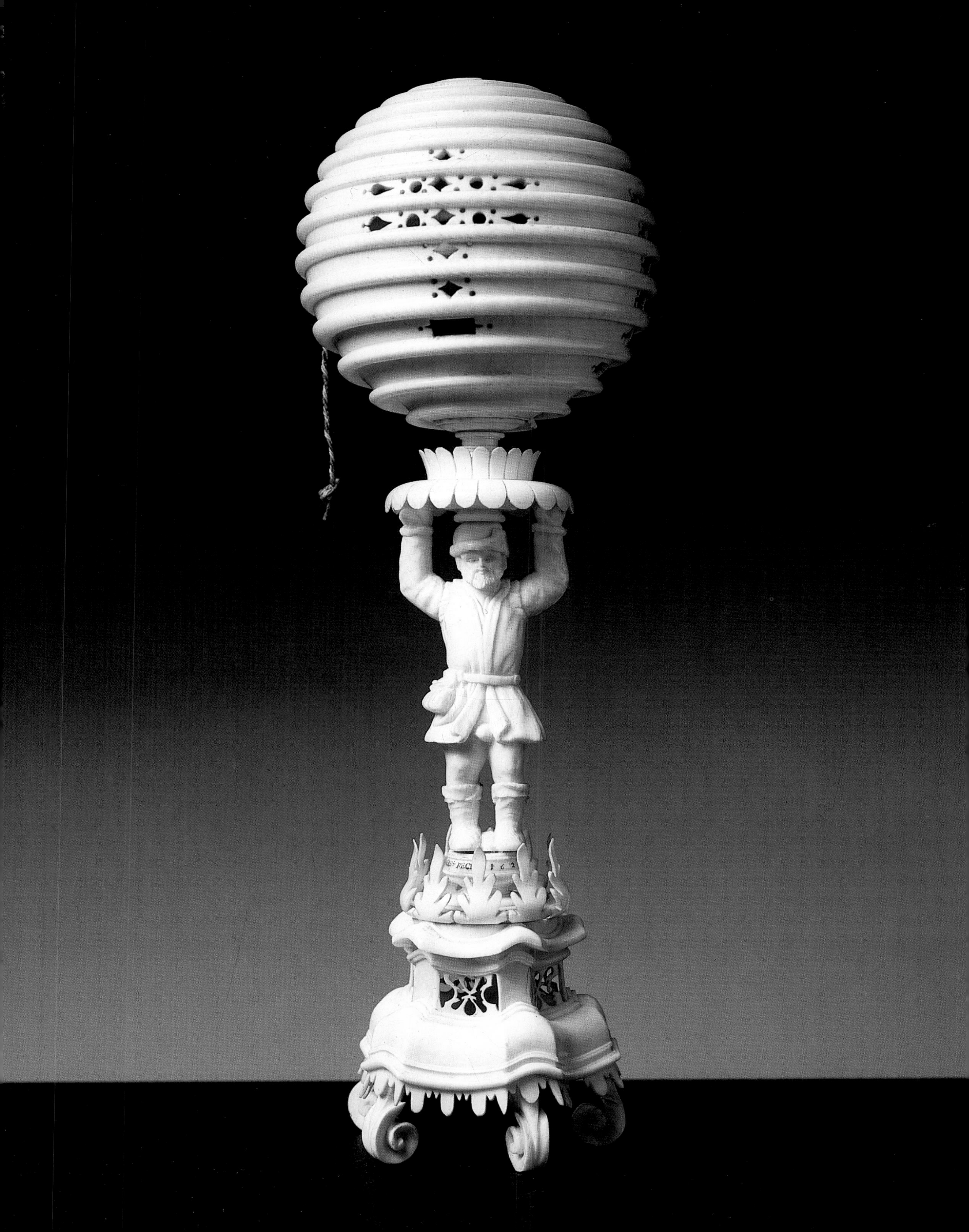

Opposite: Ivory fruit vendor embellished with a basket in enameled gold, diamonds, and semiprecious stones, on a base in agate, rubies, and pearls. Germany, 18th century. Height 4 1/2 inches; base 2 x 1 3/4 x 1 3/4 inches. Florence, Museo degli Argenti.

This small fruit vendor forms a pair with a peddler and comes from the collection of jewels and jeweled trinkets belonging to the Electress Palatine Anna Maria Lodovica. In this case, the ivory is combined with other precious materials, a technique quite customary in objects of German manufacture.

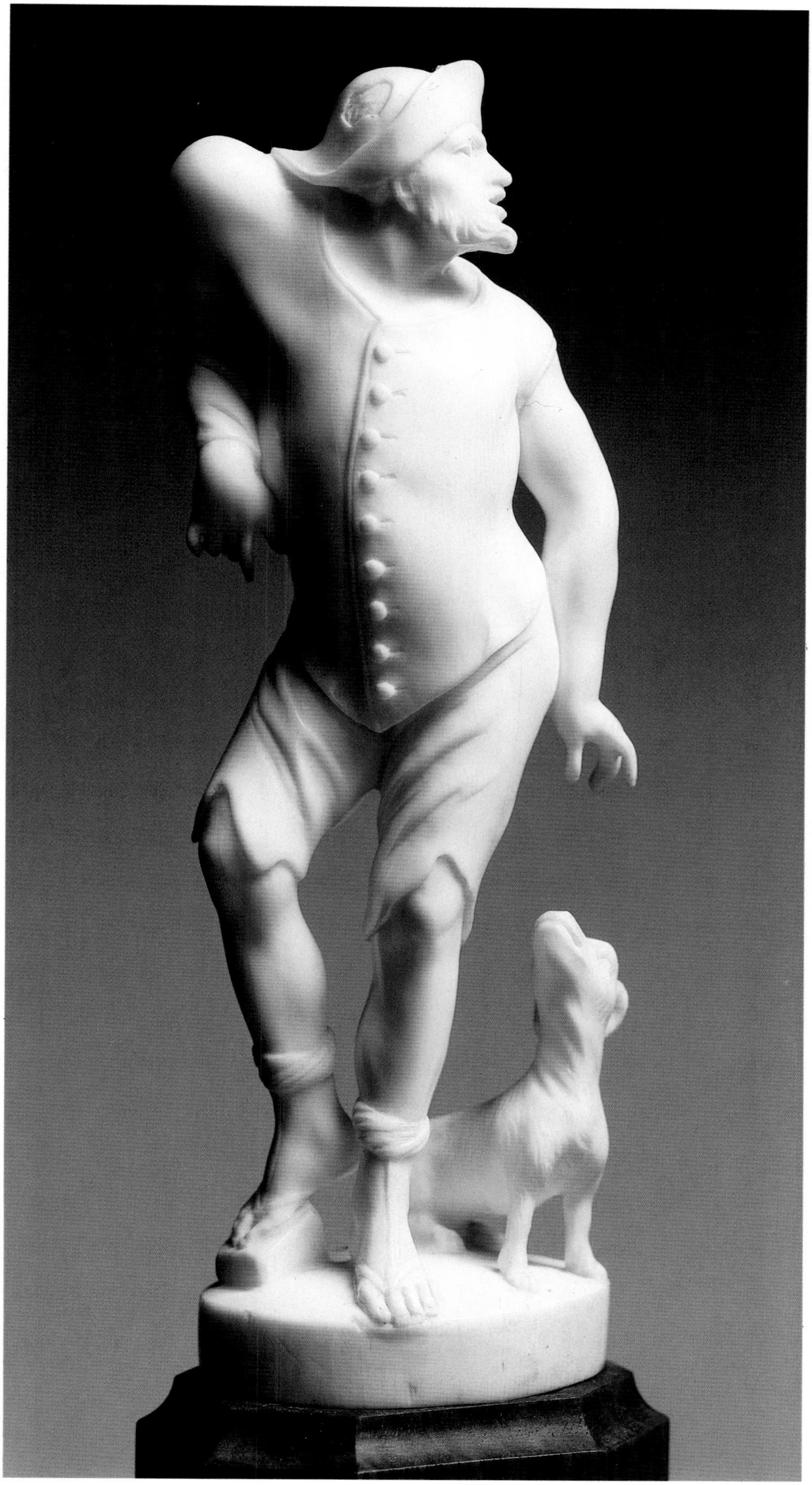

Right: Ivory commedia dell'arte masked figure (Pantalone). Germany, 18th century. Florence, Museo degli Argenti.

This Pantalone, based on a print by Callot, is one of a series of four commedia dell'arte statuettes. In this case the imitation of a porcelain figurine is evident even in the choice of subject. During the 18th century the taste for ivories progressively disappeared and was replaced by porcelain.

Below: Gold medallion with portrait of Cosimo III. Diameter 2¼ inches. Florence, Museo Nazionale del Bargello.

On the obverse is a portrait of the young Cosimo III in armor and jabot with the inscription COSMVS III D G MAGN DVN ETRVRIAE; on the reverse is a representation of Fame standing on a cloud with the inscription FAMAM EXTENDERE FACTIS. Perhaps attributable to Soldani, the medallion was made ca. 1670, perhaps on the occasion of Cosimo's investiture as grand duke.

Opposite: Bronze of the Baptism of Christ, by G. B. Foggini. Height 15 inches. Florence, Galleria Palatina.

Between 1722 and 1724, Florence's leading sculptors made twelve groups of bronzes with sacred subjects for the Electress Palatine. On March 29, 1724, Foggini was paid for his Baptism, of which another specimen is today in the Seattle Art Museum. The series constitutes an important program of small Florentine baroque bronzes.

189

Reliquary of St. Raymund in silver, ebony, and semiprecious stones, by Massimiliano Soldani Benzi. Florence, Treasury of San Lorenzo.

This reliquary, dating from 1690, is part of a series including the reliquaries of St. Louis of Toulouse, St. Pascal Baylon, and St. Alexis that modified the style of reliquaries. No longer objects for displaying a relic that took center stage and was almost always the focal point of the work, these small baroque sculptural constructions treated the relic almost as an excuse to show off the artist's virtuosity. Opposite: Detail.

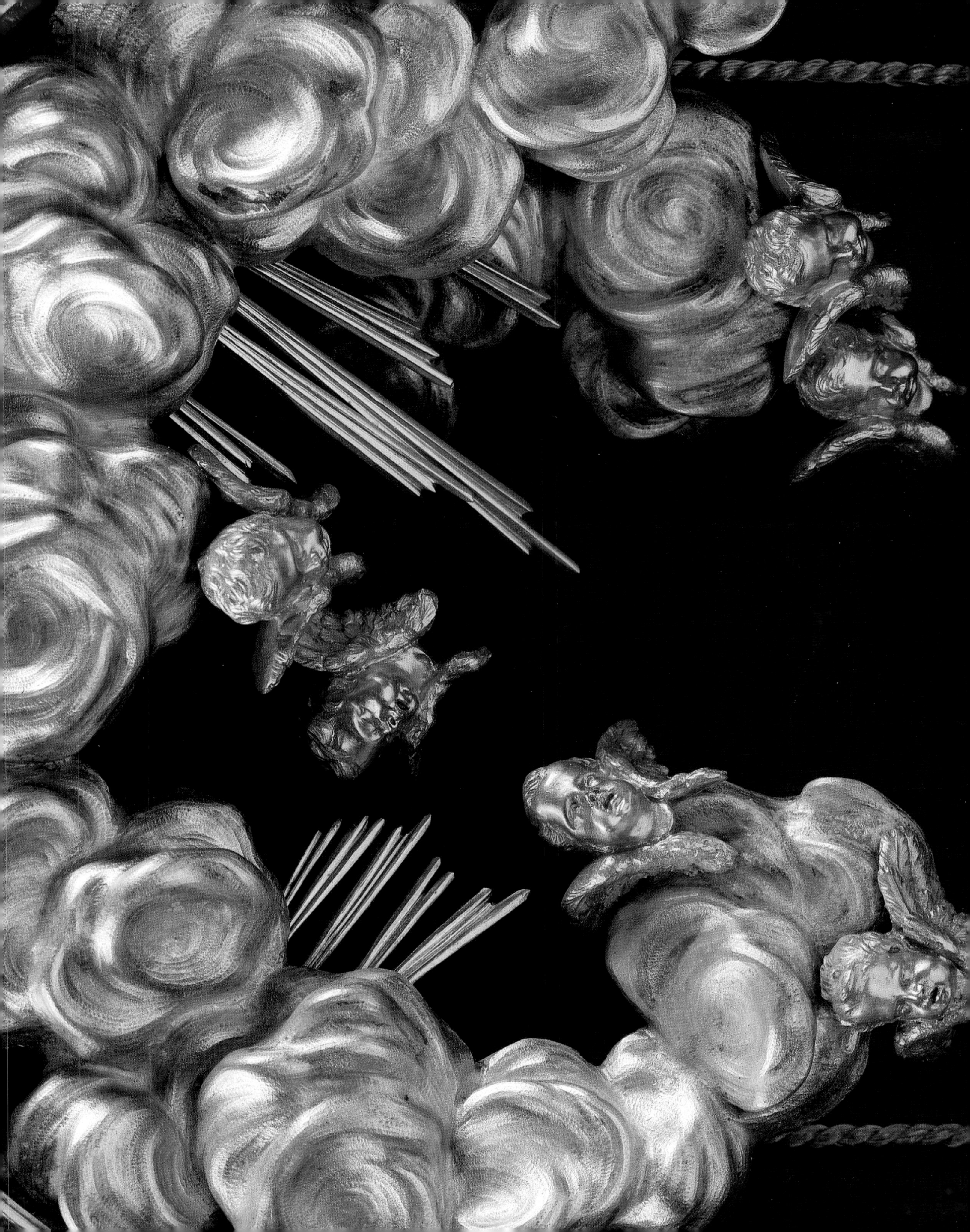

Reliquary of St. Louis of Toulouse in silver, semiprecious stones, and ebony, by Massimiliano Soldani Benzi. Florence, Treasury of San Lorenzo.

This reliquary belongs to the group made by Soldani in 1690. The contrast of silver and black, which can be found in most Tuscan furniture of this period, is used here to set off the bas-relief. The architectural composition, on the other hand, seems to have been derived from altarpieces. Soldani, whose contributions to reliquaries by Foggini were usually of secondary importance, is the undisputed protagonist in these works.

Right and opposite: Reliquary of St. Pascal Baylon in silver, semiprecious stones, and ebony, by Massimiliano Soldani Benzi. Florence, Treasury of San Lorenzo.

This, the third reliquary in the series made in 1690 by Soldani, does not differ significantly from the previous examples. Opposite: Detail.

S. PASQVALIS

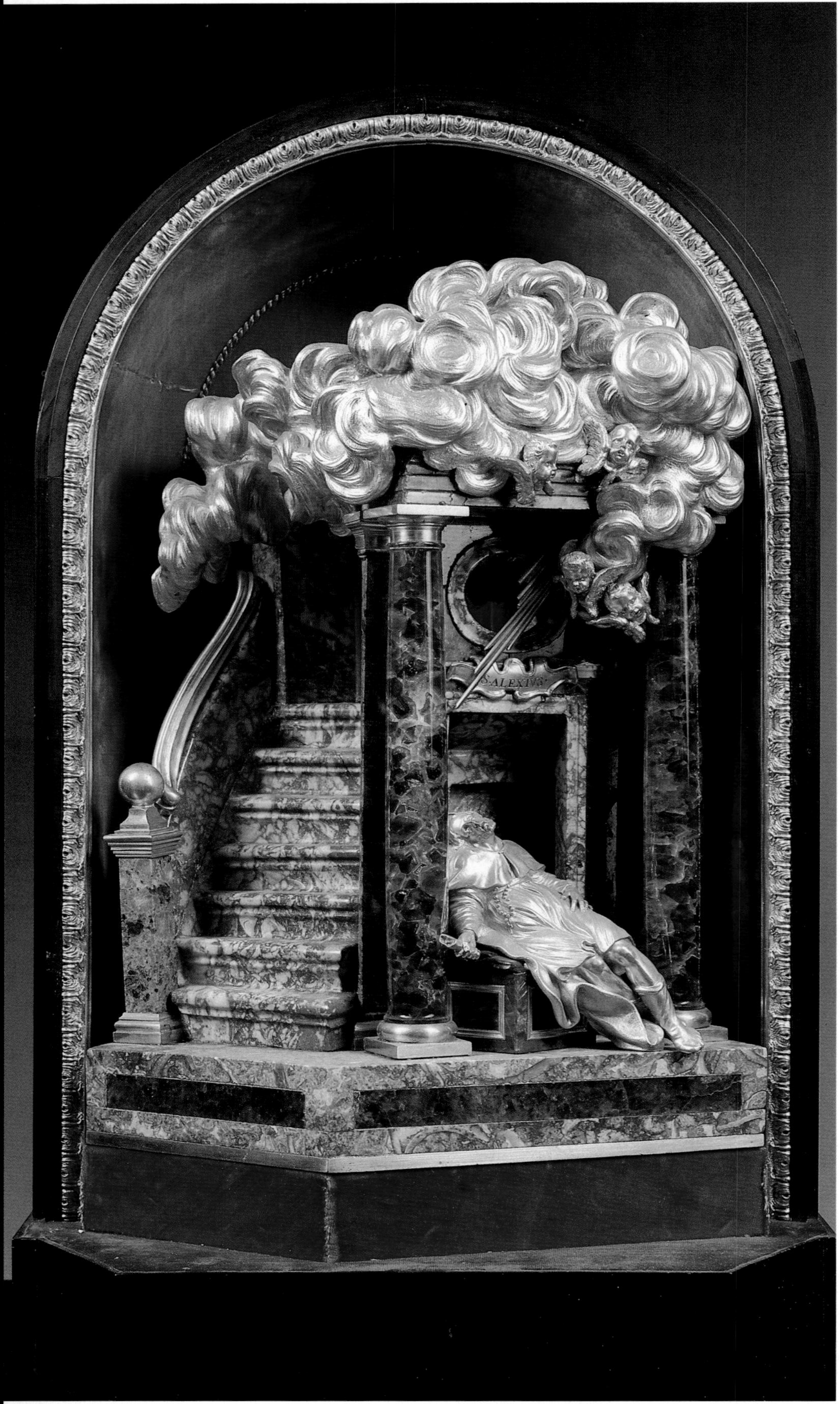

Reliquary of St. Alexis in ebony, silver, semiprecious stones, and gilt bronze, by Massimiliano Soldani Benzi. Height 21 inches. Florence, Treasury of San Lorenzo.

This reliquary contains relics of St. Alexis, the righteous young son of a 5th-century Roman patrician who gave up all his wealth to live the life of a mendicant. According to legend, he spent the last 17 years of his life working unrecognized as a servant in his father's house, sleeping in a corner under the stairs (detail, opposite). Of all the reliquaries attributed to Soldani this is the most theatrical, the closest to the canons of baroque art. The architectural structure in semiprecious stones, created with an oblique perspective, is not only a tour de force of Soldani as a virtuoso stone carver, but above all is documentation of a specific artistic expression prevalent in Florence at the time. This work is a masterpiece of its kind. This piece differs greatly from the other 1690 reliquaries because of both the large quantity of semiprecious stones and its architectural setting. These differences may be due to the fact that other artists, possibly Foggini, collaborated in its realization.

S·ALEXIVS·

Reliquary of St. Sigismond in ebony, semiprecious stones, silver, and gilt bronze. Height 22¾ inches. Florence, Treasury of San Lorenzo.

This reliquary was completed in September 1719 for the Palatine Chapel, whence it was taken to the Basilica of San Lorenzo in 1785, on the occasion of the exchange with Lorenzo de' Medici's vases. It is one of the works produced by Foggini, whose contribution was direct and not limited to design, as can be seen from evidence in the Gallery records, particularly a reference to the casting of the silver figures. The group depicts St. Sigismond, the first Christian king of the Burgundii, appearing in a vision to a wounded youth. A preparatory sketch, more elaborate than the final piece, although extremely similar in arrangement, is preserved in the Louvre. Opposite: Detail.

Reliquary of Daniel in gilt bronze, silver, ebony, and semiprecious stones. Height 26¾ inches. Florence, Treasury of San Lorenzo.

Although the scroll bears the name of St. Ambrose, the relief below it relates to Daniel in the lions' den. A number of artists collaborated on the manufacture of composite works like this. The conception of the work and its design are by Foggini, but Torricelli made the central medallion, and the goldsmith Cosimo Merlini made the silver-gilt decoration.

Overleaf: Reliquary of St. Mary of Egypt in semiprecious stones, gilt bronze, and ebony. Height 26¾ inches. Florence, Treasury of San Lorenzo.

Completed in 1704, this reliquary was made by Torricelli on the basis of a design by Foggini and is the model for an extremely successful series that included the reliquary of Daniel, that of St. Sebastian dated 1715, and even that of St. Hemeregild, although the latter is decorated in a different manner.

S·AMBROSIJ·EP.
MEDIOL·ECTÆ·DOCT

DE OSSIBVS
S MARIÆ ÆGYPTIÆ

DE OSSIBVS
S·MARIÆ ÆGYPTIÆ

Reliquary of St. Sebastian in semiprecious stones and gilt bronze, 1714. Height 22 inches. Florence, Treasury of San Lorenzo.

Completed in 1714, this reliquary is the result of cooperation between Foggini and Torricelli. At the center, the oval in semiprecious stones (detail, opposite) depicts two scenes from the Bible—the sacrifice of Isaac and Jacob's dream—that have nothing to do with the relic of St. Sebastian that the piece was supposed to hold. This circumstance cannot be explained, unless it is the use of a preexisting bas-relief that had found no other destination.

Overleaf: Reliquary of St. Hemeregild in semiprecious and precious stones, ebony, and gilt bronze. Height 29 inches. Florence, Treasury of San Lorenzo.

In the St. Hemeregild reliquary the dramatic baroque tendencies of the reliquaries of this period find different expression when compared with similar works by Soldani and Foggini. Giovanni Antonio Torricelli was without doubt a specialist in three-dimensional inlay, of which this is an outstanding example. The wooden base is almost an accessory to the upper portion of the reliquary, whose gilt-bronze halo and cloud of semiprecious stones are created with masterly lightness. Completed in 1717, the reliquary shared the fate of many others that were transferred from the Palatine Chapel to the Basilica of San Lorenzo. It has been rightly noted that the kneeling figure of the saint recalls the posture of Cosimo II in the famous ex-voto in semiprecious stones, which may be a forerunner of this piece along with the even older portable altar-front belonging to Ferdinando II. Detail on page 206.

S. SEBASTIANJ M

Opposite: Reliquary of St. Casimir of Lithuania in silver and silver gilt, from the grand ducal workshops, 1680–90. 33½ x 23 inches. Florence, Treasury of San Lorenzo.

The reliquary of St. Casimir presents a certain originality in comparison to others made in Florence at the end of the century. The sculptural component, so evident and dominant in the works of Soldani, is attenuated here in the rich foliate decoration. Also original and rare is the absence of semiprecious stones and ebony so characteristic of works from the Florentine workshops of the time.

S CASIMIRVS MAGNVS DVX LITHVANIAE

Cabinet of the Elector Palatine in ebony and various woods, bronze, mother-of-pearl, and semiprecious stones. 9 x 5 1/3 x 1 3/4 feet. Florence, Museo degli Argenti.

This cabinet was made in the grand ducal workshops between 1707 and 1709. The design, statuettes, and bronze decorations were made by Giovanni Battista Foggini, head sculptor and architect of the Florentine court between 1694 and 1725. The structure of this piece of furniture is in ebony, fir, poplar, oak, walnut, and mother-of-pearl, and it is decorated with mosaic panels and reliefs in semiprecious stones. In the central niche is a statuette of gilt bronze and semiprecious stones showing Johann Wilhelm, Elector Palatine and husband of Anna Maria Lodovica de' Medici, daughter of Cosimo III. The grand duke himself commissioned the work and sent it as a gift to his daughter in Düsseldorf. In 1717, she returned to Florence a widow, bringing with her this piece of furniture. Opposite: Detail of the central statuette.

CAPVT.S.BRIGIDÆ

Opposite: Reliquary of St. Bridget in ebony, silver gilt, rock crystal, and enamel, from the grand ducal workshops, first half 17th century. 12 x 13$^3/_4$ x 7$^3/_4$ inches. Florence, Treasury of San Lorenzo.

This reliquary box seems to repeat, in a less rich and elaborate way, a model that had its prototype in that of St. John the Baptist, with inlaid semiprecious stones, donated by Ferdinando I to Genoa.

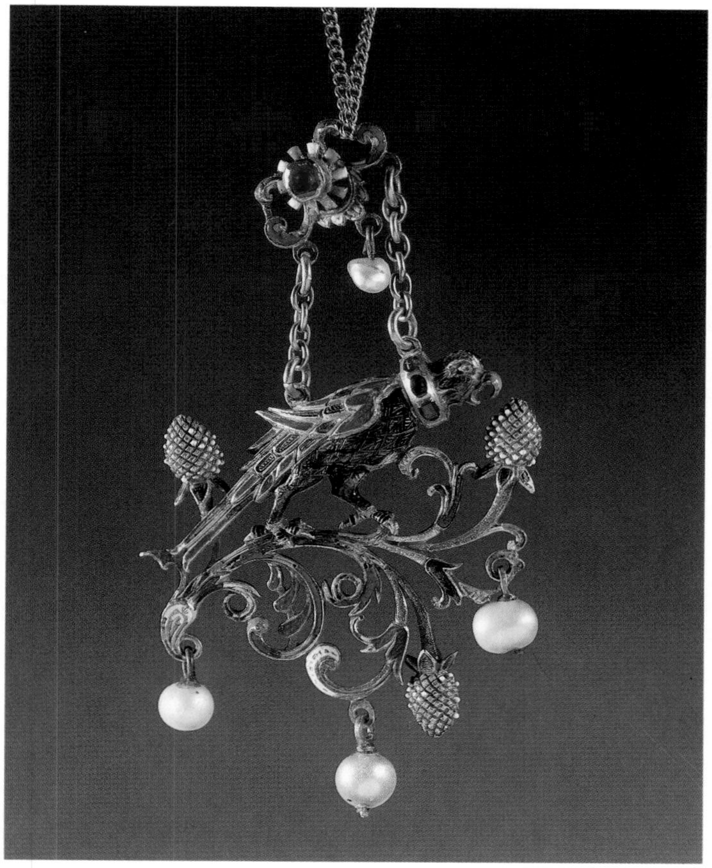

Pendant of a parrot in enameled gold, pearls, and rubies. Flanders, 1580–90. 2$^1/_2$ x 1$^1/_2$ inches. Florence, Museo degli Argenti.

This parrot sits on a branch of enameled gold that represents a stylized strawberry plant. This is one of the few pieces of its kind in which the body of the animal subject is not made from a baroque pearl; in this case the polychrome coloring of the bird may have suggested the chosen solution.

Pendant of a dragon fighting with a bee in enameled gold, pearls, and rubies. Flanders, 1580. 2$^1/_2$ x 1$^1/_2$ inches. Florence, Museo degli Argenti.

The bee is almost hidden on the stomach of the dragon, under whose left wing a golden chain prevents the monster from sinking its fangs into the insect. The symbolism of the bee is often used to call up the image of hard work and good government.

Below: Pendant of a mermaid in enameled gold, baroque pearls, white and rose-cut diamonds. Netherlands, 1650. 2 1/2 x 1 1/3 inches. Florence, Museo degli Argenti.

This pendant has lost a few of the pearls that decorated the lower part and still shows traces of enamel on the tail. The subject seems to allude to the mystery of beauty and the difficulty in attaining it.

Below right: Pendant of a gondola with masked figures and lovers in enameled gold, pearls, rubies, diamonds, and emeralds, attributed to Giovanni Battista Scolari, Munich, 1568. 2½ x 2 inches. Florence, Museo degli Argenti.

Two masked characters from the commedia dell'arte, Pantalone and Zanne, play a serenade to two lovers sitting in a gondola made from a baroque pearl. The mount suggests waves on the sea. It is probable that this jewel was made at the time of the first performance of the Italian commedia dell'arte at the court of Albert V of Bavaria, on the occasion of the marriage of his son Wilhelm to Renata of Lorraine.

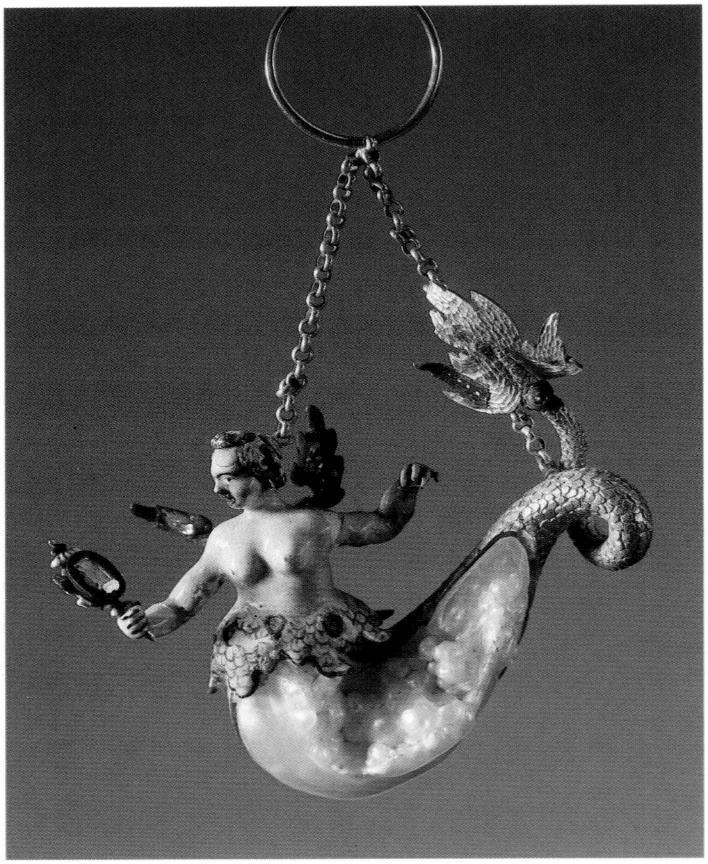

Opposite: Pendant of a ship with lovers under a tent in enameled gold, pearls, rubies, diamonds. Germany, 1570. 3 x 2 3/4 inches. Florence, Museo degli Argenti.

This pendant is similar to the one shown above right. It would not seem unreasonable to consider this also to be a work made in Germany during the second half of the 16th century.

Opposite: Pendant of Venus and Mars in enameled gold, pearls, rubies, and emeralds. Germany, 1600. 2¾ x 2¼ inches. Florence, Museo degli Argenti.

This jewel is made from joining two different objects: in fact, the two central figures have no relation to the mount, which has several holes indicating a later adaptation. However, it is recorded in this form in the inventory drawn up at the death of the Electress Palatine.

Below: Pendant of Cupid and a seahorse in enameled gold and pearls. Netherlands, 1650. 2 x 2½ inches. Florence, Museo degli Argenti.

The value of this extremely simple pendant is based exclusively on the enamel and goldwork. The horse and spirited figure of the Cupid riding it allude to amorous themes, as do the majority of jewels from the first half of the 17th century.

Preceding left-hand page: Pendant of Triton in enameled gold, pearls, rubies, emeralds, and garnets. Flanders, 1580–90. 3 x 2 inches. Florence, Museo degli Argenti.

Pendants such as this, in which a baroque pearl is used to form the central part of the jewel, invert in a certain sense the relationship between stone and mount. What is important is the fantastic rendering and the use of the pearl for a curious and original subject. In this case a garnet, almost parallel to the club studded with precious stones, is used in addition to the pearl.

Preceding right-hand page: Pendant of a mermaid in enameled gold, pearls, diamonds, and rubies. Germany, 1580–90. 4 1/4 x 2 1/4 inches. Florence, Museo degli Argenti.

In this pendant, a small baroque pearl is discreetly used, barely underlining the roundness of the mermaid's breast. Note the symmetrical relationship among the stones, which seems to ignore the anthropomorphic design, almost repeating the representation of the constellation made by joining various stars to one another.

Left: Pendant of Pegasus attacked by the Chimera in enameled gold, pearls, and rubies. Flanders, 1570–80. 2 1/2 x 1 inches. Florence, Museo degli Argenti.

When the pendant is made almost exclusively of gold, the goldsmith can do what he likes without having to use stones in a symmetrical manner. In this case, the effect of the object is created by the use of gold and enamel. The symbolism of the jewel is connected to the image of Pegasus as Virtue, attempting to defend itself from the assaults of the Chimera (Vice), a type of symbolism not infrequent in Renaissance jewelry.

Right: ***Pendant of a wounded lion in enameled gold, pearls, and rubies. Flanders, 1580. 3 1/2 x 2 1/4 inches. Florence, Museo degli Argenti.***

This lion, formed almost entirely from a baroque pearl, has been wounded by a golden arrow. Its gaping mouth holds a ruby, representing the blood of the wounded animal. It is probable that, in the theme of the wounded beast, the motto, extremely appropriate for a luxury jewel, "Omnia Vincit Amor" *is to be understood.*

Overleaf left: Statue of Marcus Curtius in enameled gold, diamonds, silver, and pearls. Flanders, 1700. 12 1/2 x 6 1/2 inches. Florence, Museo degli Argenti.

The theme of Marcus Curtius is not frequent in the repertoire of the jeweler, as it is taken from Roman history. The underlying motif is moral strength. The base shows some signs of restoration, as does the tail, which is excessively simple and bears mediocre enameling when compared to the body of the horse.

Overleaf right: Button of a flautist in enameled gold, diamonds, and pearls. Netherlands, 1590. 1 1/2 x 1 1/4 inches. Florence, Museo degli Argenti.

This decorative button forms part of a series of nine extant examples in Florence, to which a tenth, in Vienna, must be added. They represent various soldiers from a Netherlands regiment and were sewn to a ribbon used to ornament a hat. Extremely fine works, they are an interesting example of men's jewels.

Swiss soldier in enameled gold, pearls, and rose-cut diamonds. Germany, 1680. Base 2 x 1½ x 1½ inches; figure 2¾ inches. Florence, Museo degli Argenti.

The figure of the Swiss soldier, like the cobbler on the right, was not a jewel to be worn, but rather a trinket that could be used to decorate a small cabinet or used as an ornament for a boudoir.

Cobbler in enameled gold, pearls, and diamonds. Germany, 1680. Base 2 x 1½ x 1½ inches, figure 2¾ inches. Florence, Museo degli Argenti.

Anthropomorphic knickknacks of this sort, tending toward the grotesque, were common in the grand ducal collections. This trinket belonged to the Electress Palatine and was probably purchased by her husband during the Medici stay in Germany.

Opposite: Muleteer in ivory, ebony, silver gilt, enamelwork, diamonds, and rock crystal. Germany, 1670–80. ½ x 2¾ x ¾ inches. Florence, Museo degli Argenti.

Among the jewels belonging to the Electress Palatine is another very like this one. Similar models were made by several silversmiths in Dresden, such as Johann H. Koechler and Johann M. Dinglinger. The original model for such groups is to be found in Oriental works of art, particularly Indian ones that show ivory elephants set in mounts of great splendor.

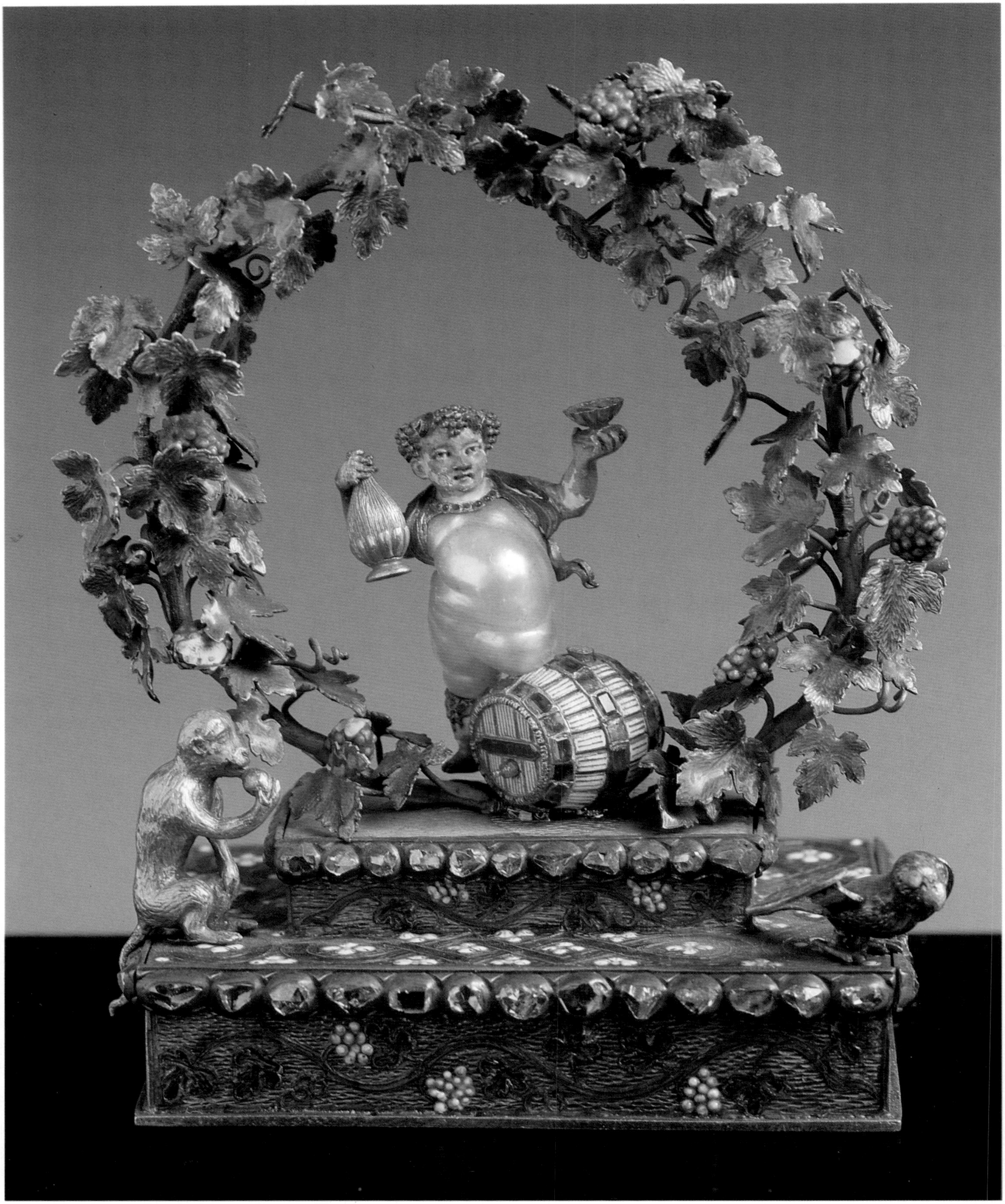

Opposite: Bacchus in enameled gold, pearls, diamonds, and rubies. Germany, 1670. 3 x 2½ inches. Florence, Museo degli Argenti.

Figurines such as this, as well as others bordering on the grotesque, made excellent decoration for a small portable cabinet or could be used to embellish a table or shelf.

Above left: Ostrich in pearl, enameled gold, diamonds, and rubies. Flanders, end of 16th century. 2 x 1¼ inches. Florence, Museo degli Argenti.

This jewel originally served as a finial for a cover. The body is formed from a large baroque pearl, the feet, neck, and tail are of enameled gold, the bird's collar is set with diamonds, and it holds a ruby in its raised left foot.

Above: Pendant of a cockerel in enameled gold, pearls, diamonds, and rubies. Flanders, 1580. 2¾ x 2 inches. Florence, Museo degli Argenti.

This jewel is not a brooch, but a pendant, from which the chain is missing. The cockerel stands on a caduceus, which gives us reason to believe the classical symbolism was suggested by the Ripa di Responsabile Vigilanza. Once again the jewel's symbolism is in the realm of morality, setting up beauty and affectation as virtues capable of preserving the soul from baseness.

***Left:* Turtle in pearl, gold, enamel, and diamonds. Flanders, end of 16th century. 1/2 x 1 inches. Florence, Museo degli Argenti.**

An oval baroque pearl forms the carapace of the turtle, its underside is of blue and green enamel, and its eyes and head are set with diamonds.

***Opposite:* Butterfly in enameled gold, with a baroque pearl, diamonds, rubies, and silver. Flanders, 1630. 3/4 x 2 1/2 x 2 3/4 inches. Florence, Museo degli Argenti.**

This jewel differs greatly from the other zoomorphic trinkets in the electress' collection. The unusually long baroque pearl may have suggested the representation of a butterfly, but the piece's greatest value lies in the subtle and delicate rendering of the wings, in which the enamel is the most important element.

Ox in gold, pearls, rubies, diamonds, and emeralds. Flanders, 1590. 3/4 x 1 1/2 inches. Florence, Museo degli Argenti.

This jewel and other animals are similar to those preserved in the casket belonging to Eleonora Gonzaga. Both the casket and the jewels are thought to have been made in Rome by the Flemish goldsmith Leonard Zaerles in 1584 pursuant to a commission from Cardinal Ferdinando de' Medici.

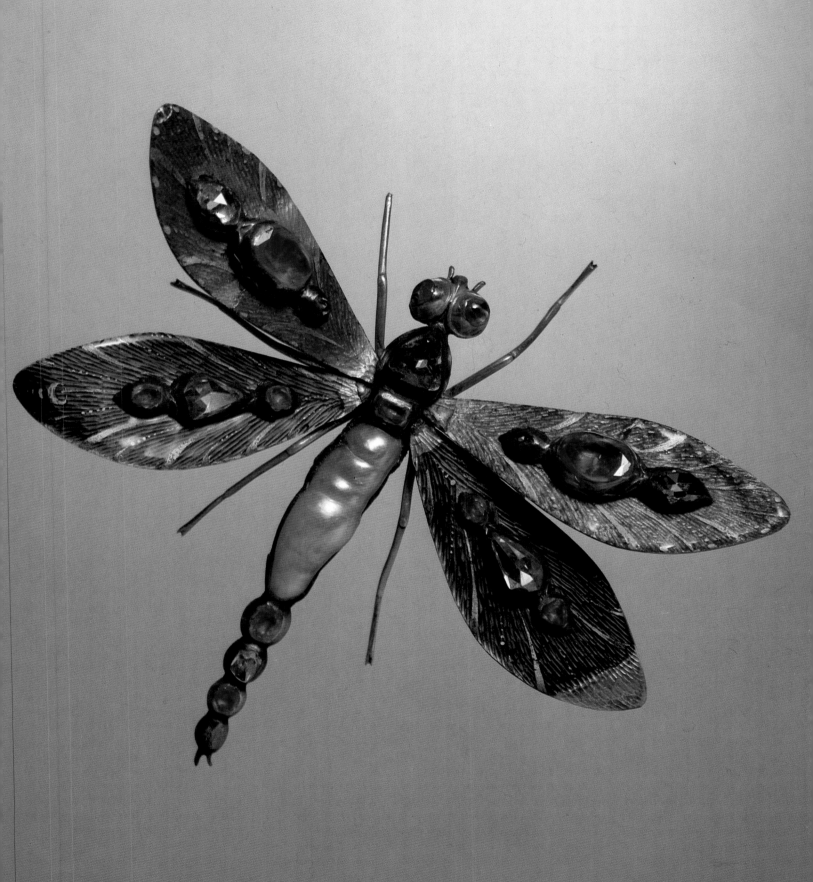

Lizard in pearl, enameled gold, and diamonds. Flanders, end of 16th century. 1/2 x 2 1/2 inches. Florence, Museo degli Argenti.

A thin pearly sheet forms the back of the animal, and its body is of enameled gold, with diamonds set in its claws, tail, and head.

Perfume case in painted ivory, gold, diamonds, crystal, and silk. Germany, 1680. 2⅓ x 2¼ inches. Florence, Museo degli Argenti.

This ivory perfume casket, painted red, contains three tiny crystal bottles. The electress also owned a similar piece, now in Vienna. Unusual in both shape and material, this object may well have been made in Dresden. It represents an exotic variant of the little nécessaires, *usually in gold and semiprecious stones or (later) in porcelain, produced in the German city's workshops.*

Documents

From the inventories of the Medici treasures

Inventory of the jewels and precious objects kept, on the death of Cosimo I (1574), by his second wife, Camilla Martelli, and in part given to her daughter, Virginia Medici, on February 7, 1585 (State Archives of Florence, *Miscellanea Medicea* 12, ins. 1b)

"- One belt of gold with twenty-four divisions, in twelve of which are three large pearls to each division, in four are four flat rubies, in four are four emeralds, in three are three white sapphires, and in one a faceted pebble diamond.
- One golden collar in thirty-nine divisions, in twenty of which are twenty large round pearls, in eight are eight emeralds, in seven are seven rubies, and in four are four diamonds
- One garland of gold with nineteen divisions, in ten of which are ten round pearls, in five are five emeralds, in two, two rubies, and in two, two diamonds, within it a Fortune with a large pear-shaped pearl below
- One pair of gold earrings with two pearl eagles with three little round pearls to each earring
- One pair of gold bracelets with eighteen divisions, in ten of which are ten pearls, in four, four emeralds, in one a diamond, and in two, two diamonds, and in two, two emeralds
- Two strings of pearls the size of beads with 46 pearls to each string
- One diamond mounted in a ring of gold
- One emerald mounted in a ring of gold
- One cross of balas rubies with three pearls
- One ring of gold all covered with jewels
- One pair of bracelets in gold with cameos therein
- One pair of emerald earrings
- One golden collar of 34 divisions, seventeen of which contain four pearls to each division, in 13, thirteen rubies, and in four, four diamonds.
- The head of an ermine in gold, comprising three rubies, one diamond, a star of diamonds with six pearls, twenty-three pearls, a heart of diamonds and rubies in the mouth of said head
- Number one thousand one hundred and three pearls the size of tares
- Number seventy-seven pearls slightly larger than the above
- One crystal belt with gold, it goes down to the ground with its vase
- One belt of agate and gold buttons there being 38 agates and 38 buttons with a gold vase
- Twenty-two rosettes with three pearls, one with a Cleopatra
- One perfume belt with 25 gold vases and 25 gold buttons, with a large vase at the bottom
- One string of perfume buttons 240 in number separated by little gold buttons
- One gold belt with the Knights' Cross, having 36 divisions
- Three pairs of earrings, that is Cernettini, eaglets and blue ribbons
- One large cabinet covered with leather, within which the following articles:
- Shirts of Rheims linen with embroidery in silk and gold of various kinds, 'lettuce' collars, cloths of raw silk and gold, towels, pocket handkerchiefs, large handkerchiefs, peignoirs, stockings
- One case covered with red leather and golden studs, within which:
- One basin
- One silver tankard
- One small footed table in mother-of-pearl
- One small blazing walnut chest set in gold, with coat of arms
- Seven pairs of cloth slippers with gold, including one pair of bedroom slippers
- One chest covered with purple velvet, within which the following articles for dressing the hair:
- One towel in Rheims linen worked in netting
- One peignoir worked in flesh-pink silk
- One small mirror with its back adorned with lapis and carnelian
- One cabinet trimmed in turquoise velvet covered with silver
- One pair of scissors with case wired with silver
- One silver straightener
- One flask of perfume netted in gold
- One silver funnel
- One albarello with silver lid
- Two ivory combs worked with gold."

The treasure of Francesco I at his death: "Inventory of the Wardrobe of the House and Palace of the Casino, under the custody of Piero Elmi, begun today, this eighth day of March 1587 . . ." (State Archives of Florence, *Guardaroba Medicea* 136, cc. 154-168)

"In the Gallery:
One bronze Hercules bearing Cacus in his arms, height 3/4 arm / One jewel box in rock crystal with a foot in silver gilt, 3/4 arm high / One figurine in antique bronze on a base in walnut, the figure 0/4 of an arm high / An India-nut for use as a flask with a long neck, it rests on three feet in ebony, 0/2 high / A Florence in wax by Giambologna on a base in walnut, 0/3 arms high / A bronze cherub sitting on a bronze cube with a bronze shield on his arm, on a wooden square 0/6 high / One foot complete with the claw of a great beast with ornament from the top in wood and ebony crowned with little silver stars 1/2 arms high / One small figurine in bronze on a base of painted wood 6 spans high in all / One flask of German steel outlined or inlaid with silver with its stopper in gilt copper, 0/2 arms high / Two bronze cherubs like bookends on two bases, one in wood and the other in mixed marble, 0/3 arms high / Two flasks called antique / One antique flask with in front two snails in mother-of-pearl edged with gold and various colors with a foot in worked silver / An antique flask made from an ostrich egg furnished with German steel inlaid with silver with its handle and beak, 2/3 arms high/ A bronze figure of an old man on a base in walnut 0/2 arms high / One small Hercules / One bronze horseman on a base of walnut decorated with gold and inlaid with mixed marble, 2/3 arms high / One small marble dog lying on an oval base in walnut with mixed slabs of marble set around it and bordered in gold 3/4 arms wide and 0/1 high / One marble figure of Hercules with a similar base, 3/4 arms high / One sundial with its facets painted with various colors, decorated with gold with its foot in stained wood / One naked figurine in bronze with one arm raised to its head, on a base of walnut decorated with gold, 0/2 arms high / One small lion in bronze said to be by Giambologna 0/4 arms long and 0/6 arms high / One bronze figure, said to be a Brutus, with a base in walnut in which are set plaques of mixed marble and which is bordered in gold, 0/2 arms high / A small bronze head with bust on a base of wood stained black, 0/2 arms high / One seated figure

in alabaster with head, arms, and legs in bronze / One small snail in mother-of-pearl, all pierced / One Hercules and Antaeus in bronze on a base in walnut engraved and bordered with gold, the whole being one arm high / One small head in marble with bust in bronze / One bronze bull by Giambologna of approximately 0/2 arms high / One bronze horse of approximately 0/2 arms / One celestial globe with foot and ornaments in brass 2/3 arms high / One antique bronze figure of a Bacchus on a base in bronze 2/3 arms high / One small figure in bronze on a base of stained wood, 0/6 arms high / One bronze billy-goat on a base in walnut trimmed with gold and set with mixed marble stones, 0/3 arms high / One small dog in bronze on two bronze shoes 0/8 arms in size / One marble cherub with wings 2/3 arms tall with a bow in his hand / One branch of coral with a foot in pierced silver, 0/3 arms tall / One small bronze figurine 0/8 arms tall / One writing desk in intarsia work set with ivory in little stars with its lock in silver measuring 0/3 arms in all directions / One silver Cupid on a base in engraved silver 0/2 arms tall / One bronze figurine holding one foot in its hand, of Venus cutting her nail, on a base of alabaster 0/6 arms tall / One India-nut for use as a flask with a small nut of the same sort on top of it to form the neck, with its foot and lid in ebony, 0/2 arms tall / A bronze figurine on its base in brass 0/6 arms tall / One vase in silver gilt with a silver flower dropped in it, 0/2 arms high / Two small ducks in porcelain stuck together / One bronze figure 2/3 arms tall / Another similar figure resting on a stick with wings on its head 2/3 arms tall / A silver figure with a lantern of the same kind in its hand, with a silver goose at its feet / One St. Paul in bronze on a base of walnut 0/2 arms high / One small bronze figurine resting on its hands on a base in wood 0/6 arms tall / One head with bust and base in marble / One sundial in the shape of a ball, painted with various colors and decorated with gold with its base in stained wood 0/2 arms high / One bronze figure on a base in walnut 0/2 arms high / One bronze figure with a ball on its shoulders with a base in wood 0/4 arms high / One metal mount with base in silver gilt, 0/2 arms high / One small sand-glass with decoration in ebony / One perfume holder in gilt brass worked with masks and figures on top, 0/2 arms tall with three dolphins for feet / Three snails in mother-of-pearl worked in various manners with their feet in silver 0/4 arms high / Two Venuses in bronze 0/2 arms tall / Two small figurines in bronze 0/6 arms tall / One Christ in coral on the cross with its foot in pierced silver, 3/4 arms tall / One bronze figurine on a base of black wood 0/6 arms tall / One little vase in Turkish wood worked red and green 0/8 arms high / One dish made from half an ostrich egg with ornament in silver gilt / One metal mount with twelve spoons and one knife in silver with handle made from a branch of coral 2/3 arms high / One bronze figure with base in walnut 0/3 arms tall / One bronze figurine with one foot upon a vase with base in mixed marble, 0/3 arms high / One Venus in bronze cutting her nail on a base in white alabaster 0/6 arms high /

Engraved cherry nut, attributed to Properzia de Rossi and cited (as a "button" in a bas-relief crucifix) in the inventories of the Casino di San Marco at the death of Francesco I. During the 18th century it was in the Uffizi.

Two marble heads with bust and base / One small bronze bull with base in ebony, 0/4 arms high / Two small dogs in marble with base in mixed black and white marble, each 0/4 arms high / One small bronze tiger with base in ebony, 0/8 arms tall / Two India coconuts with foot and cover in worked silver, 0/2 arms high, 0/3 arms wide / One small Cupid in bronze on a base in mixed marble 3/4 arms high / One figure in black and white marble standing on a mound of the same, 0/4 arms high / Two Cupids in marble standing one on a base in mixed marble and the other black, 0/2 arms high / Two horses in gilt brass each 0/2 arms high and one running on wheels / A bronze figurine with base part in brass and part in wood 0/3 arms high / One black mixed marble column with a bronze figure at the top, with a base in ebony inlaid with tiles in mixed marble 1 0/4 arms high / One glass ball with a base in gilt wood 0/4 arms high / A small sea-urchin vase with lid and foot in black wood trimmed with gold 0/6 arms high / One small round box from the Indies, trimmed with gold / One small box in mother-of-pearl 1/4 arms high, 1/2 arms wide / One marble figure said to be Antinous 2/3 arms tall / Two double snails in mother-of-pearl outlined and arabesqued with gold with decorations and feet in silver gilt forming two drinking cups / Two snails in mother-of-pearl engraved and white with silver foot / Two snails in mother-of-pearl gilded and figured, painted with various colors of the Indies and with worked and silver-gilt feet / A figure in bronze known as Bacchus 0/4 arms high / One marble figurine on a base in mixed marble 2/5 arms tall / Six figures in bronze lying down by Giambologna 2/3 arms long and 0/4 arms high approximately / One bronze satyr with a woman on his back in bronze 0/3 arms high / One vase in white India nut without lid with an ivory foot 0/6 arms high, or rather in bamboo / One apple in gilt brass with two leaves / One figure in bronze riding a Bacchus in bronze with a base in walnut set with mixed stones 0/2 arms high / Small walnut vase / One figure in brass on a base of walnut 0/4 arms high / One figure in German silver playing the lute 0/2 arms high which runs on wheels / One small chest in wood inlaid and turned, all pierced, 1/4 arms high / One small box in tortoise shell with its cover / One small syringe in ivory, broken 0/2 arms high with its ivory plunger / One small head in ivory, or rather in marble, with bust and base 0/3 arms high / One bronze figurine of Morgante dwarf with base in black wood 0/3 arms high / Snail in mother-of-pearl worked with a silver Neptune on top, resting on a silver dragon with silver base 0/3 arms high / One small bronze horse with a small rider on horseback with its base in ebony 0/8 arms high / a hind and dog in marble attached to one another, base in black marble 2/3 arms high / One horn in striped walnut 0/3 arms high / One small bronze animal with its base in ebony / One figure in marble climbing a marble branch, 3/4 arms high / One small black box from the Indies edged in gilt with its cover, 0/3 arms long and 0/6 arms high / One branch of coral with a Christ and two thieves on the cross in coral with foot in silver gilt and worked with similar garlands around, set in a triangle of silver gilt / One small box in Turkish wood painted and with gold touchneedle work 0/6 arms high, 0/6 arms wide / One small India nut with its foot and cover in black ebony 0/4 arms high / One snail in mother-of-pearl arabesqued with gold with foot in smooth silver / One flask in Indian tortoiseshell with foot, cover, and beak in silver / One snail in mother-of-pearl with a figure in silver gilt on a shell with its foot in gilt and worked silver 0/2 arms high / One half of an India nut to be used as a cup with its foot in silver, or rather in ebony / One India nut with cover and foot in ebony 0/2 arms high to be used as a drinking cup / Two silver owls forming cups each 0/4 arms high / One sow and one dog in marble, or lion, on a base in black marble, each 0/2 arms high / One small hourglass furnished with ivory / One black India box set with gold / One ivory spoon from the Indies with worked handle / [there follow various paintings] / One glass ball with a wool-winder in it / One Christ in silver gilt with decorations in ebony bordered with gold on mixed marble 0/3 arms high, 0/4 arms wide / One small German clock with brass case / One small mirror in silver gilt with rubies and diamonds and emeralds around it with rock crystal in the middle 3/4 arms high, 0/2 arms wide / Four branches of coral with a number of figurines, of which three with silver bases with one St. Jerome, on one a St. John, one a Christ at the whipping post and one a St. Eustachius and one with foot in solid gold / Two casket chests, one of agate furnished with silver gilt and one all in silver worked and engraved in threads with four silver feet 0/8 arms high / One vase in silky agate worked in the Spanish fashion with pearls upon it / One basket in silver thread for ordering the hair with its box inside in solid silver, within which seven small vases in silver gilt, inside three combs and one mirror, all beautifully finished with gold, and the mirror furnished with silver gilt and rock crystal, with two hair straighteners with nine irons for setting the hair with their handles in silver gilt, with its lock and small key in silver / One small casket in silver plate worked and figured with ebony ornaments and four figurines on the sides holding it 0/3 arms high, 2/3 arms wide / Two salt cellars in silver gilt, one in the shape of a dragon and one forming three satyrs with three little salt cellars in agate and one similar little salt cellar on top, it serves as an egg-cup / One small chest in silver thread with four silver-gilt feet 0/2 arms high, 2/3 arms wide / One breviary for the Madonna written in ink, illuminated and figured, with a cover in purple velvet embroidered with gold tubules and pearls / One rock-crystal vase, with its cover having two engraved handles, with two spouts decorated with four small shells in gold in a frieze with a gold border at the foot, at the binding points of the handles and around the cover / One cup in ancient style with its chalice in engraved rock crystal with a cover bound in gold and the same on the cover / Three pieces of rock crystal, that is one engraved navicular cup with one vase of similar kind with its cover, and one small salt cellar of like kind, octagonal in shape with a foot with gold buttons as ornaments and on the foot / Three small salt cellars in agate, one with foot and rim in gold / Five spoons in agate crystal, of which two in crystal, two in agate, and one in mother-of-pearl, with handles in silver gilt / One fork in lapis lazuli with an enameled gold ball / Two small vases of engraved carnelian, of which one for use to hold musk with an enameled gold decoration around it, with three pearls to each vase, and three chains from the top / One small gondola in silver gilt with a number of figurines and turquoises and emeralds around, the gondola moves on wheels / One ostrich and one ship in enameled gold with numerous diamonds and rubies and emeralds around, with an enameled gold figure on said ostrich / One Bezoar stone the size of an egg with gold decoration around it and its little bell / One small book with two figures and one glass / One small flask of lapis lazuli with foot and mouth in enameled gold and three small chains holding it / Two Agnus Dei in crystal, small, with a tiny figure of Christ within / One small picture in rock crystal showing a Christ within furnished with enameled gold / One small rock-crystal turtle with its veil in silver gilt / One small Agnus Dei in ebony with a Christ at the whipping post within / Three small vases in agate with gold ornaments with foot similar to the cover with gold chains, of which one has two harpies for handles in enameled gold / One knife with handle in latern sharkskin furnished with enameled and silver gilt, that is to say gold with enamel with many stones of rubies and diamonds / Three vases for perfume paste, of which two covered with gold net, one with three small chains, and the others furnished in enameled gold / Two small gold vases with rubies around, with their handles in enameled gold / One cross in crystal decorated with gold on the foot and enameled all over / One small book in engraved and enameled gold with a crystal mirror inside and nothing written therein / One small salt cellar in mother-of-pearl with its foot and handles and border in silver gilt / Two salt cellars in green heliotrope with cover of similar kind with border in enameled gold, with feet and covers / Two vases in rock crystal, one navicula or shaped like a shell engraved in sections with its border at the foot and with inlaid brass in the form of a chalice/ One small vase of perfume netted in gold with gold foot and cover, with a rose here and there similar, with two small heads in cameo, and its little silver-gilt chain, empty inside / A passion engraved in a square piece of crystal, on a foot of four S-shapes in enameled gold and ferrule of the same / One casket in rock crystal made from a number of pieces faceted in ovals, squares, and triangles and in points, with ornaments of ebony illuminated with gold, with its cover similarly made and chains therein of silver gilt 0/2 arms high, 3/4 arms long, and 2/3 arms wide / One clock in the shape of an elephant in worked brass in a castle and a number of figurines within it, 3/4 arms high, 0/2 arms wide / One small German watch with stand with six faces in lapis lazuli with its ornaments of silver gilt 0/6 arms high / One small slim vase of yellow amber / One small gold bucket with its handle of the same worked with enameled figures with a frieze engraved in the middle, with garlands around and little garnets and gold studs with a crystal chip in the middle, 0/4 arms tall from the bottom / One small writing desk in inlaid wood with in it a number of alabaster figures, with ends in silver gilt and bells of like kind 0/3 arms high, 0/2 arms wide / One small tortoiseshell chest furnished in silver with silver rosettes and its lock of a similar kind 0/2 arms long / One small ivory vase portraying Grand Duke Francesco, and a Christ in bas-relief with crystal above and with an engraved cherry stone for knop / [there follow a number of miniatures] / The tondo of a head in gold plate with a portrait of Grand Duke Francesco thereon in black crystal with decorations in ebony of 0/6 arms in all directions /. . . /One crown of yellow amber with large buttons in the style of a knight with a bow and tassel of gold and silver thread / One mother-of-pearl shell with a number of small snails in silver gilt thereon /. . . / One iron knife with sheath and handle in wood engraved and figured /. . ./ One ivory casket arabesqued with gold and female figures, for cosmetics, lined inside with red velvet, embroidered with gold and silver with a mirror, and in the lid there are four little crystal bottles and silver handles above / One small wooden bureau for dressing the hair, set with lapis lazuli and other things with black columns arabesqued with gold and its drawer to be pulled open and mirror therein lined with crimson velvet with a gold trimming 2/3 arms high."

The cabinet and jewels of Eleonora (1567-1611), eldest child of Grand Duke Francesco I and Joanna of Austria, who married Vincenzo Gonzaga in 1584. The gems were part of the dowry. (State Archives of Florence, *Guardaroba Medicea* 143, cc. 629-630)

"Note of the contents of the cabinet, beginning from above the mirror:

Compartments beneath the mirror, one large one in the center and three on each side:
3 on the right-hand side, in which:
1 agate cup and one small vase in silver gilt
1 prase cup and one small vase in silver gilt
1 prase cup and one small vase in silver gilt
3 on the left-hand side, in which:
1 prase cup and one small vase in silver gilt
two ivory combs set with gold
one small brush with gold handle
In the center are ten shelves, five on each side, and in the middle one space. In the five on the right-hand side, in the first seen there is:
1 wasp as a pendant with two gems on its back and one on its tail
1 butterfly with 17 gems on its wings and on its back, with pearls, to serve as a pendant
1 wasp with a pearl on the tail
Second:
4 little gold pins tipped with a bezel containing a pointed diamond in the center, and four rubies around it and four pearls
Third:
2 similar pins
1 flower with a spider
Fourth:
1 flower with a stylus in pearls decreasing in size
1 flower with a bee on it
Fifth:
2 flowers
On the right-hand side, or rather on the left, there are five shelves, and in the first of these there is:
1 wasp, forming a pendant with two gems and one pearl
1 butterfly forming a pendant with 17 gems and pearls
1 wasp forming a pendant with one pearl
Second:
4 little pins like those mentioned above
Third:
2 similar pins
1 flower in the center
Fourth:
1 flower bud with a branch in the middle with pearls
1 flower
Fifth:
1 flower with a bee
1 bunch of three white flowers
In the central space:
1 hair straightener in gold
Compartments on the front of the Cabinet, above, in the band of the two frames, there are seven compartments with their drawers, 3 large ones, 2 in the same size, and one in the middle larger and 4 smaller, and each of the three drawers in the lower layer has a secret panel.
3 compartments and drawers, in the first on the right-hand side there are:
2 oak branches for earrings, with 5 gems and 1 pearl
1 lizard with seven diamonds
2 frogs
2 small butterflies with 16 gems
1 locust
1 butterfly with 8 gems
In the center:
1 crown in plasma with one small book with its cover in engraved gold
On the left-hand side:
2 spiders
2 S-shaped diamond earrings
1 scorpion
1 small butterfly
2 wasps without gems
Compartments and drawers above and at the ends, first of those on the right-hand side:
2 scorpions for earrings
1 frog with 5 gems for earrings
1 leaf with a spider on it
Second:
6 rings with various sorts of stone
Third:
7 rings with various sorts of stone
2 snails
2 wasps
1 small dragon
Secret panels of the three compartments, one on the right-hand side:
pearls
6 gold chains
in the middle, blessed grains
Compartments under the second frame, there are seven compartments with their drawers, three on each side, and one in the middle with eight secret panels.
3 compartments on the right-hand side:
One pair of enameled gold bracelets
1 armlet of a locust with gems and pearls
1 armlet of a bunch of strawberries with gems and pearls
2 flat flowers like branches with gems
2 bunches of small flowers with gems
Compartment in the middle where the painting is:
1 perfume belt with vials and a gold net over it wrapped on a bezel covered in taffeta
Three compartments on the left-hand side:
1 pair of bracelets
1 armlet of a sea monster with pearls and gems
1 armlet of three peas with pearls and gems
2 tall branches of flowers of 5 flowers each with gems
1 small branch of flowers with gems and pearls
The three secret panels on the right-hand side:
1 one case of scissors with gold sheath
2 inkpots, 1 dusting powder box
1 gold needle case
The 2 compartments, or secret panels, in the center:
gloves, one pair with 24 little buttons and 24 studs and with a gold chain pressed around
2 large handkerchiefs
The 3 secret panels on the left-hand side:
2 leaves, on one of which there is a fly, on the other a spider
1 large frog
1 small butterfly
Three vases for musk, ambergris, and scent
One watch with chain
On the base there is one compartment, in which:
[various objects crossed out]
1 Spanish fruit dish
In the large drawer at the bottom there is a worked fruit bowl, all stitched, in silk of various colors, gold, threaded silver, trunks, foliage with various animals, and a small watch [crossed out] with its case in gold and chain. Gold pen, penknife, with its handle in gold, gold sand-box."

Bibliography

Acton, H. *The Last Medici*. London, 1932.

Allegri, E. and Cecchi, A. *Palazzo Vecchio e i Medici*. Florence, 1980.

Aschengreen Piacenti, K. "Documented Works in Ivory by Balthasar Permoser and Some Documents Related to Filippo Sengher," in *Mitteilungen des Kunsthistorischen Institutes in Florenz*, 10, 1963, IV, pp. 273-85.

——. *Il Museo degli Argenti a Firenze*. Milan, 1967.

——. *I santi protettori della Toscana. Festschrift für Ulrich Middeldorf*. Berlin, 1968, pp. 488-93.

——. "La collezione medicea di avori torniti," in *Antichità viva*, II, 1963, 1, pp. 15-25.

——. "La collezione medicea di sculture in avorio," in *Antichità viva*, II, 1963, 4, pp. 15-25.

——. "Le Opere di Balthasar Stockamer durante i suoi anni romani," in *Bollettino d'Arte*, XLVIII, I-II, 1963, pp. 99-110

——. "Note su due vasi nel Museo degli Argenti," in *Studi in onore di U. Procacci*, Milan, 1977, pp. 567-70.

——. "Two Jewellers at the Grand Ducal Court of Florence around 1618," in *Mitteilungen des Kunsthistorischen Institutes in Florenz*, 12, 1965, I-II, pp. 107-24.

Baldini, U., Giusti, A.M., Pampaloni Martelli, A. *La Cappella dei Principi e le pietre dure a Firenze*. Milan, 1979.

Barocchi, P. and Gaeta Bertelà, G. *Arredi principeschi del Seicento fiorentino. Disegni di Diacinto Maria Marmi*. Turin, 1990.

——. "Danni e furti di Giuseppe Bianchi in Galleria," in *Labyrinthos*, 13/16, 1990, pp. 321-37.

——. "Per una storia visiva della Galleria fiorentina, il catalogo dimostrativo di Giuseppe Bianchi del 1768," in *Annali della Scuola Normale Superiore di Pisa*, Series III, vol. XVI, 4, 1986, pp. 1117-1230.

Bassani, E. "Antichi avori africani nelle collezioni medicee," in *Critica d'Arte*, 1976, 143, pp. 69-80.

Bencivenni Pelli, G. *Saggio istorico della Real Galleria di Firenze*. Florence, 1779.

Berti, L. *Il Principe dello studiolo, Francesco I dei Medici e la fine del rinascimento fiorentino*. Florence, 1967.

Beschi, L. "Le antichità di Lorenzo il Magnifico: caratteri e vicende," in *Gli Uffizi, Quattro secoli di una galleria*, 1, Florence, 1983, pp. 161-76.

Bisticci, Vespasiano da. *Le vite di uomini illustri* (ca. 1482). Milan, 1951.

Bottari, G. and Ticozzi, S. *Raccolte di lettere sulla pittura, scultura ed architettura*. Milan, 1822-25.

Bruel, F. L. "Deux inventaires de bagues, joyaux, pierreries et dorures de la Reine Marie de Médicis (1609 ou 1610)," in *Archives de l'Art Français*, New Series, II, 1908, pp. 186-215.

Catena, G.B. *Lettere del Cardinal Giovanni de' Medici figlio di Cosimo I Gran Duca di Toscana*. Rome, 1752.

Chastel, A. *Art et Humanisme à Florence au temps de Laurent le Magnifique*. Paris, 1959.

Chiarini, A. "Il Battesimo di Cristo di Giovan Battista Foggini," in *Bollettino d'Arte*, LXI, 1976, pp. 262-63.

Chiarini, M. and Aschengreen Piacenti, K. *Artisti alla Corte granducale*, exhibition catalog, Florence, 1969.

Conte, G. "Altri documenti inediti sul parentado fra la Principessa Eleonora de' Medici e il Principe Don Vincenzo Gonzaga, e i cimenti a cui fu costretto il Principe per attestare la sua potenza virile," in *Bibliotechina Grassoccia*, 6, Florence, 1893.

Conte, G. *Firenze dai Medici ai Lorena*. Florence, 1907.

Conti, C. *La prima reggia di Cosimo I de' Medici nel Palazzo già della Signoria di Firenze, coll'appoggio di un inventario inedito del 1553*. Florence, 1893.

——. *Richerche storiche sull'arte degli arazzi in Firenze*. Florence, 1875.

Covoni, P.F. *Don Antonio de' Medici al Casino di San Marco*. Florence, 1892.

Curiosità di una reggia. Vicende della guardaroba di Palazzo Pitti, exhibition catalog, Florence, 1979.

Del Bravo, C. "Etica o poesia e mecenatismo: Cosimo il Vecchio. Lorenzo e alcuni dipinti," in *Gli Uffizi, Quattro secoli di una galleria*, 1, Florence, 1983, pp. 201-16.

De Nicola, G. "Notes on the Museo Nazionale of Florence, II. A Series of Small Bronzes by Pietro de Barga," in *The Burlington Magazine*, XXIX, 1916, pp. 363-73

Di Castro, D. "The Revival of the Working of Porphyry in Sixteenth-Century Florence," in *Apollo*, October 1987, pp. 242-46.

Fock, C.W. "Der Goldschmied Jacques Bylivelt aus Delft und sein Wirken in der mediceischen Hofwerkstatt in Florenz," in *Jahrbuch der Kunsthistorischen Sammlungen in Wien*, LXX, 1974, pp. 89-178.

——. "Francesco I e Ferdinando I mecenati di orefici e intagliatori di pietre dure," in *Le arti del Principato Mediceo*, Florence, 1980, pp. 317-63.

——. "Goldsmiths at the Court of Cosimo II de' Medici," in *The Burlington Magazine*, CXIV, 1972, pp. 10-19.

——. "Les orfèvres-joailliers étrangers à la cour des Médicis," in *Firenze e la Toscana dei Medici nell'Europa del '500. Relazioni artistiche*, Florence, 1983, pp. 831-59.

——. "The Original Silver Casts of Giambologna's Labours of Hercules," in *Studien zum europäischen Kunsthandwerk. Festschrift für Yvonne Hackenbroch*, Munich, 1983, pp. 141-45.

Fortuna, S. "Il parentado fra la Principessa Eleonora de' Medici e il Principe Don Vincenzo Gonzaga. Documenti inediti tratti dal Real Archivio di Stato di Firenze," in *Bibliotechina Grassoccia*, 7, Florence, 1888, pp. 282-86.

Galluzzi, R. *Istoria del Granducato Toscano sotto il governo della casa Medici*. Leghorn, 1781.

Ghiberti, L. *I commentari* (ca. 1425). Berlin, 1912.

Giuliano, A. and Micheli, M.E. *I cammei della collezione medicea del Museo Archeologico di Firenze*. Rome, 1989.

Giusti, A.M., Mazzoni, P., and Pampaloni Martelli, A. *Il Museo dell'Opificio delle Pietre Dure a Firenze*. Milan, 1978.

Gnocchi, L. "Le preferenze artistiche di Piero di Cosimo de' Medici," in *Artibus et historiae*, IX, 1988, pp. 41-78.

González-Palacios, A. *Il tempio del gusto. La Toscana e l'Italia Settentrionale*. Milan, 1986.

Gotti, A. *Le gallerie di Firenze*. Florence, 1872.

Grote, A. and Heikamp, D. *Il tesoro di Lorenzo. Le gemme*. Florence, 1972.

Hackenbroch, Y., and Sframeli, M., eds. *I gioielli dell'Elettrice Palatina al Museo degli Argenti*, exhibition catalog, Florence, 1988.

Heikamp, D. "La Galleria degli Uffizi descritta e disegnata," in *Gli Uffizi, Quattro secoli di una galleria*," Florence, 1983, II, pp. 461-541.

——. *Studien zur mediceischen Glaskunst. Archivalien, Entwurfszeichnungen, Gläser und Scherben*. Florence, 1986.

——. "Zur Geschichte der Uffizien-Tribuna und der Kunstschränke in Florenz und Deutschland," in *Zeitschrift für Kunstgeschichte*, 26, 1963, 3-4, pp. 193-268.

—— and Anders. F. *Mexico and the Medici* (Quaderni d'Arte. Studies in Art History), Florence, 1972.

Langedijk, K. *The Portrait of the Medici*. Florence, 1983.

Lankheit, K. *Florentinische Barockplastik am Hofe der letzten Medici*, 1670-1743. Munich, 1962.

Lanzi, L. *La real Galleria di Firenze accresciuta e riordinata per comando di S.A.R. l'Archiduca granduca di Toscana*. Florence, 1782.

McCrory, M. "An Antique Cameo of Francesco I de' Medici: An Episode from the Story of the Grand-ducal Cabinet of Anticaglie,'" in *Le arti del Principato Mediceo*, Florence, 1980, pp. 301-16.

——. "Some Gems from the Medici Cabinet of the Cinquecento," in *The Burlington*

Magazine, CXXI, 1979, pp. 511-14.
Mascalchi, S. "Giovan Carlo de' Medici: an Outstanding but Neglected Collector in Seventeenth Century Florence," in *Apollo*, CXX, 4, 1984, pp. 268-72.
Massinelli, A.M. *Bronzi e anticaglie nella Guardaroba di Cosimo I*, exhibition catalog, Florence, 1991.
——. "I bronzi dello stipo di Cosimo I de' Medici," in *Antichità viva*, I, 1987, pp. 36-45.
——. "Due rovesci di medaglie disegnati da Emilio de' Cavalieri per Ferdinando de' Medici," in *Antichità viva*, XXVIII, 1989, 1, pp. 41-43.
——. "Identità di Pietro Simoni da Bargas," in *Critica d'Arte*, 12, 1987, pp. 57-61.
——. "I gioielli di Eleonora," in *M.C.M.*, 3, 1986, pp. 17-21.
——. "Magnificenze medicee: Gli stipi della Tribuna," in *Antologia di Belle Arti*, New Series, 35/38, 1990, pp. 111-34.
Millar, O. *Zoffany and his Tribuna*. London, 1966.
Monaci, L. *Disegni di Giovan Battista Foggini* (1652-1725), exhibition catalog, Florence, 1977.
Morassi, A. *Il tesoro dei Medici*. Milan, 1963.
Mostra Medicea, exhibition catalog, Florence, 1939.
Müntz, E. "Les Collections d'antiques formées par les Médicis au XVIe siècle," in *Mémoires de l'Académie des Inscriptions et Belles-Lettres*, XXXV, 2, Paris, 1895.
——. *Les Collections de Médicis au quinzième siècle*. Paris, 1888.
——. *Les précurseurs de la Renaissance*. Paris, 1882.
Natura viva in Casa Medici, exhibition catalog, Florence, 1985.
Palazzo Vecchio. Committenza e collezionismo mediceo, exhibition catalog, Florence, 1980.
Pieraccini, G. *La stirpe dei Medici di Cafaggiolo*. Florence, 1921.
Pollard, G. "Il medagliere mediceo," in *Gli Uffizi, Quattro secoli di una galleria*, Florence, 1983, pp. 1-19.
Il Seicento Fiorentino. Arte a Firenze da Ferdinando I a Cosimo III, exhibition catalog, Florence 1986-87, Florence, 1986.
Siponta de Salvia, M. *Gli arredi sacri in San Lorenzo*. Ed. by U. Baldini, Florence, 1984.
Spallanzani, M. "Maioliche veneziane per Cosimo I de' Medici ed Eleonora di Toledo," in *Faenza*, LXVII (1981), 1981, 1-6, pp. 71-77.
——. "Medici Porcelain in the Collection of the last Grand-Duke," in *The Burlington Magazine*, CXXXII, 1990, pp. 316-20.
——. "Le porcellane cinesi donate a Cristiano di Sassonia da Ferdinando I de Medici," in *Faenza*, LXV (1979), 1980, 6, pp. 382-89.
Splendori di pietre dure. L'arte di corte nella Firenze dei Granduchi, exhibition catalog, Florence 1988-89, Florence, 1988.
Tondo, L. and Vanni, F.M. *Le gemme dei Medici e dei Lorena nel Museo Archeologico di Firenze*. Florence, 1990.
Tuena, F.M. "Cosimo I e le pietre dure," in *Antologia di Belle Arti*, New Series, 35/38, 1990, pp. 135-47.
Twilight of the Medici, exhibition catalog Florence-Detroit, 1974, Florence, 1974.
Varchi, B. *Istoria fiorentina dal 1527 al 1530*. Florence, 1547.
Vasari, G. *Le vite de' più eccelenti pittori, scultori et architettori*. Florence, 1568.
Weinholz, G. "Zu Bergkristallarbeiten von Giovanni Battista Metellino," in *Jahrbuch der Staatlichen Kunstammlungen Dresden*, 1967, pp. 131-38.
Young, G. F. *The Medici*, 2 vols. London, 1909.
Zobi, A. *Notizie storiche sull'origine e progressi dei lavori di commesso in pietre dure nell'I. e R. Stabilimento di Firenze*. Florence, 1853.

Documents

Chapter 2

State Archives of Florence:

Guardaroba Medicea 65: General inventory of the Wardrobe 1560-67

Guardaroba Medicea 136: Inventory of the Palazzo del Casino di S. Marco, 1587 (partial transcription on pp. 230-33)

Guardaroba Medicea 143: Drawing of the chest and list of the jewels of Eleonora de' Medici, 1584 (transcription on page 233)

Guardaroba Medicea 1292, c. 241 v.: July 29, 1726, delivery of a silver Labor of Hercules to Francesco Bianchi, custodian of the gallery (see p. 70)

Miscellanea Medicea 12, ins. 1b: Inventory of the jewels owned by Camilla Martelli (partially transcribed on page 230)

Miscellanea Medicea 474, fasc. 3 and fasc. 9/1: Jewels, pendants, and other ornaments belonging to Her Highness (Christine of Lorraine) . . .

Miscellanea Medicea 6377: Prince Don Francesco de' Medici's trip to Spain, 1562

Depositeria Generale antica, 389, c. 24 v.: Members of His Serene Highness' household for whom the following provisions are made (the sculptor Pietro da Barga, see page 67)

Library of the Monuments and Fine Arts Service of Tuscany:

Ms. 71, 1634: Inventory of the Sala di Madama

Ms. 95: Inventory of the Gallery, 1753, nos. 883/893: description of the cases with the Labors of Hercules by Giambologna (see page 70)

Filza XXVIII, fasc. 40: Movement to the Wardrobe of the Labors of Hercules by Giambologna

Chapter 3

State Archives of Florence:

Miscellanea Medicea 12, ins. 11: Inventory of the Wardrobe of Vittoria della Rovere, 1639

Miscellanea Medicea 31, ins. 17: Inventory of the jewels of Grand Duke Ferdinando II, 1621

Library of the Monuments and Fine Arts Service of Tuscany:

Filza V, 1772, fasc. 33: Transfer of Francesco Susini's bronze of a Dying Gladiator and Sleeping Hermaphrodite from the Villa della Petraia to the Uffizi

Index of works

THE FRASER VALLEY: A HISTORY

THE FRASER VALLEY: A HISTORY

John A. Cherrington

HARBOUR PUBLISHING

Published by
HARBOUR PUBLISHING
P.O. Box 219
Madeira Park, B.C. V0N 2H0

Design by Roger Handling
Cover painting by Jack Campbell

Printed in Canada
Published with assistance from
the Canada Council and the BC Cultural Fund

Canadian Cataloguing in Publication Data

Cherrington, John A.
The Fraser Valley

Includes bibliographical references and index.
ISBN 1-55017-068-6

1. Fraser River Valley (B.C.)—History.
2. Fraser River Valley (B.C.)—History—Pictorial works. I. Title.
FC3845.F73C5 1992 971.1'33 C92-091516-7
F1089.F7C53 1992

DEDICATION

To Dee, for her patience, tolerance, and valuable comments on the manuscript.
And to Lara Jane, Wade, and Brandon — the legatees of our Valley heritage.

CONTENTS

NOTE TO THE READER

This book overviews the history of the region extending from Hope to the mouth of the Fraser River, excluding the broad Burrard plateau comprising Burnaby and Vancouver. It is not intended to be an encyclopedia of data about the Fraser Valley or a recital of every important settler who arrived in each community. For the scholarly inclined, a bibliography is provided so as to leave the text unencumbered.

PREFACE

How well I remember my valley. In 1960, I was a boy of ten, born and bred in Vancouver. Every second weekend, my Dad drove our family out to Maple Ridge to visit my grandparents on the farm.

It wasn't really a farm; just a couple of acres, with flower gardens, fruit trees, a vegetable patch, one cow, and two noisy geese. For years my brother and I called the farm "Grandpa and Grandma's at Two Gooses."

The old Lougheed Highway was narrow, winding and dangerous then; and you had to pass by Essondale on your way through Coquitlam. That was fun and a little mysterious, staring up at the barred windows and hoping to see a "lunatic" or two—those being the days when neither children nor their elders knew much about mental health.

The old farmhouse.

Once you were past the asylum, you knew you were really in the country. I always got a thrill as we approached the Pitt River Bridge, for just to the west of the span was the Wild Duck Inn. Dad told us that there were always holdups and wild brawls in the beer parlour there, and I imagined scenes from "Gunsmoke".

Beyond the bridge, it was on past Hammond, Pitt Polder, and lush farmland, much of it reclaimed from marsh and lake by the persistent efforts of Dutch settlers. Grandpa's farm was about three miles from Haney, in the shadow of the Golden Ears Mountains. I lived in awe of those towering peaks, and on warm summer nights at the farm we would watch the setting sun cast a pink glow on the tips of the Ears.

Grandpa always sat under the big walnut tree by the garage, smoking his pipe and contemplating what chores remained undone. He was a big strapping man who immigrated from Gloucestershire in 1906 at the age of eighteen, alone and with only a few shillings in his pockets. It was popular in England at the time for peasant children to seek a new life by emigrating to a colony. The Canadian government encouraged settlers by advertising in Britain its offer of a free land grant of 160 acres. Grandpa wanted that land.

Under the walnut tree, Grandpa told me stories of his pioneering days in Alberta; how he'd auctioned off all his farm goods and livestock before enlisting to fight for king and country in 1916. Since he loved horses, he joined up with the Fort Garry Horse. At the Battle of Cambrai in 1917, he participated in cavalry charges alongside tanks—and rode straight into the hell of German machine gun nests. Two horses were shot from under him, and when the madness stopped for a moment, he found himself wounded and on his way to convalescence in England. Most of his company were dead; and never again would the "civilized" nations of the world use cavalry in warfare.

Grandpa loved Canada with a passion. After marrying my grandmother in Winnipeg, they moved to the foot of the Old Yale Road in South Westminster, near the present-day Pattullo Bridge. Dad grew to his teens there, and in summer he would swim in the Fraser, dodging stray logs brought by the swift current. He watched bar fishermen casting for salmon, while on the river, multitudes of fishboats plied back and forth. Across the channel at New Westminster docks, there was always heard the clank and chatter of freighters, barges, and assorted river craft; and the musky dank odour of the river mingled with the sharp tang of fish and the belching smoke of the sawmills.

The author in foreground with his (l. to r.) father, brother Frank, grandfather Cherrington and mother.

My Dad knew old Bill Murray in the 1930s. Murray was a river pilot who had arrived as a baby on the Royal Engineers vessel *Thames City* in 1859. Murray lived in retirement in a houseboat on the river. In earlier years he had ferried prospectors to the head of Pitt Lake to search for the famous Slumach lost gold mine. When one trio emerged from the rugged mountains at the end of a third summer of futile searching, the prospectors gave Murray a crude map of the mine's location which, they said, had originated with Slumach. Murray never had much use for the Slumach quest himself, but when he died, his widow reported that someone had ransacked the houseboat and stolen it. From memory, Mrs. Murray redrew the map for my Dad and uncle.

When I was a teenager, my uncle and I would hike all over the Pitt Lake and Alouette region, imagining that we might find the Slumach mine. In the one hundred years since Slumach was hanged for murder in New Westminster, hundreds of prospectors and hikers have ventured into the vast area north of Pitt Lake—and many have never returned. The treacherous terrain is full of towering peaks, box canyons, and quicksand. Still, it was easy for a boy to succumb to dreams of a hidden gold mine, even if the Murray map proved useless.

Grandpa moved his family to Maple Ridge just before World War II. He was tired of coping with the whims of the Fraser every spring when, during a big freshet, most of his land would be flooded. He built three houses, farmed a little, and worked in the peat bog for extra cash.

I loved to pick Grandpa's strawberries and plums, and then sell them door to door. One day, Grandpa sent me by bus to Vancouver to deliver a huge bag of his golden plums to my Great-Aunt Nell and Captain Barney Johnson. By the time I reached their home on Comox Street, the bag had burst and I was scrambling for plums all over the bus.

During summer holidays, Grandma and I would tramp each Sunday to the little St. John The Divine Anglican Church near Haney. Grandma told me that Grandpa never went to church because his hearing aid acted up too much; but I knew that Grandpa just couldn't tolerate anyone preaching at him. I never realized it then, but that simple little church was somewhat famous. The structure had been floated across the river in the 1880s from Derby - site of the first Fort Langley - and was then and still is the oldest functioning church in British Columbia.

Grandma and I played cribbage, bingo, and whist until all hours of the night; and I drank gallons of her raspberry vinegar concoction. During the day, we played croquet—and we played it with a passion. One summer night I awoke with a start from a deep sleep around midnight. Outside my window in the pitch black I could hear the familiar sound of a croquet ball being struck with a mallet. I stood at the window, transfixed, unable to see a thing. Then I ran into Grandma's bedroom to wake her; but by the time she reached my room the mysterious noise had stopped. We heard only the peaceful symphony of crickets. Grandma smiled sleepily and patted me on the head before returning to bed.

Ten minutes later the croquet game started again. This time, Grandma flew into my room, wide-eyed. "I hear it!" she spluttered. We ran to turn on some lights. The noise suddenly stopped, and we never heard it again. But in the morning we carefully inspected our croquet mallets in the garage, and I swear that one mallet and a ball were covered with wet grass. Forever after we spoke of the ghost who enjoyed croquet.

The days flew by on those farm holidays, and all too soon it was time to return home to the city. Grandpa and Grandma would stand waving in the driveway until our Nash Rambler was out of sight. It was always good to come home, but it was also wonderful to have a country sanctuary, away from the city's bustle.

I thought the farm would always be there, like Grandpa and Grandma. Now the farm, like them, is no more. A townhouse subdivision has submerged all that, and little suburbanized children run and play on curbed cul-de-sacs by the little stream where I used to float my boats down to the highway....

ACKNOWLEDGMENTS

I am indebted to numerous librarians for their assistance in researching the materials for this book, and particularly to the reference staff of the New Westminster Public Library, who are truly dedicated professionals. My thanks as well to the staffs of Fraser Valley College and the University of British Columbia Special Collections Division.

A special debt is owed to Jamie Morton, a historian working with the Parks Division of Environment Canada, who made valuable comments upon the early chapters of the manuscript. The Superintendent of Fort Langley National Historic Park was also generous in allowing me access to the Park Library and the historic Fort Langley Journal.

The staffs of both the Langley Centennial Museum and the MSA Museum Society were most helpful in expediting photographs; while aerial photographer and writer Don Waite, whose enthusiasm for Fraser Valley history is contagious, filled some crucial gaps in my photograph requirements.

The Public Archives of British Columbia personnel provided their customary courtesy and assistance respecting numerous research materials.

Finally, I express my thanks to David Lee, my editor, for his patient, thorough, and thoughtful comments on the manuscript.

INTRODUCTION

Rapid change epitomizes the panorama of today's Fraser Valley landscape. Home to almost one-third of the province's population, the Valley embraces two and a half million hectares of rich alluvial land which is increasingly becoming an extension of Vancouver's suburbia.

Yet the valley is also home to industry, agriculture and millions of migratory birds and aquatic animals. Instead of the former little fishing villages dotting the Fraser River's shores, there are now modern port facilities, bustling towns, and fully automated farms. Five percent of the working farms in the province produce more than 50 percent of the total commercial food crops—and most of these plots are situated in the Fraser Valley, truly the provincial breadbasket.

Conflict in the region is inevitable. The environmentalist battles river pollution and tries to save Terra Nova farmlands. The fisherman fights Ottawa for greater salmon catch limits and fewer river closures: at stake, the largest sockeye

The Fraser River looking east, with Annacis Island in foreground, New Westminster beyond to the left, and Surrey to the right.

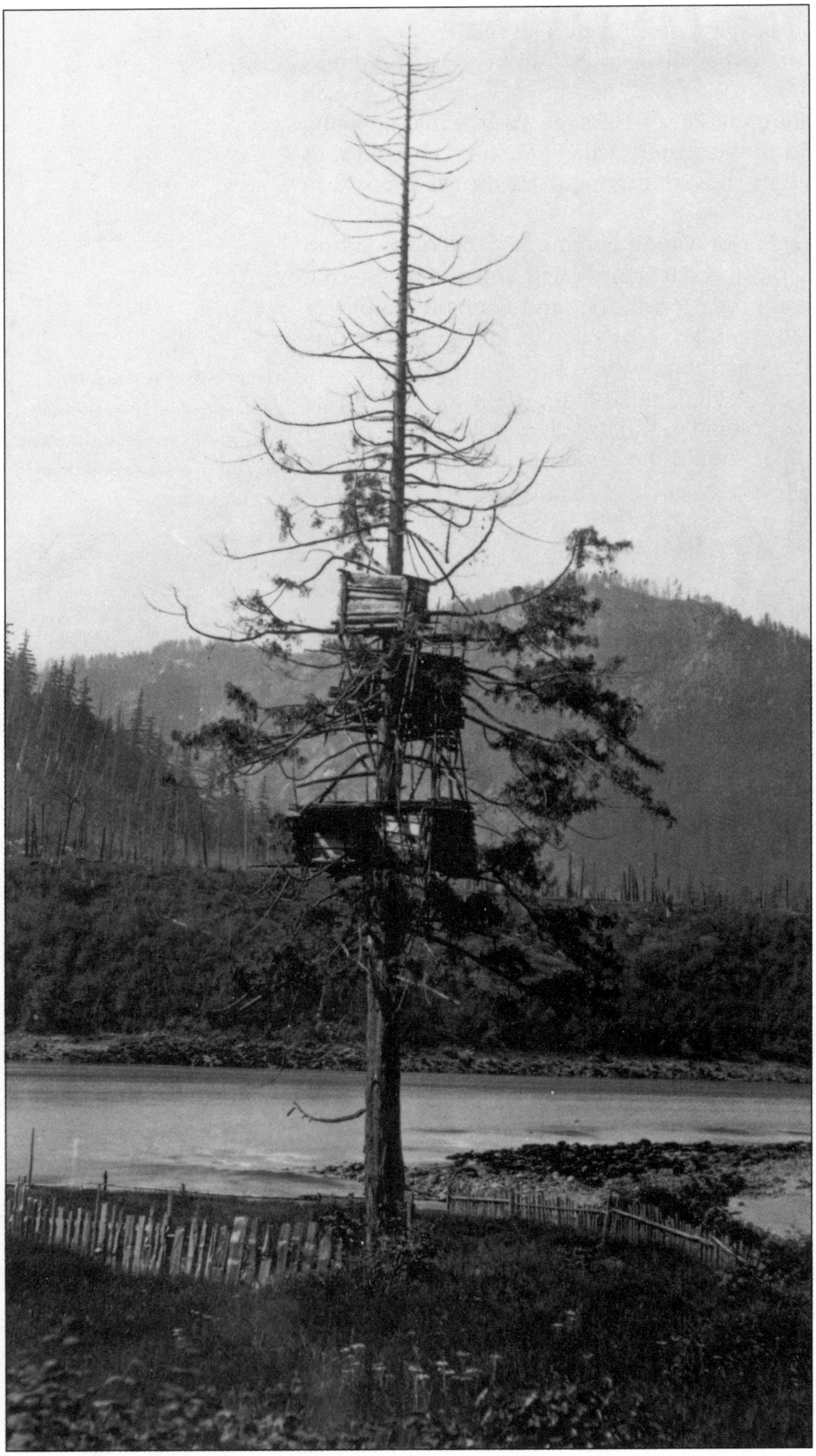

runs in the world. The Indian struggles to retain identity and ponders land claims. The farmer and town resident strive to maintain a unique lifestyle. Everywhere there is heightened recognition that there must be resistance to the vast urbanizing forces which inexorably submerge the once quiet forest floor.

It is traditional, of course, for there to be rural resistance to urbanization. For over a century, it has been country versus city. The rural resident compares verdant farms, clean air, and peaceful towns and villages to the polluted, crime-ridden coastal metropolis. (Even though the air pollution count is often higher in Langley than Vancouver, and north Surrey is referred to as the drug capital of Canada.)

The city comparison has always meant Vancouver. Historically, New Westminster was viewed benignly as the guardian of valley affairs. The *Columbian* newspaper, after all, began publishing in the Royal City in 1861, long before Vancouver was born; and the only market with any stature for close to a century was the New Westminster Farmer's Market, a key feature of the city's waterfront. Vancouver only became an important destination for valley folk after improved highway facilities slashed the travelling time from Langley to downtown Vancouver to a mere forty-five minutes.

Traditional Salish burial tree along the shores of the Fraser River.

Resistance and renewal. Come to Fort Langley on Brigade Days and greet the fur traders and Indians paddling down the river, all in full costume. Visit Bradner's annual daffodil show. Discover May Day in New Westminster, celebrated in Hyack style. In Mission, go back in time at the new Fraser Heritage Park, while enjoying the magnificent view of Mount Baker and the eastern valley. Such is the revival of community traditions that little Clayburn hosts an annual Historical Days, and remote Mount Lehman boasts a fall fair.

There is in fact no composite Fraser Valley community. Each town and village has its own story to tell, its pioneers to celebrate. Yet there is a rich commonality to the whole. From Steveston to Hope, the land veritably palpitates with energy, colour, and a cultural diversity which to some degree reflects the mosaic of the Canadian nation.

Native Indian culture represents a vital part of that mosaic. As George Woodcock notes in his history of British Columbia, "That such people should be left out of history is no longer tolerable." Nor should the oneness of native culture be assumed. There existed, for example, fundamental differences between the sedentary way of life of the Stalo river people and that of the colourful but more aggressive Nootka and Kwakiutl tribes of Vancouver Island.

Since the first humans made their way down the Fraser Canyon more than ten thousand years ago, the Fraser Valley has exuded restlessness and excitement rather than complacency. Perhaps this is inherent to any community given birth by a mighty river. An angry river. The churning, silt laden waters cascade through the canyon above Hope and then sweep around in a broad curve before making a final lunge to the sea. Islands in the stream, such as Barnston, McMillan, and Lulu, are constantly awash, their alluvial boundaries endlessly redefined by the muddy current. At the estuary, the river spews forth its life as brown sediment meets a sea of green. The Fraser seems reluctant to end its journey.

Fishermen bless it, commuters curse it, the Indians respect it; and more than one hundred thousand people rely upon the river, working in Fraser ports in marine related industries.

Yet the Fraser is foreign to most Canadians. Although one of the paramount rivers shaping the destiny of North America, there exist only a few snippets of lore about its early Indians, the gold rush, and its first white settlements. By managing to avoid the lawlessness which characterized the settling of the American West, we have left few heroes for our schoolchildren to compare with the likes of Davey Crockett or Daniel Boone.

In 1950, that venerable sage Bruce Hutchison sketched the life of the entire Fraser River, ending with a lament to the past:

> "How fast the time has gone! How little of the river life we knew in our boyhood, yesterday! All crushed beneath the marching foot of progress, improved beyond recognition, civilized in shape and spirit alien to us. Do not grudge the memories of old men, helpless to stay the birth of the new time and entitled, surely, to the past, which no one else will covet."

Forty years later, we begin to covet that past. For there are songs, myths, and river heroes worthy to celebrate. From James Murray Yale to John Oliver to Chung Chuck, special breeds of pioneers have nurtured and spawned their dreams in the vast lower basin of the Fraser.

Pioneers hard at work clearing fields.

To covet our past is not to seek naively for its return. In our fast-paced society, we speak of the "good old days," of lost values and traditions; of church, family and respect for elders. Old-timers speak of box socials; sleigh rides; of sternwheelers churning slowly up the river; of a time when one was proud to fight for king and country; of law and order. An era when "men were men," and the only liberation women knew of was when arduous farm chores were eased by modern conveniences and babies grew up to help work the land.

The reality of the valley's past also included terrible, backbreaking toil under primitive conditions, clearing out swamps and blasting endless stumps; of smallpox, tuberculosis, the 1917-18 Spanish influenza, and crude medical facilities; of swarms of mosquitoes; of suicides, drownings, and frequent farm accidents; of murders and assaults, sexual repression and abuse; of racism and persecution; of great floods, ice storms, and ravaged crops; of raped forests, polluted streams, haphazard growth—and ultimately, urban sprawl.

Each spring something wondrous occurs in the Fraser Valley. Suddenly there is a stirring. The earth comes alive with greenery; the wind is gentle and the welcome sun beats warmly on the spreading fields. Farmers rev up their tractors; everyone else dashes off to garden centres. There is this inexplicable urge to work the soil, to somehow be at one with the land. The Stalo river people understood this phenomenon. They recognized spring as a time of renewal and hope. The deeper awareness emerging today about both our natural environment and cultural heritage may yet help reconcile men and women to their precious river valley—before it is too late.

CHAPTER ONE

THE RIVER PEOPLE

The year was 1800. The river lay quiet in the dusk of a late October evening. Chief Whattlekainum stood motionless on the riverbank at Skaiametl (present-day New Westminster), the main village of the Kwantlen people.

The breeze blew a shower of yellow leaves from the alders and cottonwoods above, scattering them across the water. To his right, the young chief caught a reflection downstream. Dark shapes were coming up the river. Presently he could make out the high projected bows of the dreaded northern canoes. His heart stopped.

Whattlekainum knew instinctively that these were Yuculta warriors. Sixteen large canoes, each about thirty feet long, swept up the river; he could discern at least twenty pairs of hands in one vessel wielding maple paddles in a rhythmic cadence that barely rippled the water.

The chief thought in anguish of his sleeping village. Since the smallpox epidemic a few years before, three-quarters of the Stalo population along the river had perished. Some Cowichan visitors told him that the disease was spread by strange white sky people from the south. For years, the Yucultas had come on warring parties to plunder villages, kill the men, and abduct the women and children as slaves. Now it was much easier for them, he thought bitterly; the smaller villages were virtually defenseless against these ruthless invaders from the sea.

The chief was about to sound the alarm when he realized that the canoes would pass by the village. He breathed a sigh of relief. The Yucultas were apparently proceeding to an upper Stalo village. The warriors travelled by night to escape detection, no doubt aided in navigation by a Musqueam guide picked up at the river's mouth. At their fierce pace, no messenger sent by him could reach the

Salish canoe beached along the Fraser River.

upper tribes in time to give a warning. The following day in late afternoon, the black flotilla arrived at the mouth of the Chilliwack River. The war party clambered ashore, leaving their canoes on the sandy bank. The warriors trudged a distance up the river to where the woods were thick and then penetrated a few yards into the trees, where they fell exhausted to the ground and slept. But they were seen.

Two young Chilliwack natives had been hunting when the war canoes paddled into the cove. They raced back to their nearby village. "Yucultas! Yucultas!" they shouted. The village chief called the elders together. The women, the infirm, and the children must go deep into the forest, he told them. But the two teenage hunters refused to go. The chief regarded them for a moment and nodded.

"You and your fathers shall have the most important task," he said. "Go back to the river and destroy the canoes and take their paddles."

Several of the village men accompanied by the two hunters raced down to the cove, where they smashed to bits several canoes and cast others adrift—without the Yucultas even stirring.

At dusk the invaders rose with their weapons and filed stealthily up the river toward the sleeping village. The dying flames of many bonfires illuminated the shed-roofed plank houses ringing the village square. Alder smoke and salmon oil filled their nostrils, as the perspiring warriors raised war clubs and, on a command,

Native tribal areas.

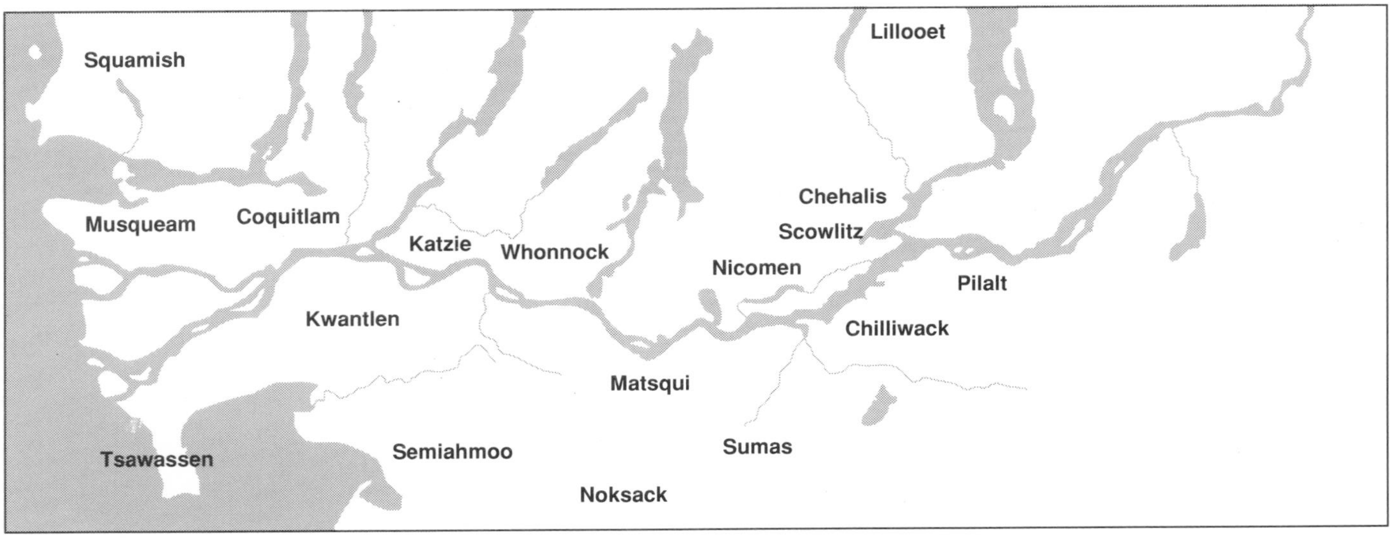

rushed in pairs into each house, clubbing viciously at the motionless shapes on the straw beds.

Soon the Yucultas realized they had been tricked. The beds were empty. The villagers had fled. So the warriors proceeded to plunder the huts and hungrily devoured the food. Then out of the shadows there suddenly came whooping cries. Arrows were unleashed mercilessly into the huts, followed by Chilliwack braves wielding five-foot clubs.

The carnage was hideous. Only about fifty of the Yucultas managed to flee to the river, where they searched in vain for their canoes. About twenty braves eventually reached a canoe adrift further downstream and escaped. The bodies of other Yucultas were found that harsh winter by Chilliwack hunting parties; five skeletons alone were discovered in a large hollow cedar tree. But the Chilliwack people knew that although they might be spared for a time, there would be other raids in the future.

Anthropologists trace the beginnings of human life in the Fraser Valley to about 8000 B.C., when the ice packs which had covered the land receded and the ocean dropped to its present level. The most interesting ancient sites have been found at the river mouth and at Locarno Beach on Burrard Inlet.

Between about 1500 B.C. and 500 A.D. there evolved a society advanced in the use of sophisticated tools; intricate carvings, well-built canoes, and massive planked houses were made from the precious red cedar which abounded along the river banks. For reasons unknown, this society regressed somewhat in the millennium prior to European contact, while the Kwakiutl and Haida nations experienced a sustained momentum of progress.

Gradually some Stalo natives fanned out upriver to build new villages, while from the Lilloet and Thompson regions a number of Interior Indians migrated to occupy the area between Hope and Chilliwack.

Chief's tomb and effigy, opposite New Westminster.

In time, the tribes east of the Musqueam villages became rather isolated from their Coast Salish brethren. Mountain peaks more than five thousand feet high tower over many sections of a valley which seldom rises more than four hundred feet above sea level. The Coast Mountains chain forms a solid wall to the north, while to the east and southeast sprawl the jagged fingers of the Cascades. Stalo contact with the Cowichan peoples was largely limited to the annual salmon runs, when the Cowichan came by the thousands to camp in summer villages along the river as far east as present day Langley.

It was during such contact periods that the Stalo first encountered European trade goods and heard stories of sky people.

The annual fishing forays by Stalo families to the Fraser Canyon area near present-day Yale afforded the natives some contact with Interior Indians, some of whom intermarried into upper Stalo villages. However, the most important communication route to the outside world was the Salmon River. The Indians paddled down the Salmon, portaged over to the Nicomekl River, and then floated down to Mud Bay to greet their Nooksack cousins and engage in trade.

The Coast Salish people were far from homogeneous in language or culture. The Stalo spoke a common language known as "Halkomelem"—meaning "river"—but there were differences in dialect between upper and lower river inhabitants. Upper Stalo tribes, like the Chilliwack and Tait, lived in smaller houses than lower Stalo natives, and depended more on hunting.

But, to all tribes, fishing provided the main sustenance and the fish, like the river itself, were sacred. The spring and sockeye salmon runs were the climactic events of the year. The very first salmon caught in each village was ceremoniously cooked in a basket or roasted over a fire and then carved into many small pieces for each community member. The mid-summer runs were immense,and the Indians, like later whites, spoke of the river being so thick with fish that one could "walk on their backs."

Spears, harpoons, and hooks were used by natives, as well as nets made principally of cedar bark and stinging nettle fibre. Dip nets were used by Upper Stalo fishermen in the canyon area, the men standing on the bank and letting the nets float slowly downriver in the swirling side eddies. Alternatively, the net would be held in place in a constant position, well braced against the current. Occasionally, weirs were placed across the smaller streams feeding into the Fraser.

The Stalo also fished for the inimitable white sturgeon, a strange species of fish which even today fascinates biologists. The sturgeon can grow up to twenty feet in length and weigh over one thousand pounds. According to ancient Katzie legend, the sturgeon will not die unless killed by a human. Scientists are uncertain as to the longevity of these antediluvian monsters, but a seven hundred-pounder was dated at 132 years in 1977. The fish resembles a cross between a shark and a catfish, is toothless, inhabits murky depths, and has not changed much in over two million years. Indians relate stories of sturgeon rooting the Fraser's bottom with its powerful snout and of the fish surviving for days out of water in the rain.

University of British Columbia zoologist David Randall, who has studied the white sturgeon intensively, has discovered that the fish is unique in being able to enter a state of suspended animation by just "turning itself off." Unlike hibernation, there appears to be no cyclical process to this phenomenon; nor do sturgeon replace oxygen like other fish. The roe of the white sturgeon has been used as a source of caviar.

The Stalo fished for the sturgeon with spears attached to handles up to sixty feet long; fishermen probed the river bottom with such devices, the sensitive hand of the native driving the spear home upon encountering the fish. The handle was then pulled back. The sturgeon would exhaust himself until the fishermen could tow the creature ashore. Frequently the fishermen would align as many as thirty canoes along the river and drift down with their spears in place, dragging the bottom. A large sturgeon might drag canoes several miles at a fast pace before tiring.

The yearly cycle of a Stalo family began in May or early June. At that time, families travelled round and about in groups. The men hunted deer, bear, and water fowl, and fished for sturgeon and the odd spring salmon. The women gathered salmonberries, dressed deer hides, and stored away rushes for future mat and basket weaving.

Salish woman gathering reeds.

By July, the first major spring and sockeye runs were well under way. Most villagers refrained from scooping up fish from the first heavy runs and even kept their children from playing close to the river banks, out of respect for the sacred purveyor of life. The Katzie people of the Pitt River region believed that the salmon were really humans who had transformed themselves into fish. Since the needs of the natives were limited and the runs large, there was no need to squander.

The real fishing occurred in August. Then the men netted fish with ardour. Women dried the salmon on racks set at angles toward the sun. Dried, the fish were temporarily stored in either rush baskets or wooden boxes. The fish entrails were never thrown back onto the river—unlike the cannery practices of later years. Salmon were usually smoked only in wet years for better preservation. Oil was extracted from the sockeye and was used for all culinary needs. The remaining dried fish were placed in a storehouse, elevated on poles, or deposited in trees. The native's greatest concern was to keep the fish dry and free from foraging animals and insects.

The close of the sockeye season in September was marked by a great feast. The men then resumed their hunting activity, concentrating upon ducks and geese as autumn wore on. Dogs were used to hunt both deer and fowl. The women gathered cranberries and Indian potatoes, various different rhizomes and bulbs which grew wild.

Indeed, Salish ethnographer Wayne Suttles believes that the use of the Indian potato originated with the Stalo Indians, and that the tuber's popularity as a staple food item among the Salish of the northwest coast occurred as a result of Stalo contact with neighbours such as the Nooksack. Camas were a special favourite, and were either boiled and eaten like potatoes or mashed into a thick soup. The women also wove garments at this time and firewood was amassed by the children in huge quantities for the winter.

The months of November and December were spent entertaining visitors and holding potlatches. Fish and meat were boiled and roasted for feasting. In most villages along the Fraser this was a time of great merriment.

The Stalo were an hospitable people. The notion of sharing the bounty of a good season was well developed, as was the desire for ostentation and prestige. The natives shared their goods as they shared their land; there certainly was enough of it to go around. There was no land ownership in the European sense, and members of other tribes were seldom denied the right to fish or hunt on traditional tribal territory. Wilson Duff states that the "concepts of ownership of resources were not well developed beyond the level of family ownership of fishing stations."

Salish woman digging roots ca. 1900.

The winter religious dances began in January, and continued almost nightly for two months. The spirit dance represented the epitome of native religious expression. The spirit song was the key part of the dance ceremony, and individuals acquired a personal spirit song in one of several ways. Usually it came to the Indian while attending the nightly dance—in a sudden flash or seizure. The afflicted one would suddenly get up and sing and dance wildly. The singer's family would then spend four days training the initiate, learning his "song" and refining both it and the dance. On the fourth day, the initiate would be led around the village, and was expected to perfect his new song; later that evening he was brought into the village hall to the sound of beating drums. After various rituals, the native proceeded to sing his personal song, and dance with feet bound.

Spring came in March. Sturgeon, trout, and steelhead were plentiful. In the Pitt Polder area, sandhill cranes by the thousands arrived to feed and nest. In April, the silvery oolichan, or "candle-fish," arrived upriver. Prized for its oil, the small fish, also known as eulachon or oolachon, was sought by all the river people.

Keith Keller, who accompanied Mike Waska on the 1988 oolichan fishing trip, noted the following entry from James McMillan's Journal of April 28, 1828: "The little fishes which the Chinooks call ullachon begin to make their appearance here, and are joyfully hailed by the Indians of the river." Such was the intense netting activity that it was uncommon for the runs to make it past the Chilliwack

Musqueam totem poles 1898.

River mouth. A canoe was usually filled within an hour using a dip net, or the fish just scooped aboard in loose woven baskets. Taken home, the fish were quickly placed on a rack and smoked over an oil fire. Several months' supply of fish oil would be stored for use by the fisherman's family, while the remainder was set aside in sealed cedar boxes for use as a trading item.

By May, the first spring salmon appeared, as did myriads of water fowl. And so the yearly cycle ended. Death, disease, and hunger were interruptions in an otherwise harmonious life. A mild climate, ample food supply, and firm social and religious customs allowed for a balanced life—in short, the Stalo native worked hard and played hard.

The Stalo population consisted of about 3,500 persons in the early 1800s. The natives lived in a clearly regulated environment, with the river dictating their life cycle. The river people consisted of numerous tribes, including the Katzie, Coquitlam, Whonnock, Nicomen, Pilalt, and Tait; the largest tribes, however, were the Musqueam, Kwantlen, and Chilliwack.

The Musqueam occupied the Vancouver area and part of Richmond, with their village life centred at Marpole. The Kwantlen extended from Marpole on the north arm and Ladner on the south arm of the Fraser, all the way east to present-day New Westminster. The Chilliwack tribe was centred in the Chilliwack River region.

It should be noted, however, that these tribal boundaries were constantly shifting, due to disease and the ravages of invading Yucultas. An entire village might be decimated, allowing a neighbouring tribe to extend its domain. In the first decades of the nineteenth century, only the villages located at the site of future Yale, Hope, and Fort Langley were considered permanent; the changing fortunes of hunting, fishing, and climate compelled tribes to relocate.

The Stalo village chief was known as a "siam." Although the siam's position was hereditary, he could be deposed if he failed to attend assiduously to his duties as director of the care and order of the village. Nevertheless, the siam was considered in a class apart, with the next ranking class composed of nobles who had acquired much wealth and, by common consent, were viewed as elders capable of assisting the siam in councils. The common people comprised the remaining members of the village—aside from slaves, who were rare in the Fraser region.

Coast Salish longhouse.

The dwellings of the river people were sophisticated affairs. The pit house was used by many segments of the Tait and Chilliwack tribes; this structure consisted of a circular, partly subterranean cedar frame, which was commonly entered via the roof. The small detached shed-roofed plank house was also common in the upper Fraser region; whereas larger plank houses prevailed along the lower Fraser. The latter were popular as summer dwellings.

In winter, families in many areas lived in communal long houses. The long house was partitioned and might run to over six hundred feet in length. Typically, a family might be allotted fifty square feet of living space, separated from other rooms by hanging mats. It was none too private.

The natives were resourceful. Beds were made of reed mats, supplemented by dog hair or mountain goat wool. The modern sauna was anticipated by the sweat-house, a domed hut framed by vine maple and fir boughs, and lined by leaves inserted between poles. The vapour caused the leaves to stick together, forming an air-tight wall. A small hole was dug in the floor, hot stones dropped in, and water spread to produce steam. Sweat bathing was used effectively to treat minor maladies such as colds, and for general purification. Not blessed with the luxury of a swimming pool, the bather would sweat inside for twenty minutes and then dash outside and plunge into the icy river.

Marriage customs resembled those of the European nobility. Although girls usually married very young, their partners were chosen for them by their parents if they belonged to a high ranking family. Among the common people, it was considered quite fair for a young brave to press his suit by turning up daily on the doorstep of his chosen maiden's home and to sit there patiently for a hearing—all the while being ignored by the girl's parents, or even having dishwater thrown in his face. Eventually, the parents might welcome him in and reward his persistence with their daughter's hand. Marriage was not taken lightly and it was considered most déclassé to sneak into a girlfriend's home to sleep with her, even if in the morning the couple pronounced marital union.

On death, a spouse was officially mourned by his or her partner for one year, and the survivor was prohibited from eating with others. Marriage formed a sacred life partnership. The Stalo believed that "when your wife dies, part of you

Salish woman spinning wool.

dies with her, and you are different from what you were." The bodies of the dead were placed in cedar coffins which were perched in trees.

Stalo women, although subservient to their husbands, were generally self-sufficient, hardy, and equal in much of the decision-making process. Divorce was common among the lower class, but abhorred by the nobility. A wife who left her rich husband would be returned by her parents to the husband; but a commoner's bride would be taken back by her family without question.

Large families were preferred by the Stalo and the midwives of the village were always busy. A newborn infant was subjected to having his face massaged, legs bandaged, and—if born into nobility—his soft forehead would be bound to a padded board to flatten it. The baby was dressed in cedar bark diapers and tightly wedged in a cradle carried on his mother's back. Often a hollow elderberry tube was attached to a male infant's urinary tract and extended through a hole in the cradle bottom—thus keeping baby's bed dry.

In Stalo lore, the blanket beating wives of the upper Fraser will always be revered. During a bleak winter long ago, a Chilliwack tribe suffered greatly from famine. The males of the village decided to abandon the starving women and the younger children and set off downstream in search of fish. One teenage boy travelling with the men became determined to prevent the desertion and sneaked back to the village. Upon hearing the boy's tale, the village women struck their beds with bark in rage. Then they gathered their spouses' blankets and feathers together and headed downriver on rafts to the encampment, all the time beating their blankets and wailing against their men.

Legend says that when the blanket beating women approached their husbands, they threw clay powder mixed with feathers at the men and thus turned them all into birds; white powder birds became seagulls and black powder birds became ravens. And the women? The women missed their husbands after a time and transformed themselves into oolichans!

Coast Salish Potlatch.

Europeans misunderstood the roles of the potlatch and the shaman more than any other aspect of Indian life. The potlatch was a gift-giving ceremony; the higher his social rank in the village, the more gifts would be distributed by the villager. Although it is true that some potlatches left families destitute, the village looked upon the gift givers as being rich, as having great status, and of being worthy of any future favour.

Among the Stalo people, the potlatch was on a smaller scale, less frequent, and less economically traumatizing than was the case among the more northerly coastal tribes. In fact, the most common potlatch of the river people was the paying-off ceremony, held when a family was able to repay years and often decades of indebtedness—including debts incurred for previous family potlatches. For such an event, the largest dwelling house in the village was rented. The ceremony would last for up to four days. When all the debts were repaid, the elderly man presiding would announce a "scramble," inviting all the young people to gather below a raised platform from which he threw assorted goods down—buckskin hides, blankets, moccasins, and numerous tools and weapons; all the while the steady beat of drums pounded away and villagers danced themselves into a frenzy outside the house.

The shaman was a man blessed both with the ability to detect spirits and to influence the souls of villagers. Although he was the chief spiritual leader in the community, there were other seers and prophets who were only slightly less important. Neither the potlatch nor the first salmon ceremony were dependent upon leadership by the shaman, and spirit dancing was conducted by one or more village elders in frequently disorganized fashion.

The popular notion today of the shaman as an all powerful religious leader who mesmerized his people, holds no basis in fact among the Coast Salish. The shaman rarely interfered with the ebb and flow of village life as presided over by the siam. A religious seer was respected or revered only if he used his powers to protect hunters and ward off famine, and he might easily be displaced for failure to perform or for misconduct.

Rhythm played a vital role in the life of a Stalo native. A brave beat the sides of his canoe with measured cadence when on an important journey. The beat of the drum was endemic to village life. Spirit dancing honed the rhythmic skills of even the clumsiest village brave. Missionaries who later frequented the Valley were appalled at the frenzied dancing and advised the siams that all such gyrating was sinful and must cease.

In an adroit reply which signifies the differing purposes of dancing in the two cultures, one siam replied, "Oh, the white man's dance is worse than the Indian's dance. Indian man alone, dance all around the house and sit down—and then Indian woman, she dance all around the house and she sit down. But white man take another's wife and hug her all around the house!"

Natives associated deep religious feeling with features of the landscape and sources of sustenance. Hence the "evil rock" (Lady Franklin's Rock, just above Yale) in the Fraser Canyon and the venerated salmon. Inherent in his set of beliefs was the notion that rational spirits possessed all objects, both animate and inanimate.

Each native sought his or her own guardian spirit. Rather than a single supreme being presiding over life, the Stalo believed that the Transformer—an ancient god—had given every Indian a choice to acquire spirit knowledge, and if the native lived in harmony with the natural features of the environment, he or she would prosper. Everyone possessed a soul in the world of the river people. But when the soul left the body at death, it floated endlessly through the universe and did not go to heaven, hell, or elsewhere. Shamans mediated with the ghosts and kept them at least neutral in the affairs of the world.

The concept of good versus evil and original sin did not develop until encounters with white missionaries. However, it does appear that in the decades preceding the arrival of Europeans in the valley, the idea of one god more powerful than any other—perhaps the Transformer—took root. Duff believes that the "greater god" concept was introduced to Stalo culture through more southerly tribes that had already had contact with white society. Certainly in both the pre- and post-colonization era the Stalo adapted the idea of a supreme deity to their existing layer of beliefs.

Intriguing Stalo legends abound. One of the most popular is the story of a great flood in ancient times—a theme ubiquitous in other cultures. The story is told of a valley which at one time was overcrowded with natives who lived along the river banks. The morning and evening bonfires were so numerous that a smoky pall hung over the land.

Then the rains came. For weeks and weeks it poured. The river and all the little streams overflowed. Summer fish houses were swept away, then the main villages flooded. Many natives were drowned; others moved their families frantically into the mountains, taking with them their dried salmon and berries. The rising waters followed them.

Soon only the peaks of the Golden Ears and Mount Cheam remained above water. The remaining Stalo tied their canoes and rafts to these peaks and waited for the flood to subside. Several canoes broke loose from their lashings and the Indians huddling in them were hurtled in every direction; many of these canoes eventually came to rest in far away places, and as a result tribes such as the Nooksack and Bella Coola were formed.

When the flood waters receded at last, the remaining Stalo of the valley clambered down the steep peaks to the river and rebuilt their villages. Indians still talk of their ancestors recovering rope fragments and cedar sticks—which crumbled to dust at their touch—from the top of the Golden Ears.

Other legends revolve around the fearsome Slalakums—strange, supernatural creatures which dwell high in the mountains, deep in the forest, and underwater at various traditional locations. Such creatures include the two-headed snake of the Chilliwack River, the cannibal woman of Yale, and the underwater bear of the Fraser Canyon. Strange creatures are to this day said to inhabit Jones Lake, Cultus Lake, and the Ruby Creek area.

The most famous Slalakum, however, is the Sasquatch. This hairy giant is reputed to stand eight to nine feet tall in full maturity, and is covered with a thick coat of body hair. Countless sightings, altercations, and even kidnappings of Indians are related in native lore.

A newspaper report in 1882 appeared to confirm the capture of a young Sasquatch, described as having a body covered with inch-long glossy hair, but otherwise resembling a human, though possessing a very long forearm and incredible strength. The creature is presumed to have escaped before scientists had an opportunity to study it. Indeed, British Columbia's best-known Sasquatch authority, the sober and learned John Green of Harrison Hot Springs, has criticized anthropologists for dismissing Indian accounts of the Sasquatch without adequately collating and analyzing the data, a criticism which ethnographer Wayne Suttles believes is justified.

Is it possible, then, to actually grasp a clear picture of the Stalo natives as they existed prior to European contact? We do see fleeting glimpses of one or two ancient chiefs; we hear reminiscences of elderly natives told in comparatively modern times. Yet we do know enough from the first years of contact by explorers, missionaries, and fur traders to be able to discern a few real men—and very few women.

There prevailed no bloodthirsty Maquinna in the 1800s to colour the history of the river people. The Stalo were relatively peaceful people and fought chiefly in self-defence. Whattlekainum of the Kwantlen tribe was himself initially only a subchief, though of royal blood. His ancestors included Princess Tsawassa, who had ultimately become chief of the Tsawassen tribe, a grouping of natives who had journeyed down the Fraser from the Hope area seeking a warmer climate.

As a youth, Whattlekainum had been raised on a spartan regimen, being wakened daily at dawn to steel his body by diving into the icy river, and then practising his prowess at fishing, hunting, and the use of weaponry. The only time he is ever said to have retreated from danger was the day he encountered a strange lizard on Lulu Island.

In time, Whattlekainum's tactful diplomacy would become the critical attribute with which he would serve his people. For the valley of the Stalo was about to change forever.

CHAPTER TWO

THE ODYSSEY OF SIMON FRASER

The year 1792 saw two important developments for the future British Columbia. In May of that year, the one-eyed Captain Gray from Boston rediscovered the mouth of the Columbia River, earlier named the Rio de San Roque by the Spanish in 1775. This was the fabled great river of the west, which was to become the means whereby a vast trading empire was established.

Meanwhile, another captain named George Vancouver was sailing north from Cape Mendocino to map, survey, and explore. The careful, conscientious Vancouver had shipped with Captain Cook on Cook's second world voyage, and he was now racing the clock in an effort to arrive on the northwest coast before the expedition commanded by the Spanish explorer Bodega y Quadra.

Vancouver lost the race, but aside from the Spanish names pinned to a few landmarks, we remember and extol Vancouver as the greatest navigator of the north Pacific coast. On June 13, 1792, Vancouver landed at Point Grey, having failed to notice the Fraser River. From there, he continued up the coast in tandem with Quadra's two forty-five ton vessels, establishing an amiable relationship with Quadra, despite Vancouver's intense disappointment in having been beaten by the Spaniard in his quest for the honour of completing the first survey.

The British government's interest in surveying the northern Pacific coast was largely commercial. The northwest region was becoming a focal point for fur trading companies. Since Captain Cook's voyages of discovery, a steady stream of British trading vessels had arrived off northern California and the Columbia River region, the latter destined to become the strategic cornerstone of a vast fur empire.

By 1794, the British presence on the coast had dwindled, due to the preoccupation of the British government with the Napoleonic conflict, and Yankee fur trading vessels gained hegemony in the region. This was all the more unfortunate for Britain, since one year later the Spanish threat was largely removed when, pursuant to the Nootka Convention, the surviving Spanish post on eastern Vancouver Island was abandoned. The Spanish never returned to the region as serious contenders, leaving the Boston ships to contend only with the coastal Indians, with whom they clashed regularly and in bloody fashion.

To the east, meanwhile, the Hudson's Bay Company and its North West Company rival were battling it out for supremacy over half a continent. In July of 1793, the rugged Alexander Mackenzie became the first European to reach the Pacific Ocean by an overland route north of California. This accomplishment was at first ignored by his North West Company employers. After publication of his journals in 1801, however, the company decided to send another explorer to establish trading posts that would form an extension of the Athabascan system of the prairie region. The man chosen for this task was a red-haired, well-built, firm-chinned Scot of dour expression named Simon Fraser.

Fraser was born of United Empire Loyalist parents and served the North West Company some sixteen years before being called upon to embark on his journeys. He is described as "inured to hardship; versed in woodcraft and the lore of the savage; strong in danger; of unconquerable will and energy; unlettered, not polished, it may be, but true to his friends and honourable in his dealings." Fraser had been appointed a full partner of the company in 1801.

Simon Fraser.

At the annual meeting of the North West Company in 1805 at Fort William, Fraser's partners railed at American expansionism toward the Pacific. The Lewis and Clark expedition was on the move that year, although it was not known where the explorers might be bound. Stories of the lucrative maritime fur trade had reached the ears of the partners and they were determined to exploit the Pacific regions for themselves—particularly since their traditional forays into the American heartland of the Mississippi and Missouri Valleys were now barred as a result of the 1803 Louisiana Purchase and Yankee trader inroads.

The assignment handed to Fraser was twofold. He must establish posts in the Pacific region beyond the Rockies and then strike south for the mouth of the Columbia River, finding a passage through the rugged mountains. So one year ahead of his friend, David Thompson—a defector from the Hudson's Bay Company, who had been charged with similar instructions—the stubborn Scot set about his task with resolution and determination. History records Fraser's earlier success; Thompson however negotiated the Kootenay River, and then turned back with a load of furs. He did not reach the Pacific Ocean until 1811.

Fraser's father had died as a prisoner of war in a Yankee jail during the American Revolution, and Fraser seethed with indignation at the thought of Jefferson claiming the entire Pacific coast for the United States. He also had become enthralled with the wild pristine lands which Mackenzie had first traversed; the entire northern area west of the Rockies was officially named New Caledonia after the Scottish ancestral homeland shared by most North West Company partners.

Upon landing at Stuart Lake in 1806, Fraser proceeded to establish Fort St. James. He had impressed the natives by having his men fire a volley into the air with their muskets, causing the Carrier Indians lining the shore to fall prostrate to the ground. Then the white men disembarked and offered tobacco to the natives—which they promptly tasted and spat out in disgust. Fraser also distributed soap to native women, who placed the substance between their teeth, grinding it and producing foam and bubbles from their mouths.

The Fraser Canyon.

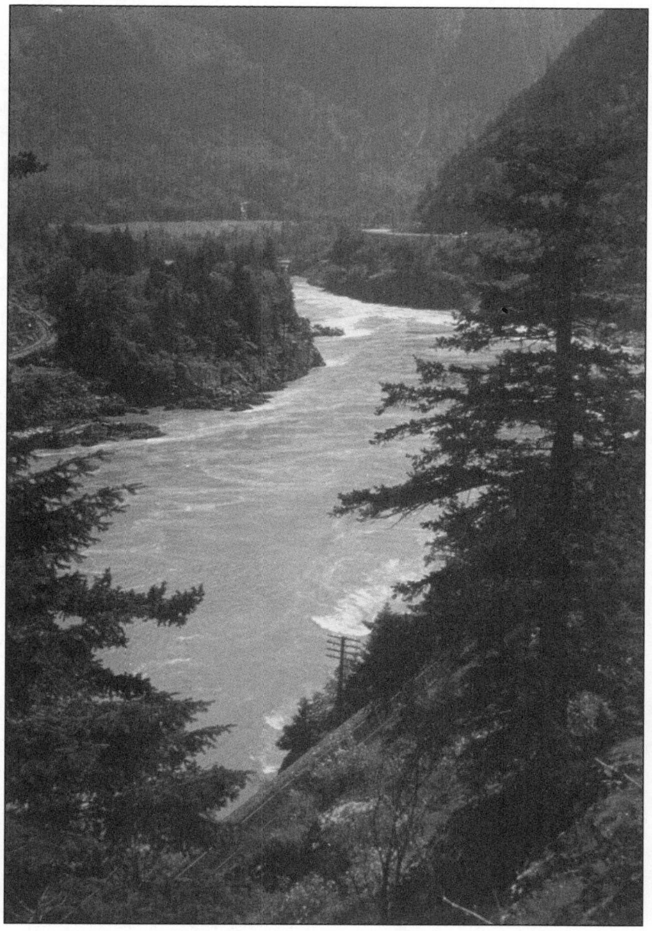

In the autumn of 1807, the explorer built a second post at the mouth of the Nechako River, named Fort George. Here Fraser sojourned over the harsh winter, a period of boredom ameliorated somewhat by his marriage with a native woman who was reputed, according to his own letters, to have provided him with a most "extraordinary courtship." He seems to have had an earlier wife and progeny in the vicinity, for he wrote to a friend that winter asking that his children be cared for, and their needs charged to his account.

On May 28, 1808, Fraser set out from Fort George with four canoes and twenty-three men, including two Indian guides. Resident natives in the area through which the party passed spread word up and down the river of strange men in canoes. The whites traded, gave gifts, and sought information along the way, firing their guns at each disembarkation point so as to impress potentially hostile villagers.

Between Lilloet and Lytton the canyon became so narrow and treacherous that Fraser abandoned the canoes and began walking with his men. At Lytton, where the clear waters of another great river meet the muddy swirl of Fraser's stream, the explorers were invited ashore to a great Indian camp. Fraser named the clear river after his friend David Thompson; and Thompson returned the favour by naming the muddy stream after Fraser.

Soggy and spent, Fraser and his voyagers nevertheless made the rounds of the assembled natives, shaking some 1,200 hands.

"We have every reason to be thankful at our reception at this place," Fraser wrote in his diary. "The Indians showed us every possible attention and supplied our wants....We had salmon, berries, oil and roots in abundance, and our men had six dogs." The explorers experienced some difficulty, however, in obtaining the use of two canoes they sought for the journey ahead. This was in part attributable to the fact that the natives claimed the whites were crazy in believing that they could navigate the great river through the canyons below.

Simon Fraser had been instructed to descend the river to its mouth, and he was determined to press on. He set off next morning with confidence, but soon found that the canoes had to be pulled into shore every few miles in order to avoid being swept into whirlpools; at these junctures the men would drag the canoes and provisions up steep banks, grumbling aloud. Often, hostile natives would hurtle rocks down from above. At one point, Fraser's own canoe was rent asunder when the black cascading waters thrashed it against the rocks; Fraser was thrown onto the slippery shore, where he collapsed in exhaustion. The intrepid—or mad—explorer had in fact drifted over three miles through the rapids and whirlpools in only half a canoe!

Simon Fraser's men traverse treacherous canyon walls.

The Indians saved the day. The Thompson chief accompanying the expedition took the whites to a lower canyon village, where they were all fed, sheltered, and soon taught how to walk along the very walls of the canyon, building ladders of trees and proceeding up and down ledges, with Indian arms performing much of the work.

Fraser described this stage of the journey: "I have been for a long period among the Rocky Mountains, but I have never seen anything equal to this country, for I cannot find words to describe our situation at times....We had to pass where no human being should venture. Yet in those places there is a regular footpath impressed, or rather, indented, by frequent travelling upon the very rocks...."

More than one hundred years later, in *The Rivers of Canada*, Hugh MacLennan wrote of this terrible stretch of the Fraser: "....the Fraser does not flow at all. It seethes along with whirlpools so fierce that a log going down it may circle the same spot for days as though caught in a liquid merry-go-round. It roars like an ocean in storm, but ocean storms blow themselves out, while the Fraser's roar is forever."

At Spuzzum, the party stopped to examine Indian burial tombs, which Fraser described as being superior to anything he had yet seen among natives. Then it was on to the evil rock above Yale. From there, the river was at last navigable once again, broadening out and making a sweeping turn to the west. Fraser's relief at leaving the dark canyon behind was tempered by the sudden realization that this was not the famed Columbia River which he was seeking and that his claim on behalf of the North West Company to the territory westward to the sea would be somewhat to the north of the Americans.

The expedition came upon two Indian camps near Hope containing three hundred persons, whom Fraser described as fairer than the Interior Indians, with flattened heads and unpronounced facial features. "They make rugs of dog's hair that have stripes of different colours crossing at right angles resembling at a distance Highland plaid. Their fishing nets are of large twine, and have handles of 20 feet." Here Fraser also observed a large copper kettle and an English hatchet, undoubtedly obtained, he concluded, from coastal trading vessels.

The explorers passed by Sumas Mountain, where they observed seals swimming, and cedar trees lining the shore measuring thirty feet in circumference. The going was tough. They were regularly engulfed in swarms of mosquitoes and morning mists on the river. Fraser also had much difficulty in obtaining fresh canoes. Near the site of present day Fort Langley, he observed a gigantic long house, some 640 feet in length.

The tired voyagers decided to disembark for the night and made camp beside the long house. There they were repasted and entertained with a "feast of fish, berries, and dried oysters in troughs, followed by songs and dances." The whites were alarmed by the constant beating of drums against the cedar walls of the long house. They were reassured, however, when the chief exchanged gifts with them and even consented to loan Fraser his own large canoe for the voyage downriver.

The next morning, Fraser was aghast to find that the chief had changed his mind. The explorer was determined to hold the chief to his promise, and there ensued a comic episode in which Fraser's men hauled the big canoe to water's edge, and the chief had it carried back by the natives. Finally, Fraser harangued the chief with an exposition of his tribal greatness and the chief not only ordered the canoe put at Fraser's disposal, but clambered aboard himself for the journey.

The party encountered Indians at a smaller village who vigorously attempted to dissuade the explorers from proceeding further, warning that Cowichans at the river's mouth would kill them all—sufficiently frightening the braves from the upper river accompanying the party to disembark.

Fraser pressed onward. Near present-day New Westminster he observed on the river's south bank, Kikait, the small summer fishing camp of the Kwantlen, who resided at the larger village of Skaiametl on the north shore. Above Skaiametl rose a hillside covered with the densest fir stands ever seen by European eyes. A little further on, the river divided into several channels and Fraser steered down the north arm. The explorers anxiously noted at this point that they were being followed by several canoes of heavily armed natives, who were singing war songs and beating their paddles upon the sides of their canoes. Fraser's men made threatening gestures and hastened onward.

The native gestures were misinterpreted. At Kikait, the Kwantlen sub-chief Whattlekainum watched with startled eyes as the party passed by. No such strange white travellers had ever been seen on the river before and although he had heard of white gods on the sea, these men had come from the east! One of his fellow chiefs, Staquist, describes the reaction of the Kwantlen people:

> "I was there when Simon Fraser came. All the people were frightened. They called out and ran around. Some picked up their bows and spears. Others just stood still and looked. It was seen that some of the people in the canoes were just like those who had come in the white-winged canoes. They were not like any of the people who lived on the river, or like those who came when the salmon ran thick in the summer. The faces of some were pale; others had big beards. They wore strange clothes. They were the Sky-people, we thought."

Near the village of Musqueam, at the mouth of the river, Fraser gazed out at the Gulf of Georgia. He observed high rocky islands in the distance. The party landed and were shown the inside of a Musqueam cedar house, but were urged by the natives there to leave quickly in order to avoid attack. The canoes by now were high and dry, the tide having ebbed, and as the explorers hastily dragged them down to the water, dozens of hostile Indians suddenly appeared, brandishing weapons and screaming war cries.

The river as Simon Fraser and his men would have seen it.

The party escaped in the nick of time and rounded Point Grey. Fraser was disappointed in not being able to view the main ocean, adding to his bitterness over failing to navigate the Columbia. He made a final bearing and noted the latitude at nearly 49°, while the Columbia's mouth was known by him to be closer to 46°. "The river is therefore not the Columbia!", he wrote. "If I had been convinced of this when I left my canoes, I would certainly have returned." Two years of preparation and effort had been wasted on a river which no one wanted.

Wearily, Fraser and his men turned back. Now the danger was great. Angry Musqueam natives pursued them up river. The explorers paddled furiously through most of the night and dropped ashore at Kikait. There they rested and in the morning recovered some goods stolen in the night. Some of Fraser's men kicked the natives suspected to be the guilty culprits. This enraged several Kwantlen men, and Whattlekainum had to quieten his younger braves' war chants.

Staquist, whose own village was at the site of the great long house, relates that Fraser became angry: "They took the things from the young men and kicked them. That was bad. It is all right to kick a squaw, but not a warrior. It makes him ashamed. So the hearts of the young men grew black inside of them." And so it was resolved to pursue the whites and kill them later that night.

After Fraser's party had left, Whattlekainum discovered the plan of the young warriors to kill the whites, and forbade them to give chase. He warned them that, as sky people, they came from the sky and there were as many of them as stars in the heavens. He referred to their smoking pipes and their guns, and cautioned them that if they killed Fraser and his men, more whites would return and massacre the Kwantlen people. Then he bestowed the warriors with many of his own possessions in order to assuage their pride.

The chief's intervention undoubtedly saved Fraser and his party; Fraser had earlier made a great impression on Whattlekainum by firing his gun at some crossed sticks and knocking them down; when the chief took the weapon and fired, he missed the sticks.

The by now ragged party of explorers reached the canyon of the great river, only to be faced with marauding Indians pelting them from above with boulders and arrows. Some of Fraser's men rebelled at this point and demanded that they abandon the canyon route and head overland to the east. Fraser remonstrated with them and after much debate, they all shook hands and struggled northward along the canyon walls. Miraculously, nobody was killed or seriously injured, and the shabby, hungry men fought the current by canoe wherever they could make headway, singing voyageur songs to soothe their misery.

Thirty-four days after reaching the sea, the voyagers straggled through the main gate of the palisade at Fort George, having actually bettered their journey time downstream by one day. The disgruntled Fraser—whose partners did not mask their disappointment—had unwittingly established the future boundary line of two sprawling nations stretching from sea to sea.

CHAPTER THREE

THE BIRTH OF FORT LANGLEY

Simon Fraser's river valley reverted to the Stalo and their seasonal cycle of activities. To the south, however, momentous events in the white man's world were unfolding. Lewis and Clark had reached the sea via the Columbia River in 1806, but they did not lay formal claim to the territory.

In 1811, John Jacob Astor established Fort Astoria at the mouth of the Columbia. This New York fur merchant and shipping magnate had been rebuffed by the North West Company when earlier he had proposed a grand alliance between them and his Pacific Fur Company. Now he was determined to make his own company supreme on the northwest coast. Unfortunately, his principal employees were unable to trade peacefully with the local Indians; and after completing construction of Fort Astoria, many of Astor's personnel and the crew of his trading ship *Tonquin* perished, along with two hundred Indians, in a bloody incident at Clayoquot Sound, off Vancouver Island.

Ironically, most of Fort Astoria's resident fur traders employed by the Pacific Fur Company were former Nor'Westers who had remained British subjects. When word reached them in 1812 that war had broken out between Britain and the United States, they found themselves in a serious conflict of interest. For a time they sat tight; but when a British naval blockade of the Pacific coast prevented supplies from reaching them, they resolved to abandon their post.

Unknown to the Astoria personnel, the North West Company itself had dispatched some seventy men via Forts Kamloops and Okanagan in a bold gambit to take possession of the Columbia post in the company's name. Before the Astoria traders and clerks had decamped, the Nor'Westers arrived by canoe down the Columbia.

For a short time a stand-off ensued outside the palisade of the fort. Then a deal was struck which seemed eminently sensible to the commercially minded men on both sides of the wall: The Astorians would sell their employer's fort and all of its furs and trade goods to the North West Company! And so the Stars and Stripes came down and the Union Jack was hoisted up the flagpole. For a price of $80,500, everyone on the scene was satisfied.

Neither John Jacob Astor nor the British government were very enthralled with these developments. In December of 1813, Captain William Black of the Royal Navy arrived off the Columbia River bar under orders to capture Astoria for the British Crown. Great was his dismay and bewilderment when he learned that the upstart fur company from Montreal had already purchased the fort with all of its treasures. Black, who had dreamed of easy plunder, grumbled that he could "batter the fort down with a four-pounder in two hours."

The captain marched ashore into the fort attired in his best gold-braided uniform, where he was wined and dined by the officers of the North West Company. It was during the main course of the dinner that Black announced that he wanted an inventory of the entire fort taken immediately since, although he had decided not to take the fort by force of arms, a prize court in London might well award it to him and he needed to establish its proper value.

Clerk James McMillan shook his head in disbelief when Black ordered that the Nor'Wester engagés must drill with muskets in his presence in order to form a proper guard of honour. The eccentric captain capped his strange performance by lowering the Union Jack, raising the Stars and Stripes, and then hauling down the American flag and raising the Union Jack once more, smashing the flagpole with a bottle of Madeira wine. He then rechristened the post Fort George in honour of the King. Back aboard his ship, Captain Black sent a coded dispatch to the British Admiralty proclaiming "mission accomplished."

The final irony in Captain Black's Astoria caper was that the post had to be returned to the United States in 1818 pursuant to the Treaty of Ghent, after the Americans successfully argued that since Black had officially captured the post during wartime, it must be returned; whereas had he not performed his antics, the North West Company purchase may have been valid and saved Astoria for Britain!

In the same year that Astoria was returned to American control, Britain and the United States signed an agreement allowing for co-occupation of the Oregon Territory, which comprised the Columbia and New Caledonia regions west of the Rockies.

It was at this time that the 49th parallel was first tentatively advanced as a possible latitude for an international boundary. The two nations also adopted an unwritten understanding that whichever side colonized with more vigour or established the greatest number of trading stations in this vast region would have the greater claim to sovereignty in future negotiations.

In 1821, the Hudson's Bay Company merged with its arch rival, the North West Company. The merger was as much related to imperial policy as it was to commercial self-interest. The British Colonial Office was anxious to extend the Crown's influence to the Pacific coast of North America and therefore assured the two companies that if they could agree on union, the government would not only sponsor the Parliamentary bill, but would grant the amalgamated company exclusive trading rights in the region extending west of Rupert's Land to the ocean.

Instead of hammering each other into oblivion, the two fur trading giants could now combine their respective talents to thwart American commercial ambitions, exploit the rich Pacific fur market, and consolidate posts in the area west of the Great Lakes to the Rockies—an area being steadily encroached upon by settlers.

The man chosen for the task of heading the new commercial leviathan was a Scottish-born clerk named George Simpson, dubbed by many "The Little Emperor" of the fur trade. Simpson was to dominate the Hudson's Bay Company for forty years, displaying throughout his tenure as governor an indomitable spirit and inexhaustible stamina.

Like Whattlekainum of the Fraser, Simpson began each day by plunging into the nearest stream or lake. He outpaced all of his men in lengthy excursions around his continental empire, in one trip wearing out two hundred horses, which he left behind as food for the wolves.

Simpson's insatiable sexual appetite was renowned. His unions with Indian women produced five illegitimate children. In this respect, however, the governor was pragmatic. After he ultimately married his British cousin, Frances Ramsey, he let it be known that "country" marriages of Hudson's Bay men with Indian women were frowned upon by the Company. As for his policies toward Indians generally, Simpson proclaimed in 1822, "I am convinced they must be ruled with a rod of iron, to bring and to keep them in a proper state of subordination and the most certain way to effect this is by letting them feel dependent upon us."

Sir George Simpson.

In August of 1824, Governor Simpson embarked by canoe from York Factory on Hudson Bay, bound for Astoria—known now as Fort George to the Company men—on the Columbia. His mission was urgent: To determine the prospects for holding the Columbia and New Caledonia regions for both the Hudson's Bay Company and the British Crown in the face of steady Yankee penetration.

The two regions were ill-defined. Generally, the Columbia Territory extended from northern California to the latitude 51 degrees N and all of the British Columbia coast. New Caledonia stretched from latitude 51 degrees N to latitude 57 degrees N. Together, the two areas were known simply as the Oregon Territory.

While traversing the rapids on the big bend of the Columbia River, Simpson first broached the subject of a possible lower Fraser River trading post in conversation with chief trader James McMillan. Simpson raved that it was a disgrace that sixteen years had passed since Simon Fraser's voyage to the sea without any follow-up mission. Moreover, he stated, there was great benefit in having a fort located at the mouth of a major river far to the north of current American territorial ambitions.

Noting McMillan's noncommittal reaction to his tirade, Simpson said he would go explore the Fraser himself and establish a post—whereupon McMillan offered to undertake the task.

Simpson arrived at Fort George in early November. He immediately turned the establishment on its ear. Scorning the leisurely, slothful life of the Columbia traders, he raged at his clerks for failing to establish farms around the fort - instead of becoming self-sufficient, he steamed, the traders simply imported food and luxury items from California; among the supplies in the fort's warehouse Simpson had discovered silk stockings, umbrellas, jewellery, and ostrich plumes. He noted, moreover, that no efforts had been made to construct or purchase ships to compete with Yankee traders operating along the coast.

After venting his venom on his Columbia River employees, Simpson immediately turned his attention to the goal of reconnoitering the lower Fraser River. Without allowing for more than one day's pause after his and McMillan's record-breaking transcontinental journey, Simpson ordered McMillan to assemble a party of men and prepare to embark northward.

McMillan and his clerks—François Annance, Tom McKay, and John Work—were not timid men; but they were furious at having to tramp northward in the cold, drizzly damp of the west coast rain forest, with the certainty of missing the festive Yuletide season at Fort George. McMillan, nevertheless, worked feverishly with his men in outfitting supplies, preparing boats, and planning his route. Ten days after arriving at the fort, he set forth with forty men in marching order out of the main gate, under the Governor's benign eye.

Among the French-Canadian "voyageurs" and Kanakas (Hawaiians who had boarded British ships and subsequently found employment with the Company in the Oregon Territory), was one Jean Proveau, who had accompanied Simon Fraser on his 1808 trip. Only Proveau returned a nod and a smile to the governor as they tramped off into the mist, for it was he who was anxious to revisit the lower Fraser and give learned advice to his masters.

The expedition travelled on three flat bottomed boats along the coastline amidst fierce winds and then up the Chehalis River. Rainsoaked, chilled, mud splattered, the men hauled the boats along two portages and finally arrived exhausted at Puget Sound. They dined at night by campfire on peas, pork, rum and oatmeal.

The party reached Semiahmoo Bay on December 11, found Mud Bay, and proceeded up the Nicomekl River, guided by Indian interpreters picked up on the way. They were now travelling on the centuries-old Semiahmoo Trail which the Stalo and their southern neighbours used as their chief communication link. But to the Hudson's Bay boatmen, the stream was too narrow, sluggish, clogged with driftwood, and "closed up with willows so uncommonly thick that it was both laborious and tedious to get the boats dragged through them."

McMillan noted the rich soil of the river plain through which they passed and, more significantly for his employers, the profusion of beaver dams. One final backbreaking portage through the mud took the party to the Salmon River. At 1:00 P.M. on December 16, the scraggly party emerged from the meandering little stream near Derby, later site of the first Fort Langley, about 1.5 miles from the second fort and present village, and gazed upon the broad brown waters of the Fraser. Here Proveau whooped excitedly and pointed toward the Golden Ears, then to what is now known as McMillan Island, where he said that he had camped with Simon Fraser. The men bivouacked for the night, too fatigued to listen any further to Proveau's excited babble of stories about his 1808 adventure.

The expedition spent the next few days exploring the Fraser, first up river to Hatzic and then down the river to its mouth. It rained incessantly. McMillan traded axes, beads and fish hooks with Stalo natives in exchange for a few beaver pelts. John Work observed that the Indians seemed to know the worth of goods and refused the tobacco which was proffered them. He was much impressed with one particular chief, described as a "fine tall good looking man, but his people are of low stature. Their elderly men generally have beards. All their heads are a little flattened. Their clothes consisted of blankets of their own manufacture, some white and some grey or black brown, with variegated bands of different colours, mostly red and white. They wore mats to keep off the rain and conical hats."

On December 19, McMillan's voyageurs landed at an abandoned summer fishing village on the island later known as Annacis, and there carved the initials "H.B.Co." in large letters into the bark of a huge cedar tree, officially claiming the valley for their employer.

The party then proceeded down the river for the homeward journey, McMillan having decided to avoid the Semiahmoo Trail in favour of an all coastal

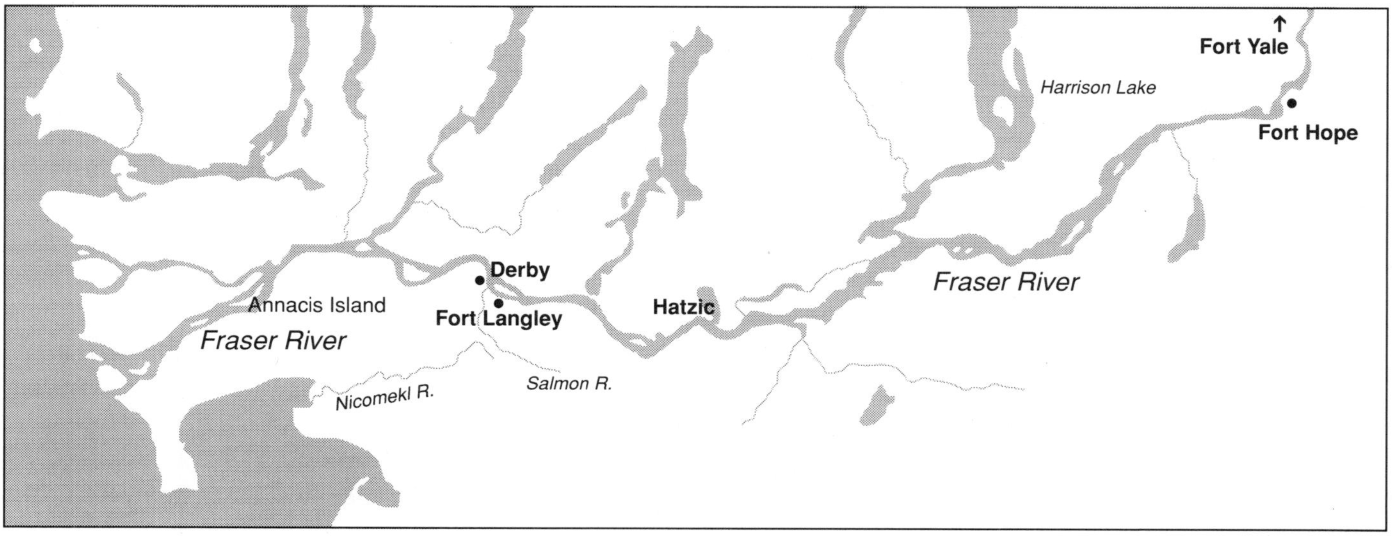

route. At the Fraser's mouth, he took a few tentative soundings of the channel depth. McMillan quickly became sceptical as to the river's entrance accommodating any ship exceeding two hundred tons, and he noted that the ocean tide ran up the river for sixty miles, beyond which he doubted that the Fraser would be navigable at all.

McMillan found a large Indian population in the Musqueam area. He wrote that the Indians were "overjoyed" to see them. "I distributed a few presents among the natives which were gratefully acknowledged, and by every word and gesture they evinced their anxious wish that we should settle among them, holding forth as an inducement the assurance of their bringing us large quantities of Beaver with which I have ascertained their country is richly stocked. It appears extraordinary that Vancouver should not in the careful survey he made of the coast have discovered a River of such magnitude...."

Returning swiftly to the Columbia via the coast route, McMillan and his party filed into Fort George in time for the New Year's Eve celebrations and were greeted by a delighted George Simpson. The governor lavished praise upon the explorers and big Jean Proveau beamed. The returning men were regaled with rum and steaming plates of salmon, beef, and desserts.

Simpson wasted no time in ordering Fort George's new chief factor, Dr. John McLoughlin, to send a return expedition to the Fraser River to take detailed soundings of the channel at its mouth. The governor was determined that the lower Fraser River should become the focus of a new policy of supply and security arrangements respecting all the forts of New Caledonia, free from the threat of American penetration and strategically located as the terminus for an overland route from the chain of Hudson's Bay posts in the Interior.

Governor Simpson had either not read, or discounted Simon Fraser's journal describing the perilous Fraser Canyon route, for he concluded that there would be a great advantage in outfitting the interior posts from the Pacific side of the mountains instead of from York Factory on Hudson Bay. As he wrote, "important benefits would result from making but one Department of all the establishments on this side of the mountains and that the mouth of Frazer's River should be its Depot."

Although convinced of the ultimate superiority of the lower Fraser region for his Pacific hub, Simpson wished also to retain a strong Hudson's Bay Company presence on the Columbia River. The fur trade potential in the region was still considerable. During the winter at Fort George, however, he had reconnoitered the area and determined to relocate the fort some eighty-five miles up the Columbia, where he selected a site more defensible from potential Yankee attack, and which was surrounded by fertile lands suitable for cultivation. Simpson was adamant that the post become wholly self-sufficient, primarily in order to reduce operating costs, about which the frugal governor was admittedly obsessed.

The new fort upstream on the Columbia was officially opened on March 19, 1825, on which date an elegantly attired Governor Simpson smashed the flagstaff with a bottle of rum and christened the post "Fort Vancouver."

Before leaving on his journey overland to the east, he slashed personnel in the region from 151 to 83 men; then he exhorted Dr. McLoughlin to keep his costs down, and gave express orders that the entire Columbia region be shorn of every last beaver pelt. This achievement, he assured his chief factor, would both ensure the Company of its profits and keep the hungry American traders at bay. Content, the governor clambered into his waiting canoe and embarked up the river.

Governor Simpson pursued his objective of a lower Fraser River depot when he met in London with the Hudson's Bay Company ruling committee in December of 1825. There he painted a glowing portrait of a new supply post servicing the inland string of forts of New Caledonia, coordinating the Pacific fur trade, and opening up China to commerce. Even the Indians were friendly toward the Company, he asserted, and had pressed for a fort to be established.

The committee was impressed with Simpson's presentation and issued an immediate directive:

> "We wish Fraser's River to be established next season if possible, and that Mr. McMillan should be appointed to the charge of it, as his re-appearance among the natives may have a good effect. From the central situation of Fraser's River we think that it will be found to be the proper place for the principal depot, but not until we have passed at least one winter there and acquired a knowledge of the character and disposition of the Natives and ascertained whether the navigation of the River is favourable to the plan of making it the principal communication with the Interior."

On the morning of July 22, 1827, the sailing ship *Cadboro* entered the Fraser River. Lining the shore were hundreds of apprehensive Musqueam natives; never before had the white-winged canoes come into the river. Aboard the ship were twenty-five Hudson's Bay Company employees, led by James McMillan. The vessel had attempted for several days to enter the shallow, silted channel, but kept grounding. Now the schooner groped its way slowly upriver, and by noon had reached the great tree emblazoned with the Company symbol near Kikait. The ship anchored for the night at the entrance to Pitt River.

McMillan's orders were clear. He and his party were to establish a fort on the banks of the Fraser, and it was to be named Langley, after a Company director. As McMillan paced the deck that night casting nervous glances at the anchor chain, he wondered whether Langley had been a swing vote for Simpson in persuading the committee to vote for this fantasy of a depot on a muddy river with shifting shoals in an isolated valley full of Indians. The chief trader could see native camp fires glowing in the night up and down the river. Below decks, six of his men were seriously ill with gonorrhea, and all but three of the expedition's horses had died during the difficult ocean passage from Fort Vancouver.

Meanwhile, Chief Whattlekainum had observed the great winged canoe on the river and spread the word among his people that no hostile acts were to be committed against the sky people.

Early next morning, Whattlekainum and some Kwantlen braves set out in a canoe laden with beaver skins and cautiously approached the *Cadboro*. They were warmly welcomed by McMillan, who noted in his diary, "Whattlekainum, a Quoitle Chief, was on board this morning, and was kindly received. He traded a few Beaver skins for knives."

Later that day a different scenario occurred when more than 150 natives, armed and hostile, surrounded the *Cadboro* and attempted to board the vessel. Cannons were hurriedly swivelled into position and muskets and sabres distributed to the crew and the passengers. Upon a few warning shots being fired, the Indians withdrew.

On July 30, McMillan moored his ship near the south bank, just below the mouth of the Salmon River, where he had first viewed the Fraser in 1824. There he chose the location for the new fort: "The schooner was brought close to the shore and the horses landed by slinging them off to the bank. The poor animals appeared to rejoice heartily in their liberation. Our men at noon were all very busily employed in clearing the ground for the establishment. In the evening all came aboard to sleep, a precaution considered necessary until we are better assured of the friendly disposition of the natives. A few Indians and Indian women were alongside for a great part of the day and were quiet and peaceful. One of the ship's company was this day put in irons for making use of language calculated to promote discontent and create disorder among the crew."

The Hudson's Bay men toiled in the thick underbrush, their broad axes, mattocks and saws striking a virgin forest of gigantic cedars and rotting logs underfoot, interwoven with brambles, briars, and stinging nettles.

As McMillan reported to Dr. McLoughlin, many trees were two hundred feet high and eighteen feet in circumference. Indians brought them sturgeon and a few pelts to trade. An axe was stolen, and an elderly native apprehended and forced to return the implement. This produced a major conference between the whites and some fifty natives, among whom were Whattlekainum and other sub-chiefs, who conveyed friendly intentions. McMillan was cautioned, however, by Shashia, the great southern Salish chief who had journeyed with the *Cadboro* to interpret, that the Stalo in the region were in fact divided in their reaction to the white interlopers, and that one large group led by Chief Punnis was determined to prevent the Company men from settling on their river.

Throughout the summer the Scottish, French-Canadian, Iroquois, and Kanakan workers laboured in the hot sun. Natives by the hundreds plied up and down the Fraser, some intent on salmon fishing during the peak run, others more curious about the interlopers' activities. Some bolder souls stopped to come ashore and trade fish, furs, and cedar bark, the latter being useful as a thatch for buildings.

Then one day the forest suddenly burst into flames. Men cutting pickets fled for their lives, as the fire burned hot and fierce for several days. McMillan was told by Shashia that hostile Kwantlen had set the fire to drive the whites away.

The fire was finally extinguished and work resumed. The palisade and bastions were completed, and McMillan mused that the natives appeared somewhat awed by the size of the emerging structure. By September 8, the exterior defences were complete, and McMillan could breathe more easily. "The picketing of the Fort," he recorded, "was now completed, and the gates hung. The Rectangle inside is 40 yards by 45, and the two Bastions are 12 feet square each, built of 8 inch logs, and having a lower and upper flooring, the latter of which is to be occupied by our artillery."

The Company men could now sleep within walls on shore. Their toil, however, continued apace and construction began on a warehouse, store, and wintering quarters. In the hazy light of dawn on September 18, the *Cadboro* weighed anchor and raised sail; the morning calm was shattered by a booming salute from the fort guns, which was instantly returned by the schooner's captain. Then the men were left alone to contemplate their fate.

McMillan surveyed his new post with grim satisfaction. Here he was, isolated from civilization with a motley group of exhausted men. Bitterly he wrote to McLoughlin that he was surrounded by Indians, his men were ill, and the trees were so huge that it took a day to fell one forest giant. Nevertheless, on November 26, the fort was deemed officially complete and the Hudson's Bay Company ensign was proudly raised. McMillan ordered that the cannons be fired and muskets flashed black powder—causing two of the garrison's hunters to come scurrying from the woods in alarm at the noise..

All that evening and well into the early morning hours, McMillan regaled his men with dried salmon, peas, bread, and rum. However, both he and his superintendent, François Annance, kept watch on the many flickering shadows moving about outside the palisade. Both men were well aware that they were intruders in a native land. Only their guns, and Whattlekainum's moderating influence, had saved them from probable massacre.

McMillan was grateful to Whattlekainum for having tracked down native thieves who had broken into the fort one night and stolen tools. In appreciation for return of the implements, he gave the Kwantlen chief two axes. Whattlekainum was also responsible for the few beaver pelts which were brought to the fort.

The garrison faced a food shortage that winter. The dried salmon which the Company men had obtained from the natives had mildewed and spoiled in the damp climate. As autumn wore on, only a few Indians straggled into the fort to trade, as the Stalo busied themselves with their own winter preparations.

Meanwhile, the whites were unnerved by the all too frequent spectacle of Yuculta war canoes passing up and down the river on missions of plunder and slave raiding. McMillan was particularly revolted one day by the sight of several canoes returning from a raid, loaded with captured women and children, stolen goods, and the head of a male victim suspended on a pole above the bow of the lead canoe.

Late autumn rains turned to sleet and the sleet to snow by December. Life inside the palisade became "dull and monotonous—everything has taken on a winter appearance." Some men put in time rooting out stumps or building furniture; others roamed the woods, hunting for beaver and deer, led by the skilled forager Pierre Charles. Firewood was cut furiously. A wharf was built on the river below the fort. Many men were still ill; some complained of the constant diet of mildewed salmon. The two horses, which had survived the sea voyage and were much needed for hauling logs, both perished in a swamp.

The days shortened. All along the river the Stalo hunkered down in their winter dwellings. The river was barren of traffic. The cold cut to the quick of the men who toiled; the loss of the horses meant that the labourers had to struggle mightily to drag heavy timbers to the fort. Men became distraught and easily spooked. "Last night," noted McMillan, "a noise was heard by some of the men, resembling the sound of distant cannon. The houses were shaken a little at the time, which makes us suppose that it was a slight shock or earthquake."

By December 18, the Fraser had frozen solid and men walked across the channel to try hunting on the north bank; there Pierre Charles was successful in bagging four deer. Christmas approached. The men shivered and cursed the heavy snow which now began to fall continuously. They thought of their friends at other forts, of great eastern cities they had known; the Kanakas dreamed of soft oceanic breezes and warm nights. McMillan made no plans for celebrating the normally festive Yuletide season, other than hosting a venison dinner.

Then, on Christmas Eve morning, the sentries on duty noticed two figures running upriver along the frozen ice. They squinted. Two Indians emerged puffing at the main gate, one of them waving a dirty piece of paper. Annance met them and received a scrawled note from one Alex McKenzie, a Hudson's Bay trader of the Columbia region, who advised that he was stranded a few miles down the Fraser, surrounded by hostile natives. McMillan quickly dispatched Annance and a party of ten armed men.

François Annance was described by George Simpson—who rated all of his men—as a "half breed of the Abiniki tribe near Quebec: well educated and has been a schoolmaster. Is firm with the Indians. Speaks several of their languages—is a good shot and qualified to lead the life of an Indian...Is not worthy of belief, even under oath—a useful man." Annacis Island is named after him.

Near the confluence of the Fraser and Pitt Rivers, the Fort Langley party found McKenzie and four other Bay employees among a large group of Musqueam Indians camped there. The Fort Vancouver traders had been en route to Fort Langley when they were accosted by natives and robbed; they managed however to persuade a friendly Kwantlen man to take a message to the fort. Annance had little difficulty in freeing the traders, regaining their possessions, and then marching them triumphantly back to the fort three hours upstream, where they were met by a beaming McMillan.

The visitors acted as a wonderful tonic to the Fort Langley engagés. McKenzie and his comrades had fought their way through the snow to Puget Sound and from there embarked in a small canoe by sea to the Fraser, hugging the coastline as the blizzard-like flurries lashed their cheeks. They bore letters, parcels, and news of the outside world.

All that Christmas Eve the bonfires were piled high with cedar limbs as the visitors joined with their fellow Company comrades in singing hymns in both English and French; violins screeched; rum overflowed; stories, laughter, and men dancing the jig continued well into the early morning hours.

McMillan sighed contentedly after the last of the revellers had retired to the bunkhouse for the night. He made the rounds of the compound, ensuring that all the bonfires were thoroughly doused. Overhead, the skies cleared and the stars shone brightly. Tomorrow, he mused, the Company tradition would be ritualistically observed, with all of the men calling upon him as chief trader to pay their respects. He would respond by giving each man his ration of rum and telling a jest.

And so the first Christmas passed at Fort Langley. New Year's Eve ushered in a new year of expectation and promise as the Hudson's Bay men of the Fraser settled into their winter quarters. Downriver at Skaiamatl, Whattlekainum argued with old chief Punnis about the white intruders. As much as he pondered, he could not fathom the meaning of the coming of these sky people. Their arrival might bode both good and ill, he thought. But of one thing he was certain—they were here to stay.

CHAPTER FOUR

LONELY OUTPOST OF EMPIRE

James McMillan was a steady Scot; a resourceful but not too brilliant fur trader who had served his time as a clerk, and then as chief trader, at various posts both east and west of the Rockies, including old Astoria. There, in 1813, he had signed as a witness to the fort's purchase from the Pacific Fur Company by the Nor'Westers. He came to Governor Simpson's attention in 1824. His chief objectives during the first year of his Fort Langley tenure were to collect furs, complete the interior buildings, and protect his employees from Indian attack.

On the morning of January 2, 1828, Alexander Mackenzie and his men embarked down the Fraser on their return journey to Fort Vancouver. They were accompanied by an ebullient McMillan, who had decided to report personally to Dr. McLoughlin that he had not only erected a fort, but had collected an impressive 1,182 beaver and otter skins.

Tragedy intervened. The party became stormbound at Point Roberts for a week and McMillan decided to return to Fort Langley. Over a month later, his Cowichan Indian friend, Chief Shashia, landed at the fort with the news that Mackenzie and his companions had been massacred by Clallam Indians on the Hood Canal. McMillan winced and prayed that this was just an idle rumour, but Shashia's reports were all too true. The Hudson's Bay Company exacted revenge by raiding a Clallam village, killing twenty-one people. This was the one time that the Company departed from its custom of punishing only the guilty parties, instead adopting the American strategy of a wholesale reprisal.

During the spring of 1828. Annance was continuously on the move, obtaining a good canoe in trade with the Katzies, who were moving to their Pitt

Lake camp, fearful of a major Yuculta raid. McMillan sent a party of eight well-armed men to Fort Vancouver to ensure that his report to McLoughlin had been received. Shortly after they departed, Whattlekainum arrived at the fort to trade beaver and relate further information from Shashia about the Mackenzie massacre.

The fort personnel plodded doggedly onward in their endeavours. That spring, they planted some two thousand bushels of potatoes; the idea came in part from McMillan's observation that the Indians grew wappatoes, a potato-like root which thrived in marshy areas along the river. Fish sheds were erected, stables built for future livestock, and additional accommodation constructed for the men. Sawing, cooking, fish curing, rooting, hunting, and trading furs kept the men of the post busy.

Overshadowing all of this activity, however, was fear of Indians. With the McKenzie massacre fresh in their minds, the sentries watched with concern as war parties of Yucultas in full regalia paddled up the Fraser on their annual plundering expeditions. "They are 150 men in ten canoes, and ugly looking devils they are," wrote McMillan. Natives skulking outside the fort at night also unnerved him. The effect of the constant Yuculta threat upon peaceful trade with the Stalo was a factor militating toward white intervention:

> "This warfare keeps the Indians of this vicinity in such continual alarm that they cannot turn their attention to anything but the care of their family and that they do but poorly; while the powerful tribes from Vancouver's Island harass them in this manner, little hunts can be expected from them and unless the Company supports them against those lawless villains, little exertions can be expected from them."

War parties of Yucultas defiantly waved war clubs at the Company men as they passed by on the river; at night, hostile natives threw stones at the sentries. The men were continually on edge as a result of persistent rumours that they were about to be attacked. Hence the collective relief when the "express" brigade sent to Fort Vancouver returned safely.

The *Cadboro* also paid a return visit at this time, loaded with sorely needed supplies. The traders were having difficulty with convincing the Indians to part with either fish or furs—a problem blamed on the presence of Yankee trading ships, which plied the coast and paid much more than the Hudson's Bay Company for Indian wares. This became a vexing issue that was to plague Fort Langley for years to come.

"We hear from the Indians," wrote McMillan, "that there is a ship at the Clallams trading skins. I have no doubt the Yankees will pay that quarter another visit, which will injure our trade much, and will furnish these rascals with their wants, especially ammunition...The Indians about here laugh at us when we ask them 5 skins for a blanket."

The Hudson's Bay Company motto, Pro Pelle Cutem, meant literally "a skin for its equivalent." But under penny-pinching George Simpson, orders were that nothing useful, such as tools, should be given to natives unless in exchange for pelts. This meant that it became extremely difficult for the Fort Langley traders to interest local natives in trading them the salmon they required for winter sustenance.

In 1828, so many Indians established encampments near the fort, and nearby McMillan Island, that the main Kwantlen tribe eventually became known as the Langley Band. This movement from the Skaiametl area was led by Whattlekainum, who decided that the sky people could offer protection to his people from the constant Yuculta depredations. McMillan himself was cynical regarding the Stalo. When Indians seeking protection from invaders arrived en masse at the fort in May of 1828, he allowed them shelter inside the palisade. He later cursed himself for allowing them in, after several natives began pilfering foodstuffs and carting them off, obliging him to "stick to the good old custom of keeping them to the bank of the river" and outside the fort itself.

Numerous Stalo tribal groups now visited the fort, constantly milling around; they were allowed inside the palisade in controlled numbers during the day and ushered out for the evening.

The Hudson's Bay men failed to realize the shrewd trading habits of the natives. The typical Indian family went about its annual fishing and hunting activities to secure a sufficient winter food supply. Natives resented the poor quality of goods which the traders offered for salmon and sturgeon, and, like any good businessmen, preferred to sell to American traders at higher prices. Only if there was a surplus of fish or furs would they trade for lesser quality items like beads, an old Company favourite, preferring useful tools such as axes, saws, and at a later date, rifles.

Indians gathered at Fort Langley for social and ceremonial purposes, as well as to trade. Incidents of violence and confrontation outside the palisade walls were common. McMillan describes one occasion:

> "A dispute arose betwixt a Musqueam woman and a Kwantlen young girl about their virtue. The women continued the dispute for some time, then the men took a share in the quarrel. Several speeches were made upon the occasion by both parties—the Musqueam went off for their arms—the Kwantlens remained about the fort but sent a canoe off for reinforcement... In a few minutes about 50 men of the Musqueams came across armed and began haranguing...."

About forty Kwantlen braves arrived and orators from both sides railed on at each other for some time, but it all ended without bloodshed—McMillan being "sadly disappointed that it ended so, as it would give us an opportunity of seeing their mode of fighting."

The sentries in the bastions were continuously entertained, and occasionally frightened, by the constant flow of Indian traffic both along the river and around the fort. Canoe loads of Stalo would sing and even dance in their canoes by river's edge. Upper Stalo natives would pass by on their way downriver, their canoes loaded with what appeared to be all of their worldly possessions, only to return the next day, bound upstream without their household goods, but with a wife or children freshly ransomed from the slavery of a temporary Yuculta camp.

The staple rations for the men of the fort continued to be salmon, supplemented by berries, some venison, and the odd sturgeon. Pierre Charles manufactured a seventy-two-foot spear handle in order to hunt sturgeon "Cowichan fashion." In August 1828, the post was blessed with a huge supply of fresh salmon, which was properly dried and preserved this time. The run was heavy and so the natives were willing to accept the traders' terms. McMillan prayed for salt so as to be able to cure the fish within the palisade walls.

In general, the fishing attempts of the whites were clumsy and unsuccessful, forcing heavy reliance upon the Indians—and, it can be assumed, a bending of Simpson's policy of trading only beads for food.

On July 2, 1828, the Indian wife of a fort employee gave birth to a son, who was appropriately named Louis Langley. Whattlekainum, Shashia, and many other Stalo natives came to marvel at this first child of mixed blood born on the river; they all opined that this was a good omen. Many of the Company employees had established liaisons with native women; others brought wives to the fort from the Columbia region. Since 1823, Company policy required employees living with native women to sign marriage agreements, and if the employee abandoned his wife, he must either pay support or find her another male provider for her and any children of the union.

Ten days after Louis Langley uttered his first cry, George Simpson left York Factory, on the western shore of Hudson Bay, accompanied by chief trader Archibald McDonald, his "country wife" Margaret, and a party of voyageurs.

Two months and 3,200 miles later, the governor marched triumphantly through the gates of Fort St. James on the headwaters of the Fraser, having set yet another transcontinental speed record. Simpson's entry was preceded by booming cannons, bugles, and bagpipes, with the expedition's guide leading the procession, bearing the Hudson's Bay Company ensign, and the voyageurs acting as bandsmen. The party was met at the main gate by James Douglas, a young clerk temporarily in charge of the post.

James Murray Yale.

Simpson sojourned one week at Fort St. James, making a note to remember James Douglas as a man of ability. Then he prepared to depart on the tortuous trip down the wild Fraser River to Fort Langley, Simpson being anxious to determine whether the Fraser route could serve as an alternative to the lengthy trek from Fort Vancouver, via the Interior, to the northern posts.

Another young clerk serving at Fort St. James, James Murray Yale, was so awed by the legendary governor that he begged Simpson to accompany him to the lower Fraser; the governor, ever on the watch for lap dogs, assented to the request.

At 2:00 A.M., amidst swirling river mist, the party began its great descent of the Fraser. To relieve monotony, Simpson encouraged the voyageurs to sing. In fact, he railed at his best paddler for not singing loudly, although the poor fellow suffered from a miserable sore throat. Rebuked, the voyageur sang like a bird thereafter.

Simpson described the Thompson as "exceedingly dangerous," and a whirlpool nearly overturned his canoe. Near Lytton, the governor and his wife literally were flopped ashore by the rapids, drenched and shivering, surrounded by curious natives and a concerned James Murray Yale. Simpson recovered and from Lytton down he even outdid Simon Fraser. Spurning all advice to leave the river at dangerous spots, the governor insisted on travelling by water the entire way regardless of risk. Even this titan, however, was awestruck by the hellish waters:

> "The banks now erected themselves into perpendicular Mountains of Rock from the Water's edge, the tops enveloped in clouds, and the lower parts dismal and rugged in the extreme; the descent of the stream very rapid...the Rocks...overhanging the foaming waters, pent up, from 20 to 30 yards wide, running with immense velocity and momentarily threatening to sweep us to destruction...we were frequently hurried into rapids before we could ascertain how they ought to be taken, through which the craft shot like the flight of an arrow, into deep whirlpools which seemed to sport in twirling us about, and passing us from one to another...."

By the time the foaming river spit out the canoes into calmer waters near the evil rock, the governor had the answer to his burning question: the Fraser trading route was an impossible dream, and hence Fort Langley could never be the chief Pacific depot for the Hudson's Bay Company. In his journal, he wrote: "Frazer's River can no longer be thought of as a practicable communication with the interior; it was never wholly passed by water before, and in all probability never will again." Simpson was the first white to navigate the entire canyon south of Lytton—and indeed was one of the last, until the advent of white water adventures on large rubber rafts.

Meanwhile, at Fort Langley James McMillan and his men were oblivious to Governor Simpson's pending arrival. The chief factor found life tedious and exasperating, and longed to return to the Columbia region. He was continually confronted with disorderly natives, particularly during the summer months, when Cowichans from the upper coast and southern Vancouver Island arrived to fish, barter goods, and sniff out the fort enclave. McMillan wrote: "Indians about us every hour of the day, but they provoke us to harsh measures towards them in spite of all our endeavours to be on friendly terms....Indians rather saucy...The Musqueams are always rather impudent when they come to the Fort."

Annance, in particular, was tested by native encounters and became a frequent arbiter of disputes. The unruly behaviour of visiting natives required tact and guile. McMillan, as "Chief White Eagle," lacked the needed temperament to deal with these situations, and he was unable to establish a personal rapport with even the most peaceable Kwantlen leaders.

At 8:00 P.M. one clear October evening, the sentries at Fort Langley were surprised to hear the sound of singing from upriver, followed by a shrieking blare of bagpipes which startled natives and whites alike. Out of the shadows emerged the lead canoe, bearing a scarlet frocked figure. The helmsman docked the craft and Governor Simpson stepped ashore, his dark eyes peering intently at the silhouetted salmon sheds, above which towered the bastions and walls of the palisade.

Simpson was pleased by his survey of the fort during his week long stay. He observed well-constructed buildings, a full larder, fireplaces, cellars, and three fields of potatoes outside the walls. He also took a passionate delight in entertaining curious natives with his musical snuffbox.

Simpson commended McMillan on his progress. Although disappointed with the Fraser's potential as a trade route, he wrote to his London superiors that he anticipated the post would become a valuable asset to the Company, particularly in securing the coastal trade.

The governor was renowned for making and executing quick decisions. Before he had even retired to his bed on the night of his arrival, he decided to take McMillan down to Fort Vancouver with him for furlough, and place Archibald McDonald in command at Fort Langley, assisted by the eager Yale. McDonald was a rugged, energetic and well-educated man of thirty years, who had served as secretary to Lord Selkirk at Red River. He is credited with having written the most historically reliable account of the destruction of the Red River colony.

Archibald McDonald.

Weary from his journey across the continent with the frenetic governor, McDonald was yearning to settle down to the challenge of a new post. He was married, and planned to bring his wife and children up from Fort Vancouver in the spring of 1829.

The founder of Fort Langley departed with Governor Simpson with nary a glance behind him, so eager was he to shed the tedium of the Fraser and its problems. But his successor was already analyzing the situation of the fort and planning energetically for its future. He noted that the low bank site was subject to periodic flooding; that there stood two dwelling houses, one for the gentlemen clerks and officers, and the other for the labourers, apprentices, tradesmen, guides, and hunters—a total complement of twenty men.

Within a month of his arrival, McDonald had enlarged the compound, harvested a good potato crop, and traded enough salmon with the natives in a four day period to equal the entire previous stock, fish which was immediately dried, salted, and stored by deft native women who welcomed employment. Soon the rafters in the salmon sheds were lined with row upon row of fresh fish curing in the smoke.

McDonald studied the notes about the Indian troubles left by McMillan, and discussed with Yale the constant state of fear and anxiety both the whites and the Stalo experienced concerning the Yucultas and other raiding war parties. The new chief factor had no immediate solutions, but was confident that he could promote the interests of the post in both fur-trading and food procurement by living in harmony with the Stalo.

The fort employees found McDonald to be fair-minded, but a strict disciplinarian. One evening a servant of Annance slipped out of the main gate in the night to visit an Indian maiden and was retrieved in the morning back to the fort, where he had to "run the gauntlet and was hung up to the flagstaff."

McDonald was determined to impress upon his men the criminality of opening the main gate at night. On another occasion, an employee hauled a native woman up the wall and through a porthole during a New Year's Eve celebration; for this, he was penalized by the loss of half of his annual wages and deprived of all liquor. The blacksmith was punished one day with a ruler across his skull, for insolently demanding time off work after having gorged himself sick on oolichans.

Archibald McDonald also directed the matrimonial policy of the fort. Shortly after his arrival, he discussed with Yale the prudence of the latter taking a "country wife." Yale was a diminutive but passionate man. At Fort George, on the upper Fraser, he had experienced rejection of his affections toward young ladies on more than one occasion. In 1824, while temporarily absent from the post, his Indian wife renewed her intimacy with a former Indian lover. When Yale's two servants threatened to report the affair to Yale, they were both murdered by the lover, and Yale's wife fled with her paramour into the hinterland.

In 1827, both Yale and fellow clerk James Douglas were vying for the hand of the mixed-blood daughter of Chief Factor William Connolly, a beautiful maiden named Amelia. Again Yale was unlucky. He had injured his hand and had to travel all of the way to Fort Vancouver for medical treatment. While he was gone, the wily Douglas married Amelia, who later became the initial and esteemed first lady of the colony of British Columbia. The rivalry between the two young clerks was to leave lasting scars.

Lady Amelia Douglas.

Yale was specifically "encouraged" by McDonald to find a wife in Whattlekainum's village. "These, being the principal Indians of this neighbourhood and who all exert themselves to collect Beaver, we have thought it good policy in Mr. Yale to form a family connection with them, and accordingly he has now the Chief's daughter after making them all liberal presents." So McDonald wrote in defining his new Indian strategy.

For his part, Whattlekainum was overjoyed; he believed that union of whites and Indians in marriage would assure the long-term welfare of his tribe, and he proudly offered his daughter's hand.

The first year of marriage appeared to be a happy one for Yale and his bride. A daughter named Eliza was born, whom Yale adored. Shortly thereafter, however, his wife left him without warning, returning to her Indian husband of another tribe.

Yale was morose, but did not pursue her. Whattlekainum panicked; he was terrified that Yale would blame him for trickery. In his zeal to cement the relationship between Kwantlen and whites, he had carelessly assumed that his daughter would never breathe a word of her Indian husband. Miserable, he appeared at the fort one morning to face Yale's wrath. But Yale quietly assured the chief that he sought no retribution; their relationship, he said, was too important to be destroyed by a matter of marriage.

Whattlekainum left the fort greatly relieved. McDonald viewed the affair with equanimity, observing that in Yale, the Company had found its ultimate dedicated servant.

McDonald and Yale became great friends. McDonald could be gruff and harsh on occasion, but Yale respected the fact that all of the chief factor's actions were cold-bloodedly calculated to serve the interests of their mutual employer–such as the time when the chief factor ordered all Indian women out of the fort compound when he perceived that his men displayed greater interest in pursuing matters of the heart than in procuring furs. Simpson described McDonald as "full of laugh and small talk," contrasting sharply with the sober McMillan, who was "all work and no jaw."

The two senior officers took a break from their weekly labours each Sunday and spent time canoeing on the river and rambling in the woods, here and there marking timber areas and future agricultural plots of promise. At a river flowing into the Fraser they later named "The Stave," McDonald and Yale discovered magnificent stands of white pine, which they soon engaged labourers to cut and haul for use as staves in making barrels for storing and shipping salmon and other food products.

McDonald burned with energy; he would need all of it and more. His orders from Simpson were to make Fort Langley completely self-sufficient; to develop the potential for marketing food for export; to increase fur production; and in the latter regard to aggressively compete with and set his own policy against the Yankee traders plying the coast, an endeavour made more important by the increasing possibility of a Russian withdrawal of claims to the northern regions. Fort Langley was viewed by Simpson as the fulcrum for implementation of this new Pacific policy of the Hudson's Bay Company.

The fort, looking east upriver.

McDonald was determined to break the siege mentality which gripped both the Stalo people and the fort personnel each spring and summer when the northern warriors appeared on the river. Hardly a week passed during these seasons without the alarm being sounded of an imminent Yuculta attack. Men, women and children would race to the fort gates on these occasions and would be admitted until the threat passed. McDonald believed that a showdown was necessary. He reluctantly gave guns and ammunition to Whattlekainum's Kwantlen warriors to better defend against the invaders.

In March 1829, McDonald dispatched his canoe express comprising Yale, Annance, and ten voyageurs to Puget Sound, carrying the annual reports of trade, correspondence, and extracts from the Fort Journal. From Puget Sound, an Indian runner would carry the documents to Fort Vancouver. The express had no sooner disappeared down the river when Whattlekainum reported to McDonald that a flotilla of thirty Yuculta canoes containing twenty-five men per craft was closely following the express. McDonald anticipated the worst and prepared for an attack on both the departed men and the fort. Women and children living at the fort were ordered to remain inside the palisade, and defences were bolstered.

Meanwhile, Little Yale and his men had delivered their package at Puget Sound unhindered. The next day, on their way home, they spotted ahead of them on the Fraser nine huge Yuculta war canoes, containing an estimated three hundred howling, painted warriors, their craft strung across the river to bar passage. The voyageurs paddled furiously. Yale and Annance shouted to each other and their canoe sped toward the Yuculta line, surprising the warriors, who had expected a retreat.

The Company canoe pierced the line, causing the Yucultas to turn their canoes hastily around, spraying the water with bullets and arrows. The gap between Yale's craft and the Yucultas narrowed as the Company men tired.

Better armed, but vastly outnumbered, the twelve Hudson's Bay men appeared to face certain annihilation. Then Yale abruptly angled the canoe toward shore. Near Annacis Island, the Bay men clambered clumsily ashore and plunged into the forest for cover; then they turned and began firing on the Yucultas as the Indians charged toward the shore in their canoes.

For some twenty minutes the battle raged as the whites kept up a rapid fire fusillade, killing and wounding dozens of warriors. Finally, the Yucultas turned their canoes round and headed back down the river. The muddy Fraser's waters flowed red with blood.

Stories of the first battle between whites and Indians flashed up and down the river. McDonald was exultant. "All the Indians hereabouts collected into the Fort today," he wrote, "and seem amazed at the victory gained over the invincible Yucultas; and that too by a handful of men—they wish very much to be in league with the whites and if possible to be under their wing in case of battle."

The immediate consequence of the skirmish was the heightened prestige of the Company men and the permanent movement of most of the remaining Kwantlen families still living in the Skaiametl area to the Fort Langley vicinity. The Yucultas, however, exacted revenge by murdering a popular Kwantlen Indian friend of the Hudson's Bay Company known along the river as "The Doctor." The unfortunate native was caught at the mouth of the river by the enraged Yuculta party which had attacked Yale. His dismembered body was brought to the Fort wharf accompanied by wailing relatives and friends. The river valley was not yet safe—certainly not for the Stalo—but the Yucultas never again seriously threatened fort personnel.

Salmon export became a pet project of McDonald. He wrote enthusiastically to Simpson in 1830 that he had succeeded in packing two hundred barrels of salmon the previous year; unfortunately, most of these barrels leaked. But by 1831, three hundred barrels were successfully shipped abroad, including one hundred to Hawaii. Thereafter, salmon export quantities increased steadily. Trade with Hawaii expanded to include Fraser River shingles and timber. One unforeseen effect of this trade was the settling of a number of Kanakas in the Fraser Valley over the years, most of whom worked for the Hudson's Bay Company and married Stalo women.

By 1832, the beaver returns at Fort Langley had nearly doubled to 2,500 skins, despite stiff American competition. The going rate was now twenty skins for a gun; two skins for a blanket. A cooper arrived to help with the barrel making, which facilitated another increase in salmon exports. Outside the palisade, the fort farm grew in size, though the land remained subject to floods and the ravages of caterpillars. Once a year, a sailing ship would bring goods and letters from Fort Vancouver. This was the only contact which the men of the fort maintained with the outside world.

Within the palisade, McDonald, his wife Jane, and their children installed an oasis of learning and laughter into the remote outpost. The family members studied Chinook, a form of pidgin English which permitted limited communication between whites and natives. Always a man of letters, McDonald sought no fame or glamour in his life, being content to diversify production in any manner which assisted his employer. "I have descended to oil and blubber too," he wrote, "so that whatever others may think of Fraser's River, I am well satisfied with its proceeds."

On Sundays, McDonald read prayers to the eighteen fort employees and their families. Births, marriages and deaths were duly recorded in the Fort Journal. Travel was restricted due to the Yuculta danger, and aside from the odd exploratory mission, the employees were confined to the immediate fort area. Relief from daily routine was provided by the constant Indian gossip, the flow of colourful war canoes along the river, and the occasional celebration.

On New Year's Eve day, the men were ushered into the Big House, where McDonald doled out half a pint of rum—enough to cheer the engagés, but insufficient to ruin their sobriety for the evening festivities. Alas, the New Year's Eve celebrations were often followed by several days of frolic, debauchery, and hangover; while all the while the Kwantlen locals continued with their own festival outside the palisade and the fort guns boomed each day to salute the holiday spirit.

McDonald made allowance for these good times, partly because he cannily chose the first days of the new year to sign renewal contracts with his men, frequently at reduced wages.

In 1833, the Fraser outpost was threatened from a new quarter. Simpson had concluded that despite McDonald's successes with fur and salmon, the post should be moved to a deep water location so that Hudson's Bay trading vessels could better compete with Yankee traders. Fort Langley's existing site was viewed as being both too far upriver and its wharf area too shallow to permit large vessels to dock or anchor.

However Dr. McLoughlin, at Fort Vancouver, opposed abandonment of the fort, arguing that its salmon fishery was showing valuable promise. Nevertheless, McLoughlin acceded to Simpson's demands and prepared to establish a new post on Puget Sound to be called "Nisqually." But he wrote to the governor:

> "In regard to Ft. Langley and Nisqually, there is no place on the coast where salmon is so abundant and got so cheap as at Ft. Langley; and if we find a sale for salmon, it would alone more than pay the expense of keeping up that place."

McDonald himself had explored Puget Sound in 1832 after a visit to Fort Vancouver, and was credited with locating the Nisqually site (near present-day Tacoma, Washington). He doubted the wisdom of the Puget Sound location replacing Fort Langley. Working in tandem with the rebellious Dr. McLoughlin, McDonald strove to increase both fishery and fur returns from his Fraser outpost and so succeeded in this endeavour that McLoughlin decided to ignore Simpson's letters urging him to close Fort Langley.

Dr. McLoughlin was so impressed with chief factor McDonald that he ordered him to report with his family back to Fort Vancouver the following spring for re-assignment. McDonald was reluctant to depart. "I regret leaving Langley—it is a snug, comfortable place." He did, however, yearn to enrol his children in a proper school.

On the day of his departure both whites and Indians lined the wharf to see him off. The fort guns boomed a salute as he embarked in his canoe. McDonald looked back smiling, content in the knowledge that he had succeeded in laying the groundwork for a diversified post of plenty. He went on to handle several assignments for the Hudson's Bay Company. It was on one of these that he discovered massive quantities of lead ore on Kootenay Lake, where the legendary Bluebell Mine would eventually function until 1972. He retired in the year of the mine's discovery, and died in Ottawa. His epitaph reads: "One of the pioneers of Civilization in Oregon."

James Murray Yale was left as the clerk in charge of a reduced complement of thirteen men. He was in a gloomy state. His wife had left him, his best friend was now gone, and the future of the fort was still much in doubt. Yet the indomitable little man was determined to make his mark yet. He carefully set about the steady expansion of salmon exports, initiated the raising of cattle, and began cultivation of new fields he had cleared on a large prairie seven miles south of the fort.

Although furs were still important, the years ahead were to witness a gradual decline in returns of pelts, as the post assumed an increasingly pivotal role as food supplier for other Company forts, as well as chief food exporter for the foreign trade.

Yale brooded. For years after McDonald's departure, he continued to retain the lowly title of chief clerk of Fort Langley, when it was customary for most forts

The SS *Beaver* plied the Fraser River and Pacific Coast, delivering supplies and trading with the natives.

to at least have a chief trader as their head. Meanwhile, his old rival James Douglas was lounging in luxury at Fort Vancouver as McLoughlin's right hand man, already a chief trader. Although much experienced in the wilderness and proven fearless in the face of danger, he knew that many of his men scorned him behind his back, calling him "Little Yale." Only his daughter Eliza gave him comfort, and he clung to her, reading her bedside stories and locking her in her room at night in the little house he had built for himself between the fort and the new Langley farm.

In 1836, the steamer *Beaver* arrived at Fort Vancouver. The ship had been launched in 1835 at London as a sturdy little vessel of 109 tons, equipped with a huge elm keel and, best of all, a new form of power.

The *Beaver* was Simpson's answer to Pacific trade problems. He had harangued his London superiors for some time about the need for a steam vessel on the northwest coast, stating that it would provide "incalculable advantages over the Americans, as we could look into every creek and cove while they were confined to a harbor."

In short, the very shallow draft and speed of a steamer might make such a difference to coastal commerce that Simpson believed that the Americans could be ousted entirely, and the Hudson's Bay Company made "masters of the trade."

The *Beaver* made an enormous impression upon the Indians. Word spread up and down the coast and along the Fraser that a strange craft belched smoke and churned the waters angrily with its huge paddles.

Over the years the *Beaver's* varied roles were to impact significantly upon the history of the future British Columbia. Not least of these roles was her peacekeeping function. The only drawback to the steamer's efficiency was the enormous amount of effort required to keep her running. It required six axemen cutting steadily for two days to supply enough wood for the vessel to steam along for one day.

At Fort Langley, Yale fought battles on several fronts during 1837. First, Dr. McLoughlin ordered him to move the fort inland from the Fraser along the Salmon River, an order he promptly refused to obey, stating that this move would interfere with the post's valuable salmon industry. McLoughlin demurred. Then, later that year, Yale faced criticism for the decline in fur returns. The strutting clerk blamed the *Beaver* for this, claiming that the vessel had traded guns and ammunition to Queen Charlotte Indians, who had in turn peddled them at low prices to the Stalo tribes along the Fraser, thus undercutting Fort Langley.

One early evening in 1837, the Fort Langley cannon boomed in anger for the first and last time. Over a thousand Yucultas streamed up the Fraser to attack Stalo villages. This time, however, instead of proceeding far up the river to prey upon the Chilliwack settlements, the fleet turned suddenly southward toward Whattlekainum's peaceful Kwantlen village near the fort.

The attack came just before dusk. The sentries yelled. Quickly, Yale ordered the cannon loaded, the swivel guns on the walls armed, and muskets readied. Kwantlen villagers fled for safety into the forest.

When the war canoes came into range, Yale signalled his gunners to fire. The surprised invaders had little time to react. Canoes were blown apart; warriors spilled into the water and swam frantically out into the river channel, where many drowned. The Kwantlen who had fled now emerged from the woods and with knives and clubs massacred dozens of Yucultas. The remnants of the huge war party escaped downriver.

The *Beaver* required enormous amounts of cordwood for fuel.

Yale surveyed the bodies lying on the river bank through a pall of smoke. He personally deplored violence, but knew this showdown had been inevitable. Although for several years raiding parties would harass tiny Upper Stalo villages and single family units caught unawares, never again would the Yucultas be an important factor in the life of the Fraser Valley.

Yale was developing other strengths in the face of adversity. Across the river from the fort he had discovered an Indian maiden whom he wished to marry. She and her father readily consented to his proposal, but the independently minded young woman advised Yale that, unlike other Indian wives of Fort Langley men, she wished to continue living with her tribe in the village. Yale was taken aback, but consented. The ceremony was performed in the village itself, with hundreds of Stalo from the length of the Fraser attending the all-night revelry. Yale's slight figure became an accepted part of village life as he came and went each week for evening assignations in his wife's little cedar house.

By 1838, both Simpson and Douglas were acknowledging Yale's stellar performance at Fort Langley. The governor wrote flatteringly to Yale that his services were well known and appreciated in London, but exhorted him to develop a butter industry; while Douglas advised that he and Dr. McLoughlin were gratified with both the explosive expansion of the salmon industry and the new farm production, stating that Fort Langley was being relied upon now to supply all of the future salt provisions for the entire northwest coast.

Fort Langley's reprieve as a post was strongly influenced by the increasing success the Hudson's Bay Company was having along the coast north of the Columbia river. In 1839, the Company concluded an agreement with the Russian American Company which gave it its long-desired monopoly on coastal trade. The key element in the treaty which affected Fort Langley was the requirement that the Company provision Russian colonies with foodstuffs, including salmon, pork, beef, and butter.

Yale had now decided on a new site for his fort, about two miles up the Fraser on a high river bank. The new location was free from flooding, easier to defend, and closer to the expanding Hudson's Bay farm pastures. Soon Yale had the carpenters busy erecting the new larger stockade and internal residences, cooperage, blacksmith's shop, food sheds, and officer's quarters. Some timbers were moved from the old fort, while pickets were cut upstream and floated down the river.

By October of 1839, the seventeen Hudson's Bay employees and their families were ensconced within the new premises—and Indians were already tearing apart and hauling away the remnants of the old fort. The first fort site became known as Derby. The second location is the site of Fort Langley National Historic Park.

So ended the first phase of white habitation in the Fraser Valley. Stolid McMillan had laid the foundation; McDonald had broadened the scope. Now it was all Yale's show—and he fully intended to run it well.

CHAPTER FIVE

THE WORLD OF JAMES MURRAY YALE

"We are traders, and apart from more exalted motives, all traders are desirous of gain. Is it not self-evident we will manage our business with more economy being on good terms with the Indians than if at variance."

Dr. John McLoughlin, 1843

Ethnologist Wilson Duff estimated that the 1839 Stalo population of the Fraser Valley was 2,074 persons—down somewhat from the 3,500 thought to be present at the time of Simon Fraser's first contact in 1808. This decline was attributable to two principal factors—the white man's diseases and the depredations of the Yucultas. The fur trade activities of the Hudson's Bay Company had little impact on the traditional Stalo culture and economy. The Indians and Company men became involved in a mutually beneficial commercial relationship, in which the whites were actually the more dependent party.

Greater respect and influence were gained by the Fort Langley traders when their superior weaponry eliminated the Yuculta peril; but, with the exception of the Langley tribe of Whattlekainum, the traders were neither able nor inclined to obtain subservience, much less servility, from the Stalo. As Duff notes, the fur trade brought to the Indians "prosperity, and an increase in wealth in a society already organized around wealth." This is not to say that increased wealth did not alter the Stalo lifestyle; but until 1858 this was a self-directed trend.

James Douglas, who under Dr. McLoughlin at Fort Vancouver had become increasingly powerful in managing the Columbia and New Caledonia regions, owed his rising star in part to the fact that Governor Simpson had lost confidence in the independent and liberal minded McLoughlin. He held mixed opinions about the Stalo, and in particular the Langley tribe. In a letter to Simpson in 1839, Douglas scorned the fort natives as lazy in their hunting habits, but he credited Yale with "dunning them into something like exertion." (Beaver returns were up from 398 pelts the previous year to 1,025 in 1839.) He went on to report, however, that these same natives were beginning to farm the land in most civilized fashion, having with great perseverance cleared forests and planted many acres of potatoes.

Yale was viewed by his employer as a loyal, plodding workhorse, and he was constantly pressed by both McLoughlin and Douglas to accomplish greater things. He was aided in his endeavours by the arrival in 1840 of Ovid Allard, a genial, hardworking hulk of a man who was very experienced in the Indian trade, a capable interpreter, and an invaluable handyman. Also arriving at this time was a rosy cheeked Scottish woman, Mrs. Finlayson, who was to become the fort's first butter-maker.

Ovid Allard.

When Dr. McLoughlin paid a visit to the Fraser post aboard the *Beaver* in December 1839, he brought with him twenty-nine wild California dairy cows and delivered them to Yale with the explanation that he wanted Fort Langley to produce large quantities of butter. Yale sniffed, but quickly built a creamery. He confided later to Simpson that he would try his hand at making butter, but that he'd had a mind to ask the good doctor how much butter Fort Vancouver had made and salted during the cold winter of 1827, when McLoughlin "made us eat our cakes without butter" at Fort Langley.

On the night of April 11, 1840, fire erupted in the Fort Langley blacksmith shop. As the dazed men and their families emerged from their beds, they beheld flames to the sky engulfing several of the buildings. Yale yelled for his men to haul the black powder barrels to safety. Others fought smoke and flame to save trade goods in the store.

Mrs. Finlayson was as overwrought as Yale. She ran around screaming for someone to save the cream she had set out during the day, frantically pounding on one man's back until he turned and rescued her big pans from the creamery. Meanwhile, she had in her excitement forgotten that her baby was still asleep inside her residence, which was now aflame. Allard, however, rushed into the building, emerging with his eyebrows singed and a crying infant in his arms.

Yale surveyed the charred ruins the next morning. Smoke, ashes, and blackened boards were all that remained of the fort buildings. The staff had saved most of the trading goods, the powder, and a few barrels of salmon. But all of the furniture, most foodstuffs, barrel staves, tools, and almost one thousand pounds of furs had been lost.

Fortunately, a large quantity of pickets intended for use on the farms were stored intact outside of the palisade and Yale proceeded to have work proceed immediately on a new stockade. The little clerk strutted about inspecting every aspect of the rebuilding activity, while Allard showed his mettle by ably directing the technical requirements, managing the men, and still finding time to trade with the Indians down at the wharf.

At Puget Sound, James Douglas was aboard the *Beaver*, on his way to the Stikine River to take over a Russian trading post, when he learned of the fire at Fort Langley. He panicked, fearful that he must defer occupation of the northern post now that the Fraser station would be likely unable to supply provisions to the Russian fort. He ordered the captain of the *Beaver* to alter course immediately, and headed up the Fraser River to inspect the damage.

Little Yale, meanwhile, had worked wonders. Douglas stepped ashore on May 1 and was escorted by Yale around the new fort, the stockade of which was larger than the old and fully completed. The buildings were also taking shape. Peppery Yale told Douglas bluntly, "All I want from you is six good axes and be out of here!" Douglas, however, assigned twenty men from the *Beaver* to finish a bastion and to cut and square logs for other buildings. After a few days, satisfied that the post was on its way to full recovery, Douglas steamed away for the Stikine.

Ten months after the conflagration, Yale reported to Simpson that matters were proceeding at the fort as if there had never been a fire, "with a fort far more spacious than the old one, and things inside nearly as far advanced" as the old Fort Langley which Simpson had visited in 1828. Yale, however, became paranoid—perhaps with some justification—that a conspiracy existed to downgrade or even eliminate his Fraser post.

When Douglas returned on the *Beaver* in September, he bore orders from Dr. McLoughlin to remove "as many young cattle from Fort Langley as the steamer would take." McLoughlin believed that Yale had his hands too full with rebuilding to give attention to expanding dairy production.

But Yale became apoplectic when Douglas informed him of his orders. He heatedly advised Douglas that he could provide food for three times as many cows as were on hand. Douglas empathized, but knew from the hierarchy of things—including McLoughlin's temper—that the little chief clerk of the Fraser was not to be consulted. He placated Yale by boarding only eleven cows on the *Beaver*, even though the vessel was quite capable of carrying twice that number.

It was more than possible that Yale's outburst was occasioned by the fact that Douglas had been appointed by Simpson as a chief factor in 1840. Yale could not help but be bitter that his former colleague—and husband of Amelia—was

The cooperage at the restored fort, scene of bustling activity during the early decades of trade.

advancing fast in the Company, while Yale was not even a chief trader. He was not promoted to that rank until 1844.

The new fort was indeed spacious and commanded a fine view up and down the Fraser. The workers and officers lived very well, their diet consisting of rations of salt pork and beef supplemented by venison, geese, turkeys, ducks, salmon, and sturgeon—all cooked in numerous different ways over an open fire. There was even a pigeon house installed on each side of the fort bastions, pigeon pie being a favourite dish. The family quarters were comfortable, but quite small, measuring fifteen-by-twenty feet with a fireplace, and partitioned off from other quarters in similar fashion to the Stalo longhouses.

Life at Fort Langley hummed with bustling activity all year long. Allard spent much of his time at the wharf beside trunkfuls of trade goods, which included blankets, tools, tobacco, and vermilion used by Indian women as make-up. During the peak salmon run season the pace was frenetic:

> "Cromarty would be at the big cauldron making brine, and ever so many boys and a man or two would be running from the wharf with salmon, which they piled before the women of the fort and others who were seated in a circle in the shed where they cut the salmon. No rest for the boys! They had to continue their running; this time with the cut salmon to the men in the big shed where they were doing the salting. So they worked all the week; early in the morning until late at night, until the salmon run was

over."

By 1848, the fort's salmon production surpassed furs and Yale's post became the largest fish exporter on the Pacific coast. Agriculture remained important, but by 1845 rainy weather and frost had so ravaged crops that Dr. McLoughlin and Douglas decided to downscale the farming operation and concentrate on the fishery.

Life was improving for Yale. In 1839 and 1840 his wife had given birth to two girls, Aurelia and Isabella, both of whom resided with him in the Big House of the fort with their half sister Eliza.

The Big House was reserved for Yale and overnight guests.

Yale still visited his wife across the river, but concentrated his affections upon his three daughters. As they grew, he fussed and doted over them, still locking them in their rooms at night, and seldom letting them out of his sight. He especially had to watch Aurelia, who loved to run down to the river bank and mingle with Allard and the natives. Yet he proudly canoed them up and down the Fraser and paraded them into Stalo villages, where the Fort Langley master's daughters were well known and welcome. Yale personally tutored Eliza, who in turn taught her half-sisters from the books which Yale stored in his library.

Inside the Big House, Yale's office was situated just to the side of the front door, from where the chief trader could view through his window all of the fort's activities and the river beyond. There he lived his days and kept his account books; there he wrote his letters and received guests. It was from there, also, that Yale dispensed wages for the employees, although common labourers and Indians were seldom admitted to the Big House.

Indians were hired by the Hudson's Bay Company to perform many assorted tasks, including planting, harvesting, and acting as messengers. They were paid in consumer goods at the Indian trade shop, where there was a constant milling around, and nervous young clerks kept consulting their directional manuals to determine the value in trade goods of a particular fur or load of fish.

All calculations of value were made to a "made beaver" scale; for example, one beaver pelt was worth two made beavers, and ten raccoon skins were worth one made beaver. Trappers were given wooden tokens for each made beaver and these in turn were used for the purchase of goods in the store. Company voyageurs travelling with the annual brigade had to be very careful in choosing their goods from the store for the return journey, since a Company rule limited purchases to items filling no more than a ninety-pound (forty kilogram) bale, so the packhorses would not be unduly strained.

At the end of each day, Allard would call out for the Indians to leave the fort and he would lock the gates with his keys, returning them to Yale before retiring for the night.

All work in the fort began at 6:00 A.M. and ended at precisely 6:00 P.M. Wages varied from £30 to £50 per year. The half-day off on Saturday which Yale gave to his staff was to be used to tidy and scrub one's living quarters. At noon on Saturday, the employees were given four ounces of rum and allowed to purchase a pint per man for the usual Saturday night party. Teetotallers often bootlegged their rations on Sunday to drinkers who had run dry, obtaining fancy shirts, silk handkerchiefs, and tobacco in exchange for the precious liquid.

On Christmas Eve, the men of the fort were permitted to buy presents for their families at the sales shop. Christmas morning dawned and all of the employees filed as a body into the mess hall of the Big House; here Yale greeted them and hosted a smoker where rum and other spirits passed freely. The men then chose from a selection of turkeys, ducks, geese, and venison for their family dinner.

In the afternoon, the ladies were invited to the Big House, and Yale went about the room filling their baskets with cookies, jam, and biscuits; the decanter was passed around, and dancing ensued until the wee hours. Nor were the local natives ignored. Chiefs from nearby villages were always invited to a New Year's fete at which Yale distributed blankets, tools, and foodstuffs.

The dances held in the Big House were rollicking affairs. The violin was the favourite instrument and the rafters shook to all manner of dance steps, including the Scottish jig, reels, waltzes, and the "dance ronde." The latter commenced with Yale or his assistant clerk dancing around the costumed women who sat along one wall, with the host suddenly throwing a coloured handkerchief over the neck of his favourite lady, whereupon that lady would in turn designate her favourite male by the same gesture, until everyone in the room had been selected.

The couples then danced about the room in a circle with one participant singing a typically old French-Canadian melody, while the first lady chosen entered the circle and, at the appropriate words from the song being spoken, kissed a gentleman of her choice, which gesture signalled the turn of the next chosen lady to perform. It is not surprising that on several occasions much jealousy was aroused among the sexes by this popular dance event.

Many local Indian women participated in social events of the fort, since most employees were married to Stalo wives. These ladies donned European clothes on such occasions, but adorned themselves with traditional native ornaments and make-up. White visitors from beyond the Pacific Northwest were impressed by their appearance and demeanour. Charles Wilkes observed:

> "Many of them have a dignified look and carriage; their black eyes and hair, and brown ruddy complexion, combined with a pleasing expression, give them an air of independence and usefulness that one little expects to see. As wives, they are spoken of as most devoted, and many of them have performed deeds in the hour of danger and difficulty worthy of being recorded."

Despite the entry of Stalo women into white society, friction was ever present among the wives of the different ranks of staff personnel at the fort. In addition to the rivalry between the wives of tradesmen or labourers and the spouses of gentlemen, there prevailed a fierce jealousy between Stalo and Kanaka women. Kanakas were regarded as being at the bottom of the class hierarchy within the Hudson Bay Company's labour structure.

At one Christmas ball, Kanaka and Stalo women began taunting one another and then a full-fledged battle ensued—with much punching and hair pulling—until the spouses of the ladies intervened in the mélée and sustained more than a few blows and scratches before restoring peace.

The first missionary to visit the Fraser Valley was the Roman Catholic priest Father Demers, who journeyed to Fort Langley in September 1841. Ascending the Salmon River via the old Nicomekl portage, Demers arrived exhausted at the Hudson's Bay farm, where he was met by a horseman sent by Yale. As he neared the fort, the missionary was given a cannon salute. "The welcome that Mr. Yale extended me was such as would be expected by a man of merit and distinction," wrote Father Demers. "Five or six hundred savages instantly surrounded me and I had difficulty getting out of their midst to enter the Fort."

Father Demers, first missionary in the Fraser Valley.

Father Demers was a gifted linguist, who had travelled from Red River in 1839 to the Columbia region with the Oblate Father Blanchet. Blanchet invented the famous Catholic Ladder, which was a kind of long scroll—resembling a modern-day wall history chart—that portrayed key events in the Christian religion. For more than a century, the Ladder would be used with great effect throughout the Pacific Northwest.

At Fort Langley, Father Demers studied the situation keenly: "A score of men are employed as labourers, eight of whom are Canadians, one Iroquois, and the others Kanakas...all have wives and children in the manner of the country. I baptized 15 children, including those of Mr. Yale, and gave instructions to others, who did not even know the Lord's Prayer."

For one week, Father Demers preached and proselytized on the prairie outside the fort to over 1,500 Indians—including Yucultas and Cowichans from Vancouver Island. They sang hymns, watched as the Catholic Ladder was explained, and learned to make the sign of the Cross. Over seven hundred children and a few adults were baptized, including Whattlekainum. The rite of confession was introduced, and it is perhaps significant that many natives who arrived with weapons laid them at the feet of the priest, and abandoned them altogether when they left for home.

Father Demers was ecstatic with his reception. His arms ached at week's end with the joy of so many baptisms. "All these natives had forgotten their hatreds and their projects of vengeance to come to listen to the Holy Word...they repeated what they had understood and retained of the explanations of the historic Ladder. In short, there was universal zeal, ardor, enthusiasm."

The missionary reluctantly prepared to return to the Columbia region; before he departed, he distributed religious trinkets and much tobacco. A huge smoker was held and the priest finally left in high spirits to the well wishes of hundreds of aroused natives.

Even the sober Yale was wide-eyed at the priest's impact and success, particularly when the dreaded Yucultas arrived to mingle in harmony with the Stalo.

Although it would be nearly twenty years before permanent missions arrived in the Fraser Valley, key aspects of Catholicism, such as confession, prayer, and hymns were to permeate native culture from this experience, reinforced by word of mouth spiritual messages from Columbia River tribes, so that gradually the Stalo and Christian supernatural beliefs began to coexist in the scattered villages along the Fraser.

Events in the Columbia region now moved toward a climax. American naval vessels began anchoring on the Columbia River in 1841, in which year the recently knighted Sir George Simpson dined in a tense atmosphere with Dr. McLoughlin and his Yankee guest, Commodore Wilkes. Simpson suspected Wilkes was surveying the area in preparation for a claim by the United States to the entire coast up to latitude 45 degrees N. Sensing that Britain might not win the entire Columbia Territory, Sir George ordered McLoughlin to establish a major depot on the southern tip of Vancouver Island, choosing a location recommended by James Douglas, known to the natives as Camosun.

The relationship between Simpson and McLoughlin now deteriorated into a vicious feud. Simpson had ordered most of the northern coast forts to be closed, as well as the abandonment of the San Francisco post commanded by McLoughlin's son-in-law; both of which moves were vehemently opposed by the doctor.

The situation turned ugly when McLoughlin's own son, John, was killed in a brawl at Fort Stikine, whence Simpson journeyed a few days after the mishap. Cooly taking sworn statements from four witnesses, Simpson cursorily determined that the younger McLoughlin had been armed and drunk, and ruled that his slaying was justifiable self-defence. The father was mortified; the Hudson's Bay Company's London Committee later decided that young John McLoughlin had been murdered, and reversed Simpson's findings.

Douglas meanwhile proceeded to erect a fort at Camosun, which was named Victoria, quietly ignoring McLoughlin's directive to "build it small." Douglas deemed a large fort necessary in order to meet Simpson's objective of transferring the main depot on the coast from Fort Vancouver to a new deep-water port, which he hoped to command. Usually rather phlegmatic, Douglas waxed euphoric over his chosen site:

> "The place itself appears a perfect Eden, in the midst of the dreary wilderness of the North west coast, and so different is its general aspect from the wooded, rugged regions around, that one might be pardoned for supposing it had dropped from the clouds into its present position...."

American settlers poured into the Columbia region. In 1844, President Polk was elected on a platform which included an emotional plea for United States occupation of the whole of the Oregon Territory—which position a panicking Great Britain feared meant a grab for the entire Pacific region stretching to Alaska. "Fifty-four forty or fight!" became the Yankee war cry often heard, and the British responded by sending several frigates to the west coast.

Lord Aberdeen, the British foreign minister, was not prepared to commit his country to war, however, and concentrated upon ensuring that the new international boundary was fixed at the forty-ninth parallel. Vancouver Island was saved, in order to ensure that both a deep-water port and a defensible depot for the mainland's interior posts would be achieved. The government and the Hudson's Bay Company regarded Fort Langley as destined to serve the dual role of a brigade terminus and supply centre.

In 1845, Dr. McLoughlin was rudely shuffled aside by the Company he had served so long. Control of the Columbia department was given in that year to a triumvirate of James Douglas, John Work, and Peter Ogden.

To Douglas fell the task of building Fort Victoria into the main Hudson's Bay Company depot; Fort Vancouver was thenceforth downgraded and ultimately would be closed. In 1846, the Treaty of Washington was signed and Britain's chief aims achieved, with the fixing of the boundary at the forty-ninth parallel and the recognition of Vancouver Island as British territory. Despite the loss of the Columbia Territory by Britain, the Hudson's Bay Company continued for a few years to operate Fort Vancouver and other posts in the area.

Just before the Columbia region became American territory, Dr. McLoughlin resigned from the Hudson's Bay Company, an embittered man. He had worked all of his life in the service of a company which now blamed his generosity to American settlers and missionaries as the key reason for the loss of the southern region. He became an American citizen, was shunned and disregarded by the new Yankee authorities—who even deprived him of title to his land—and he died in 1857, heartbroken. Posthumously, he was honoured in future American history texts as the "Father of Oregon."

Back at Fort Langley, Yale pushed himself to ever greater heights. He realized that the status as chief trader, accorded him in 1844, represented both a grudging recognition of his accomplishments and an indication of his bailiwick's future importance. He might never achieve the status of chief factor like Douglas, nor have his post become the chief depot, but he resolved to make his fort the best in the region.

Yale's staff salted six hundred barrels of salmon in August of 1844 alone for shipment to Oahu, and when Douglas arrived in 1845, eight hundred additional barrels were ready to be shipped and Yale gloated over the fact that neither the *Beaver* nor the vessel accompanying it carried large enough holds to accommodate all of the fish and hence were obliged to make a return trip. Yale even manufactured a gelatin compound called isinglass from the float bladders of sturgeon, and made caviar from a Russian recipe.

The Hudson's Bay Company scrambled in 1846 to find new brigade routes via the Fraser Valley to service its interior posts, so as to avoid the Columbia River passage, which now entailed stiff American tariffs.

In May 1846, Alex Anderson left Kamloops with five men and traversed the Fraser from Pavilion to Lillooet. From there, he travelled along Seton and Anderson Lakes to the Lillooet River, down Harrison Lake, and thence to the Fraser, arriving at Fort Langley on Queen Victoria's birthday to a cannonading salute. Anderson reported to Yale that the route was better than the tortuous canyon, but not suitable for fur brigades.

The explorer made a return trip via the Coquihalla River pass; the following year he made another reconnaissance, this time portaging around the most difficult part of the Fraser Canyon via Nicola Lake.

Yale was unimpressed with the routes discovered by Anderson. Both Douglas and John Work, however, were becoming frantic in their search for a new brigade trail. In September 1847 the two men arrived at Fort Langley to pick up Yale and travel up the Fraser to make a final assessment. The three veteran Hudson's Bay servants tramped all around the canyon area above the natives' evil rock.

Like Simpson before him, Douglas was surprised and aghast at the formidable barrier imposed by the canyon, particularly one thirteen-mile stretch of foaming rapids. "Before he reached the head of the falls," Yale wrote to Simpson of Douglas, "he was convinced that Fraser's River was not quite that placid stream he had before seemed to imagine."

Douglas, nonetheless, ordered Yale to commence construction of a portage at Spuzzum and a road up the Fraser Canyon. A small post with a store was established in November 1847 by Ovid Allard near the evil rock, to be known as Fort Yale. Work on the canyon road was hastened by news of the Cayuse Indian War in Oregon, which had been precipitated by the November 29 murder of missionary Dr. Whitman, his wife, and twelve other whites. This event the Company men feared might seriously jeopardize their employers' further activities in the

Yale, 1865, with sternwheeler in foreground.

Columbia River region. Douglas abruptly advised Yale that the new Fraser route must be ready in time for the June 1848 brigade.

Yale scurried about on his new assignment, delegating his other duties to assistant clerks. A boatbuilder arrived at Fort Langley to construct four large bateaux for use on the river. Huge stocks of supplies and dozens of men were steamboated to the fort, from where they were dispatched to Fort Yale for roadbuilding.

In June, Alex Anderson and Don Morrison led the fifty men of the fur brigade down from Kamloops, along with four hundred packhorses that had to be ridden, pushed and pulled along narrow ledges and rough trails, and then transported across the Fraser at Spuzzum by a make-shift ferry.

After depositing their furs at Fort Langley and sipping claret with Yale, the men returned to the Interior via the same route, only to lose seventy horses in mishaps, and one rider to suicide. In addition, large quantities of goods were stolen by Indians who swarmed throughout the canyon for the fishing season. Some eighty natives, however, came to the aid of the brigade by shouldering much of the freight, thereby easing the burden on the horses.

The Fraser Canyon brigade route was abandoned in 1849, when Fort Langley labourers, assisted by Indians, constructed a trail from the Fraser River via the Coquihalla mountain pass to the Interior.

Once again, Ovid Allard was appointed by Yale as the field manager in charge of operations; this time Allard was ordered to construct a post to be called "Fort Hope"—aptly named in view of the desperation of the Hudson's Bay Company to find a practical inland brigade trail.

In June 1849, the brigade travelled down the canyon route for the last time and returned via the Coquihalla, stopping over at Fort Hope base camp to assist Yale's weary men complete trail construction. For 10 years thereafter the famous Fraser fur brigades were to use this route, dropping their furs off at Fort Hope and then returning to Kamloops with supplies.

James Douglas was unstinting in his praise for Yale and the Fort Langley trail-blazers. "The preparations for opening the new road to the interior for the passage of the summer Brigade," he wrote, "threw much additional work upon Fort Langley...which required no common degree of energy and good management in chief trader Yale to accomplish with 20 men in the course of a severe winter."

At last the Hudson's Bay Company had established an all-British route free from the American threat. To culminate matters, Douglas learned that Queen Victoria had signed a proclamation in January 1849 which granted all of Vancouver Island to the Hudson's Bay Company for seven shillings per year, subject to the Company taking active steps to colonize the territory. The grant would be revoked in 1859, when the Hudson's Bay Company Charter regarding trade west of the Rockies came up for renewal.

Yale and his staff shivered through the coldest winter on record in 1847-48. Old Chief Whattlekainum died quietly and, in the traditional Stalo manner, his body was enclosed in a cedar coffin and placed among the boughs of a tree. Few whites were aware of the enormous contribution the Kwantlen chief had made to the success of the fur traders—first saving Simon Fraser from massacre; then safeguarding the first fort of James McMillan and facilitating its trading activities.

Indeed, the chief's policies helped to lay the groundwork for acceptance by the Stalo of later white settlement in the valley.

The interdependence of traders and natives at Fort Langley was demonstrated during that harsh winter, when Kwantlen villagers saved many of the Hudson's Bay Company cattle by sheltering them in their own houses from the cold. Of other Indian leaders who had offered their assistance to the traders, Chief Shashia of Puget Sound was still alive, having acted as interpreter, mediator, and friend to James McMillan, Archibald McDonald, and James Murray Yale successively. Without such aid, Hudson's Bay Company tenure would have undoubtedly been bloody and much less lucrative.

Upon the abandonment of the Fraser Canyon brigade route, Allard was ordered to close Fort Yale. One day, just before leaving the site, Allard was surprised by a band of canyon Indians who attacked the store and tied him up inside.

A Kanaka servant escaped and ran outside the fort to the Allard home, where Mrs. Allard—a sister of Chief Shashia—was working in her garden. The Kanaka yelled at her to flee into the woods; instead, the steadfast woman picked up her hoe and charged into the fort store, where she beheld several natives looting the place, while her husband Ovid sat bound to a chair.

Mrs. Allard raised the hoe over the head of the leader of the raiding party, who was bending intently over a barrel of goods. In a shrill voice, she advised him that, unless Ovid was freed and the goods restored, she would not only hack off his head, but the Hudson's Bay Company would send troops back to destroy his village. The invaders promptly fled.

Shortly after the Fort Yale incident, Mrs. Allard gave birth to a son named Jason at Fort Langley; she was rejoined there by Ovid in 1849 after fully completing construction of Fort Hope. Like most employees who took native wives, Allard was forced by Yale to legalize the liaison by participating in a Christian marriage ceremony; James Douglas somewhat disdainfully agreed to the ritual being performed by the newly arrived chaplain of Fort Vancouver, the Reverend Herbert Beaver, after Mrs. Beaver refused to speak to his wife Amelia until the ceremony was performed.

One of Yale's eccentricities was his refusal to perform the marriage ceremony himself, despite the fact that he held legal commission to do so. Employees were forced to travel by canoe to Fort Victoria for the solemnization rites unless favoured by a passing missionary. Yale, like his predecessor McDonald, was very keen on his men marrying well into key Stalo families of high rank. He himself appears to have abandoned his village wife by 1850.

In 1852, Allard was beset by the great cranberry controversy. Captain James Cooper arrived up the Fraser that year and began trading for potatoes and cranberries with the Katzie Indians. The market for cranberries was excellent in San Francisco, and the cranberries plentiful in the river's marshy lowlands. Cooper initially made a good profit, but then ran headlong into the will of James Douglas.

Hearing of an interloper in his realm, Douglas ordered Yale to purchase all of the cranberries that the Katzies had collected and to sell Fort Langley barrels to Cooper at three dollars each, though they cost only thirty cents apiece to manufacture. Cooper quickly retreated from the region; Douglas gave Yale a tongue–lashing for allowing Cooper to trade; and Yale passed on his old rival's wrath to Allard, who was still his chief Indian trader.

There was more trouble to come for Allard, and it all had to do with dogs, specifically, James Murray Yale's dogs. Yale loved his dogs, and would fastidiously feed them himself. His favourite canine was a rather large specimen kept on a leash outside of the Big House residence. One early morning, Allard came as usual to the Big House to pick up the keys to the fort in order to open the buildings. The dog on duty growled and strained at its leash as the big trader approached. Without hesitating, Allard raised his musket and shot the dog dead.

Sir James Douglas, father of British Columbia.

Yale stood speechless at the door. For days he paced the Big House floors in an agitated state. Finally, he called Allard inside and advised him that he was to be transferred. "You are a good, capable man," Yale told him, "but I cannot work with one who would commit such acts against my dogs."

Allard piled his family and goods into a canoe and paddled all the way to Fort Victoria, where he went to see Douglas personally in order to tender his resignation from the Hudson's Bay Company. But Douglas valued Allard's abilities and persuaded him to stay on in a new capacity at Nanaimo, where he was quickly placed in charge of all Indian labourers at the coal mines. He was sorely missed at Fort Langley, and for months the children of the fort would ask their parents when the beloved trader was going to return.

In 1849, the Hudson's Bay Company had formally moved its headquarters from Fort Vancouver to Fort Victoria, as operations on the Columbia were gradually being wound down. By virtue of character, perseverance, and fate, James Douglas became the undisputed emperor of the entire region west of the Rockies remaining in British hands.

Although Vancouver Island became a colony in 1849, the power exercised by Douglas, as lord of the company holding a monopoly on trade, was immense. London did appoint a civilian governor of the fledgling colony in the form of Richard Blanshard, but he proved so impotent in the face of Douglas' iron will that he scurried back to England after just one year – only to be replaced by Douglas himself.

Governor Douglas now bore the distinction of being the ruler of the only colony west of Upper Canada, while he was, at the same time, chief factor of the Hudson's Bay Company's mainland territory. After a few rumblings of discontent from frustrated gentlemen settlers on Vancouver Island, the British government did appoint a Council to "advise" Douglas, and the rudiments of parliamentary democracy were established in 1856 with the election of a Legislative Assembly based on a very limited property franchise. But Douglas overwhelmed his critics on all but a few occasions.

Douglas's accumulation of all this power disturbed Yale greatly. Aside from his personal resentment of his superior, it was clear that Douglas treated him as his chief "gopher," to perform all manner of tasks on the mainland. If roads were to be built, new industries developed, coal to be discovered, Yale was the man to do it. When Douglas heard an Indian report describing a great plain near Burrard Inlet, stretching to the Fraser, he asked Yale to send out a party; Yale duly reported back to Douglas as to the flora and fauna of the future site of Vancouver. When Fort Vancouver ceased to supply the Interior posts with flour and grain, it was Fort Langley which was ordered to remedy the deficiency.

Poor Yale poured out his heart to his old benefactor George Simpson, whom he much regretted no longer travelled to the west coast on those famous transcontinental treks of old. He advised the governor that he was aging and tired, and wished some assurance that he would be granted some free land for his retirement years. Simpson replied by advising Yale that he would have to deal with Douglas in the matter of a land grant for retirement.

Yale criticized Douglas for constantly depleting his staff at the fort for assorted assignments. The years of pressure and responsibility were wearing down the graying chief trader. But when he was offered a choice of a new post or a leave of absence by Simpson, he demurred, stating proudly that he would stay on for a time and keep Fort Langley prosperous.

Yale took his daughters to Fort Victoria in 1850 to board there with the Reverend and Mrs. Staines in pursuit of a proper education. However, he held a disdainful view of the Vancouver Island capital. His employees were regularly travelling to Fort Victoria for wild weekends of debauchery with prostitutes and rough-edged prospectors. When Yale complained to Douglas of these bad influences on his men, his superior tersely advised him to keep a tighter rein on his employees. So Yale returned to Fort Langley, lonely without his girls to dote on, increasingly reclusive in his Big House.

Yale's letters to Simpson frequently sounded a tirade of paranoiac anger against Douglas and Fort Victoria:

> "The greatest evils here seem to spring out of Vancouver's Island. It would be ungenerous and cause no salutary consequences to cast reflections derogatory to the business of Fort Langley. It has resisted many tendencies to obstruct its course, and tho' much depreciated, old Langley stands still stable, the main prop of the Company's commerce on the North West coast of America and cannot... be reproached for anything, except perhaps that of affording maintenance to a rising Sodom on Vancouver's Island...."

Yale claimed that the Indians received better prices for their furs at Fort Victoria than at Fort Langley; he believed that this was part of Douglas' plan to show up his post, and that after depositing their furs in the island capital, native "wives and daughters are disposing of their rather more smutty commodities to still greater advantage and after seeing the world and tasting its sweets...they come home loaded with goods."

The 1850s were full of colour and excitement along the muddy Fraser. In July of each year the day dawned when every employee at Fort Langley would drop tools upon hearing the distant crackle of muskets sound up river. Bateaux piled high with baled furs would first stop near Whonnock, where the voyageurs donned ceremonial regalia and then paddled madly down the river to the fort, singing boat songs and firing their small arms.

The brigade was given a booming welcome by the fort cannon as the bateaux approached the wharf. Employees, Indians, and guests alike all streamed down to greet the boats. The cargo was unloaded, and the men of the brigade marched up past the salmon sheds to the main gate and on to the Big House, where chief trader Yale stood with folded arms, legs astride, ready to greet the bearers of fur.

The welcome was followed with the traditional drink, with Yale carefully measuring from a decanter exactly half a gill (two fluid ounces) of rum for each man. The formalities over, the fort succumbed to several days and nights of wild drinking, feasting, dancing, and fighting. Yale detested the debauchery, but was canny enough to realize that the men needed an outlet after months of toil in the wilds.

The voyageurs usually stayed at the fort for a month, during which period they selected goods at the sales shop. The general equipping of the brigade with trade goods for the new fiscal year was attended to by the busy clerks. James Douglas often travelled to Fort Langley just before the brigade's departure for the Interior, to receive reports, renew contracts, and formulate mainland trading strategy.

Douglas was renowned for his persuasiveness in keeping men employed who wished to move on, or retire. If an employee was tiring of the brigade life or found the climate of an interior post too inhospitable, Douglas would suggest that the man stay on at Fort Langley. "Stop with Mr. Yale here—he is always good to his men," he counselled. The Hudson's Bay Company under Douglas invariably kept its man.

Despite the excitement of the annual brigade arrival, Yale and his staff resented the flaunting airs of many voyageurs who invariably lolled about for most of the month long layover; many such men chased after native women, wore gay costumes bedecked with feathers, and treated the fort staff generally with derision. Yale complained to Simpson about a "motley set of renegades" who possessed no scruples.

The fort employees, for their part were kept hopping, as they rushed about provisioning the "outfit" for the coming year, selling personal goods to the brigade men, and packing the newly received furs for shipment to Fort Victoria. This process involved placing the furs in 250-pound bales wrapped invariably in large, low quality bearskins. The furs had to be dried well and cleaned, and were frequently sprinkled with a mixture of rum and tobacco before being loaded into barrels known as puncheons.

Prince Albert, consort of Queen Victoria, effectively triggered the decline of the world beaver trade in 1854, when he appeared in public wearing a silk top hat instead of a beaver headpiece.

Soon all of Europe was following the new fashion, much to the relief of James Murray Yale. The chief trader never did like hunting the "silly little animal," and it was he who had proven that the salmon fishery could be more lucrative for the Company than furs.

Yale, in fact, was concentrating anew on the fort's farm production. Hay and grain were transported from distant fields of the rich prairie by barge down the winding Salmon River, to be stored near the site where James McMillan had first stepped ashore to view the Fraser in 1824. To work some 2,200 acres of farmland, Douglas kept sending Yale a steady supply of labourers, few of whom worked hard enough to satisfy the chief trader.

The cranberry incident 1852 inspired Douglas to push Fort Langley into the San Francisco trade in a major way. Yale was ordered to obtain large quantities of the berries from the Indians, and to increase barrel production accordingly.

Yale made no attempt to hide his sarcasm to Douglas: "I presume it was not intended that we should relinquish the salmon trade and keep our coopers employed throughout the year making kegs for cranberries," he wrote.

Douglas ignored the jibe. "Pray my friend," he replied, "do not despair of the future, but get as many more cranberries as you can, and try to make those savages wait till they are ripe before they pick them."

The Hudson's Bay Company made a profit from this new trade, although major commercial production was to cease in 1858.

Fort Langley thus reached its apex in activity and importance during the 1850s, serving the triple function of brigade terminus and depot for furs, operating a major salmon fishery, and exporting agricultural products. It was the pivotal post on the mainland of the Pacific coast north of the new boundary, and served as the base and linkage point for access to the interior forts. Patterns of communication for the future new colony and province were determined by the Fraser River and its lone little fort, cast as an island in a sea of Stalo villages.

Already settlement was encroaching upon Indian lands near Fort Victoria. During the decade prior to 1858, Douglas became increasingly preoccupied with striking a balance among the trading interests of his employer, the colonization requirements of the British Colonial Office, and the Indian land claims. When in 1849 he had sought instructions from the Hudson's Bay Company respecting Indian land rights, Douglas was advised that the Company recognized only "qualified dominion" of the Indians over the lands, the criteria being that the native family or village must have built dwellings on or cultivated a particular plot in order to establish title—and, moreover, to have done so before 1846.

Douglas negotiated numerous land claim treaties with Vancouver Island tribes and was somewhat more liberal in his allowances for reserves than required by his instructions; he did, however, often lump together numerous claimants without regard for tribal distinctions.

The entire history of native land claims dating from 1849 was characterized by the refusal of successive governments to recognize the right of individual native families to obtain ownership of specific lands in the manner of Europeans. Yet vast territories were surrendered by the Indians in exchange for a blanket or two, the grant of a small reserve, and the right to hunt and fish in areas not occupied by whites.

There is no evidence that the natives were aware of what they were giving up, since they did not comprehend notions of European land ownership, particularly at this early stage, when there was so much land and so few settlers.

The irony for governments of a later day in the future province was that in settling Indian land claims for nominal consideration, Douglas and his council were implicitly recognizing some form of native sovereignty over the soil.

Although no settlers had yet reached the Fraser Valley, Douglas knew that the Indian claims issue would have to be faced on the mainland soon as well. He wrote to Yale of his treaty negotiations: "The price paid will come on average to about 15 shillings in goods. I mention this circumstance because no doubt your Indians will be claiming payment for their lands also; but that can be settled bye and bye."

In June 1857, Douglas journeyed to Fort Langley to officiate at the double wedding of Aurelia and Isabella Yale, to John Manson and George Simpson's son of the same name, respectively. (Eliza had married Henry Peers in 1849.)

Yale proudly gave away his two daughters, remaining only momentarily at the front of the room where he was obliged to stand next to the six-foot two-inch governor. (Douglas loved to stand over Yale, who would always find an excuse to sidle off.) Following the recital of the vows, the fort cannon boomed and the wedding party proceeded down to the wharf for a canoe ride on the river, with Douglas, Yale and the bridal party in one large canoe, and staff in a second craft lagging behind for safety. They paddled up the Fraser on a wonderful summer's day, to the melody of voyageur boat songs and the chant of Indians on the shore.

After a pleasant ride, the canoes turned and were swept gently downstream by the current. Yale beamed; above him on the hillside the bastions of the fort loomed, their presence denoting security, stability, and success. He felt his age, yet relished his triumphs in these twilight years as master of the Fraser Valley. Little did he know that his hard-won valley paradise was about to explode.

CHAPTER SIX

GOLD RUSH

James Houston ran away from his Scottish home in the 1830s with his best school friend, Andrew Carnegie. The two youths separated; Carnegie landed in the United States, where he apprenticed to a Pennsylvania blacksmith; Houston was shipwrecked and taken prisoner by Maoris off New Zealand, later escaping from his captors by swimming out to a passing trading vessel.

Carnegie went on to make a fortune in the steel business. Houston, meanwhile, spent many years wandering the South Seas and Latin America until arriving in San Francisco for the gold rush of 1849.

James Houston. His discovery of gold near Kamloops in 1857 may have triggered the Fraser River gold rush.

Unsuccessful in his hunt for the yellow metal in California, Houston booked passage to Puget Sound in 1856 and, hearing of a gold strike near Fort Colville on the Columbia River, drove a herd of cattle to the mining camp, where he sold the animals at a handsome price to the hungry gold seekers. He then prospected with a partner along the Pend Oreille River, was attacked at night by Indians, and escaped with an arrow in his back—his partner dead.

Houston decided to head north to British territory, where he understood the Indians to be peaceful. Just south of the international boundary, however, he was robbed of everything he owned by another hostile group of natives.

Finally, Houston straggled into Fort Kamloops, where he was promptly locked up by chief trader McLean, who pegged the dishevelled prospector as a Hudson's Bay Company deserter. Houston soon persuaded McLean that he was really a ship deserter, whereupon the chief trader released him to enjoy the hospitality of the fort.

In 1857, Houston struck gold nuggets at Tranquille Creek and paid for his Fort Kamloops board. Another prospector, Peter Baker, then arrived in the area and the two men together taught the local Indians to hunt for gold. McLean enthusiastically processed the nuggets and sent them down to Douglas at Fort Victoria; from there the gold was shipped to the assay office in San Francisco.

McLean himself soon began providing Thompson Indians with iron spoons with which to dig the gold out of crevices. It was only a matter of time before word of a strike leaked out in San Francisco, prompting a handful of prospectors to migrate northward to the area.

The Thompson Indians were paid well for their gold, and resented the intrusion of American prospectors. Reports reached Douglas that the Indians were harassing and attacking the white miners. At first, the governor chuckled, "I cannot help admiring the wisdom and foresight of the Indians." Then he sobered. A white–Indian war threatened to erupt as the number of prospectors steadily increased.

Douglas held no authority over anything on the mainland other than the Hudson's Bay fur trade. Ignoring this technicality, he repeated an action he had taken in 1852, when gold was struck on the Queen Charlotte Islands. On December 28, 1857, he proclaimed that any person removing gold from mainland streams without a licence would be prosecuted. The licence fee was fixed at ten shillings per month. Douglas then travelled to Nanaimo, where he persuaded Ovid Allard to embark for the Fort Yale site, to attempt to prevent any further clashes between Indians and miners in the Thompson-Fraser region. Allard agreed to go, provided that he was allowed to report directly to Douglas, and not to Yale at Fort Langley.

In March 1858, a party of California prospectors journeyed up the Fraser by canoe, stopping at Fort Langley and Fort Hope for supplies and information about the goldfields. The Hudson's Bay men were tightlipped, giving them no encouragement. Undaunted, the party moved on up the canyon and there, on a sandy bar, each man filled his pan with colours. Then quantities of gold nuggets were found. They staked claims, and when one of the party reached Puget Sound for supplies in April, word leaked out of a big strike at "Hill's Bar."

The news spread like wildfire. Thousands of San Franciscans deserted jobs, closed businesses, and threw an outfit together. Billy Ballou, a storekeeper from Olympia, boarded a steamer for San Francisco, determined to form there an express company which would transport the gold from the mines to Fort Victoria.

On April 25, devout Victorians emerged from church service to witness the American side-wheeler *Commodore* unloading 450 motley, pack-burdened prospectors, who immediately began pitching tents and looking for sailing craft to take them across the Strait of Georgia to the Fraser River. Many miners were drowned when hastily built skiffs were wrecked or capsized in the sea.

Throughout the year 1858, some thirty thousand miners poured into the Fraser region. Douglas took further action in May by prohibiting American ships from carrying weapons, ammunition, or liquor on the Fraser River, and requiring the prospectors to buy all of their supplies from Hudson's Bay Company outlets. Later, he replaced that last edict with a ten percent tariff on American goods. In order to enforce these regulations he dispatched officers to Fort Langley, where many seizures of prohibited goods were made.

Up and down the Fraser Canyon swarthy, red-shirted miners toiled on their

The Hudson's Bay Company fort in Victoria in the 1860's, a launch point for gold miners heading up the Fraser.

claims. They also brawled raucously. Self-appointed leaders among them decreed "miner's law" to prevail throughout the camps, a form of rough justice formalized during the California gold rush days. Prospectors earned between $8 and $50 per day at the diggings, and names such as American Bar, Boston Bar, Sacramento Bar, and China Bar were repeated in homes and taverns throughout North America.

Both Douglas and Yale were overwhelmed by the size and suddenness of this intrusion into their realm, a migration perhaps without precedent in history. Douglas complained, "They are represented as being with some exceptions a specimen of the worst of the population of San Francisco; the very dregs of society."

But the Vancouver Island governor was cautiously optimistic after he personally toured the bars of the canyon. In May, he and Allard mediated between miners and Indians, lecturing, threatening, and cajoling hotheads of both groups, and warning them of the sternness of British justice. Douglas even tactfully hired a local Indian chief as a government agent. He warned the prospectors that British law only would prevail in the region and that the rights of native peoples would be enforced "no less than those of the white man." In this, he was bluffing, since he could marshal only six naval recruits and a few Company employees to enforce his laws in the camps.

One of the ways in which the intrepid governor impressed the miners was his practical approach to their problems. Sensing that winter snows might trap the prospectors in the canyon, Douglas told them that a road must be built that could be used for transporting supplies to the mining camps. He persuaded five hundred of their number to work on constructing such a road via the Harrison Lake-Lillooet route earlier discovered by Anderson. He then hired Anderson to supervise the trail blazing. Each of the miners placed with Douglas a twenty-five-dollar good conduct deposit, money which was used for immediate construction requirements, and was returned to the miners in due course in the form of camp supplies, at Company mark-up prices, of course. By November, freight was pouring into Lillooet and the mining camps were made secure.

By June, a few steamboats loaded with goldseekers were venturing up the Fraser as far as Fort Langley, where the men were unloaded to buy supplies at the fort. From there, the miners made the journey up the Fraser in canoes or bateaux. During the first week of June, about fifty craft containing an average of six miners each reached Fort Hope. Numerous canoes were dashed to pieces or overturned in the river and countless lives lost.

A brash Yankee captain brought his sidewheeler *Surprise* to Fort Langley in early June, laden with miners, and determined to take his boat all of the way up the river to Fort Hope. Yale's officials argued that the river was too treacherous for a bulky vessel, and that he would be swept onto a sandbar or suffer a worse fate. The captain shrugged off these warnings and employed a Kwantlen Indian named Speel-set to act as pilot. Speel-set negotiated a price for his services of $160, boarding the side–wheeler erect, barefoot, and clad only in a blanket. The *Surprise* smoked and grunted and chugged away, while an amused Yale looked on, certain that the vessel would not get very far.

Sternwheeler tied to the shore on the Fraser.

Two days later, the shrill whistle of the *Surprise* was heard once again at Fort Langley, as the sidewheeler anchored in triumph.

Speel-set sauntered off the ship, now dressed in a fancy nautical suit, with high black boots, and gold coins jingling in his pockets. He had successfully guided the vessel through the sandbars and eddies, proving that the Fraser was navigable to Fort Hope. Speel-set became known thereafter as Captain John. He served for many years as a river pilot for Fraser River steamboats.

A sister ship to the *Surprise*, the *Sea Bird*, was less fortunate. Arriving at Fort Langley in late June of that chaotic summer, the vessel boarded passengers and freight, then struggled her way up the river, eventually turning back within one mile of Fort Hope, her engines too weak to cope with the swift current.

A few days later, the steamer finally reached Fort Hope, after being tossed about like a cork for several hours. On her return to Fort Langley, the *Sea Bird* grounded on a sandbar and lay wallowing there for two months until finally being hoisted up and refloated.

Dr. Carl Friesach, a noted Austrian mathematician, was one of hundreds of interested tourists who flocked to the goldfields of the Fraser in 1858. Friesach was anxious to observe the tumult and excitement of the diggings, and his account of what he saw gave a vivid picture of life in the Fraser Valley at the time.

Friesach boarded the *Sea Bird* in August at Fort Victoria, shortly after the sidewheeler had been refitted. Nearing Discovery Island, the ill-fated ship burst into flames. Thick smoke billowed, while the passengers ran frantically to the lifeboats. The captain gunned all engines to speed the vessel into a sandy beach of the island, where the passengers leaped into the water and reached shore. Two men died in their cabins; the rest of the passengers and crew watched from the beach as the vessel burned to the waterline.

A passing steamboat rescued the *Sea Bird's* stranded survivors and carried them to Fort Langley, where they boarded the *Umatilla* for the final leg of the journey. The conditions on board were filthy and crowded. Dr. Friesach lay down on a dining table after refusing to join the snoring miners whose sprawling forms littered the coal-dusted saloon floor. Unnerved by the day's traumatic events, the professor found it impossible to sleep, what with the constant roar of the engines, the filth, and the strong wind, which blew sparks from the boat's funnel onto him, causing burns to his skin and holes in his clothes.

Nevertheless, the *Umatilla* gained fame that summer by becoming the first sternwheeler to travel up the Fraser beyond Fort Langley, and then to Fort Yale. The *Umatilla* measured about 124 feet in length and 25 feet on the beam; she drew just over two feet of water. For river passage, she was more suitable than a side–wheeler, because her stern paddlewheel allowed her to ram headlong into soft landing banks, with passengers disembarking via a gangplank from the bow. Her success heralded a new era, in which steamboats would bring colour, adventure, and practical transportation to the lower Fraser.

Meanwhile, Dr. Friesach was in no mood to be impressed by the *Umatilla's* historic achievements. At 8:00 A.M., the sternwheeler was still two hundred feet from the Fort Hope landing bank; the current was so strong that it took a further half hour to reach shore. The professor noted a vast sea of Indian and miner tents surrounding the Hudson's Bay Company stockade. He straggled ashore, where, upon learning that Governor Douglas was in residence, he hurried off to pay his respects.

The following day, Dr. Friesach arrived at Fort Yale. He called upon the officer in charge, Ovid Allard, and received a promise that Indian guides would be provided for a tour of the goldfields.

The professor was not greatly impressed with the bearded trader, who used to dance on the tables at Fort Langley: "He has become half savage by living so long in the far West; he has almost forgotten his mother tongue, has never properly known the English language and makes himself best understood in Chinook. He has married a full-blooded squaw, who gave him a number of children, who in their appearance take far more after the mother than after the father."

Dr. Friesach cut short his conversation with Allard in order to feed his famished stomach. "As we wandered among the tents we noticed a large cabin, displaying the sign 'American Restaurant,'" he wrote. "The only table was occupied by three wild-looking men." One of these men was known as Captain Pocahontas and, although the professor did not normally consort with uncouth types, he and his companion hungrily sat down at their table, thereafter spending a miserable time rebuffing the trio's attempts to have them join in a drinking party. The professor records that he managed to get rid of the characters only after casually brandishing his firearm.

Despite bad characters, some of whom had been exiled from California by the San Francisco Vigilante Committee, Friesach found the miners and their camps fascinating. Although Americans predominated, he noted Germans, Frenchmen, Chinese, Italians, Spaniards and Poles, many Indians, and only six women. "In spite of the rough life and the privations arising from such a life in a new land, almost all had a healthy and happy appearance," he observed. "The tents stood in groups...the river, which flows here between a double wall of very high and rugged mountains, runs with many windings and whirlpools...Hardly a day passes without some life being lost in the strong current."

At Hill's Bar, Dr. Friesach found the river banks covered with miners for over a mile, some of them digging in the sand, while others worked at rockers and sluices. He was told that miners there averaged $30 per day and earned $100 on very good days.

While Dr. Friesach toured the gold workings, Douglas paced the floor at Fort Hope. He was in a vile mood. A few days earlier he had hurried to the canyon region with thirty-five armed men upon hearing of a full-scale war erupting between miners and Indians. Trouble had begun when white miners began driving natives off the bars; native women were also molested and Indian burial grounds desecrated. Arrows and bullets flew in mélées throughout the canyon. More than sixty-one dead miners were recovered from the Fraser above Hope in early August, and numerous headless corpses floated down the river to the sea.

By mid-August, Allard was beset at Fort Yale with hundreds of panicking miners, who began to organize militia units. Some Indian chiefs risked their lives to come to Allard's office in order to attempt to arrange a truce. Allard and a justice of the peace from Hill's Bar just managed to save one chief from being lynched, by persuading an angry mob of prospectors that he and his native companions were good Indians whose lives, and nearby village, should be spared from destruction. The chief posted a white flag above his home in the village and avoided the violence.

A veritable slaughter of natives ensued, as enraged miners hunted down over five hundred canyon Indians; the prospectors were armed with double-barrelled shotguns and Kentucky rifles. The Indians who were not killed in the carnage faced starvation when the miners denied them all access to the river, and to the salmon runs so necessary to provisioning them for the coming year. Finally, a tentative cease-fire was agreed to by the miners, who allowed the few remaining natives to return to their villages near Fort Yale.

Douglas methodically went about an investigation into the hostilities. The Indians he interviewed convinced him that, although much blood had been shed by natives, the fault lay chiefly with the miners. He found the swirling new town of

Yale to be a filthy, unholy place: "A city of tents and shacks, stores, barrooms and gambling houses. The one street crowded from morning till night with a surging mass of jostling humanity... miners, prospectors, traders, gamblers and painted ladies mingled in the throng... A worse set of cutthroats and all-round scoundrels never assembled anywhere... Night assaults and robberies, varied by an occasional cold-blooded murder or a daylight theft, were common occurrences."

The beleaguered Douglas adopted several measures which he hoped would lessen tensions. He prohibited the sale of liquor to Indians, levied a licence fee of six hundred dollars for each saloon—accompanied by licensing restrictions—and ordered townsites established at Hope and Yale, offering transitional ownership rights. Thereafter, most of the burgeoning towns developing around the Hudson's Bay Company stockades would no longer include the prefix "fort"—only Fort Langley would retain its old name.

Finally, Douglas appointed a chief of police and five constables at Yale, a measure laughed at by miners and visitors alike, before returning to Victoria to ponder his next move.

Help was on its way. In England, the new colonial secretary pushed a bill through Parliament to create the Crown Colony of British Columbia. Although he criticized Douglas for the unilateral restrictions imposed upon American vessels and goods on the lower Fraser, Lord Lytton recognized the Vancouver Island governor as the man of the hour. Provided Douglas would divorce himself from the Hudson's Bay Company forthwith, the British government was prepared to appoint him as governor of both colonies.

Colonel Richard Moody.

Lytton worked assiduously to provide the machinery needed for an efficient administration. He chose an élite corps of men to come to the new colony as part of a Royal Engineers contingent, fulfilling a promise made to Douglas earlier in the year that he would sent military and engineering assistance.

In seeing off the advance group of Engineers at Cowes, Lytton told the assembled men: "Christian cities will dwell in the land of which you will map the sites and lay the foundations. You go not as the enemies, but as the benefactors of the land you visit, and children unborn will, I believe, bless the hour when Queen Victoria sent forth her sappers and miners to found a second England on the shores of the Pacific."

The mission of the Royal Engineers was twofold: first, to build roads, lay out townsites and conduct surveys. Second, to provide a military defensive force that was less likely to provoke American miners than full soldiers.

Lytton was brilliant in his selection of three key leaders to set out for the new colony. Colonel Richard Moody, commander of the Scottish Royal Engineers, was to be in charge of all Royal Engineers in British Columbia. Lytton's hand-picked chief of police and gold commissioner was Chartres Brew, dependable and scrupulously honest, who was to arrive in Victoria December 2, 1858, closely followed by Moody on Christmas Day.

But Lytton's tour de force was his choice of Matthew Baillie Begbie as the chief judge of the new colony. Begbie was cultured, fair-minded, and shrewd—a giant of a man, standing six feet four inches, and very dashing with his clipped Van Dyck beard and long flowing black robes. Single-handedly, Begbie would do more to bring law and order to the chaos of the mining camps than an army of policemen ever could do.

Typical of the men of the engineer corps was the tall Scot, John Maclure, who, upon hearing of the call for volunteers, rushed home to his wife Martha and asked, "Martha, how would you like to go to New Caledonia?" "Where is it, John," she replied. "I don't know," he said, "but they are calling for volunteers. There is gold, wild animals, and Indians. I think it sounds interesting." The Maclures came—with their two-year-old daughter Sara in tow.

Judge Begbie boarded the ship *Niagara* and left England on September 11, 1858, at about the same time that Douglas received word of the royal proclamation creating British Columbia, which would only become official when Begbie arrived and swore in Douglas as the new governor. In the interim, Douglas received welcome aid in the form of HMS *Ganges*, an aging warship equipped with seven hundred sailors and marines. In the Fraser Valley, sixty-eight Royal Engineers arrived to work with their American counterparts in surveying and clearing the international boundary.

The first Sappers spent the summer camped on Sumas Prairie, a low meadow area adjoining Sumas Lake, a shallow body of water home to salmon, sturgeon, and thousands of ducks. For an hour at dusk the men would go for a shoot and bag between twenty and forty ducks. The tents of the engineers were pitched on a tranquil stream which teemed with fish, while their horses munched on rich knee-deep grass. Above the camp rose Mount Cheam and the peaks of the Cascades. The party's naturalist, John Lord, commented:

> "We were in a second Eden! Silvery-green and ever-trembling cottonwood trees, ruddy black-birch and hawthorn, like a girdle, encircle the prairie, and form a border of Nature's own weaving to the brilliant carpet of emerald grass, patterned with wild flowers of every hue and tint...stretching away for about 3 miles is an open grassy prairie, one side of which is bounded by the Chilukweyuk River, the other by the Fraser. At the junction of the two streams, at an angle of the prairie, stands an Indian village: the crude plank sheds and rush-lodges; the white smoke, curling gracefully up through the still atmosphere from many lodge-fires; the dusky forms of the savages, as they loll or stroll in the fitful night, give life and character to a scene indescribably lovely."

Not all was bliss for the surveying party. By day they travelled to and from the boundary line, clearing brush and placing four-foot iron posts every mile and a half. At night they encountered the ubiquitous Fraser Valley mosquito: "Night and day the hum of these bloodthirsty tyrants was incessant; we ate them, drank them, breathed them; the thickest leather clothing scarcely protected one...lighting huge fires, fumigating our tents, trying every expedient we could think of, was all in vain."

Eating and drinking became difficult, it was impossible for men to read or write; faces turned to swollen masses; mules and horses raced madly about, plunging into the lake for relief; and many of the engineers began showing fever symptoms. Vanquished, the contingent retreated into a hilly area and waited for late autumn before resuming work.

For Yale and his staff at Fort Langley, the spring and summer of 1858 were tumultuous times indeed. Hundreds of miners waiting for transport to the diggings encamped near the fort in tents and little make-shift shanties. *London Times* correspondent Donald Fraser reported that the Yankee prospectors were intrusive, impertinent, and lawless, invading the post's cornfields, eating the green peas, stealing oats, and tearing down fences for firewood.

At first, Yale had welcomed the unruly miners as a boon to the fort economy. "The arrival of so many strangers is unpleasant," he wrote, "but until Her Majesty's government authorizes me to prevent their entrance into the country we are obliged to make a virtue of necessity and to turn them to advantage."

Yale mistakenly believed that the influx of miners would not affect the fur trade. He constructed a larger store to accommodate the increased business and had Douglas send him two thousand blankets. By May 10, the fort had receipted 336 gold ounces and $5,000 cash. Two months later, sales averaged $1,500 per day, consisting chiefly of flour, bacon, beans, mining tools, blankets, and woollens.

Some confusion existed as to how to cope with United States coinage, and Douglas reprimanded William Newton, clerk of the sales shop, for overvaluing the ten-dollar American Eagle coin—ordering him to value it at eight dollars. The fort blacksmith shop made pick-axes, which sold like hot cakes.

The editor of *Harper's Weekly* described activity in the Fort Langley sales shop that summer: "The door is scarcely opened when the small space allotted to customers inside the building is filled with people and from that moment, trade is unceasing and a continuous stream of coin flows into the till of the Company until noon, when a bell rings and business ceases at once."

After an hour's lunch break, the frenetic activity at the sales shop resumed until 6:00 P.M. American prospectors, accustomed to the unshackled entrepreneurial customs of Californian mining towns, found the whole experience very tedious but often amusing.

One journalist observed that "inside this trading warehouse there is a look of venerable antiquity that would be difficult to match in any other portion of the world today." Even the weighing scales used old fashioned upright and beam with trays of merchandise suspended from one end and the weights on the other, much like in the quaint old towns of New England.

Fraser River bateaux were in great demand at Fort Langley for use by prospectors anxious to reach the canyon mines, and construction of these boats continued even after the sternwheelers began travelling on the upper river. Samuel Robertson was a Columbia River veteran who handcrafted the bateaux, ensuring that each boat was sturdy and of just the right buoyancy. These craft carried up to

York boat on the Fraser, similar in design to the "bateaux" used by the fur traders. Of sturdy construction, the flat-bottomed vessel could withstand the river's swirls and eddies, but was hard to row upstream.

three tons of freight, measured thirty feet in length with a beam of five to six feet, and were crewed by eight men. The flat oak timbers used in construction were bent to shape by heating, then bolted to a flat keel.

The arrival of the fur brigade on June 30, 1858, represented the end of an era for both the Hudson's Bay Company and Fort Langley. Never again would the brigade travel to the fort, or play a pivotal role in the unfolding economic and social history of the new colony of British Columbia. But the swaggering fur traders left the stage in grand style.

The voyageurs arrived as usual in their gaudy attire, prefaced by the familiar crackle of firearms, and greeted by the return salute of the fort guns. On disembarking, they viewed with some surprise a tent village sprawled outside the palisade; crude shanties were also visible, and one log cabin displayed a shingle advertising itself as "Miner's Home Restaurant."

One Prince Edward Island prospector attended the welcoming ball for the voyageurs, and expressed wonder at the diverse mixture of races represented at the gathering. "The ball was conducted with the best possible decorum," he wrote. "The music was sweet from the violin, and the dancing was performed in the most graceful manner by the Indians and the half-breeds, who took a very prominent part on that occasion."

Murray Yale played the gracious host, acutely aware that with steamers plying every day to Hope and the growth of that post into a town, the days of Fort Langley as brigade terminus and major supply depot were ended. Already Company supplies were being sent directly to Hope and Yale to serve the miners.

Yale, in fact, longed for retirement now. His world was crashing down on him. Still, he was mesmerized by the hustle and bustle, sensing that his fort's glory days were over, but captivated by the glamour of these explosive moments in history. He was also at this time joined in the Big House by senior clerk William Newton and his wife Emmeline, who were steeped in the mores of Vancouver Island's genteel social fabric.

Emmeline was decidedly the brighter and more assertive of the new couple. She had insisted upon hauling her piano from Victoria, and delighted one and all with her playing. Emmeline frequently cheered Yale with songs as he sat in his front office poring over his books of account, or staring out the window absentmindedly at the sternwheelers plodding up the river. Her husband William was of placid disposition, possessed limited ability, and spent most of his leisure time collecting and sketching butterflies.

Together, the Newtons supported Yale in his declining years. The chief trader frequently indulged in quiet sneers at Douglas, his jealousy no less intense, his self-pity obsessive. His small staff lapsed into redundancy, as Fort Langley began to be bypassed by the miners and abandoned by the fur traders. One American visitor described the fort employees as dullards who had spent too long serving a monopolistic employer: "Time, whiskey, the rough and secluded life which they have led, intermingling with aboriginal society in all the everyday relations of life, have all done their work upon them, and fattened and developed the animal part of their natures." The visitor also claimed that the employees lived only for the purpose of obeying orders and getting drunk at all idle intervals on "Hudson's Bay lightning."

The gold rush had the immediate effect of ruining the trade relationship which had flourished between the Hudson's Bay Company and the Stalo river people since 1827. Hundreds of Indians opted to sell fish and other foodstuffs to the miners directly in return for cash and trade goods; to guide the prospectors along the river; and to pan for gold themselves. The natives also deserted the Chilliwack fishing station that year, being so lured by the mining fever that many families caught insufficient quantities of salmon to tide them over the winter season.

Although not approaching the scale of riotous life in the Fraser Canyon, lawlessness prevailed in the growing shanty town of Fort Langley. As chief port of entry, the town boasted revenue officers, but no police. Miners would often arrive from the canyon area sick and undernourished, some even dying. Boats were stolen and brought by thieves to Fort Langley for resale to miners willing to pay a big dollar for any vessel available. One Joe Miller was beaten up in a friend's shack and robbed of $340 in gold dust. The Hudson's Bay farm was regularly plundered by transients. The two revenue officers were utterly incapable of coping with crime, and also had to divide their time between the fort and the growing village of Derby down the river.

The most important occasion in British Columbia's history occurred on a rainy morning on November 19, 1858. Judge Begbie had arrived in Victoria four days previously and was taken in hand by an impatient James Douglas, who was anxious to officially take charge of his new colony. The two men, ceremonially clad, alighted from the *Beaver* below the river bank at Fort Langley, and walked in procession up to the main gate of the fort, accompanied by an honour guard of

November 19, 1858. The swearing-in ceremony at the Big House in Fort Langley gave birth to British Columbia. Judge Begbie is on the left, with James Douglas facing him to the right.

Royal Engineers. At the entrance, an eighteen-gun salute from the *Beaver* boomed out, sending echoes reverberating back from the hills north of the river.

More than one hundred people crowded in and around the Big House to witness the proclamation of the colony of British Columbia and the swearing in ceremonies. Douglas eyed the sodden grounds of the fort, then stood stoic as the Hudson's Bay Company ensign was lowered and the Union Jack raised on the flagpole. A brief delay in the proceedings ensued when, upon opening the official box of letters, it was discovered that the mace was missing. Within thirty minutes, a crude substitute was fashioned by the fort blacksmith.

Douglas turned to Judge Begbie, delivered to him the address of commission as chief judge, and received in turn the oath of allegiance from the towering Scot. Begbie then swore in Douglas as governor of the mainland colony and read the Queen's Proclamation. Begbie also declared that, henceforth, English law would prevail, and all exclusive trading privileges of the Hudson's Bay Company were revoked.

Yale had stood mute on the sidelines until the ceremonies were concluded. Then he went through the motions of entertaining his distinguished guests, ably assisted by Emmeline Newton and her piano. After a restful night, the official party departed early next morning to the salute of seventeen guns from the fort. Yale stood at the wharf for a time, watching as the *Beaver* faded into the morning mist along the river.

CHAPTER SEVEN

THE SAPPERS OF STUMP CITY

For months, James Douglas had walked a tightrope of bravado, bluster, and illegal edicts to prevent anarchy and Yankee jingoism from prevailing on the mainland. A lesser man would have fumed, fretted, dithered, and perhaps lost everything. Already he was beset by American officials who travelled to Victoria to "protect the interests of United States citizens," including one lawyer who demanded to be authorized to practice law in the mainland colony in defence of miners accused of crimes. Douglas sent the advocate packing.

Immediately following the November 19 proclamation ceremony, Douglas ordered the Royal Engineers—or "sappers," as they were known—to construct administrative buildings at Derby, on the site of the old McMillan fort; for this was Douglas's chosen site for the first capital of British Columbia.

Complications arose. Several Kanaka employees of the Hudson's Bay Company lived on the proposed site for the buildings, and Sam Robertson, the boatbuilder, ran the What Cheer House Saloon there. As well, Douglas learned that several Victoria land speculators claimed title to much of the townsite; these claims he promptly and angrily declared to be null and void. The governor then sent J.D. Pemberton to survey the area into 183 blocks of eighteen lots, complete with streets and alleyways. Of these, the Hudson's Bay Company later claimed sixty as its own property.

In late November, Douglas held an auction in Victoria of all lots—343 of which were sold at prices varying from \$40 to \$725. The auctioneer was later quoted as stating that the prices paid were "foolishly excessive."

The choice of a capital for the colony was the governor's to make, but Lord

Lytton had instructed Douglas that he must make that choice in consultation with Colonel Moody of the Royal Engineers. Moody did not arrive in Victoria from England until Christmas Day, well in advance of his main body of sappers.

Moody's advance man, Captain Grant, had inspected the Derby location and warned Douglas against proceeding with the sale of lots; he viewed the site as unacceptable for a capital because of its low bank location and its proximity to the Salmon River leg of the Semiahmoo portage route, both of which factors made it indefensible against an American attack.

Colonel Moody himself arrived at Fort Langley on January 6, 1859, but before he could inspect the Derby location, he and Begbie had to grab twenty-two sappers and rush up the Fraser by steamer to Yale, where serious trouble brewed. But massive ice floes delayed the *Enterprise* by several days. Meanwhile, Murray Yale harangued five Indians and four half-breeds to take a messenger, Lieutenant R.C. Mayne of the Royal Marines, by canoe to Hope to advise Moody that reinforcements were on their way from Victoria to help him.

Moody scoffed at the idea of requiring additional men in support, and proceeded to Yale with only Begbie and Mayne, leaving his sappers behind in Hope. "I had great confidence in myself and always consider soldiers as the very last dire necessity," he wrote.

Arriving at Yale, Moody conducted the first church service ever held there, then proceeded to investigate the troubles which had stemmed from the assault upon a white miner by a black. The assault provoked a Hill's Bar magistrate to trade blows with the Yale magistrate, into which fray stepped the notorious Ned McGowan, a well-known criminal from California, who led a posse of twenty men to arrest the Yale magistrate.

It took but a few hours for Moody to calm the waters; but just when it appeared matters were firmly in hand, McGowan caused a major uprising by assaulting an old enemy from San Francisco. Mayne then took a canoe supplied by Ovid Allard and paddled down to Hope to summon the sappers to the scene. Mayne kept paddling down river to Fort Langley, where he secured Marine reinforcements, but by the time these men reached Yale, Moody once again had the situation in hand.

Judge Begbie fined McGowan heavily for the assault. McGowan responded by inviting the judge and Moody to Hill's Bar for some hospitality. Moody demurred because of a cold, but Begbie and Mayne attended to "a collation in his hut, where we drank champagne with some 12 or 15 of his Californian mining friends." Mayne later said that he had rarely lunched with a pleasanter, more well-spoken group of men. McGowan's War thus ended. Ned McGowan became henceforth a loyal British subject, and the Royal Engineers never again had to act in a military capacity on the Fraser.

The situation at Fort Langley and Derby now pre-occupied Moody. He found that lawlessness abounded, noting that the towns were full of riotous Americans, and that two men had just been shot to death without any prosecution of the culprit. He cursed Douglas for having authorized the Derby lot sales prior to consulting with him about the site for the new capital, although Captain Mayne and others had purchased lots there on speculation. Moreover, he observed that

American soldiers had travelled to the Fraser recently via the Semiahmoo Trail, and that smuggling along the route was rife.

Moody prepared for a confrontation with Douglas over the capital selection issue. His own choice was either on the north side of the Fraser at the confluence of the Pitt River—present-day Mary Hill—or at the old Kwantlen village of Skaiametl, across the river from the big tree marked with the Hudson's Bay Company initials. He travelled to Victoria to make his case before the governor.

The military consideration finally won the day for Colonel Moody. His planned city of "Queensborough" on the Skaiametl site was situated on a high slope with a deep harbour below—ideal for firing at Yankee warships coming up the river. Douglas reluctantly agreed, and proclaimed the Queensborough location as site for the new capital on February 14, 1859. He also announced that those who had purchased lots at Derby would be refunded all of their money.

Two months later, the main body of sappers arrived at Victoria on the ship *Thames City*; their numbers consisted of 122 men, 31 women, and 34 children. This group immediately travelled to the chosen site on the Fraser and, together with the vanguard sappers from Derby, commenced the clearing of a townsite on the hill; their camp was known as Sapperton, and was later to be occupied by the B.C. Penitentiary.

The Engineers built a barracks, Customs House, Treasury building, Public Works offices, a small church, and a residence for the lieutenant-governor—the latter office being filled by their commander, Colonel Moody himself. The colonel worked alongside of his men and women, and wrote to Douglas that the thickets in the woods were the "closest and thorniest" he had ever seen. His clothes were ragged, and his men's hands were torn and scratched. He begged for some stout, strong leather gloves for the sappers. "The woods are magnificent, superb beyond description," he wrote, "but most vexatious to a surveyor and the first dwellers in a town." To add to the discomfort, it rained in torrents that spring and Moody ordered large supplies of Indian waterproof boots.

On June 2, 1859, Douglas proclaimed Queensborough as the sole port of entry for all vessels having ingress on the Fraser River. He also imposed tonnage,

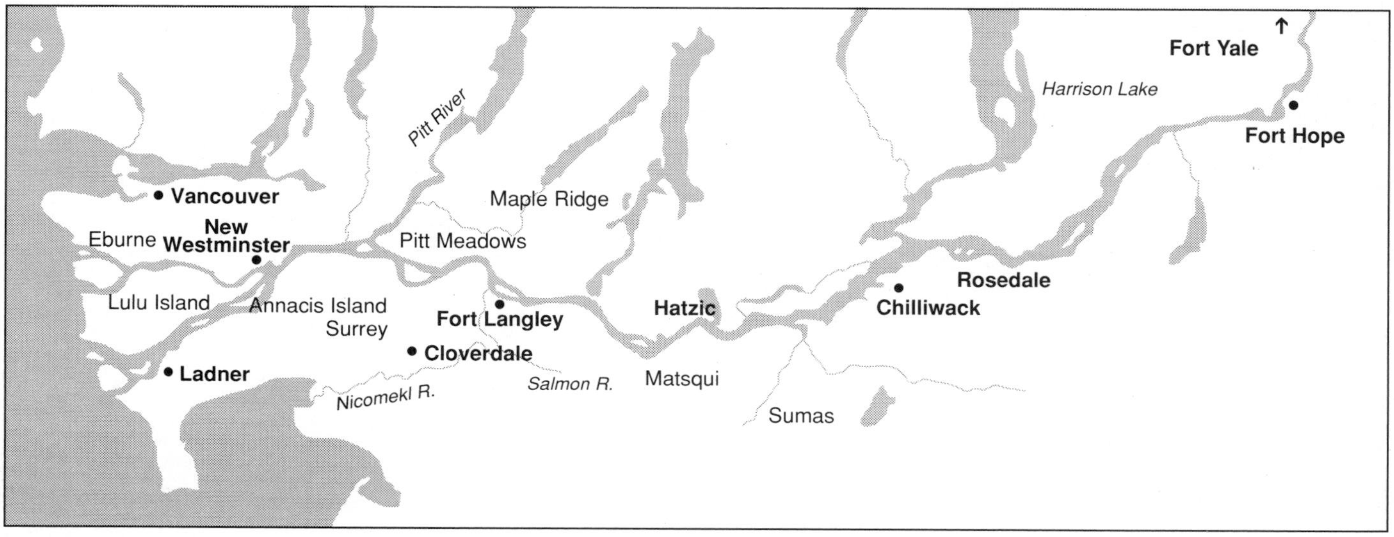

pilotage, and harbour dues at the port. Town lots were offered for sale and quickly purchased at an average price of two hundred dollars each.

On July 20, the name of the capital was changed to New Westminster at Queen Victoria's personal request. The *Victoria Colonist* complained that "Queensborough is not only genuine Anglo-Saxon, but also appropriate and avoids confusion. We had hoped for better things from the Colonial Office."

For his part, Douglas was still upset over losing out on the Derby location, and hoped that Derby might yet develop into the largest commercial centre on the mainland. To the Reverend Burton Crickmer, first rector of the Derby Anglican Church, he wrote: "I feel a deep interest in the place, and a higher degree of confidence in its development as a commercial station."

The diameter of many cedar trees at New Westminster measured close to ten feet. Worthy axemen were hard pressed to topple one of these giants in a single day. Once felled, the trees were too large to haul away and had to be sawn and cut into blocks. The extensive root systems posed an equally great problem.

Soon a sea of stumps appeared along the hillside, which "outnumbered the houses built for 20 years and more," causing Victorians to refer derisively to the new capital as "Stump City" for many decades. The Reverend Sheepshanks, first resident Anglican clergyman, described one evening experience: "In the neighbourhood of the huts and stores the mud was deep and sticky. I floundered

Early New Westminster. Government buildings were very prominent in the Royal City, and even included a bakery.

about in the darkness, occasionally tripping over a stump, and now and then I heard voices of the men in the drinking bars...and the light gleaming from the saloons fell upon the black mud and castaway playing cards that I was treading underfoot."

Land clearing proceeded apace throughout the year 1859, with Indians assisting the sappers in making way for the new town. Settlers and merchants erected shanties near the river and by October, the land was fully surveyed and more lots were for sale. A saloon, butcher shop, general store, lumber office, and church all appeared.

The Reverend Edward White arrived from Victoria as the first Methodist minister, and preached an open air service in April under maple trees on the river to a group of fifty men and one woman. White travelled by canoe regularly to Derby, where he also held services. His life was varied—preaching to sappers at their barracks, holding temperance meetings, serving as juror, and burying anonymous men whose corpses floated down the Fraser from unknown canyon sandbars. A Methodist clergyman, the Reverend Ebenezer Robson, took charge at Hope.

By 1861, over 125 houses, shops, and government offices had been built at New Westminster, many of them of brick. The streets were so rough that a number of lot owners threatened to sue the governor and his council. The townspeople, however decided to take a more constructive approach by securing in incorporation status in July of 1861.

The top priority of the new municipal council was to proceed with grading of streets and chopping of trees, but the groundwork was laid as well for schools, a fire department, and a municipal hall. A government assay office was completed and put to immediate use in receiving and appraising gold from the mines—averaging one hundred thousand dollars worth of gold per month in 1862. A government wharf accommodated large vessels.

Miners, merchants, and workers, including many Chinese, were flocking to the stump city, and the affluent were erecting fine Victorian style homes on the hillside. The 1862 population was 204 persons; not included in the census were dozens of Indians who lived in town. By 1870, there were still only 600 permanent residents, compared with 3,000 in Victoria. On February 13, 1861 the first issue of a community newspaper, the *British Columbian*, was published.

The Royal Engineers served as the stabilizing force in the new colony. The sappers also became the hub of all social activity, organizing clubs and events and engaging the citizenry in such refined sports as cricket and croquet. Each Sunday morning the sappers marched in uniform from their barracks to the different churches they attended, where many of them sang in the choirs, or brought violins and brass instruments for musical accompaniment.

During the five years they were to toil in the colony, the sappers designed buildings, published maps, built roads, directed land auctions, and kept order. Colonel Moody even had them construct an underground powder-house—connected by a tunnel to the river—as a precaution against American attack. When the British Columbia Penitentiary was built in the late 1870s, workers discovered this storage chamber. One carpenter from sapper days attested to the building of the underground tunnel, though the passage has never been found.

On May 1, 1862, the first May Day in the Fraser Valley was celebrated at New Westminster. Following a cricket match between sappers and citizens, the players withdrew to a bower built of fir and cedar branches and began drinking spirits.

In the midst of their revelry, someone remembered that it was May Day and quickly erected a fir trunk, which was stripped of branches and adorned with wild flowers. Then both sappers and citizens—surely a most conservative lot—joined hands and danced around the May pole singing the song which most had learned as children in England. One wonders if any Indians viewed this pagan ritual. Certainly, in the years to come, many natives would attend the white man's spirit dance, and the New Westminster May Day has continued in uninterrupted fashion to the present day.

Picnickers often travelled to Fort Langley from New Westminster by river boat for a Sunday outing.

What manner of men and women were these Royal Engineers and their wives? We know that they were intrepid, industrious, pious—and generally a stubborn lot. When sappers working on the international boundary in 1859 could not secure packed frozen beef, they killed their camp cow in desperation, despite the availability of fish and fowl. Sappers were plucky, but had trouble felling trees. One engineer's wife said she had to teach her husband how to kill and dress wild animals for food—but then, her husband had to send her to a bachelor friend to learn how to make clotted cream and the quintessential plum pudding!

What New Westminster lacked in refinement and decor it compensated for with colour. All manner of characters inhabited and visited the fledgling town—prostitutes, smugglers, opium dealers, and horse traders. Politics of the day were brash and chaotic. Aside from Colonel Moody, the power élite of the two colonies was detested. Douglas was viewed as a dictator who travelled to the mainland only in an emergency and still was said to prefer Derby to New Westminster; who gave patronage to Victoria merchants and to his own church; and who refused to provide badly needed funds for municipal works projects.

In an effort to burnish his image, Douglas invited the stump town's social leaders to an excursion up the Pitt River on the occasion of Queen Victoria's birthday. The partygoers had a rollicking good time, but next morning they all unabashedly presented the governor with a petition that he be removed from office "because he was unfitted for the position."

Beloved by historians, respected in the wilds, Judge Matthew Begbie was hated in New Westminster. Seen as the right hand of Douglas, the "hanging judge" heard all important cases and went on assize circuit throughout the colony, ably assisted by his registrar, Thomas Bushby, who was married to one of Douglas' daughters.

The incident which alienated Begbie from the affections of the New Westminster citizenry was rather unusual. In November 1862, the fiery editor of the *British Columbian* newspaper, John Robson, published a letter from a reader which alleged that Begbie had received a gift of twenty acres at Cottonwood, near Barkerville, in exchange for overruling a local magistrate's decision to deny the donor an improvement certificate for his quarter section of land. Such accusations were not uncommon—even Police Chief Chartres Brew was accused of feathering his own nest by engaging a chain gang to clear his private lot.

Judge Matthew Begbie.

Begbie denied the allegation and ruled that Robson was guilty of contempt of court for publishing the letter. When summoned to Begbie's courtroom the next day for an apology, Robson, a true journalist, qualified his atonement by advising that he regretted publication only if the reader's charge was untrue. Begbie angrily threw the editor into jail for this impertinence, where Robson wrote editorials for his paper under the byline of "A Voice From the Dungeon."

Citizens rallied in defence of the editor. A mass meeting was organized and hundreds of townspeople marched to the gaol and delivered three cheers for Robson and "three groans for the tyrant judge." Robson finally relented and gave a full apology, but continued after his release to attack both Begbie and Douglas relentlessly.

On the judicial circuit, however, Begbie quickly established a reputation of fairness and impartiality which preceded him to every nook and cranny of the vast wilderness. At his first murder trial in 1859, Begbie presided over a jury trying one Matt Nial for a barroom killing. The deceased had fired first—and some evidence suggested that he had aimed wide just to scare Nial—but Nial had fired three shots in retaliation which killed the other man. The jury, comprised of American miners, could not reach a verdict.

Begbie harangued the Nial jury exhaustively, and advised it that a verdict of manslaughter might be appropriate. The jury took the hint and delivered its verdict accordingly. The occasion was notable in that Begbie used an American legal text to speak to the jurors so that they might better relate to him, although he followed British law. More importantly, as the San Francisco newspapers reported, the verdict and subsequent four-year sentence appeared much more sensible than the naked choice between acquittal, and a murder conviction for which the sentence would certainly be hanging.

Judge Begbie cited the Nial case in his campaign against gambling and drunkenness, the vices to which he attributed most crimes in the mining camps. He awed his jurors with colourful lectures on evil and its consequences, in effect becoming an itinerant preacher who claimed both heavenly and earthly authority.

The Indians were no less impressed than the whites. At Hope in 1860, a white miner assaulted an Indian, cutting the native's eyebrow open with a sharp blow. Strong feeling prevailed in the land that a white person should never be convicted on the testimony of Indians only. Begbie, however, convicted the miner on the strength of native witnesses. An outcry ensued, with a delegation of miners travelling to Victoria to protest the judgement before the governor. But Douglas stood firm in defence of the judge; and word spread that, although Indians might be treated inhumanely on other fronts, in the eyes of the law they were equal.

Chief of Police Chartres Brew was hard pressed to maintain order in New Westminster, and much crime went unpunished in the Fraser Valley hinterland. On several occasions, he and his constables were called up the river to Derby and the shanty-town of Fort Langley to quell drunken brawls at establishments such as the What Cheer Saloon and Fort Hotel. In January 1860, a group of American officers unlawfully proceeded across the border from Semiahmoo and portaged via the Salmon River to Fort Langley, where they seized two fugitives—brazenly defying any British authority to stop them. Neither Brew nor Moody even knew of the intrusion until several days later.

After the initial round of gold fever had subsided and the bars picked clean of the easy nuggets, the first settlers began to trickle down from the diggings to establish farms in the Fraser Valley.

Ironically, the man often credited with triggering the Fraser Gold Rush became the first independent farmer in the valley. James Houston married Agatha Cusham, a Nanaimo Indian princess, and cleared a farm on the outskirts of Derby on the Salmon River. He also began a tradition that was to endure for over a hundred years by delivering his potatoes, carrots, peas, and other produce to New Westminster to market—paddling the distance with his wife and little son Alex in a Stalo canoe. The Houston family also exported cranberries and hemp, made milk pails from birch bark, and brooms from birch branches.

The proclamation of 1858 decreed that all land on the mainland belonged to the Crown, subject to claims of the Hudson's Bay Company to its principal assets consisting of trading posts and the lands around them. Only surveyed land was initially offered for sale to the public; country plots outside towns were sold at $2.50 per acre.

The need of Douglas for settlers had to be carefully balanced against his need for funds—the only source of which came from land sales, customs duties, and sale of liquor and mining licences. The governor's goal was to attract sturdy British settlers who would pay a nominal amount to live under the Union Jack, despite the free land being made available to settlers in the United States.

To facilitate land sales, Joseph Trutch was commissioned in July 1859 to survey much of the western Fraser Valley into 160-acre tracts, using as bases for his survey the coast meridian, the International Boundary, and the first standard parallel running twelve miles north of the boundary. The lands included much of Lulu Island, half a block of Hall's Prairie (the future Surrey), and some land in Pitt Meadows. One week after Trutch completed his survey, Douglas held an auction of the huge areas. It was a dismal failure.

Judge Begbie and Victoria editors exhorted Douglas to lower the price of surveyed land in order to compete with the Americans. He complied, offering land at $1.25 per acre in 1861. Meanwhile, the governor also took alternative measures by proclaiming the first Pre-emption Act. The statute was the precursor of the kind of legislation which would open up the entire Canadian West.

A male British subject or alien swearing allegiance to the Crown could preempt 160 acres of vacant unsurveyed land for the total sum of $2.00, subject to providing a magistrate with a rough plan of the property. In the 1870s, the preemption system was replaced by a "homestead" policy of free land grants, whereby improvements on the property entitled one to a certificate of title.

Though preemption was attractive to farmers, no flood of settlers ensued. Between 1860 and 1864, only 450 tracts were obtained by way of preemption, most of them near New Westminster along the Fraser River. These lands were to form the nuclei of early settlements that were to grow into the communities of Surrey, Langley, Maple Ridge, Pitt Meadows, Mission, Matsqui, Chilliwack, and Hope. Most of the settlements which emerged at this time possessed a steamboat landing, and all southern bank communities were ultimately connected by trails to a track which became known as the Old Yale Road.

By 1871, the population of the six principal rural communities of the Valley was still only 440 persons, most of them retired miners and Royal Engineers who chose to stay in the new land, along with a few former Hudson's Bay Company employees, such as Sam Robertson, Ken Morrison, and a handful of Kanakas. Of these rural centres, none became incorporated until the 1870s, so that the settlers

A river in transition: Salish canoe in foreground, burgeoning town on hillside. New Westminster, 1871.

depended solely on their own resources and community spirit to survive. Langley and Chilliwack were incorporated in 1873; Richmond and Surrey in 1879. The population of the six centres, excluding Hope and New Westminster, was as follows: Ladner—60; Lulu Island—40; Mud Bay—40; Langley—90; Sumas—80; Chilliwack—130

The first settlers faced enormous hardships. Due to the proximity of the Fraser, their acreages were subject to periodic flooding, particularly at freshet time in June. The land had to be cleared and in many areas drained before it could be worked. One pioneer remarked that by the time his farm was ready for production, he was too old to work and his sons too sick of the toil to remain on the land.

The mosquitoes alone were enough to drive many away from the land. Then there was the lack of transportation. In the early colonial period, the only track resembling a road in the valley ran from New Westminster to the Pitt River north of Mary Hill. It was not until 1865 that the Telegraph Trail was blazed from New Westminster, via Langley, Matsqui, and Chilliwack, to Hope—and this pitiful track was useless for practical carriage of goods and people. As John Gibbard notes, prior to Confederation all "commerce on the lower Fraser was confined to river steamers and to boats and canoes on river and slough."

The big losers in the preemption game, were of course, the Indians. Douglas instructed Moody in 1861 to survey sites for native reserves. He specifically requested that Moody be generous and include all established "village sites, cultivated fields, and favourite places of resort," and also fishing stations, cemeteries, and even berry patches. Unlike the land holdings of whites, however, all Indian reserve lands were to be held as joint and common property of the entire tribe.

McMillan Island Indian Reserve opposite Fort Langley, looking north toward the Golden Ears.

Governor Douglas also departed from his earlier policy of entering into treaties with native bands, such as he had done on Vancouver Island. No land treaties were ever signed with mainland Indians, the governor instead pursuing a policy of reserves, preemption, and native assimilation. Douglas believed that the reserves would protect traditional native villages; preemption would be open to Indians and whites alike; and missionary activity would surely assimilate and Europeanize the Indians.

University of British Columbia professor Paul Tennant, although sharply critical of government policies toward natives, concedes that in the case of James Douglas "there can be no doubting his desire to ensure not merely the physical survival of the Indians, but also their attaining individual equality with the Whites. At a time when aboriginal peoples everywhere were routinely being forced from their lands and often actively exterminated, Douglas displayed a spirit of tolerance, compassion and human understanding."

Many of the reserve areas set aside for natives were inadequate for the preservation of the tribal way of life. Douglas was consequently beset with a constant barrage of petitions from Indian bands requesting enlargement of their reserves. Coquitlam natives complained in 1863, for instance, that their fifty-acre reserve was not large enough for them to cultivate enough food to become self-sufficient. The governor immediately ordered the reserve size expanded.

Fraser Valley reserves were generally quite small compared to those in the interior of British Columbia. Wilson Duff attributed this to the fact that "not being farmers, Indians did not ask for very much, in no case more than 10 acres per family." Douglas, however, genuinely believed that the reserve was to be a sort of temporary buffer to the eventual entry of Indians into the mainstream white society. He walked a tightrope in his quest to act in the best interests of natives, since Colonial Secretary Lytton enjoined him not to allow reserves to interfere "at a future date with the progress of the white colonists."

Colonel Moody and his sappers were in an even tighter position than Douglas on Indian land questions. When natives complained about the small size of reserves, Moody retorted that the "interests of the Indian population are scrupulously, I may say jealously regarded by myself and every officer and man under my command."

Settlers protested that the government represented lands as open for preemption, then later made them part of Indian reserves. Indeed, some confusion reigned for a time. A few white settlers occupied prime reserve land in the hope that they could either buy it from the tribe, or eventually gain title by way of prescription. Robin Fisher has argued that the key reason for Douglas retaining title to the reserves in the name of the Crown was to prevent unscrupulous whites from extorting land from natives.

When Peter O'Reilly was surveying the Hope township in 1858, he recommended to Douglas that a "trifling remuneration" be made to the Indians occupying an adjacent village so that the reserve could be moved away from the town proper. Douglas responded that the Indians were not to be disturbed. At Fort Langley, some Kwantlen village members wished to reestablish their reserve across the river in Maple Ridge and were granted a new reserve of 160 acres in 1863.

Very few Indians chose to preempt land. This was attributable, in part, to the natives' general lack of interest in a farming lifestyle. A second factor was that natives felt secure in the belief that Governor Douglas would treat any of their grievances fairly.

In 1862, for example, a Squamish Indian desired to purchase a lot near New Westminster. Moody's argument to Douglas in favour of the purchase was that the land was "some distance from the town, so that it cannot prove an annoyance." The governor responded by reproving Moody for his comment, and delivering a lecture on the Indian's equality with whites, and his inalienable right as a British subject to both preempt and purchase land at will.

British Columbia remained a gold colony until Confederation in 1871. The Cariboo Gold Rush of 1862 witnessed a mad dash of thousands of prospectors to the

Barkerville area. A few participants in this and the 1858 rush were interested in servicing the miners.

Billy Ballou was one such individual. Ballou became the colony's first mail carrier, packing the mail on his back from New Westminster and Hope to the mines, and back again. Frank Barnard later operated a mail service, and ran a stage line as soon as the Cariboo Road became passable.

Colourful, bearded, red-shirted Billy Bristol worked for Barnard's Express. His job was to carry passenger and freight up and down the lower Fraser River. In inclement weather when steamboats ceased activity, he ferried mail between New Westminster and Yale, paddling in a dug-out canoe equipped with a shovel nose to pass easily over ice.

Bristol employed only Indians as crew, and scoffed at white passengers who complained about having to eat his dried salmon. Each time he landed at New Westminster, he created quite a stir, packing his mail sacks on his shoulder and carrying his paddle through the town streets to fend off stray dogs.

Other entrepreneurs opened guesthouses and tried their hand at farming on the side. Given the high cost of importing beef, flour, and even potatoes from the United States, it was inevitable that a few of the thirty thousand people who entered the colony during the 1858 rush would come to view agriculture as a potential source of profit in itself.

These first farmers were very much tied to activities in Hope, Yale, and Port Douglas, because it was these towns in the early 1860s which were depots for the gold mines; farmers could make good money tending to packhorses in winter, cutting wood for sternwheelers, and growing farm produce for hungry prospectors.

The town of Hope was gradually becoming a residential centre. Edgar Dewdney, who built the Dewdney Trail to the Similkameen country, lived there, as did Billy Bristol. Hope boasted two churches, but no school. At Maria Slough, near Hope, lived Thomas Hicks, who had served with Davey Crockett in the United States' Indian Wars. Later, he helped stir up trouble on the disputed San Juan Islands, worked on the Whatcom Trail from Sumas to the Fraser, and finally married an Indian princess, thereafter retiring to raise many cattle and children.

Hope postmaster Louis Agassiz preempted a claim in 1862 at a site later to bear his name. Unable to leave his job, he sent his son down the Fraser on a raft to clear a farm.

Mary Agassiz and her children found Hope to be an exciting town in the early sixties. Throughout spring and summer they watched pack trains filing to and from interior points, and the children took delight in standing by when the horses were loaded up with provisions, for the animals reared, bucked, and kicked against their new burden. Another colourful sight were the thousands of miners passing through town—particularly the Chinese jogging single file, with mat sacks full of supplies hanging from each end of a pole balanced on their shoulders.

The Agassiz family learned to speak Chinook with the local Indians, which came in handy when they moved to the farm they named "Ferny Coombe," where they employed native labourers. Many Upper Stalo Indians still wintered in pit houses which the Agassiz children loved to visit:

"Keekwillie holes, a large, deep round hole in the ground, covered by a large roof topped with branches of trees inter-woven with a layer of clay and earth on top, making an immense mound. Here the whole tribe lived all winter. They had an open fire in the center and a hole in the roof through which both the smoke and the Indians had exit."

On a chilly October afternoon in 1859, several miners were paddling down Harrison Lake from the Lillooet portage. As they approached the south shore, one man jumped into the water to pull the canoe up, stumbling into the shallow water. Instead of jumping up in a shiver, he lay instead basking in the water and shouted for his companions to join him for a hot bath.

And so, Harrison Lake's hot springs were discovered by whites. (They were known to the Stalo as "warm chuck.") Two principal springs were found, one sulphur and the other potash, having temperatures of 150 and 120 degrees Fahrenheit respectively. The famous St. Alice Hotel was later built at the springs; the structure was destroyed by fire in 1920 and replaced by the Harrison Hotel.

The St. Alice Hotel at Harrison Hot Springs. Mount Cheam in background.

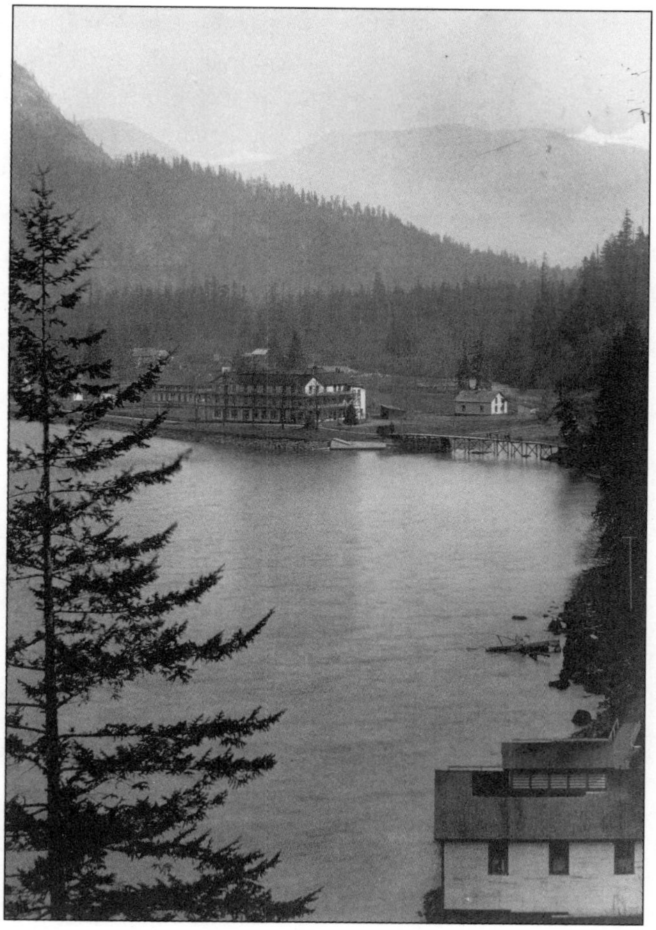

The oldest and largest agricultural settlement in the Fraser Valley began at Chilliwack, whose name came from a word spelled several different ways in the Halkomelem language, and meaning either "head of a people," or "as far as we go up a river." Yet the earliest farming settlers there were not whites, but Indians. When the Royal Engineers surveyed the area in 1858, they passed through magnificent potato fields of native families.

Miners often struggled up the arduous Whatcom Trail from Bellingham Bay to avoid Governor Douglas's customs duties, many of them half-starved by the time they reached the Fraser near the mouth of the Chilliwack River.

Jonathan Reece, a Hope butcher, imported some 200 head of cattle via the Whatcom Trail in 1859. When he arrived in the Chilliwack Valley, he was so impressed with the fine pastures that he decided to leave his cows there with a hired hand and bring them to Hope as they were needed. Two years later, however, when he attempted to repeat his feat, he lost over 200 head in the deep winter snows.

Two of Reece's cousins, Isaac and James Kipp, typified the conduct of many miners who ran out of money and abandoned the gold fields in search of employment. The Kipps began wintering cattle and oxen for Reece and others on fine rushes which grew on islands in the Fraser River, becoming in 1870 the first men to register cattle brands in British Columbia. They established a farm adjacent to Reece, ploughing the land with a twenty-four-inch share, seven yoke oxen, and a harrow with wooden teeth.

Other settlers trickled into the upper valley below Hope and settled on the rich prairie. By 1867, the *Columbian* reported numerous flourishing farms, and that farmers now "can and do supply our wants." At Sumas, the Chadsey family planted various crops, including 1,700 tobacco plants, and made two thousand pounds of butter which they sealed in cans and delivered to the mining camps by ox-team, where it sold for one dollar a pound.

James Codville established the first rural post office in British Columbia on Nicomen Island, where he farmed and operated a guesthouse. On Nicomen Slough settled Joe Deroche, a Cariboo teamster who wintered his horses and oxen there each year, until he finally settled down.

Nearby Hatzic Prairie was not inhabited by whites until the late 1860s, and then only sparsely. The area remained a paradise for hunters, harbouring large herds of deer and wild goats, animals which continued to be stalked by local Stalo. The prairie was still used by the natives, who gathered wild carrots—known as "haskinskills"—which were dug with sharp sticks by native women, carried back to the reserve in huge baskets, and served either raw or cooked in hot ashes.

Huddled in his shack on the river flats west of Hatzic Prairie was Mortimer Kelleher, the first settler in the Mission area. He was later joined by James Trethewey, one of the first rural tradesmen, who built a grist mill which later served the mission school, and who established mills at Sumas and Pavilion Mountain.

Reverend Crickmer preaching on the street at Derby, 1859.

Across the river from Kelleher was Matsqui Prairie, one of the most flood-ravaged areas in the Fraser Valley. There the Fraser makes a sweeping curve; at spring freshet time, the river usually rose up to twenty-three feet and would flood most of the ten thousand fertile acres until dykes were built in the 1870s. The earliest settler in Matsqui would not arrive until 1865.

In the Langley and Maple Ridge areas, settlement was stimulated by retired Hudson's Bay Company employees; these included Sam Robertson, Ken Morrison, and John McIvor, all of whom joined in the lifestyle of James Houston. Morrison and McIvor had deserted from a Hudson's Bay Company brigade and were imprisoned by Murray Yale when he discovered them hiding in the woods near the fort. Unsure of what to do with them, he released the men to work in the fort cooperage. When their term of service ended, the two men journeyed to the Cariboo goldfields, later returning luckless to Fort Langley, where Morrison preempted the very land where he and McIvor had been hiding when discovered by Yale.

A traveller in late 1859 described Fort Langley and Derby:

> "The Fort at Upper Langley is one of the most notable features, and recalls old times when such protections were deemed necessary. To the back of the Fort the land stretches away in an undulating fashion for some 10 or 15

miles...At Lower Langley there is a neat Church and Parsonage house, though the population is few and scanty and perhaps not of a churchgoing character. Still, there are always a few, and one sees with pleasure the first church built in British Columbia. The population is very fluctuating and is supposed to be chiefly supported by smuggling and supplying the infernal poison to Indians; a group of these benighted treasures may be seen every night on the sand flat at Langley, in every state of intoxication and madness. One feels but little anger against them compared with those who supply them...."

At Derby, the Reverend William Crickmer preached to what few churchgoers could be found. Prior to completion of his church, he placed his pulpit in half-finished barracks and even on the streets.

A sketch preserved of one of his street services portrays the good cleric standing on a barrel, with the bow of a boat anchored on the river he faces; Sam Robertson's What Cheer Saloon and other buildings are behind him; and in the street a group of Indians—one of whom wears the tunic of a Royal Engineer—stand next to a yoke of oxen drawing a cart; white settlers stand about as well; a sow and her litter wander along the street; a Chinese man lounges in front of a billiard hall and restaurant; chickens scratch about; and an old-timer whittles wood while all around are strewn empty whiskey bottles.

St. John the Divine Anglican Church was completed and consecrated at Derby on May 1, 1859. It was the first permanent church in the colony of British Columbia. Ironically, due to the lack of sawmills, the church was built of California redwood which was floated up the Pacific coast. The Reverend Crickmer was jubilant. "The cloth for the Communion table I compounded of the red cloth and lace tassels traded by the Hudson's Bay Company to the Indians for salmon," he wrote, "as also the desk and pulpit cloths."

St. John the Divine Church at Derby. The structure was later barged across the river to Maple Ridge, where it is still in use today.

The Reverend Crickmer's euphoria was short-lived. Derby died as a town. Sam Robertson closed the What Cheer and opened a new saloon near the fort palisade. The Reverend Crickmer moved on to Yale, making his last entry in the Derby church register on January 8, 1860. The little church was used as shelter for transients until 1882, when it was floated across the Fraser to Maple Ridge.

Farmers who preempted land in the vicinity of New Westminster found a ready market for their produce and livestock. Thus, the farms in Maple Ridge, Pitt Meadows, and Surrey were the first agricultural endeavours to cater exclusively to urban needs, as opposed to the requirements of mining camps or the export market. William Howison of Maple Ridge harvested five hundred bushels of "large, dry and well flavoured potatoes" in 1862, which gems he transported by canoe to

New Westminster every ten days for sale.

The first settler in Surrey was James Kennedy, who preempted land in 1860. He and his family lost much of their livestock to bears and cougars. The Kennedy children were required to wear little cowbells outdoors, in order to ward off dangerous animals and to prevent them from becoming lost in the dense woods. Kennedy not only farmed, but made a lasting contribution to the valley by blazing an oxen trail from the Fraser River to Mud Bay. When the Fraser froze over in 1862, American entrepreneurs drove cattle along the Kennedy Trail to New Westminster when the steamboats were unable to penetrate the ice.

Lulu Island was attractive to settlers for its rich alluvial soil. The delta lands were covered with peat bogs, mixed timber, wild roses, crabapples, and wonderfully rich long grasses, and a home to beaver, muskrat, and mink. Colonel Moody named the island upon impulse while travelling on the sternwheeler *Otter* to Victoria with Lulu Sweet in 1861. Moody was smitten by Lulu, who had caused a sensation in New Westminster with her superb acting and dancing performances at the theatre built by the sappers.

The first settler on the delta was Hugh McRoberts, whose colourful past typified most of these early pioneers of the soil. Born in Ireland, McRoberts had travelled to Australia, California, and then the Fraser River mines in 1858. He was unsuccessful as a prospector and obtained a contract from the Royal Engineers to build a stretch of the canyon road from Yale to Boston Bar. He used the scrip he earned in this task to purchase from the government more than half of Sea Island and part of Lulu Island, where he planted wheat and fruit trees, imported cattle from Oregon, and erected the first dyke at the mouth of the river. McRoberts also constructed a trail from New Westminster to Musqueam, following much of the present day route of Marine Drive.

McRoberts and his family encountered hardship, but they also found a paradise of deer and waterfowl—snow geese, widgeons, pintails, wood ducks, mallards, teals, and Canada geese. They also stumbled across the odd Indian midden, for the Musqueam band had used the delta islands for burial and food gathering purposes for millennia. McRoberts named his farm "Richmond View" after his previous home in New South Wales, Australia.

William and Thomas Ladner arrived at the mouth of the Fraser in an Indian canoe in May 1858, having persuaded a Songhee chief to take them from Victoria to Fort Langley for the sum of fifty dollars. The two brothers wished to avoid the customs duties levied on miners entering the Fraser River, and so arranged to be dropped off at a Tsawwassen Indian village. Although they did avoid paying duty, they discovered to their chagrin that Fort Langley was not nearby, but some fifty miles up the river. Hiring another Indian for the journey, they were so impressed by the south bank of the Fraser, as they travelled up the river's South Arm, that they promised to each other that they would return there to settle.

The Ladner brothers kept that promise. After ten years of gold mining, operating a pack train which ran from Yale to the Cariboo, and then conducting a feed and grain business in New Westminster, they preempted 1,300 acres of the very land which they had first admired along the Fraser.

Many preemptions were never fulfilled by the original owners, who seldom even saw their land. Prominent men, including Governor Douglas, Bishop Hills of Victoria, and Captain Grant of the Engineers, purchased lots or preempted acreage on sheer speculation. Trappers, squatters, derelicts, and drifters often occupied land without securing lawful authority.

Some preemptions changed hands a number of times within a short period, and not always legally. A settler who left his cabin for several months might return to find a trespasser there who would not hesitate to use force to keep the lawful owner out. Land was so plentiful, and the police so distant, that the owner sometimes just shrugged and moved on to another plot.

In 1861, Henry Bates petitioned Moody, Douglas, and Brew for redress, after he returned home with his wife from Canada to find two strangers occupying his land and cutting timber for sale to river steamers. He received no justice beyond an offer of equivalent land by the governor, despite his holding a certificate of title signed by the commissioner of Land and Works.

The twilight years of Fort Langley as a trading post began on that fateful day in November of 1858 when the colony had been proclaimed. The fur brigade travelled thereafter only to Hope, from which steamers carried the wealth of the interior directly to Victoria. The salmon packing industry was never profitably revived once the Indians' traditional ways of trading were disrupted by the huge influxes of miners, then settlers. The loss of exclusive trading rights exposed posts such as Fort Langley to fierce competition, which, in turn, affected the viability of the Hudson's Bay farm. Finally, the rejection of Derby as the capital of the new colony was a bitter blow to the prestige of the Fraser's first white settlement.

All of this was too much for James Murray Yale. He purchased a farm near Victoria and retired there in May of 1859, occasionally sharing a fireside evening

Neglected old buildings at Fort Langley's original HBC site, ca. 1890.

with Alex Anderson, the old trailblazer, and John Work. Yale was a forgotten man, swept off the stage of history by the tide of events. He is said to have returned just once to his post on the Fraser, only to find it as deserted as a cemetery. "In the evenings," he lamented, "came reminiscences and sadness that none of my fondest hopes, though always seeming fair, have availed."

William Newton assumed control of the fort as chief clerk after Yale's departure. A mere seven employees were left in his charge. Minimal activity prevailed, though the blacksmith shop still made beaver traps and axes. The Chilliwack fishing station continued to salt salmon; and Cromarty, the cooper, still manufactured barrels for storing and shipping food. The Indian sales shop was eliminated. Natives were allowed to come and trade in the main store, previously the exclusive preserve of white Company employees.

The fort buildings became dilapidated. Discipline suffered; efficiency waned. In 1861, James Houston even successfully sued the Hudson's Bay Company for £40 after an employee shot his prize bull—although it took three juries to reach a verdict. Yale would have settled the dispute himself and never exposed the Company to such publicity.

Newton was a poor manager. Emmeline, however, compensated for her husband admirably, as the visiting Malcolm Campbell reveals:

> "Mr. Newton, the agent in charge, was absent, but his good lady did the honors of the house most handsomely. The party was bounteously regaled with wines and fruit, after which they indulged in a waltz, Mrs. Newton playing the piano."

Both Fort Langley and New Westminster were honoured in 1861 by the visit of Lady Franklin, widow of the lost Arctic explorer, Sir John Franklin, and her niece, Sophy, who were touring the Fraser Valley. However, the two women entered the Fraser River by steamboat more interested in the human scenery aboard than the natural landscape:

> "Most of them had their pack of baggage, consisting of a roll of blankets to the cord of which was slung a frying pan, kettle, and oilcan. Some possessed the luxury of a covering of waterproof cloth to the package. Every man had his revolver and many a large knife also, hanging from a leather belt. I should say that this mining costume in 'highest style' consists of a red shirt (flannel), blue trousers, boots to the knees, and a broad brimmed felt hat, with beard and mustaches ad libitum. There was also a party of theatrical ladies and gentlemen."

The two lady visitors were received at Colonel Moody's home at Sapperton by both Moody and Governor Douglas. Lady Franklin noted that delays in construction of the home had occurred due to the plagues of mosquitoes. "People who can leave New Westminster in the summer," she wrote, "always do so, to escape this terrible scourge: but happily it is curing itself by degrees, as the forest is being cut down."

The ladies proceeded from New Westminster to Yale, a town the visitors termed as "dreary, in a perfect sop of mud." They were piloted by Captain John Irving, who experienced some difficulty against the rapids with his *Maria*, his lady passengers convinced that the craft would sink or ground after striking a rock.

Along the shore they observed mining bars which had been abandoned by whites, and were now being worked by Chinese.

The Reverend Crickmer hosted the ladies at Yale. From here they visited an Indian burial place, where a naval officer accompanying them broke open cedar chests containing native bodies. A Yale grand jury later criticized the man's actions thus: "He opened three coffins, in which were deposited the bodies of the dead, some of which had been recently interred; and not content with this, he tore off the shrouding of blankets and left the bodies exposed, thereby greatly arousing the indignation of the half-civilized Indians...."

Harper's Weekly **portrayal of Fort Langley, ca. 1861.**

The following day Lady Franklin and Sophy were paddled by canoe a distance up the canyon to a narrow point where, suspended from the beams of a salmon drying shed was a white banner, made and hung by Ovid Allard's son Jason, with the words "Lady Franklin Pass" etched in large letters. The narrow pass and the great evil rock of the natives that Simon Fraser noted in 1808 have borne Lady Franklin's name to this day.

Lady Franklin visited the Allard home at Yale and commented on Ovid's wife and children: "He has however thoroughly civilized her, and their children are very nice looking and well mannered." The party then boarded the steamer for the return voyage down river. At Fort Langley, the ladies paused for tea with the Newtons and inspected Mr. Newton's huge collection of butterflies. Sophy described the scene at Fort Langley:

> "Old Langley consists of little more than the Hudson's Bay Company's buildings, within and without the Fort, 3 eating and drinking houses (or rather huts) on the high sand bank to which we made fast, and a little wooden chapel...When the water is high, these houses stand in the water, being placed upon wooden supports, and boats run actually alongside of the counter over which the drink is served out."

In the midst of the swirling events of the colonial period, the Stalo people struggled to maintain their way of life. To the settler's mind, nothing contrasted more vividly with the gentility of Lady Franklin's visit than the barbaric potlatch. A very large one was in fact held at Fort Langley in 1861. Some four thousand Indians from throughout the Fraser Valley camped on McMillan Island and exchanged blankets, muskets, skins, and hatchets. The *Columbian* described the blanket throwing portion of the ceremony:

> "The blankets were thrown down with 15 or 20 Indians obtaining a hold upon them and clinging desperately thereto, while the contestants struggle

on the ground like so many dogs in a fight, until an aged warrior, sword-nife in hand, steps forward and divides the blanket... this dividing process frequently results in cutting and slashing of the hands of those who have hold of the blanket...Some of the blankets are torn into shreds by the donor and cast into the midst of the admiring crowd. Muskets and other articles are also sometimes broken in the same manner. This is done to show their contempt for the value of property, or to prove they are not niggardly. These proceedings are interlarded by a sort of music produced by Kloochmen, dressed in the most fantastic costumes, the heads and faces besmeared with fish oil and covered with downy feathers...."

The potlatch concluded with the "savage and revolting ceremony" whereby a dog was placed in a circle of warriors; at a prearranged signal, "they snatch up, tear in pieces and devour the animal, while the hot blood of their victim bespatters their persons." When the revelry ended, the tribes left in hundreds of canoes and the little Kwantlen village settled in for the long winter. There were many stories to tell, many moments of this great potlatch to be cherished and shared with grandchildren.

A few hundred yards to the south of the channel separating McMillan Island from the main shore, the junior clerk closed the squeaky main gate of the fort, yawned, and took one final look at the still smouldering Indian fires glowing in the distance. Never again would he or any man or woman witness such a large potlatch, involving all of the major Indian bands of the Fraser Valley. Missionaries would attack the tradition; the law would ultimately forbid it.

Like the fur traders who came after them, the Stalo people had never sought to own their valley; now, like the fur traders, they had lost it, to the inexorable forces of civilization.

CHAPTER EIGHT

TELEGRAPH TRAIL

Max Fifer of Yale was the most renowned medical doctor in British Columbia during the heady days of the Fraser Gold Rush. Whether or not he possessed a legal medical diploma or licence was a moot point: the miners loved him. He had practiced his healing art in San Francisco and his reputation preceded him to the new colony. In June 1860, he was elected chairman of the first Yale town council. Governor Douglas liked him and appointed the doctor to tend to the needs of the destitute.

On the afternoon of July 5, 1861, Dr. Fifer was shot and killed in cold blood at his office by one Robert Wall. Wall had been told by another doctor that Fifer was a quack, and that some medicine Fifer had given him for an ailment was poison. After the shooting, Wall fled down the Fraser in a canoe and disappeared below Hope.

Word spread throughout the Fraser Valley of the shocking deed. Several days later, Jim Houston spotted Wall ditching his canoe at the mouth of the Salmon River, and heading overland into the bush via McMillan's old Semiahmoo Trail. He quickly paddled to New Westminster, where Chartres Brew collected together a posse; Houston and several men then travelled by canoe down the Fraser and around Point Roberts in an attempt to head off the fugitive.

All night long, the posse waited at the mouth of the Nicomekl River to intercept its man; but when Wall failed to appear by morning, the armed men struck up the stream, where, three hundred yards away, they found a tired, bedraggled Robert Wall. The fugitive drew his revolver, but Houston knocked it from his hand. Wall was soon under tight escort back to Fort Langley. On August 23, 1861, he was hanged for his crime at Yale.

For eight weeks in 1862, New Westminster was isolated from the world by river ice that prevented steamers from penetrating the Fraser above Lulu Island. Cattle and horses died along the upper river, and some settlers starved to death. Indians declared the winter to be the coldest in history, and the first time that anyone alive had seen the Harrison River frozen solid. Horse-drawn sleighs travelled up and down the Fraser.

Perhaps more significantly, the game of hockey was introduced to British Columbia. Hockey sticks were fashioned from cedar, and the male portion of the population - bureaucrats, parsons, storekeepers, woodsmen, and Indians alike were all engaged "in this exciting game upon the broad river."

The Reverend John Sheepshanks was one of those who played hockey that winter: "I cannot easily comb my hair," he wrote, "for it is frozen together...All the bed-clothes near my mouth are stiff with ice. When one proceeds to breakfast, the cups and saucers are stuck hard to the cupboard. The bread is frozen, and must be put in the oven before it can be eaten."

In the midst of the harsh winter, Fraser Valley residents observed smoke emanating from the snow-covered cone of Mount Baker to the south, and feared an eruption from the volcano, which was thought to be extinct. Mortimer Kelleher's son Cornie stated that the mountain glowed at night so strongly that he could read a book outdoors on a moonless night.

Captain Moore's *Flying Dutchman* finally broke through the river ice on March 12 and travelled to Victoria, but sustained a broken stern-wheel. The grateful citizens of New Westminster raised $350 to replace the wheel, happy as they were to be rejoined with the outside world and its treasures. As late as mid-April, explosives had to be used to break through the ice from Hope to Yale.

One of the paramount achievements of the Royal Engineers was the construction of the Cariboo Road from Yale to Soda Creek, which was later extended to

The Cariboo Road at Jackass Mountain, Fraser Canyon.

Barkerville. The Fraser Canyon section represented an engineering feat which to this day amazes experts in the field. The canyon road facilitated miners travelling to the Cariboo goldfields after 1862, supplanting the old Harrison-Lillooet portage route.

The sappers' achievements are too numerous to list here. We have seen their contributions to roads, surveying, construction, and the laying out of townsites. But they also drew the first official maps, established the first printing office, social club, theatre, and observatory. Add to this the first private hospital and library; the corps even designed the colony's coat of arms.

Alas, the days of the Royal Engineers as an official body in British Columbia were numbered. Douglas viewed the mounting expense of maintaining the sappers and their families to be prohibitive. Moreover, he was arguing constantly with Colonel Moody and his deputy, Captain Gossett, treasurer of the colony, respecting the state of finances. Gossett was in charge of the assay office at New Westminster, where gold was both measured and converted into bars and ingots by smelting. The office was a benefit to the colony, but continually ran a deficit.

Captain Gossett also had the temerity to defy Douglas. Despite orders from the governor to the contrary, he continued to stamp the gold ingots with valuations expressed in English pounds and pence, rather than dollars and cents. Finally, he refused to stamp the ingots at all, with the result that the gold bars were left unmarked and their owners were forced to go to private assayers to confirm their value. Gossett further incurred the enmity of the governor by minting a few attractive $10 and $20 gold pieces against instructions.

Busy river traffic, New Westminster, 1865.

Mrs. Moody wrote her mother in May 1863 to say that her husband Richard was "looking very old just now, and is not quite well. He requires change, but I fear he won't get away far, as the Governor won't sanction his travelling expenses."

On July 8, 1863, Colonel Moody received word that his corps was to be disbanded, a decision in which Douglas and Lord Lytton concurred. Moody paraded his men and gave them the sad news. Each sapper was offered a free land grant of 150 acres, should he choose to stay in the colony. Most remained; of the 165 men and their 32 wives who had arrived with the main body in 1858, only 22 men and 8 wives returned to England—including Colonel Moody.

New Westminster's citizens were devastated. On November 5, they gave a huge banquet in honour of the corps at the Colonial Hotel. Emotions ran high as Moody delivered the keynote speech and thanked his officers for their efforts and the citizens for their support. On November 14, residents from throughout the Valley gathered at the docks to say good-bye to Moody and his few departing men.

The reporter on hand described the scene thus:

> "The concourse of people upon the wharf was such as to make one wonder where they all came from... Incessant shaking of hands was kept up until the steamer began to move. The Royal Engineers Band all the while played those beautiful and touching airs—'Home Again,' 'Auld Lang Syne,' and 'God Save The Queen.' In every direction, from window and balcony was to be seen the waving of handkerchiefs and hats, accompanied by many a truant tear. But oh! the reaction. When all was over ...a feeling of sadness and gloom seemed to pervade the entire community."

One month after disbandment, the Royal Engineers' stores were sold at a gigantic auction which "probably attracted the entire population of the lower mainland...There was a magnitude of stuff, from a portable sawmill down to a cambric needle." The sappers themselves dispersed into a wide variety of occupations, mostly as farmers in the valley, or tradesmen in New Westminster.

Philip Jackman typified the stalwart breed of Royal Engineer who remained in the colony, and he later became prominent in his community. Jackman had arrived on the *Thames City* and helped clear the Sapperton camp. He later worked on the Harrison-Lilloet portage route, laid out New Westminster streets, and laboured on both the Cariboo Road and the Dewdney Trail. Upon discharge, he sought his fortune in the Cariboo mines, nearly starved to death, and later returned to help build a road from New Westminster to False Creek under private contract. He capped these early endeavours of his life by serving as the entire police force of New Westminster for nine years, many nights packing drunks home in a wheelbarrow.

His life still not complete, Jackman and his wife homesteaded for a time in Langley, where he ran a store, surveyed for the railway, served as reeve of Langley, and was employed as a fisheries officer for fourteen years. In order to detect illegal fishnets, Jackman rowed along the Fraser in his boat with a long pole fastened to the bow with which to probe the river's depths; when the pole struck a net, he would haul it aboard, confiscate it, and deliver the fish found trapped in the webbing to needy families.

On January 21, 1864, the recently knighted Sir James Douglas presided at the abandoned sapper barracks over the first session of the Legislative Council of British Columbia. This throne speech stressed the three priorities of his administration: roads, settlement, and good relations with the Indians. In the latter regard, Douglas followed up on his speech with instructions to his surveyors that in the case of land claimed by the Indians, the natives "were to have as much land as they wished, and in no case to lay off a reserve under 100 acres."

Paul Tennant points out in *Aboriginal Peoples and Politics* that Douglas also referred in his speech to ten acres per Indian family as a maximum allotment. Douglas later claimed that he intended to say that ten acres was a minimum per family. Certainly his retirement utterances support the latter position, but future administrations seized upon the "maximum" statement to justify their policies of meagre allotments to natives. A few months after delivering the throne speech, the governor resigned from office.

Douglas yearned for retirement. He was tired of the venomous assaults upon his character and policies, led by John Robson and the leading lights of New Westminster. The growth of Victoria was confronting Douglas and his government with demands for better roads and more facilities. Economic recession loomed. He was a Hudson's Bay man from another era; he had founded Fort Victoria, launched the new mainland colony, and done his best to placate and protect the Indians.

Governor Frederick Seymour.

On April 8, 1864, Douglas was feted at a retirement banquet held at New Westminster, and Lady Douglas was presented with a plaster medallion portrait of her husband. When Douglas was given a testimonial document lauding his years of tenure, signed by more than nine hundred British Columbia residents, he was overwhelmed. He responded, "A pyramid of gold and gems would have been less acceptable to me than this simple record. I ask for no prouder monument and for no other memorial, when I die and go hence, than the testimony here offered - that I have done my duty."

So James Douglas left the stage of history, surely deserving the title, "Father of British Columbia." Despite the warm send-off, however, Fraser Valley residents eagerly awaited their new governor, Frederick Seymour, particularly when it was learned that he would preside solely over the mainland colony, and live in grand style at New Westminster. To assist him in this objective, the British Colonial Office promised Seymour a large salary and a Government House to be built at the colony's expense. His new quarters are described as elegant:

"An extensive suite of apartments has already been added to Government House, including a spacious and handsome ballroom, capable of

Steamboats docked at the wharves of the growing Royal City.

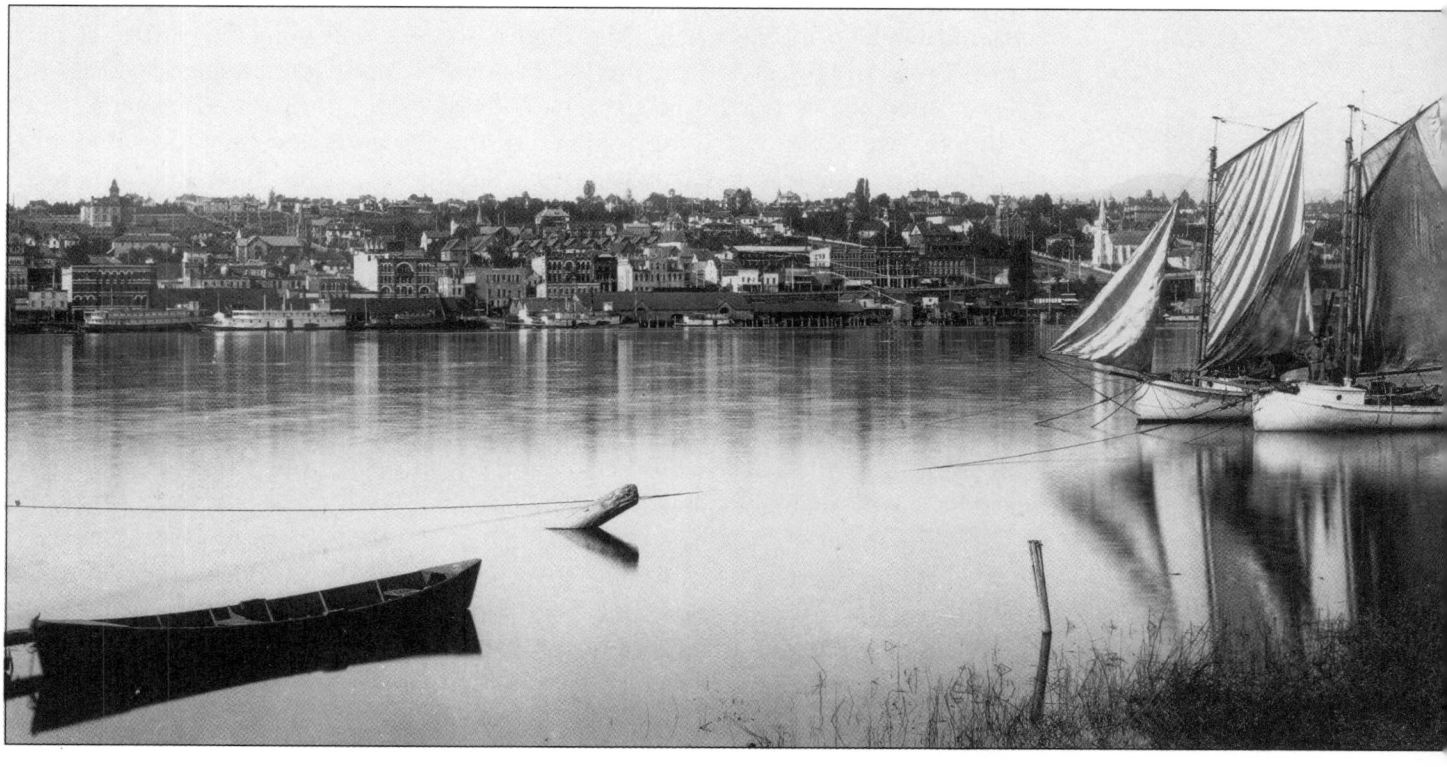

accommodating with ease 200 dancers. Adjoining this are the supper rooms, and elegantly furnished apartments. Extensive improvements were made to the grounds by the chain gang."

Governor Seymour was a native of Belfast and had most recently served as governor of Honduras. He was genteel, full of good cheer, and well educated. On April 20, he arrived on the gunboat *Forward*, the vessel's cannon booming the approach, answered in turn by bugles of the New Westminster Volunteer Rifle Corps.

A delirious crowd met Seymour at the wharf, where an address of loyalty was read, and he was then taken to Government House. The next morning, Judge Begbie in his red robes swore in the new governor. The city band played the national anthem; and church bells were rung throughout the city.

Seymour was not impressed with the aesthetics of his new environment. "I had not seen even in the West Indies," he wrote, "so melancholy a picture of disappointed hopes as New Westminster presented on my arrival.

"Here, however, there was a display of energy wanting in the tropics, and thousands of trees of the largest dimension had been felled to make way for the great city expected to rise on the magnificent site selected for it. But the blight had come early. Many of the best homes were untenanted. The largest hotel was deserted, decay blocked up most of the streets. Westminster appeared, to use the miners' expression, 'played out.'"

The new governor loved parties and socializing, giving such lavish balls that when he racked up a huge deficit for social affairs and dipped into his private funds to defray costs, the colony's Council promptly increased his salary by £1,000.

Within weeks of his arrival, however, Seymour was confronted with the Chilcotin Indian War. The affair began when nine roadbuilders and a ferryman were massacred while working on the Bute Inlet road. Seymour immediately dispatched Chartres Brew and a force to pursue the murderers. Misadventures and wild goose chases ensued. Governor Seymour personally set forth with reinforcements, and five Indians were eventually apprehended and hanged, despite Judge Begbie's opinion that the ringleader, Klatsassin, was "the finest savage I have ever met with yet."

The whole episode cost the government £18,000. It also reflected upon Seymour's inexperience with native matters and failed to address the causes of the massacre, chief of which were land claims and the molestation of Indian women by some of the road workers. Veteran Hudson's Bay Company trader John Tod reflected that in the relationship of mutual respect and interdependence that existed between the early traders and most Indian groups, an episode such as Chilcotin affair would have been quickly and cheaply ended by "a mere handful of fur traders," working together with friendly natives.

In the midst of the Chilcotin uprising, Governor Seymour hosted the annual Queen's birthday celebrations at New Westminster, which, variously referred to as Empire Day or Victoria Day, became a traditional festival of colour and ceremony for decades to come. He wanted particularly to establish as good a rapport with the Indians as Douglas had enjoyed, and so he summoned the Stalo along the river through the auspices of Roman Catholic missionaries.

The fiery but gentle Father Léon Fouquet.

The key Catholic figure in this regard was Father Léon Fouquet, who organized a group of nearly seven hundred canoes carrying some three thousand natives. The flotilla assembled at Mission and swept down the Fraser singing hymns, and carrying some sixty red and white flags aloft bearing the words, "Religion, Temperance, and Civilization." All of the city's residents stopped to stare as the Indians approached the docks and disembarked in the most orderly fashion.

The Indians participated keenly in the sports activities organized by the governor, excelling in canoe racing and track events. Residents were impressed and comforted by the religious overtones to the gathering, as described by one observer who attended an open air Mass:

> "We proceeded with them to the vicinity of the altar, and at eight o'clock the service commenced. The arrangement of the large crowd was perfect.The main body with women and children were close to the altar...The appearance of this assemblage kneeling was most awe-inspiring. One could not help being impressed with the fact that these Fathers and Brothers connected with the Roman Catholic Church had implanted in the hearts of the children of the forest the spirit of religion, and through its influence could control a large number of otherwise savage people as if they were lambs in a flock."

At the end of the week-long festivities, Governor Seymour handed out gilt-headed canes and Union Jacks to the chiefs and invited them to return the following spring.

In a later year, Captain William Irving transported settlers along the Fraser to New Westminster for the Queen's birthday celebrations free of charge. A new event was featured in 1870 called the Indian Scramble, whereby many goods, such as clothing, knives, and ornaments, were thrown from the upper storey of a dockside building and the Indians all scrambled about to fetch them. A reporter commented: "The crushing, crowding, tumbling, and screaming that ensued baffles all description."

The scramble, of course, crudely resembled a part of the potlatch ceremony, and was thought to give the Indians more pleasure than the "blow-out" on roast beef and plum pudding that had been offered them in earlier years.

Father Fouquet had arrived in New Westminster in September of 1860. Like Father Blanchet, whose Catholic Ladder was instrumental in converting Indians in the Pacific Northwest, Fouquet belonged to the order of the Oblates of Mary Immaculate. The order was dedicated to the aid and conversion of the poor, and in the Fraser Valley, the Indians soon became the chief focus of its priests' endeavours.

Fouquet himself was a fiery, dedicated preacher who gave up a distinguished literary career in France in order to work with natives. He thought nothing of travelling anywhere by canoe; in 1859, he paddled five hundred miles up the coast, as far as the Queen Charlotte Islands, to preach to natives.

At New Westminster, Fouquet constructed two small churches—St. Peter's for the whites and St. Charles's for the natives. Always a man of action, he represented for the early Catholics what Douglas was to the Hudson's Bay Company: "Wherever he saw evil he immediately attacked it head on and with invincible obstinacy, completely disregarding the obstacles in his way and occasionally stubbing his toe on them."

The burning ambition of Father Fouquet and the Oblates was to found an Indian boarding school, where children could be converted not only to Christianity, but made to abandon their traditional ways and be given a basic European education. Fouquet canoed up the Fraser some thirty-five miles in 1861 and found a slope covered with blackberry bushes on the north bank, facing Matsqui Prairie and the white dome of Mount Baker beyond. On this site he built St. Mary's Mission, named not for the Virgin Mary, but in honour of an Egyptian prostitute who had converted in Jerusalem and done penance in the desert for forty-seven years.

Natives and priests at worship on a Mission hillside, 1868.

The Oblates quickly garnered the respect and loyalty of key Stalo tribal leaders, reinforcing the earlier work of Father Demers with his rendering of the Catholic Ladder. Abstinence pledges called "billets de la temperance" were taken by watchmen in each native village, who kept notes of each Indian's conduct for the missionaries.

The priests laboured at St. Mary's to complete buildings and plant crops. They learned the Halkomelem language, although they forbade its use by the children. By the fall of 1863, Fouquet and his assistants had completed several buildings, aided by natives who delivered shingles and heavy base timbers. The first Indian boarding school in British Columbia opened that year, with an enrolment of forty-two boys.

The missionaries especially abhorred drunkenness. Father Fouquet also denounced prostitution among the Stalo and viewed common-law relationships of native women with whites as vile. In 1863, he claimed triumph prematurely in his struggle against these perceived vices, stating that "drunkenness has completely disappeared, and with regard to morality, the change has been almost as consoling; someone wrote to us, saying that the squaws are all leaving the white men; there is the greatest excitement." Yet many Indians visiting New Westminster continued to spend their money on bootlegged liquor, and acts of prostitution in exchange for alcohol remained common.

Father Fouquet despised false pride and high-handedness, and had a genuine way with children. On Christmas Day of 1862, he told his brothers at St. Mary's, "It is good for us to become as little children." He and Father Grandidier preached at Indian reserves throughout the week, conducted temperance meetings, administered to their two churches at New Westminster, and attended to the affairs of the mission school.

In 1864, Fouquet vaccinated some four thousand natives against smallpox—virtually the entire Stalo population of the Fraser Valley. Although editor John Robson constantly complained of Indians roaming and camping on the streets of New Westminster, he applauded the work of the Oblates in tending to the health of the natives and sheltering drunken and unruly urban Indians. Governor Seymour also appreciated these efforts and toured St. Mary's in 1865 to encourage and support the school's endeavours.

The Indian students at St. Mary's received both practical and academic instruction, often spending several weeks in agricultural pursuits. Father Gendre wrote in 1863, "The children and me, for 3 weeks, have not worked in class, but at agriculture...We have planted cabbages, turnips, and potatoes. The total amount of cabbages is a good ten to twelve thousand. This is a real treat for the Indians for the next winter, because they are fond of cabbage soup."

The Oblates shared the government's belief that the only future for Indians lay in the farming way of life. Despite some notable exceptions, the missionaries were miserably unsuccessful in converting natives to the tillage of the soil.

At the close of the 1865 school year, Oblate Bishop D'Herbomez visited St. Mary's, and dispensed holy pictures and gilt-edged notebooks to each student as gifts from Governor Seymour. He was impressed with the appearance and manners of the Indian boys, but became violently ill during Mass when exposed to homemade St. Mary's incense, as a result of which the boy incense swinger, Stanislas, had to leave the chapel. The bishop and other visitors were particularly enthralled with the adeptness of Indian children at music. The St. Mary's Brass Band became quickly renowned in the valley for its wonderful performances at official functions, concerts, and celebrations.

The Sisters of St. Anne arrived in New Westminster in 1865 and immediately established a day school for girls. In 1868, they founded a girl's boarding school at St. Mary's. Sisters Lumena and Bonsecour—one Irish, the other Canadian—were permanently stationed at St. Mary's, where they emphasized sewing and cooking skills with the native girls, who were now boarded there. These early nuns faced great hardship. Initially, there was no furniture for them and they slept on sacks, packing hay around their feet for warmth. They gradually made their own furniture out of pieces of scrap wood they could scrounge. By the fall of 1869, girls were making cotton and flannel shirts, and the Mission community was gratefully enjoying the enhancements that the nuns' cooking skills brought to their traditional drab fare of dried salmon and potatoes.

A third nun, Sister Mary, joined St. Mary's in 1869, and became well known in the Fraser Valley for her indefatigable spirit and cheerful demeanour. She taught the girls English, supervised laundry operations, and hoed the fields. Father Fouquet noted: "Indeed, she is a blessing for St. Mary's and the whole mission district. Her gunny-sack apron and grub-hoe are legendary of her, and it is an edifying sight to see the old bent Sister working hard in the garden with her heavenly cheerfulness."

Father Durieu was chosen as bishop over Father Fouquet because of his greater capacity for tact.

Concurrently with Sister Mary's arrival came Father Durieu, who assumed charge of the now self-sufficient mission. Durieu would go on to become bishop of New Westminster and a powerful advocate of Stalo interests.

It is difficult to assess the immediate impact of the Oblates upon the Stalo natives. In one sense, the missionaries greatly assisted with the health and land problems of the Indians, vaccinating regularly, and petitioning successive governors and officials. The Catholic missionaries shared essentially the same view as Douglas with respect to the value of a rudimentary practical and academic education in helping natives to cope with mainstream white society.

On the negative side, the Oblates did not advance Indian land ownership claims per se; they hastened the death of the Halkomelem language; and they separated children from their parents for long periods of time. In fact, many native children were traumatized by the forceful separation from their families, and many cringed under the rigid school discipline.

One effect of the white society's attempt to "civilize" the natives was the changing face of many Stalo villages. At Cheam, Chief Alexis ordered European style cabins built around the village church. His daughter, who had attended St. Mary's, taught day school in the village. Ironically, it was believed that the more isolated the village, the greater was the potential for natives to adopt healthy white lifestyles. Judge Begbie advised that Indians be "removed from the centres of white population and induced to devote themselves to agriculture and certain manufacturing arts."

Protestant missionaries such as the Reverend Sheepshanks and Ebenezer Robson made some native converts when they cruised the Fraser, preaching to tiny clusters of settlers who lived near Indian reserves. Robson founded a small Indian day school at Hope in 1861.

However, only the fiery Methodist Thomas Crosby seriously competed with the Oblates in the field. At Chilliwack, Crosby blazed away against the old Indian ways and forbade all native dancing. At his famous church revivals, Crosby obtained many converts, including Captain John, who supplemented his river pilotage income by farming.

Father Durieu was highly critical of the Methodist interlopers, accusing Crosby of having led the Indians astray by threats and false promises. One can speculate that the wild gesticulations of Methodist preachers at these revivals, accompanied by shrieking, groans, and the thumping of chests, impressed the natives as much as the colourful pageantry of the Catholics.

Against such competition, it is hardly surprising that the stoic Anglicans and other more traditional denominations experienced limited success among the valley Stalo.

Governor Seymour was as awed by the challenges of his new office as he was by the mountainous terrain. Roads were a major problem. The only two paths designated as roads in the colony's earliest days were the North Arm Trail and the North Road, both of them virtually impassable until 1871. In 1865, the Douglas Road was completed between New Westminster and Burrard Inlet. For a time a bayside resort, "New Brighton," on the site of the future port, was a popular tourist destination for the genteel of Stump City.

The Collins Overland Telegraph Co. announced the construction of a telegraph line to Europe via British Columbia, Alaska, and Siberia in 1865, following the failure of the first transAtlantic cable attempt. To accommodate the line, Seymour commissioned a sleigh road from tidewater to Yale, to be built 12 feet wide. The road used existing trails, such as the old Hudson's Bay route along the river from Fort Langley to Hope, joined near Chilliwack by the Whatcom Trail from the southwest. The route turned southeast beyond Matsqui in order to circumvent vast Sumas Lake, and skirted the border before turning northward for Chilliwack.

Governor Seymour was so keen on the project that he lent his own steam yacht to the crew laying cable under the Fraser, and personally took command of the vessel during the operations. In April 1865, the first message to leave the Fraser Valley by telegraph was sent to London by Seymour: "Weather beautiful. All well and Indians perfectly quiet."

The line was no sooner installed along the newly completed Telegraph Trail when the project was jettisoned in 1866, when a successful cable linkage with Europe was made via the Atlantic.

The earliest settler on Matsqui Prairie was John Maclure, a retired sapper, who helped survey for the telegraph line. Enthralled with the rich loamy soils and abundance of game, Maclure moved his family to Matsqui and established a farm. A telegraph station was built on his land, as the portion of line installed in the valley continued to function.

Maclure's twelve-year-old daughter Sara became so proficient at dispatching messages that eventually she was hired by the Eastern Union Telegraph Company as a permanent operator—the first woman telegrapher in the Pacific Northwest. Sara Maclure eventually married John McLagan and went on to become manageress of the *Vancouver World* newspaper, predecessor of the *Vancouver Sun*. At the age of 65, she returned to her telegraphing skills by volunteering for duty in World War One.

Travel along the Telegraph Trail remained hazardous. Bridges were rare. The Reverend Alexander Dunn recorded a typical wet horseback ride: "The horse, instead of cantering along easily, had to wade and tug and pull...When the streams were swollen by heavy rains it was necessary to draw one's legs onto the saddle, so as to prevent even long boots from getting filled."

The year 1866 began with both British Columbia and Vancouver Island facing bankruptcy. In May, the Bank of British Columbia curtailed loans to the mainland colony. Victoria residents petitioned for union with the mainland. British Columbia opposed, saying that Victoria had been a "parasite living off the economy of the mainland," since it profited greatly from the gold business, but as a free port of entry, no import duties were charged on goods in Victoria, but were levied on the mainland.

Governor Seymour waffled on the union question. The Colonial Office, however, had decided that amalgamation of the two colonies was necessary for the well-being and indeed survival of each, and the proclamation of union was issued simultaneously in Victoria and New Westminster on November 19, 1866.

If mainlanders were not enthusiastic, Victoria was furious, for the islanders now learned that the terms of the union eliminated their city's free port status and provided for a Legislative Council of twenty-three members, nine of whom could be elected, four from the Island and five from the mainland. But the most crushing blow was the announcement that New Westminster was to be the interim capital of the united colony.

New Westminster's place in the sun lasted a scant two years. Although Seymour possessed the power to designate the permanent capital on his own volition—and favoured Stump City—he naively allowed the Legislative Council to vote on the issue without instructing his appointed members on how to cast their vote. The result was that Victoria won the contest.

Believing that he might reverse matters, the governor ordered a second vote on the issue. The decision still favoured Victoria, and the governor dared not use his prerogative to override the councillors. The civil servants who comprised the majority of the council favoured Victoria because the city could provide them more perks and amenities than the stump town in the bush. In public, however, these men argued that the Fraser was unsafe for commerce, being full of sandbars, snags, and ice in winter.

After the results of the final vote on the capital were made known in New Westminster, an angry mob appeared outside of the hotel of Dr. Helmcken, a Victoria councillor. During the two years as capital of the united colony, New Westminster residents had found a new pride, and loudly proclaimed their centre as the "Royal City." Now, all of the bureaucrats and councillors packed their bags and scurried off to Victoria. Abandoned government buildings at Sapperton were turned over to a caretaker to avoid their occupation by Indians.

The timid and by now alcoholic Governor Seymour also fled to Victoria to escape the storm of protest. Finding his reception there cool, he returned to New Westminster and buried himself in booze and self-pity. The retired James Douglas railed at the governor's ineptitude: "The whole machine is in a strange incomprehensible muddle—wanting a firm and experienced hand to bring it into good working order."

The British Colonial Office agreed with Douglas. However, before they could recall Seymour, the governor managed to literally drink himself to death while touring the northern coast. The doctor aboard the naval vessel on which he travelled reported that, aware of Seymour's alcohol problem, he had attempted to keep liquor from the governor, but Seymour had succeeded in getting hold of a bottle of brandy and "drinking it off."

The press announced that Seymour died of dysentery. He was given a lavish state funeral in Victoria. Judge Howay gives us a fitting epitaph to the man: "A genial, pleasant gentleman, fond of good living, of society, and of social functions, but vacillating, lymphatic, procrastinating, anxious to do what was right, but lacking the firmness to carry it through."

Seymour's weakness was most pitifully displayed in his failure to further his predecessor's policies towards the Indians. Although strong on ceremony and outward manifestations of good will, he failed to prevent the withdrawal of native preemption rights in 1866. In February 1867, the truculent editor and councillor John Robson moved that the Lower Fraser reserves be "reduced to what is necessary for the actual use of the Natives."

Lands Commissioner Joseph Trutch agreed with Robson, reporting to the council: "The Indians really have no right to the lands they claim, nor are they of any actual value or utility to them; and I cannot see why they should either retain these lands to the prejudice of the general interests of the Colony, or be allowed to make a market of them either to government or to individuals."

Trutch himself was unabashedly racist in substance and tone, terming natives as "bestial rather than human; ugly and lazy; and lawless and violent." Yet he epitomized the attitude prevalent among many white settlers, who were adamant that Indian land claims not hinder agricultural development which was so badly needed by the colony.

Trutch received authority to reduce the size of Fraser Indian reserves, thereby opening up some 40,000 prime acres for white settlement. While he advocated the right of a white settler to purchase 480 acres additional to his preempted 160-acre plot, he expected an Indian family to subsist on a maximum of 10 acres.

The *Columbian* reported widespread satisfaction by the white settlers with Trutch's survey and slashing: "A proper appreciation of the importance of settlement and a becoming interest to consider the interests of the white settlers has characterized the survey...In one instance a reservation of six thousand acres has been reduced to about two thousand, and in no case has the re-adjustment of boundaries disturbed the property of whites."

The Stalo of the Fraser were dumbfounded. In 1868, the lower Fraser chiefs, with the assistance of Father Durieu, petitioned the government: "Some days ago came new men who told us that by order of their Chief they have to curtail our small reservations, and so they did to our greater grief; not only they shortened our land but by their new paper they set aside our best land, some of our gardens, and gave us in place, some hilly and sandy land, where it is next to impossible to raise any potatoes; our hearts are full of grief day and night."

The disbanding of the Royal Engineers, followed by the loss of its status as a capital, sapped the lifeblood of New Westminster. The entire town was riddled with tension, strife, and bickering during these unsettled times. The townspeople even fought over churches and cemeteries. When he was not complaining about Victoria, John Robson blamed urban Indians, prostitution, gambling, and the Chinese for the failure of the Royal City to prosper.

In 1859, Douglas had set aside land for the site of the first Anglican Church within the bounds of a public park. This act exposed him to charges of religious nepotism. When the Anglicans acquired their own cemetery, the New Westminster Council demanded and received a grant from the Crown of thirty-two acres for a "non-sectarian" graveyard on Douglas Road. However, Anglicans would not use the new cemetery unless granted exclusivity to one-quarter of it; Methodists, Catholics, and Presbyterians thereupon demanded the other quarter shares. When no such allocations were made, Anglicans boycotted the new cemetery, and the grounds became overgrown for lack of maintenance funds.

Rudi Dangelmaier painted this original Harrison Mills schoolhouse and teacher's residence. Built in 1884, it is now designated a Heritage Building by the BC government.

Worse still, the public site suffered from very poor drainage. Freshly dug graves often filled with water so quickly that someone would have to stand on the coffin to hold it down until it was covered with earth.

Public education did not legally arrive in New Westminster until the first Public School Act was proclaimed in 1869. Before that date, debate frequently reached the boiling point regarding the lack of public funds for schools and the sectarian nature of instruction, as the major churches sponsored most educational activity. Many parents struggled throughout the sixties to pay the ten shillings per child per month required, even though a government grant offset some of the cost.

The schoolhouse was described in 1864 as being "in an unsuitable location with a bog on one side and an Indian encampment on the other. In fact it is disgraceful that the only means of ingress and egress is through an Indian rancherie, redolent of salmon and associated with all the usual accompaniment of filth and vermin."

By 1870, government school grants had increased, sectarianism in the public schools was eliminated, and the New Westminster School District was reduced in size, excluding finally the Sapperton and Fort Langley schools. Leading citizens, such as Captain William Irving, headed fund-raising drives to assure teachers' salaries and improved facilities. It was not until 1872, however, that school funds were raised from general taxation and user fees eliminated.

The first courthouse in New Westminster consisted of one "small, low room with a canvas ceiling in an old wooden building with no ventilation or means of warming it." The first jail was a "miserable little rookery" in the middle of the business district. Overcrowding was rife, as all serious criminals from the mainland were housed here. Theft, assault and sale of liquor to Indians were the most frequent crimes committed. In 1869, the total number of prisoners jailed comprised 145 males and fifteen females. Indians were often jailed for drunkenness. Governor

Seymour commented in 1865 that "drunken squaws have for their own protection and the public decency been locked up until sobered."

A common sight on New Westminster streets during the sixties was the chain gang, consisting of groups of prisoners bound by chains and shackles, who were set to work on local improvement projects. While working on the cricket grounds in 1866, two prisoners escaped, stole an Indian canoe, and paddled down the Fraser, only to have their craft upset in midstream. Three Indians rescued them, only to have the convicts push them into the river.

Upon recapture, a convicted murderer named Mark Dunne broke free from his chains and made it all the way to the Fraser's mouth, where he was captured by a Musqueam chief and his sons. In the absence of militia and equipped with only one or two policemen, prison and civic authorities relied heavily upon the Stalo along the river to intercept escaping convicts and apprehend criminals at large.

The mentally ill were thrown indiscriminately into jail with the other prisoners, though contact was limited during the day, since the "insane" stayed indoors while the criminals worked on the chain gang. Conditions were atrocious. A grand jury reported in 1861: "...a white and a Chinese lunatic, who are so violent as to require irons and straight-jackets. No furniture or bedding of any sort can be kept in their cells—and they actually sit and sleep upon the bare floor and often wallow in their own filth. The white man is generally in a state of entire nudity, as he tears to shreds everything...These men are confined in our Jail, not for any crime, but simply on account of insanity...and from the absence of any accommodation for such cases are dying a lingering death."

In November 1861, Father Fouquet announced that in the absence of any public facility, he was going to open a hospital himself. Within a month of his declaration, two public meetings were hurriedly held, with the result that, through citizens banding together, raising funds, and enlisting a chain gang to work as a construction crew, the Royal Columbian Hospital was opened in 1862.

Fouquet was quietly amused. Having shamed the largely Protestant community into action, he graciously declared that he would abandon his own plans.

From 1862 to 1870, 355 patients from the Fraser Valley and the Interior were treated at the new hospital. Boxes were placed on riverboats for donations, and regular benefit concerts were held. Colonel Moody even donated all of the sapper camp's hospital inventory and equipment when the Engineers disbanded, as well as his own personal "large and valuable bath with pipes and fittings."

Patients at the hospital paid fifteen dollars a week—sailors being given a special rate of two dollars per day—and two doctors made daily rounds of the wards. The hospital was constantly in debt, despite the fund raisers, largely due to the smallness of government grants. Patients were regularly admitted suffering from knife or bullet wounds, attesting to the rigours and dangers of the frontier life. Regulations were strict respecting cleanliness, and patients, visitors, and nurses alike were prohibited from chewing or spitting tobacco.

Early standards of care, however, were somewhat primitive. One patient's chart reveals: "Admitted May 18. To have 3 oz. of port wine daily. July 6. To have beer instead of wine. July 24. Left hospital at own request. July 27. Readmitted. August 5. To have as much wine as he can take. August 8. Discharged dead."

The famous Hyack Volunteer Fire Brigade was organized at New Westminster in 1861. Hyack is a Chinook word meaning "quick." Brigade members wore red shirts, black trousers, and caps. The first fire engine was purchased in San Francisco and arrived in 1863; the horse drawn tank, known as Fire King, was lovingly hauled off the wharf by fifty-eight volunteer Hyacks, who were accompanied by an admiring crowd. When fire broke out at Sapperton the following year, the Hyacks established their reputation for efficiency: "In nine minutes from the time the leading ropes were taken hold of at Hyack Hall, a stream of water was playing on the burning buildings at the camp."

The growth of commerce in the Fraser Valley depended upon numerous institutions established at New Westminster during these colonial years. Aside from acting as the primary market for agricultural and other goods after the demise of the gold mines, the Royal City coordinated mail delivery, built a Land Registry Office serving the entire valley, held the first agricultural fair in 1867, and acted as the chief shipping point for export goods and produce.

The Bank of British Columbia operated in New Westminster until 1866, followed by the British Columbia Savings Bank in 1869—the latter being the only bank doing business in the colony at the time of Confederation. From 1866 onward, the Colonial Office recognized the American dollar and cent as the official currency for British Columbia, in place of the English pound and pence.

The principal newspaper on the mainland for many decades was the *Columbian*, also known for much of its history as the *British Columbian*, which reported on Fraser Valley events and issues from 1859 until its demise in 1983. The paper served as the key voice for the valley prior to the growth of community weekly newspapers. From 1861 to 1869, Robson managed the *Columbian*. When the seat of government moved in 1868, he swallowed his pride, packed his bags, and moved both his residence and press to Victoria—the "island Sodom" he had so often decried.

Finding the economic climate in that city almost as depressed as at New Westminster, Robson ceased publication after only four months and delivered a suitable epitaph: "We thank our friends, forgive our enemies, and die in peace." John Robson returned briefly to New Westminster in 1880, bought another small paper, *The Herald*, and published it as the *British Columbian* until 1883, when he once again returned to Victoria, leaving the paper in his brother's hands. He became premier of the province in 1889.

The lack of efficient transportation facilities caused farmers, who hauled produce to New Westminster, to stay over in the city for one or two nights before they set forth on the return journey with supplies for the homestead. In 1862, there were six hotels and boardinghouses along the main street, accommodating four hundred persons. The Oro Hotel advertised "meals at all hours;" the Mansion House boasted two bowling alleys; the New Westminster Boarding-House offered room and board at $8.50 per week to "parties furnishing their own bed."

The most popular hostelry of the day was the Colonial Hotel, established on Columbia Street in 1860. The Colonial offered a billiard saloon that was billed as being "superior to anything on the British Pacific." Most of the government's lavish dinners were held at this hotel; the menu for one such banquet in 1867 included turkey, tenderloin, calves' heads, lamb, chicken, ham, tongue, and six vegetables, all washed down with champagne, beer, and fine wines.

The Chinese community in New Westminster numbered twenty-six men and one woman in 1869. Most of the Orientals had arrived in search of gold, to service the miners with laundries and bakeries, or to perform assorted labouring, cooking, and other household services.

Local white opinion was distinctly hostile to the Chinese, as exemplified by one editor:

> "It is well known that of all the foreigners, the Chinaman is of the least benefit to the community. He comes here with the deliberate intention of making as much money and spending as little, as he conveniently can; with a very few exceptions, the Chinaman is a migratory animal. He never pre-empts land...John Chinaman is certainly a very peaceable and quiet personage, and seldom troubles a Court of Justice. But he is a pagan and an idolater...he never will amalgamate with the Anglo-Saxon races, and beyond

Advertisements in The *British Columbian*, September 6, 1862.

New Advertisements.

British Columbia
STAGE COMPANY.
(LIMITED.)

THE COMPANY'S STAGES, carrying Passengers and Express Freight, run regularly between

Douglas and Lillooet,

Leaving each Town every morning.

FINE GOODS are conveyed, with dispatch, over the route in Light Four-Horse Waggons.

For further information, apply to
STEWART, MELDRUM & CO., Victoria,
HENRY HOLBROOK, New Westminster,
and at the Company's Offices in Douglas and Lillooet.
se6 1m

In the Supreme Court of Civil Justice of British Columbia.

General Order.

I. From and after the date hereof, the Rules and Practice of all proceedings in this Court shall, as nearly as may be, conform to the rules and practice of the Superior Courts of Common Law and Equity in England, and any General Order of this Court inconsistent therewith is hereby discharged.

II. From and after the date hereof the fees hitherto charged shall be discontinued, and shall henceforth be charged at the same rate as in the Superior Courts of Common Law and Equity in England, with the exception of office copies of any Documents or Records which shall be chargeable at the rate of one shilling per folio.

III. Every appeal from a Gold Commissioner, and the proceedings thereon, shall, as to the Court Fees chargeable in respect thereof, be treated as the delivery of the record at Nisi Prius, in any action at Law, and the proceedings subsequent thereto.

MATT. B. BEGBIE, J.
Quesnelle Mouth, 25th July, 1862. se6 1m

Fruit Trees and Seeds
— FROM THE —
BALMORAL NURSERY,
SALT SPRING ISLAND.

THIS WELL-KNOWN NURSERY, situated within the Colony, will have ready for the market this fall an excellent assortment of Grafted Apple, Pear, Plum and Cherry Trees. Also, Gooseberries, Currants, Strawberries, Grapes, Garden Seeds, &c., &c., which will be sold at reasonable prices for Cash. J. Begg, from the Nursery, will be at New Westminster about the 1st of October next. with an assortment of Trees and Seeds, and orders left with Mr. W. J. Armstrong. New Westminster, will receive prompt attention. Send in orders early, so as to ensure a good variety.
August 18th, 1862. au26 3m

New Advertisements.

MACDONALD'S
UNION HOTEL.

THE PROPRIETOR has just enlarged and finished in good style the above House, and hopes by strict attention to business, and the comfort of guests, to merit a share of the travelling community.

Private Rooms
fitted up with all the
LATEST IMPROVEMENTS.
Douglas, B. C., August 12th, 1862. tc

J. A. WEBSTER.
——ooo——
NEW DRY GOODS
JUST RECEIVED.
——ooo——

SILKS, Poplins, Cashmeres, Be Reges, Organdies, Princettas, Lawns, Brilliantes, Mohairs, Madonnas, D'Laines, Worsted and Dress Goods of every description. A very large selection of

HOYLE'S ENGLISH PRINTS,

Cashmere, Chenille, Woolen and Tweed Scarfs and Square Shawls, Cloth, Tweed, Black and Colored Mantles, fashionable styles, Black Silk and Lace Mantillas, Penelope, Victoria and Eugenie Collars, Laces, Embroideries and Rufflings, all widths. An assortment of

Ladies', Gents', Miss's, and Children's
HOSIERY,

Habits, Lisle Thread, Silk, Kid and Fawn Gloves and Gauntlets, Damasks, Linens, Hollands, Towelings, Sheetings, Ticks, Shirtings, Flannels, in great variety.

Curtains and Curtain Fixtures.
——oooo——
EX "SPEEDY," FROM LONDON.

English Clothing,
Embracing Tweed Suits, Tweed and Cassimere Sack and Frock Coats, Tweed and Cassimere Pants and Vests, Alpacca, Silk and Mohair Coats, Linen Coats and Pants.

A LARGE INVOICE OF
ENGLISH STRAW HATS,
Garibaldi, white and colored, and Albert Mourning Hats, Felt and Cassimere Hats, late styles.
——oooo——

BOOTS & SHOES.

English Balmoral and Watertight Boots,
" Blucher and Oxford Shoes.
" Nail Napoleon Mining Boots,
" Riding Boots

New Advertisements.

BALLOU'S
EXPRESS,
ESTABLISHED JUNE, 1858,
CONNECTING WITH
Wells, Fargo & Co.,
AT VICTORIA,
FOR ALL PARTS OF THE WORLD,
AHEAD OF THE MAILS,

Conveying Goods, Wares, Merchandise of every description, Treasure, LETTERS, Parcels, Packages, &c., with unequalled dispatch, in charge of

Confidential & Experienced Messengers,
TO ALL PARTS OF
CARIBOO,
QUESNELLE, THOMPSON, AND FRASER RIVER MINES.
——oooo——

Having no Mails to delay us, we go to every Camp,
And Sell Papers, Deliver Letters, &c.
——oooo——

We buy Goods on Commission,
" Pay Duties and Advance Money,
" Do Custom House Brokerage,
" Receive and Tranship all kinds of Goods,
" Collect Money and Rents,
" Purchase Checks from Wells, Fargo & Co., and other Banking Houses,
" Do all required of General Agents and Common Carriers.
——ooo——

Owing to the enormous advance on Government Postage, we only add the same to our charges on Letters and Newspapers, less 10 per cent. to all points above New Westminster.
——oooo——

OFFICES.
WELLS, FARGO & CO., Victoria,
LIVERPOOL STREET, New Westminster,
B. C. STAGE CO'S. OFFICE, Douglas,
W. H. SUTTON, Hope,
H. NELSON, Yale,
W. H. WOODCOCK, Lillooet.

BALLOU & CO.
July 21st, 1862. jy23

COLONIAL HOTEL,

the furtherance of his individual interests, he has no care or desire for the prosperity of his temporary home."

Wild days of gambling, prostitution, and drunkenness were prevalent in the New Westminster of the sixties, though abating slightly by the end of the decade, when the patronage of the played-out prospectors wore thin. Residents complained about the constant rattle of billiard balls and the laughter from grog shops that was heard on Sundays. Chartres Brew and his meagre police force were overwhelmed by the incidence of drunkenness and whoring along the main street of the city. The latter problem was exacerbated by the dearth of white women in the young colony.

Typical democrat (buggy) of the early colonial period.

The British Columbia Female Emigration Society was formed in order to encourage "respectable, industrious women" to emigrate to the colony, where they were expected to provide matrimony for miners and settlers, to serve as domestic servants, and to generally smooth the coarser edges of frontier life.

The first group of these women arrived at Esquimalt from England in September 1862, an event awaited with great anticipation in both colonial capitals of the day:

"Although the time and place of disembarkation were shrouded in uncertainty...a continuous stream of humanity set in towards the point indicated, which very shortly resulted in every available inch of ground from which a view could be obtained being occupied by men of all ages and colours, eagerly looking for a sight of the long looked for and much talked about cargo...in the lot there are perhaps a few that might be called good-looking, yet, as a whole, they were neat and tidy. There are a few stout looking women among them, but the majority are slender, having the appearance of girls of from 12 to 15 years of age."

The young women found employment and husbands within days of landing.

The colony's gala social life centred around the governor's mansion, adjoining which was a well-manicured croquet lawn. At formal balls, an orchestra would be thrown together from the ranks of retired sapper band members, and guests would arrive in four-horse wagons and by steamer from Victoria. The dancing lasted until midnight, when a multi-course dinner was served; then more dancing ensued until 4:00 A.M.

The colour of these gatherings was dazzling, as the scarlet, blue and gold of various uniforms mingled with the finery of the ladies. The dress of one woman was described as "rich white silk over which was a tunic of white satin ribbon, pink roses covered with white net. In her hair were white water lilies and red coral; another lady wore a headdress of white geraniums."

The growth of towns was hampered during the sixties by the lack of industries, other than agriculture and a minor service sector.

A sawmill was founded in 1860 just below New Westminster by J.A. Homer. The mill boasted a capacity of 8,000 board feet a day, and for several years Homer's facility provided most of the lumber needs of the Fraser Valley. Many settlers who lived any distance from the Royal City, however, continued to cut and shape their own cabin and barn materials. During a three-month period in 1861, Homer shipped 300,000 board feet of lumber and 100,000 shingles to Victoria. By the late sixties, the centre of sawmilling activity had shifted to Burrard Inlet, where Moody's and Stamp's Mills employed three hundred men.

An early May Day celebration in New Westminster. The social élite never seemed to worry about the pagan origins of the annual rite.

The salmon canning industry was still in its infancy. A man named Annandale did establish a fishing station across from New Westminster in 1864, on the site of the ancient Kwantlen summer fishing village of Kikait. The business failed because the employee hired to develop the station used clumsy Scotch nets instead of drift nets.

The first salmon canning attempts were made in 1867 by James Symes, who displayed samples of his efforts that year at the Agricultural Exhibition. It is ironic, and not coincidental, that Indians were banned that year from participating in commercial salmon fishing.

A brief revival of salmon curing at Fort Langley occurred in 1864, when Ovid Allard was appointed chief clerk in charge of the post. Allard transported his family and effects down the river from Yale, happy to return to his old bailiwick. He immediately caused enough salmon to be cured to allow for a shipment to Hawaii, the first in many years.

Natives cleaning salmon at an early Fraser River cannery.

Now Allard's old trading skills came to the fore. The wily clerk easily competed with the commercial operators struggling along the river by purchasing salmon from the natives at ten cents each, then packing the fish in barrels built by Cromarty, the cooper, and shipping the product to Victoria and Hawaii on a regular basis until the end of the decade.

The first functional commercial cannery was established in 1870 by Alexander Loggie & Co., one of whose principals, Alexander Ewen, a New Westminster fishmonger for many years, is regarded as the father of British Columbia's salmon canning industry. The cannery was located at Annieville, about three miles below New Westminster. The facility operated in very primitive fashion. There was virtually no machinery; the fish were preserved in the cans by boiling in large wooden vats; the cooking room resembled a Turkish bathhouse. All work was performed by Chinese and Indian labourers. The men gutted, cleaned and cut the fish, while native women packed the product in the cans. Some four hundred half-barrels of salmon were exported by the cannery in 1871. Despite this production, a competitor emerged when Captain Stamp built his own facility at Sapperton.

Despite the temporary revival of the fishing industry at Fort Langley, Allard found himself presiding as a trustee of an estate that was being slowly dismantled. In 1870, he received orders to downscale the farm, and leased all of the land except for a twenty-acre plot retained as a Company garden. The Hudson's Bay store could not compete with the New Westminster shops, partly because it did not barter goods for produce of the farmers as did the hungry urban merchants. Even the elements combined to work against the fort, as the sandbanks accreted to such an extent along McMillan Island that ships could no longer anchor within four hundred yards of the wharf.

The silting problem produced two interesting consequences over one hundred years later when plans to build a dock for a replica of the *Beaver* had to be shelved because of the constant inflow of sand and mud. The accretion process affecting McMillan Island led to a lawsuit between the Langley Indians on the island reserve and the private owner of adjoining Brae Island. The judge apportioned the accreted land between the two parties.

Still, Allard managed to have a good enough time at the old fort. For years, he had been shunted about by both Yale and Douglas, and now he was in charge—he, who in 1841 could not even read or write. He no longer danced on the table as in the old days, but Allard enjoyed life; unlike Yale, he would put his feet up on his desk in the Big House and chat with all and sundry.

Allard's former assistant at Yale, William Yates, said of him: "He was another Canadian. The old fellow would drink and I could not stop him. He would come in the store and drink and give everybody fits. I had to send him out dozens of times, but he was an old servant of the Hudson's Bay."

Indeed, the Hudson's Bay Company could and usually did overlook the excesses of its servant if that man was a valuable, efficient officer. Allard was placed in charge because his thrifty employer knew that he would do the job.

For over fifty years following the birth of British Columbia, the steamboat represented the key to commerce in the Fraser Valley. A few deep-water vessels travelled to New Westminster to load cargo for export, but the steamboat ferried the miners, settlers, tourists, and provisions between Hope and Victoria. The first vessels were the Hudson's Bay-owned *Beaver* and *Otter*, the latter operating on the Fraser until 1862.

But these craft were soon supplanted. Scottish-born Captain William Irving arrived from Oregon in 1858, and immediately formed a company which built the *Governor Douglas* and the *Colonel Moody*, both sternwheelers. Other steamboats were built by rival companies. Other than the *Surprise* and the *Umatilla*, American-owned vessels failed to penetrate to Hope, and after the 1858 gold rush only British-owned steamboats prevailed along the Fraser.

Competition between steamboat companies was fierce; accidents frequent. Boilers were often shoddily built, inspections rare, and captains were daring to the point of recklessness. Unsafe channels were plied in the hope of slashing a few minutes off the journey time, while safety valves were frequently tied down.

By 1871, four vessels had been destroyed by explosions. Norman Hacking describes the prevailing philosophy of steamboating:

> "The disasters were met with philosophy. The casualties were counted—Indians and Chinese not included. The dead were buried if enough remains could be found, and the incident was written off as an act of God. Explosions were considered one of the natural perils of navigation. If the timid wayfarer did not like them, he could stay at home."

The debut of the sternwheeler on the Fraser heralded an era of romance. One early settler recalls: "To me, a sternwheeler slapping her way through white rapids, spray cascading from bow and paddlewheel, steam and smoke belching skyward in great swirls of black and white, was a picture that once seen was never forgotten."

The typical sternwheeler contained three decks. The upper deck housed the pilothouse and officers' quarters. The middle or cabin deck accommodated

The first snagboat sternwheeler on the Fraser, *Samson*. The vessel cleared hazardous logs and debris from the river channel.

passenger cabins, dining room, and lounge. The main deck contained the engine room, boiler, fire box, cargo area, and kitchen. Some steamers were elegant and painted bright white with polished copper; others were derided as being nothing more than "floating packing crates." Stacks of firewood were depleted so quickly by the fuel-hungry engine that unless woodcutters were aboard, passengers had to jump ashore at intervals and take to the woods with axes in hand.

Speed was everything. A fast boat's reputation was worth extra fare in good times, when desperate miners fought to reach the diggings ahead of their mates. One trip from Victoria to Hope could net twenty-five thousand dollars for the vessel's owners.

Every device and ruse was used in Victoria by the steamboat companies to induce passengers to board their vessels—including the voice of jolly John Butts, the town crier. He would run madly about the city streets announcing the imminent departure of a vessel, always ending his message with a hoarsely sung rendition of "God Save The Queen." When Butts one day rather tipsily shouted "God save John Butts," he was promptly thrown in jail.

River hazards played havoc with the nerves of passengers, as recorded by R.C. Mayne:

> "Struggling up the river against the stream, the greatest risk comes from the overcharged boilers giving way; but tearing down the current at 12 or 14 knots, bumping over shoals, striking against snags, and shooting rapids, is far mor animated work...Upon one occasion when I was going up the river in the *Enterprise*, no less than 3 times after we had struggled past the snag, the strong current caught and swung us broadside across the stream; and it was only by running the vessel's bow into the muddy bank without a

moment's hesitation and holding her there by the nose...that we escaped impalement."

The typical steamboat captain was imperturbable and, of necessity, not a little eccentric. One captain ordered a cask of bacon poured on the boiler fire in order to obtain enough steam to overcome a fearsome rapid. The challenge of the river was met with courage and cool reactions, as Mayne attests:

"There was something very exciting in this struggle between the forces of steam and water. Each time, as we hung by the bank, the engineer might be heard below freshening his fires, and getting up as much steam as the boilers could—or might not—bear for the next effort...Nor is the composure with which the captain meets and remedies an accident less remarkable. A supply of tarred blankets is always kept handy for service, and if a hole is stove in the steamer's bottom, the captain cooly runs her ashore... jams as many blankets into the crevice as seems necessary, nails down a few boards over them, and continues his journey composedly."

The sternwheeler *Maria* joined William Irving's fleet in 1860 and was captained by Tim Wright. In January 1861, the vessel proceeded up the Fraser from Fort Langley, bound for Hope with a load of freight and over two hundred passengers. Encountering thick ice floes in a roaring gale, Captain Wright ordered all of the passengers below decks to stabilize the boat. But the *Maria* kept losing headway against the wind and twirled madly about in the current.

"Blow 'er up!" the captain exclaimed to his engineer, "Blow 'er up!"

The river pilot, a Kanaka named Nahu, warned Captain Wright against proceeding further, but the obstinate skipper just bellowed for more steam.

Below Mission, the *Maria* became firmly stuck in the thick ice. Night fell, and the passengers shivered in the cold. Food was scarce; children cried; many adults panicked. When morning dawned, the passengers looked out upon a frozen wilderness, with visibility limited by a driving blizzard.

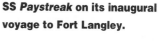

SS *Paystreak* on its inaugural voyage to Fort Langley.

Ignoring remonstrances from Captain Wright, the passengers began a rush to shore across the ice. One group headed for the north bank and the other to the southern shore. Mrs. Nahu, daughter of a Stalo chief, was ordered by Captain Wright to stay aboard the vessel; defying him, she coolly snatched a box lunch from the steward, strapped her six–year-old daughter to her back, and disembarked.

Mrs. Nahu crunched through the foot-deep snow on the south shore, following old Indian trails. She could hear the bedlam of confused cries in the woods from passengers hopelessly lost, and shuddered at the anguish of the women and children; yet she knew that the only chance to save many of the passengers lay with her; she must reach Fort Langley and summon help.

All day and well into the evening, Mrs. Nahu trudged wearily along, her progress hindered by fallen trees, deep holes, and swirling snow. Exhausted, barely able to crawl her way along, she finally reached the palisade of the old fort around midnight. Her child's cries awakened the sleeping watchman. William Newton was aroused, and upon hearing Mrs. Nahu's story, he immediately dispatched two clerks and twelve Indians, all of them bearing backpacks of hastily gathered food.

It took almost two days for the men of the fort to reach the *Maria*. They found Captain Wright in some nearby woods searching for passengers, many of whom had arrived back on the sternwheeler in a famished and demoralized condition. The searchers themselves found dozens of people in the forest, as well as clothing strewn about, blankets, carpet bags—and corpses. More than fifty passengers froze to death, and most bodies were never recovered. But Mrs. Nahu's arduous trek saved the lives of a great percentage of the travellers, who were led back to safety at Fort Langley.

On the evening of April 14, 1861, Captain William Irving was himself a passenger on a rival steamer, the *Fort Yale*, which had just left Hope, bound for Yale. When dinner was called, Irving offered to take the helm for Smith Jamieson, the steamer's master.

"No you don't," jested Jamieson, "no opposition captain will steer my boat."

Irving laughingly withdrew to the diningroom, but he had no sooner sat down when there was heard a fearsome crash "like the ring of a heavy blow on a huge Chinese gong." Suddenly the deck above collapsed onto the dining area. Splinters and glass flew in all directions. Irving crawled through the debris with several other passengers, cut and bleeding, and emerged above to behold a chaotic scene.

The pilothouse and boiler had disappeared. In the river floated firewood, boards, trunks, and injured men. Two crewmen had been blown high into the air by the force of the explosion, one of these men being thrown ashore naked, the blast having ripped the clothes from his body. A ninety-pound piece of boiler iron was found four hundred yards from the vessel, and other fragments were located half a mile away on the river bank.

The SS *Ramona* was a popular sternwheeler serving the Fraser Valley.

Within twenty minutes of the explosion, Indians arrived in canoes and removed the survivors from the sternwheeler. Captain Irving and a Ballou Express agent, H. Lee Alley, remained aboard to try and beach the steamer at Hope. After several attempts, the two men gave up, were pulled ashore, and the blackened *Fort Yale* was allowed to drift down the Fraser to a sand bar, where it grounded hard. The top of the hulk's pilothouse and the steering wheel were both found by Indians near the Harrison River.

A jury later found that the explosion had been caused by defective boiler plating and low water levels in the device. The engineer had been deceived in thinking the water level was sufficiently high because of the presence of foam caused by corn meal which someone had thrown into the boiler to plug leaks.

Other notable steamers on the Fraser during the sixties included the *Enterprise*, a sidewheeler owned by the Hudson's Bay Company, which replaced the *Otter* in 1862; Captain Irving's *Reliance*, which drew only twelve inches of water and offered a "large and airy main saloon and fine ladies' cabin;" and the *Onward*, which was commanded by William Irving's son, John. The *Onward* was one of the finest paddlewheelers ever built; measuring 120 feet in length and boasting twenty-one state-rooms, the vessel was truly state of the art.

In the year 1866, only four steamers remained on the Fraser: the *Onward* and *Reliance* owned by Irving, and the *Lillooet* and *Hope* owned by Captain Fleming. The *Enterprise* journeyed from Victoria to New Westminster on a weekly basis. By 1870, only Irving survived. The erstwhile mariner and businessman became president of New Westminster's first city council as a leading citizen, and when he died, all business in the Royal City halted for his funeral.

John Irving carried on the family tradition, buying out the Hudson's Bay Company line of ships in 1883, and founding the Canadian Pacific Navigation Company—which was later sold to the Canadian Pacific Steamship Company.

The younger Irving stood well over six feet tall, was known for his business acumen, and was popularly hailed as a "two-fisted fighter, a great social favourite, a mighty drinker—and the soul of generosity."

He was also superstitious. It was believed by many that it was unlucky for a ship to carry a grey horse and a parson. One day, Irving docked his steamer at Chilliwack. A clergyman waiting patiently on shore tried unsuccessfully to board the vessel, being curtly told by Irving that, as he carried a grey horse aboard, the man would have to wait for another boat. Passengers covered their ears in disgust as the vessel pulled away amidst a flurry of epithets and oaths from the enraged man of the cloth.

The year 1868 dealt a triple blow to many residents of the Fraser Valley. The capital was moved to Victoria; Indians saw their reserves shrink drastically in size; and the Great Fire, in October, destroyed a considerable percentage of the forests and farms. The origin of the fire is unknown, but the flames were driven southward along a broad front by gale force winds which sent blazing chunks of cedar bark spiralling through the air. The deadly conflagration crossed the international boundary and spread as far south as the Columbia River Valley. At night, Victoria residents gazed incredulously toward the mainland at a vivid glow which, as with a thick pall of smoke visible in daylight, persisted for several weeks.

The fire wreaked devastation upon valley residents. Telegraph service was severed. Steamboats ceased to operate. New Westminster was lost in a smoky cloud for several days. Indians and whites alike lost huge crops of potatoes. The *Columbian* reported: "In the Sumas and Chilliwack settlements, fences and hay to a considerable extent have been destroyed, and we hear that James Codville lost some 75 tons of hay, together with houses and nearly everything he possessed."

When the flames approached Matsqui, John Maclure was repairing the telegraph line in Langley with an Indian named Supple Jack. Just before the line was severed for the second time, Maclure's daughter Sara reached him with the message to return home at once, and the two men canoed anxiously up the Fraser. They arrived to find the family safe. For many years, however, settlement in Matsqui, Langley, and Chilliwack was impeded by charred fallen timber and matted undergrowth left in the Great Fire's wake, a factor which induced many early landowners to live in New Westminster, rather than settle on the land.

Confederation with Canada was accepted by Fraser Valley residents with a gentle sigh of relief. Since the Indians were never asked, because the franchise then was limited at the time to white male residents living in the area for over three months, the decision in the valley was made by the approximately nine hundred male white residents who clustered along the Fraser.

Guard of Honour at opening of Parliament in front of old parliament building, 1870.

The decision was made somewhat easier by Ottawa's offer to assume all of the depressed colony's debt; to provide equalization payments, and—best of all—to build a transcontinental railroad. John Robson favoured union, and it was he who represented the Fraser Valley as elected member from 1866 to 1870. Seymour's successor, Governor Musgrave, referred to Confederation as a whiff of hope that penetrated the Royal City's "ghost town atmosphere."

The year 1870 portended change. When the Yale Convention met to vote on the Confederation issue, the Fraser Valley was more heavily represented than any other area of the mainland.

Two factors were of prime concern to valley delegates at the table. Firstly, residents feared that without union with Canada, Victoria would dominate the mainland. Ovid Allard even sponsored a resolution at a big Langley meeting to petition the governor for protection from the "unbounded cupidity" of Victoria; there existed, in fact, much popular sentiment favouring secession from the union with Vancouver Island. Secondly, settlers hoped that Confederation might vastly improve the market for agriculture. The promised railway would not only link the province to eastern markets, but would likely precipitate increased settlement, thus creating a more viable local economy.

The first May Queen was crowned in 1870 at New Westminster—seated on a fire engine and drawn along by four horses to the Sapperton cricket field. The year also witnessed the close of an era, when the legendary Judge Begbie moved from the Royal City to Victoria in order to assume duties as chief justice of the new province. Begbie had lived in New Westminster for over ten years, though he was frequently absent on his hinterland circuits. He enjoyed staying at the Colonial Hotel more than his own home on the hill, for he could partake of breakfast, dinner and a bottle of claret for $2.50 a day at the hotel, with a room thrown in.

Judge Begbie was an excellent raconteur. He detested formal attire, however, objecting frequently to having to wear a dress suit at official dinners. The judge played Blind Man's Bluff at banquets, sang songs with women for charity, and played whist avidly. One New Year's Day he was present for official festivities at the crudely appointed New Westminster council chamber.

The occasion was described by a participant:

> "Our Council chamber was a large wooden building like a big barn with one American stove at one end, and it was bitterly cold. Our grand supper was all ice, chickens like rocks, jellies you could only break with a hammer, champagne bursting in bottles...We danced in our greatcoats and icicles hung from our hair...."

His bones aching from years of riding about his judicial domain in the saddle, Begbie was glad to move to the greener pastures of Victoria's gentility. He spent the remainder of his life in the capital.

Confederation was proclaimed at New Westminster with great fanfare and "flags of every shape and nationality floated from every possible pole." Royal salutes were fired by the Seymour Artillery and Volunteer Rifles, while sports activities were held at the cricket grounds, followed by a grand ball in the evening.

It is not recorded whether any Indians were present for the celebrations, but they would not have been happy to learn of the appointment of the racist, truculent Joseph Trutch as the province's first lieutenant governor.

In a mere thirteen years, the British Columbia mainland had changed from a private fur preserve to a colony, and then to a province. But the patriarch of the Fraser Valley fur and salmon trade did not live to see Confederation ushered in. James Murray Yale died in Victoria on May 7, 1871, alone and forgotten. His fort on the Fraser remained, an anachronism which reminded the toiling settlers of another age.

CHAPTER NINE

STRUGGLES OF THE SOIL

The white population of the Fraser Valley in 1871 was tallied at 1,300 persons, of whom about 400 were women and girls. Some 286 farmers cultivated 1,200 acres, in addition to pasturelands which supported 235 horses, 4,000 head of cattle, 2,000 pigs, and 22 sheep.

The formation of the Agricultural Institute in 1870 represented a determined attempt by valley farmers to promote agriculture as the key element in the future of a province which had hitherto been dependent upon gold. Settlers, such as Jonathan Reece, the Kipp brothers, Sam Robertson, and the Ladners, gave strong leadership and impetus to the Institute's activities.

One immediate effect of Confederation was a great increase in land sales in the valley. The years 1871 to 1875, in particular, witnessed the arrival of many new settlers to homestead. By 1877, the entire valley had been comprehensively surveyed into six-mile-square townships, subdivided into thirty-six sections. Railway surveying was also conducted and provided employment for several Royal Engineers, including John Maclure.

By mid-decade, however, there was widespread doubt as to Ottawa's commitment to build the railroad through to British Columbia. This caused the rate of settlement to slacken considerably. For the nine-year period of 1875 to 1884, settlers toiled simply to survive, isolated as they were from major markets for their produce. The Reverend Alexander Dunn, an early Presbyterian minister living in Langley in the seventies, commented that "many of the settlers around me would have given much to have been in a position to leave the country."

The provincial government sought to aid the stagnant rural economy by

First you had to get rid of the trees. Two hand-fallers pose on their springboards.

passing the Free Grant Act in 1874, providing free grants of up to 250 acres of unsurveyed land. To discourage speculation, the applicant was required to declare by affidavit that the land was to be for his own purposes of settlement and cultivation, and for no other use. The applicant would be issued a grant subject to twenty acres being cultivated, and a house being built within three years of application.

The 1874 act was disallowed by Ottawa for failure to adequately define "Crown Lands" and also for neglecting to take into account Indian reserves. A revised act was passed in 1875 to remedy these deficiencies.

The government was so anxious to secure settlers that it allowed the applicant to be absent from his land for more than six months of the year, so long as the land was cultivated. The free grant system was terminated in 1879, by which time 343 parcels had been homesteaded and the requisite improvements made. By this date, the most desirable Crown lands available had been set aside for the railway belt and the grant system was viewed as largely a failure.

Despite a near empty treasury, Victoria began a programme of significant road improvements in 1871. The Semiahmoo Road was upgraded from a trail to a crude road allowance in 1872 with the help of New Westminster citizens, who raised one thousand dollars for the project in the hope that it would encourage settlement. The Scott Road replaced the old Kennedy Trail in Surrey.

The key route adopted through the valley, however, was the Old Yale Road. Built in 1874, the Old Yale Road was first known as the New Westminster and Hope Wagon Road, and stretched from South Westminster all the way to Yale. This road was built well back of the tiny riverfront communities and south of the Telegraph Trail (which was now impassable), in order to provide access to the valley's southern hinterland. The Ladner Trunk Road was also built at this time to connect the Delta and Richmond areas with Hope.

The Old Yale Road was for many years the only land route connecting Fraser Valley communities.

All these projects were premature. The slashing of a route through many areas was expensive and impractical unless traffic substantially increased—which it failed to do until the late 1880s.

One tough area to penetrate was the Green Timbers, a tract of magnificent first growth firs and cedars in Surrey, which rivalled today's Carmanah Valley giants. Corduroy and planking methods were utilized, and in the swampy areas two parallel ditches were dug and soil placed between them to make a roadbed. Gravel was used for the first time on a Langley portion of the Old Yale Road.

The roads were only passable in summer and early fall. Wagons were not used extensively in this era; rather, horses, oxen and sleds, and even the occasional hayrake were used for transport. As most settlers lived near the Fraser or its feeder streams, the canoe remained the preferred mode of travel. The odd stagecoach traversed the roads, but it was not until 1884 that the demand for better transportation facilities arose, when a regular ferry service was established between Surrey and New Westminster. Farmers, tired of battling the Fraser's treacherous currents in their own small craft, scrambled to obtain wagons and teams to haul their goods to the ferry and thence to market.

Land rights became a heightened priority for natives after Confederation for two reasons. Firstly, white encroachment upon the best lands, including reserve territory, threatened to deprive Indians of the means to regain self-sufficiency. Secondly, the provincial government was viewed as being recalcitrant in meeting the needs of particular reserves. Confederation terms had conferred jurisdiction over Indian matters to the federal government, with the caveat that Indian policy continue to be "as liberal as that hitherto pursued by the British Columbia government." The problem was that, under Trutch and successive premiers, there was nothing at all liberal about Victoria's reserve policy.

Dr. Israel Powell, a Victoria physician, was appointed by Ottawa in 1872 as Indian Agent for British Columbia. Dr. Powell immediately set about creation of

Indian agencies in each area of the province and tackled the problem of creating enlarged reserves, pointing out that many reserves did not even contain five acres of land per family—hardly enough to raise crops economically. At Musqueam, for example, he found that although there were some seventy families living on the reserve, only 314 acres in total were allotted, of which 114 acres were quite useless. Ottawa decided that eighty acres per family should be the standard - but Victoria countered with the old ten-acre maximum policy. Stalemate on the question prevailed for many years.

The Oblates in the Fraser Valley played a central role in spurring on the Stalo natives to demand larger reserves. At the Queen's birthday celebrations in New Westminster in 1873, Father Durieu marched two thousand Indians down to the wharf to greet Dr. Powell, who had barely stepped off the gangplank when accosted by an Indian chief. The chief harangued the commissioner eloquently about reserve size and the lack of compensation for lands taken. Powell assured the chief that he intended to protect native rights. The St. Mary's Brass Band then played a few selections, following which Durieu bade the Indians to disperse. The priest then grabbed Powell by the arm and literally yanked him back aboard the steamer, where he pleaded that Indian land claims be resolved, before the entire Fraser Valley was fully settled by whites.

The following year, Chiefs Peter Yessik of Hope and Alexis of Cheam combined with 108 other tribal leaders from the valley to present another petition to Dr. Powell, pointing out that if Ottawa's goal was to make Indians into farmers, then Indians required as much land as whites for the purpose. "We are not a lazy and roaming-about people," they pleaded, but they felt "like men trampled on, and are commencing to believe that the aim of the white men is to exterminate us as soon as they can."

In fact, during the 1870s natives began to fully grasp the concept of land as a valuable commodity. One effect of this was a virtual abandonment of Fraser Canyon villages. Indians by the hundreds moved to the Hope area, and further down into the valley. In 1879, Seabird Island was set aside as a special Indian agricultural reserve accommodating natives between Popkum and Yale.

Even when a new reserve was established or lands promised, the Indians risked losing existing territory within the reserve if sufficient pressure was exerted by white settlers. In one incident, several whites encamped on Seabird Island itself, hoping that the government would allow them a preemption. It took the strenuous intervention of Indian agency authorities to drive the squatters away.

In 1874, Governor-General Lord Dufferin visited many Indian communities in the province. In Victoria, he criticized the provincial government in less than subtle tones, stating that "we must all admit that the condition of the Indian question in British Columbia is not satisfactory. Most unfortunately, as I think, there has been an initial error ever since Sir James Douglas quitted office...of British Columbia neglecting to recognize what is known as Indian title."

At the time, the Langley natives on McMillan Island were furious over the fact that several tracts of land promised to them had not been transferred, including some 240 acres along the Stave River. The situation became urgent when loggers began harvesting timber on the territory.

Hearing that Lord Dufferin was visiting Hope, the Langley natives gathered in canoes and paddled furiously up the Fraser through the night in one vast flotilla. They arrived just as the governor-general was about to leave; yet he lingered behind and gave them a sympathetic hearing. Lord Dufferin advised that upon his return to Ottawa, he would instruct that the conveyance of the Stave lands be expedited.

Eventually, the band received 1,100 acres of land—the total landholdings of Whattlekainum's proud Kwantlen nation, at one time the most populous Stalo tribe in the Valley.

Father Durieu became Oblate bishop for the province in 1875, succeeding Bishop D'Herbomez. He was chosen over Father Fouquet because he was viewed as possessing the same intense commitment to Indian interests, without appearing fanatical. In other words, Durieu was a more subtle political animal. The Durieu System, which emerged from his leadership, was most effectively employed in the Fraser Valley, and involved an attempt to create a state within a state by the establishment of a separate but theocratic Indian nation.

The Oblates incorporated traditional hierarchies and created some new ones for this ambitious purpose. Watchmen, chanters, village chiefs and councils were all linked with the reserve church. Law and order matters were handled internally. Traditional Indian practices and relationships were maintained—including domestic relations, marriage, and gift-giving. Potlatches were banned, but feasts could still be held for status purposes. Community law consisted of church precepts, bylaws passed by native councils, the Indian Act, and laws of the nation - provided that the secular state's laws did not conflict with church doctrine. Indian courts were regularly held, with the chief acting as judge, unless a priest wanted to preside. Punishment varied with the crime, and included the lash, fasting, fines, and community service.

For over forty years, the Durieu System exercised a major influence upon Indians and the preservation of their identity. Although stressing enlargement of reserves, rather than compensation on the basis of Indian title, the missionaries now acted as a powerful force in opposing the objectives of both provincial and federal governments to have Indians gradually "abandon their reserves and their special status and disappear into the general population."

Key features of federal Indian legislation passed in the 1870s included the requirement that only registered Indians be allowed to live and be buried on reserves; voluntary relinquishment of Indian status was permitted; and the right to vote and become a full British subject was denied to registered natives.

The Reverend Alexander Dunn arrived in the Langley area to live and preach in 1875. He became the foremost Protestant minister in the Fraser Valley. For over thirty years, Dunn established an incredible record of service to numerous far-flung settlements in the valley, galloping his horse about in all manner of weather. For many years, he rode thirty-three miles from Langley to Sumas every third Saturday in order to preach Sunday morning—and seldom met any travellers along the way. On alternate Saturdays, he rode to Ladner.

Dunn found the Langley settlers of his congregation to be outwardly rough and brash, but inwardly decent:

"When all were seated, they presented a very respectable appearance, though the garments of some were hardly fashionable or up to date. As I looked around, the upturned countenances bore an expression of seriousness and intelligence. Subsequent acquaintance with these men, through many years, confirmed my first impressions. Lacking it may be in outward polish, blunt and outspoken, as most old-timers were, they were warm-hearted, sterling characters."

The Presbyterian minister did, however, admonish pallbearers he met on a road one day, who were talking and laughing uproariously, telling them that they jabbered as if they were on their way to market.

There were only two pipe organs in the entire Fraser Valley until the 1880s. Churches were few and plain, with backless cedar benches for pews. Men and women wore gum boots to church year round due to weather and poverty. The church building served as a place of worship, as a school, and as a meeting place. For many years, different denominations shared the same building and even the same minister. Steveston's Opera House served Methodists, Anglicans, and Baptists.

The Rev. Alexander and Mrs. Dunn.

A bizarre problem arose when Anglican Bishop Sillitoe preached to a mixed congregation. The bishop was frustrated that the worshippers all knelt differently during prayer; indeed, some refused to kneel at all. Each sect's desire to preserve some measure of identity no doubt contributed an element of rivalry to these differences.

Methodists, who probably felt that as bishop Sillitoe carried out his duties with greater pomp and ceremony than they could stomach, knelt with their backs to the pulpit. Sillitoe could stand it no longer, and one day he diverged from his sermon to express his displeasure in a most caustic manner. But the Methodists kept on kneeling the other way!

The isolation of valley-dwellers during the 1870s affected the Reverend Dunn and others keenly. "What struck me very forcibly," he wrote, "was the overwhelming stillness and solitude. Immense fir

Clearing land near Chilliwack, 1880s.

trees stood within a short distance of the dwelling. The underbrush was densely thick. Pestilential mosquitoes were there in myriads. Seldom was a breath of wind felt. A whole week might come and go without seeing a traveller pass. When the short dark days of November came, with long continued rains, the picture of desolation and isolation was complete."

The compensations of such a life were the beauty of the land and the hospitality of its people. From Hope to Delta, most settlers either knew one another personally or knew of the other. Ironically, when transportation finally improved in the 1880s, this would no longer be the case.

The interdependence among households was profound. From borrowing food, medicine, and tools to helping a distant neighbour build a barn at a raising bee, settlers regarded each other with mutual respect and often affection. Fortunately, they tended to be a healthy lot, for there were no doctors from New Westminster to Hope in this period, and the Reverend Dunn is said to have conducted only two funerals during his first ten years of service.

The pioneers created their own pleasures and pastimes. Hunting and fishing were popular and served a dual purpose, the toiling farmer often needing an excuse to break away from work in the fields. Women attended quilting sessions. Very amateur concerts were held in church halls. Most popular of all, settlers loved to sit at a neighbour's table over a cup of coffee or a bottle of rum; or dance in the kitchen to the tune of a squeaky fiddle.

Women of the era acted as mid-wives in a pinch; and if a neighbour's house burned down, without hesitation the settlers in the district would help feed, clothe, and shelter the unfortunate family—and drop everything to work at erecting a new home. An early Glen Valley resident, Beulah Probert, relates, "In those days you were never alone. Your joys and sorrows, they were there to share them with you."

These early settlers were typically tough and decisive, yet warm-hearted, and often very eccentric. Isolation was sought by some, especially confirmed bachelors—of which there were many—for they could live as they wished, unbothered by the constraints of society. Alben Hawkins arrived as the first settler in Mount Lehman in 1874, where he homesteaded acreage which included both hill and lowland on Matsqui Prairie. A sample of his diary entries from 1874 provides a sketch of his life:

> "Paid $10 for oxen at Langley. Commenced ploughing. Logging back of shanty. Planted 25 lbs. of early Rose potatoes...Salted cattle in evening. Harrowing all day. Got 16 lbs. of bacon from Swords. Borrowed boat to go to Mission for supplies...Put up fence; splitting rails and 500 shakes...To Swords loan of block and tackle; killed heifer; cut up and salted beef—took some to neighbours; surveyors camping along river...Indian Charley and Supple Jack called."

Even a loan of two tobacco sticks was carefully recorded by Hawkins—and faithfully repaid.

In 1872, only 200 of some 470 eligible children were in school. Aside from the New Westminster public and private schools, there were schools at Fort Langley, Sumas, Chilliwack, and Hope. The St. Mary's Mission school served Indians and children of mixed blood.

The Public Schools Act of 1872 established for the first time a centralized, free public school system for the province, with school districts being designated wherever there lived a minimum of fifteen children aged five to fifteen years. A grant would be made toward construction costs and the teacher's salary, while the elected three-man school boards were to administer funds, raise money for maintenance and supplies, and ensure the proper conduct of the schools. The boards had no power, however, to hire or fire the teachers.

Early schoolhouse at Huntingdon.

The first superintendent of schools for British Columbia was John Jessop, a former New Westminster printer who had also tried his luck in the Cariboo gold fields. Jessop was a strong exponent of Ryerson's ideas on public education. In 1872, he set forth on a tour of inspection of every school in the province, visiting Langley on June 12, where he observed:

> "No school since last month—the late teacher as anxious to leave as the settlers are that he should do so—thought it better not to institute an investigation into the late difficulties, but to recommend the removal of Mr. Kennedy. Travelled over the district on both sides of the Fraser—No possibility of reopening school till August on account of mosquitoes. School house in very good order with comfortable dwelling attached; but no maps or blackboard—good well with pump in it, put there by late teacher and should be paid for—About 40 children in the district. Returned to New

Westminster by canoe."

A poll tax was introduced in 1876 to help defray the cost of teacher salaries. Each male resident over eighteen years of age was assessed $3.00 per year. Little revenue reached the teachers from this scheme, as the average salary was $63.10 a month in 1872 and $59.61 a month in 1890.

Schoolhouses were of wood frame construction, heated by stoves, and very rustic. Furniture consisted of crude benches, and there was often no blackboard. Each school was supplied with maps, a globe, and textbooks to be sold to the parents. Spelling, grammar, geography, arithmetic, British history, algebra, and bookkeeping were taught; and the reading books for the 1870s were known as the "Canadian Readers"—the First Reader costing five cents and the Fifth Reader, sixty cents.

The St. Mary's Mission school broadened its curriculum in the 1870s to include geography and history. Much emphasis continued to be placed upon agricultural skills for the boys and home economics for the girls. One teacher, Father Gendre, visited homes on reserves throughout the valley in order to gain a better insight into disciplinary techniques. The reward and title system worked well. Students were given many trinkets and bestowed with titles such as Captain of the Pots and Pans and Captain of the Tools. Children learned their catechism, were baptized, sang hymns, and learned to serve Mass.

The St. Mary's Mission Boys' Band attained a lasting reputation throughout the province.

Music became a key instrument in the teaching of the missionary school. Thomas Crosby had noted earlier: "Indeed, these people are naturally very musical, and in their heathen state were passionately fond of singing their own native melodies."

The Boys' Brass Band appeared annually at the Queen's Birthday on May 24 and at other celebrations. Later, reed instruments were added and the band toured the province for many years giving recitals—even entertaining at various Canadian Pacific Railway construction camps in the 1880s.

The federal Indian Commissioner visited St. Mary's in 1875 and was astounded by the school's progress:

> "At the time of my visit there were 32 girls attending the school and 22 boys, all of whom passed a very creditable examination in reading, writing, grammar, geography, arithmetic...The girls exhibited some very fine specimens of their needle and knitted work...The boys have a brass band of their own, numbering 16 instruments ...Attached to the mission are a flour mill, sawmill, carding-mill, blacksmith shop—also a farm. There are also extensive vegetable and fruit gardens, playground, everything to make the place an attractive resort for both young and old..."

The mission school was not quite a resort. Discipline was strict, though there is no evidence of the kind of physical or sexual abuse of pupils that occurred in some other Canadian residential schools. A good percentage of the pupils were in fact of mixed blood, such as Cornie Kelleher, who described bedtime at St. Mary's:

> "We used to have lots of fun going to bed. Of course, we had to go as soon as the sun went down...when we were still full of hell. An old fellow by the name of John Strong used to march up and down the dormitory to keep us quiet. So we took into our heads to pick up our pillows, and when he'd be going by we'd hit him in the back of the head, then jump into our beds and cover up. He would holler, but he wouldn't catch anybody...Father Martin came up with a switch. He opened the dormitory door and there was a boy with his shirt-tail, and he let a whack at him and the boy let a yell out and ran for his bed. I remember the old father going around. He'd peer into somebody's face, but that fellow was sleeping, he had his eyes closed...Oh, boy, we used to have lots of fun...Years afterwards, when I was married and living on Matsqui Prairie, Father Martin came over and he laughed until the ears ran down his face about the pranks we used to play."

Mary Englund recalls how the nuns at St. Mary's forced the girls to speak English; for serious infractions—such as running away—a big razor strap was used.

Mary remained a strong Catholic all of her life and appreciated the kindness of most of her mission teachers. But in later years, she viewed her education more critically, stating: "They were always degrading us because we were Indians. We didn't come from homes, we came from camps, and we didn't know how to live. We ate rotten fish, so they didn't seem to be particular in what they gave us to eat. They never let us forget that we were Indian, and that we weren't very civilized, that we were more or less savages."

In 1872, the newly elected Provincial Legislature passed the Municipality Act. One year later, Chilliwack and Langley were incorporated as the first rural municipalities in British Columbia. They were followed by Maple Ridge in 1874, and Surrey, Delta, and Richmond in 1879.

Communities also sprung up during the 1870s at Mission, Pitt Meadows, Nicomen Island, and Mud Bay. Although the number of farms did not increase significantly from 1875 to 1885, their size and productivity did, thanks to the sweat of settlers, who cleared, dyked, drained, constructed and planked. Small general stores doubling as post offices were established at this time in each community, setting the pattern of settlement for future generations.

In 1871, Hope faced a future as a ghost town, due to the decline of gold mining and the improvement of the Cariboo Road which, in streamlining travel to and from the Interior, no longer made it essential to rest or obtain supplies from the old HBC town. Parents were forced to petition Lieutenant Governor Trutch to use the courthouse as a school, only to abandon it in 1876 when strong winds threatened to blow it down. A grant was obtained for a small new school accommodating sixteen pupils.

Bill Bristol lived on an island in the Fraser near Hope with his Indian wife

Mary. He continued to carry the mail by packhorse and boat well into the 1880s, finally being replaced by the railway. He was a familiar figure on the river, and occasionally rescued people in trouble on the water. "The children adored him," recalled one settler, "for he always remembered his little friends."

When he retired from the mail service in 1886, Bristol settled down to farming on his island, but every year lost money. One day, when an interested buyer asked him for what price he would sell his island, Bristol replied, "How much money do you have?"

The prospective purchaser said, "Enough to pay a reasonable price." "That's not what I am interested in," retorted Bristol, "I want to know if you have enough to support it." The old mail carrier never left his island, dying there in 1909.

Growth in the Chilliwack area centred around Five Corners, later known as Centreville, and finally as plain "Chilliwack." Chilliwack, like Langley and Mission, was to have both a rural and urban municipality of the same name, confusing matters greatly for non-residents.

Of these three municipalities, only Langley City and Langley Township still battle out in neanderthal fashion the question of amalgamation, the others having merged. The amalgamation issue currently absorbs Abbotsford and Matsqui politics; whereas Port Coquitlam still retains separate status from Coquitlam District; and Haney, once a separate entity, has been absorbed by Maple Ridge.

Though the dust was so thick in summer that people on Chilliwack's main street choked, and the mire halted traffic during the rainy seasons, the town slowly developed along the Old Yale Road. St. Mark's Church represented the centre of the new community; the structure was transported in pieces on six Indian canoes from the abandoned Port Douglas to the townsite in 1875.

Chilliwack is dominated by Mount Cheam, the Fraser and the Chilliwack Rivers, and Cultus Lake. The Fraser was the community's lifeblood, connecting it to

Mount Cheam was a popular destination for adventurous hikers.

the outside world—meaning New Westminster. Mount Cheam was favoured by generations of avid hikers; and in Stalo legend the mountain was the proud wife of Mount Baker. (The three children of Mounts Baker and Cheam are Mounts Hood, Shasta, and Shuksan.) The Chilliwack River led to hunting, fishing and wilderness. Cultus Lake was everyone's destination for genteel picnics and water sport. In 1881, Violet Sillitoe accompanied her husband, the bishop, on an eight-mile journey to the lake of legends:

> "A very slow and jolting ride over rough ground brought us to the Chilliwhack River, a rushing, foaming, mountain torrent. It was decided to have lunch there and I was considerably surprised to hear that we were to proceed by canoe up the river. This seemed hardly possible. Soon 2 canoes appeared, each manned by 2 Indians, who had long poles for punting the canoes along. Very gingerly we got in, and I was much amused by one of our Indians remarking "hyas cumtax." (She very much understands.) It was very exciting...The poles with which the Indians punted bent till one thought they must snap in two. We had to land about a mile before the lake was reached, as the canoe could proceed no further. Following a narrow trail, across which many trees were lying, we were not long in finding Cultus Lake...The 'canoe ride,' as it is termed in this country, was the principal feature of the return journey. We seemed almost to fly through the water and the skill with which the Indians turned and guided the canoe was simply wonderful."

Chilliwack soon began developing its reputation as a centre of what is vernacularly termed the "Bible Belt." Methodism swept the area in the wake of Thomas Crosby. Renewals and camp meetings became a way of life for several years, until churches were built. The Methodists even controlled the quality of settlement. When a prospective resident appeared in the region, he was quickly referred to A.C. Wells, a Methodist pioneer. Wells would invite the gentleman to dinner, probe gently into his religious leanings, and, depending upon the man's responses, would either encourage or discourage the would-be settler. As community leader, justice of the peace, and deputy sheriff, Wells was a formidable deterrent to anyone not exhibiting suitable religious fervour.

Settlers off to church in Surrey.

The dominance of strict religious views resulted in the refusal by Chilliwack's municipal council to issue liquor licences until well into the twentieth century. In 1885, a 186-signature petition implored council to revoke a Mrs. Bartlett's restaurant licence because she was selling liquor with meals, thereby "bringing a blightening curse on our community." The council went further and voted to fine Mrs. Bartlett

The Rosedale General Store.

fifty dollars. Only forty-three people could be found to sign a counter-petition.

The construction of the Old Yale Road built a backbone along Chilliwack's hinterland, encouraging the settlement of outlying areas such as Rosedale, Sumas, and Popkum. Settlers grumbled, however, about the land tax of twenty-five cents per acre and two days of statute labour for male residents. In 1874, a new tax on personal property was levied; outraged, men demanded the right to work it off by being credited the same $2 per day for their volunteer road work as they were getting for their statute labour.

As well as mosquitoes, every summer settlers had to contend with the flooding of both the Fraser and Chilliwack Rivers. In 1875, a record flood on the Chilliwack tore out bridges and submerged farms. A comprehensive diversion and dyking scheme submitted by Edgar Dewdney merely caused bickering and protest from the adjoining communities of Sumas and Chilliwack, for residents in each district believed that the other was trying to divert rivers and streams to their detriment.

The A.C. Wells farm near Chilliwack was known as Edenbank, and it was there that the Fraser Valley's first creamery was built. It was also at Edenbank that Crosby arrived in 1869 to establish Methodism. One of his first converts was Chief Halalton of the Chilliwack tribe.

When the chief died in the early seventies, his son Sepass became chief. A close friend of A.C. Wells, Sepass worked at Edenbank in his youth. He was fluent in the Halkomelem language of his forefathers, as well as Chinook and English. For many years, Sepass was the leading spokesman for Stalo tribes. Although he had converted to Christianity, Sepass retained for his people some of the ancient ceremonial rites and traditions, including the potlatch, though of necessity such rites were practiced on a limited scale.

On Matsqui Prairie, few pioneers joined John Maclure on the land, as the ravaging Fraser's floodwaters discouraged settlement. To avoid the annual floods, some settlers established farms on Alben Hawkins's Mount Lehman, which was a high forested plateau containing about ten thousand acres, and lying between northeast Langley and Matsqui.

In 1878, the Sumas Dyking Act was passed and Colin Sword acquired all unclaimed acreage on Matsqui Prairie, subject to his completing a comprehensive dyking system. The massive barrier which Sword built stretched from Sumas Mountain to the Fraser, and consisted of cedar piling and planks, soil, and gravel by the ton. In 1882, a great flood destroyed much of this structure, despite expenditure of over seventy thousand dollars, and it had to be rebuilt—only to be breached many more times by *ta coutchi*—the Fraser's fury.

In Maple Ridge, Thomas Haney arrived in 1876 to a community which had spread from the cluster of Kanaka cabins on the Fraser westward to the present sites of Haney and Hammond. By 1882, there resided in the district forty-four farmers, two storekeepers, two teachers, one hotel proprietor, and two loggers. Haney was a brickmaker who explored both sides of the Fraser searching for high quality clay suitable for processing. He found a rich deposit on the river's north bank, and there decided to build a brick plant. A native of Cape Breton raised in Ontario, Haney brought his wife and children to Derby in 1877, where they stayed in the unused church parsonage while Haney built a fine home near his brick factory. The plant was to operate successfully for nearly a century, and helped lay the foundations for the commercial centre of Port Haney.

Thomas Haney.

Mrs. Haney was typical of many pioneer women of the day, who had left a more comfortable lifestyle in Eastern Canada to forge a new home in the wilds of the West. Theirs is an untold story of hardship, endurance, self-sacrifice, and toil; of days of insufferable cold spent in uninsulated cabins; of illness and the giving of charity to the poor and the sick—including the nursing of neighbours and acting as midwife on many occasions; of planting gardens and fruit trees; scrubbing clothes on washboards with water hauled from a stream and heated on the stove; knitting and sewing all of the family's clothes and quilts; making Christmas special with a tub of mincemeat for pies and puddings; dragging the family to church on Sundays over miles of muddy trails. These are the unsung heroes of pioneer days in the Fraser Valley: they never sought recognition, but deserve more than written history has offered.

Few pioneer women would have had an experience similar to Mrs. Haney's when she first arrived at her new home, although they would have shared her consternation. Upon disembarking from the steamer at Derby after her weary journey from the east, Mrs. Haney entered the parsonage and found a human skull adorning the fireplace mantle.

Later, in her new home, high on the hill, Mrs. Haney was startled one February afternoon in 1880 by a loud rumbling. Then before her eyes some thirty acres of river bank slowly slid into the Fraser, causing an enormous sixty foot high tidal wave to sweep across the river.

Local teacher James Sinclair—a great-great-grandson of Dr. John McLoughlin—was just closing his school for the day when he felt the ground trembling and dove for cover. William Edge was out clearing land and was caught by the wave of water, which catapulted him across a field. He was thrown into a tree, and later died of his injuries. Trees toppled like matchsticks. Roaring eddies swept down the river past Barnston Island. The disaster shaped much of the future landscape of Haney; a geological phenomenon caused by repeated thawing and freezing in winter which had unsettled an already unstable bank.

Maple Ridge struggled mightily to raise funds for a road to run along the high river bank from Kanaka Creek to Hammond. It was exasperating for local council members—for many people defaulted on their taxes; fences were deliberately erected in the path of road construction; some swamps seemed impassable. By 1885, however, a road was completed and a town hall built for community use. There also prevailed a Sunday observance bylaw and a bounty of $2.50 for bears' heads. Receipts in October of that year totalled $132.00 and expenditures $256.00.

Settlers poured into Maple Ridge in 1881, as construction began that year on the Canadian Pacific Railway right-of-way through the municipality. Anglicans now clamoured for a new church, causing Bishop Sillitoe and his wife to row across the Fraser to Derby to examine the abandoned church of the Reverend Crickmer in the hope that the structure might be moved. The boat they rowed leaked so badly that they had to bail furiously for the entire crossing.

They landed and found that the church was still sound, although they decided to leave the parsonage building where it stood.

Samuel Edge was contracted to dismantle the old church and transport it to its new home. (Edge was the first non-native person to climb to the summit of the Golden Ears; Edge Peak is named in his honour.) The structure was moved on rollers to the river's edge and loaded onto a scow built from the church's own timbers; it landed down river on the north bank, where it was hauled with great difficulty by means of rollers, windlass, and oxen some three hundred feet up a steep slope, and finally re-erected at the corner of Laity Street and River Road.

The church was redecorated, a brick chimney added, and a new roof installed. For years, children in Maple Ridge believed that their church was stolen by good Anglicans from bad Anglicans of Derby. It sits there still, quaint and fully functioning as the oldest church in the province.

Victorian morals were outwardly strict and prudish; beneath the surface, however, outrageous—even criminal—behaviour could thrive without social restraint. The case of Julia Apnaut is a tragic example.

A step-grand-daughter of Ovid Allard, a direct descendant of Chief Shashia, and the first child to travel the Cariboo Road, Julia was orphaned in 1863 at the age of two, and was placed in St. Ann's Convent in Victoria. In the mid-seventies, a Sophia Nelson connived to have Julia released from the care of the nuns and come to the Nelson farm in Maple Ridge. Her aim was to have the girl help with the chores and, she hoped, to marry her son George; this would guarantee that the Nelson family would partake in the modest inheritance which Julia would receive when she turned eighteen.

Julia greatly assisted Sophia on the farm and even gave her "benefactor" an education, for Sophia was illiterate. The Nelson home was used by the Catholic priest, Father Ponz, to hear confessions of nearby Katzie Indians. Julia believed it improper to give confessions so publicly and refused to help translate, which infuriated Sophia into beating the girl mercilessly with a birch stick. To further break the teenager's spirit, she forced Julia to work naked in the vegetable garden on limited food rations.

Again and again, Julia tried to escape from her misery, only to be hunted down like a slave and dragged back to the farm. In desperation, she married George Nelson, only to face another living hell from his brutal sexual advances. Fortunately, she was released from her torment by a young Canadian Pacific

Railway worker who boarded with the Nelsons and one morning smuggled her onto a Victoria-bound steamboat. Julia headed straight to the convent and had her marriage annulled. Years later, she celebrated the sudden death of her former husband by purchasing a red dress, instead of black.

At Fort Langley, Ovid Allard lived out his twilight years at the fort. In 1872, the Big House was reconstructed following a visit from Chief Factor Dr. William Tolmie. Allard had complained for years that when the storms lashed his fort, the Big House would creak and groan from one end to the other. While Tolmie slept as a guest at the post one spring, a tremendous gale struck the fort at 2:00 A.M. Tolmie left his room with candlestick in hand and rapped loudly on Allard's door. But the chief clerk pretended to be asleep.

"Allard! Allard!," shouted Tolmie above the din of the wind. "Wake up man! How can you possibly sleep in this commotion? I'm afraid the house is going to blow down!"

Allard sleepily answered, "Oh, go to bed, Doctor, you'll get used to this."

"Allard!" yelled Tolmie again, "can't you find me a place of safety and quiet?"

"Why yes, Doctor," replied Allard, "in the potato cellar." Tolmie grunted and retreated angrily back to bed. The next morning at breakfast the chief factor gave orders to Allard to erect a new building without delay.

Two years later Allard was dead. All of Langley mourned, and even the flags in New Westminster were lowered to half-mast for the funeral. His son Jason settled on a farm near the fort and provided interpretive services in the courts for many years. William Newton succeeded Allard as chief clerk at Fort Langley, but died in 1875.

Sir James Douglas died of a heart attack on August 2, 1877, at home in the arms of his wife Amelia. Testimonials poured in from friend and foe alike. The *Colonist* gave tribute: "Truly, he has set an example of goodness and patriotism worthy of being copied by future generations of British Columbians." His death marked the passing of the last of the old Hudson's Bay veterans from the scene.

The Fraser Valley has had its share of both corrupt and pious politicians. The colorful William Gibbs was elected reeve of Langley in 1877, at a time when the district included both Fort Langley and the growing community to the south called Langley Prairie. Gibbs was a co-owner of the Fort Langley Hotel, a landmark for its free flowing liquor. In fact, when Gibbs ran for office, he did so partially in retaliation for his conviction for unlawfully selling liquor in a "dry" district.

One day, Gibbs found a Hudson's Bay pig perched on his hotel steps and he stuck a pitchfork into the animal. He was promptly charged and convicted at New Westminster of killing the pig, pleading unsuccessfully that the porker had actually died of starvation. He was frequently seen strutting about the Fort Langley steamboat landing area dressed in a black suit, wielding a fancy cane. His remarks to women were so insulting that one day the brother of an offended lady arrived on the daily steamer and punched him in the face. Gibbs regained his feet and made a sarcastic remark, only to be drubbed again. After this blow, he remained on the ground for some time.

The new reeve's first act was to issue himself a new liquor licence for his

Cloverdale post office, 1899.

hotel, despite the objections of his council. Tempers flared at council meetings, and the district was soon divided into two hostile camps—those supporting Gibbs and expecting patronage, and those advocating "fair, clean, municipal government." Matters were resolved abruptly when councillors discovered one day that Gibbs had doctored council minutes. The flamboyant Gibbs was literally run out of town.

When new Chief Clerk Henry Wark tried auctioning off more of the Hudson's Bay farm in 1877, there were few buyers. Land was cheap and plentiful. Alexander Dunn, however, believed in the valley's potential and purchased two 100-acre lots, stating: "Having once seen Langley Prairie, with its 3,000 acres of rich, black soil, having seen Pitt Meadows, Lulu and Sea Islands, Sumas and Matsqui Prairies, together with the great stretches of splendid bushland extending from Chilliwack westward to the upper end of the delta, I felt and often said that the Lower Fraser was destined to become, sooner or later, great and populous, and that those who possessed houses or lands there would one day deem themselves fortunate."

Surrey in the seventies was—and remains today—not one community, but a collection of scattered settlements. The district consisted of centres at Brownsville—or South Westminster—on the river, Mud Bay, Hall's Prairie (which was settled by a man of that name who was driven from there by packs of fierce wolves), and Cloverdale, initially known as Clover Valley.

The entire municipality sheltered only fifty-five farmers, most of whom were bachelors living in small clearings which they had hacked from the dense forest.

The outside world for these settlers consisted chiefly of visits to neighbouring farms, trips to Blaine, or treks to New Westminster to market produce.

Saturday was market day, and a man of the soil might haul his wares to town, barter for goods, and stop for a drink or two. Another attraction was the horse races, which for many years were held along New Westminster's Columbia Street on Saturday afternoons. On the way home, there was Jim Punch's hostelry and saloon at South Westminster, where settlers might imbibe some more, staying over if they were too inebriated to resume the journey home.

Surrey was home to many characters in the seventies. One interesting pioneer was John Oliver who, as a member of the school board, attended its inaugural meeting held on a cedar log in the forest. Oliver and fellow board members excitedly took possession one day of the abandoned shack which served as Surrey's first school. Hog Brown was another early settler, a man obsessed with raising and eating porkers. His cabin floor was littered with old harnesses and other junk, but in one corner sat a finely tuned piano which he played with skill and expression.

Settlers living on Semiahmoo Bay were ferried across to a store on the

Early logging operations at Alouette Lake.

American side by Dick the Ferryman. Dick had no wharf; one had to wade out to the ferry, clamber aboard and pay ten cents. The boundary was ignored by residents. American cattle grazed on south Surrey fields, and dozens of Canadians flocked to the July 4 festivities to partake of free food spread on tables in an orchard. The Yankees ultimately discontinued these picnic celebrations because hungry Canucks vastly outnumbered patriotic Americans, and ate up all of the food.

Surrey has traditionally had a more transient population than any other Fraser Valley district. Trappers and squatters abounded, many of whom took native wives whom they abandoned with their children. (Surrey Family Court officials might testify that nothing has changed over the years in the field of matrimonial responsibility.) Transient white fishermen also lined the Fraser, setting up summer fishing camps in Stalo fashion.

By 1884, logging had become a major industry, and large companies acquired timber rights to huge tracts. Logging camps operated as self-sufficient mobile units, complete with skid roads, cookhouse, living quarters, stable, blacksmith shop, ox teams and equipment. Unfortunately, the areas worked were completely stripped of all marketable timber and left in a disgusting, chaotic mess of stumps, branches, and debris, called "slash."

Loggers built skid roads to the Serpentine, Nicomekl, Campbell, and Fraser Rivers. At first oxen, and later horses and donkey engines, hauled the timber to water's edge; then the logs were floated downstream to the mills along the Fraser. Settlers made little money from sale of their own timber, since they were taxed heavily if they tried to sell the wood; logging companies simply paid a small royalty to the government in exchange for exclusive rights to an area. A few farmers worked in the camps to supplement their agricultural income. As for the blighted land remaining after the loggers departed, the farmers had to work arduously to burn the waste and blast stumps before preparing the land for cultivation.

The Delta and Richmond districts split into separate municipalities in 1879. The most prominent settler and first reeve of Delta was William Ladner, whose fine cattle, horses, and seven-foot-girthed oxen became legendary. Ladner mingled frequently with natives of the nearby Tsawwassen reserve, and employed Indians on his own and brother Tom's farms; later, Indians worked for him in the salmon canneries.

The river delta soil was incredibly fertile, but subject to flooding of up to fifteen feet. The land was required not only to be drained, but coated with lime and phosphate. The only significant portions of land unclaimed by the late seventies consisted of peat bog, which nobody wanted until the peat industry developed many years later.

Despite his prominence, William Ladner failed to escape chastisement by fellow councillors in 1881, when an entire council meeting was devoted to discussion of Ladner's use of a public road as a dung heap. The road went by the reeve's cow shed, and Ladner demanded twenty-five dollars compensation for expropriation of his traditional right to dump dung on the right-of-way. Council refused.

In fact, the majority of councillors became so overwrought that they passed a Protection of Highways Bylaw which forbade many common practices, such as obstruction of public roads, leaving unhitched wagons on roads for more than twenty-four hours; dumping dead animals within 300 feet of a highway; trotting or running animals on bridges; destroying fences, or building fires within 100 feet of a road—and yes, leaving manure and other "noxious and offensive substances" on roadways.

Farmers in the delta region suffered from problems similar to those of their neighbours upriver. Oxen teams were vital for ploughing and transport; fences were split by hand; finished lumber was obtained by barge from New Westminster. Dyking efforts proceeded apace, but the earth barriers were constantly undermined by muskrats. For many years, the water supply was dependent upon rainwater, collected from eavestroughs and stored in barrels. Cattle roamed all over the prairie, eventually to be sold as beef to New Westminster and Victoria butchers. Farm implements were scarce, but a plough, drag harrow, and stoneboat on runners were considered necessities, supplemented by shovels and hoes, homemade garden rakes, and a mattock for chopping out rotten stumps.

Harvesting oats on the David Thompson farm, Terra Nova, 1890s.

Even after completion of the Ladner Trunk Road, linking the delta with the eastern valley and New Westminster, the sternwheeler remained the dominant means of commercial transport. At Ladner's Landing, there was room for one steamer, and children would stand on roofs to watch for boats like the *Enterprise* and the *Wilson G. Hunt* arrive from Victoria.

The *Enterprise* was the most popular of the vessels, with its "lower deck used for the carrying of freight, Indians, and Chinamen, while her closed-in upper decks were comfortably equipped with state-room, dining room, and lounges for passenger service." The competition between vessels remained fierce and men placed bets on which steamer might arrive first; people congregated at the wharf as soon as they heard the roar of the paddlewheel well out on Georgia Strait.

Delta and Richmond farmers who could not afford the steamer would convey their produce to New Westminster by farm barge, poling the crude affair up the river with the help of the incoming tide. When the tide ebbed, the farmer pulled the barge to the river bank and rested, often spending many cold nights before reaching market. In the mid-eighties, a passenger and freight road service was begun by Joe Jordan between Ladner and New Westminster. In winter, Joe offered sleigh carriage, making the trip once a week. But for many years yet the steamer reigned supreme as the favoured mode of commercial transport.

The future of Richmond was fated to become linked more with the Vancouver hinterland than with New Westminster; whereas Delta was to maintain close ties with the Royal City and the valley region south of the Fraser. New settlers in Richmond included Harry Eburne, Sam Brighouse, and Manoah Steves. Today's Marpole area was known as Eburne, after the pioneer of that name who established a general store. Part of Brighouse's farm now accommodates a large racetrack; and Steves farmed at the site of present-day Steveston. In 1881, a small steamer service was inaugurated between river delta points, Eburne, and New Westminster, by means of the scow *Alice*, which was equipped with a paddlewheel driven by a threshing machine. By the close of the eighties, the clamour of Lulu Islanders for a direct link to the mainland resulted in the opening of the first bridge across the river's North Arm.

Lulu Island road ditches averaged seven feet in depth and formed part of an extensive dyking and drainage system.

Residents of the two river mouth municipalities became known jokingly as "mud-flatters." Ida Steves noted the interesting fashion differences between Richmond and Delta residents: "People from Ladner dressed up to go to New Westminster. People from Steveston didn't dress up for the trip. Steveston people

The Sea Island side of Eburne.

were plain country people. Somehow or other the Ladner people looked as if they had just come from the hairdressers, and their clothes were just so."

One can only speculate on the source of such differences. The founders of Ladner, such as the two Ladner brothers, were "English country gentlemen" farmers; whereas Steveston's roots were in the fishing industry—a much more rough-and-tumble occupation, where individuals held perhaps fewer pretensions.

The most important commercial development of the period was the growth of the fishing industry. All of the Indians and most farmers on the lower Fraser were engaged at least part-time in fishing, although no Indian was permitted to fish commercially, except as an employee of a cannery. The homemaker's stand-by was salmon. Hunting was too time-consuming, beef was not always in supply, and most small farms could not afford to use up their domestic fowl at the table. In river delta areas, especially, farmers also used fish heads, tails, and offal as fertilizer. Farm equipment, hinges, and harness leather could be oiled with fish grease, and the natural lubricant was even smeared on skid roads to help with log haulage.

The proliferation of salmon canneries caused an upsurge in the numbers of commercial fishermen on the river. The early experiments of James Symes and Alex Ewen now bore fruit. Between 1871 and 1882, thirteen canneries opened at New Westminster, South Westminster, Ladner, Coquitlam, Sapperton, Lulu Island, and Canoe Pass.

In 1882, these canneries packed 250,000 cases of four dozen one-pound cans and employed up to five thousand people. The location of a majority of canneries near the mouth of the river also encouraged for the first time a dispersal of non-agricultural workers from New Westminster to outlying communities.

Pioneering Alex Ewen led the pack. His modernized cannery, situated on Lion Island, five miles south of New Westminster, eventually caused its site to be renamed Ewen's Island. Here he introduced the packing of salmon in one-pound

Fishing boats near Steveston on the Fraser River, one of the greatest salmon fishing grounds in the world.

flats, while other canneries still used the more expensive vertical cans. Ewen's innovation gave him a competitive edge of a dollar a case. His new plant allowed for fish to be dumped from the boats at one end, and loaded in cases from a warehouse at the other end. He even bought two steam tugs for the operation.

New Westminster experienced its last boom years as the seat of mainland commerce in the early eighties. Even the Burrard Inlet lumber magnates were bringing their products to the Royal City for sale and shipping. As railway construction began in the Fraser Canyon, and then in the valley, thousands of workers passed through the city, a few staying on to open businesses. The Chinese community grew from 28 in 1869 to over 300 in 1880, many of its members finding work in the canneries. On the eve of the railway's arrival, the annual shipping volume amounted to 180,000 tons.

Canners, pier, and fishboats at Steveston, 1890s.

One of the results of Confederation was the construction of the British Columbia Penitentiary on the Royal Engineers' old Sapperton site. On a bright autumn day in 1878, Warden Arthur McBride marched twelve shackled prisoners from the *Enterprise* at the New Westminster wharf to their new home on the hill. The first stone structure consisted of three storeys and seventy-nine brick cells, five of them reserved for solitary confinement. There were two chapels.

Although built to last, the new penitentiary suffered from serious defects in construction. Locks failed to work; bars on windows were not properly embedded, but simply rested on the sill and painted over; chimneys and stoves were deficient; baths, water closets and sinks malfunctioned. Even the penitentiary crops suffered from a simple lack of fencing, which was needed to keep out neighbouring cattle.

The provincial government matched Ottawa's zest for incarceration in 1878 by building the mainland's first mental health centre at the site of Woodlands School. A member of the Legislature reported that Ottawa had declined to assume responsibility for "lunatics" in British Columbia because it would be too large an undertaking. Some thirty-seven patients were admitted to the only partially finished facility, most of whom were transported from Victoria.

During a Legislative debate over moving the patients to an unfinished building, Member of the Legislative Assembly Dr. Ash remarked that "it was unwise to make the asylum too comfortable so that people who had no right...would flock in." MLA Smith added that he "had always regarded New Westminster as the proper place for lunatics."

When Lord Dufferin visited Government House in 1874, a chain gang of twenty convicts, watched over by guards carrying shotguns, prepared the reception by polishing floors, arranging flowers, and plucking fowls. With the advent of the British Columbia Penitentiary, the chain gang was abolished, since there was plenty of manual labour to occupy convicts on the new prison grounds. But Government House was right next door, occupied now by John Robson in his capacity as paymaster for the Canadian Pacific Railway gangs, and this angered the new warden, who had been promised the large ornate building for his prison area.

The public used the grounds of Government House, however, for picnics and gala events, and combined with Robson to thwart reversion of the house to a prison purpose. The 1879 penitentiary report notes: "It needs no argument to show how incongruous...it were to have games, music, dancing, and other amusements, with all the attendant boisterous mirth, within easy earshot of convicts undergoing their allotted punishments. There is no benevolence, no philanthropy in this picnic project...the proposition involves a strange degree of selfishness, nay, heartlessness." But these pleas were to no avail. Robson and the Canadian Pacific Railway stayed, and the picnics and public events continued for many years on the site.

Laying CPR tracks in the Fraser Valley, 1884.

In the year 1878, British Columbia threatened to secede from Canada unless railway construction to the Pacific coast was begun immediately. Ottawa complied. Chief contractor Andrew Onderdonk established his headquarters at Yale, and the old gold town boomed once again. Just below Yale, at Emory's Bar, steamboats plied busily back and forth, depositing huge quantities of men, materials, and equipment at the Canadian Pacific Railway's warehouses.

On May 4, 1880, the first dynamite blast at Yale signalled the commencement of Fraser River construction activity. The sound of the blast was heard some distance down the lower valley. A solitary whistle from a steamboat broke the silence which followed, for Captain John Irving was on hand to observe the occasion, perhaps conscious that the railway's debut would eventually render his craft redundant.

The route of the railway pleased few Fraser Valley residents. South bank settlers had hoped that the line would be laid along their side of the river; New Westminster, in turn, had hoped that it would serve as the terminus. Delta and Richmond saw little direct benefit to their districts. The Royal City was pleased, however, that the Port Moody terminus designated was very close; council had feared that a southern valley route could connect by bridge to Marpole, allowing Vancouver to grow and supersede New Westminster as both the chief commercial centre of the mainland and marketplace for Fraser Valley agriculture.

The actual process of railway construction involved three phases. First, the route must be slashed clear of all natural growth. For this phase, 300 Indians and a number of white labourers were hired. After the line was cleared, the grading began in preparation for the third phase of rail laying.

For this task, the Canadian Pacific Railway initially imported 1,000 Chinese, sparking a heated debate that would lead to much bitterness, rancour, and racism in the province for several decades. The accommodation for these Chinese labourers in the camps was atrocious. A near riot occurred in New Westminster in 1882 when 900 workers were herded onto a dock for an overnight stay "like so many cattle."

By the fall of 1882, track had been laid from Yale to Harrison River. Westward to Burrard Inlet, construction proceeded in several sections. Lots of twenty-five thousand ties were laid in each section between camps. All sleeper and cross ties were to be sawed smoothly, squared at both ends, and cut into eight-foot lengths.

Tie contractors were required to haul their own timber out of the woods and to arrange the timber in tidy piles along the right-of-way. A total of 3,355,000 cubic yards of material was removed along the eighty-five mile stretch between Port Moody and Harrison River by Chinese working with picks, shovels, and wheelbarrows—all for very low wages. The average cost of the Fraser Valley portion of the railway line was thirty thousand dollars per mile.

The Canadian Pacific Railway hired many pioneers who possessed particular expertise, including Edgar Dewdney, John Maclure, Jason Allard, and the inimitable John Robson.

As in the gold rush days, many people benefitted indirectly. Hotels did a roaring business, so much so that James Sinclair resigned his teaching position in Maple Ridge to manage a hotel at Port Hammond. Sawmill operators made small fortunes, and farmers could not keep up with the sudden demand for meat and produce. The craving for beef was so great that Levi Cartier of Harrison paid Indians to raise large cattle herds; he then resold the beef to the hungry men of the construction camps.

Once the right-of-way was graded, masses of Chinese arrived to lay ties and rails. These workers assembled at river landings at Nicomen Island, Hatzic, Mission, and Port Hammond, where steamboats dumped the rails; then groups of six to eight coolies hoisted a rail and packed it on bamboo poles up the embankment.

Many Chinese were injured or killed. Mrs. James Trethewey played a Florence Nightingale role, attending to the nursing of injured workers along the line from Port Moody to Kamloops. It was common for her to leave her bed in the middle of the night and travel sixty miles by handcar to reach an injured man. She also found time to raise a family and operate a small store on the Mission flats.

More than seventy men died from accidents occurring along the Fraser Valley section of the railway,

Railway workers washing up.

most of them Chinese. Many casualties were caused by landslides occurring in Maple Ridge. A few pioneers had tried to convince the railway company that the river banks were unstable and that the route should be diverted away from the Fraser, but the company was obdurate in its choice of route.

In one incident, a Chinese crew refused to return to work after a slide killed three of their mates. Wellington Harris, the Canadian Pacific Railway foreman, finally forced them back to the job by threatening them with a loaded revolver. (As a child in Ontario, Harris had been told by the retired Simon Fraser to go West and buy land in the Fraser Valley where the hoped for railway was most likely to pass through. Harris followed the old explorer's advice and obtained tidy compensation from the railway company when its line cut through his farm. Harris became first reeve of Maple Ridge.)

In another incident, a group of Chinese were killed in an explosion apparently planned by a subcontractor who sought to avoid paying their wages.

In February 1883, after special constables arrested two Chinese accused of assaulting a foreman, the constables were chased, prisoners in tow, by an angry mob of Chinese armed with shovels. The constables holed up in a general store, where a stand-off ensued. The mob got larger. Finally, the storekeeper persuaded the constables to release their two prisoners, who immediately fled from the scene. The mob dispersed, the two accused were recaptured by Katzie Indians, and were later fined fifteen dollars each by a local magistrate.

For many residents along its right-of-way, the railway was a mixed blessing. The Agassiz farm was cut in half, but Mary Agassiz took advantage of the situation by running a store in her home from which she sold food supplies just as fast as she could stock them. Her bread was $1 a loaf and eggs were $1 a dozen.

The Oblates of St. Mary's, however, had to completely relocate the mission school half a mile northward on the densely wooded hillside; there they laboured

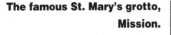

The famous St. Mary's grotto, Mission.

arduously to clear one hundred foot firs from the ground—the victims of forest fires—as well as standing timber. The priests and nuns set aside here in a corner of the acreage a heritage cemetery for all of the pioneer missionaries and their successors.

High on the hillside, the Oblates erected a beautiful six-sided chapel with a white cross on its silver dome; this Grotto On The Hill became a landmark in the Fraser Valley for more than seventy years. Valley residents on whose land the railway was constructed received compensation, and many took advantage of the compensation scheme. William Perkins of Hatzic, for example, managed to plant an orchard in time to collect five thousand dollars from the Canadian Pacific Railway.

On November 8, 1885, the first train chugged through the Fraser Valley to Port Moody. All clean-up work along the line ceased that day, as men in bright red work jackets stood and waved to the dignitaries flying past. Both new settlers and old pioneers also waited and watched for that first train, many of them lining the south bank from Langley to Chilliwack, hoping to catch just a glimpse of Engine No. 148 as it wended its way westward.

At last, the Fraser Valley was truly part of Canada. Somehow, the river, with its treacherous currents and friendly steamboats, had diminished in importance. To men and women toiling deep in the bush, there was little immediate impact. But the true frontier was now past. As Alexander Dunn declared, "When the people of Langley could see the right-of-way being cleared on the north side of the Fraser, the last vestige of doubt in the minds of reasoning men as to the future greatness and prosperity of the country utterly vanished."

CHAPTER TEN

RAILWAY BOOM

When the speeches and hubris were over and that first Engine No. 148 made its return journey from Port Moody eastward, the excitement in the Fraser Valley remained. New Westminster City Council became frantic upon learning that the Canadian Pacific Railway did not intend to build a line to the Fraser, but instead planned to extend the tracks to Coal Harbour.

On November 9, 1885, council passed the Railway Bonus Bylaw, by which the Royal City in effect bought the spur line they sought, by granting a huge bonus to the railway company for quick construction of the extension.

The CPR played coy. The company was really more interested in pushing on to the fledgling town of Vancouver, where Sir William Van Horne believed a deep-water port facility would assure that centre of future commercial predominance on the mainland. When John Robson raised $37,000 in the Legislature as a further contribution to the New Westminster spur line, he subjected the bequest to a requirement that no Chinese labour be used to build the line.

Construction immediately stalled. Impatient citizens met and burned Robson in effigy, raising $51,000 at meetings and declaring that they could care less who the railway employed, provided that the tracks arrived in New Westminster soon.

Early locomotives such as "Curly" in this photo aided logging activities. Port Kells, 1891.

Several landowners caused further complications, however, by resisting expropriation for the right-of-way, including one Sam Greer, who defended his property with an axe.

On August 28, 1886, Royal City residents at last heard the whistle of the locomotive. Daily passenger service soon began between the city and Westminster Junction, later known as Port Coquitlam. "This ought to infuse new life into our city," trumpeted the city editor.

But the jubilation was short-lived. A few months later, the Canadian Pacific Railway terminus was moved to Vancouver, which within seven short years would be transformed from a small lumbering town of 500 souls to a bustling metropolis of 13,685 people.

But all was not lost for New Westminster. It was to lose commercial hegemony on the mainland to Vancouver, but by 1891, its Front Street would boast eleven wharves, a woollen mill, a foundry, steamboat offices, hotels, a stage coach office, general stores, bootmakers, watchmakers, barbers, canneries, fish dealers, grocery merchants, and a butcher. New Westminster was to remain the centre of Fraser Valley trade for many decades.

Evening scene along the Fraser River. Lulu Island on left, Sea Island on right.

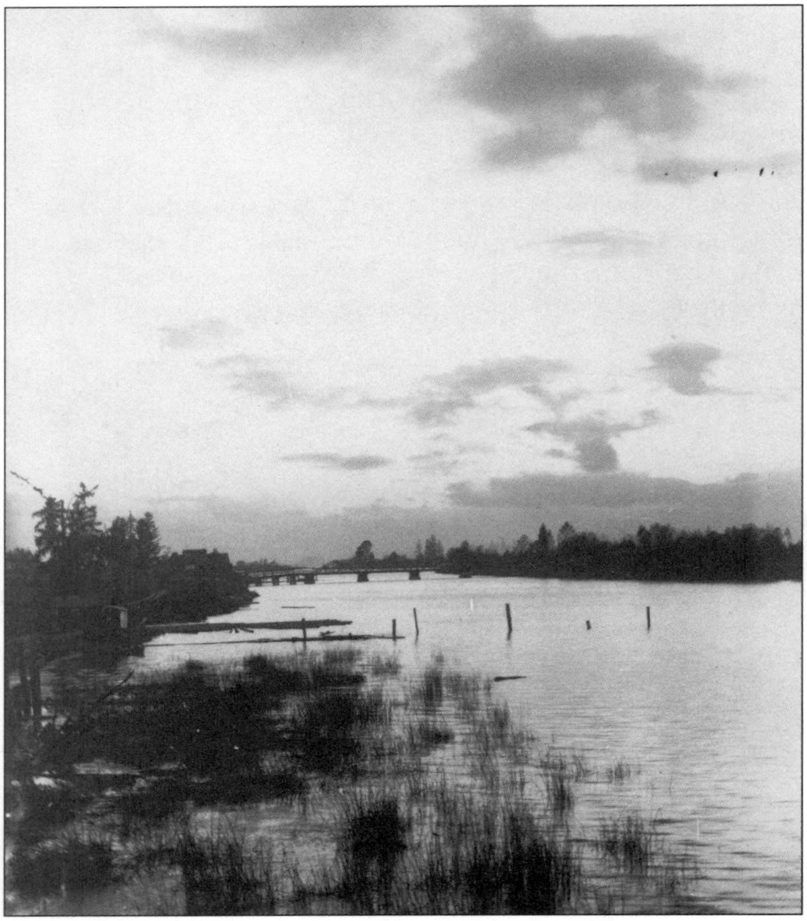

The entire valley became consumed with transportation fever, as every community clamoured for roads, bridges, and railway spur lines. In 1889, two North Arm bridges were constructed between Richmond and Marpole, though the final timbers were scarcely in place when ice floes crashed through the swing span of one bridge, preventing its use until late 1890. Bridges at this time were delicate wooden affairs and were often closed for repair. Teams of furiously driven horses ruined the surface, and complaints were made about the wild speed of Billy Mellis's Vancouver to Steveston stage coach run. Richmond Council finally began prosecuting people who permitted their horses to even trot across a bridge.

Roads in many areas were still primitive muddy wagon tracks. Every young man over the age of twenty-one was compelled to work on road maintenance by the Statute Labor Act; but lack of a gravel base and inadequate equipment made such measures insufficient to the task of ensuring year-round traffic flow.

Meanwhile, legislators discriminated against slow travellers in favour of speed with the 1892 Highway Traffic Act:

"No person shall race with or drive

furiously any horse or other animal upon any highway... In case a person travelling a highway in charge of a vehicle, or on horseback, is overtaken by any vehicle or horseman travelling at a greater speed, the person so overtaken shall quietly turn out to the left and allow the said vehicle or horseman to pass."

The year 1891 was a watershed for transportation in the valley. No less than four major projects were completed that year and in 1892, including the Queensborough Bridge. Some three hundred boats passed beneath the span each month and the bridge was rammed so many times that it had to be rebuilt. However, the Reverend Lennie of New Westminster expressed the optimism of the times: "The tide of immigration is rolling in and there are numerous inquiries for places of residence. Lots are advancing in value. Soon we shall have a bridge connecting our city with Lulu Island, one of the richest agricultural districts in the Province. The road bed is being prepared between this city and Vancouver, and before many months go by, we expect to make the trip between the 2 cities in half an hour."

The first Central Park tram leaves Carrall Street for New Westminster, October 7, 1891.

But while roads, bridges and railways were under construction, upriver residents clamoured for better ferry service between Harrison Mills and Chilliwack; for many years old Mac MacDonald carried travellers in his canoe for "four bits, and you pull an oar yourself."

The opening of the Westminster and Vancouver Tramway Co. interurban electric railway line between New Westminster and Vancouver in 1891 was followed by regular passenger tram service the following year; the line was taken over by B.C. Electric in 1897.

Completion of the Fraser Street Bridge assured Vancouver of three access routes to lower valley points. Major festivities occurred on February 14, 1891, when the New Westminster Southern Railway was completed from South Westminster via Cloverdale to Blaine. The event was marked by a railway "wedding," whereby trains departed from New Westminster and Blaine so as to arrive at the border simultaneously. The last spikes were driven in by the two railway corporation presidents amidst cheering picnickers. The twenty-two mile stretch was said to be the only Canadian railway ever built without government subsidy.

The immediate effects of improved links among valley settlements and to the worlds of Vancouver and Washington State were momentous. The population of municipalities such as Richmond, Surrey, and Langley boomed; while overall in the valley the population grew from a mere 6,000 in 1881 to 52,000 by 1901.

Improved transport made possible the founding of new industries. Farm production increased to service burgeoning new markets. However, there was still no direct Canadian Pacific Railway line to the United States. In order to access American markets directly, the railway company constructed in 1891 a spur line from Mission to the border town of Huntingdon, where it was linked to the Sumas terminus of the Bellingham-to-B.C. Railway.

Unlike the celebrations at Blaine that year, the festivities held at Bellingham to mark the arrival of the first Montreal to Seattle passenger train almost created an international incident. American officials had organized a welcoming arch of flags and bunting—and another rather unorthodox arch comprised of cannonading water sprayed by local fire department personnel.

Unfortunately, much liquor was consumed by the firemen while they waited for the train. Friendly water fights ensued, and by the time the Canadians arrived, instead of being met with a graceful arch of water over the train, they were soaked to the skin by a fusillade of water directed into the open coach windows. A Union Jack was trampled underfoot, worsening matters; finally, the soppy, bedraggled Canadians stomped off to lunch. The entire matter was raised in both the British and Canadian parliaments.

First CPR station, Mission 1886. The station was built on the site of the original St. Mary's Mission.

Railways provoked massive land speculation. A rumour of a Canadian Pacific Railway extension to Chilliwack triggered an auction of town lots in 1891. Special excursions from Vancouver were organized by the developer, and lots sold at one hundred dollars each, a large sum at the time. These investors lost their collective shirts.

In Matsqui, John Maclure purchased a quarter section near the proposed railway line as an investment. While traversing the property, his son Charles discovered a wizened old man living in a cedar tree. The hermit "saved himself the trouble of building a house by roofing a hollow cedar stump, living in the base of it, and had climbing pegs set in the sides to his sleeping loft above. He brought his own supplies from New Westminster, taking two days to walk each way." The squatter was finally ousted by Maclure after a year of argument and the transfer of a one hundred dollar bill.

A train station was built near the Maclure farm and named Abbotsford, after Henry Abbott, a Canadian Pacific Railway general superintendent for the pacific region. Around it, fifty acres of land were subdivided into town lots. The new rail line to Huntingdon had an immediate impact upon farming, for now the settlers could transport produce to either the Abbotsford or Mission stations for shipment to Vancouver and points east.

The beginnings of Abbotsford. Looking west on Essendene, 1900s.

The Matsqui, Abbotsford, and Mission districts proved ideal for fruit growing. The rail bridge at Mission was also used by pedestrians, and Mission became for a time the shopping centre for south bank communities. Matsqui was incorporated in 1892 and Abbotsford in 1924.

James Welton Horne was a wealthy Vancouver financier who had made a fortune by anticipating a town developing along the rail line in Manitoba. He bought the site which looked most promising, divided it into lots, and sold them. The city of Brandon was thus born.

In 1886, Horne rode the railway to Vancouver, where he acquired numerous landholdings and served as an alderman. In 1890, he purchased all of the land surrounding the Mission railway station, carving a townsite from the mud on a grid system - unmindful of hills, ravines, or gushing streams. The tycoon named the main street Horne Avenue and, in order to reflect the cosmopolitan nature of the city of his dreams, graced other avenues with names like Washington, Seattle, and California.

Huge advertisements appeared in New Westminster, Victoria, and Vancouver newspapers heralding the "Great Sale of Mission City." Bands were imported for the scheduled auction, and on May 20, 1890, a special train of seven Canadian Pacific Railway coaches departed from Vancouver carrying the cream of the city's social élite.

At Mission Station, the St. Mary's Brass Band led the visitors down Horne Avenue, which was bedecked with flags. Groups of visitors then wandered about the townsite to inspect the empty and hastily erected stores and shops. Then the

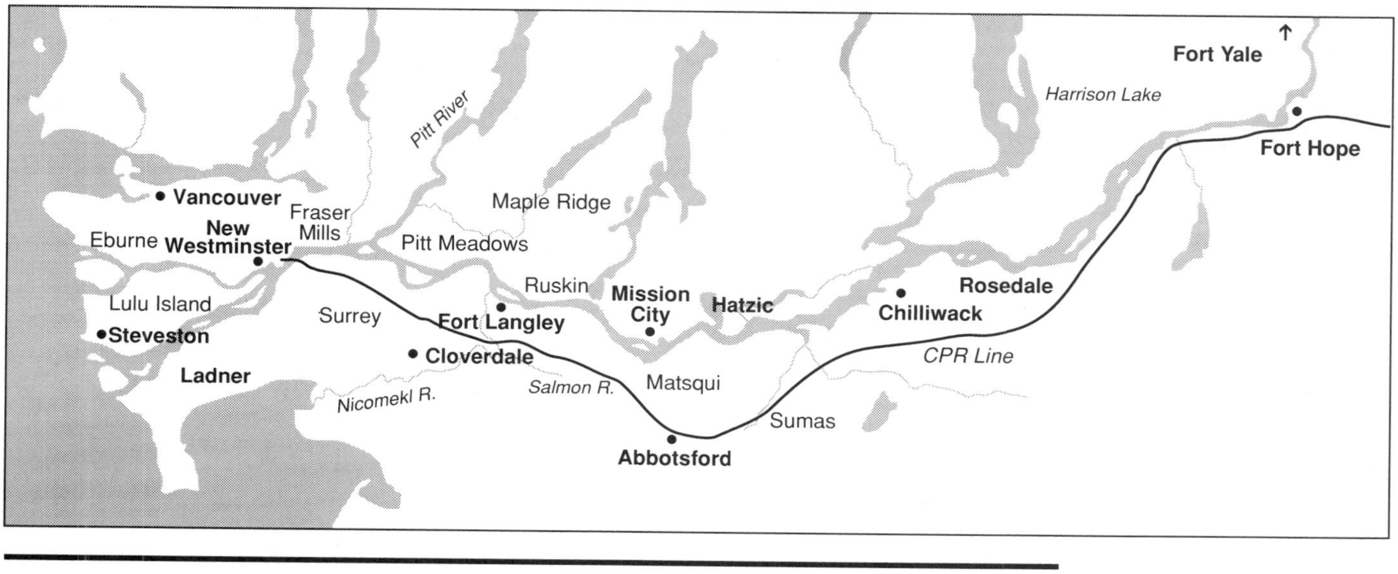

The Great Sale of Lots.

whistle of the *William Irving* blasted out its arrival, and the procession was again marched along by bands to the wharf to greet the New Westminster contingent.

The crowds were ushered into a large auction hall built for the occasion, where the local legislative member, Colin Sword, extolled the virtues of Mission, as did the auctioneer who followed him.

"It's Mission City!" bellowed a man in the audience, not just "Mission."

The bidding began. Within four hours, half of the lots were sold. Visions of instant capital gain flashed through the minds of buyers, and everyone present seemed to be imbued with unbounded optimism as to the future great city on the site. The one exception, perhaps, was a well-dressed lady from Vancouver who fell off a high board sidewalk into the mud.

Horne, in fact, experienced difficulty in disposing of the remaining town lots. A town did begin to grow from the nucleus that he had established, but it could hardly be called a boom. A few months after the auction, disgruntled settlers and shopkeepers met again at Horne's vacant hall to complain about Victoria's inaction respecting road improvements.

Two women pioneers present were asked to rise and be recognized at the meeting.

"These women," said the chairman, "have the fortitude to walk along a six inch cedar log and ford foaming, icy mountain streams on horseback. They put to shame some of our lofty legislators who, ensconced in luxurious homes, tread with slippered feet the nicely paved footpaths on the shores of James Bay."

The meeting then resolved to raise funds locally to build roads. In 1892, the Municipality of Mission was incorporated to finance such local improvements.

A most unusual experimental community in the woods emerged in 1896 at Ruskin, on the west bank of the Stave River. Where Murray Yale's barrel-makers used to cut staves, the Canadian Co-operative Society established a settlement based upon the socialist principles of John Ruskin. The centrepiece of this experiment was a large sawmill, accompanied by a store, school, and residential cottages. The residents agreed to share and share alike, regardless of effort or production.

In 1899, the Ruskin co-operative community experienced financial woes when the river level dropped so much that logs could not be floated down to the mill. Moreover, a number of co-op members became disgusted with having to support their lazier brethren. That year, the co-op sold its assets to E.H. Heaps & Sons Ltd, which rebuilt the mill and made British Columbia history by powering it electrically.

The now defunct Ruskin co-operative had ironically paved the way for large-scale commercial sawmilling activity in the region. Heaps built a twenty-two bedroom hotel for its employees, boardinghouses for Chinese workers, dining-room, general store, stables, brickyard, blacksmith shop, and even tennis courts. A company doctor lived on site.

The early nineties witnessed many improvements to Fraser Valley dyking systems. At Sumas, Matsqui, and in the delta areas, fortresses of rock and earth were confidently erected to counter *ta coutchi's* threat.

In east Delta, a leading figure in dyking efforts was John Oliver, who moved from Surrey to the shores of Mud Bay in 1882. This gruff farmer found a quarter section still available for homesteading because the land was unwanted - low-lying, riddled with salty sloughs, and covered with driftwood. Oliver was undeterred. He ignored the warnings and advice of other settlers and moved into his well-crafted cabin.

The Oliver farm was cleared first of driftwood by oxen and chain; then Oliver toiled for months on end in mud-caked rubber boots, ploughing, digging stumps, and erecting temporary dykes of sod and earth. He devised a system of underground drainage by means of sluice gates, which helped solve flooding problems, and drained away the white salty brine which had prevented the growth of cereal crops.

Fraser River floodwaters obliterate the CPR track at Hatzic, 1894.

Oliver developed a reputation for integrity and hard work. He served as alderman, reeve, and in 1900 as member of the Legislative Assembly for Delta, being known far and wide by the nickname of "Honest John."

Oliver was not too proud to get his hands dirty if the job demanded it. One day, while baling hay for William Ladner, he was asked to help rescue a cow that was stuck in a slough. Unless pulled loose quickly, Ladner explained, the animal would be drowned by the incoming tide.

Without hesitation, Oliver grabbed a rope, rushed to the slough, and plunged head first into the water, with his feet held by a companion. A minute later, a rather undignified John Oliver emerged spluttering from the depths, black with mud from head to foot. But he had managed to secure a rope around the cow, and the animal was rescued.

Sumas and Chilliwack had still failed to agree on common dyking measures to combat the annual depredations of the Chilliwack and Vedder Rivers. In early 1894, a Chilliwack resident clandestinely dynamited a log-jam on the Vedder, causing a surging wall of water and debris to be hurtled onto Sumas farms. The militia had to

Flooding at Chilliwack, 1894.

be called in from New Westminster to prevent the longstanding feud between the two settlements from escalating into civil war.

But the mischievousness of man paled beside the awesome power of nature that same year. Heavy snow, a cold winter, and sudden warming in May combined to cause the Fraser to rise to alarming levels. On May 28, an angry, foaming river swept away railway bridges in the Fraser Canyon. Onward in a broadening tide swept the floodwaters. Nicomen Island was entirely submerged; houses and livestock were carried away. At Hatzic, three hundred yards of railway track disappeared.

Nor did *ta coutchi* respect Colin Sword's fortress dyke at Matsqui. By midnight on the first day of the flood, thousands of acres were inundated. At New Westminster wharf, crowds gathered to watch piles of driftwood, debris, and even two live sheep on a hayrack float by on their way to the sea.

Rowboats tied up at the front door of Fort Langley's two hotels, at one of which the waters rose above the windows. Embankments near the fort itself disintegrated and were washed away. Mary Ann McLellan fled upstairs when a wall of water crashed into the main floor of her home. A few minutes later, she went into labour and was delivered of a baby boy by neighbour Agnes Towle, who had to tie Mary Ann's other son to his bed to prevent him from drowning downstairs.

Delta was saved from total destruction thanks to settlers who worked furiously to reinforce the dykes. Even church services were cancelled and clergymen toiled in the mud along with their congregations. In the areas near the river's mouth, the worst damage was caused by salt infiltrating the soil, and the lack of high ground where farmers might protect their cattle from the rising waters. A subsequent tuberculosis outbreak decimated the herds. Delta residents, however, were angry with the steamboats: "Much damage has been done to the dykes by steamers passing down river at full speed, their wash sweeping over the dykes and letting much water inside. The wash from the *Islander* last evening cut the top off the Delta dyke in places, and swept logs clean over the embankment."

Mission was completely inundated by the 1894 flood.

The steamboats' hurry had some justification. The *Gladys*, *William Irving*, *Transfer*, *Samson*, and *Bon Accord* worked day and night to save lives, livestock, and possessions. One poor fellow near Silverdale pleaded with his pigs to follow him to higher ground, even splashing through the water ahead of them holding high a plate of food—but to no avail. The *Gladys* plucked him aboard after assuring the farmer that his pigs would be saved. Many settlers were rescued from their rooftops and taken to higher ground at Mount Lehman and Sumas Mountain.

Relief camps were established by the provincial government. Only two people drowned—a small boy at Langley and a terrified Chinese, who flung himself into the river strapped to a barrel. Canoes navigated village streets, cattle bellowed pitifully, and small farmers were bankrupted.

Amidst this deluge, however, the settlers proved themselves a tough breed. Chilliwack residents, for example, paddled to church in canoes and tied their craft to pews while they prayed for deliverance. Even Chilliwack's newspaper editor showed gutsiness: "We have no telegraphic and very little postal communication; we have to perform...on foot, boat, canoe or raft; and to add to our discomforts the floor of our office is under water, and staff...have to stand on the precarious foundation of planks laid on blocks of wood. We are going to get out the paper however—if we have to build a scow."

For one week the Fraser Valley was paralysed. Many cases of selfless aid by neighbour to neighbour were recorded. St. Mary's opened its doors to refugees and Indian children delivered food, blankets, and medicine to beleaguered settlers. Some homes were destroyed; others filled with river sediment. When the waters finally receded, parents scolded their children for picking up dead fish from the mire. Crops were ruined. Some centres, such as Mission City, even relocated entirely to higher ground.

There was a silver lining to the tragedy. The rich river mud proved bountiful for farmers who replanted crops, and for years thereafter, almost freakishly large vegetables were grown, such as the monster turnips from Silverdale.

The flood also awakened government to its responsibility. "The magnitude of the dyking task," said Premier Davie, "places it beyond the ability of private enterprise and makes it clearly the duty of the state to undertake."

Dyking activity near Chilliwack, 1899. Local farmers contributed teams of horses.

A flood gauge was quickly installed at Mission Bridge and remains to this day the official bellwether of river trouble. Even so, government was slow in funding dyking repairs and projects. Local residents continued to bear the brunt of cost and labour. Alas, *ta coutchi* would return.

The "gay nineties" were a time of consolidation of trading patterns in the Fraser Valley. The nucleus of commerce was the New Westminster Farmers' Market. Opened in 1892 in a large shed west of the wharves, the market catered to farmers and urban shoppers hungry for fresh produce and meat. The official opening was attended by reeves and pioneer settlers from throughout the valley. So much trade was conducted at the market that a Vancouver alderman complained in 1896 that two-thirds of the produce sold in the Royal City was purchased by Vancouver residents. Frustrated Vancouver merchants even subsidized a steamboat company to make twice-weekly trips between Vancouver and Chilliwack to deliver farm goods and other wares.

Going to market was often a trying ordeal. Farmers in Langley would spend all night plodding along muddy roads with horse and wagon to reach the ferry landing at South Westminster in early morning, where the *Surrey* would transport them across the river. Steamboats brought produce and farmers from the more

The New Westminster Farmers' Market.

The Steves family residence under construction at Steveston, 1890. Note large wooden stave tank for domestic water supply at rear.

outlying areas such as Matsqui and Chilliwack, right to the market shed, which overhung the river. Delta produce was boated upriver—crates of chickens, cartons of eggs, sacks of vegetables, boxes of fruit, and even live pigs and chickens.

At the market, farmers rented stalls for displaying their goods. Teams of horses and cattle herds were auctioned in a big square. Chinese merchants flocked from Vancouver to buy as many as one hundred crates of chickens each week. Major sales of beef and lamb were made to St. Mary's Hospital, Vancouver's European Hotel, and numerous food stores. The market became such an integral part of valley life that when the buildings were destroyed by fire in 1898, Surrey and Matsqui Councils donated over $1,200 toward reconstruction.

The contours of New Westminster were changing. The stumps had disappeared; beautiful Victorian-style homes dotted the hillside; the muddy streets gave way to fine roads subject only to potholes. The harbour accommodated larger ocean-going vessels, thanks to improved navigation devices on the Fraser. In 1891, 128 households possessed telephones, and two years later a cable was laid across the river to South Westminster, and from there to Ladner. South Westminster was still under the jurisdiction of New Westminster, though later forming part of Surrey. Telephone service was established from New Westminster to Chilliwack in 1896.

On the evening of January 2, 1891, Columbia Street was bathed in light from a newly installed lighting system, though the power plant was fuelled by sawdust. The *Columbian* noted: "The streets were thronged with people for several hours who inspected with interest and delight the new electric lights...ladies and children made at least two-thirds of the throng and all appeared charmed with the effect and brilliancy of the new illuminator."

New Westminster was the hub of British Columbia high society. Fancy carriages carried the élite to gala balls in mansions replete with cut glass, horsehair sofas, and antimacassars. Grand opera was performed every Saturday night, and

Pauline Johnson often came to town to read her poetry. There were picnics to Derby and Harrison Lake by steamer; and exotic Chinatown. Moonlight cruises by sternwheeler on the Fraser were a favourite pastime. It was for the pleasure of these citizens that pioneer coffee maker John Murchie rolled his wagon down city streets, vending his special blend of brew.

The seedier side of life centred around the waterfront, where robberies, brawls, and prostitution were still rife. Japanese and Chinese girls were imported and sold as slaves for about five hundred dollars apiece.

The police were largely ineffectual. One police blotter of the day records: "Told all the women on Ramage Street they must keep their window blinds down at night." The inspector noted: "Will the police on night duty see that the above orders are strictly enforced."

The 1896 May Day parade, New Westminster.

Alas, they were not. A few days later a sergeant reported in shocked tones that French Lucy had stood at her door "in a low neck dress," and would not budge.

The modern pleasures of life could all be sampled in New Westminster by Fraser Valley settlers. Genuine Havana cigars were purchased for 10 cents each, and cigarettes were regarded as déclassé—smoked only by lower class elements and the underworld. Gentlemen paid $5.00 for their own gilded shaving mugs to be permanently on hand at their favourite barbershop, an establishment which, in the nineties at least, offered much more than a mere haircut. Jake Coon provided the works: a cut and shave, followed by a singe, egg and lemon shampoo, massage, and dandruff cure. For his more affluent customers, the barber might procure some good rum from a café upstairs, served discreetly to the customer in a teapot.

The clash of primitive and modern conveyances was a common occurrence. The *Columbian* reported: "A milk dealer's team took fright at a tram car on Columbia Street today and tore down at great speed, sprinkling the mud with rich milk and dropping the odd milk can on the road. The mad gallop ended with the team hitting an electric light pole—vehicle much damaged." Dogs frequently scared horses into bolting; and juvenile delinquents often loosened nuts on carriage wheels, an act which sometimes resulted in injuries to the occupants.

Sanitation was still a major problem in the Royal City. Constable Miller noted one day that "an overflow from the WC in rear of the city hall is running down over the square, the odour of which speaks for itself." Author Frances McNab travelled through the Fraser Valley in the nineties and recorded her impressions of New Westminster:

> "I spent the following night at New Westminster—a second-rate little town with a vile inn. All night the inhabitants sang songs in the streets; and as I was dressing the next morning, I saw a dray and two horses drive into a plate-glass window."

Criminals crowded into the penitentiary. This was an era of fakery and con artists—the inevitable trash of civilization—and phoney doctors, self-proclaimed ministers, and philanderers abounded. But more serious crimes kept cells occupied as well.

The story of Slumach, the Katzie Indian, is now legend. In the 1880s, Slumach discovered gold nuggets in the wild region north of Pitt Lake. He allegedly came to New Westminster with his gold and spent freely at saloons and gaming houses. When he returned to the wilderness, he generally took with him some white woman he had picked up in the city—who would never be seen alive again.

Molly Tynan was the ninth woman to disappear with Slumach. She was also the first of the missing females whose body turned up—face up and floating down the Fraser with a knife through her heart. Slumach was questioned, but there was insufficient evidence to charge him.

Records show that Slumach was hanged for the murder of Louis Bee on January 16, 1891, at the provincial gaol yard. It was thought that Bee had tried to follow Slumach to his gold mine, but the evidence at trial established only that there had been an altercation between the two men, and that Bee had borne a grudge against Slumach from an earlier incident. In today's courts, Slumach would in all likelihood have been acquitted, but the all white jury decided otherwise. Before his death, Slumach allegedly said, "When I die, my mine dies with me—and all those who try to find it will die also."

As Slumach was awaiting trial, he gave the location of the lost mine to his nephew, Peter Pierre, an Oblate catechist and medicine man of the Katzie reserve. Pierre went looking for the gold cache and promptly broke his hip. He is said to have given a map of the mine to an old prospector, but today, one hundred years after Slumach's death, the lost gold mine legend is still very much alive in British Columbia—as is the curse. At least twenty-five gold hunters are said to have perished looking for Slumach is gold, many of their bodies never found. Katzie Indians still say in Chinook, "Mine memloose": It is a dead man's mine.

Opium, diamonds, and Chinese labourers were the prime components in a large smuggling ring operated by swashbuckling Jake Terry and Larry Kelley from a waterfront office in New Westminster in the nineties. "Cowboy Jake" used the old Semiahmoo Trail to smuggle Chinese into Washington.

Following the completion of the Mission to Huntingdon rail line, Terry stole handcars in the middle of the night. The Chinese did the pushing. On the evening of July 24, 1891, Terry was caught by three customs officers at Sedro Wooley. When commanded to halt, Terry opened fire; and when the shooting stopped, Cowboy Jake lay badly wounded, a customs officer was dead, and Terry's Chinese clients had escaped to their comrades in San Francisco. Terry served a long term in San Quentin. When he was released in 1906, he returned to New Westminster to continue his life of crime.

Jake Terry used female accomplices on several occasions. One day, a well-dressed lady boarded the train at Sumas, Washington, leading a large, shaggy dog on a leash. After some argument, the dog was placed in the baggage car, where it attracted the attention of a customs officer because of the frantic manner in which

Charlton's General Store, Haney.

the canine tried to scratch its back. The officer inspected the dog's back carefully, and to his surprise he discovered razor slits, in which were found several glittering diamonds.

The dog was given immediate medical treatment and became the mascot of a railway section crew. The dog's mistress was apprehended and soon shed her fur coat in prison.

Larry Kelley smuggled Chinese on his motor cruiser at fifty dollars apiece via the San Juan Islands. The famous China Caves which boaters visit on Sucia Island are so named for the Chinese who were dropped off there by Kelley and other smugglers. Often, Kelley's American counterpart vessel failed to rendezvous, with the result that unknown numbers were left to starve to death on the isolated island.

Even more cruel was Kelley's practice of bundling each Chinese passenger in a weighted gunnysack at embarkation, on the understanding that if a customs vessel should approach, the Chinese would be instantly thrown overboard. Apparently, many drowned in this fashion; on several occasions, tips from reliable sources led customs officials to Kelley's boat, only to find it empty of cargo.

So efficient were both Terry and Kelley that they carried on their illegal activities for some thirty years, interrupted only by Terry's San Quentin sentence and the odd short stay in jail for Kelley.

The banner year of 1891 also witnessed the opening of a proper courthouse in New Westminster. But the public's attention continued to focus upon the penitentiary.

Alex Houston, son of James, was serving fourteen years for killing an eighty-year-old Indian woman at Fort Langley when he escaped from the prison grounds while hoeing in a field. Recaptured, Houston was tried before Judge Begbie and a jury in 1893 for shooting at his jailors when they pursued him. Begbie ordered an acquittal when evidence proved that the gun used could not be fired with accuracy beyond five yards.

When Houston pleaded guilty to escaping custody before another judge, Begbie was asked his opinion on sentence and responded: "...the poor devil had forfeited all remissions previously earned; and the prosecutor in the last case had riddled him with buckshot after Houston had complied with the command to throw up his hands." Begbie recommended a concurrent rather than cumulative sentence, showing a leniency rare for the age.

On June 11, 1894, Judge Begbie died in Victoria and was buried near the grave of James Douglas. A simple, self-authored epitaph was inscribed on his tombstone: "Lord be merciful to me a sinner." Tributes were manifold, and the sadness was shared by several needy Fraser Valley families whom Begbie had quietly assisted financially.

Steveston's main street, ca. 1908. The well known Commercial Hotel is to the left.

John Robson became premier of the province in 1889. The veteran newspaperman continued to lead a colourful life, running for both the New Westminster and Cariboo seats in the 1890 general election, winning in each riding, and being kidnapped during the course of the campaign by some political opponents.

As premier, Robson pressed his many strongly held views, including his fierce opposition to oriental immigration and liquor—making him a favourite speaker on the temperance circuit. His last year of office, in 1892, was punctuated by bitter attacks upon his government, including a vicious diatribe by the Kennedy brothers, who owned his old newspaper, the *Columbian*, known at that time as the *British Columbian*. The Kennedy editorial attacked the government for rejecting legislation to incorporate the interurban railway between New Westminster and Vancouver. The government rammed through a Legislative Assembly Privileges Act in response, pursuant to which Robson had the Kennedy brothers arrested in New Westminster and taken to jail in Victoria. They were soon released. Robson had apparently forgotten the lesson from his own days as "A Voice From The Dungeon."

Robson became obsessed with a scheme to import a number of Scottish crofters to British Columbia to work in the fishing industry, hoping to displace the Chinese who worked in the canneries. For this purpose, he travelled to Britain in June of 1892. Somehow his finger was crushed in the door of a cab while he was in London, and three days later he died of blood poisoning. He, too, was buried near

Douglas in Victoria's Ross Bay Cemetery.

Robson's death failed to silence the hysterical anti-Chinese sentiment expressed by so many whites. A Chinese was accused of stealing a Chilliwack cow in these terms:

> "Our celestial friends from the Flowery Kingdom have developed a "heap likee" for the white man's chickens, turkeys, pigs, etc. and now... beef. One of these pig-tailed and rascally bipeds became so enamoured of G.W. McKeever's cattle that he determined to place himself on the outside of it...G.W.objected and Johnnie will probably languish for some time in the New Westminster jail...Some of these marauding Mongolians will come home missing one of these nights—or a band of irate ranchers may clean out a few of our opium dens...."

Excellent gardeners and very thrifty, the "threat" that the Chinese presented to the white farmer was less that of thievery and vice than it was of honest competition. The Chinese were also different, speaking a strange tongue and wearing strange clothes. Young James Kipp and his friends in Chilliwack would pelt Chinese with snowballs and pull their queues, but think nothing of asking the same Chinese for firecrackers, nuts and candy on Chinese New Year's Day.

Chinese businessmen in front of their New Westminster shop, 1895.

Graft and corruption at Chinese expense were a common occurrence. For many years, some Chinese railway labourers had to pay three dollars to a Canadian Pacific Railway supervisor for the privilege of working. When paycheques were handed out at Mission Wharf to railway coolies, the cheques for any absent workers were often forfeited to the paymaster. These practices and public pranks would gradually wither in frequency over the years as the Chinese learned to protect their rights, and the majority of whites came to accept their presence. But it was a long and difficult road.

Those who employed Chinese found them to be invariably conscientious, honest, and neat. Judge Begbie surveyed the situation well:

> "Industry, economy, sobriety and law-abidingness are exactly the four prominent qualities of Chinamen as asserted both by their advocates and by their adversaries. Lazy, drunken, extravagant and turbulent: that is...exactly what a Chinaman is not. This is, on the whole, the real cause of their unpopularity. If Chinamen would only be less industrious and economical, if they would but occasionally get drunk, they would no longer be the formidable competitors with the white man."

The growing Chinese community in New Westminster was located in a low-

Hogs being driven to market on Front Street, New Westminster 1904.

lying waterfront area known as The Swamp. Here more than one thousand Chinese lived when not employed in valley canneries, sawmills, or railway construction camps. The squalor was dreadful; makeshift boardinghouses were crammed in among livery stables and Indian shacks.

New Westminster native son Richard McBride assumed Robson's role in railing stridently against the Chinese taking "white" jobs. Only white British subjects should be allowed to fish, he argued; and his slogan "No aliens need apply" became a rallying cry for many bigots thereafter. McBride's election as Dewdney member of the Legislative Assembly for the Conservative Party in 1898 was a narrow victory, undoubtedly secured by his popular anti-Oriental views.

Significant Chinese communities also existed in Vancouver, Victoria, Steveston, and Chilliwack, where mass meetings of the Asiatic Exclusion League were held from time to time. In Steveston, the murder of Police Chief Alex Main by two Chinese raised a clarion call for action. Main had set out in search of stolen goods at a Chinese shack. When his badly mutilated body was found near the dwelling, Yip Chuck and Chanyu Chung were arrested. The Vancouver *Province* created the ultimate Chinese bogeyman:

> "Yip is one of the ugliest looking specimens of a bad Chinaman ever landed in British Columbia. His face is of the blackest of his race, his upper teeth protrude, his eyes are fierce and his hair is like that of a barbarian."

Steveston whites, and even a mob of Japanese, threatened to lynch the

Chinese defendants. The accused were finally removed to safety. Yip Chuck was hanged after a proper trial, but his ghost lived on in the minds of white settlers.

In Ladner, police regularly raided Chinese gambling dens, where fantan games were popular. Opium was frequently seized, although in many towns it was common to see Chinese contentedly smoking opium pipes in and around their cabins.

Chilliwack aldermen raged over unsanitary Chinese huts—never bothering to consider that the starvation wages paid to their occupants by good corporate citizens like the Canadian Pacific Railway did not allow for better living quarters. The very tidy gardens complementing the Chinese dwellings were ignored.

In Hatzic, the literary aspirants of the Corn Cob Club, who met in a cave overlooking Hatzic Prairie, effusively compared Orientals to lepers. Segregation was the rule at public functions in the Valley. At a typical Dominion Day celebration in New Westminster, a reporter noted that "the whites and blacks drank all the beer, the Indians ate all the fruit, and the Chinese looked on and did not pay a cent." White comments about Chinese thrift were usually tinged with bitter envy, although grudging admiration developed as Chinese grocers gradually came to dominate the fresh vegetable stalls at the Farmers' Market.

The Chinese gained a solid reputation in the canneries, where they came to dominate the work force. Yip Sang originated the Chinese contractor system, securing wages for cannery workers of some $30 per month, with Chinese overseers receiving $45.

During the peak salmon runs, canneries employed hundreds of workers. As the runs slowed, workers were laid off and returned to live at New Westminster and other towns, where they barely subsisted on two meals of rice per day.

Indian women performed an important role at the canneries. Their work involved the cleaning of fish, making web for the nets, and stacking boxes. They were paid eleven cents per hour. Musqueam and Chewasin natives arrived early in the season at Delta canneries. Katzies and other upriver Indians usually worked at New Westminster area canneries. The Haidas, and other Vancouver Island tribes, arrived by canoes, often racing their craft in friendly intertribal competition up and down the Fraser. It was common for entire families of natives to reach the cannery barefoot and in a state of near starvation.

Native family buying ice cream at Imperial Cannery, Steveston.

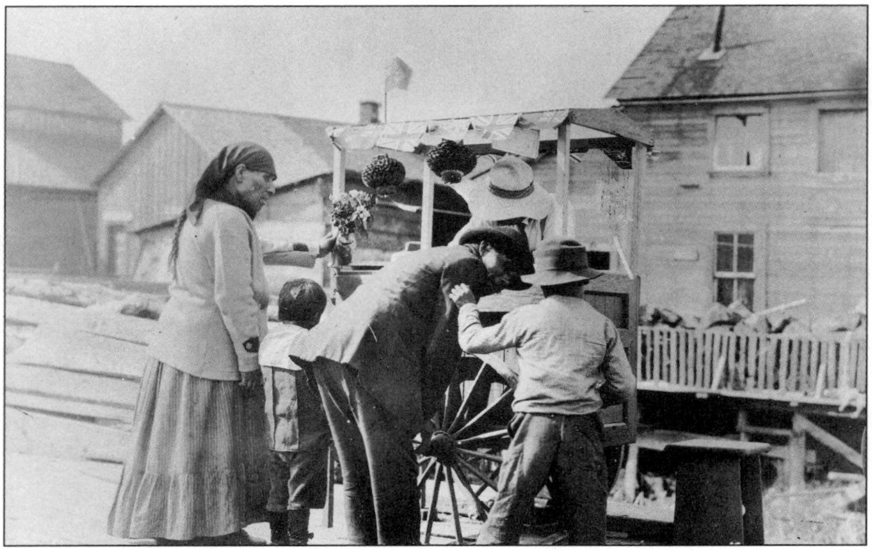

A "rancherie" was designated at each cannery, where Indians built cedar summer dwellings in the fashion of their forefathers. The difference, of course, was that they were no longer free to earn a living independently, and legally fished only as employees of the cannery, for lower wages than their white counterparts. The credit which the cannery store extended to Indian workers at the start of each fishing season only compounded their dependency on their employers.

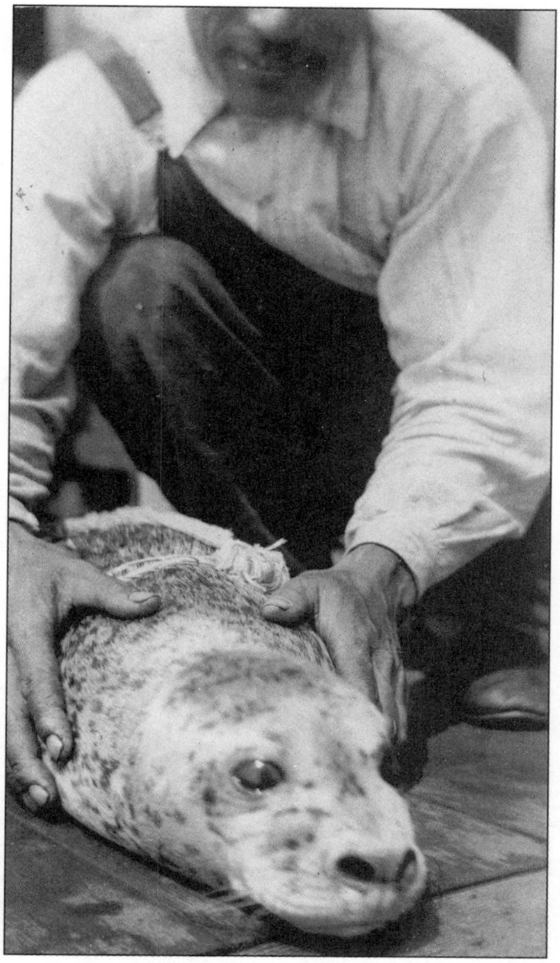

Baby seals were often caught in fishermen's nets on the Fraser River.

Seals were often caught in fishermen's nets. White fishermen would knock the animal on the head and throw it back into the river. Indians, however, would frequently bring the seal onto the boat, fasten a rope to it, and take it back to the rancherie as a playmate for the children. The seal would then dine well on a diet of salmon heads. On occasion the seal would become so tame that Indian children would take their pet out in a canoe on the Fraser and allow it to romp about.

T. Ellis Ladner was haunted by the songs of the seal and the Indian on the river:

> "Two sounds I have never forgotten are the seal's cry at night and the song of the Indian inducing fish to swim into his net. The cry of the seal closely resembled that of a dreaming infant; the Indian's song was a composition of his own—a tune of a few bars, sometimes with improvised words. On a quiet, moonlit night, with the stillness so absolute as to be heard, the cry of the seal or the song of the Indian broke through with a suddenness both weird and startling."

Japanese fishermen began arriving in strength in British Columbia during the late 1890s. Unlike the Chinese, the Japanese were not subject to the immigrant head tax. In much the same way in which Chinese agricultural skills upset white farmers, however, the Japanese fishermen's abilities were soon seen as a threat by their white counterparts.

In 1893, the Fraser River Benevolent Association was formed by 1,500 white fishermen to protect their share of the fishery from resident Japanese, as well as American fishermen. Later, the powerful Fishermen's Union, based in New Westminster and Vancouver, emerged to fight for higher fish prices and reduced government regulation of the fishery—a battle still being waged today. (The Fraser River Benevolent Association changed its name to the Fraser River Fishermen's Protective Union. The Fishermen's Union was later known as the United Fishermen & Allied Workers' Union.)

By 1896, there were forty-seven Fraser River canneries producing 601,570 cases of salmon, of which nearly 539,000 cases were exported. In 1897, sockeye salmon entered the Fraser in such numbers that the canneries could not handle the flow. Tom Ladner gazed on seventy-five thousand glistening salmon piled high on his Delta Cannery wharf and overflowing the scows. Marco Vidulich, a Ladner fisherman, described the wealth of fish that season:

> "My biggest set was 900 sockeye at one time... Catching 500 was nothing, and we used old linen nets 45 fathoms long...We'd leave at four in the morning in our big, 25 foot rowing skiff. Four hours hard work out to the net; pull it, take out the sockeye. Throw away all the coho, chum, pinks,

and big, big springs. Canneries wouldn't take those fish, but we'd have about 500 sockeye. There would be just room for us to row."

Sturgeon fishing was also popular, and, for a few years, American canneries paid four cents per pound for the antediluvian creature of the deep. Agents of these canneries came up the Fraser with scows and derricks equipped with block and tackle to haul in the five hundred pound monsters. Cross line nets across the river bottom were initially used, but they were soon banned, with the result that poaching at night became rampant. Cornie Kelleher caught one sturgeon near Mission Bridge which weighed in at 1,010 pounds. He had to hail the steamer *Gladys* and have his fish hauled aboard by a steam winch and then transported to a cannery at New Westminster.

The independent white fisherman lived a solitary existence, often occupying a vacant shack or lean-to along the river. Such fishermen sold fish to hotels, canneries, and the Farmers' Market. Frances McNab observed a typical dwelling of one such "river rat":

"Two small canoes lay moored to a single plank... As we drew near, a dog rushed out to the canoes from the heavy screen of maples and aspens. Almost concealed in the dense greenery I saw a small shack, in front of

Fishing boats at Steveston, "after the night watch."

which there burnt a fire upon the ground, with a black pot suspended above on cross-sticks. Inside the cabin, through the open doorway, I caught a glimpse of the fisherman sitting on a settle before a table, enjoying a solitary meal. There was just room in the cabin for himself and his dog - a kind of black collie...."

Many year-round Fraser fishermen lived on houseboats—usually ramshackle cabins perched on rafts. A tug carried these craft upriver in autumn, sometimes to Harrison Lake. In the spring, they floated down with the current to a chosen base for the season's fishing activity.

The most disgusting practice of the canneries was their dumping of fish offal into the Fraser. This assumed special importance near the river's mouth, where the incoming tide swept the decaying matter into sloughs and over lowlands, resulting in contamination of both pasture lands and water supply. The reeking odour also did nothing to enhance Ladies' Aid picnics.

Following a petition by William Ladner and John Kirkland in 1893, the Fisheries Commission ruled that the disposing of offal, dead fish, sawdust, and mill rubbish into the Fraser was harmful to both the water and people. The canneries ceased the practice, and the Delta dairy industry began to prosper once more.

Despite the destitution of many Indian families, the canneries and other seasonal employers made Fraser Valley Indians more affluent than their brethren elsewhere in the province. At the end of August, most Indians would leave the rancherie and proceed to hop fields in Washington, Sardis and Agassiz. The natives also laboured in mills, shipyards, and on railway maintenance crews. This rotating pattern of seasonal activity was consistent with the Stalo heritage, which was first seriously studied in 1892 when anthropologist Charles Hill-Tout began examination of relics from the Great Fraser Midden, a 4.5-acre site discovered by road workers at Marpole.

Quarters for native workers, Imperial Cannery, Steveston.

The failure of Indians to engage in economically viable farming activities unsettled the Catholic missionaries, since the bedrock of federal government and their own policies toward native education was the plan for transition from a nomadic to an agricultural lifestyle. Of some 47,492 acres of Fraser reserve lands gazetted in 1897, only 3,705 acres were under cultivation. The priests and nuns of St. Mary's were particularly concerned, as they were now receiving annual government subsidies to operate the mission school, so confident was Ottawa in their successfully promoting the agricultural objective.

Still, the Oblates were proud of their successes in the general education and religious training fields; Bishop Durieu could report in 1898 that of 3,185 Indians in the Fraser Valley, 2,073 were Catholic, 194 Protestant, and 178 pagan. (The remaining 740 were presumably agnostics.)

The Indian population was still steadily declining. Within British Columbia, the total number of natives was reduced from 46,000 to 26,620 in the twenty-year period of 1871 to 1891. Much of this reduction was attributable to diseases such as smallpox and tuberculosis, the former less common in the Fraser Valley due to the assiduous vaccination efforts of the Oblates.

The Methodists were not to be outdone by Catholics, and so founded an alternate Indian residential school in 1886 on the Squihala Reserve near Sardis, named Coqualeetza Institute. The first buildings were destroyed by fire in 1891, and replaced by a brick structure which accommodated an average of 150 Indian students for many years to come. The typical enrolment period for a Coqualeetza student was two years and ten months.

The Coqualeetza Institute.

The secular instruction at Coqualeetza was similar to St. Mary's, with a heavy emphasis upon agriculture. Truancy was common and "boys ran away from the fields where they were digging potatoes and were found fishing in Luckakluck Creek." The school developed a tradition of round-table discussion and dialogue respecting native issues; prior to the 1960s, the Coqualeetza Friendship Society was unique as the only province-wide non-political Indian organization in existence.

The impetus given to agriculture by improved transportation facilities was bolstered further by advances in technology on the farm and improved techniques of cultivation. Fall fairs were organized in each district, and communities competed keenly to win prizes at the annual Provincial Exhibition held at New Westminster. The tradition of the fall fair became embedded in the culture of the Fraser Valley, involving schools, churches, and service groups of all persuasions.

The Dominion Experimental Farm was established on 1,400 acres at Agassiz in 1888. Here trees, shrubs, fruits, nuts, and grains from all over the world were cultivated. Unique crossbreeds of many varieties were developed, and intensive work was performed to improve the health of cattle and the quality of their milk and butter. One cow, named Segis May Echo, set a world record when she produced 30,886 pounds of milk and 1,345 pounds of butter in one year.

The first Holstein cattle arrived in the late eighties, and soon proved to be ideally suited to the valley's rich, wet pasture lands.

The refinements of civilization percolated slowly into the scattered farming settlements. The first British Columbia child born by caesarean section was delivered by Dr. George Drew in Fort Langley in 1896. No longer was New Westminster the only base for professional medical treatment. However, local facilities remained primitive until communities obtained enough of a population to support hospitals.

In Chilliwack, young men formed a business transporting ladies who wished to be taken on local fishing expeditions—offering to carry women of all ages over streams and sloughs. Dances moved out of family kitchens and into community halls, where the Highland Fling, eight hand reel, Red River Jig, and numerous quadrilles were performed to the tune of two or three fiddles. Whiskey flowed, although serious drunkenness was rare; and young people literally danced the night away until a dawn "home waltz" signalled that it was time to leave. The many bachelors living on the land were reminded at such jamborees of the tradition that whoever refused a lady's Leap Year proposal of marriage must buy her a silk dress. The Christmas celebration was a community affair which centred in the 1890's upon the local school.

Port Haney in the 1900s.

In 1893, the Haney school Christmas concert was held at the new town hall. The settlers arrived by horse and buggy with their children, the snow crisp underfoot. A few souls even rowed across the Fraser from Langley. The women wore long dresses and high buttoned blouses, and carried baskets of homemade food. The men wore dark suits. Inside, a huge Douglas fir glimmered in the dimly lit hall, bedecked with decorations, little presents nestled among its branches.

The settlers ate upstairs at three long tables made of cedar planks laid on saw-horses. Following the meal, the school concert was performed, with some forty pupils acting and singing their recitals. Then the coal oil lamps were dimmed and the Christmas tree lit up by dozens of tiny candles. This was the signal for Santa Claus to appear. The little children and babies were soon bundled off to bed, and the dancing began to the tune of two screeching Albion fiddles. Dances like the quadrille and cotillion involved a frequent change of partners, and soon settlers who had not seen one another for weeks or even months were experiencing a joyful spirit of camaraderie. A general recession prevailed at the time, but nobody present at that 1893 festive occasion in Haney Hall considered themselves very deprived.

Crude schoolhouse near New Westminster. The school board preferred to hire women teachers from rural backgrounds.

Most rural schools were still rustic affairs—basic shacks with long rusty box stoves, blackboards, scarred and battered double-desks, and a rickety table for the teacher. If a playground existed, it was usually patchy, uneven and barely fit for goats to frolic upon. Keeping a school open was challenging, for the law required that a minimum number of pupils attend regularly, failing which the school would close. One teacher piggybacked a two-year-old toddler to school every day to meet the quota.

John Duncan MacLean, a future minister of education, taught in Mission City schools, and declared "Happy and contented children, well educated, and surrounded by a clean, wholesome environment, are the foundations of a nation's success." Someone should have enlightened Old Man Moore, also a Mission teacher, who used a coiled razor strap measuring one foot long and two inches wide to discipline his class. The strap was kept in the teacher's pocket until a pupil misbehaved, when Moore whipped the weapon out and threw it at the offender. The strap wrapped around the victim's neck like a python and left a red streak for several days.

Another teacher in the district, nicknamed "Old Billy-gut," wielded a large cedar stick in class and on days after nights of heavy drinking, he would lash out at students for the slightest misdemeanour—real or imagined—using, in his own words, "stunning, crushing blows" to the hands and legs.

The road to truly refined town living was long and arduous, as the *Chilliwack Progress* editor lamented:

"Our citizens can take steps to clear the streets of rubbish piled up outside our stores. We can surely insist on the owners of cattle to have them properly fed and fenced in, instead of being turned adrift to annoy their neighbours...to prowl around and damage our gardens or soil our drying clothes...Surely too we are to blame for dozens of dogs which visit from house to house and thieve what they can, when these mongrels might just as well be kept at home, or better still, shot....Who hasn't experienced the annoyance of being nearly run over by a group of frantic horses...which go tearing along our streets in the afternoons imperilling the lives of our little ones. These are things which may be expected and overlooked in an Indian rancherie, but surely we ought to aspire to something better...."

The editor realized he may have gone too far about shooting dogs, when several canines were poisoned to death shortly after his comments were published. His next crusade was against cruelty to animals.

Away from the rural centres, settlers toiled in the woods with cross cut saw, broadaxe and grub hoe to carve a home and farm out of the wilderness. Wild animals abounded. Farm wives were often left alone with children for lengthy periods, when they might encounter bears in the back yard and bearded strangers calling at the house for a meal. Meanwhile, the ceaseless chores of cooking, preserving, knitting, quilting, washing, and tending to children and their ailments consumed all of a woman's energy—God help the farm wife who ever fell ill.

Accidents and pranks were common occurrences. A Canadian Pacific Railway foreman in Langley ordered a worker one day to remove the carcass of a dead horse from the tracks, only to return later and find the body dangling twenty feet overhead in a tangle of telegraph wires. The worker had decided to employ dynamite to destroy the carcass and had used an excess of powder.

In another Langley incident, a farmer told two teenage boys to steal a turkey from a neighbouring farm. An hour later, the boys returned with the body of

Logging operation, Langley, 1890s.

a twenty-pound turkey, which the farmer happily roasted and served. Next morning, the farmer realized that his prize pet, Old Tom, was missing, and that he had cooked and eaten his own bird.

The site of the old Hudson's Bay fort in Fort Langley was sold to Alex Mavis in 1888, and the Company store in the village was closed in 1896 due to continual losses. Never known for sentimentality, the Hudson's Bay Company paid no further attention to the area until, almost a century later, it opened a department store in Langley City. The fort site, like Derby, was left for the cows to enjoy. Today, however, the site of the fort is managed by the Fort Langley National Historic Park.

The Derby site of the first fort was farmed by Alex Houston after he was finally released from prison. It has since been acquired by the Greater Vancouver Regional District.

The abandoned buildings of the Hudson's Bay Company's Fort Langley site. The building on the right, now restored as the trading store, is possibly the oldest intact structure in British Columbia.

The Fraser Valley's links with its past were being severed by the deaths of all of the earliest pioneers. Another old friend departed in 1888, when the *Beaver* grounded on the rocks off Prospect Point. Legend has it that as the historic steamer was chugging out of Vancouver Harbour, the captain realized suddenly that the liquor supply had been left behind in Gastown and ordered an immediate turn of the vessel back to port. The pioneer ship was lost forever. However, shortly before the accident, Hudson's Bay veteran John Work had rescued the ship's bell as the vessel underwent repairs, and had delivered it to Fort Langley, where it was hung in the belfry of Alexander Dunn's St. Andrew's Presbyterian Church.

The large sternwheelers which had served the Fraser Valley so well since the sixties were now being displaced by smaller vessels intended to concentrate on servicing the local trade.

The rate of attrition of the larger vessels was accelerated on the evening September 10, 1898, when fire broke out in the New Westminster wharf area and quickly consumed the steamers *Gladys, Edgar*, and *Bon Accord*. The night watchman on the *Gladys* dangled for his life from the paddle wheel of the vessel until rescued by a crew manning a rowboat from another harbour ship. The three steamers, fully ablaze, were cut loose from their moorings and drifted downriver in the night in a bizarre procession.

The waterfront blaze gained momentum as it devoured hay stored on the docks. Soon flames spread to the Farmers' Market, and onward through the business district, destroying all in its path. A northeast wind fed the raging inferno, as it wound up and around the hillside, consuming Alex Ewen's fine home among others, as well as such landmarks as the *Columbian's* office, Number One Fire Hall,

The devastation wrought by New Westminster's Great Fire of 1898.

the Young Men's Christian Association building, the public library, and various salmon canneries and business establishments.

Royal City residents ran terrified up the hill, clinging to their possessions; others drove wagons or carts before them. Adding to the danger were flaming shingles which were carried by the wind over the city, as well as exploding ammunition and blasting powder stored in warehouses. Amidst the smoky chaos there were heard explosions from blazing canneries, as cans of salmon blew apart, hurtling shredded fish and shards of tin through the air.

The efforts of the Hyacks and Vancouver Fire Department saved some blocks of the downtown core and prevented the fire from proceeding west beyond 10th Street. But the major portion of the city lay in ruins: "In the sickly sight of Sunday's dawn, thousands looked down on the smoking remains of what, six hours before, had been as beautiful, well built and well kept a city as there was on the coast."

The stunned populace met Sunday afternoon to form a relief committee. Some five hundred homeless residents were fed at relief centres and Royal City homes were thrown open to shelter them. Donations poured in from across Canada during the next few weeks and months. The Victoria Chinese Benevolent Society sent $1,500 to aid burned out Chinese, and the Chinese community led the way in commencing reconstruction of brick buildings forthwith. Valley communities contributed to the rebuilding of the Farmers' Market.

Investigation into the cause of the fire centred upon the dock area, and the popular theory had it that the *Gladys*, or a spark from a passing sternwheeler, was responsible. Others reported the curious sight of three male strangers hoisting a skull and crossbones to the top of the Public School flagpole one hour before the blaze erupted. The strangers were never found or identified.

Most of the city's business section was rebuilt within a year. The *Columbian* reported: "The new Royal City with pluck true and gritty rose, phoenix-like from the wreck." Many new buildings were of sounder construction, and improvements were made to the previously jammed, dilapidated waterfront streets and structures, including the layout of the Farmers' Market.

And so the century closed in the soft twilight of the Victorian era. Many believed the age would never end. In celebration of the Queen's Diamond Jubilee, Judge Norman Bole orated to some five thousand ecstatic people in Queen's Park in 1897, citing the principal accomplishments of Queen Victoria's rule—Empire, progress, and the triumph of Anglo-Saxon culture.

Floods, famine, and war were faraway problems. The mainstream white population of British Columbia wanted roads, railways, and growth, and successive provincial governments were determined to give it to them. The more affluent were now purchasing buggies with rubber tires. There was even talk of a new, motorized contraption which would render old Dobbin obsolete.

CHAPTER ELEVEN

THE GOLDEN YEARS

In July of 1900, valley fishermen staged a huge strike against the Fraser River Canners Association. The canners had sought to control salmon prices and the number of fishboats, whereas the fishermen sought better prices for salmon and free access by independent fishermen to the canneries of their choice.

Caught in the middle of the dispute were some 1,700 Japanese fishermen, comprising one-third of the entire fishing industry, the vast majority of whom spoke no English.

For twenty-three days the strike continued. During this period, some members of the Japanese Fishermen's Benevolent Society defied the strike by openly fishing. They did this partly for their own survival, since many lived at the canneries and were told that unless they fished, the canneries would cut off their food supply. Nets and sails were slashed; tempers flared. The militia were called in by the canneries, and troops travelled from Vancouver to Steveston, where violence threatened. A week later, the strike was settled when the canneries agreed to pay fishermen nineteen cents per fish.

The real winners were the salmon. Enormous numbers escaped the fishermen's nets that year; but in 1901, one of the largest salmon runs in history ascended the Fraser and eclipsed the loss to the industry. Nearly a million cases were packed.

The new era of industrial relations, however, portended trouble for the Fraser Valley's top cash trade.

Fisherman deliver their catch to a New Westminster cannery, 1905.

Interior of Pacific Coast Cannery, Steveston 1905.

Negotiations during the early years of the new century were difficult and many acts of violence occurred during strikes. At Steveston, there was hand-to-hand fighting on fishboats, net slashing, sabotage, and gunfire.

The labour strife was related to and accentuated racial tension, as "competition among the major racial groups provided the first important stimulus to organize." The Japanese were excluded from the white unions; the Asiatic Exclusion League became vogue; and Victoria childishly attempted to flout federal control of immigration by illegally imposing a head tax of five hundred dollars on each Japanese entering the province.

Richard McBride fitted well into the maelstrom of the new century's politics. On June 2, 1903, he became the first native-born premier of British Columbia, and at thirty-three years of age, the youngest.

McBride's first act as premier was to announce the advent of party politics and the end of factionalism. "Glad Hand Dick" was amiable, polished, and well liked. His astute exploitation of anti-Oriental sentiment and mastery of the art of Ottawa-bashing assured him a long term in office.

McBride also kept a boyish sense of humour, which was demonstrated on one occasion when he and Stuart Gifford "borrowed" a streetcar they found empty one night in New Westminster after attending a political meeting. A policeman chased the runaway tram up Columbia Street, and caught up with it only to see two shadows flee into the black of the night.

The Conservative premier mirrored John Robson in many respects, though with greater suaveness. They both came from the Royal City, were of similar political beliefs—McBride using sugar to get his way, where Robson used vinegar—and their fathers were both prison wardens. (Arthur McBride was suspended as penitentiary warden in 1894 in the wake of a Royal Commission Inquiry into prison operations. He was alleged to have received hams for favours.)

For a short time, McBride had even owned the *Columbian*. As premier, he managed government finances soundly; he also improved transport facilities, established a provincial university, and passed legislation which required most timber cut from Crown lands to be processed within the province.

Japanese workers with dried salmon at Steveston wharf, 1908.

The Canadian Pacific Railway's Vancouver & Lulu Island Railway from Vancouver to Steveston was completed in 1905. This line was followed in 1909 by a branch railway connecting Eburne to New Westminster. These interurban tramways were patronized heavily by Vancouver shoppers who purchased produce and fish at Steveston and New Westminster markets. Hundreds of urban dwellers also travelled on special excursion trains to watch the fishing fleet go out. Indians rode the rails in profusion during the canning season. New Westminster merchants no longer complained about Indians in the streets, reserving their animosity now for Orientals, who were said to never spend their money—whereas the Indians patronized their stores freely.

The opening of the New Westminster Bridge, the first bridge across the Fraser, 1904.

The Sockeye Special from Vancouver to Steveston offered a fast, thrilling ride along the Richmond flats. The old handbrake cars had slippery seats in which children would slide and jerk about and occasionally be thrown into the aisle. Moustached conductors wore dark blue suits adorned with big shiny brass buttons, and the interior of the coaches glistened with stained glass and polished wood, the gentility of which contrasted vividly with the garish ads on the walls for liver pills and Heinz apple butter.

A key event for Premier McBride and the Fraser Valley was the opening of the New Westminster Bridge across the Fraser on July 23, 1904. Forty boats passed under the main draw span of the million dollar structure, tooting their whistles while the crowds above waved and shouted.

The bridge was unique in its double railway approach, with a 2,850-foot-long upper deck roadway. Far into the night the torchlight parades and revelry shook the Royal City. So many Japanese lanterns twinkled from river craft that South Westminster residents slept not a wink. Of course, the bridge meant the demise of the old paddle wheel ferry; the *Surrey* was given an official wake and permanently berthed.

Adding to the colourful mosaic of cultures being woven into the life of the valley were two new groups of immigrants in the 1900s, Sikhs and French-Canadians. Both groups were to play a vital part in the development of the fledgling forest industry.

Sikh troops had visited Canada in 1897, the year of the Queen's Jubilee, and liked what they saw. Significant numbers arrived to settle in three major centres of the province - South Vancouver, Mission, and Abbotsford. With their turbans, beards, and saris, the Sikhs became a target for ridicule, but fortunately they were not viewed as a significant threat to whites other than by the trade unions, who resented their influx into the sawmills.

Early Maillardville.

French-Canadians were recruited from lumber camps in Eastern Canada. Several hundred settled with their families at Maillardville, east of New Westminster, and these skilled workmen found employment at nearby Fraser Mills, site of the Fraser River Sawmills, the largest lumber mill complex in the British Empire. The capacity of the mill on a single shift amounted to 350,000 board feet.

A town soon flourished at Fraser Mills as well, as the employer offered quarter-acre lots plus timber to build homes on an instalment plan of five dollars per month. A French-Canadian band was assembled, an ice hockey team formed, and social functions, such as square dances, were frequently held in the vacant upper storey of the general store. The mill employed 850 men at an average wage of $2.50 a day. The constitution of the work force was reflected by the 1910 population figures: 877 French-Canadians and a few Europeans, 168 Sikhs, 57 Japanese, and 20 Chinese.

Prior to settlement, some 20 billion board metres of marketable timber stood in the Fraser Valley. Much of this was destroyed by forest fires and land clearing. Until 1930, the valley timber stands were under Ottawa's jurisdiction as part of the twenty mile wide Railway Belt stretching north and south of the main Canadian Pacific Railway line.

Timber rights were acquired by licence sold by auction. Companies made a killing cutting near the railway tracks, for the wood was easily accessible and the annual rental of five cents per acre, plus royalty, was cheaper than that charged by the province. The rates and profits were so good, in fact, that American timber companies stripped much of the Surrey forests in the year 1908 alone.

The New Westminster Insane Hospital expanded from 284 patients in 1901 to 690 in 1911. Principles of "Moral Treatment" were applied now for the first time, with an emphasis on varied patient activities. Diagnosis was still in its infancy, and the principal causes of insanity were thought to be heredity, disappointing love affairs, religious excitement, alcohol, masturbation, and sexual excesses.

In 1904, the government purchased one thousand acres of land near the confluence of the Coquitlam and Fraser Rivers for expansion of the hospital facility. The first project was the creation of Colony Farm in order to grow produce and raise stock in a bid for self-sufficiency, as well as to provide a healthier environment for some of the less serious cases.

Horse-drawn wagon carrying load of shingle bolts along Eburne Road, Sea Island 1908.

British Columbia's miniature version of Alcatraz was established on tiny Goose Island on Pitt Lake. In 1906, the island was deeded to the British Columbia Penitentiary for use as a prison camp. Convicts erected a forty-foot cell block that year and were put to work cutting cords of firewood.

On May 28, 1908, a carrier pigeon flew into the penitentiary grounds at New Westminster, bearing the message: "Send up the gas boat, 25 cons have made a murderous assault on self and an inmate..."

Prison guards rushed to the scene and the riot was quickly quelled without loss of life. Several men escaped, however, by means of makeshift rafts. The camp supervisor, Bill Patchell, pursued two convicts to the shore at Raven Creek, and from there he tracked them through the dense forest beneath the Golden Ears for several days, finally capturing them at the Haney rail yards.

Patchell's reputation as a tracker later became legendary, and he went on to become the first man ever to rise from the lower ranks to become a penitentiary warden. As for Goose Island, the camp was abandoned to fishermen and hunters, who continued using the blockhouse as a shelter for half a century.

On the evening of September 10, 1904, Mission City lay enveloped in a thick fog. The occasional resident groped his way along the main street, lantern held high, while trains shunted back and forth at the station. Jim Reece, station-master, glanced at his watch. The No.1 Transcontinental was due shortly. At 9:00 p.m., the shrill whistle of a train pierced the night as the Vancouver-bound Canadian Pacific Railway passenger express approached Mission station. On board, Engineer Scott was weary, and could barely stifle his yawns.

The Gentleman Robber, Bill Miner, immortalized as the "Grey Fox."

The train slowed to a stop; passengers peered out of their windows, seeing little in the pea soup of the night. Judge Bole pulled out a cigar. Outside, fireman Harry Freeman mounted the tender, depressed the huge spout, and filled the reservoir tank with water. Then the train moved slowly away into the blackness.

Only five minutes had elapsed when Engineer Scott felt cold steel against his cheek. He turned around and found himself staring into the faces of three men wearing floppy hats, each of whom brandished a revolver.

"Do what we say and you won't get hurt," snarled one bandit. "Stop the train at Silverdale Crossing."

Scott nodded and began slowing the engine. When they came to a stop, the lead bandit led Freeman down the track, where he was ordered to uncouple the passenger cars from the front of the train.

Once this was done, one bandit remained positioned outside of the passenger car, unnoticed until Conductor John Ward poked his head out the window to see what was happening. The outlaw raised his revolver and told Ward to put his head back in or lose it. Ward jerked back, and then ran through the passenger cars shouting "Holdup! Holdup!" Mothers and babies screamed and cried. Judge Bole sat alone in pensive meditation.

Meanwhile, the lead bandit—a grey-haired, moustached man with twinkling blue eyes—ordered Scott to shunt the engine, coal and express cars away from the passenger coaches.

In the express car, train messenger Mitchell was unaware of events and was busy counting money and stuffing currency and gold dust into bags in preparation for arrival at Vancouver. Suddenly a heavy knock sounded and a gruff voice yelled, "Open up or we'll blow the door down with dynamite!" Mitchell hesitated. A moment later shots were fired. Mitchell opened the door, was quickly bound with rope, and the money, gold dust, and mail was stuffed by the outlaws into a large travel bag.

Back in the passenger cars way down the track, the pandemonium continued. Men and women peeled off jewellery and watches and hid them in nooks and under seats, hoping to deny the bandits their valuables. Judge Bole finally took command and addressed the travellers. "Is there any gentleman present who has a weapon?" he asked. Nobody responded. "Then," said the judge, producing a revolver, "I am the only person here in a position to defend us all from these wretches. How many of you men will help me prevent the bandits from entering these cars?" Every man rose. The judge's first move was to send the porter running eastward down the track to Mission City for help. He then took up a position near the front compartment door, ready to shoot the first robber who entered.

The outlaws had no intention, however, of meddling with the passengers. Once the express money was secured, the bandits ordered Scott to speed the train westward. Just past the Stave River at Whonnock, they had the engineer stop the engine, bid him a cheery adieu, and jumped off. "Be careful when you back up for the passengers," chided one outlaw, "it's very foggy." The bandits clambered into a rowboat and disappeared across the Fraser.

Canada's first armed train robbery caught everyone off guard. The railway company's Police Superintendent George Burns was dining late that night with the Vancouver police chief in a downtown Vancouver Chinese restaurant. The chow mein was just being served when a messenger rushed in and informed Burns of the holdup.

The telephone and telegraph wires buzzed with the news, as customs officials were informed. The next few days were hectic with the mounting of a large-scale manhunt. A special train was dispatched to Silverdale, where officials searched for clues. A Whonnock man reported his boat stolen. At Mount Lehman, residents reported horses had been heard galloping in the night, and empty mailbags were discovered in an abandoned shack by the river.

On May 8, 1906, a second holdup of a train occurred near Kamloops. The bandits were followed, and on May 12, Bill Miner, Louis Colquohoun, and Shorty Dunn were arrested and arraigned in Kamloops for the interior robbery.

Miner had been released from San Quentin in 1901 after serving nineteen years for grand larceny. Known as the "gentleman bandit," he pulled off so many stagecoach robberies over the years that Pinkerton's detective agency had made note of his exploits on a large map of the American West. Released from prison, he decided to head north to Canada and try his hand at robbing trains. Using the alias "George Edwards," he inhabited abandoned cabins throughout the Chilliwack, Mission and Haney areas, making friends with everyone he met. In fact, one posse leader swore that he ate breakfast with the kindly outlaw on the day after the Mission robbery.

Miner and Dunn were sentenced at Kamloops to life imprisonment, and Colquohoun to twenty-five years. As the train carrying the convicts rolled into Sapperton Station, Miner took what would seem to be his last drink of whiskey.

"Well, luck to you, and here's where I sign the pledge," he told his guards. Then the men were ensconced behind prison walls.

In prison, officials regarded Miner as a feeble, kindly old man who complained of sore feet. A constant visitor to his cell was Katherine Bourke, daughter of the deputy warden, who befriended him and dedicated herself to educating him with books and art. She and other friends persuaded the warden to make Miner's life easier by transferring him to the prison brickyard. There the wily old fox shunted his wheelbarrow full of bricks to and from the yard to the drying kiln, while unknown to his guards, he was slowly digging a hole beneath the yard fence.

On August 8, 1907, Bill Miner escaped with four inmates when a guard briefly left the yard to get a cigarette. Shots were fired at the escaping prisoners and the prison bell sounded a general alarm. But Miner had vanished. Police forces everywhere were alerted; Pinkerton's reluctantly reopened their files. The prison warden was incredulous. Old Bill Miner was virtually a cripple—how could he just disappear? Worse, public sentiment was oddly on Miner's side. The press mocked police efforts to recapture the elderly inmate, and one headline read, "Chase of Bill Miner a howling farce."

The cries of criticism penetrated even the House of Commons, where allegations were made that Miner's lawyer and railway officials had connived in Miner's escape in order to have the robber reveal the location of valuable bonds missing from the Mission holdup. Deputy Warden Bourke—who was retired in the escape aftermath—revealed that Miner had been offered a pardon in exchange for turning over the bonds.

The main street of Mission City, 1907.

As for Miner himself, the man who has been immortalized on film as "The Grey Fox" staged the first train holdup in Georgia in 1911—and his last. Twice escaping from state prison after arrest, Bill Miner requested that he be transferred back to the New Westminster penitentiary to live out his life where he had been "treated so kindly." But time had at last run out for the gentle outlaw, and he died in prison on September 8, 1913.

When Royal Engineer veterans and other pioneers congregated in New Westminster in 1909 to celebrate the fiftieth anniversary of the gold rush, few greybeards from the old era were alive. James Houston died in 1902, followed by John Maclure and Billy Bristol. On his deathbed, Bristol retained his sense of humour, saying, "Well, doctor, I think I'll be goin' on a long trip today." Of the Engineers, only nine who had come out from England in 1858 survived.

Interior of general store, New Westminster, 1912.

One by one, too, the gold rush forts and ancient sites of Indians outside the reserves were ploughed under—including native pit-houses along the upper Fraser and the old Hope stockade of the Hudson's Bay Company.

The new pioneers of the valley were solidly linked with agriculture, merchandising, or one of the resource industries. Acton Kilby ran the quintessential community store at Harrison Mills. Charles Miller and his family came to the Ruskin area in 1903 to build a legend of rough and wild logging and mining exploits. Charles Pretty of Harrison River formed the Pretty Timber Exchange in 1908 to coordinate the purchase, sale and exchange of timber limits and forestry assets. These men exemplified rugged individualism at its finest.

The entrepreneurial Pretty family were typical of a handful of family dynasties which have continued to be prominent in the valley to this day. Charles Pretty, Jr.—who passed away at the age of 102 years on May 1, 1992—told of watching his father leave an absconding partner helpless at the New Westminster wharf one day when the scoundrel attempted to claim as his own a boatload of salmon, half of it actually owned by Pretty, only to find that Pretty had bought up all of the ice in town. Pretty was now able to dictate his own terms to the reprobate, whose alternative was to watch all of the fish rot on the dock.

Side by side with the Pretty family in the Chehalis area lived many Indians and mixed bloods. Relations with white settlers were usually cordial, often warm. Henry Pennier was a boy of mixed blood who enrolled at St. Mary's and served as an altar boy. But he left school early and learned to cut bolts for a shingle mill, slashing brush, and using blasting powder on stumps.

Pennier also learned the sting of humiliation. One day he and several men were hoeing turnips for a farmer, who had offered twenty-five cents an hour. When the men collected their pay, the farmer looked at Pennier and told him, "Half man, half-price." The lad received only twelve and one half cents for each of his hours.

But Pennier's greatest fears as a boy were of the myriads of hoboes who travelled the railway and might be seen wandering aimlessly about every river settlement. Pennier spent most of his working life at one end of a ten-foot cross cut saw in the woods, and told of his experiences in his book, *Chiefly Indian.*

Charley Miller grew up in the wild Ruskin area, a child of fishing streams, hunting forays, and logging camps. During summer holidays, he worked for twenty cents an hour at the Stoltze Shingle Mill where he learned to ride logs and boom sticks. He also came into contact with many Indian families, as the Langley band possessed a reserve along the Stave River.

One night, the Indians heard a baby's cries near the Fraser; there beside the railway tracks they found a white male infant wrapped in a blanket. He was taken in by an elder of the tribe, cared for, and later went to Ruskin School as part of the Indian contingent. Another night the Cheer family home burned down on the reserve and Charley sheltered the family. He then gathered a group of Indians and whites who rebuilt the home within a month.

It was common during these years for Charley Miller to stumble across Indian graveyards. One day he was slashing bush when several Whonnock natives approached him and advised him to cease at once, as he was standing on an old burial ground. The Indians were so concerned that they accompanied Charley to the Ruskin store, where they spoke with the proprietor, who turned to Charley and told him in a quavering voice never to touch another twig in the vicinity again.

But Charley was still young and defiant. On another occasion, he and a friend found some rotting cedar coffins by the Stave River and decided to arrange the bones found inside in a skull and crossbones pattern similar to those he had seen on medicine bottles. The boys removed two thigh bones and a skull, carried them up to the road, and set them in place. Around a corner came a lady in a democrat who raised her horsewhip and tongue-lashed the boys into returning the sacred remains to their coffins. Charley developed a healthy respect for Indian places, but many burial grounds were destroyed by vandals, souvenir hunters, and whites who marketed the artifacts.

Recluses abounded, tucked away in backwood crannies, many boasting a colourful past. Captain Dick Ward was known as the Harrison Hermit. A distant cousin of American president Abraham Lincoln, Ward commanded ships on all seven seas, was shipwrecked, and left the ocean for a quieter life on Harrison Lake. There he built a twenty-two ton custom yacht and catered to tourists staying at the St. Alice Hotel, carrying as many as one hundred passengers on cruises around the lake.

Ward's homestead on the Harrison River also attracted tourists, as he possessed a huge collection of arrowheads—which he periodically sold to pay taxes and obtain goods. From his farm, he supplied the hotel with butter, milk, eggs, and poultry. (The hotel refused his bread because it was so hard, the proprietor saying it was only useful for doorstops.)

Captain Ward was a man of few words. When he proposed to his housekeeper in 1900, he simply showed the lady the ring he had purchased and said "Huh." She replied, "Uh huh," donned a black silk dress, and clambered into the captain's rowboat. They floated down the Fraser into New Westminster, were married, and headed back the next morning.

Ward was a great storyteller, however, and repeated legends he had heard from Indians about the Great Flood, secret caves, and middens where the bones of Sasquatches were buried. The captain also took tourists to see what is known today as The Doctor, an engraved stone image lodged in a crevice thirty miles up Harrison Lake. The lake waters are rough there and Indian tradition requires that gifts be thrown overboard to cause the Doctor to give safe passage. The relic is very ancient and was a traditional site for Indian potlatches.

One recluse named Bergemeist lived in a shack on Allen Lake in Hatzic. A retired miner, Bergemeist kept his gold and banknotes in a baking powder tin, enclosed in another tin, placed in a box he kept buried behind his dwelling. When he required money, he would tell visiting children that he had to go to his "bank,"

The Vancouver side of Eburne, later known as Marpole, 1912.

and he would go outside to dig up his cache. "Well, I guess that'll last me for so long," he would say as he reburied the box.

Another hermit, Billy Martin, was illiterate and pleaded with children to read to him. The man was renowned for his violin playing. He would also sit for hours on his veranda playing Scottish folk songs on the hornpipes. When he died, his violin was found to be a Stradivarius, which was sold for the then enormous sum of $1,200.

The pioneer's view of illness differed from the modern perspective—you were either healthy, frail, or died of an accident. Captain Ward lived out eighty-nine healthy years. In her *Healing Waters*, Belle Rendall summarizes the view from Ward's era: "People generally died of old age. An age in which galloping consumption [tuberculosis] and heart disease were about the only fatal ills. There were no psychiatrists, virus infections, airplanes or television. Taxes were nothing to speak of. People did not worry about diet... and a middle-aged woman who was not comfortably bolstered was a bad advertisement for her own kitchen." Needless to say, cholesterol was not recognized as a health problem, and most farm families gorged themselves on beef, eggs, and fresh cream.

Although medical doctors were now beginning to appear in the larger valley centres, even they depended upon naturopathic remedies to a considerable extent. Surrey doctor G.G. Fife practiced in the Port Kells area, where he gathered herbs and roots and made his own liniment and cough syrup; in his saddle bags he carried bottles of whiskey for anaesthetic although, since he usually referred all surgery to New Westminster, rumour had it that the bottles were not strictly for medicinal purposes.

However, the population did use a variety of patent medicines, most of them sold completely unregulated, without description of contents. At H.J. Barber's drug emporium in Chilliwack, bottles of glycerine, cascara, and Seidlitz powders were sold, while the druggist made his own special blend of cough medicine.

One could even purchase a complete set of teeth from a dental firm in New Westminster for five dollars. A Mission City drugstore advertised, "To prevent smallpox, use Chemically Pure Cream Tartar; also get Hydrogen Peroxide Pure Sulphur." George Abbott reminded readers of the *Fraser Valley Record*: "Remember, we are sole agents for Hanford's Balsam of Myrrh—guaranteed to cure rheumatism, grip, pimples, or any ailment due to extreme changes in the weather."

In 1906, legislation was introduced to ensure that the labels of medicinal products showed a complete list of ingredients, and that certain compounds were marked "Poison."

The problem was viewed as grave. Wrote one editor: "There are many in every community who continue to 'dope' themselves with these mixtures through ignorance of the real nature of the stuff...Women and men of strong temperance and moral principles continually use 'medicines' containing from 10 to 30 and even 40 per cent alcohol, yet if their local doctor should prescribe even 4 per cent, they would be scandalized." Perhaps the populace was blissfully ignorant!

Young Dr. Ben Marr established his practice in Fort Langley. He kept a large stable of fine horses and gave each one quite a workout with daily gallops over long distances. Although he was a fine rider, he was once nearly killed by a horse and buggy. On his wedding day, he was racing to the church with his best man beside him when the buggy wheels jammed. The vehicle flipped over and his companion was thrown clear. Marr, however, was dragged along by the horses some distance, and suffered a broken collarbone, three cracked ribs, and severe lacerations. Undaunted, he arrived at the church on time, shocked his beautiful bride, Isabel Drew, with his appearance, and following the ceremony had to check into Royal Columbian Hospital before proceeding on his honeymoon.

Sea Island side of Eburne, 1905.

Like most country doctors, Marr had to perform dental and veterinary services in addition to his other duties. Some incidents were bizarre. In the middle of one stormy night he was awakened by a pounding at his door. He rose and ushered in a young man hobbling in considerable pain. Upon examining the man, Marr found that the lad's big toe on one foot was a bloody pulp. He cleansed and bound the wound, and then inquired as to its cause.

"Well," drawled the patient, I always sleep with my rifle under my pillow. When I woke up suddenly in the dark, I thought I saw something moving at the foot of my bed—and shot at it. Guess I made a mistake." The good doctor could barely restrain his laughter.

If hockey is the national sport of Canada, then surely lacrosse belongs to British Columbia. An Indian game originating in Québec, lacrosse came into its own in the 1900s, and nowhere has it been more popular than in the Fraser Valley. The first New Westminster Salmonbellies team was formed in 1889. Up to twenty thousand fans crowded into Queen's Park for key games, and interurban trains put on extra runs to accommodate spectators. These matches, played at a feverish pitch with a hard ball, make modern hockey roughness look tame—fights, injuries, and crowds tearing down fences to raid the field were regular occurrences.

With the exception of two years, the Salmonbellies won every provincial championship from 1896 to 1904; and in 1908, they won their first national prize, the Minto Cup. When the team returned from Eastern Canada following the national match, "the Royal City stood on its head to welcome home the conquering heroes, and they hung a gold locket around the scarred neck of each player."

The competitions between Vancouver and New Westminster were as charged with emotion as today's Montreal/Toronto National Hockey League battles. For some inexplicable reason, Vancouver players were called "crab eaters" by Royal City fans, and pesky little children would yell this epithet at the players as they entered the arena for the game.

Hockey, cricket, soccer, and other sports were also played. Gun competi-

An early lacrosse match at New Westminster Exhibition Grounds.

tions were very much in vogue during the era, and turkey shoots were held regularly. The Delta racetrack did a roaring business and high stakes gambling prevailed. Soccer matches in Chilliwack got out of hand from time to time, and Bible Belt newspaper editors railed at "unclean" spectators, who hurled insults and openly guzzled whiskey at games.

Bowling and billiards were blamed for truancy from school, and bowling alley revelry often kept residents awake at night.

Chilliwack Council passed a curfew bylaw in 1909, requiring all children under fourteen years to be home by 9:00 p.m. Councillors believed that this would stop youths from congregating outside town stores at night, and encourage homework to be completed. (Valley store owners' 1991 solution to the teenage loitering problem is to play loud elevator music.)

To enforce the curfew, an original method of determining age was formulated, by which all children wearing knickers would be ruled to be under fourteen years, whereas those wearing trousers would be allowed to roam at large. "Of course it is understood," joked council, "that tourists and golf players will be allowed their liberty and freedom after 9 o'clock if in the charge of their parents."

Controlling the social mores and behaviour of residents was for many decades a primary concern of municipal councils. Successive provincial governments prevaricated on issues such as the liquor question, and allowed individual municipalities to decide whether they wished to enact temperance oriented bylaws.

The procuring of a liquor licence depended often upon the applicant obtaining the signatures on a petition of at least two-thirds of a town's adult citizens. Temperance and church groups frequently charged that councils looked the other way and failed to enforce their own liquor control bylaws. Taverns called simply "barrooms" were present in all hotels, and there a thirsty patron could purchase hard liquor by the glass or the bottle. A customer would sit down and be given a bottle with a two-ounce glass, into which he poured his own drink at fifteen cents a shot. Drinking, like voting, was considered a man's business, and women were prohibited from both endeavours.

Steveston was a lively centre during fishing season. Nicknamed "Salmonopolis," the town boasted six hotels, and several of these offered a free drink to the first patron of the day. A bar was even located outside the dyke on the river to service thirsty fishermen. Every Saturday night, the Salvation Army paraded down the main street past all of the bars and gaming houses, seeking to lure miscreants and boozers back into the fold of decency. Steveston police regularly turned back suspected rowdies who arrived on the Sockeye Run from Vancouver for weekend revelry.

Prostitution was now conducted in bawdy houses in valley towns, usually at the lower-class hotels. Most citizens ignored the issue, but the odd arrest incensed the moral élite—particularly if the ladies pleaded guilty. As one citizen complained, "When three of four brazen faced women come forward and unblushingly plead guilty to a charge of this kind, it is time the public got astir and made some united move towards making the place so uncomfortably hot that they would find it more pleasant to live outside the valley. Chilliwack does not want creatures of this stamp within its limits."

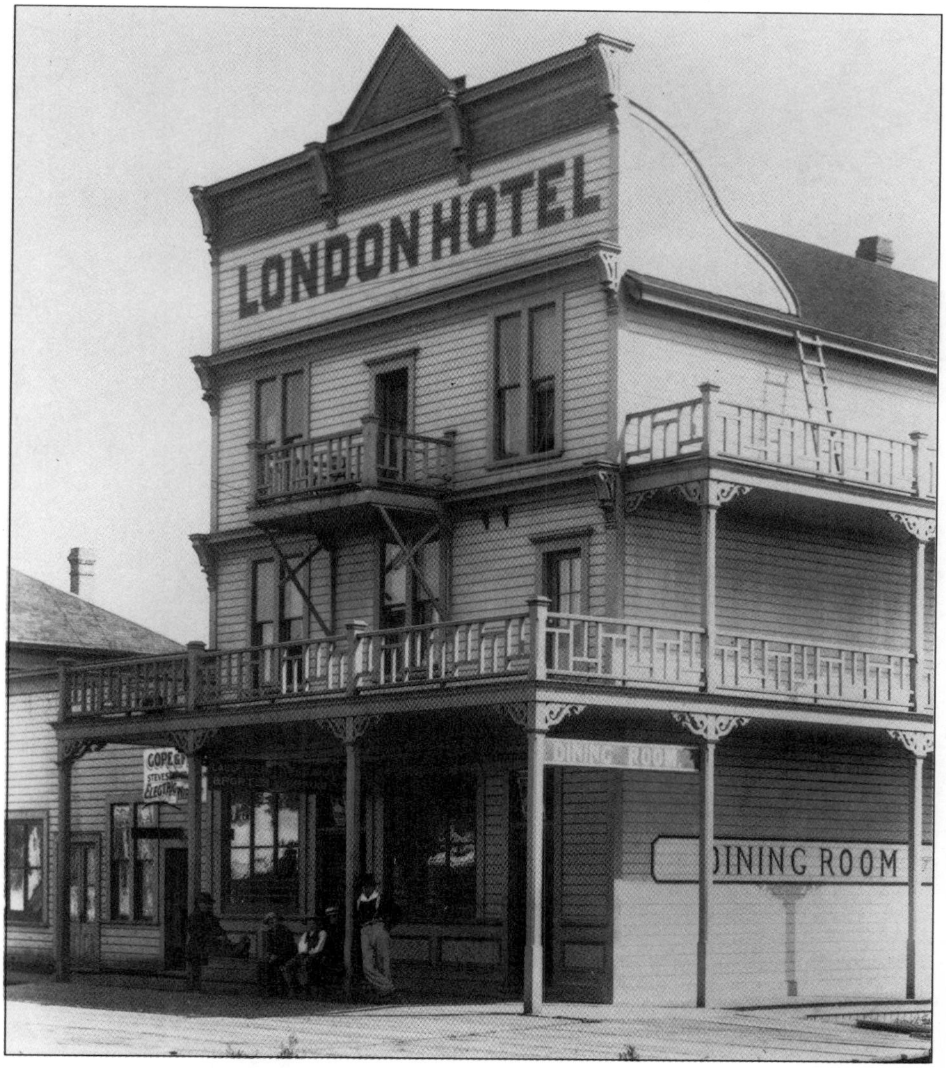

The London Hotel, Steveston 1908.

Stylish Edwardian homes were spreading from city to country, characterized by rambling structures with steep slanted roofs, symmetrical window placement, wall dormers, and off-centre porticos on the front porch. The parlour was usually kept closed and the blinds drawn, except for special occasions. An organ or piano sat in a corner, pictures made of hair hung on walls, and prickly horsehair chairs and sofas cluttered the room. Some parlours held spittoons, at which the more déclassé took frequent aim.

Before radio and television, games were enjoyed by guests on Sunday afternoons following church, and skits were performed by schoolchildren for their elders. Occasionally, favourite songs were sung, such as "Queen of Angels," "A Farmer's Boy," and "Yes, Let Me Like A Soldier Fall."

Dominion Day excursion on the SS *Beaver*, 1905.

Fraser Valley residents were paying more attention to fashion. Mail-order catalogues kept everyone current. For women, bustles were out and the hourglass figure was in, as were dainty blouses, tiny silk-clad waists, and ornate skirts. The well-dressed man might appear in a Homburg hat with suit and vest, starched white shirt, bow tie, and a Fiscal Policy two-inch collar, which sold for fifteen cents in New Westminster.

Boys in flannels and girls in long white dresses graced the tennis courts. Sailor suits accommodated young children, and those who believe that hippie hairstyles began in the 1960s will be surprised to learn that it was stylish for young boys to wear their hair not only very long, but with beautiful curls and tresses—not to mention their being dolled up in velvet shirts with frilly lace collars. Of course, beneath all of this, mother was still fashioning underwear out of Five Roses flour bags.

The advent of New Westminster's first movie house in 1904 allowed valley residents to travel by democrat over the new Fraser Bridge to enjoy a film after patronizing the market stalls and Columbia Street shops. Frank Kerr featured western movies, using a crude projector; when the film broke—which happened frequently—he would quickly get out his glue pot. One later theatre was reconstructed from an old livery barn; customers indignantly complained about the lingering smell of horseflesh.

Kerr also travelled around the valley with a hand-cranked projector, papering an area during the day with his ads and playing at night to a full house with films like *Desperado Jim.* (If you didn't care for Westerns, you could take the tram to Vancouver and take in *When Women Love* at the People's Theatre.)

Kerr broadened his enterprise to include opera performances in New Westminster, where he featured Amateur Night on Mondays at his Edison Theatre; here would-be actors and actresses entertained in the hope that their acts would be good enough to avoid the Hook—a long crooked pole which could appear from the theatre wings at any time to yank one offstage. Other valley stage activity of the era included smoker clubs such as Harrison House and Chilliwack's Silver Cornet Band, featuring virtuoso soloist Billie Dusterhoeft.

Significant changes to rural education occurred in 1906 with the establishment of rural municipal school boards. The new act provided for consolidation into one entity, administered by a single three-person board, of the many school districts operating in a municipality. The funding system was also changed to provide for local assessment accompanied by a provincial grant of $480 for each teacher.

The problem of securing stable, qualified teachers was now exacerbated by a developing rural-urban rivalry. A 1907 Surrey School Board report echoed these sentiments:

> "Our rural schools are largely in the charge of young women from the cities who seldom remain more than a year...The remedy for this growing evil is more country-bred teachers. Far be it for me to say anything derogatory of the young woman from the city. In many instances, she has brought to the classroom a cultured and well-trained mind, excellent bearing...and genuine zeal for the progress and advancement of her pupils. At the same time the country girl may and often does possess all these qualities, with the addition that she becomes more identified with the life of the community, knows more of the requirements of rural children, and above all, remains longer in charge of the school."

The settler's historical preoccupation with survival on the land was giving way here and there to a few thoughts about conservation. It is difficult today to grasp the reasoning process whereby every towering old growth fir and cedar tree in the Fraser Valley was destroyed. However, trees were a nuisance to farmers, and few were in a financial position to preserve valuable timber for aesthetic reasons. The few forest giants which were spared inevitably succumbed to forest fires, high winds, or the depredations of loggers.

In 1906, Charles Hope of Fort Langley purchased a number of California Redwoods which he planted along the road, hoping to increase appreciation of large trees; these specimens still stand today bordering Hope's Deep Creek Farm, near Fort Langley. The farm was passed on to son Alex Hope and now grandson Phil Hope. Sandwiched in a nearly isolated pocket of a growing suburban residential area, the farm typifies the plight of farmers trying to work productive ground

Shingle bolt camp at Aldergrove, 1913.

amidst a changing environment.

In Surrey, waste water and flooding challenged the local council, as residents grappled with the tragic effects of clear-cut logging practices which had decimated the forests. In Chilliwack, leading citizen A.C. Henderson gifted land for a city park, and council lobbied Victoria for a large park site to be created at Cultus Lake. It was not until 1925, however, that Chilliwack finally acquired sixty-four acres plus foreshore at the lake.

Greater cultural awareness of the Fraser Valley was also stirring. New Westminster County Court Judge Fred Howay became a distinguished advocate for appreciation of valley history. Author of numerous articles and books, the erudite Judge Howay travelled the province lecturing and writing about the fur trade, Simon Fraser, and the events of 1858. His accumulation of valuable historical materials caused him to once remark, "The distance from the bibliophile to the bibliomaniac is very short, is it not?"

Together with his many literary contributions, Judge Howay's initiatives with countless historical preservation projects—including the restoration of old Fort Langley—created enormous interest among the citizenry, and sparked creative contributions from journalists such as Bruce McKelvie.

Many of the Stalo oral traditions were preserved in the early years of the new century by a unique circumstance.

Eloise Street was the granddaughter of pioneer Methodist missionary Edward White, who had arrived in New Westminster in 1859. As a young girl of the 1900s, Eloise was sitting on a log one day at Cultus Lake, when an Indian suddenly emerged from the forest. Eloise recognized the native as her family friend, Sepass, great chief of the Chilliwack tribe. Chief Sepass was convinced that his people would gradually be exterminated by disease, particularly tuberculosis.

Natives arrive by canoes at Pacific Coast Cannery, Steveston, 1905.

As Eloise Street watched, enthralled, Chief Sepass addressed the waters of Cultus Lake in song, and after a time turned to her. Would she, he asked, agree to preserve in writing the sacred myths and songs of his people? She immediately assented, and, together with her mother, Eloise laboured for four years with pen and paper, carefully recording the ancient lore of the Stalo people, preserved today as *Sepass Poems*.

Other visible vestiges of Stalo culture were suppressed by law or co-opted by white culture. A potlatch was held at Kilgard near Abbotsford in 1900, and spirit dancing continued on a minor scale on the reserves.

The largest celebrations, however, were held under the auspices of the Christian church, with the Oblates at St. Mary's wielding the greatest power. Easter and Christmas were occasions for thousands of natives to congregate for catechism,

Passion play performed on hillside at St. Mary's Mission, 1901.

singing, and processionals in a week-long festival which featured grand vestments, brilliantly lit altars, and fine musical voices. Most spectacular of all was the *Passion Play*, a colourful and moving reenactment of the crucifixion of Christ. This event received national media attention in 1901 and was to attract tourists from Vancouver and Victoria well into the 1920s.

The *Passion Play* typically commenced with Stalo leaders organizing the participants at the bottom of the hill near St. Mary's School. Silently, the native throngs wound up the hill of Calvary, chanting and singing hymns in Chinook. Inebriated with excitement, they threw back their heads and waved their arms, their voices attaining a shrill pitch. When the procession reached the crest of the hill, the natives halted before the first of the play's eight tableaux. Many of the thousands of Indian spectators broke into sobs, wails and groans at scenes which followed.

The climax of the *Passion Play* came when the procession was joined by a native who portrayed Christ bearing a cross, with a waxen life-like figure then being raised upon it. Fifty native actors played their parts; soldiers mingled about, their swords discarded on the ground. The chanting of the Indians reached a crescendo and then suddenly died. A hush fell for several minutes. Then five chiefs rose and each in turn called out in a different Indian dialect: "Jesus is dying!" Three thousand natives fell to the ground, writhing in agony.

Finally, the presiding priest raised his arms and the spectators rose and filed humbly past the crucifix, returning slowly to their tents, which dotted the hillside. Such was the performance that was reviewed as "the amazing product of the combined efforts of cultured missionaries and raw Indians."

The 1900s have been described in history as "The Boom Years" or "The Golden Years." In this era, culture was viewed as secondary to material progress, whose possibilities seemed limitless. Mechanization was leading to greater production in agriculture, and crops were more diversified. Two Chilliwack creameries produced

Threshing outfit near Chilliwack, 1910.

five hundred thousand pounds of butter in 1906. Milk sold for five cents a bottle, and by the end of the decade milking machines had become commonplace. Automatic creamers, hay mowers, binders, seed drills, potato sprayers, and hay balers were changing the face of the farm. Farm buildings even changed in style, as the flat pioneer barns were replaced by larger dairy barns with silos.

Fruit canneries appeared and soon Fraser Valley strawberries and raspberries were being shipped all over the world—though farmers raged against discriminatory Canadian Pacific Railway freight rates. In 1908, the largest agricultural fair ever held in the province opened at New Westminster, and the many specimens displayed by farmers were a source of immense pride, causing politicians to refer to the valley as "The Garden of Canada."

Chinese market gardeners introduced the concept of smaller, intensively cultivated farms when they began leasing plots from Delta and Richmond farmers. The hard-working Chinese obtained extraordinary yields of vegetables; whereas Japanese strawberry farmers gained fame for the exceptional size and quality of their berries, and their propensity to cultivate every square inch of land which white farmers had often abandoned as being of marginal fertility.

The efforts of these farmers were aided by the improvements to dyking in the valley, particularly in the delta regions: "Thirty years or so ago these islands were great swampy tracts overgrown with coarse grass and rushes, the happy haunt of wildfowl of every description, but useless as they stood for the purposes of Man. Today, 20 miles of dykes, erected at a cost of $115,000, keeps the sea in check."

New water systems tapped the mountain streams north of the Fraser to supply Vancouver and many valley centres with some of the world's softest, purest water. In 1906, the Stave Lake Power Company expanded its plant at the Stave River dam site to supply power to Maple Ridge, Mission, and Port Coquitlam.

At the foot of Sumas Mountain, John Maclure's son, Charles, found some whitish lumps of clay on his farm which led him to discover one of the most interesting series of clay deposits in western Canada. With the assistance of his brother Samuel - a renowned architect - Charles built a town and mining complex which he named Clayburn. The clay was transported from Sumas Mountain by a narrow gauge steam railway.

The original Clayburn brick plant, 1913.

Until that time, only red common bricks had been made in British Columbia, while heat resistant fire bricks were imported. The Clayburn brick became nationally known. Landmark buildings, such as Vancouver's Hotel Vancouver and Victoria's Royal Jubilee Hospital, were constructed of the buff-coloured brick, and by 1909 some thirty thousand bricks a day were being produced from the grimy, smoky, and noisy plant across the road from the quaint little village of colourful gardens and white picket fences.

The first automobile recorded in the Fraser Valley was a 1896 Wolseley. In 1907, there were 175 registered car owners in the province, most of them living in Vancouver and Victoria. The *Columbian* confidently advised readers that no car

An early commercial truck at Mission City, 1900s.

would ever travel faster than eight miles per hour. In Surrey, the only passable motor routes were the Scott and Old Yale Roads.

Gravel was not used abundantly on roads until 1913; village streets were so dusty in summer that water and, later, oil were regularly poured on their surfaces. Amused settlers hitched their horses to rescue many a beleaguered motorist from mudholes.

In 1910, car dealer H. Hooper made a record trip from Chilliwack to New Westminster in two hours and ten minutes: "The trip is a most remarkable one considering the state of the roads and it is a practical tribute to the qualities of the Hupmobile as a utility car. Across Sumas Prairie, in places, the axle of the car dragged through the mud and water."

The automobile was viewed by rural residents as more of a rich man's toy than a practical means of transportation. The decade ended with an event which, at the time, held far more promise—the inauguration of the B.C. Electric Railway.

Following the opening of the Fraser Bridge, residents to the south of the river demanded their own railway. In 1906, Surrey, Langley, Matsqui, Sumas, and Chilliwack passed bylaws to authorize the B.C. Electric Railway to operate light, heat, power and tramway systems.

The company's right-of-way ran from New Westminster to Cloverdale and on to Abbotsford via Langley, Bradner, and Mount Lehman. The company briefly floated a scheme to drain Sumas Lake and thereby open up thirty-five thousand acres of farmland, but this idea was abandoned when the cost of the project was estimated at 1.75 million. Hence the line passed to the south of the lake, straddling the international boundary at Huntingdon, rounded the base of Vedder Mountain, and proceeded northeast to Chilliwack. Along the way, numerous train stations and power substations were erected.

Laying rails on CNR line near Chilliwack, 1910.

The power substations, huge four-storey concrete structures resembling medieval castles, were equipped with machinery for domestic power and lighting, in addition to converters for train service. Overhead wires and feeders were strung over the track, carrying six hundred volts direct current. Sub-stations were built at Cloverdale, Coghlan, Clayburn, Vedder, and Chilliwack.

On October 3, 1910, a special train left New Westminster carrying various dignitaries, headed by Premier Richard McBride. All along the B.C. Electric Railway route, mayors and councillors of the districts were picked up; everyone was in high spirits until the train rounded a bend at Vedder and found a power pole lying across the track. The engineer learned that there was no power for the line from this point to Chilliwack, and a steam engine that had served as a work train had to back up several miles to haul the stranded express cars to Chilliwack.

When the official train arrived in Chilliwack in this undignified fashion, the two thousand people assembled were surprised by the clanking rods and belching smoke of the work train. But nothing could spoil their party. Premier McBride detrained and quickly drove home the last spike to the deafening cheers of the multitude, who proclaimed through mayor and media that "this was Chilliwack's greatest day."

Thereafter, three trains daily commenced to run in each direction along the line, and by the end of the year, nine hundred passengers per week were travelling the railway throughout the valley.

Although the B.C. Electric Railway impacted upon the travelling habits of residents south of the Fraser, its greatest effect was upon the economy of the region. With the commencement of regular freight service, Edenbank began selling milk and cream directly to Vancouver.

BCER streetcar leaves Kitsilano Station bound for Minoru Park races in Richmond, 1909.

By mid-1911, the dairy industry reached such dimensions that the railway company initiated a special milk and vegetable train. The forest industry also expanded rapidly, with ten sawmills, three single mills, and two logging camps along the line by 1912. The steamboats were bypassed by farmers, who now found it faster to ship their produce by train. The last two commercial steamboats quickly folded operations, though one steamer, the *Skeena*, entered the field, the last survivor of an earlier era.

Country stores with post offices appeared all along the new railway line at stations like Sullivan, Bradner, and Mount Lehman. These became the centres of new communities, where it was part of the daily routine to amble down to the store, pick up mail and wait for the train, all the while catching up on local news with one's neighbours.

The advent of a comprehensive rail network shrunk distances overnight. Fraser Valley farmers were now able to tap the lucrative Vancouver market directly, and Vancouverites in turn discovered the valley, as special Sunday excursion trains brought hundreds of urban dwellers out every week to enjoy the verdant land, visit country cousins, and perhaps sample such delights as homemade ice cream—made with fresh strawberries, farm eggs, and real cream.

CHAPTER TWELVE

FOR KING AND COUNTRY

The legend of Slumach and the lost Pitt Lake Gold Mine grew over the years. A San Francisco prospector, John Jackson, had arrived in New Westminster shortly after Slumach was hanged in 1891. There he had listened to all of the stories circulated about the gold cache, and then he set out for the Pitt Lake mountain region. He returned after several months with his knapsack full of heavy nuggets, exhausted and suffering from exposure.

"I've toughed it out all my life," he said, "but never before have I experienced conditions anything like this; barely found any fish or meat, and enough flies to eat a man alive. And the rough going—I was forcing my way through snow breast high; and the natural hot springs in there make for mist and fog all the time. I seemed to be all alone in another world."

It is unclear whether Jackson had obtained a map of the Slumach mine from the Indian's nephew, Peter Pierre, or if he had simply discovered the cache on his own; but he revealed to a Seattle friend that he had found the Slumach lode and drew a map for him of its location.

In 1912, Jackson's friend and three other prospectors arrived in New Westminster and commissioned Hugh Murray to transport them to the head of Pitt Lake to search for the gold. For three successive summers, the prospectors continued their search until, battered by injuries and in failing health, the foursome wearily handed Murray their crude map in 1914, and abandoned their quest. Murray quietly stored the map away, amused to hear of the many gold seekers who continuously headed into the Pitt wilderness in search of the lost mine.

British Columbians have never quite severed their attachment to their romantic gold rush past. Prospectors have proliferated in every era; most miners never found gold, and if they did, kept careful counsel. Valley prospectors like James Cromarty—son of the old Fort Langley cooper—were followed into the mountains, like Slumach, and more than one tracker was threatened with a Winchester into turning back.

A gold dredge was even commissioned to work the sandbars above Hope, but the amount of gold dust retrieved was hardly sufficient to justify a farm labourer leaving his $3.50 a day job to help work the barge.

In 1910, two American businessmen arrived in Hope carrying gold quartz which they claimed they had discovered on a nearby mountain in Skagit country. Soon hundreds of prospectors were flocking to Steamboat Mountain to stake claims. No gold was ever found, and in 1911 the two con artists fled back to the United States with $80,000 of profits realized from selling their phoney claims. Thousands of naive investors lost their savings in the scam.

Early Fraser River sawmills at Eburne, 1908.

The Golden Years had spawned the growth of crime and exacerbated social stresses. New Westminster was described in the pre-war years as reeking of vice, and a record number of criminal offences occurred in 1910.

On the early morning of September 15, 1911, five masked men entered the Bank of Montreal, broke into the vault, and blew open the safe with nitroglycerin. Inside, they found $250,000 in cash and 150 pounds of gold. Most of the cash was to be paid that day to salmon fishermen, Fraser Mills workers, and Indian hop pickers.

The bank robbers escaped in T.J. Trapp's "powerful motor car," found abandoned a block away. Some bills were discovered by workmen tearing up an old wooden sidewalk six weeks later. Although several suspects in possession of the stolen money were eventually arrested, only one John McNamara was ever convicted, and at that was only found guilty of auto theft. The bulk of the money was never recovered.

The *Columbian*, ever anxious to put the Royal City on the map, waxed euphoric: "It was the neatest, cleanest, best-planned job and the biggest cash haul ever pulled off in the Western Hemisphere, and will go down in the annals of crime as a classic."

In Coquitlam, a vagrant thief had the temerity to break into the inner office of the chief of police, where he stole the chief's revolver. He then moved on to steal three pairs of pants from the Commercial Hotel. Upon the thief's apprehension and conviction, the *Coquitlam Star* reported: "All concerned are now where they should be: the revolver is on the wall at the police station; the pants are back at the Commercial; and Coady is in New Westminster serving three months 'hard.'"

Murders were also on the rise. In 1911, young Dearborn Probert was shot to death by a thief while he slept in an apartment adjoining the Whonnock Store. The case was never solved. In White Rock, meanwhile, an immigration officer was killed in the course of apprehending three bank robbers from Sedro Wooley.

Crimes of passion, with booze as a factor, were at least as common as today. An Indian constable named Peter, very active in fighting alcohol on reserves, was murdered by Louis Victor when he arrived to squelch a drunken spree at Agassiz Slough.

While he was being tried for several axe murders, one Ah Wooey demanded to take the Chicken Oath instead of the usual method used at the time. Wooey was granted his request, and the oath was taken in the traditional Chinese manner, by signing a yellow paper, then cutting off the head of a chicken, after which joss sticks were burned. Such apparent gestures of liberality by the New Westminster Court did not save Wooey from the hangman's noose.

The province's hangings took place at the New Westminster jail. Frequently, journalists flocked to watch the hooded hangman drop the trap door, which sent the victim plunging to his death below. The body occasionally twitched and writhed for several minutes, all of which was reported in great detail.

Flogging was regularly carried out at the penitentiary as part of a sentence. More primitive devices of punishment such as the Oregon Boot, a heavily weighted metal stirrup enclosing part of the prisoner's leg, the triangle, and the dark dungeon were being phased out. "Hard labour" in this era did not mean crafting licence plates. The prison fields and yards were places of backbreaking toil.

Squatters, hoboes, and wayward boys occupied the attention of many local councils. Judge Howay ruled against several squatters at Chilliwack who claimed title to lands by virtue of lengthy possession, pointing out that prescriptive rights in the province had been abolished. A school even lost its access when it was ruled that, despite decades of use, a pathway did not establish a legal right-of-way over private land.

In Mission, a band of hoboes broke into the local pound and jubilantly set free all of the dogs and cats; while Chilliwack wrestled with a teenage stowaway who arrived from Ireland and begged from door to door. The reeve was asked to have the lad deported, but he advised the complaining residents that he had no such power, and that they should stop bothering him about the matter, as the council was not a "foundling asylum."

The rugged church fathers of early days were now being replaced by more town-oriented ministers. Alex Dunn retired; Thomas Crosby died in 1914. As for Father Fouquet, he travelled the countryside until his last days, crippled by asthma and rheumatism, but still not averse to walking his soles off through the backwoods.

Father Fouquet often visited young Peter Legacé's home, at Durieu on Hatzic Prairie, to conduct Sunday Mass. Ever playful, he would allow Peter to bring refills of wine to his table all evening, as the boy tried valiantly to get the old priest drunk. Playing the game, Fouquet covertly dumped his wine into a jug under the table. When he had no appetite for fish on Fridays, he would eat beaver tails, claiming they were not meat.

On August 15, 1910, the Oblates gathered at New Westminster to celebrate their fiftieth anniversary in British Columbia. Premier McBride presided as the provincial Indian Agent presented Father Fouquet with a portrait of himself. The jubilee event wound up at St. Mary's Mission, where all of the priests, nuns, and Indian children walked silently over to the Oblate cemetery overlooking the Fraser. There the participants stood around a crucifix in the brilliant sunshine, remembering the missionaries who had lived out their lives in the service of their faith.

Two years later, in 1912, Father Fouquet was found dead at the Grotto, still crouched in prayer. The pioneer priest was laid to rest beside his old friend, Bishop D'Herbomez, near a huge fir tree.

The welfare of the Stalo people was the primary concern of the Methodists who founded Coqualeetza, as it was to the Oblates of St. Mary's. These institutions may be criticized for their suppression of Indian language and culture, as well as their misguided attempts to force an agricultural lifestyle onto the Stalo.

In her 1986 study of St. Mary's, however, Jacqueline Gresko concludes that, contrary to the claims of certain radical Indian leaders, there existed no uniform attempt to emasculate Indian culture in the school. Native children resisted many school programmes and retained dancing and other traditional customs. Indeed, when St. Mary's finally closed as a residential school in 1984, Indian dances performed by native staff had become part of the chapel liturgy. The proud traditions of the St. Mary's Brass Band and athletic teams in later years fostered the Mission War Dance Festival.

Wilson Duff estimated that the total Stalo population in the Fraser Valley had decreased to only 1,401 persons by 1915, an all time low. At this time, the McKenna-McBride Commission was conducting an inquiry into the size of Indian reserves. Although Ottawa assured Indians that reserves would not be reduced without the consent of the male majority, natives were apprehensive, given the great clamour of white settlers for Indian land.

Fraser Valley member of Parliament F. Stacey told the House of Commons: "I presume that these Indian reserves were granted years ago on the premise that

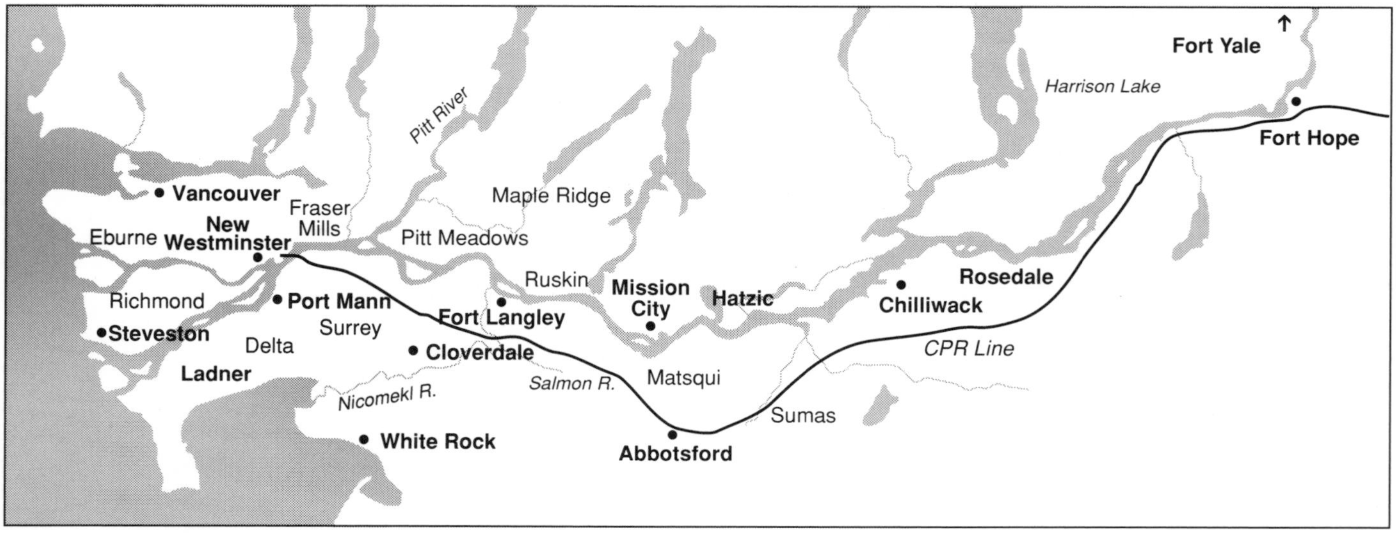

the Indian was the ward of the government...and that therefore a wide sweep of land should be given to him on which he could hunt and fish. In the course of time the Indian population has decreased, the hunting...is a thing of the past, and the result is that in many parts of southern B.C. we have large areas of the finest land being utterly wasted." Stacey demanded that these good reserve lands be opened for public sale.

The federal government broke its promise to Indians by passing the British Columbia Indian Lands Settlement Act, which authorized the implementation of the commission's 1916 report recommending the deletion of some 47,058 acres of land from reserves without native consent. Although 87,292 acres of new land were added to reserves, the acreage removed represented some of the finest and most valuable land craved by white settlers, much of it in the Fraser Valley.

Fishermen work with dried salmon at Steveston wharf, 1908.

This assault upon Indian reserves was accompanied by the prosecution of Indians who sold fish which they caught by means of nets. Natives were allowed to fish in the traditional manner only for their own food consumption, unless they were supplying a cannery in season. In 1913, even the right to fish for food was prohibited on the Fraser above Mission Bridge.

Ironically, valley settlers reserved their real animosity in the fishing controversy for Chinese and Japanese fishermen. At a 1914 rally in Fort Langley, a public meeting voted to reserve the Fraser River exclusively for whites and Indians! To further aggravate matters, the provincial government passed an amendment to the Game Protection Act in 1913 which subjected Indians to similar restrictions as other citizens respecting hunting, fishing, and trapping. The legislature believed that it would be to the "eventual benefit of the Indians if there was less reliance on traditional food sources."

In an election fought on the free trade issue in 1911, Sir Wilfrid Laurier's Liberals were driven from power and replaced by the tariff-favouring Conservatives —a result reversed when the parties switched platforms seventy-seven years later. The Fraser Valley witnessed a battle between Tory J.D. Taylor and Liberal John Oliver for the federal seat. Oliver had recently retired as provincial Liberal leader, but after a stint on the farm with his cows and pigs, he charged back into politics, genuinely believing that free trade was ultimately to the farmer's advantage.

The farmers thought otherwise. Even with a tariff in place, American fruits and vegetables were being dumped on the lucrative prairie market. Growers argued that Yankee farms were larger, more intensively cultivated, and better established, whereas the valley industry was still in its infancy and should be protected. A New Westminster journalist capsulized Oliver's dilemma: "Politics is a queer game. There is old John Oliver stumping the Fraser Valley in favour of a policy that is dead against his own interests and that of all his neighbours. He hasn't a chance."

Oliver was soundly trounced. Unperturbed, he unsuccessfully contested the provincial election in his Delta riding. The indefatigable farmer returned to his farm and small sawmill once more, where he contentedly worked "in overalls and with an old straw hat on his head, slogging away with his men, lifting logs and pitching out poles with the best of them."

In 1911, Premier McBride stood at the pinnacle of power. His reelection provincially was followed by a trip to London for the coronation of King George V and a knighthood; he was the first and only British Columbia premier ever to be knighted. The gadfly from Stump City acted as confidant to Prime Minister Robert Borden, and was heralded in many quarters as Borden's heir apparent.

In 1912, however, the frantic boom years turned to recession. Labour unrest seethed, railway subsidies rankled, and British Columbia borrowed $1.5 million from England. For McBride, the roller coaster of politics now headed irreversibly downward.

The orgy of prewar railway construction was capped in 1911 by the commencement of the Canadian Northern Railway line between Hope and Port Mann, on the south bank of the Fraser. Another speculative spree ensued with a two thousand acre townsite being cleared at Port Mann and lots sold at inflated prices. The location was heralded by railway company brass as the future Liverpool on the Pacific.

Alas, the new railway's terminus never quite blossomed, for, despite construction of a hotel and a few houses, nobody seemed to want to live at Port Mann. A Christmas promotional concert was held in 1912, with Maggie and Grant Kinney singing "Won't You Come Over To My House."

Children play on salt barge dock in Surrey near Fraser River bridge, 1913. Fish nets drying in background.

The Canadian Northern Railway hurriedly moved its terminus to Vancouver and crushed executive Donald Mann's dream. Surrey acquired most of the town lots for unpaid taxes, and, by 1930, one could buy twenty-four-lot blocks for $800—a little over $33 apiece. Today the Port Mann area is known for a bridge, dusty railway yards, and a major garbage dump.

The Canadian Northern Railway workers who toiled along the Fraser met similar hardships as their forbears. At one point, all workers marched off the job on a twenty-four-mile hike to escape marauding bands of mosquitoes. Living conditions along the line were pathetic—up to forty-eight men slept in one boxcar without sanitation facilities. The track layers, many of whom were Chinese, finally converged on Chilliwack, refusing to sleep in the cars any longer. There many slaked their thirst and eased their bones with beer and whiskey. When large numbers became routinely drunk, the railway union was asked by the local police to assist in stemming the flow. The union replied that the workers preferred the comfortable sanitary quarters of the local jail to the boxcars. During this period the story made the rounds that there were always three track gangs working on the line: one coming, one going, and one in jail.

Disruption of valley life along the river by the Canadian Northern Railway right-of-way provoked the outrage of many settlers, for the line blocked access to the Fraser at many points, and cut through historic farms.

At Fort Langley, the foreshore where Ovid Allard had traded with Indians was separated by rails from the old fort site. Fort carpenter William Brown was offered title to the Commercial Hotel by the railway company as a gift, after the company had acquired the building for demolition. The catch was that Brown had exactly twenty-four hours to move the hotel off the right-of-way. Brown rushed into the hotel's saloon and offered a case of whiskey to anyone who would bring a team of horses to help with the relocation. The old structure was soon pulled off its foundations by five teams of horses and deposited some fifty yards away. It cost Brown five cases of whiskey, but he went on to operate the historic hotel for many years.

First airplane flight in BC. Minoru Race Course, Lulu Island, March 25, 1910.

White Rock began its historic feud with the Great Northern Railway at this time, residents being upset over fires in the district allegedly set by railway workers; the tracks running along the beach are a major irritant in the town to this day. In Port Coquitlam, a Saint Bernard dog boarded the New Westminster bound Canadian Pacific Railway passenger train every morning and jumped off at the new Essondale hospital facility, where he waggled his way to the kitchens, enjoyed a most delicious fare, and then boarded the next train passing back to Port Coquitlam, where he detrained for home.

Hatzic residents became incensed one day when a Canadian Pacific Railway train derailed and railway personnel proceeded to burn food and other contents of boxcars damaged in the mishap. An old hobo living in a cedar stump managed to pilfer the grocery car and filled his humble home with coconuts, currants, and raisins. When darkness fell, a group of youths filed down to the boxcars to see what could be salvaged. All they found were a few huge barrels full of red paint. For years afterward, travellers in the north Fraser region would remark at the sight of red fences, red barns, and red farmhouse porches seen all along the river.

Unlike the B.C. Electric Railway, the Canadian Northern Railway did not significantly impact upon the Fraser Valley economy. The line became used predominantly as part of the transcontinental passenger service linking up with eastern points, whereas the B.C. Electric Railway served as a primary conveyor of agricultural and forestry products, augmented by passenger service. The towns of Chilliwack, Matsqui, Abbotsford, and Cloverdale were literally put on the map because of their association with the provincial railway company. Improvements to the Old Yale Road through Abbotsford, and the construction of the Pacific Highway in 1911 from Cloverdale to the border, further assured the two centres of a thriving future.

White Rock has always beckoned weekend tourists.

Centres which were completely dependent upon a railway were gradually displaced over time by towns strategically located upon the major highways. Hence, Matsqui Village was displaced by Abbotsford; while the previously thriving Port Hammond deferred to Haney.

Automobiles were now to be seen on valley roads with persistent regularity. In 1911 there was one car for every 116 people in the province; by 1921, the ratio had dropped to an incredible 1:16. The Vancouver Auto Club took a keen interest in promoting tours of the valley and initiated directional signs from New Westminster to Hope.

Road travel on the north side of the Fraser was greatly boosted by the opening of the Pitt River Bridge in 1914. Travel to Bellingham, Washington was in vogue for the wealthy and adventurous, although drivers had to adapt to driving on the right side of the road when crossing the border; it was not until 1922 that British Columbia switched from driving on the left to the right side of the road.

The leading pioneer families in each district were usually the first to purchase cars. This was not just a matter of affluence, but of social standing. Community leaders were expected to innovate; others followed. Al Deroche, son of Joseph the gold miner, bought a car in 1911 which was without a top, so that "the wind blew like blazes and the ladies had to wear big scarves."

The Hill-Touts of Abbotsford travelled in 1912 to Bellingham in a large Napier: "Preparations for this safari were thorough. The trunk was filled with tins of gasoline, lanterns, ropes, tow chains, water, food, and blankets. The expedition left in mid-afternoon...What with narrow dirt roads, no road signs, a rainy evening, and smooth treadless tires, troubles did develop. The car slid off the slippery, muddy roads at least three times, then nearby farmers had to be hired to hitch up a team of horses to pull them out."

The last sternwheelers to ply the Fraser were sailing into the sunset. The *Ramona* sank near Harrison River in 1909 and was abandoned. The *Transfer* was converted into a cannery power plant. The *Samson II* was a steamer commissioned to travel the Fraser solely as a snag-puller. Successors of the *Samson* plied the river until 1980, when New Westminster purchased the *Samson V* and refitted the craft as a museum. It now rests at New Westminster Quay.

By 1914, there was only the *Skeena* left for commercial carriage, commanded by the indomitable Captain Charles Seymour. She carried goods and passengers and, as the Vancouver *Province* noted: "As she sails week after week past the low shores of Surrey, Langley, and Matsqui, of Coquitlam, Pitt Meadows, Maple Ridge and Mission, she seems to carry some of that nearly dead romance of the river. Even when crowded with holiday makers...she wears still that air of simple dignity particular to the pioneer."

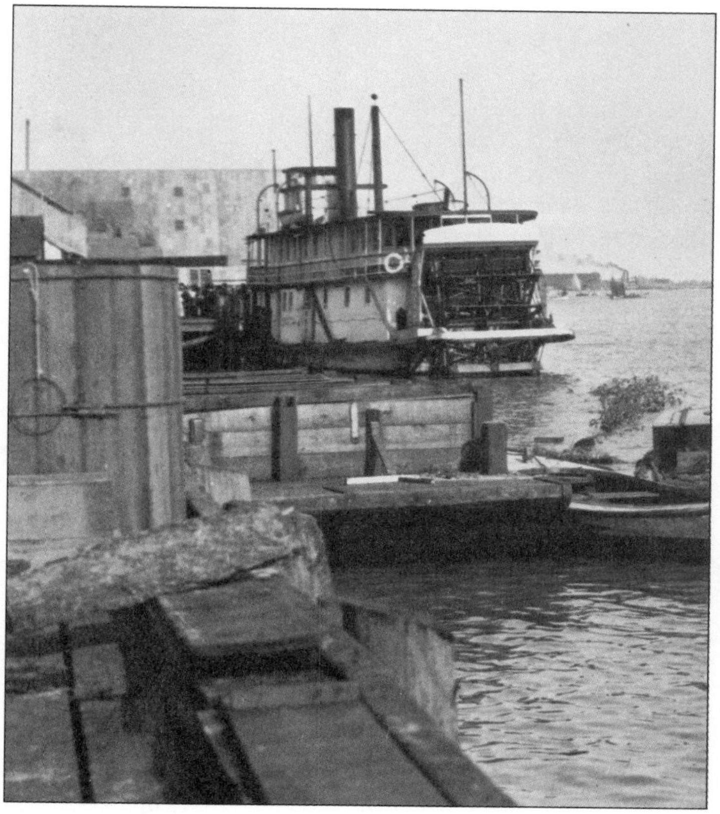

Steamboat docked at Steveston Cannery, 1913.

In August of 1914, war intruded upon Fraser Valley life suddenly and incomprehensively. The vast majority of citizens were of British origin, and feeling for Empire ran high. Volunteers rushed to enlist. Farmers offered their best horses for use in cavalry brigades, little realizing that the same technology which had hatched the motor car had also produced machine guns and tanks.

The Westminster Regiment, officially named the 104th Regiment, Westminster Fusiliers of Canada, proudly turned Queens Park into a barracks and trained 6,500 men for combat. Once overseas, the 104th dispersed into different units of the Canadian Expeditionary Force. These men—most of whom had spent their working lives behind a plough—marched smiling to the train depot. At each station along the rail line east they were met with cheering throngs who presented

Westminster Regiment troops in New Westminster ca. 1914.

them with food packages, handshakes, and good wishes. The filth and stench of death and mass destruction were inconceivable to these enthusiastic young men to whom the politicians gave assurances that "the Huns" would be beaten within six months.

Even when casualties mounted and the war bogged down in the mire of trench warfare, the cause was viewed as irrefutably just. The *Columbian* lectured, "There are those who think with a cheery optimism that the road of Life is ever upward and always leads to progress; it never leads to progress when a great civilization collapses...Today, the British Empire is a circle of light illuminating the darkness all around the globe. Who dares to say that this circle of light can be extinguished?"

At a huge rally in Queens Park in 1916, Sir Charles Tupper heaped scorn on the few able-bodied young men who refused to fight, while the New Westminster Symphony Orchestra played patriotic music, and Alex Wallace sang The Death of Admiral Nelson. Empire concerts were regularly sponsored; while Victory Loan Drives raised the handsome sum of $2.3 million. Nowhere in Canada did the fervour for the British cause exceed that of Fraser Valley residents.

Women formed the backbone of the war effort in Canada, right down to supplying the box lunches for each departing soldier. Acting under the motto of "For Home And Country," the Women's Institute acted as the key coordinator in organizing patriotic teas, holding concerts, knitting clothes, and packing food and tobacco for shipment overseas. Red Cross units worked to supply bandages, dressings, and quilts.

Given their already onerous duties on the farm, women were placed under intense pressure. The shortage of men in the fields provoked a call for women to save the crops and pick fruits and hops. Many Fraser Valley women responded to this call as part of the patriotic effort at an average wage of one dollar a day.

Antagonism erupted towards German and Chinese residents during World War I. Provincial police rounded up Baron Carl von Mackenson and two compatriots at the baron's splendid cattle ranch near Port Kells. The baron was suspected of aiding German-Canadians to cross into the United States and from there to join the German armed forces. Documents were rumoured to have been found in a buried can which detailed the baron's plan to divide land among important German citizens after the war. In 1918, the baron was deported to Germany.

The Chinese were scorned both for refusing to fight, and for taking jobs left behind by departing troops. At Cloverdale, a Chinese named Peters was seized by some returning soldiers for having failed to contribute to a patriotic fund. The soldiers escorted the frightened man to a wharf, where he was given the choice of kissing the Union Jack or being thrown into the chilly waters of the Fraser. Peters kissed the flag and was then dragged off to a Victory Loan Office, where he was forced by his captors to subscribe five hundred dollars towards the war effort.

Despite their strong presence as market gardeners, the Chinese suffered a drastic decline in New Westminster. The large Chinatown area was depopulated as a result of the continuing recession and the demolition of most of the older shops and restaurants, which were condemned by building inspectors. Chinese merchants sold their properties to white proprietors and the old Swamp became the home of light industry, gas stations, and car lots. New Westminster's Chinese population decreased from 900 in 1910 to 400 in 1941. In Chilliwack, town fathers began a drive to oust Chinese by condemning their shacks. The Japanese, meanwhile, fared slightly better, being well ensconced in the fishing trade; they were even given permission to plant flowering cherry trees in Queens Park as a symbol of their loyalty.

East Indian immigration was successfully opposed by provincial politicians, culminating in the infamous *Komagata Maru* incident of 1914, when 370 Hindus on board the ship were refused permission to land and had to be turned away by a gunboat. Several hundred Sikhs lived and worked at sawmills in the Mission and Abbotsford areas, however, worshipping at the valley's only Sikh temple, a shrine still a centre for worship today. The Sikhs suffered from similar restrictions on immigration as Hindus, being unable to bring their wives to Canada until the early 1920s.

Early mechanization at the J.W. Berry farm, Langley, 1917. This silage cutter, with motor and blower, was owned collectively by the local farming community, with shares based on acreage under cultivation.

In 1906, Finnish socialist Matti Kurikka founded a cooperative community, Sampola Farm, on 159 acres at Websters Corners in Maple Ridge. There he gathered together families who had originally immigrated during the 1890s to Sointula, Malcolm Island, off the northeast coast of Vancouver Island. In addition to agriculture, the families engaged in fishing and cutting shingle bolts. Traditional Finnish customs such as sauna bathing, folk dancing, and cross-country skiing added a colourful dimension to community life.

Sampola Farm was abandoned in 1913 in favour of individually owned plots, which were subdivided from the main parcel. The cooperative spirit persisted, however, and for several decades the Finnish-Canadians not only assisted one another as family, but organized a common waterworks supply and pooled grocery orders; two farmer cooperativess resulted, which sponsored numerous recreational activities, such as softball, basketball and lacrosse teams that made their presence felt within the wider community of the Fraser Valley.

The war years witnessed an expansion of cooperative efforts in the dairy industry, an endeavour becoming dominant in the valley because of the availability of excellent pasture, stock, and the success of the modern methods employed by farmers. However, the farmers found it difficult to obtain a fair price for their products from Vancouver milk distributors, who kept prices down by bargaining

Upper Sumas Creamery, 1900s.

with the farmers individually. Sometimes, too, shady dealers would steal a farmer's milk cans, disappearing with them.

On June 18, 1913, several leading dairymen who met in New Westminster became charter members of the Fraser Valley Milk Producers Association. Among the first directors was John Oliver, who participated in a whirlwind tour of farms which resulted in 90 percent of valley dairy farmers buying stock, on the basis of five shares of $10 each for every can of milk delivered to the association.

Operations were hampered by the war, but by 1917, 848 members resolved not only to cooperate in the sale of milk products, but to involve the association in broader facets of the production and distribution process. Accordingly, the Edenbank and Chilliwack creameries were purchased and a central distribution depot was established in Vancouver.

By 1919, several Vancouver dairies were purchased by the Fraser Valley Milk Producers Association, and Fraser Valley Dairies Ltd. was incorporated as the central processor. An orderly system of supply was devised, whereby lower valley farmers supplied the Vancouver headquarters and the Ladner Pacific Milk Condensary, while upper valley farmers hauled their product to the nearby creameries. The association never looked back. Unlike many cooperatives, it was to

Boating the milk to market on the Fraser River, 1900s.

survive the Depression and adapt successfully to the modern era, while fighting to this day a rearguard action against non-member farmers who sell independently.

Cooperative marketing of other agricultural products was slower to evolve. However, communities came alive in late August or early September for the fall fair. This was the occasion for every farming household to exhibit anything from honey to pigs in preparation for the annual provincial exhibition in New Westminster. Other activities such as egg-laying contests between districts bonded farmers in friendly rivalry. Delta even held a monster celebration after sending winning entries to a New York potato contest. Farmers, however, could not agree on Daylight Saving Time, which was inaugurated in 1913. Fifty years later, many farmers still refused to change their clocks from Standard Time.

Mechanization revolutionized the forest industry. In a few brief years, logging evolved from relatively primitive oxen and horse methods to steam donkey engines and narrow gauge railways. The Forestry Act of 1912 created at last a Forest Branch of the Department of Lands. The new department began to supervise logging practices, collect royalties and stumpage fees, and help to prevent forest fires. Fir was in heavy demand for frame construction, railway ties, and boom sticks, lumber from 22 to 24 feet-long, which were used to hold log booms together while they were floated downriver to the mills. Cedar was used for shingles; and maple and alder were cut for firewood.

The Canadian Western Lumber Mills, Fraser Mills 1923.

The basic equipment used in logging included a strong cross cut saw, double-bitted axe, broad axe, shovel, picaroon, chain, blocks, cable, and saw files. A hand-held peavey was often utilized in the woods for moving small logs.

All along the Fraser, mills expanded production and upgraded equipment. It was the heyday of the independent mill operator. Although the huge Fraser Mills facility dominated as the largest lumber manufacturer, the Port Hammond Lumber Co. flourished, as did innumerable sawmills, such as the giant E.H. Heaps Mill in Ruskin. Logging camps dotted the shores of Stave, Harrison, and Alouette Lakes, employing a rugged breed of woodsman and entrepreneur.

A colourful figure in the woods during the war years was Jesse James, nicknamed "Paul Bunyan" for his stature. James decided to move his operation from Washington in order to log along the Stave River. He was forced to transport his donkey engines from Sedro Wooley in the middle of the night after state highways officials denied him a permit, fearing damage to the roads. It took his crew eight hours, but when James reached the Sumas border station at 7:00 A.M.,

Washington officials could only splutter obscenities as they watched the long line of machinery parading its way north. When he reached the Fraser, James barged the equipment across and on up the valley of the Stave.

The James Logging Company employed some of the finest loggers on the Pacific coast and paid the top wages. The company also utilized the most modern equipment. A locomotive and four railway "trucks" ran along tracks stretching from the cutting operation in the woods to the Stave. These vehicles had no air brakes; two brakemen who rode the train would jump off to slow it when the engineer whistled. They did this by running alongside the train and inserting a hickory bar into a small wheel attached to a chain which operated the truck's wheel brakes. Accidents were frequent and a brakeman who failed to respond quickly enough could cause the train to plunge out of control into the river.

Jesse James often sweated it out in the woods with a broadaxe. His face was disfigured from a dynamite explosion, from which his doctors prognosticated he would never recover. He lived on to dance in his hob-nailed boots on the restaurant tables of Mission. His reckless automobile exploits left tongues wagging. One morning, he raced his shiny Stutz car to Vancouver. Near Essondale, Jesse lost control and crashed through a fence, bounced across a field and landed upside down in a haystack. On another occasion, he careened recklessly into the path of an oncoming car near his camp. When the shaken driver left to summon the local constable, Jesse brought some loggers to the scene, who helped him to lift and carry the other driver's car to the other side of the road. Photographs were then taken. In the subsequent court case, James collected damages in full from the hapless driver after he smilingly presented his photos of the doctored accident scene to the judge.

The country store.

The Fraser Valley country store was for many years a sacred institution. Farmers brought in produce to barter; the post office did a flourishing business, supplementing the storekeeper's income. Settlers congregated around the old potbellied stove in winter to escape the monotony of a home bound life. Sometimes farmers would even compete in spitting contests—with the winner being judged on the basis of the spitter who caused the greatest sizzle from the stove. At the Dewdney store, 10 cents bought lunch and one could buy molasses at 25 cents a jug.

Although many country stores carried

everything from shoes to patent medicines, settlers still journeyed to New Westminster or even Vancouver for most of their dry goods. Others shopped by catalogue or bought from peddlers. Two peddlers named Kidd and Israel regularly travelled the Old Yale Road in a covered wagon full of miscellaneous goods. As they approached a farm or settlement, one would signal their presence by blowing on a cow's horn.

Other door-to-door salesmen marketed the first sewing machines and home ranges. One rather rotund saleslady walked the muddy roads with a backpack full of spools, handkerchiefs, embroidery, and other items, including hat pins, which some people believed were a sure cause of blood poisoning.

Young boys and girls created most of their own toys. Bows and arrows and balls made of rags wrapped in yarn were fashioned by children. A truly wonderful gift for Christmas would be a pocket knife for a boy and a hand carved wooden doll for a girl. Chewing gum was obtained from spruce stumps. Popular games included blindman's bluff, prisoner's base, fox and hounds, lacrosse, baseball, and shinny.

Farm chores occupied children from an early age. Girls were expected to assist their mother full-time until marriage; if a girl made it through high school, it was expected that she would become a teacher. Boys herded cattle, managed the horses, harvested crops, and learned to hunt, shoot and wield a woodsman's axe. If a lad did not become a farmer, he was likely to drift to the logging camps, which he might well do by age thirteen in any event, in order to supplement family income.

The clash of town and country inevitably occurred, as rural centres strove to achieve the dignity of modernization, cleanliness, and sophistication. Town councils railed constantly against unsanitary shacks, litter, and noxious weeds. Animal-related issues were a major preoccupation. In 1915, the Chilliwack Beautification Association erected a special railing for use by farmers who persisted in tying their horses to posts along the main street. Roaming cows were also a problem: "The old habit of using streets as stamping ground for the village bovine seems hard to shake off and bossy is continuously getting into trouble on the newly made boulevards, browsing on the young grass shoots and shrubbery...."

One Chilliwack resident lamented that the town had prematurely eliminated the watering troughs for horses, and recommended that a public garden be established "with shade trees and seats for the men who have been here for over forty years to go and rest and ponder over their past follies."

The council, meanwhile, met to consider a pound bylaw which covered everything that walked, flew, or swam; any animal caught straying on the streets could be executed. Just as council had begun debate on the measure, however, terrible cries and yowls which were heard by councillors coming from deep in the dungeons of the dog pound cells which were located in the basement of city hall. The cries persisted so loudly that the bylaw was quickly amended to provide for administration of chloroform to the noisiest canines.

Premier McBride gained one final moment in the sun in 1914, when he purchased two submarines from a Seattle shipyard and then handed them proudly over to the federal government for the war effort. The three-day interval during which British Columbia possessed a navy perhaps inspired a later premier to create a ferry fleet.

But in 1915 McBride resigned. He was in poor health and beset by recession, suffragettes, and prohibitionists demanding a ban on liquor sales. He secured for himself the sinecure of Agent-General to Great Britain—every British Columbia politician's fantasy—and died in 1917.

The new premier, Billy Bowser, called an election in 1916. For many years the liquor issue had dominated local politics throughout the province. Although a local option plan was approved by plebescite in 1909, the McBride government declined to implement it, leaving municipal councils to fight the liquor trade by withholding licences from hotels, prosecuting drunks and bootleggers with vigour, and sniffing out stills. Premier Bowser announced that referendums on the issues both of prohibition and women's suffrage would be held on election day.

The wet and dry forces readied for battle. The wets were a disparate group, bankrolled by hotel, distillery, and brewery owners. The dries were composed of various church, youth, service, and women's club members. Emotional debates, lectures, and rallies were held in every centre. Shrill advertisements appeared, denouncing liquor, with some persons even identifying the liquor barons as the "B.C. Whiskey Huns," and arguing that liquor consumption detracted from the war effort.

In the valley's Bible Belt, religious leaders dominated the dry front, although one Sardis hop farmer quoted Scripture to show that Christ counselled moderation, and in fact drank wine himself. This sparked a fierce debate as to the proper interpretation of "wine" in the Bible.

The 1916 election overthrew the governing Tories, and Harlan Brewster became the province's first Liberal premier. Women's suffrage was overwhelmingly endorsed and prohibition passed by eight thousand votes. As a result of voting irregularities, the soldier's ballots which arrived late—and which would have defeated the dry forces—were in part discredited by a provincial commission, and prohibition became law in the province on October 1, 1917. The temperance pledge was taken by large numbers of Fraser Valley residents: "For self conquest, the sake of others, and for love of Christ and country, I do hereby pledge myself to abstain from the use of all alcoholic liquors as a beverage, from the use of tobacco in any form, from the use of profane language, the reading of bad books, and to devote earnest efforts to securing the prohibition of the liquor traffic."

Bootlegging immediately became an industry. Speak-easies and "blind pigs" proliferated by the hundreds. The medical profession came to be viewed by prohibitionists as a veritable bartender's union, as doctors freely prescribed liquor for medicinal purposes. A concoction known as near-beer was sold in the saloons still in operation; liquor the quality of anti-freeze reached home and hearth as government regulations disappeared. Municipal councils had to levy new taxes to compensate for the loss of liquor revenue. The courts were clogged with liquor offence cases. To top it all off, British Columbia's Prohibition Commissioner, W.C. Finlay, was sentenced to two years in jail for bootlegging.

The upheaval of war contributed to the social unrest which divided the population on Prohibition and led to the enfranchisement of women in 1918. Avid debate also ensued on key issues affecting women and the family, such as equal guardianship, minimum wages, deserted wives legislation, and mothers' pensions. Langley Council gleefully amended its Road Tax Bylaw by changing reference from "male" to "person"—but not because of any compunctions over gender discrimination. The change ensured a doubling of tax revenue, since theretofore only adult males were subject to a two dollar levy.

The slaughter of war created a horror of conflict, but it did not immediately alter the settler's pride in Empire. Schoolgirls still skipped their ropes and sang:

"When I was a girl guide dressed in blue
These are the actions they taught me to do;
Stand at attention; stand at ease;
Bend my elbows; bend my knees;
Salute to the King; bow to the Queen;
And never turn my back on the Union Jack."

Conscription, which began in 1917, hardly affected the Fraser Valley. Most able-bodied men left at home were too old, or considered racially unsuitable for service; while others were exempted as being food producers. It is ironic that this and other heavy-handed legislation was passed in Canada at a time when the country was fighting for freedom and democracy. For in the same year, Ottawa also enacted a "temporary" income tax measure and proposed anti-loafing legislation requiring

Wellington Avenue, Chilliwack. Early 1900s.

every man to "regularly be employed in some useful occupation, in the absence of reasonable cause to the contrary."

When the town bells tolled out the peace in November 1918, the celebrations were quiet, even muted, in the Fraser Valley. In Cloverdale, a religious service was held, then townspeople gathered in a field and burned an effigy of the Kaiser, ceremoniously burying the corpse. Several valley families had lost more than one son, brother, or husband. Of the 6,500 Westminster Regiment recruits, 753 died and 1,718 were wounded.

Labour unrest prevailed in the province, and the first inklings of doubt trickled into people's minds about the nobility of having waged, and ostensibly won, the "War to end all wars." Like most politicians of the day, Fraser Valley member of parliament F. Stacey misread the postwar ferment of ideas, when he lectured: "If there is one thing that Canadians need to keep permanently in their minds...is that they must keep busy. It is almost an actual crime for loyal citizens to rock the boat."

The jubilation over war's end was further tempered by the outbreak of Spanish influenza. Usually referred to as an epidemic, this form of influenza, which baffled doctors and killed more people in a shorter period of time than any war or disease to date, was more properly called a "pandemic," as its effects were worldwide. In fact, it was the worst pandemic in world history. In British Columbia, at least 30 percent of the population were afflicted.

From October 1918 to March 1919, the "Spanish Flu" raged, killing twenty-eight patients at Royal Columbian Hospital during the month of October alone. Doctors collapsed from exhaustion, while nurses were infected, and their working ranks decimated.

Fraser Valley towns obtained quarantine orders from Victoria. All offices closed; schools shut down, and all public gatherings were banned. Returning soldiers who had escaped German bullets died by the score. There appeared to be little pattern to vulnerability, although people in their thirties sustained the greatest number of fatalities. Influenza drugs, masks, and veils were mass marketed to a desperate and frightened population. The price of camphor rose from 40 cents to $6.50 a pound in one week. When the disease finally abated, hundreds of valley residents lay dead. Precise fatality figures are not available. Vancouver sustained 900 flu-related deaths out of a population of 100,000. However, given the reduced opportunity for contagious contact in rural areas, it is unreasonable to presume a fatality rate as high as 1 percent in the Fraser Valley.

At church, temperance meetings, and around country stoves, residents emerged from quarantine to hear war stories of valour and sacrifice. Chilliwack piper Jimmy Richardson was posthumously awarded the Victoria Cross for rousing the troops to storm a German ridge, playing his bagpipes amidst a storm of lead. His body was never found. Even his commanding officer shattered public notions of chivalrous conflict thus: "The Somme state of mind was a state of foreboding evil overhead...Such devastation, such huddled heaps of dead; such death in life. Man, created in God's image, was indeed shrivelled up in an abjectness of being. The Somme was hell."

Gassing, trench warfare, tanks, and machine guns contrasted vividly in the minds of residents with the smiling young faces who in 1914 had paraded about the valley in their fancy uniforms on fine steeds. In Langley alone, more than thirty native sons perished; of the two hundred soldiers who returned, men like Dr. Marr and William Brown would bear the war's physical and emotional scars to the grave.

AKERY
"QUALITY"
Vancouver B.C.
Prince Albert
TAXI
CO.
Sey.
299
Always at your Service

CHAPTER THIRTEEN

FLIVVERS, FLAPPERS, AND JITNEYS

When Premier Brewster died in February 1918, John Oliver was elected leader of the Liberal party and hence became premier. Honest John changed little with his new job. He still wore his old tweed suits and square-toed boots, and would, if he fancied, drink tea out of a saucer at a formal gathering, much to the chagrin of his sophisticated urban colleagues. He seemed equally at home talking to the Prince of Wales or a Delta pig farmer. His rusticity was deceiving, for beneath the country clothes and well-trimmed white beard was a shrewd, astute politician—the epitome of Kipling's hero, who "could walk with kings nor lose the common touch."

The new premier was a nineteenth century liberal who believed in social reform, but only for the truly needy. Thrift and hard work governed his own life and he opposed extending welfare to the lazy. He did pass a Mother's Pension Act, however, to assist widows and orphans, inaugurated old age pensions, established an eight-hour working day (which did not apply to farm labourers), and appointed Mary Ellen Smith to his cabinet—the first woman cabinet minister in the British Commonwealth.

The thousands of soldiers returning from World War I, who sought employment at a time of recession, constituted a great problem in Canada. The federal government sought to alleviate the problem by setting up the Soldier Settlement Act; the provincial government passed the British Columbia Soldier Settlement Act, which reserved some land for veterans, but gave no financial assistance; and Oliver, who dreamed of founding cooperative farming settlements for the soldiers, and immigrants who might follow, created in 1918 the Land Settlement Board.

Of the three attempts to aid repatriated men, Oliver's was the least successful. His board was given awesome powers by the British Columbia government to award Crown lands and to finance farmers, but it did not function in the Fraser Valley, other than at Sumas. The province's largest and most fertile agricultural area, therefore, fell outside the board's jurisdiction. Furthermore, in areas where it did operate, the lands available were of poor quality, and insufficient financial assistance was offered by follow through programmes.

In the valley, the best agricultural option open to the returning troops was offered by the federal Soldier Settlement Act. Under its terms, soldiers were encouraged to settle on existing or abandoned valley farms by an offer of a $5,000 loan to purchase land, and an additional $3,000 to acquire livestock, equipment, and improvements.

Bureaucrats were appointed to supervise applications, provide free transportation, and offer farm training courses for applicants and their wives. The Fraser Valley received 802 soldier settlers under this scheme, who settled chiefly in the districts of Surrey, Langley, Matsqui, and Chilliwack. The average size of the soldier's plot was 29.4 acres.

The toil of farming was too much for many returning veterans who had worked in cities before the war, or whose injuries rendered them unfit. These men quickly drifted away from farms to urban centres, and their land reverted to the Soldier Settlement Board, to be resold. In 1926-27, an Empire Settlement Scheme brought nearly 3,000 British families to Canada under government sponsorship; of these, 54 purchased board holdings which had reverted in the Fraser Valley.

Valley residents welcomed soldier settlers with open arms. The young troops were pitied as much as honoured, as the gruesome details of slaughter continued to unfold amidst a storm of ridicule of incompetent British generals alleged to have squandered the cream of the Empire for the sake of a few hundred yards of French mud. Judge Bole of New Westminster even granted 102 acres to the Settlement Board as a gift for disabled veterans.

Each in his own way set about remembering fallen relatives and friends. Charles Perkins of Surrey quietly built a little natural park on his farm with ivy, ferns, and vine maples, as his own tribute to his many comrades who had not returned from the front. Cenotaphs proliferated in every town, and the November 11 ceremony became one of the few traditions which bore deep and personal meaning for the majority of Canadians.

More than ten thousand Canadians and Americans gathered at the Blaine border crossing on September 6, 1921, to dedicate the Peace Arch, which was claimed at the time to be the first memorial of its kind in the world.

Blocks of wood from the *Mayflower* and the old *Beaver* were sealed in the Arch's masonry. Flags, bands, and speeches made the dedication a most impressive spectacle. The crowd rejoiced in the outpouring of sentiment of peace and international friendship. "Brethren Dwelling Together In Unity" was inscribed on the Canadian side of the monument, while "Children Of A Common Mother" was engraved on the American segment. Several references were made to the civilized relationship prevailing between the two nations, in contrast to European states, which eulogized the victories of past wars. Washington's Lieutenant-Governor Coyle said, "Never will these highways resound to the tramp of marching men from the south and the north, nor these roads of concrete bear the rumbling wheels of destroying engines of war."

Perhaps the most ambitious endeavour of the British Columbia government under Oliver was the draining of Sumas Lake. This huge expanse of shallow water was eyed hungrily by farmers, who recognized the rich potential of the loamy soil beneath.

The great flood of 1894 had enlarged the lake by altering the course of the Chilliwack River. Successive governments had refused to undertake the huge costs of reclamation. John Oliver's treasury was bare; but the stubborn farmer in him argued that, once recovered, the huge acreage would be easy to cultivate and could render the province less dependent upon American vegetables and dairy products.

A key proponent of the Sumas drainage scheme was Chilliwack farmer Dodsley Barrow, Oliver's minister of agriculture. A three-pronged plan was instituted by Barrow in 1920 for the reclamation of some thirty-three thousand acres: new dykes along the Fraser between Sumas and Chilliwack; construction of a dam and pumping station at the base of Sumas Mountain; and the diversion of the Chilliwack River via canal.

Sumas Lake prior to its drainage.

Construction began in 1921 on a budget based on an estimated cost of $1.8 million for the project. The price tag was to be recovered through levies on existing Sumas Prairie farmland, which would benefit from the flooding protection afforded by the new dykes.

The Marsh Bourne Construction Company employed 150 men on the drainage project over two years. Fifty-four-inch pumps capable of pumping three hundred thousand cubic feet per minute were installed, the largest in Canada. Sumas Lake was fully pumped out by the fall of '22, exposing the unique sight of hundreds of dead and flopping fish. It was said that even a few sizable sturgeon were found beached in the mud.

Marsh Bourne grossly overran its budget. The total cost amounted to $3.7 million, more than double the original estimate. A flurry of lawsuits ensued, as angry Sumas farmers refused to pay the additional per acre levy for the overrun. Eventually, Victoria provided relief to landowners, but rancour persisted toward the government.

The Sumas accomplishment was considerable. The reclaimed lands did prove fertile and crops of timothy, oats, and wheat proved bountiful, notwithstanding the proliferation of willows which choked out much of the grain in the first season. But the rich lake bottom was difficult to market. The government divided the lands into plots of forty acres and offered these for sale at the exorbitant price of two hundred dolars an acre. Buckerfield's, Canadian Hop Growers, and British Columbia Tobacco purchased parcels at these prices, but small farmers were unable to afford it. The government finally reduced the price to $125 per acre in 1928 and sales became brisk.

In time, Sumas Prairie was to become the richest, most efficient dairy, berry, and hop-growing region of the province: "Wide acres of green are dotted with brown hay shocks and where cattle are feeding, their udders are brushed by the luscious grass." Even the mosquitoes, which had so tormented the Royal Engineer survey parties in earlier days, all but vanished from the dry prairie.

The booze question challenged Premier Oliver's first administration. Between March and October of 1919 alone, doctors in the province wrote 118,120 liquor prescriptions for their thirsty patients. Bars flourished in Vancouver and New Westminster in open defiance of the law.

Wet forces, including leaders of the British Columbia Moderation League, claimed that liquor smuggling and trafficking was linked with the drug trade, white slavery, and the illegal immigration of Chinese and Hindus. The moderationists opposed bars, but endorsed a proposal to have the government run a monopoly of liquor stores. In a 1920 referendum, prohibition was discarded by a twenty-five thousand-vote majority in favour of the government run scheme with only Chilliwack and Richmond against it. "John Oliver's Drugstores"—as the liquor outlets were called—were to provide a comforting source of revenue for every succeeding provincial administration, although sale of beer by the glass was not allowed in Chilliwack until 1950.

In order to qualify for a permit to purchase liquor from a government store, a citizen was required to have his or her character approved by the Liquor Control

Board. A purchase was stamped with the patron's permit number and, if one were caught with unauthorized bottles, one could be charged with unlawful possession or bootlegging. Each municipal district could vote whether or not beer could be sold in hotels.

Once again the fight was on between wet and dry forces. One Mission resident extolled the value of beer in this debate: "To the working man, beer is no more injurious mentally, physically, or morally, than afternoon tea is to the ladies; moreover, there are many Missionites who make as big an ass of themselves on tea and water as others do with booze."

The penalty for operating a "blind pig" or illegal bar was a minimum of six months in jail. Prosecutions were rife throughout the Fraser Valley. After the passage of the Volstead Act by the United States Congress in 1919, bootlegging of Canadian booze into Washington became widespread. All along the border in Surrey and Langley, midnight exchanges of contraband kept customs officials hopping. On one occasion, a teenage runner driving a car loaded with twenty cases of Scotch was approaching his rendezvous when a dozen loggers appeared out of the woods and relieved him of his cargo. The youth's employer raged over his eight hundred-dollar loss, but dared not pursue the matter.

In Mount Lehman, 250 full bottles of whiskey were found by a resident one day dumped in sacks in a ditch. It being the Christmas season, local farmers came from far and wide to scoop up bottles for home and hearth. Shortly after all of the liquor was removed, three high-powered black cars were observed idling beside the ditch where the cache had been dropped, and well-dressed businessmen stood around muttering angrily. The cars then roared away, leaving a trail of dust.

American prohibition made for some interesting incidents. Popular millionaires George and Harry Reifel were indicted in 1927 for smuggling liquor into Seattle via a motor launch. Vancouver police band pipers were playing at a Bellingham tulip festival when United States federal agents gave their bus a shakedown and removed eight dozen bottles of beer and three crocks of Scotch. The bus was also seized. The long distance telephone lines were kept sizzling by threats of the Americans to arrest the pipers. A compromise was reached to avoid an international incident, but the piping men in blue returned home in a parched state.

Surrey customs house at Pacific Highway crossing, 1927.

The king of the bootleggers was a man named Frank Palmer, who was wanted in Washington for robbery and murder. New Westminster police discovered that he rented a home from a Royal City alderman. Six officers arrested Palmer on the street and marched him to his house to search for evidence. Unfortunately, one of the more corpulent officers got stuck in a trap door and Palmer escaped. He was not apprehended until many months later.

Washington residents flocked to the Fraser Valley in search of beer from legal saloons and hard liquor from government stores. Overnight, Huntingdon became a bustling centre; its bars and nightclubs played host to more than three thousand Americans every weekend. At the request of United States Customs, provincial police intervened one night without warning and removed all women from the bars. While the ladies waited on the street, their male companions brought out glasses of beer. The police were not upset by the women drinking on the sidewalk, for it was the evil influence of the bars themselves which was said to lead to female corruption.

Haney residents dished out stiff medicine to a Dry Squad officer in 1926. When hapless enforcer Tom Sheaves tried to break up a lively dance at Ruskin Community Hall, he was jostled and defied by the fun-loving crowd. Later, some of the party goers went so far as to lay a charge against Sheaves for causing a disturbance at the dance. At the Haney hearing, buzzing residents packed the courtroom. Defence lawyer George Cassady and Prosecutor Genge traded barbs, witnesses snarled retorts, and Magistrate Drain ejected Constable Stad from the courtroom for interrupting the proceedings by yelling excitedly that witnesses outside the courtroom, who were about to give testimony, had been listening at the door.

As soon as he was ejected, Constable Stad became involved in a scuffle with the witnesses outside. This caused Police Inspector Tuley to remark to the judge, "This courtroom is a disgrace to the British flag!"

Magistrate Drain turned beet red. "Stand up, Inspector," he barked. Tuley meekly explained that he had meant no disrespect to the judge, but was only referring to the spectators.

Magistrate Drain threw his hands up and then slammed down his gavel. "Thomas Sheaves, I find you guilty." The fine imposed was ten dollars - and the audience of wets loved it.

Enforcement of liquor laws was erratic and the bureaucracy was riddled with graft and corruption. In some locales, police confiscated regular samples of near-beer to ensure their low alcohol content. In other areas, illegal outlets operated freely. Beer parlours were supposed to have only one entrance and curtains were never to be drawn on the windows. New Westminster Constable Walter Bremner gave evidence in a 1925 trial against a hotel operator, testifying that although he drank eight glasses of Scotch and three bottles of beer in the course of one evening's investigation, defence counsel's suggestion that he may have been drunk while on duty was absurd. "The glasses have thick bottoms," he argued; "regular bootleg glasses, they don't hold much."

The postwar blues gave way to the brash, boisterous spirit of the new American culture. Slang abounded. Young ladies were called "darlings"; boldly dressed young ladies were "flappers"; while know-it-all young men were "whippersnappers." Jazz bands were the rage. Cheek-to-cheek dances like the one-step, the fox trot, the Charleston, and the jig fired young people with a sense of liberation. Men shaved their beards, whiskers and sideburns and replaced their stove-pipe trousers with bell bottoms. Women bobbed their hair, shortened their skirts, and spent much time

Fashion-conscious Fraser Valley youth, 1920s.

in front of mirrors applying rouge and lipstick and pencil-lining their brows.

The growing assertiveness of women in society expressed itself on several fronts. The older women in the community often involved themselves in groups such as the Women's Institute, which had now broadened its activities to include seminars on egg marketing, mental hygiene of schoolchildren, the benefits of prohibition, and womanly ideals.

But these ladies were not prepared for the individual self-expression emanating from younger women - represented by such dangerous trends as smoking; bathing suits which exposed more than ankles; high heels and make-up; and the propensity of some young women to surrender to the lure of the dance floor saxophone on the arm of some whippersnapper. Surrey ratepayers, in fact, railed against the dance halls and cabarets on the Pacific Highway at this time, which staged drunken orgies and raucous all-night dances.

Youngsters discovered baseball in the twenties. Babe Ruth popularized the sport, and it swiftly superseded soccer as the summer activity of most valley youths. Little boys read Gasoline Alley and traded birds' eggs for the copper wire useful as radio antennas.

Theatres appeared in most towns and Peter Pan was all the rage, as were all-night marathon dances which lasted until only one couple was left on the floor. Big city bands came to valley centres to play not only jazz, but fox trots and waltzes, on Saturday night at the roller-skating rink. For the more cerebral, crossword puzzles made their debut, and were so popular that many teenagers strapped miniature crossword dictionaries to their wrists.

The first radio station in the Fraser Valley was founded by Fred Hume at New Westminster in 1924. The predecessor of CJOR, Radio CFXC broadcast out of a coat closet. In 1927, Earl Streeter began transmitting from Osborne's Ice Cream Parlour in Mission City. Streeter ran madly about town streets asking people for records to play on the air, and coaxing children's choirs to perform. Casey Wells purchased the station's assets after only a few months and hauled the equipment away on a Model T truck - miles of wire, storage batteries, and a beat-up old transmitter removed from a World War One submarine.

At Chilliwack, Wells named his new station Radio CHWK. Often he operated for only one hour a day, as Wells spent most waking hours travelling about the town and countryside selling radios. "You couldn't catch the farmers in the daytime," he said. "The only time to sell to a farmer was after he'd finished milking and had his supper." CHWK slowly developed in importance as an outlet for news and entertainment in the eastern Fraser Valley. Correspondents along the river phoned in local news every day. Even stock market quotations were broadcast. Children's programming included dialogues such as "The Preacher" and the "Bear and Two Black Crows," the latter consisting of a comedy act between two white boys posing as Negroes.

Health fads swept the province, thanks chiefly to the influence of American dietitians like Bernard McFadden. Children mockingly recited "Every day in every way I am feeling better and better." Diet was proclaimed as a cure-all, even for influenza and middle-age spread.

Many people responded keenly to the ever more abundant and smartly advertised curatives available at the drugstore counter. Some samples are instructive: "A pimply skin needs sulphur; turn hair dark with sage tea; break a chest cold with Heat of Red Peppers; at meal time snap into it—your box of Stuart's Dyspepsia tablets enables you to face a big banquet with delight." Older pioneers stuck with traditional remedies and ridiculed dieting and nutrition.

Grandma Rambo of Mission continued to extol the virtues of plain roast beef and potatoes, but also cooked her own dishes of glazed calf's head, fried frogs' legs, and stewed dandelions.

The old-fashioned barber shop fell victim to health concerns in the twenties. Sanitation regulations under the 1925 Barbershop Act banned sponges and vaseline pots; vaseline now had to be applied from squeeze tubes. Towels were to be used for only one customer and then washed, and hairbrushes must be disinfected with lysol. "Before passing from one customer to another," read the new law, "the barber shall wash his hands, using soap...all barbers shall wear a coat of washable white material." The common practice of spitting by customers was also outlawed.

The accelerating incidence of automobile ownership overshadowed and in turn influenced changes to the social fabric of the province. Electric starters were installed in the popular Fords and glass windows replaced flapping side curtains. The *Columbian* ran ads which, then as now, avoided mention of the total cost of a new car: "Fords On Easy Payment—Buy a Ford Touring Car complete with starter, electric lighting, one-man top, demountable wheels, non-skid rear tires, extra rim and tire carrier for $295.80 down, with balance at $50 per month." Major roads in the valley were being paved—such as the Pacific Highway—allowing cars to reach speeds of up to fifty miles per hour.

Early transport truck, 1927.

The police could only regulate this new age of speed if their own vehicles could keep up. Motorists started keeping an eye out for the shiny red bike of the province's first motorcycle patrolman, Surrey's Bill Mortimer.

At 2:00 a.m. on January 1, 1922, British Columbia switched from driving on the left to the right side of the road. The first casualty of the change was Surrey municipal worker Claude Harvie, whose car was struck at 3:00 a.m. by a driver oblivious to the switch, while he was en route home from a night spent moving all of the highway signs. Harvie's car was wrecked, but he was uninjured.

White Rock beach and pier, 1924.

Country residents favoured "flivvers"—cheap, used automobiles. Weekend touring became a pastime, though in rainy season cars would bog down or even partly disappear in great clay boils, huge mudholes which defied gravel and devoured logs and boulders. The completion of the Lougheed Highway and the bridging of the Harrison River connected all north bank communities by road and provided a new route for urban tourists travelling to Harrison Hot Springs.

The most popular excursions, however, continued to be the trips to White Rock, considered to be the province's premier resort. There holiday cottages on the beach could be rented for six dollars a week per family. The Great Northern even ran a camper's special train known as the Dinky Run on summer evenings from New Westminster to White Rock, so that Vancouver and Royal City residents who worked in urban centres during the day could join their families at their rented cottage for the night. Visitors could enjoy a stroll on the beach, eat fish and chips, and see the white rock—which vandals painted black one day. For a time, they could also marvel at Ocean Park's collapsible six-foot-square post office which Ripley's Believe It Or Not claimed was the smallest functional post office in the world.

Large Model T Fords were sometimes used as jitneys—a kind of taxi-bus which toured the valley offering rides for five cents. The schedules were somewhat erratic, but a call ahead of time assured one of eventual transport. The Blue Funnel Jitney Company based in Port Coquitlam operated one of the more efficient services.

Mission school bus, 1923.

In Maple Ridge, a Model T was converted into a school bus to convey Whonnock and Ruskin students to Haney High School. The multi-purpose Ford was even used as a cordwood cutter by stripping the vehicle and attaching a circular saw to one side of the frame.

Although the rise of automobiles increasingly consigned trains to the role of carrying freight rather than passengers, the railway continued to play an important part in Fraser Valley life.

On September 21, 1927, the Canadian Northern Railway and Canadian Pacific Railway got a little carried away in their competition with one another. Each company loaded a train with several carloads of raw silk at Vancouver. The first train to reach Montréal stood to earn for its owner the long-term contract for all future shipments of the product. After leaving the urban area behind, both trains thundered through the valley, reaching speeds in excess of sixty miles per hour.

Just above Yale, the Canadian Pacific Railway train derailed. Nine rail cars full of silk hurtled down the steep canyon embankment. Four of these cars rolled into deep water near the Lady Franklin Rock. Dozens of bales of silk were strewn all about. The Canadian Pacific Railway brought explosives to the scene and dynamited the river where the cars had disappeared, hoping to blast them open and retrieve the contents. A tremendous blast reverberated down the canyon, but more dead and stunned fish floated up from the depths than silk. One man dragged ashore an eight hundred pound sturgeon as a result of the blast and shipped it to Vancouver by rail, receiving $145 for the carcass. Fishermen were paid $5 for every silk bale salvaged.

The Canadian Pacific Railway increased the salvage price of the missing silk to $20 a bale by winter. An estimated 4,250 bales had disappeared into the murky depths of the Fraser, and an unknown quantity recovered. The evidence suggests that valley residents preferred the silk to the reward money. Word flashed the length of the Fraser about the missing cargo and boats of all description soon prowled the river. A mob of noisy townspeople jostled each other on both sides of Mission Bridge, casting fishing lines for the silk bundles and perturbing the regular greybeard fishermen who frequented the bars. A number of bales were "caught" there, and for years after the accident one could purchase Indian sweaters made of half wool and half silk.

Community spirit in the Fraser Valley reached its zenith during the twenties, as the family's greater mobility facilitated travel opportunities within districts, yet road conditions prevented quick or frequent jaunts into the larger urban centres.

The Fall Fair, May Day, Dominion Day, and Victoria Day blossomed into large, ever more colourful events for young and old. In this period, volunteer labour erected an unprecedented number of community halls, in which were held dances, bridge tournaments, and political rallies. Langley and Surrey even inaugurated an annual municipal picnic. As many as six hundred residents packed lunches, climbed into their flivvers, and headed to the Fraser, where they boarded the *Skeena* for an all-day cruise on Pitt Lake.

When the *Skeena* was retired in 1925, motor launches replaced her, and the picnics remained popular well into the next decade. The *Skeena* was auctioned to a cannery upon Captain Seymour's death and ignominiously converted into a floating boardinghouse. Thus ended the career of the last commercial steamboat on the Fraser.

In June 1925, the Fraser renewed its war on Valley farmers. A thirty-five-foot hole in the Matsqui dyke was breached, and a solid wall of muddy water eight feet high poured onto the rich farmlands. The alarm was sounded and soon farmers arrived in force by horse, in cars, by rail and on foot—many of them jumping onto trains from as far away as Huntingdon and Chilliwack. Lumber camps sent help; Clayburn brickyard crews arrived with tools; and hundreds of women came with sacks for sandbags. War veterans worked up to their knees in mud and water and human chains were formed to pass sandbags along the dyke. Sikhs, Japanese, Chinese, and even Minister of Agriculture E.D. Barrow worked side by side to heal the breach.

Flooded streets in Cloverdale.

Dozens of women took over the Matsqui Hotel and larger houses possessing big stoves, and began cooking for the army of toiling men. All night long, flares and lanterns lit up the big gangs of men and the waters they strove to dam. With the assistance of pumps and pile drivers, the dyke was finally sealed.

All along the upper river, at Nicomen, Sumas, and Chilliwack, farmers lost crops, livestock, and equipment to the flood waters. It would not be the last battle, but modern communications, technology, and cooperative effort had contained *ta coutchi's* fury and prevented wholesale devastation.

Strangers to rural areas are viewed warily and with suspicion until they establish an acceptable reason for their presence. It is a paradox of country living that while the rural resident may be stridently independent in thought, he is not very tolerant of those who fail to conform to community custom and vocation. Thus, a band of gypsies encamped in Langley were ostracized for their wayward life and means were sought to oust them from the district. Salesmen, also, were now touring the valley in force, many of them unscrupulous. Several Matsqui farmers were sold phoney shares in a company marketing life preservers, after a salesman

CPR tracks and Fraser River at Port Hammond, looking east, 1928.

demonstrated the efficacy of his product by donning a life suit and plunging into the Fraser—emerging warm and dry minutes later. But the company did not exist, and the salesman was later sent to jail for fraud.

Indigent transients were an incessant problem for Fraser Valley municipalities. In pre-Medicare days, local councils had to foot the bill for hospitalization of their residents. Resentment flared from taxpayers who were assessed increased taxes in order to help care for transients having no roots in the community. Matsqui council debated at length the propriety of paying the burial costs of a tramp who fell ill in Matsqui and died in Mission Hospital. The body was finally interred in Mission, and Matsqui angrily passed the funeral bill on to the Provincial Police.

The clash of the modern and the traditional in fields such as transportation was sharp, bitter, and frequently amusing. People walking along Mission Bridge had to watch for trains; if a freight came along, one might have to hang from a girder over the river until it passed.

In Haney, council and the police force fought over the right of councillors to permit school trustees to bring their members to board meetings in the police car. Councillor Martyn opined: "What are they kicking about? It is our car." Councillor Hilder added, "It would not harm the car, anyway." The reeve pasted the police with a final shot: "They seem to object even to its use by the Council in looking over the roads. It is not used for fun, either."

The automobile provoked controversy in every region. Much livestock was killed by speeding motorists. Conversely, a Mount Lehman resident unsuccessfully petitioned Council for compensation for his damaged radiator after hitting a cow on the highway. At Whalley's Corner in Surrey, a circular wooden track called a "Whoopee Dipper" was built for young drivers to speed around in their flivvers at twenty-five cents a crack. Business grew so brisk that the bridge to New Westminster became regularly backed up with traffic and Surrey Council closed the raceway.

The obdurate independence of farmers was frequently reflected by their resistance to the growing number of governmental ordinances and red tape. Government had banned the narrow rimmed tires of farm wagons. Highway regulations favoured fast travellers, requiring the farmers' wagons or slow-moving tractors, to turn out so cars could pass. Milk and produce were subject to rigid scrutiny by Department of Agriculture inspectors. Amidst such intrusions upon their lifestyle, countrymen gave vent to their frustrations. One Chilliwack farmer, George Clarke angrily fired his shotgun to drive off municipal employees who arrived to cut wild thistles in his fields pursuant to the Noxious Weeds Act.

The increasing ties of the Delta and Richmond regions to Vancouver served to diminish the preeminent position of New Westminster as queen city of the valley. The beaver had all but vanished from Richmond by 1910, and although muskrat and waterfowl remained, the glory days of trapping and hunting were over. Most valley politicians bitterly opposed Ladner's bid for a road bridge across the Fraser, fearing that it would interfere with the deep-sea ocean freighters destined for Royal City wharves.

Charles Hope of Langley noted, "What Burrard Inlet means to Vancouver, the Fraser below the present Westminster Bridge means to New Westminster and the Lower Fraser Valley; and if a high level bridge 180 feet high and with a 1500 foot span might be a detriment to navigation, then what is a low level bridge with a 300 foot span going to be?"

The farmers of the upper valley demanded that New Westminster continue as a deep-sea port which could ship their produce.

When the main water pipes burst in the line running from Coquitlam Lake in 1928, New Westminster lost water pressure. Richmond residents fared worse. Under a 1909 agreement, the Royal City was to supply Richmond with its water. But when the pipe burst, New Westminster officials turned off the main valves of the Richmond line, turning them back on when pressure was restored. In the interim, Richmond appealed to South Vancouver for help and duly received some water from the urban community. However, Richmond officials turned off the valves they controlled at the eastern end of Lulu Island to prevent New Westminster from receiving any of this Vancouver water!

Unaware that the water pressure from the New Westminster line had been restored—the valves still being shut—Richmond issued a Supreme Court Writ demanding compensation and restoration of supply. New Westminster Alderman McAdam then asked Richmond Reeve Miller, "Are your gates open?" The reeve replied, "I'll make sure of that," and the flow of water was promptly restored. In 1930, Richmond residents voted to join up with the Greater Vancouver Water Board.

Charles F. Pretty envisioned Steveston as expanding into a major west coast port. The Board of Trade planned for docks and industrial pockets to expand over an area of fourteen square miles, at a cost of $35 million, to include a tunnel beneath the Fraser linking Richmond and Vancouver.

The Richmond *Record* noted in 1926, however, that the municipality lacked the financial base to build and sustain such an industrial empire: "What would be the good of being all dressed up with docks and tunnels and factory chimneys and nowhere to go?"

In fact, the eastern half of Lulu Island had by 1930 become one vast terminal and industrial area. Eight thousand residents participated in a heady prosperity which included establishment and growth of a major flour mill, Brighouse and Lansdowne Racetracks, and numerous businesses and industries efficiently linked by roads, river, and railway. Eburne, renamed Marpole in 1916, retained strong links with Richmond, and prospered as a crossroads community.

Municipalities faced awesome problems of funding and growth at a time when their taxation powers were limited and provincial budgets were tight. But councils were feisty. In 1919, Richmond adroitly sold to South Vancouver the foreshore it had retained on the north bank of the Fraser's North Arm, in exchange for seven hundred dollars a year for thirty years and a promise from the urban district that it would pay the cost of maintaining the Eburne Bridge. In 1927, Surrey Council successfully petitioned Victoria to take South Westminster into its jurisdiction, much to the chagrin of the Royal City.

In an era of freewheeling growth and a "subdivide as you please" mentality, numerous configurations of land parcels were created which were to plague future town planners. Roads, roads, and more roads dominated council agendas. Court actions were threatened daily against municipalities by irate motorists who lost their cars in mudholes. Council meetings were frequently so raucous that blows were struck. In Mission, a peace pipe was smoked around the council table at the first meeting of the year as a reminder to councillors that they should hold their emotions in check.

Higgins Farm at Eburne from foot of Granville Street. Sea Island in background. 1908.

Community newspapers, including the Chilliwack *Progress*, Mission's *Fraser Valley Record*, the *Maple Ridge & Pitt Meadows Gazette, Abbotsford, Sumas, & Matsqui News, Surrey Gazette, Coquitlam Herald, Langley Advance, Richmond Record,* and *Delta Optimist*, emerged throughout the Fraser Valley.

Their editorial stances were those of the majority - white, Anglo-Saxon, Protestant, and proud of it. Yet despite biases, bigotry, and the favouring of tradition, these weekly papers served as an important outlet for differing views and they were avidly scanned by politicians seeking to gauge the pulse of their constituents.

Even the Vancouver *Sun* had kind words for the country newspaper:

> "The throne of democracy is in the small town. And usually it is the small town editor who holds the sceptre. The country newspaper has reduced the essence of news to its simplest values. The sickness of Mrs. Jones' baby, the birth of a new son to the postmaster, the fire in Jim White's barn, and the meeting of the local debating society contain the germs of all human joy and tragedy...The big city daily deals with world events so vast as to be beyond full human comprehension. In a few scattered columns, the country weekly tells the same story of life and death—but infinitely more poignant, infinitely more real, because it has all happened not a thousand miles away, but around the corner. The country newspaper presents a picture of life reduced to its simplest terms...."

Rural residents tended to vote Conservative and favoured nationalistic measures, such as tariffs and enforced Canadian content. The clash of rural nationalism and urban-based liberalism came to the fore during the twenties in debates over the education system.

Professor G.H. Sedgewick, head of the University of British Columbia English Department, preached that true education crossed all boundaries; Minister of Education Joshua Hinchcliffe argued that Canadians should resist American influence by ensuring that all textbooks were British and Canadian in content.

Schools should only order books printed in Canada, he said.

Valley schools were still underfunded and ill equipped. Inspector F.D. Sinclair reported on a number of Surrey schools:

"Springdale—no urinal for boys; consequently boys foul the seats. Environment poor, trees about the building shade the light; no playground, heating unsatisfactory; Mud Bay—building unsuited for school use; Anniedale—children drinking water from road side ditch; Clayton—air space totally inadequate, building unsuited for school purposes; Strawberry Hill - water foul, 25 yards from a big latrine; White Rock—it is absolutely necessary to condemn the Division Three Room—the room is overcrowded, lighting totally inadequate, and the air is foul; South Westminster—no water at this building; odor from closets in basement permeated the building."

New Westminster students at Trapp Technical School were trained in the manual trades and domestic arts. The school was founded in 1921 at the site of the old city jail, and was to serve generations of Royal City young people.

To the students, their reconverted jail was full of ghosts. The solitary confinement cell in the basement was a source of mystery, having been lost when the basement was partially filled in during renovations. Stories abounded of prisoners having died while chained in that cell, and shackles were said to have been hung from the iron staples which were still to be seen in the basement's brick walls. The students also talked of the hangings of men like Slumach, which had occurred on the site of the school's boiler house. Trapp Tech girls capitalized on the macabre atmosphere one day by fabricating a grave in which they enclosed an art class skeleton and then charging all the boys five cents each for a look at their gruesome "find."

Compared to Trapp Tech, descriptions of life at Essondale sound positively Eden-like. Dorothy Bell of *The Province* described the inmates and their environment:

"This great family lives in the cheery red brick buildings surrounded by

Essondale Mental Hospital, 1932.

rolling green lawns on the side of a broad hill overlooking the Coquitlam River. In the smiling valley below, nestled in the fertile well-tilled fields beside the stream, are buildings of a less institutional appearance, modern farm buildings of grey and red. In and around these barns moves a little colony of happy workers in their daily routine."

By 1925, the province's mental health hospital was centralized at Essondale, with the old Provincial Health Institute facility in New Westminster becoming a mere satellite.

The rosiness of Essondale life was somewhat exaggerated. Overcrowding was the norm, sanitation still a problem. The government announced a $2 million expansion plan in 1927 which included a budget for a 750-bed chronic care facility for long term confinements.

The showpiece, however, was Colony Farm, where former Agassiz Experimental Farm director Pete Moore took charge. Under his astute leadership, Essondale quickly began producing all its own food—milk, mutton, potatoes, and all manner of fresh vegetables. Patients participated fully in all aspects of farm activity. One patient even spent ten years building a beautiful stone wall around the grounds. Others canned fruit, peeled potatoes, and worked with livestock. The dairy herd, consisting of one hundred purebred Holsteins, was one of the finest in Canada.

The cooperative movement in agriculture gained momentum during the twenties with the founding of the British Columbia Poultrymen's Co-op Exchange, the Surrey Farmers Co-op, and various fruit cooperatives. The Surrey organization was formed in 1921 in order to provide a cheaper source of feed for farmers. The cooperative purchased a building in Cloverdale, and by 1923 the feed business had expanded to the point that a general manager was required. When applicants for the job demanded salaries of at least $300 a month, a board director offered to take the post at $150. Shortly thereafter, Henry Bose became general manager, ably managing the co-op for the next twenty-five years.

Annual Plowing Match, Chilliwack, 1926.

The farmers fought battles on many fronts. Leon Ladner and Gerry McGeer took up the cause of farmers in their struggle against discriminatory Canadian Pacific Railway freight rates on produce shipped east. Combines such as Mutual Brokers were prosecuted for fixing fruit prices throughout the Canadian West, depriving berry growers of fair prices.

Valley dairymen began their own war against oleomargarine, which was becoming a popular substitute for butter. In an ironic twist, British Columbia

Dairymen Association president, H. Shannon, praised the wisdom of the Japanese government for banning margarine in that country; Tokyo viewed any substitution of other fats for butter as contributing to the "deficient" physical stature of its people. But valley dairy farmers had to settle for colour restrictions on the hated butter substitute.

Farms were becoming modernized and mechanized on a grand scale. Most large poultry barns were electrified by 1929. The Pacific Berry Growers factory in Haney was one of the most advanced on the continent, with an efficient pre-cooling plant which stored the berries pending shipping by refrigerated rail car to prairie markets, or conversion into jam. Prohibition created a great demand for fruit juices and contributed to the diversification of the fruit industry.

Politicians exhorted the urban unemployed to travel to the Fraser Valley and pick fruit, with the slogan "From Skid Road To Jam Pail." Alas, Skid Road paid no heed. The only consistent pickers were teenage girls from the valley, who donned overalls and wide-brimmed hats, and the Indians, who kept up their tradition of congregating in the Sardis area for the annual hop-picking season.

Increased Oriental immigration in the postwar years sparked renewed racial tensions; the 1921 Census reported a total of 38,539 Orientals in the province. Nowhere was antagonism more virulent than in the Fraser Valley, where white farmers feared competition from Japanese and Chinese farmers. For many years, white settlers had happily employed cheap Oriental labour, but when former labourers began leasing and purchasing their own land for intense cultivation, the white majority balked. As one farmer expressed it: "The proportion of Orientals to whites in British Columbia is too great, but only in one sense, and that is owing to the fact that they are in business for themselves and are not, as they should be, working for white men."

Chinese men at Imperial Cannery, Steveston.

Cries of "Oriental Menace" were heard at farmers' meetings everywhere, and demands were made to halt immigration and to prevent Orientals from acquiring any further land by purchase or lease. Dozens of Chinese were prosecuted for hoeing their gardens on Sundays—as if superior Oriental industry might be thwarted if only they would abide by white rules!

Police also charged many Chinese, like Leu Hum of Haney, with failing to pay the prescribed minimum wage. In Ladner, Chung Chuck operated a store and farm and defied the British Columbia Marketing Act rules restricting the selling of potatoes, thus beginning a long and colourful battle with the law and bureaucracy.

The Japanese established prosperous berry farms in Maple Ridge and Surrey. Surrey farmer Jim Ardiel recalled: "The Japanese did make competition very difficult. Men, women and children all worked in the berry patches. The rest of us didn't work at their pace, and we also hired outside help. The price of berries began to fall."

Racist rhetoric in Maple Ridge claimed that returning soldiers were unable to farm there because all of the choice land had been grabbed by Japanese. The *Columbian* reported that white settlers were being driven out and that "little brown men are rapidly taking over; the situation is becoming intolerable to whites...."

The Japanese were undaunted by the paranoia. Several of them had served with Canadian forces in the World War I, and, in fact, at the 1919 Haney peace celebration, the Japanese community erected a huge arch, decorated the hall, and provided an evening lantern parade with band and fireworks. Surrey farmer Z. Inouye fought at Vimy Ridge, was seriously wounded, and returned to carve out a prosperous farm from a poor quality, overgrown stump ranch. Inouye also established a Japanese Berry Co-op—inviting whites and non-whites alike to join.

The historically anti-Oriental *Columbian* could not help but marvel at Inouye's indomitable spirit: "Inouye and his brother have a team and each have a wife. They have no money, but they have done more real land clearing and good farming in the limited time they've been on the land than any other settler...At first they carried water from South Westminster in buckets; then they dug a 24 foot well...He has no road access and he certainly deserves one. He has made a part of Surrey on which few Europeans would have ever set foot, a veritable garden. A Jap can start on uncleared land and be independent in five years, say the old-timers. Inouye, despite his very heavy handicaps, will do it in less than that."

The growing population made the tradition of hunting in the valley more and more hazardous. On the opening day of the 1922 duck hunting season, a Chilliwack man was shot in the leg, a Ladner youth lost an arm, two Chinese were wounded with pellets in their feet, and numerous farm animals were hit. (A quantity of ducks and pheasants were also shot.)

Motor vehicle accidents reached staggering proportions, due to poorly banked roads, primitive brakes, and reckless drivers. Crime proliferated and "yeggs" —robbers, thieves and bandits—overwhelmed meagre police forces; officials were kept so busy prosecuting liquor transgressions, Lord's Day Act violations, and vagrancy offences, it is a wonder they could cope at all with more serious crime—and there were plenty of murders and rapes. When the fifteen year old daughter of a Matsqui farmer was sexually assaulted on her way to Sunday School, police involvement was largely peripheral, as a one hundred-man posse quickly hunted down the suspect.

On the religious front, a wave of evangelism swept the Fraser Valley during the twenties; tents and tabernacles drew large crowds night after night. In 1925, the Presbyterian, Methodist, and Congregationalists merged to create the United Church of Canada. In Yarrow, the first Mennonites arrived, the vanguard of thousands more who were anxious to leave Europe. These new settlers were industrious, upright, and thrifty, and were to have a lasting impact upon the valley's cultural mosaic.

Perhaps it was the turbulence of the twenties which stirred a revival of religious interest in the population. Certainly there were as many violent crimes and suicides recorded in this decade as in any era since. One afternoon in 1927, motorists on the Pacific Highway near Whalley's Corner found the body of an elderly man dangling from a tree. In the man's pocket was found a note reading, "J. Mellon, of Devon, England, born 1856, lived in this country 48 years...I had two sons in B.C., but they could not get work and had to go to the U.S."

Whalley's Corner was then, as now, a rough place. Murders, robberies, and muggings influenced most valley folk to give the area a wide berth.

Industrialization was accompanied by ongoing labour strife. New Westminster teachers went on strike in 1922. Some 300 women workers staged a brief strike at the Broder Cannery in 1926, appealing for better wages. A foreman advised the women that if they did not go to work forthwith, they would all be fired. All but eleven women trudged sullenly through the doors. The eleven hold-outs were fired and appealed to New Westminster Council that they were simply trying to earn a living wage—finding it difficult to make even one dollar a day, since the piecework they performed was not covered by the Minimum Wage Act. Council was powerless to assist the women, instead proceeding against the cannery owner for having breached one of the conditions of his lease with the city by employing Orientals.

Imperial Cannery.

Turbulence rocked the Fraser River fishing industry on several fronts. In 1923, anti-Oriental rhetoric succeeded in reducing by 40 percent the number of licences issued to Japanese and Chinese fishermen. In 1928, fishermen staged a strike over salmon prices, idling some 1,500 boats. That year, a new treaty was drafted between Canada and the United States to help conserve the Fraser salmon fishery, for the first time empowering an international commission to ensure an equal division of fish between American and Canadian fishermen. The treaty stalled in the United States Senate, but the groundwork had been laid for future action.

Many canneries were closed in the twenties as a result of consolidation efforts by the now dominant B.C. Packers Limited. Terra Nova Cannery, built in 1892, was the sole survivor from the early era of fishing, although it was fated to change functions over the years and would be ultimately used for net storage and later as a fishing station.

The search for the lost Slumach Mine took a new twist in 1926, when a colourful old prospector known as Volcanic Brown obtained a copy of the famous map from Hugh Murray. Brown had gained a reputation in 1892 for staking valuable claims at Princeton's Copper Mountain—and some earlier notoriety for performing abortions as a means of financing his prospecting trips. Brown was in his mid-seventies, obtusely self-reliant, and absolutely indomitable.

Brown disappeared into the wilderness area north of Pitt Lake in search of Slumach gold. Caught in a blizzard while crossing Stave Glacier, Volcanic slept in the open air for several nights. When his toes froze, he amputated one and cut the gangrenous flesh off of several others. A search party found him hobbling out on his own. Undaunted, the old prospector headed back to the region a second time a few years later, vowing that he would discover the lost mine or never come back. When months passed without his return, Constable Spud Murphy captained a search party. On Stave Glacier, the searchers discovered Brown's last camp—a piece of blackened bear meat, his pup tent, utensils, shotgun, and a notebook full of herbal remedies. They also found a glass jar containing eleven ounces of gold. The prospector's body was never found.

John Oliver lost his seat in the 1924 provincial election. His government squeaked in to govern as a minority, and after regaining a seat in a Nelson by-election, the premier had to woo both the radical fringe in the Liberal party and the malcontents representing the new Progressive party. He expanded his earlier social welfare legislation, aided by good economic times and a strong fiscal position.

The old Delta farmer died in office, however, on August 17, 1927. Like his predecessor McBride, Oliver left a legacy of stability and economic progress. The province would miss his grandfatherly guidance, honesty, and common sense.

Port Haney, 1930. River Road looking east.

John MacLean, Oliver's successor, is remembered less as premier than as a prominent education minister. He worked indefatigably to improve rural schooling and was the driving force for the creation of the University of British Columbia. He and his party were defeated in the 1928 election by the Tories, who were led by Fraser Tolmie.

Tolmie was the largest premier the province has ever known, weighing well over three hundred pounds. He was also the son of Dr.William Tolmie and, hence, the last link in the Hudson's Bay Company chain. Tolmie would enjoy only one year in office before his world came crashing down in the face of economic forces far beyond his comprehension.

Conservation of resources was still not in vogue. Life had not yet achieved that stage of comfort and luxury which civilizations seem to require before they heed the warning signs of damage and depletion. The magnificent firs of the Green Timbers in Surrey were gradually cut down by the King Farris Lumber Company. Pollutants from sawmills fouled the Fraser. Some positive steps were being taken by the government to preserve the fishery, through the initiation of seasonal salmon quotas and hatchery programmes.

In the hills and mountains around Chilliwack, Chief Sepass still roamed, finding peace in the high places as he gazed down on Cultus Lake and the broad verdant farmland beyond. Chief Sepass continued to observe his people's ancient customs, but he knew that the old way of life was destined to fade away completely.

In 1924, a huge forty-year-old Nootka canoe was paddled down the Fraser from Harrison Mills to the sea and around to Stanley Park, where it was mounted near the totem poles. In 1927, Ottawa ruled that British Columbia Indians had established no land claims based on aboriginal title, and the entire matter was regarded as closed.

Chief Sepass was weary of it all; let the younger generation of natives fight for land; he had the mountains and the streams to give him solace in his advancing years. He was comforted too in the knowledge that the Stalo population had stabilized and the *Sepass Poems* would help to preserve their many myths and songs.

Judge Howay and Dr. Ben Marr organized the Fort Langley Preservation Society in 1923. This group became instrumental in acquiring the site of the 1858 fort piece by piece, and conveying it to the Crown for a national historic site and public use. In 1927, the Langley Chapter of the Native Sons of British Columbia was formed, which took over care and management of the site until a later era, aided eventually by the Native Daughters of British Columbia.

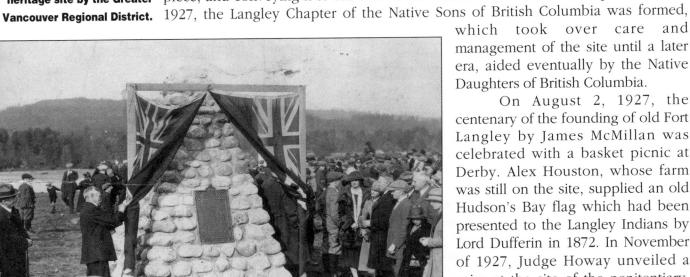

Unveiling of cairn marking original Derby fort site founded by James McMillan, May 2, 1925. The site is now owned and preserved as a heritage site by the Greater Vancouver Regional District.

On August 2, 1927, the centenary of the founding of old Fort Langley by James McMillan was celebrated with a basket picnic at Derby. Alex Houston, whose farm was still on the site, supplied an old Hudson's Bay flag which had been presented to the Langley Indians by Lord Dufferin in 1872. In November of 1927, Judge Howay unveiled a cairn at the site of the penitentiary, commemorating the first Royal Engineers camp. Children and grandchildren of early pioneers stood round, Union Jacks fluttered gaily, and not a few greetings in Chinook were exchanged. That same year, the last surviving member of the Royal Engineers, Phil Jackman, passed away.

The largest logging company in the province during the twenties was the A&L, operated by George Abernethy and Nelson Lougheed in Maple Ridge near the base of the Golden Ears. Major camps were established at Mike, Marion, and Alouette Lakes, in the area which now comprises the University of British Columbia Forest Reserve. There modern equipment operated with a most efficient system of railways, skidders, and huge elaborately constructed trestles.

Abernethy & Lougheed Logging Co. train north of Haney, 1928.

In 1929, the A&L, a showpiece for modern logging, hosted a visit from Winston Churchill. Churchill was amused to watch a logger top a spar tree, then stand on his head atop the pole. The camp cook was less amused when Churchill turned down a piece of his famous lemon pie he had prepared for the occasion, favouring instead a slice of the plain apple pie which the cook had reserved for himself. In late 1929, a monster fire devastated much of the A&L area and caused a downscaling of operations. All activity ceased in 1931.

In the twilight of a tumultuous era, Churchill also visited New Westminster in September of 1929 to preside at the Provincial Exhibition. The fairgrounds and buildings had been destroyed by fire in July. Stubborn Royal City boosters began to rebuild, improvising with circus tents to uphold the annual fair tradition. The *Columbian* opined that "no more brilliant function has ever been staged in New Westminster than the luncheon given on Labor Day to Winston Churchill on his visit to open the Provincial Exhibition. The Great Armouries were filled end to end with guests eager to see and hear."

Churchill spoke of his close friendship with Richard McBride, and how moved he was to be greeted with several bars of "Rule Britannia" upon his arrival—a tradition accorded First Lords of the Admiralty in Britain.

One month later, on October 29, 1929, Canadian stock markets crashed. Hemlines fell, soup kitchens appeared, and the heady materialistic idealism which had followed the postwar blues gave way to a grim pessimism.

On an individual level, rural residents were better prepared than their urban counterparts to meet economic hardship; farmers were at least able to raise their own food. Traditionally apprehensive of change, older country folk still looked back fondly to the gentility of the pre-war era. Perhaps it was time to call a halt to extravagance. Few were prepared, however, for the gut-wrenching sorrow and human suffering of the Depression, which were to exhaust community resources, and eventually give birth to the welfare state.

R.P.W.U.

CHAPTER FOURTEEN

DEPRESSION

The immediate effect of the stock market crash was a slackened demand in all production sectors except the domestic agricultural market. As George Woodcock has noted, even the salmon industry suffered, as English families could no longer afford the luxury of "high tea with tinned sockeye." Breadlines had formed in Vancouver by the end of 1929. British Columbia unemployment increased threefold by 1930, with the ranks of the jobless swelling to one hundred thousand by 1933.

The national crisis was exacerbated in British Columbia by the tendency for the most restless of Canada's unemployed to head west to Vancouver, where at least the climate was mild. "Riding the rails" became a way of life for these men, who were often derided as "transients," "hoboes," or "bums." Ottawa and Victoria established 237 relief camps to combat the inflow, most of them in remote areas of the province where their inmates were put to work building roads. The combination of hard, dull work and the camps' remoteness and poor facilities turned many of these camps into hotbeds of strikes and riots, where workers were liable to turn to radical Communist agitators for leadership.

Premier Tolmie was, like most politicians, paralysed by the suddenness and extent of the Depression. His most ambitious response was to borrow $7 million to provide 7,200 men with work on road construction. It was not enough. The relief camps were being filled with large numbers of men from other provinces, but, at first, it was up to the municipalities to cope with those of their own citizens who were in distress.

Fraser Valley residents were generous, but fiscally conservative. *Fraser Valley Record* editor Lou Cumming wrote: "One of the chief causes of world depression is the high standard of living—too much extravagance when times were

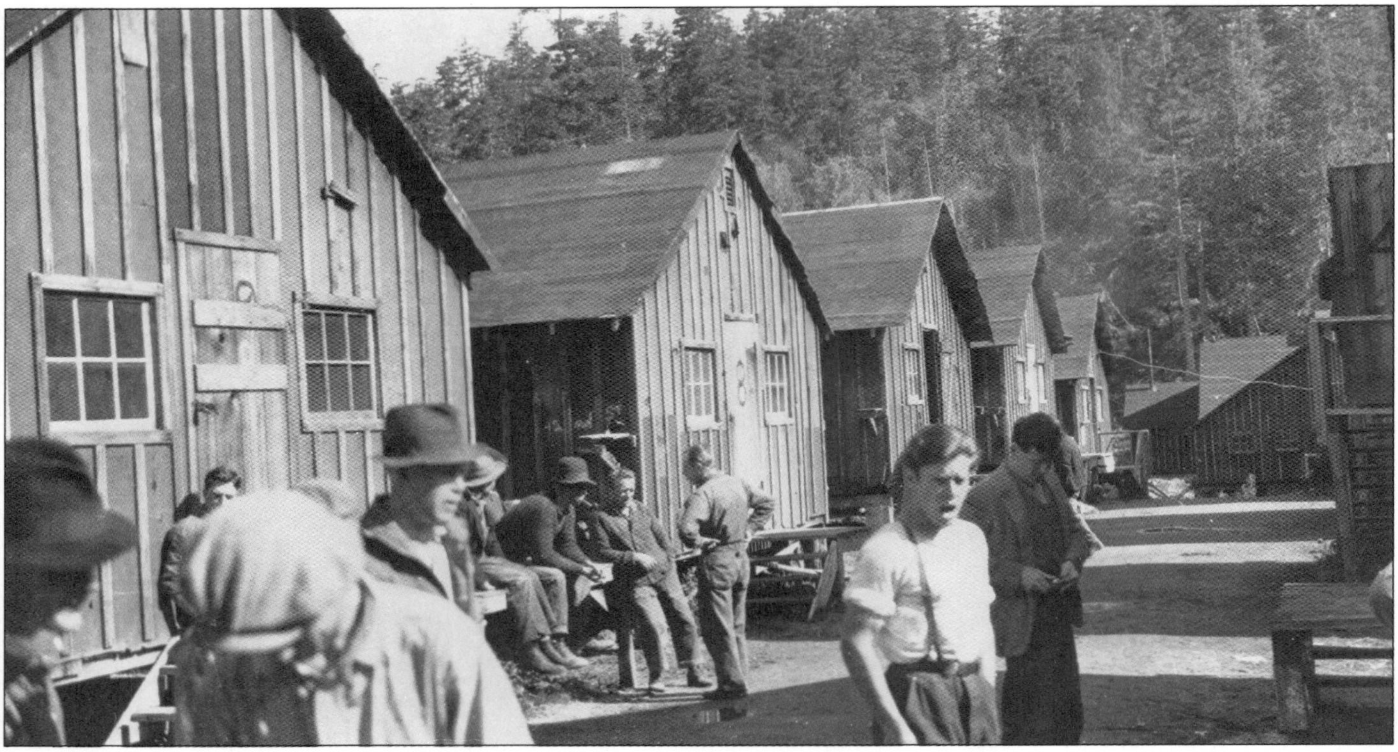

Harrison Mills relief camp, 1937.

good. We spent all our own money, borrowed the other fellow's money, spent that too; we mortgaged our homes and salaries in the insane urge to buy. When we didn't have the money, we bought on the easy payment plan...A good beginning to end the depression would be to muzzle all high pressure salesmen, jail all human sharks and make it illegal to buy on the time payment plan."

Valley municipal councils expressed initial hostility and cynicism toward the transients in their midst; farmers and townspeople alike were suspicious of men who left their own neighbourhoods. Others were fearful.

In 1933, 275 men marched along the Lougheed Highway to Vancouver from Deroche relief camps. Along the way, the men were routed around Mission City and ate in a gravel pit west of town, the food being hastily gathered from town merchants by police.

At another work camp near Deroche, one hundred men suffering from venereal disease were thrown together. When eighty-five of the afflicted began a march toward Vancouver, protesting low wages and the firing of their chief cook, in December 1934, people fled before them and locked their doors. Provincial Police Corporal Renner tried in vain to persuade the men to return to their camp.

The "VD men" marched onward—glum, sullen, but determined. At Dewdney, they tried to take shelter for the night at the community hall, but were blocked by police. Renner phoned New Westminster for instructions and was simply told, "Move cautiously, for Victoria is concerned." A truck arrived to carry the marchers' baggage and the men followed it along to Mission City. A few townspeople stood on sidewalks staring; the marchers scowled back. The group headed to the Canadian Pacific Railway station, where they spent the night, exhausted, sleeping on the floor.

At six a.m. next morning, Corporal Renner roused the marchers and ejected them from the station. The men resumed their trek. Near Vancouver, the group leader asked Renner for a meeting with Dr. J. McGammon, the health officer in charge of provincial hospital camps.

McGammon was quickly brought to the scene. After listening to the men's grievances, he promised to work toward rectifying the camp injustices—including the reinstatement of the cook. The marchers then voted to return to the camp. Government trucks were hastily fetched and the men rode back, much to the bewilderment of residents along the Lougheed Highway.

Transients riding the rails would pitch camp close to the tracks and cook whatever fare was available.

In the Chilliwack area, forty-six relief camp inmates were arrested and tried on charges of commandeering government trucks from Hope in order to ride to Chilliwack. Ironically, the men had been allowed to ride in the trucks for a distance by the camp superintendent after announcing their intention to leave camp. When told that they must get off at Hope, they decided to take over the vehicles by force and drive to Chilliwack in order to board the freight train to Vancouver the following morning.

Magistrate Johnston sentenced the two ringleaders in the caper to five months in jail, stating, "You will go to a place where you will work for nothing and do what you are told, which has not been the case in the past—and it will do you a lot of good." One wonders how the two convicts rated the city jail as compared to their crude mountain camp.

At relief camps in Surrey, police made regular searches for firearms, fearing violence from communists and other malcontents.

Muggings were reported all along the railway line in the valley, and transients were blamed for any unsolved crime. An English gypsy couple lived under the Marpole Bridge, telling fortunes and weaving baskets to earn their living, until the wife was arrested and sentenced to fifteen days in jail, for telling fortunes and selling baskets without a license.

Hobo camps emerged on the fringes of rural centres, two notable ones being established at South Westminster and Ladner; while along the river west of the Royal City there existed a vast hobo jungle of shacks and shanties. These living quarters were of variable design. Some were mere lean-tos with no walls other than blankets; others resembled ancient Stalo fish drying huts. A favourite beverage among hoboes was Vin Supreme, a loganberry wine which sold for sixty-five cents a gallon. Serious violence among the "'boes" was really quite rare, although an angry Ladner man crushed the skull of a fellow hobo who secured an unloading job at the wharf ahead of him.

Dock violence occurred in New Westminster. Many arrests resulted from several beatings of "scabs" by irate workers during a longshoremen's strike. At Fraser Mills, workers struck in September 1931 after repeated wage rollbacks. Windows were smashed and police were called in, forming a line at the mill entrance.

The strikers were dispersed, but a second and more serious confrontation occurred in October. When strikers stood in a line to prevent scabs from unloading cargo at the mill wharf, several Royal Canadian Mounted Police officers on horseback charged into the throng, wielding whips. A report noted, "They were harried by the mounted men over the creosoting company grounds...until they scattered in all directions and sought refuge in the bush." Two strikers were hospitalized with serious injuries.

Even British Columbia Penitentiary inmates caught the Depression virus and "struck" in 1932 in opposition to a new exercise programme. In 1934, seventy-eight convicts refused to work unless they were paid wages, and they then proceeded to go on a rampage, which ended with the destruction of tables, chairs, beds, toilets, and 182 windows. The disturbance was the first of any note at the prison and presaged many years of bitter turmoil ahead.

Ironically, prison life had been liberalized in 1932 to provide for cigarettes, lights in cells for reading, more inter-prisoner dialogue, and the replacement of close cropping of hair with a military cut. Flogging was abolished, except where agreed to by the superintendent.

Before the Depression, local community groups, churches, and families had tended to the poor and needy. By 1930, however, most rural districts were desperately slashing budgets for road maintenance and other amenities in order to help their masses of destitute people. Matsqui applied for four thousand dollars under Ottawa's new Relief Act in 1930 and matched the sum with its own treasury funds.

By 1936 - the climax of the Depression—one-half of Matsqui's budget was allocated for relief. Civic workers were laid off; there was no money to pay them. This, in turn, added to the burden of relief payments. People defaulted on property taxes, further reducing revenue.

As a solution for white unemployment, the reeves of Matsqui, Sumas and Abbotsford devised a unique plan. These illustrious leaders gathered twenty-five businessmen together and met with officers of the Abbotsford Lumber Company, the area's largest employer. The group "encouraged" the company to fire all of its Asian workers and replace them with whites. This the company duly did, but closed down anyway in 1931, due to slumping markets and declining local timber supplies. It is not recorded whether or not the fired Sikhs and Orientals claimed relief.

Although agriculture gained absolute hegemony over forestry in the early thirties, the prices paid to farmers often did not cover the cost of transportation. Many farmers fed milk and eggs to their animals while hungry people stood in long lines at dreary Vancouver soup kitchens. Municipalities were offered $200 per family in 1932 for each household they would accept under a federal-provincial resettlement scheme. Most districts refused to participate, stating that $200 would hardly cover the annual relief costs to families unable to become self-sufficient.

Tolmie's government refused to be thwarted by the objections of rural councils, however, so it barged ahead and offered Crown grants of twenty-acre parcels to settlers on generous terms, using relief camp workers to clear access roads and build crude temporary shacks for the newcomers. In Matsqui, the council tried to block one such planned new community at South Poplar, arguing that the costs of supporting it would bankrupt the municipality. Large rallies were held in protest; councillors claimed that as many as nine people were living in eight-by-twelve-foot shanties, many without food.

Matters in Matsqui reached a boil in 1933, when the reeve halted all municipal work relating to the government-sponsored subdivisions, and advised Victoria that Matsqui would cease all relief payments to any new settler. The government convinced Matsqui Council to keep paying the relief recipients by promising to reimburse it.

Tension and ill feelings pervaded until 1936, when the province finally assumed primary financial responsibility for relief payments to people who had moved to the district within the previous year. Over the ten years of Depression, the population of Matsqui increased by 47 percent to 5,601 persons, a phenomenon repeated in other rural districts.

One immigrant group which required little assistance were the Mennonites, who began a settlement at Yarrow in 1928; another small settlement also began at Agassiz, but it was abandoned in 1930.

These new settlers were people of German extraction from the Soviet Union. With the onset of communism, many Mennonite families began emigrating in the early twenties, and by 1929, some twenty-one thousand persons had reached Canada. Most of these settled initially in Manitoba, where there existed an earlier Mennonite community. The general movement westward during the Depression carried many of these agriculturally oriented people with it, and in the Fraser Valley, many Mennonites discovered the wondrously fertile farmland of their dreams.

Mennonite settlers near Yarrow.

The Mennonites were divided into two religious subgroups: the General Conference and the Mennonite Brethren, the latter being regarded as slightly more liberal than the former. The Yarrow community survived early problems and erected its first church in 1932. The community was cooperative to a considerable degree. The property owners formed a council and elected a chairman, known as a Schultze.

The typical Mennonite farm at this time was unpretentious; paint and decorations were frowned upon. Little land was used for yard or grounds - the estate concept was taboo - and every portion of cleared land was planted with crops. A co-op store was opened in 1937 near Abbotsford which, together with Chilliwack, became a centre for a large Mennonite community.

Relief payments during the Depression averaged $15.00 per week for a family of five, at a time when the average weekly industrial wage equalled $23.50. In most districts, relief recipients were barred from owning cattle or dogs; and if they owned land, it was required that they plant and tend a vegetable garden. Sometimes a district would give seeds to landless people and allow them to plant vegetables around the municipal hall. Firewood could be cut from public property at 25 cents per cord.

When relief funds dried up, councils issued special scrip, redeemable at stores in the district. In Surrey, a near riot occurred in 1937 when several hundred indigent men invaded the council chamber and refused to leave until cheques were cut for them. The councillors were physically prevented from leaving the room and nervously hand wrote cheques well into the night.

The generosity of rural residents was sorely tried by the controversial relief question, and the work camps in their midst. The Langley Farmers Institute proposed disenfranchising men on relief. One Mr. Shewitt threw rocks at Langley councillors and smashed windows at a meeting in 1933, after being denied relief unless he agreed to work. An ambulance driver refused to pick up a sick Langley resident and take him to Royal Columbian Hospital unless payment for the trip could be guaranteed in advance. One Mrs. Overn requested a permit to make tea for indigent men and women waiting outside the municipal hall for their cases to be called; but "members of Council were doubtful whether or not they could issue such a permit, as this came under control of the Provincial fire wardens."

The misery experienced by the unemployed was intensified by their degradation within the community. Car owners were required to turn in licence plates to the municipal council in order to qualify for relief, even when serious job hunting required the retention of driving privileges. Children of parents receiving social assistance were allowed to have teeth extracted for free, but not filled! Relief applicants were spied upon by neighbours and investigated by bureaucrats. Women appeared at council meetings to beg for work for husbands who were too embarrassed to plead for themselves.

Rural residents reverted to the practice of trading and bartering goods and services with their neighbours. Shoes were made to last longer by applying bits of old inner tubes to the soles. Efficient vegetable gardens and an ample supply of dairy products mitigated the distress of most farm households; so much so that in 1936, when terrible drought afflicted the prairies, valley residents sent fruit, vegetables, and clothing to Regina by boxcar, to be distributed to needy families.

Still, the plight of some backwoods residents was heart-rending. One Durieu mother scrawled a plea to the provincial constable:

> "We have had 3 feet of water in the house, which left it very damp. The children have all got bad colds...we have no money and are writing to ask if anything can be done for us. We would like a bottle of Buckley's Mixture, a jar of Vick's Vapo Rub, and 1 large tin of Mustard for plasters... We had to live on the beds for one and a half days until the water came over them - then we were taken out by boat. Our mattresses have all gone to pieces. Our barn has gone down, losing all our feed...All the cows have gone dry on account of standing in water so long. Would it be asking too much for a

bottle of Rubbing Alcohol for my leg, as the stump is all raw through being wet so long..."

The reputation of banks and large corporations suffered irreparably during the thirties, not so much because Canadians blamed these powerful bodies for causing or failing to cure the Depression, but rather because they were frequently heartless.

The Canadian Pacific Railway set a poor example of citizenship when it refused to pay the burial costs of a transient who was decapitated in a fall from a freight train at Mission. The local council castigated the railway giant for its callousness, instructing the local police henceforth to let people lie injured, commit crime, or die on railway property.

Bankers, for their part, rarely hesitated to take steps that would put municipalities into bankruptcy, and only the intervention of Victoria saved the day. Ironically, most councillors frowned upon retail credit and were more fiscally conservative than the bankers themselves.

Individuals and governments alike developed ingenious ways to cope with hard times. A Cloverdale relief applicant presented Surrey Council with a sack full of empty medicine bottles to show he was physically weak and unable to work for wages. The Langley *Advance* encouraged newspaper subscriptions thus: "Send in a few spuds, apples, carrots, or any other garden produce, together with your name and address."

Land was so worthless that Haney discontinued its practice of giving away free building lots to prize winners at the annual fair, because winning recipients caused problems with the land title system by failing to bother to claim the prizes through registration of their deeds.

Riding the rails.

The 1933 provincial election resulted in a fundamental realignment of political forces in British Columbia. The Tories were crushed, returning just one member. They would never again become a potent provincial force. The Co-operative Commonwealth Federation won seven seats and 31 percent of the popular vote, capitalizing on the helplessness of the main line parties in the face of the prevailing economic catastrophe.

Into the breach stepped Dufferin Pattullo, a suave, astute, and experienced politician, who had served John Oliver as Minister of Lands. Though something of a dandy, like McBride—he spent hours on his coiffure—Pattullo was well read and converted quickly to the Keynesian and New Deal views of overcoming recession through deficit financing. The Liberals captured thirty-four seats to help him follow through with his mandate for change.

The new premier swiftly instituted measures to deal with municipal unemployment, raised the free education age limit from twelve to fifteen years, ordered a mortgage moratorium for hardship cases, and laid the groundwork for a medicare programme. Roadbuilding and forestry camps were funded and joint financing schemes were arranged with Mackenzie King's government.

The trend from 1936 onward was one of an evolving welfare state supported by the two senior levels of government, leaving the municipalities free at last—though underfunded—to concentrate upon local improvements.

Fraser Valley residents were saturated with the entire range of cranks, religious zealots, and political hacks who toured the country. Communists extolled Stalin's Five Year Plan. The local Orange Lodges wired R.B. Bennett to prevent Bolsheviks from entering Canada. Robert Cromie of the Vancouver *Sun* explained to audiences that Technocracy and science would solve all problems. The big tents of evangelists proliferated everywhere and curious children were caught peeking under canvas in fascination.

Premier Duff Pattullo.

Even as the Depression clouds gathered in late 1929, the Fraser Valley was being prepared for a silver lining. After the death of gold miner James Houston's old friend, Andrew Carnegie, Carnegie's multi-million dollar estate established educational trusts and legacies. The Carnegie Corporation of New York chose the Fraser Valley as the location for an experimental rural library project which would institute a travelling bookmobile system.

The sum of one hundred thousand dollars was granted by the Carnegie Corporation in 1930 toward the purchase of twenty thousand books, a large bookmobile, and the founding of a depot and administration centre at Chilliwack and New Westminster respectively. Dr. Helen Stewart ably supervised the project and soon the bookmobile was travelling regularly down one side of the valley and up the other side every two weeks. Branches were opened at Abbotsford, Langley, Cloverdale, Ladner, Haney, and Mission, with sub-branches located at Hope, Port Coquitlam, and White Rock.

The Carnegie project was an overwhelming success. The bookmobile stopped at fifty-five ports of call, and residents from the backwoods walked miles to meet the van. By 1932, 15,637 adults and 700 students were registered as members. After the grant monies were fully expended, residents were polled as to whether they wished to pay a new local tax to sustain the library system. In the midst of the worst depression in history, 20 out of 24 library areas in the valley voted "yes" to the new tax. The Fraser Valley Union Library emerged as the first regional library in North America. In 1951, its name was changed to Fraser Valley Regional Library.

The eagerness with which residents lapped up the library service - nonfiction was more popular than fiction - was not matched by the same concern for improvements to the school system. Although high schools were built in all of the rural centres, facilities were greatly lacking, and teachers were underpaid and ill-equipped to deal with preparing rural students for a career. Dean F.M. Clement of the University of British Columbia's Faculty of Agriculture lamented that of about 1,000 rural students who began high school, only 100 reached university. Moreover, a large number of students dropped out of school before graduation.

Fraser Valley residents were unwilling, however, to pay increased taxes to fund badly needed school improvements. One Langley principal asked, "What does

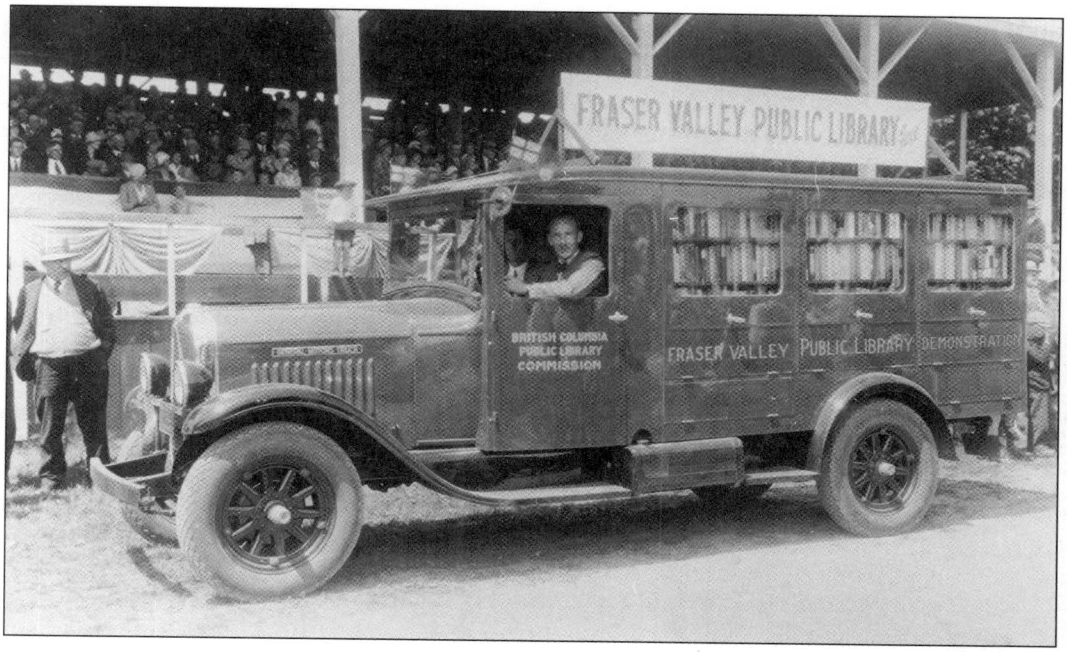

The bookmobile, a favourite with valley residents.

it profit to attempt teaching of Physics and Chemistry when there is no Science room equipped for this purpose—and no gas at all and insufficient water, if there was one?"

Alas, schools were much more adept at enforcing community behaviour standards than in preparing students for the world of work. Cloverdale's elementary school principal banned ankle socks in 1931 with the spirited concurrence of the school board.

Dr. G.H. Raley served as principal of Coqualeetza Residential School from 1914 to 1934. During that period, he achieved a good degree of success with native children. Although farming was still emphasized, Dr. Raley also took pains to prepare children for practical occupations in various fields. He also took a keen interest in Indian heritage; he not only encouraged children to remember their culture, but collected a large number of artifacts which he donated to the University of British Columbia.

Dr. Raley's encouragement of Indian children to attend high school in the community angered both the federal Indian Affairs Department and the Toronto-based United Church headquarters, which ran Coqualeetza. Dr. Raley resigned in 1934, upon learning that the school was to be closed. Yet all was not lost. As a result of Raley's success in operating one small building at Coqualeetza as a centre for tuberculosis treatment for Indians, the entire facility was eventually converted to a tuberculosis hospital, serving the province's native people.

Considerable prejudice arose during the thirties against married women teachers, since it was felt that they should be supported by their husbands' income, rather than take jobs from a single man or woman in need. Single women, particularly older spinsters, were also believed to be more dedicated to education. All rural teachers were grossly underpaid compared to their urban counterparts, and were not to reach parity until 1945.

In the interim, battles over salaries waged in Langley and elsewhere among municipal councils, school trustees, and teachers, resulted in a 1939 binding arbitration award in Langley. When the Langley School Board fired the teachers after the award displeased them, the provincial government had to intervene to obtain reinstatement.

Premier Pattullo's most memorable achievement was the construction of a new four-lane road bridge across the Fraser at New Westminster in 1937, at a cost of $4 million. The initial euphoria of valley residents was somewhat tempered when it was announced that the bridge would exact tolls. Howls of protest ensued. Proponents of the toll stated that tourists would contribute to paying off the bridge debt, but Langley's municipal council performed a quick on-site study at the old bridge and counted 2,926 vehicles licenced in British Columbia and only 84 American cars in one twenty-four hour period.

Pattullo Bridge, New Westminster.

Alas, the tolls were levied, and for several years farmers derided the structure with the phrase "Pay-Toll-O Bridge." The top deck of the old bridge was eventually removed; the lower span is still used as a railway bridge. The tolls remained until 1952.

Transportation by air received a boost in 1930 with the announcement that construction would be started on Vancouver Airport. By 1936, there were thirty passenger planes based at the Deas Island facility. The single runway measured 2,400 by 100 feet, and there were taxi lanes, a grass landing area, pumping station, administration building, and a hangar. An aircraft plant provided employment and built, among other models, the popular Catalina PBY prop plane.

The road improvement work performed by relief camp inmates proved to be an unexpected benefit to Fraser Valley communities. Both the Trans-Canada and Lougheed Highways were upgraded and paved in 1935 and 1937 respectively.

Pacific Stage Lines emerged as a subsidiary of the B.C. Electric Railway in 1923, and was soon offering regular passenger bus service along the Lougheed Highway to Agassiz. Another subsidiary, British Columbia Rapid Transit Co., offered similar service between Vancouver and Hope south of the Fraser. The electric railway company itself, feeling the competition from trucks carrying commercial freight, began its own Fraser Valley Truck Lines to complement its daily rail runs.

The B.C. Electric trains still performed a valuable service to Fraser Valley farmers. Despite the increased popularity of freight trucks, the daily milk run continued until 1939. For years, farmers waited at each wayside station in the morning and loaded their milk cans, eggs, butter, chickens, pigs, and produce onto the boxcars for delivery to Vancouver and New Westminster. Up to 250 ten-gallon cans of milk were picked up each day along the line. Upon unloading the farm products in the city, the train would reload with groceries and other merchandise destined for valley stores.

One of the worst storms in history hit the Fraser Valley in January 1935, causing massive destruction, death, and loss of livestock. A combination of heavy snow followed by an ice storm—known in the valley as a silver thaw—caused thousands of trees to topple, power lines to be severed, and highway and rail lines to be flooded. Slides blocked the Lougheed Highway.

In Mission City, virtually every tree and pole was reported down, with tangles of telephone and hydro wires askew on the sleet-covered streets. A bedraggled relief camp worker hobbled into Chilliwack to report that his camp, fifteen miles away, had run out of food and was isolated from the world.

The original Vancouver airport, 1928.

The Pacific Highway and other major roads in Surrey were under water at many points; some twenty-five Mud Bay families had to be removed from their homes by rowboat. Dr. Sinclair of Surrey strapped a canoe to the top of of his car and paddled down driveways to attend to patients. When the Fraser froze, some Mount Lehman residents were walking across the river to a barn dance in Ruskin when they were startled to hear an engine behind them. Turning, they watched in wonder as a Model T Ford sailed past them on the ice.

Flood waters destroy CPR track at Dewdney.

At the height of the storm, ten homes were swept away by a mudslide at the Kilgard site of the Clayburn Brick Company. The structures were hurtled down Sumas Mountain into the brick plant works, killing two people. All rail lines remained closed for several days, and at Sullivan in Surrey, the Bear Creek rampaged over the B.C. Electric line, severing track and leaving one hundred feet of rails suspended over a fifteen foot chasm.

Archie Barker, owner of Chilliwack's City Dairy, hauled milk to a shivering New Westminster with a wagon attached to a Caterpillar tractor. When a B.C. Electric employee froze to death at Sardis during the storm, Barker loaded an empty coffin on top of the milk bottles in his wagon, grabbed the undertaker, and set off on his tractor to fetch the corpse.

Flood and slide victims were cared for in homes, schools, and community halls. At Abbotsford, three hundred people were brought to town by boats and rafts. Sumas Lake returned to reclaim its former territory, until pumps could restore the farmland. An elderly Chinese, Lee Chew, was found dead in a foot of water near Cloverdale. Although the Fraser did not flood to 1894 levels, the death toll in the valley rose to a dozen; the economic loss was horrific, and it was several weeks before power, telephone service, and transportation links were restored with the outside world.

The Depression years were a time of mixed gains and losses for agricultural producers. The Fraser Valley Milk Producers Association suffered a serious reversal in 1931, when the Supreme Court of Canada found the Produce Marketing Act to be unconstitutional. Under the Milk Board established by the provincial government in 1930, control of milk prices and practices was invoked. This caused eleven Vancouver dairies representing 94 percent of all retail outlets to amalgamate under the name of Associated Dairies, a company controlled by the association. After the Supreme Court ruling, independent producers and dairies immediately increased in number and for a time after 1936, supplied nearly 80 percent of the fluid milk market.

Berry growers in the Mission area joined forces in 1923 to form the Pacific Co-op Union, establishing a plant at the site of the first St. Mary's Mission on the flats. John Shimek was the driving force behind the co-op—cajoling, writing, and speechmaking until he was hoarse. By the late thirties, the co-op was handling $500,000 worth of berries every year. About 90 percent of the area's growers belonged to the co-op, including Japanese growers, who enthusiastically participated at all levels, including the board of directors.

Young George Grauer milks cow the old fashioned way.

The industry was helped by a new method of preserving berries, known as the SO2 technique. Berries were heated in a solution of sulphur dioxide gas and calcium powder; this preserved the fruit longer while it awaited conversion into jam.

At the Pacific Co-op Union plant, excess sulphur from the process was thrown daily into the Fraser. One day, billing clerk Ethel Burnham was startled at her desk by plant workers who ran into the office laughing uproariously.

"It's Windebank's pigs!" one of them exclaimed, "they're all drunk out there!"

Ethel ran outside. Sure enough, pigs had broken out of their pen and were flopping about all over the place - onto the railway tracks, into the river; there was even a pig lying prostrate on Mission Bridge. The pigs had evidently tasted some sulphur which a careless worker had tossed onto the riverbank, and the chemical had produced an intoxicating effect.

The plight of many farmers who watched the price of their product drop and co-operative associations wither was desperate. About two hundred milk producers converged on a Hatzic road in 1933 to blockade a truckload of "bootleg" milk en route to Vancouver. The Fraser Valley Milk Producers Association farmers had warned one Whieldon—a defiant independent producer—that he was weakening prices and hurting others by selling to an independent Vancouver dairy. When the Whieldon truck failed to appear on the main road, the mob marched to Whieldon's home, where the farmer was harangued by several spokesmen. Despite threats, Whieldon refused to agree to haul his milk to the association's mainland dairy.

The morning after the Hatzic confrontation, another group of association dairy farmers chained two trucks together and blocked Whieldon's driveway. Whieldon and his wife were threatened with violence; police were called. Officers told Whieldon that he should avoid potential injury and agree to the farmers' demands. Under duress, Whieldon then trucked his load to mainland dairy.

A few days later, however, Whieldon obtained a court injunction preventing the association farmers from "procuring the plaintiff's customers to break milk hauling contracts, from watching and besetting the plaintiff's premises and trucks, and from barricading public roads." The battle over control of milk marketing, however, was far from over.

The potato industry faced problems just as chaotic. Marketing and licencing regulations angered many farmers in the thirties, not a few of whom were Oriental. The Chinese Agricultural Association was dominated by Chung Chuck of Ladner, who, with cunning, alacrity, and dogged determination, defied every legal measure which interfered with his freedom to do as he pleased.

Arriving in Canada as a young boy with his family, Chung had worked hard, operated many enterprises, and built a thriving farm. In 1929, he was charged with selling potatoes without the permission of the Mainland Potato Committee of Direction.

Chung filed a writ seeking prohibition against the New Westminster magistrate hearing his case, pending his constitutional challenge of a previous conviction, scheduled to be heard by England's Privy Council, Canada's final court of appeal at the time. Magistrate Johnson observed that Chung's agricultural organization existed "for no other purpose than to make it as difficult as possible for the Committee of Direction to do its duty—in fact, to break the Produce Marketing Act." When Chung failed to appear in court on another related charge, a warrant was issued for his arrest. He was later convicted and fined three hundred dollars.

A very prosperous citizen—he was allegedly involved in the opium trade—Chung Chuck had the advantage of access to the finest barristers in Vancouver for his constant skirmishes with the law and government officials. After the British Columbia Coast Vegetable Marketing Board was formed, officials blocked Chung's trucks as they attempted to cross the Fraser Street Bridge in July 1936. One officer, baton in hand, seized fifty-two sacks of potatoes, and a number of smaller loads the following day.

The eminent barristers Alfred Bull and G.E. Housser argued later in court that Chung and his associates had every right to transport potatoes to a Vancouver warehouse for export purposes, as the governing act only affected domestic sales. An injunction was granted against any further interference by officials with Chung's trucks, although it was limited to potatoes for export. Chung would continue to do battle with officialdom until his dying day.

New Westminster ratepayers voted to kill the annual Provincial Exhibition in 1930. It was never revived. Although the Royal City continued to act as the valley's commercial trading centre, local agricultural fairs grew in size and importance as the focus of community pride. Other events, such as the annual Bradner Flower Show, also prospered.

In 1928, Fenwick Fatkin staged an innocuous display of daffodils at Bradner in conjunction with local growers; known as a "parlour show," the event was held at the local community hall. Fatkin imported many daffodil varieties from Europe, including the King Alfred type, which became the most popular daffodil in the world. Fatkin discovered that the Bradner area soil was ideal for the commercial growing of flower bulbs.

In 1932, the Bradner Show was attended by huge crowds, and concluded in the evening with a grand concert and dance. In time, Bradner became known as the daffodil capital of Canada—if not the world. Every March, flower stands abound along its roads and byways, their marvellous displays of sunshine gold telling us that spring cannot be far away. Among the bulb growers attracted to Bradner was the Dutch farmer William Vander Zalm, Sr., who first visited the area in the 1930s; he purchased an area farm, grew bulbs there, and brought his family to the farm from Holland at the end of World War II. It was there that Vander Zalm's son, also named William, a future premier of British Columbia, spent many boyhood years.

The strong community spirit, which had prevailed in the Fraser Valley during the twenties, matured and strengthened during the Depression years. Only a very few could afford new cars, and although technology and industry had made available many new devices, the first Massey-Ferguson rubber tired tractor did not appear until 1938; and the first powered combine in 1939.

Many of the new settlers of the land were prairie families seeking a

Greybrook Dairy Farm, Pitt Meadows, 1935.

drought-free farm. Fern Treleaven wrote of the farmers arriving in Surrey, "They piled their families and a few cherished possessions into old cars or trucks and left farms that had become drifting deserts of sand." In Delta, more than one hundred families arrived from Saskatchewan to purchase one and two-acre parcels offered for sale by the Delta Manor Holding Company. The families had responded to advertisements acclaiming the poultry-raising potential of these plots.

The settlers from the praires struggled hard with their chickens, but just could not make a profit on their small holdings; instead, they had to take odd jobs working on the roads or in the Richmond, Surrey and Haney peat bogs in order to feed their families.

Along the Pacific Highway, between Whalley's Corner and Port Mann, newcomers of varied backgrounds eked a bare living from the soil. These included a young unemployed ironworker from Vancouver, who blasted out stumps to build an Angora rabbit farm; a former bureaucrat, inexperienced in carpentry, who built a five-room bungalow; a Lancashire carpenter, who raised cocker spaniels and wire-haired terriers among the stumps; and a Japanese mill worker who planted strawberries.

Meanwhile, a new breed of worker was contributing to the development of the suburbs: the daily commuter, who, with the opening of the Pattullo Bridge, found that he could avoid high city taxes by walking or driving across the bridge every day, from a home in Surrey to a job in New Westminster.

The turbulence of the times bred a new kind of tolerance. A resident farmer, who could lapse into a catatonic fit over a neighbour receiving welfare, might now make positive remarks about Orientals, earlier excoriated as misers. The Orientals were now viewed in a different light as they seldom became a burden upon the public purse. Even dens of iniquity, known to house opium and gambling activities, were ignored if they functioned behind closed doors and made no bid to attract white youths.

Hop's Store in Ladner was a fascinating place. Inside, the acrid scent of incense prevailed; two illegal slot machines stood in the shadows; elderly Chinese sat on boxes smoking opium pipes. There, one could purchase fresh roasted peanuts from Hop, have one's clock repaired, and purchase firecrackers, lady fingers, and torpedoes for Hallowe'en.

In 1937, Hope still had no hospital. One dark rainy night that year, a pregnant white woman began to have labour pains. The local Chinese laundry owner offered to drive the lady and her husband to Chilliwack Hospital, but near Rosedale, it was evident that the birth was imminent. The driver stopped his car. While the nervous husband provided light from matches, the Chinese delivered the baby, using his black bow tie to tie the umbilical cord. So a crying infant, wrapped in a blanket, was carried into Chilliwack Hospital that night wearing only a bow tie. The launderer became a hero within the Hope community.

The era witnessed a loss of faith in production, progress, and politicians. Residents often took matters into their own hands. When the government failed to provide

Bridge over Fraser River at Hope, 1929.

running water for Mount Lehman School, the Parent-Teacher Association installed a pipe underneath the road, built connections, and provided fixtures to ensure a supply of running water for the school.

In Fort Langley, the village's bachelors and spinsters alternated in sponsoring old-time balls and dances in order to raise money for the needy. Women's Institutes in all locales comforted and cared for the sick, the homeless, and deserted mothers.

The original Hard Times suppers flourished, as did Robbie Burns Nights. Many mothers made bathing suits from flour sacks so that their children wouldn't swim nude—unaware that, once soaked, the clinging fabric was rather revealing. Families huddled around radios listening to "Orphan Annie," "The Green Hornet," "Jack Benny," and the sound of the big bands. Crosswords, jigsaw puzzles and a new game called Monopoly were played passionately.

Passion was also expressed in the lacrosse box. In 1933, the Coquitlam Adanacs and Abbotsford Hotel lacrosse teams fought it out in the courts after a contentious ruling by the referee in a play-off game. Less intense was a baseball game played by the Mission Board of Trade in 1936, when adults and high school students played each other while riding on the backs of donkeys, thus inventing the sport of donkey baseball. The game developed into a hilarious free-for-all when several donkeys refused to go around the bases and others travelled around in the wrong direction.

Reporter Alan Morley toured the Fraser Valley by bus in 1937, and he made these observations: "They talk the same language, they fly the same flag as we do in Vancouver, but they are a different folk that live in those little towns within an hour's drive of the city." The boundary between city and country was passed "when the first roadside pedestrian raises his hand in greeting to the bus driver; your bus has ceased to be a ripple and is now an event."

Observing serious flooding at Fry's Corner in Surrey, Morley was staggered by the farmer's reticence: "You are amazed at their calmness...they plod smilingly through the mud and wait patiently for the withdrawal of the waters...There you see the difference in our characteristics. In Citiana, we know the value of Time, and pursue Him relentlessly from minute to minute. In Ruralia, they know the value of patience and they wait for Time and trap him as he passes by."

Morley noted the friendly banter on the main streets of Langley and Abbotsford and commented upon the ability of valley residents to amuse themselves and work toward common social goals:

> "They have an odd way of getting together to do things without any preliminaries, such as pep talks and publicity campaigns. In Abbotsford they wanted a place for badminton and the acting of plays, so the government that makes (or does not make) the roads, gave Abbotsford some lumber. From far and near gathered these farmers, labourers, lawyers, teachers, and grocers with their hammers and saws and bevels, and lo! It was but a few days and such a hall was built as Citiana rarely sees. They even thought of the school children and put in a room for manual training and one for domestic science with benches and ovens...and just a week ago, they held an amateur show in their new hall with 21 acts; an audience of 1500 overflowed and they never had such a good time."

There were many who had soured on society, of course, and they sequestered themselves. An old pioneer, known as Napoleon, lived in a floathouse on the south shore of the Fraser in Surrey; visitors were admitted when they brought along a bottle of wine.

Then there was the Dog Man, George Bramfield, formerly a prominent city lawyer, who now lived in a tar paper shack near the Pattullo Bridge. George slept without blankets, cuddling his beloved dogs for warmth. The dogs so unnerved a telephone lineman one day that he clung to a pole for some twenty minutes, the dogs howling below him, until Bramfield called the canines home.

Beneath the veneer of Victorian propriety, many Fraser Valley folk were rugged, boisterous and fiercely independent. Laws were not always respected; yet there is much evidence that police and prosecutors failed to exercise discretion in cases which today would never be pursued.

Vendors of strawberries, particularly the Japanese, were repeatedly fined for selling baskets of fruit allegedly arranged so that the largest, most luscious berries were placed on top and smaller, less ripened berries were hidden beneath.

In Pitt Meadows, John Gray was charged with nonpayment of the $1 library tax imposed for the new library facility. Pleading poverty, Gray apologized, but told the court that feeding his wife and three children came first. When Magistrate Sparling imposed a fine of $5 upon him, a sympathetic crowd gathered outside the courthouse and collected enough money to pay the fine for Gray, but defiantly left the $1 tax unpaid.

The entire Richmond police force of three was fired one day when the municipal council determined that they were unable to cope with drinking parties of male youths in Steveston's "blind pigs." A new police chief was appointed - the same man who had resigned from the position a short time before because he said he was unable to cope with the area's rowdies.

In Langley, the judge and lawyers played poker in court between cases. Police Chief Macklin, however, was urged to attend the district's popular moonlight dances, which were so upsetting to parents. The chief was told that all of the lights were turned off at these affairs, and much beer was consumed. Chief Macklin complained to council that he would need an extra gas allowance if he was to act as chaperone at such events. Council agreed.

In another Langley incident, a group of residents who objected to the reckless driving habits of a local store employee, tarred and feathered the man's automobile, which was owned by his employer. The vehicle was made to resemble a big black fearsome-looking owl, but the employee continued to drive the befeathered beast about. Horses and cows bolted at the sight of the apparition; puzzled residents called police. The big bird was finally apprehended. The store owner complained of $150 damage to his car, but the police found no clues as to the identity of those responsible. The unpopular driver was fired.

Out of the tumult of the early Depression years there emerged a profound respect for the human condition. The Liberal party became temporarily dominant federally in the Fraser Valley, representing a switch from the Conservatives; the majority of residents believed that the Grits combined conservative economic values with necessary social programmes.

The hoboes and transients who rode the rails were becoming more acceptable, and there were fewer of them. The proprietor of Bowie's Bakery in Mission was touched one day when a well-dressed young man appeared at his store and handed him a one dollar bill. "When I was here in 1934," said the man, "tired, hungry, and penniless, you gave me some bread rolls. Now I want to repay you."

In a 1939 tax referendum campaign, Chilliwack voters were exhorted by their newspaper editor to vote for a new hospital facility to better care for the ill and injured:

> "Since the days that Chilliwack Hospital made its first appearance, the Model T, the Brush, The Chalmers, The Baby Grand, and numerous other model automobiles have come and gone; telephones and radio receiving sets have become general; paved roads, garages and filling stations are everywhere, as well as short skirts, no skirts, and beauty parlors and permanents, lip sticks and rouge. The silent movie has given place to the technicolor. The popular tram line is a back number and streamlined trucks haul milk, hogs, and cattle... Children are carried to school in comfortable coaches, while parents turn a switch and have their cows milked mechanically...The world has moved forward or backward according to the point of view. Chilliwack ratepayers are not going to allow the cost of a new hospital building hold out on those who need their thoughtful care and consideration the most—the ill and the injured."

The hospital was approved by a healthy majority.

Romance and mystery, always part of the Fraser Valley's history, flashed to the fore every now and then. On March 23, 1934, a few Indians were quietly fishing at Morris Creek near Harrison River when rocks began to fall around them from the cliff above. They looked up to see a gigantic hairy man—or beast—preparing to roll a huge boulder over the edge. The natives scattered.

In 1935, two giant "two-foots" were seen in the same area leaping down a mountainside. Their guttural, animal grunts were heard by several Morris Valley residents. The creatures crossed the creek and clambered up the opposite hillside into the forest. Huge human-like footprints were found, and the incidents were added to the generations of Sasquatch lore which dates back into the mists of time.

A Langley stroller discovered an ancient, weather-beaten cabin in the woods one day and was taken back to another age:

> "As I approached the doorway, I stumbled over something on the soggy ground. I turned it over with my foot; it was only the decaying skull of a cow. I turned the handle of the rotting door which creaked upon its rust-stiffened hinges... An odor reminiscent of a catacomb greeted me. Scattered about the room was a conglomeration of old clothes, boots, honeycombs, and pails. A large bull-necked cauldron with some green stuff in it sat awkwardly upon the stove. On a wall hung 13 storm lanterns and 11 massive frying pans. From the sagging ceiling dangled a pimpled side of mouldy bacon. In another room was a bookshelf loaded with musty

Green Timbers portion of the Pacific Highway.

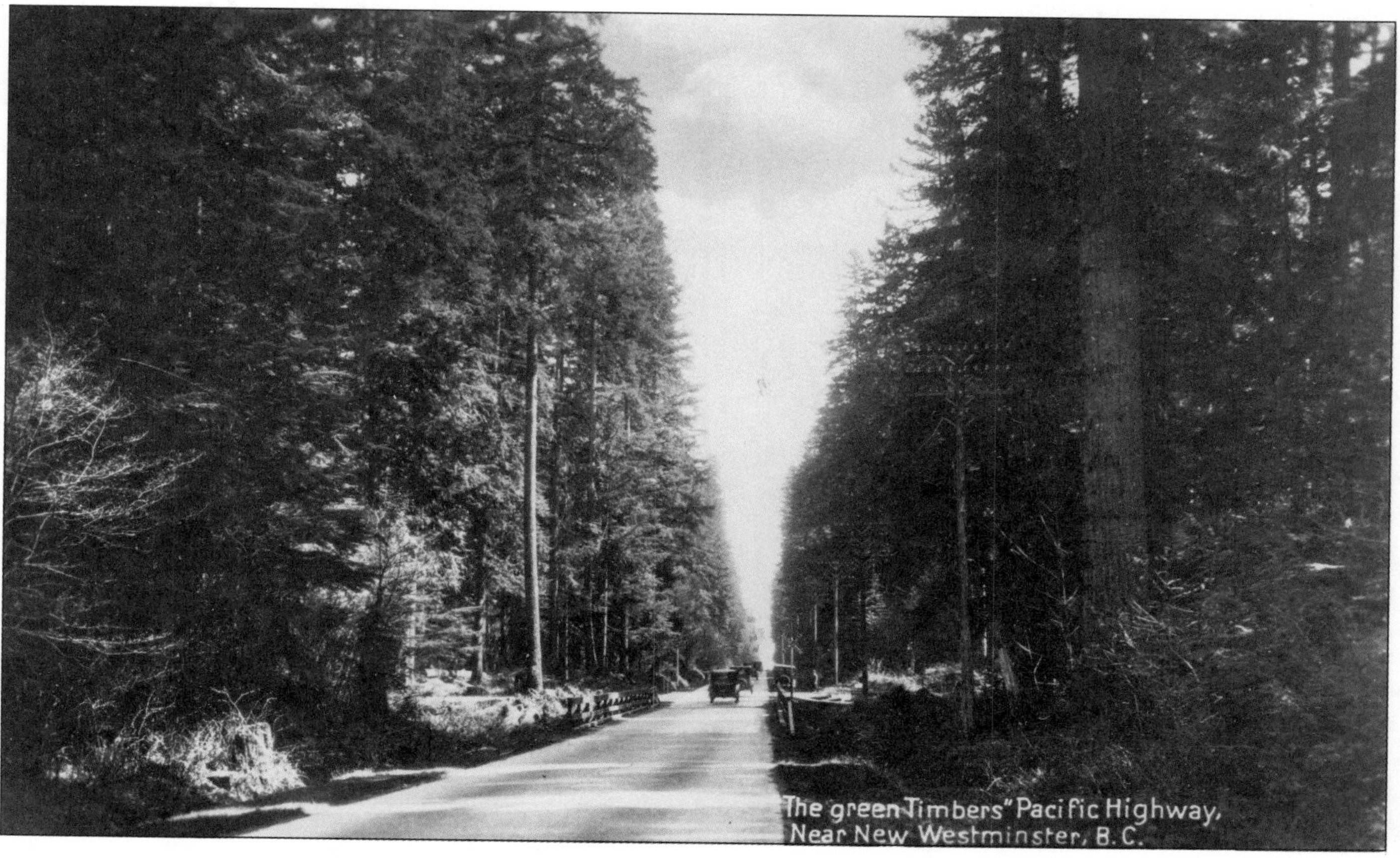
The "green Timbers" Pacific Highway,
Near New Westminster, B.C.

books...In between the yellow leaves of one book I found a few hand-written sermons. I realized that I was invading a hidden sanctuary, the memorials of a dead man. The cracked walls, broken windows, the gnarled trees outside, all seemed to breathe the romance of a hardy, rugged, God-fearing pioneer...."

Judge Howay's speeches about the early fur trade and gold rush days continued to kindle pride in local heritage. Commencing in the mid-twenties, an annual gathering of several hundred Fraser Valley pioneers took place, providing a time to reminisce and a place to dance the quadrilles and reels of a bygone age.

In 1935, the National Parks Board announced plans for the restoration of the old fort at Fort Langley at a cost of thirty-five thousand dollars. The village of Fort Langley, meanwhile, had reverted from a bustling centre to a sleepy, rustic museum of lost dreams. Even the Canadian Northern Railway station closed for lack of business.

Resource conservation still suffered in the face of utilitarianism. In 1930, the last giant old growth fir crashed to the ground at Green Timbers. The Abbotsford Lumber Company had asked the government to set aside the last old growth fir stands on the Pacific Highway for a park, but Victoria ignored the request. The company even advertised in newspapers, warning people that they would regret the destruction of the ancient trees.

King George VI and his wife Queen Elizabeth toured the Fraser Valley in 1939, receiving a tumultuous welcome at every stop.

Nobody responded. "Farewell," eulogized the *Columbian*; "there it stood, a magnificent specimen of Douglas Fir, towering above a desolate sea of stumps...This one bit of the highway was unique to the traveller. Especially on a hot day in summer it was with a keen sense of pleasure that one entered its shade and breathed in the invigorating atmosphere...But regret in vain; Green Timbers is gone."

Nonetheless, a block of twenty-five acres of Green Timbers was set aside by the provincial government for reforestation, and replanting began in 1932.

The largest crowds in the history of the province gathered in 1939, when King George VI and Queen Elizabeth toured the lower mainland. If the greeting delivered by Vancouver residents was grand, Fraser Valley residents became delirious in their display of affection for the Royal couple. The streets of New Westminster were bedecked with flags, bunting, and arches; thousands jammed into Queen's Park.

When the official car appeared at city centre, the roar of the crowd and the bands reverberated across the Fraser, while on the river more than 150 fishboats, tugs, and yachts shimmered with Union Jacks in the warm June sun.

The king was dressed in a blue naval uniform; the queen wore a redingote, beige stockings, and a mauve hat. When the king asked Mayor Hume the size of New Westminster's population, he was told it was 22,000, but that the cheering crowds present were estimated to contain 150,000 people.

As the royal couple boarded the blue, silver-panelled train taking them on their journey east, Queen Elizabeth smiled and waved vigorously at the vessels below the Pattullo Bridge; the engine whistle blew, and the train slowly proceeded across the bridge, while the boats blew their horns unceasingly.

All along the train's route, people gathered to catch a glimpse of their king and queen. At Fort Langley, where the train was scheduled to slow down, but not stop, two thousand schoolchildren waited. Throughout the morning, cars, trucks, and buses unloaded passengers, and numerous Indians and Japanese mingled with the predominantly white Anglo-Saxon crowd.

The crowd sang and sang, and in the midst of "Tipperary," the royal train suddenly appeared round the bend. Mackenzie King stood and gestured toward the rear coach observation car, where the king and queen stood smiling. Across a small ravine near the old fort, residents had strung a banner reading "Fort Langley—original capital of British Columbia, November 19, 1858. Langley greets their gracious Majesties."

The exultant scenes were repeated in Chilliwack, where the train stopped for a time. There the king broke precedent by jumping down from the platform and mingling with the crowd. Those who caught a glimpse of the royal couple were to recount the event to their children and grandchildren.

As the world lurched into war, people of the Fraser Valley would look back sentimentally to that very special day in their lives, when roots and patriotism, pride and splendour, came together to unite one and all with a sense of bonding and community of interest, a moment which for sheer fervour would never be repeated in our history.

CHAPTER FIFTEEN

WAR AND FLOOD

It was a golden September evening in the Fraser Valley. The pungent tang of fresh cut grass pervaded the country kitchen, mingling with the aroma of dinner. The birds sang, and in the distance a train blew its whistle at one of a hundred unmarked crossings. The farmer glanced outside at a rabbit dashing across a field, lit his pipe, and flicked on the radio.

The news was grim. "Canada," proclaimed the announcer, "declared war on Germany today. The declaration follows the lead of Great Britain...." The farmer abruptly turned the radio off.

Across from him sat his twenty-year-old son, his eyes eager with anticipation.

"It's no good," harumphed the farmer, as he fingered his scarred thigh, thinking of the bullet which had shattered the bone at the Battle of Cambrai.

"War, that is," he continued. "This will be a mean business, Geoffrey, mark my words."

The farmer stood up, nodded to his wife Sarah, and stomped outdoors to tend to his cows. Sarah sat motionless, tears welling in her eyes. Geoffrey was in the militia and eager to fight. For months now, he had been training with D Company of the Westminster Regiment at Mission—one parade a week, and a few weekend field manoeuvres. She had been proud of her son, and had even laughed when he'd told her of the old lumbering truck that the boys rode in that always overheated, coughing and spluttering all the way to the rifle range. Now the war games were over.

Canada had delayed its own war proclamation for nine days following Britain's September 1, 1939, declaration in order to demonstrate its independence. In

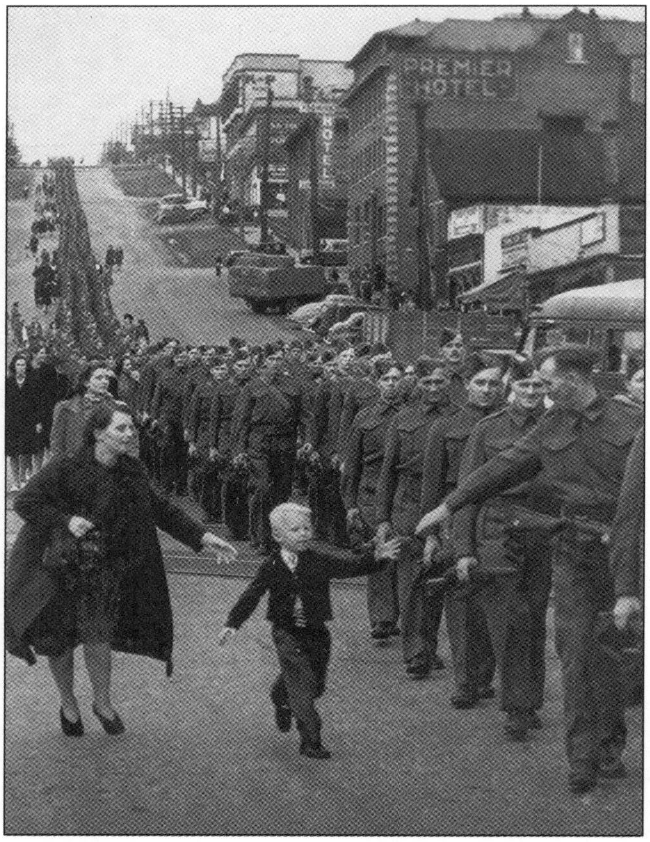

Troops march off to war in New Westminster.

English, and particularly rural, Canada, there was a rush to the colours. The Fraser Valley's own Westminster Regiment was deluged with recruits. Young men of British descent predominated, but many other nationalities were also represented.

Hobo camps were thinned out rapidly as men joined the armed forces to gain a job and escape the dole. One seventy-year-old Chilliwack veteran demanded to participate and when refused admission to the Canadian Army, he flew to Britain, where he was placed in charge of a production department.

The Depression seemed to disappear overnight. In fact, by 1940 there was a labour shortage, and farmers made desperate pleas for help in harvesting crops. District councils cut relief payments. In Surrey, all relief was denied to employable single men under the age of forty-nine and married men under thirty-nine; the food allowance was halved for qualified recipients having access to vegetable garden plots.

Boundary Bay was established as a flight training base and residents were treated to the sight and sound of Harvards, Hawker Hurricanes, and Tiger Moths tearing up the skies or, in several instances, crashing. Mink farmers were furious, complaining that their animals killed one another in fright provoked by the din overhead. In Delta, heavy army trucks killed so many chickens and pheasants that paper boys regularly picked up freshly killed birds in ditches and presented the carcasses to their mothers for dinner.

The Westminster Regiment trained in Saskatchewan from May 1940 to November 1941. They were then billeted for six months at the Hotel Vancouver, of all places, before sailing for England.

The Red Cross, the Women's Institute, and numerous community groups began fundraising, packing medical supplies, and knitting socks, as many of them had done in World War I. The first valley troops were barely overseas when a Chilliwack teacher distributed names in a hat and had girls draw for a soldier to write to and supply with woollens. Communities competed for the distinction of attaining the highest subscription quota for Victory Bonds. Air raid drills were practiced; high school boys and older men joined the Pacific Coast Militia Rangers, a home defence corps which roamed about the countryside on manoeuvres with unloaded rifles and bombs made of flour bags filled with sand.

The December 7, 1941, attack on Pearl Harbour greatly heightened the fears of invasion. On December 8, the entire valley was blacked out, and regulations provided that all lights were to be extinguished thenceforth by 5:00 p.m. The militia, previously derided as "a bunch of old men and boys playing soldier," was accorded newfound respect.

Even air drills were now taken seriously, particularly after the Japanese shelled a Vancouver Island lighthouse. For the first time in British Columbia's history, women trained with live ammunition in a Canadian Women's Training Corps. Sugar rationing was implemented, followed by wage and price controls.

One evening in June 1942, Richmond residents became convinced that the Japanese were invading when they saw bright streaks in the sky, followed by strange noises, then silence. It transpired that a fleet of military balloons had broken free from their moorings and dragged eight hundred-foot cables through the air, which produced sizzling noises, flashes, and radio static when they struck house roof aerials.

Amidst the increasing paranoia, roving bands of policemen patrolled the streets of Ladner and Steveston, checking for invaders; at Fort Steveston, soldiers manned two eighteen pounder field guns designed to fire upon enemy ships entering the Fraser River.

The threat of invasion prompted frantic outcries from most provincial and federal politicians for the removal of Japanese persons from coastal areas. Unfortunately, this was a popular sentiment. Despite the fact that the vast majority of people of Japanese descent were Canadian-born,or naturalized citizens, their heritage made them natural targets. Unlike German-Canadians, they did not assimilate easily into the mainstream of society.

Moreover, just as the Chinese aptitude for agriculture had stirred racist sentiments in the farming community, the Japanese were envied and resented for their abilities as fishermen and farmers, consistently outperforming their white counterparts. Many of those who were not racist wanted Japanese jobs, and everyone else was just plain scared, imagining that every Japanese home with a radio tower housed a den of enemy spies.

On January 14, 1942, Ottawa announced that all Japanese would be removed from coastal areas and sent to government camps. All Japanese fishboats were confiscated and towed to Annieville, near New Westminster. Steveston was the fishing capital of Western Canada, and it was here that most of the 1,800 Japanese fishermen of the province lived and worked. (Japanese-Canadians held 12 percent of the outstanding fishing licenses in British Columbia in 1939.)

One of the infamous anti-Japanese edicts.

NOTICE

TO ALL PERSONS OF JAPANESE RACIAL ORIGIN

Having reference to the Protected Area of British Columbia as described in an Extra of the Canada Gazette, No. 174 dated Ottawa, Monday, February 2, 1942:-

1. EVERY PERSON OF THE JAPANESE RACE, WHILE WITHIN THE PROTECTED AREA AFORESAID, SHALL HEREAFTER BE AT HIS USUAL PLACE OF RESIDENCE EACH DAY BEFORE SUNSET AND SHALL REMAIN THEREIN UNTIL SUNRISE ON THE FOLLOWING DAY, AND NO SUCH PERSON SHALL GO OUT OF HIS USUAL PLACE OF RESIDENCE AFORESAID UPON THE STREETS OR OTHERWISE DURING THE HOURS BETWEEN SUNSET AND SUNRISE;

2. NO PERSON OF THE JAPANESE RACE SHALL HAVE IN HIS POSSESSION OR USE IN SUCH PROTECTED AREA ANY MOTOR VEHICLE, CAMERA, RADIO TRANSMITTER, RADIO RECEIVING SET, FIREARM, AMMUNITION OR EXPLOSIVE;

3. IT SHALL BE THE DUTY OF EVERY PERSON OF THE JAPANESE RACE HAVING IN HIS POSSESSION OR UPON HIS PREMISES ANY ARTICLE MENTIONED IN THE NEXT PRECEDING PARAGRAPH, FORTHWITH TO CAUSE SUCH ARTICLE TO BE DELIVERED UP TO ANY JUSTICE OF THE PEACE RESIDING IN OR NEAR THE LOCALITY WHERE ANY SUCH ARTICLE IS HAD IN POSSESSION, OR TO AN OFFICER OR CONSTABLE OF THE POLICE FORCE OF THE PROVINCE OR CITY IN OR NEAR SUCH LOCALITY OR TO AN OFFICER OR CONSTABLE OF THE ROYAL CANADIAN MOUNTED POLICE.

4. ANY JUSTICE OF THE PEACE OR OFFICER OR CONSTABLE RECEIVING ANY ARTICLE MENTIONED IN PARAGRAPH 2 OF THIS ORDER SHALL GIVE TO THE PERSON DELIVERING THE SAME A RECEIPT THEREFOR AND SHALL REPORT THE FACT TO THE COMMISSIONER OF THE ROYAL CANADIAN MOUNTED POLICE, AND SHALL RETAIN OR OTHERWISE DISPOSE OF ANY SUCH ARTICLE AS DIRECTED BY THE SAID COMMISSIONER.

5. ANY PEACE OFFICER OR ANY OFFICER OR CONSTABLE OF THE ROYAL CANADIAN MOUNTED POLICE HAVING POWER TO ACT AS SUCH PEACE OFFICER OR OFFICER OR CONSTABLE IN THE SAID PROTECTED AREA, IS AUTHORIZED TO SEARCH WITHOUT WARRANT THE PREMISES OR ANY PLACE OCCUPIED OR BELIEVED TO BE OCCUPIED BY ANY PERSON OF THE JAPANESE RACE REASONABLY SUSPECTED OF HAVING IN HIS POSSESSION OR UPON HIS PREMISES ANY ARTICLE MENTIONED IN PARAGRAPH 2 OF THIS ORDER, AND TO SEIZE ANY SUCH ARTICLE FOUND ON SUCH PREMISES;

6. EVERY PERSON OF THE JAPANESE RACE SHALL LEAVE THE PROTECTED AREA AFORESAID FORTHWITH;

7. NO PERSON OF THE JAPANESE RACE SHALL ENTER SUCH PROTECTED AREA EXCEPT UNDER PERMIT ISSUED BY THE ROYAL CANADIAN MOUNTED POLICE;

8. IN THIS ORDER, "PERSONS OF THE JAPANESE RACE" MEANS, AS WELL AS ANY PERSON WHOLLY OF THE JAPANESE RACE, A PERSON NOT WHOLLY OF THE JAPANESE RACE IF HIS FATHER OR MOTHER IS OF THE JAPANESE RACE AND IF THE COMMISSIONER OF THE ROYAL CANADIAN MOUNTED POLICE BY NOTICE IN WRITING HAS REQUIRED OR REQUIRES HIM TO REGISTER PURSUANT TO ORDER-IN-COUNCIL P.C. 9760 OF DECEMBER 16th, 1941.

DATED AT OTTAWA THIS 26th DAY OF FEBRUARY, 1942.

Louis S. St. Laurent,
Minister of Justice

To be posted in a Conspicuous Place

(top) Japanese homes in Steveston just prior to evacuation, 1942. (bottom) Japanese men leave Vancouver by train for unknown eastern destinations, 1942.

One day in early 1942, Mounties appeared at the doors of Japanese homes, giving the inhabitants notice and directions as to evacuation procedure, including the weight limits on suitcases. On February 27, the bulk of the twenty-one thousand people affected by the government decree were rounded up and escorted to Vancouver's Hastings Park; from there the Japanese were shipped by train to the British Columbia Interior or prairie internment camps. Married men under forty-five years of age were separated from their families and trucked to separate work camps, where they were made to build roads and clear brush.

No distinction was made among Nisei, (those born in Canada), Issei, (naturalized Japanese-Canadians), and Japanese citizens. Even World War I veterans like Masumi Mitsui, who had been decorated at Vimy Ridge, were interned and had all of their property seized.

The Japanese Fishing Vessels Disposal Committee was quickly formed to auction off Japanese boats and gear. The vessels had deteriorated from sitting unattended at Annieville, lashed together in winter weather like one vast flotilla of so much flotsam and jetsam. Many boats had been damaged while they were being towed; others were vandalized, while still more suffered cracked blocks. Although the Japanese owners were initially consulted as to price, most boats were sold for only a fraction of their value.

Word spread fast that Japanese compasses, spotlights, batteries, and fishnets could be acquired cheaply at the "Jap" fishboat auction. One Japanese internee later remarked bitterly, "These navy guys were looting our boats of everything they could tear off, and selling it for beer."

The removal of the Japanese greatly affected the fishing and agricultural industries. Steveston became a ghost town, a condition from which it has never recovered. School enrolment at the town's high school dropped from 500 to 137 students. Many of the auctioned fishboats were bought by novices who had never fished commercially. The canneries became so desperate for salmon that the government released convicts to help on the fishboats!

The valley's berry industry was crushed when Japanese farmers and their

Japanese fishboats were rounded up and impounded in Annieville.

families were evicted. A few kind neighbours tended to crop planting and tried to keep the vacant homes from deteriorating. But most farms quickly became run down and overgrown. Pursuant to the War Measures Act, Ottawa passed Order-in-Council 1665 on March 4, 1942, which vested title to all Japanese property in the "protected area" of British Columbia into the name of the Custodian of Alien Property. Initially, it was explained by the government that the intent was to preserve Japanese homes and farms by leasing them. But all that changed after only three months, perhaps in part because tenants clamoured for government subsidies to compensate for "bad weather and poor soils" that had not fazed the Japanese.

On June 29, the Director of Soldier Settlement was given control of all Japanese real property and authorized to lease or sell all lands without the consent of the owners. In short, since these peaceful Japanese farmers and fishermen constituted the enemy, it was only just that their property should be bought up to facilitate the resettlement of returning veterans!

By June 1944, 769 Japanese farms, most of them in the Fraser Valley, were acquired by the director at fire sale prices. The lone Japanese-Canadian member of the Rural Property Committee directing Fraser Valley acquisitions, Mr. Yamaga, resigned in protest over the low prices paid. The properties remaining unsold were bought by neighbours and speculators.

In Ladner, Chung Chuck acquired the Maeda family's home and barbershop, including equipment and fixtures, for eight hundred dollars. This ended a long, proud struggle to prosperity for a family whose chief breadwinner had arrived in Canada, penniless, in 1903.

A number of Japanese farms were purchased by Mennonites, a large number of whom were conscientious objectors, who refused to take up arms out of religious conviction; most young Mennonite men did not seek exemption from military service, but preferred support tasks which did not involve the actual firing of weaponry.

The Fraser Valley Boards of Trade unanimously passed a resolution in 1943 demanding a halt to Mennonite farm purchases. President Gordon Towers stated, "The Mennonites are a menace...They are exempt from military service and do not live up to our Canadian laws of citizenship."

Another editor frothed, "For these slackers and so-called conscientious objectors to be permitted to exploit the war to their own advantage in obtaining homes and farms in the best parts of this country is nothing short of stabbing our loyal Canadian youngsters in the back." The sting of prejudice would taint relations with the Mennonite community for many years.

Canadians of Austrian and German descent were more readily tolerated than the Japanese, particularly after Pearl Harbour. In the Hatzic area, a naturalized Austrian-Canadian named Harry Kluck went broke operating a shingle bolt camp. Kluck had previously been the drill sergeant in an Austrian regiment. "Adolf Hitler," he told the *Fraser Valley Record*, "came up for his training in the army; because his parents could afford training costs, Hitler had to serve only one year—others had to do three years. Adolph Hitler was under me for eleven months of 1905 and 1906, and one month of 1907. Hitler was of a sharp temper, but slow to learn, and there was hardly a day that I did not have to bawl him out for not doing things right...I trained Hitler; now I'm broke and he's running a country. How come?"

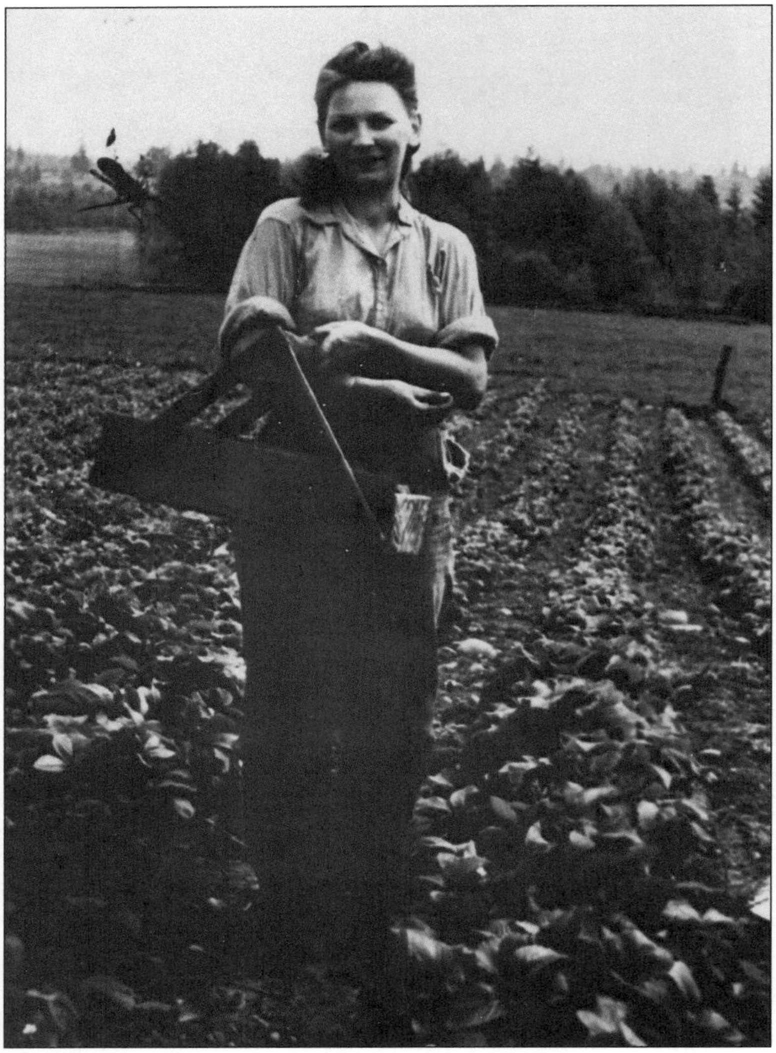

Nellie Jansen poses in a strawberry field, 1947.

War, like politics, makes for strange bedfellows. The heretofore "wily, lowly Chinese" were now accorded equal opportunity to buy Japanese homes and farms. Even more astounding was the huge China Aid drive which commenced in the Fraser Valley in 1943, as a result of the Japanese invasion of mainland China. Hundreds of shops and stores acted as depots for donations to the relief fund in the wake of reports of Japanese atrocities.

A similar phenomenon occurred in the valley when the Soviet Union was attacked by Germany. More than three thousand dollars was raised for the Russian Relief Fund in such right-wing municipalities as Langley—five times its requested quota. Reeve Alex Hope, whose vitriolic anti-Japanese outbursts were legend, pleaded that money was urgently needed for medical supplies and clothing for Russian soldiers, stating: "The mother of the Soviet aviator feels just the same as the mother of the RCAF pilot when that message comes which says her son will not come back...and of the dead soldiers, almost every one of them had a family in which there was the same kind of love as among any family in Canada."

The motorized Westminster Regiment attained considerable distinction on the fighting front. During the Italian and, later, European campaigns, the regiment "never failed to obtain an objective and never yielded a position to the enemy." Major John Mahoney of New Westminster won the Victoria Cross, and thousands of other valley lads served their country with gallantry and pride. Although several hundred local men were killed, the casualty rate was in fact 4 percent, considerably less than the previous war's 10 percent.

The course of British Columbia politics took a new turn in 1941 when Premier Pattullo resigned after his Liberal party, having attained only twenty-one seats in the October election, went against his wishes by forming a coalition government with the Conservatives.

The new government was headed by his former colleague, John Hart, a careful, cautious financier who assumed office two days after Pearl Harbour. Hart fulfilled his duties prudently during the war years, initiating road projects, promoting electrification of rural areas—"a bulb in every barn" was the current motto—and improving the quality of education. He was aided by a booming economy which was seemingly restrained only by wartime restrictions on the supply of such products as gasoline and rubber.

Scow full of salmon being iced down at Imperial Cannery dock, Steveston, pending unloading and processing, 1942.

Amazing technological changes aided the boom. Quick-freeze storage facilities allowed for mass shipping of frozen berries for export. Rapid processing assembly lines speeded production. Roads were paved by a new blacktop machine invented by the Columbia Bitulithic Company. Even the rural post office progressed, with the introduction of automatic stamp cancelling machines. The New Westminster waterfront hummed with activity, as huge quantities of lumber were loaded onto deep-sea ships. Plywood was much in demand, and booms of pulp logs were towed from Ruskin mills to Powell River to be converted into newsprint.

The huge sockeye run of 1942 was a boon to Fraser fishermen and fisherwomen. At the unique Delta community of Sunbury, houseboats mingled with dwellings on stilts in a picturesque array of colourfully painted structures, graced by window boxes, weather-beaten docks, and even chicken coops. There widows, and wives of absent husbands, like Elma Holmes, Alva Iverson, and Mrs. Sjoblon, mended their nets and set out after salmon. Elma supervised the catch of 400 salmon in just twenty minutes, her nets sinking under the weight of the wriggling mass. The Sjoblon boat delivered 30,000 salmon in two days to the canneries.

Farmers and shopkeepers suffered from wartime price controls and red tape. Petty bureaucrats strutted about checking up on proprietors, producing dozens of forms and regulations; they paid no heed to whether the merchant was receiving a fair return at the time that prices were fixed by the government, neither did they allow for hidden increases in production costs. In 1944, the Wartime Prices Board commenced wholesale prosecution of Fraser Valley grocery merchants—usually for charging prices in excess of those prescribed by wartime regulations—enraging community leaders. There were many convictions, but only petty fines were imposed as punishment.

Woman on tractor threshing field, 1940.

Nearly six long years elapsed before the clouds of war in Europe cleared. Upon learning of the German surrender of May 7, 1945, special thanksgiving services were held in New Westminster and other valley towns. The outpouring of gratitude was so great that in Chilliwack, the Reverend John Scott had to hold services at the fairgrounds, where some five thousand people gathered. The spectacle was repeated on VJ Day in August. Boys raced through the streets on decorated bicycles, and the din of car horns and church bells was deafening. In the middle of Chilliwack's busiest intersection, a drummer, a banjoist, and a fiddler suddenly appeared, while citizens danced in the streets. Victory parades were held in other centres.

Some celebrated the peace in a quiet but meaningful manner. In a remote country area, a grey-haired woman dashed from a wooded trail and planted a Union Jack on the roadside.

A truck approached round a bend and the driver slowed to a stop. Pointing at the flag, he asked the woman, "Is it over, then?"

"Yes," the woman replied, smiling expansively. "I just heard; I am so glad, for I have two boys over there. Thank God!"

The driver opened his door, climbed out of the vehicle and embraced the woman. And so, two strangers on an isolated country road experienced a spontaneous release from fear.

The Westminster Regiment was fêted in London at the ancient city of Westminster, in honour of its contribution to the war effort. In early 1946, the troops headed home. Some fifty of the Fraser Valley men left behind their British war brides. In what was surely a most rewarding task, Canadian Lou Fell also remained behind in England for many months to coordinate the paperwork facilitating the war brides' emigration to Canada.

The last leg of the soldiers' journey was via the Canadian Pacific Railway through the Fraser Valley to New Westminster. A reporter captured the mood aboard the train:

> "For the first time the strain, the suspense, the deadly weariness lifted...Rolling west, every man could feel the change, could sense the feel of his home countryside; for the first time the hard impassive shell of the fighting man began to dissolve. Hands trembled as they adjusted webbing, and eyes peered eagerly: 'Those are Coquitlam willows,' said a sergeant. 'There's Maillardville,' cried another veteran, dancing in the aisle. 'I want to walk across New Westminster Bridge,' declared a Surrey private."

Thousands lined the streets of the Royal City as that very special train pulled into the Canadian Pacific Railway depot. The troops detrained and began the last march to their barracks, erect and proud, led by the popular Lt.-Col. Gordon Corbould. But after a block of marching, discipline cracked. Friends and relatives yelled greetings; faces turned. An entire family rushed into the street and pulled their khaki-clad soldier out of the ranks; two small boys found their father and marched along with him, as did a number of wives.

VE Day, Vancouver, 1945.

At Queen's Park, Commander Corbould accepted the Freedom of the City from Mayor Mott and addressed his men for the last time. "The commanding officer does not win battles," he said. "It was you men who made our record of never losing a battle." The speeches were cut short and the ceremony ended as tearful families swarmed over the field and mobbed the troops.

Many of the returning servicemen purchased farms—not a few of them confiscated from Japanese-Canadians—from the Soldier Settlement Board. At Webster's Corners in Maple Ridge, veteran Ray Reynolds built a series of pools near Kanaka Creek and established a frog farm. He found a good market at hotels and Chinese restaurants, being paid one dollar a pound for the amphibians' meat. "Contrary to popular belief," said Reynolds, "frogs are humanely killed by a knock on the head before being parted from their edible legs." The frog farmer's giant breeder bull frogs measured sixteen inches from toe to toe.

Of course, less exotic ventures occupied other new farmers, some of whom found it uneconomic to work smaller farms without the extensive family infrastructure that had enabled the former Japanese owner to make a profit.

It might have been thought that the war's end would have ended the acute distress of Japanese-Canadians. Such was not the case. The federal government remained under intense pressure from local politicians to deport all persons of Japanese extraction to Japan. Ottawa compromised by setting April 13, 1945, as the date on which those Japanese interned in British Columbia camps must decide to return to Japan or settle in Canada east of the Rockies. At the Tashme camp, near Hope, the inmates could hardly believe their eyes when notices were posted telling them that they would be unable to return to the Fraser Valley.

The Nisei were still inclined to remain in Canada; however, many of them desired to find out what had happened to relatives abroad, and so they went by ship to Japan. Others were too disheartened at losing their farms or fishboats to start a new life in another province.

According to Hideo of Steveston, some 1,200 Japanese were aboard the ship on which he sailed to Japan with his wife and children. Hideo and his wife had been separated for four years before their reunion in Vancouver at the war's end; despite this they continued to be separated during the voyage, and were permitted only short conversations each day. The men and women remained below decks at night, cramped in separate quarters, sleeping on canvas hammocks slung one atop the other. As of 1948, out of the 21,000 Japanese-Canadians deported to camps in 1942, only 3,964 returned to Japan.

Japanese-Canadians sued the federal government in a test case to determine the validity of orders-in-council which allowed their lands and possessions to be sold. Although the courts upheld Ottawa's authority, the government was clearly embarrassed, particularly since no Japanese-Canadian had ever been convicted of any act of disloyalty.

In 1947, the British Columbia Legislature extended the franchise to Chinese residents, and then to Japanese residents in 1949. Finally, the Nisei who had resettled east of the Rockies were allowed to return to their home province. Some came back to Steveston and worked for wages until they could save enough money to buy fishboats. Steveston's old Japanese hospital had disappeared, as had the Japanese department store, noodle shop, and restaurant.

Most former Japanese fishermen returned to fish the Fraser, though they were now dispersed throughout many communities. Those who resettled in Steveston, like Asamatsu Murakami, faced much initial hostility. The Fishermen's Union agreed not to oppose the granting of licenses to Japanese fishermen, as long as their numbers were restricted to 150.

Japanese spokesmen were forced to accept this quota, but many other hurdles remained in their struggle to regain economic self-sufficiency. Several canneries, including those run by the giant Canadian Fishing Co., refused to hire Japanese fishermen. B.C. Packers and a few small canneries did hire them, however, and the high production of these experienced fishermen had such an impact on the catch that Canadian Packers was soon pleading for Japanese employees.

During their first season back on the sea, the Japanese fished from dilapidated boats loaned to them by the canneries. By the following year, the fishermen had done so well that the canneries gladly loaned money to allow them to purchase new boats.

"When we first came back," recounted Murakami, "we found that if we left our boat unwatched, all our gear would be gone right away. We couldn't do anything about it. So we got permission to tie our boats at North Arm. They wouldn't let us hang our nets in Steveston, either...So we took our nets and all our gear to Terra Nova Cannery."

Hideo returned to Steveston and lived his years in search of the glistening sockeye. He, like others, was hardened by the internment experience, a little bitter. In place of the old low-slung dory with white sails, he now operated a noisy, gas-powered craft. Although the gulls and the wind and the river still beckoned, the fisherman's life was just not the same.

The 1945 provincial election witnessed a victory for John Hart's coalition forces. People could hardly complain amidst a postwar economic boom. This was a rocketing age of gadgetry for rural folk. People rushed out to buy the latest radios. A.E. Easingwood's electronics store on Langley City's main street represented the sort of progress which every valley town sought to emulate. CKNW was the most popular commercial radio station, and held the distinction of being the only station in Canada which broadcast twenty-four hours a day. Jack Cullen was hired by the station in 1949, and soon became the Lower Mainland's favourite disc jockey.

With the lifting of wartime restrictions, people hurried to buy cars. Some young men purchased two used cars—one for parts, and used their vehicles to explore valley roads, such as the old logging tracks around Alouette Lake, a favourite haunt.

One day a Maple Ridge teenager whisked through the woods in an old Chevy. Rounding a corner, the lad realized too late that the bridge over the Alouette River was out. The car catapulted into the water and was swept downstream. The driver managed to escape to shore. Gasping for breath, he watched his beloved coupe float out of sight down a canyon. He never saw the vehicle again.

On Sea Island, the airport expanded towards its goal of becoming a truly international facility. Crop-dusting planes made their debut. Langley's Art Sellers, a founder of Skyway Air Services, blitzed mosquitoes from the air with DDT, dusted crops, and donated his time to drop one thousand pounds of grain on the Mud Bay flats to feed several thousand starving ducks who were threatening to destroy sugar beet and clover seed crops.

At Abbotsford's airport, schoolboys collected souvenirs from scrapped Royal Canadian Air Force planes: bent and burned machine guns, old ammunition belts, and fascinating electrical panels and gauges.

Changes in the valley's vital statistics indicated the continuing influence of the war on its residents, as well as reflecting the effects of the postwar boom. Marriages were down; naturalizations were up. Increased life expectancy came in tandem with old age pensions. Yet 50 per cent of rural residents refused to pay compulsory premiums for a government hospital insurance scheme.

This is not to say that residents neglected the importance of hospitals. By the end of the decade, Chilliwack, Surrey, White Rock, and Langley had their own hospitals, although valley inhabitants relied upon New Westminster's Royal Columbian for more complex surgical cases.

Fuller Brush salesman called at every door; five and dime stores prospered. Farm freezers and nylon stockings enthralled housewives. Cigarette smoking was ever more fashionable. Coke and ice cream sold for a nickel, gasoline was eleven cents a gallon, and country doctors all made house calls. A mechanic known as Grindstone drove a big truck around Surrey, Langley, and Delta year round, repairing anything and sharpening everything from a "delicate finger nail clipper in a beauty parlor to the most obstreperous old lawn mower."

Main Street of Langley City, 1940s.

All, however, was not rosy. Grateful as North Americans were to have survived the war, the extent of its devastation left a legacy of disillusionment. This, along with the erosion of the traditional farming society, and the independence that the automobile gave young people, made juvenile delinquency a reigning concern in the valley, as it was elsewhere in North America. In all but the eastern Fraser Valley, the church as an institution experienced an accelerating decline. Community leaders desperately sought to marshal an organized attack upon vandalism, vagrancy, and increasing sexual licentiousness. In Chilliwack, Rotary Club members were shocked by the Reverend David Somerville's announcement that their youth counselling program had utterly failed.

The Teen Town movement did enjoy limited success. These clubs sponsored sports activities, dances, and plays. They were entirely self-governed by a teen executive. Ping-Pong tournaments were a favourite pastime. Membership rose to eleven thousand teenagers in 35 provincial groups, 20 in the valley. Unfortunately, the clubs lacked financial support, and the Teen Towns withered and died by the early fifties.

Nonetheless, the Saturday night dance remained ubiquitous throughout the valley. Teens dressed in loose-fitting sweaters, colourful patched pants, sports shirts, and bobby socks. Boys were "snazzy" and girls were "slick chicks." Prevailing slang included "What's cooking, handsome," "hubba hubba," and "for corn's sake."

The social intimacy of earlier eras had disappeared. During the Depression, valley residents satisfied themselves with fireside chats, bridge games and house parties. Almost everyone could sing or play an instrument. One Langley farmer complained, "Today everyone has his favourite program and crawls away into a corner by himself with his own radio and scowls like a mad dog if anyone should interrupt him. Keeping up with the Joneses is a regular pastime - and no-one stays put anymore."

Throughout the forties, the New Westminster Rotary Club raised money with its annual barrel contest. Once a year, a gaily decorated, cork-filled cask was dumped into the Fraser at Lilloet. Club members placed bets as to the length of time the barrel would take to reach the Pattullo Bridge, with the closest time earning a five hundred dollar prize. Middle-aged, normally dour businessmen sped along the river in boats, shouting and whooping like children as they watched the barrel's progress.

The first Cloverdale Rodeo was held in 1945. It was to become the largest annual event of its kind west of Calgary. Rodeos appealed to people throughout the valley and replaced the quaint but parochial municipal picnics of old. In Mission, residents initiated an annual Strawberry Festival in 1946, complete with a soap box derby, a downhill race involving boys aged 10 to 16 in orange crates mounted on wheels. Vancouver Mayor Gerry McGeer opened the festival in 1947 and proclaimed Mission City the strawberry capital of the Pacific coast.

Fraser Valley etiquette had its own set of precepts, not all of which followed Emily Post. It was bad manners for a farmer to ask anything personal about a stranger, particularly an urban visitor; the farmer might talk for an hour over a fence with the stranger, tell him all of his troubles, but never once ask the person his name.

New Westminster's Trapp Technical School teachers authored their own thirty-eight-page etiquette manual; illustrated by student Bruno Gerussi, which contained many apt pointers:

"Boys, don't sing or let out the wolf call and never hail a girl or whistle across the street; for a girl or woman to smoke on the street is extremely unbecoming; don't be a little Lord Fauntleroy, don't be a bully—both types are equally repulsive; do not ask a girl to dance with 'May I have the pleasure of your company?'—she is worthy of respect however so do not ask her with 'Say, babe, how about the hop next Friday?'"

Ever increasing mobility allowed for new forms of recreation. In 1940, the King George Highway to Blaine opened and shopping in Bellingham, and even Seattle, became popular. People tented at Semiahmoo Park in White Rock. Young men and women drove from Haney to Essondale, where they could play on beautiful tennis courts, even if they might have to endure the taunts of inmates watching from their barred windows.

The romance of the B.C. Electric's star passenger tram, the Red Bullet, was replaced by buses. A Bradner

BC Electric's popular passenger tram, the "Red Bullet."

farmer protested that the train was still needed: "We've got roads out here in the spring that a mule wearing snowshoes couldn't wade through." In 1949, the Hope-Princeton Highway opened, allowing quick access to the Okanagan.

Accommodation for travellers improved with the construction of Surrey's Turf Hotel on the Pacific Highway in 1949. The hotel was capable of lodging thirty-eight persons and it embodied the latest and finest in design.

For ambience, the Lougheed Highway's rustic Wild Duck Inn on the Pitt River, and the Sasquatch Inn near Harrison River, gateway to the Chehalis region, were well worth visiting. The seventy-year-old proprietor of the Sasquatch Inn, Charlie McNeil, catered to loggers, miners, and tourists, and ran a very tight ship. Rowdyism was prohibited, and Charlie would throw out any patron who demanded more booze after Charlie figured he'd had enough. One patron complained, "In the Sasquatch bar I waited so long between drinks that my stomach thought my throat was cut."

Rural-urban conflict, encroaching subdivisions, and zoning debates coloured postwar horizons. The very concept of town planning was ferociously attacked by those who believed in the sanctity of private property. However, decades of unrestricted subdivision practices had led to serious problems, including traffic bottlenecks caused by ridiculous road jogs.

Aerial view of Marpole Bridge, 1954.

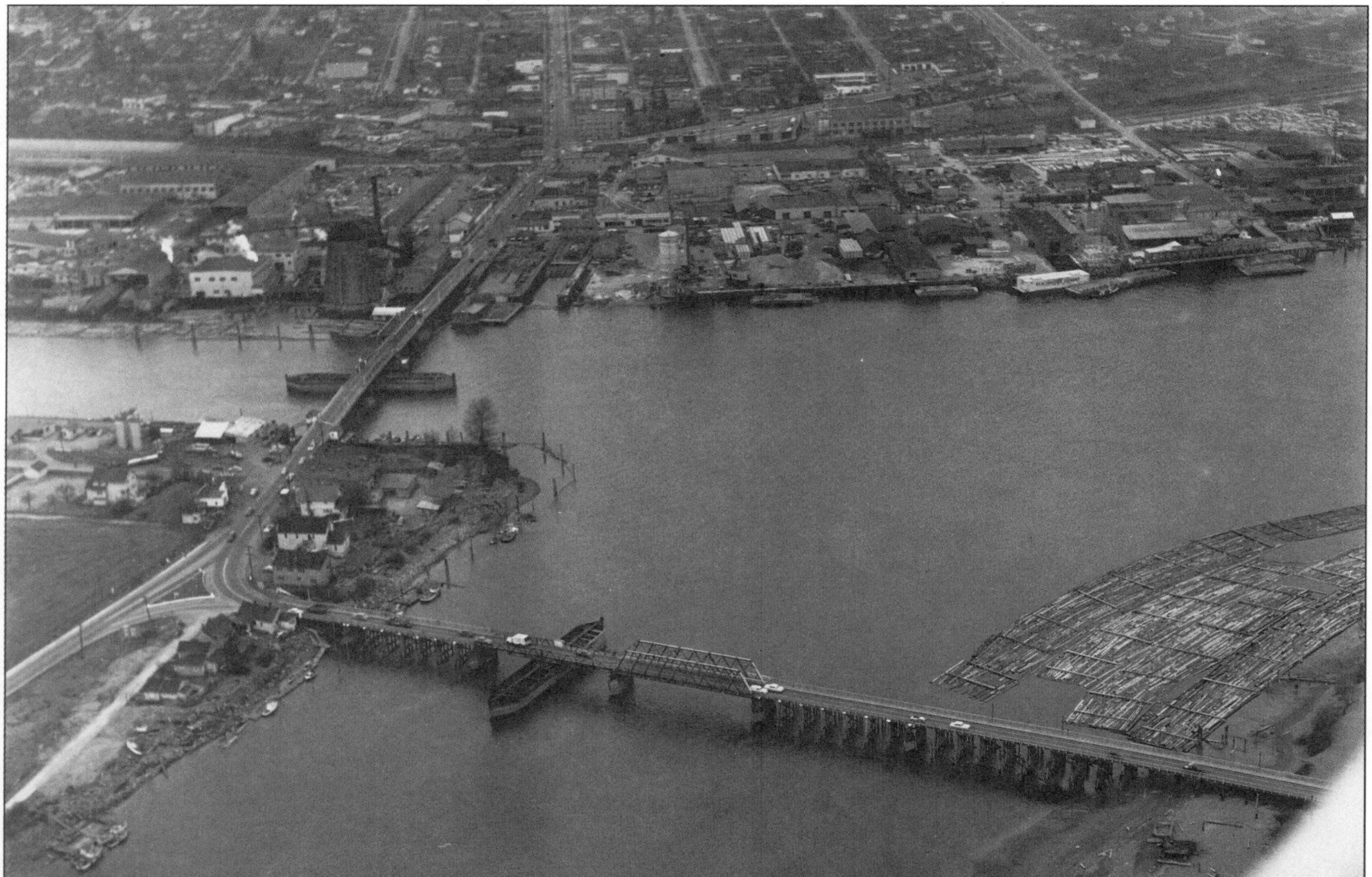

In White Rock, taxpayers complained of chicken and mink farmers operating in contravention of local bylaws. In Richmond, the town planning commission took the lead in the Fraser Valley by dividing the municipality into various zones of usage, its action prompted by the rapidly disappearing farm acreages which were now being subdivided for industrial, commercial, and residential purposes. The new "mudflatter" lived in Richmond and commuted to work in Vancouver.

Throughout 1948 and 1949, higher American prices for beef led to widespread cattle smuggling from Langley to Whatcom County, Washington. Farmers continued to debate the pros and cons of berry and egg marketing boards, and continued to protest the legality of margarine.

The Farmers Market still functioned in New Westminster. A sampling of stall activity there indicated the wide variety of wares available on a typical Saturday:

> "Miss F. Steele has added a sideline to her business of selling dogs. Two Flemish grant rabbits occupied the lower part of a kennel... The display of daffodils mixed with greens at the stall of Cooper the Florist caused favourable comment from many...Top price for a cow was $52...Giant Monument chrysanthemums made their appearance for the first time, at Mrs. Annie Wood's stall. Mr. and Mrs. Len Patterson of Cloverdale were selling netted gems at 6 lbs. for 25 cents and small spuds at 9 lbs. for 25 cents. Mrs. P. says women object to peeling small potatoes if they have large families. English soft shell walnuts were on sale at 50 cents per lb. by the Misses Cooper, Ladner...Mrs. Mary Lay of Pitt Meadows was selling Cowichan sweaters and socks. Mrs Storopada of Haney had vegetables and her garlic was 50 cents a pound."

Science and technology were becoming increasingly important factors in valley agriculture. Through improved quick-freezing methods, the Delnor plant in New Westminster preserved vegetables and berries in a healthful manner that retained the vitamins.

Planting potatoes, 1940.

The Brackman-Ker feed company employed skilled trouble-shooting field analysts to attend at farms where livestock were experiencing dietary problems. Another company, called simply "Mc and Mc," provided mobile mechanical and diagnostic services to farmers—much more sophisticated than Grindstone's operation—as farmers utilized ever more complex equipment.

In 1948, agricultural history was made when the artificial insemination farm at Milner, in Langley Township, shipped bull semen to Hong Kong. The practice of exporting high quality calves to other parts of the world would soon be curtailed as a result of this feat, as "test tube" calves were born better acclimatized to foreign environments.

Ever since the great flood of 1894, Fraser Valley residents had anticipated the river's spring freshet in May with apprehension. Once or twice a decade, high water caused minor flooding, but the dykes were strengthened over time in key areas such as Matsqui Prairie and Glen Valley.

At Mission Bridge, a concrete blockhouse sheltered the famous Mission Gauge, a device which was built to measure the rise of the river. Mission zero reading was actually 8.27 feet above sea level on the sandheads at the Fraser's mouth. Two pipes extended into the swirling river waters; an ink pen attached to a counterweight moved in response to the water rising up and down in the well on which the gauge rested. The gauge was accurate to one-hundredth of an inch.

There were three key ingredients for a major flood: a winter of heavy snowfall, a late spring, and a sudden stretch of very warm weather. In early May 1948, old-timers on the river mumbled that trouble lay ahead. Matsqui Indians spoke of *ta coutchi's* return. Logs and other debris began appearing on the lower Fraser. Then the temperature went from a low of 37 degrees Fahrenheit on May 18 to a high of 80 degrees the following day.

Joe Poirier manned the Mission Gauge and announced his readings to the public each day. By May 23, the river neared the 20-foot level—just five feet lower than the 1894 high water mark. The usually boisterous May 24 celebrations along the river were subdued. At Agassiz, a warm evening's dance was suddenly interrupted when a policeman appeared at the door and spoke in hushed tones to the young men. The hall quickly emptied. Men rushed to the river and began piling sandbags. Farmers moved cattle to higher ground. At 2:00 a.m. the following morning, the deluge broke loose. Dirty brown water cascaded across the land, inundating Agassiz, and sweeping away everything in its path.

The Agassiz Indian reserve and dozens of farms in the area became one giant lake. Three miles west of town, 185 evacuees set up camp at Mount View Cemetery, where cattle grazed and children played among the tombstones. The local Red Cross, under Mrs. W.A. Jones, brought blankets and helped cook. Other refugees headed west on a Canadian Pacific train. At Harrison Hot Springs, the lake's clear waters were muddied by the flood, joining it with the Fraser in one long brown swathe.

Ta coutchi's next victim was Nicomen Island, where shiny white barns and sleepy farmhouses dotted the lush loamy landscape at the foot of a steep mountain. The graceful scene was shattered on May 28, when the rampaging waters breached the dyke near the Tremblay farm. Fifty sappers arrived at midnight and worked until morning in the mud throwing sandbags. When the exhausted men saw that the task was hopeless, they left for another emergency, warning residents to leave their homes. Few heeded this advice.

The frigate HMCS *Antigonish* arrived at New Westminster, where naval emergency aid headquarters were set up; and from there motor cutters and other small craft headed upriver to rescue families and livestock.

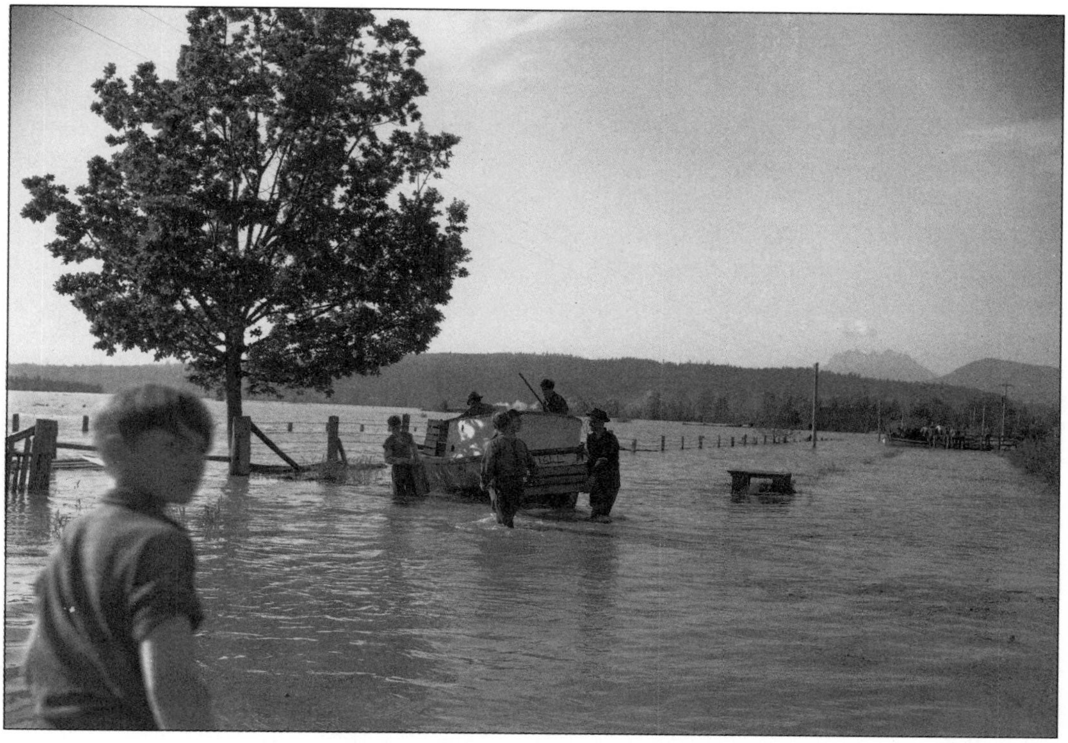

1948 flood scene.

On the evening of May 29, the main Nicomen dyke was pierced with a roar described by one farmer as like a "yard full of freight trains," immediately preceded by the sight of a tree shooting into the air with a bomb-like explosion.

An old coupe equipped with a loudspeaker careened westward into Mission with the news, blaring out a call for help. Men ran from cafés, hotels, and houses, and soon a snake-like line of more than one hundred vehicles headed east to the disaster area. Over 350 Nicomen residents were picked up, many by naval craft, and taken to shelter at Mission, where volunteers from the Westminster Regiment had established a base camp at the Armouries.

Chilliwack residents worked feverishly to strengthen their dykes. Gravel trucks dumped rocks and soil day and night. Students, farmers, clergymen, store clerks and soldiers worked side by side for as along as twenty hours at a stretch.

In the end, Chilliwack, Sumas, and Rosedale were saved, but on May 29, Glendale, Cottonwood Corners, Chinatown, and the Mennonite community of Glendale were inundated. In the Glendale School, desks clattered against the ceiling, houses collapsed, and pieces of bridges and barns floated about.

Of the 200 soldiers who worked on the dykes in the area, Mennonite spokesman A. Remple said, "We never knew the army before. The soldiers assisted us like brothers." The army later praised the Mennonite communities throughout the valley for providing a twenty-four-hour food service for the troops and cooperating at every turn with relief efforts.

This cooperative experience did much to alleviate Mennonite concerns at a later date when, in 1949, the army established a five hundred-acre instant town at Sardis, near Chilliwack, as an adjunct to the permanent armed forces base in the vicinity. The base was designed as a training centre for engineers, becoming home to 1,000 men, women, and children. Thus, at least in spirit, the Sappers of 1858 returned to the valley.

Matsqui fell on May 30. Colin Sward's old dykes trembled and finally gave way as the Mission Gauge registered 24 feet. Logs, fence posts, outhouses, barns, and animal carcasses floated in one vast lake, the waters inching toward the higher land of Abbotsford. Over 10,000 acres and 617 homes sustained flood damage or destruction. Marooned residents were boated across the river to Mission for shelter, while hundreds of cattle were boarded at St. Mary's School, where the Indian children quickly developed an efficient milking system, and even shipped the milk to Vancouver on behalf of the exhausted owners.

The crisis deepened. A span of Mission Bridge crashed into the foaming waters. The premier proclaimed a state of emergency. Some 2,600 soldiers and 700 naval personnel worked with 30,000 volunteers to save lives and property. The Fraser Valley's rail and road connection with the rest of Canada were severed. Still the river rose.

Hatzic's turn came on June 2, when "suddenly a faint tremor ran through the ground and the bridge began to vibrate. The pump house blew into the air as though hit by a bomb. Telephone poles snapped. The railroad tracks creaked and groaned under the strain, and then crumbled; then the mad waters of a rampaging river poured through a 100 foot gap." The army commander chose the Hatzic schoolhouse as a headquarters, only to find when he arrived that the structure had been swept away.

In both Glen Valley and beneath the knoll of the old fort in Fort Langley, children and soldiers filled sandbags; and all night long lanterns and headlights shone as the dykes were strengthened. Cattle, bellowing in terror, were tightly packed in trucks and hauled away. About sixty high school lads pitched in, whose grad dance was cancelled in the crisis.

When the break came, Fort Langley became an island, as the Fraser's waters swept through Glen Valley and over the Salmon River flats. Chief Alfred Gabriel and his Kwantlen tribe of McMillan Island evacuated to shelter in Langley City; at the Athletic Hall, the Indians organized their temporary living quarters in a similar manner to the early days of the large cedar lodges. Chief Gabriel scoffed at the fuss about the flood, noting that in his grandfather's day, "they just picked up their tents and moved to higher ground as the waters rose."

The battle against the river had its victories as well as its defeats. Although Pitt Meadows became a vast brown sea, Essondale's Colony Farm fought back and won, continuing to supply vegetables and milk to the inmates. At Queensborough, seventy-three-year-old Scotty McKenzie commanded the dyking forces until the army arrived, pummelling his wooden leg into rat holes which undermined the dykes. Queensborough was saved. As for the remaining down river communities, although minor flooding occurred, the major dyking systems held fast. By June 11, the Fraser's rage was spent.

In the wake of the flood, 16,000 persons fled their homes. Damage was estimated at $17 million. Ten people died; 2,000 families were left homeless, with 55,000 acres of prime farmland under water. Some 82 bridges were washed away. The tremendous cooperative effort matched the huge economic loss. Countless organizations donated time and labour, and individual acts of heroism, self-sacrifice, kindness, and courage inspired by the flood would fill a book. The New Westminster Rotary Club sponsored a "flood holiday" for hundreds of children at a White Rock beach camp. Radio stations CHWK and CKNW placed their entire facilities in the hands of the flood committee during the crisis. Red Cross workers worked day and night; one young woman searched two days in the deep woods to locate a family until she found them, hungry, bruised and battered, but still alive.

For many of the flood's victims, however, the road back was long and tortuous. Flooded dwellings could not be reclaimed until health officials had approved them for habitation. By the end of June, some twelve thousand evacuees had returned to their homes, in many cases to find "stoves rusted, kitchen cupboards warped and twisted, floors warped, carpets ruined, walls stained and bedroom suites a total loss. Water-soaked furniture crumbled in many instances at the touch of a finger." Outside their homes lay stagnant water and layer upon layer of mud, silt, and debris. Trees and bushes were silvery grey; dead foliage was covered with a fine slime. Entire regions stank, and dead fish lay entombed throughout the putrid mud.

Relief and rehabilitation moved quickly into high gear. Day and night, as much as seventy thousand gallons of water per minute were pumped back into the Fraser. The federal government agreed to pay 75 percent of the clean-up costs and dyke repair, and made an outright grant of $5 million to assist the provincial government in its recovery programmes. The Fraser Valley Rehabilitation Commission granted each affected farmer $25 per acre for replanting crops and clearing debris; plus $25 for hiring labourers and another $5 per acre for cultivation expenses. Among the classes of producers assisted were 987 dairy farmers; 266 poultry farmers; 697 fruit and nut growers, a small number of bulb and hop producers, and a few fur ranchers.

Residents set about restoring their households and farms. Chief Gabriel and his band moved back to McMillan Island and found conditions deplorable, the chief's own driveway having been washed away, and eight acres of reserve lands covered with four feet of sand. Gabriel expressed his appreciation to the touring Major-General Worthington of the assistance given his people, stating, "We were treated far better than we expected to be." Already re-seeding of fields was under way on the reserve and along the Salmon River.

Anger erupted among some bitter farmers who had warned the government for years that more attention was required for the dykes. Matsqui's Cornie Kelleher exhorted:

> "What desolation meets the eye—a brown desert! Are we going to be secure with just a big mound of dirt? I don't think so...This is a cement age; take a look at the B.C. Electric dams. If we are to build for the future, why not start right and build to last, instead of throwing up a pile of river mud and having people living inside the dykes fighting every freshet, year after year...Nothing is good enough but the best; the best is none too good—and I have lived behind the dykes for many years."

Government finally paid heed. The Fraser Valley Dyking Board began reconstruction of the broken barricades; this time, rocks, concrete and bricks were used for greater strength. In a smart move, the government of British Columbia took over control of all dyking operations from local government bodies.

The return to normalcy in the valley, everyone's goal, was hard to achieve. Depression, war, and then flood had eroded rural idealism; while the steadily encroaching pressures of urbanization threatened a way of life. Richmond had already become a bedroom community of Vancouver. Surrey was being transformed into suburbia. Even Fort Langley was threatened when construction companies discovered that massive gravel deposits lay beneath the village. "The nervous community," wrote a newspaper editor, "figures that if they keep digging much longer, something's going to fall—namely, Fort Langley."

A bylaw prohibiting further gravel removal was hastily passed to prevent the literal collapse of the village.

A few men and women of vision strove to preserve and conserve. In 1939, Oliver Wells had converted part of the old Edenbank farm into a waterfowl sanctuary. Every year, Wells had accompanied Chief Sepass on his hunting trips into the mountains. In 1943, Chief Sepass died at the age of 102 years. The Stalo people mourned. An age had passed.

Indians gained the right to vote provincially in 1949. In that year, the Native Brotherhood of British Columbia sponsored the opening of the Haig Indian Museum, one of several such projects which it initiated in various centres of the province. Among the displays were two hundred-year-old baskets and woollen blankets from the Katz reserve near Hope. Chief Peter Pete said he "hoped that the display would encourage his young people to foster the crafts of their forefathers."

Judge Howay also died in 1943. Although his hair had turned snow white, the judge's keen eyes remained lively and enquiring to the end, as he continued to play chess and read his books at his New Westminster home overlooking the Fraser. Tributes poured in from far and near to the man who exemplified justice and mercy in his professional life, and devoted much of his personal life to the valley's heritage.

Judge Howay's legacy would bear fruit. On November 21, 1946, journalist Bruce McKelvie gave the main address at the Fort Langley Community Hall, following the unveiling of two historical plaques to mark the journey of James McMillan in 1824 and the founding of the first fort at Derby in 1827.

An intriguing spectacle of the postwar years was the Indian Potlatch held at McMillan Island on Labor Day, 1947. This event was sponsored by a variety of community groups and Indian bands, and combined many elements of the traditional potlatch with Anglo-Saxon pageantry. A parade through Fort Langley was led by Scottish pipers and the famous Dufferin Coach, followed by many floats. Pioneers in a covered wagon travelled behind with fifty-five foot Indian canoes and natives dressed in traditional garb.

All day long, Indians from Vancouver and Fraser Valley reserves competed in canoe races, wrestling, and log rolling contests, while in the evening huge bonfires were lit on the island below the site of the old stockade—reminiscent of the great 1861 potlatch—and dancing proceeded apace throughout the night. The

Indian game of *Slahel*, an event in which the participants' proficiency in dancing and singing was judged by several chiefs, attracted particular attention from the crowds. Performers were gradually eliminated until one native remaining in the circle was pronounced the winner.

Since 1946, the annual Douglas Day banquet has become a tradition in Langley. November 19 has become the one day set aside to both commemorate the proclamation of the colony of British Columbia and to honour the valley pioneers.

At the 1949 banquet, Provincial Archivist Willard Ireland spoke to an audience which included Chief Gabriel. "People of Fort Langley and British Columbia," he said, " are terribly evasive of the importance of the past. The genius of the old-timers is not dead—it is still within the people of this country...We are afraid to hold up our pattern, our past, but that is the obligation Douglas Day imparts upon us." Suddenly the hall floor boards shook violently from the vibration of a passing freight train.

The speaker smiled and paused, waiting for the deafening roar to pass.

"George," sighed one old-timer in the audience to another, "these racing trains are a damned sight noisier every year—do you remember the friendly whistle of the old *Skeena*—and the *Gladys*, now there was a steamboat!"

CHAPTER SIXTEEN

TOWN PLANNERS AND SASQUATCHES

On September 30, 1950, the B.C. Electric Railway Co. ceased operating its Fraser Valley passenger service, almost forty years to the day after Premier McBride had proudly driven in the last spike at Chilliwack.

Although diesel engines offered faster, trouble-free service, the steady expansion of settlement away from the railway line spelled the death knell of the Red Bullet. Streamlined Pacific Stage Lines buses now began regular runs along the Lougheed and Trans-Canada Highways.

The Trans-Canada Highway consisted of variously-known highway sections, particularly portions of the Old Yale Road. When the freeway was built in the 1960s, planners incorporated portions of the old Trans-Canada, but also aligned much of the freeway along a more direct route from Port Mann eastward.

Fraser Valley municipalities were paid $220,000 to compensate for both the lost railway service and the increased pressure upon municipal roads. Local councils had bitterly fought the demise of the passenger tram. Freight runs would continue, but many stations were closed.

Agnes Cronkhite watched the dismantling of Jackman Road station in Langley:

> "For years that station was a sort of gathering place of the clans on Sunday evenings, when settlers met to see their commuters and week-end visitors off. When the train had thinned the ranks, we chatted awhile about all the latest news and farming short-cuts...From that old station too we saw our grown children launched on life journeys to school, to trades, and even to war."

The Canadian Pacific Railway also wrestled with declining passenger traffic. An elegant, vista-domed, steel snake named The Canadian was introduced to travellers as the fastest, most luxurious passenger train in North America. However, the railway's officials made the mistake of initially running the transcontinental train nonstop from Hope to Vancouver, thus offending Mission City residents, who successfully petitioned railway officials for a scheduled stop in their town.

The comfortable, elegant Canadian gave an important boost to the waning popularity of the passenger train.

The Canadian Pacific Railway kept William Van Horne's 1887 pledge to New Westminster of a perpetual passenger service along the spur line to Port Coquitlam. An aging, gas-lit, wood-heated coach rumbled daily over the eight miles from New Westminster to the main line; the Port Coquitlam Flyer averaged only four passengers a night and cost 35 cents for a one way ticket—20 cents if one were to detrain at Essondale.

The thirty-five-year-old coach, with its plush green seats and pot-bellied stove was a dying relic, but its wheels clicked along at fifteen miles an hour in stoic dignity until Royal City aldermen finally released the railway from its pledge and settled for limousine service to the main line. The last interurban passenger service to operate in the valley was the Marpole to Steveston run, discontinued in 1958.

The Social Credit party swept the Fraser Valley in the 1952 provincial election, as W.A.C. Bennett skilfully played small town rural interests against urban based capitalism and socialism. Even the coalition government's pre-election ploy of removing tolls from the Pattullo Bridge failed to prevent the unknown Socred Tom Irwin, of White Rock, from winning in the western valley.

The Fraser Valley would continue to be a bastion for Social Credit through successive decades of politics, with voters even electing federal Socreds George Hahn and Alex Patterson to Parliament in 1953.

Much of Social Credit's populist appeal emanated from the varied backgrounds of its candidates. Short on lawyers, the party tended to attract men and women who had made their mark in private enterprise.

Early Fraser Valley members of the Legislative Assembly included Tom Irwin, manager of the Cloverdale Legion; Lyle Wicks of Dewdney, later appointed minister of lands, who boasted membership in the Street Railwayman's Union; and Phil Gaglardi, who was raised on a farm at Silverdale, the son of a large immigrant family. He thundered at one local election gathering: "I was born on a stump ranch about a mile up the road; you people know all about me and I'm just the same as the boy who grew up here; the only difference is that now I have more than $106 million to spend!"

The core of Social Credit support over the years rested with the province's small businessmen and farmers, who were suspicious of both big labour and large corporations. Hunter Vogel, for many years Langley City mayor and legislative member, epitomized the new breed of valley entrepreneur. Vogel purchased Cloverdale Paint and Chemicals, a fledgling paint business, and built it into a large manufacturing and retail chain, which employed revolutionary methods of production, and boasted the largest wax works in Western Canada.

Vogel believed passionately in the future of the Fraser Valley, and his zeal for community service, combined with his sense of ethics and business acumen inspired many citizens to regain a measure of faith in their elected representatives. Vogel's three sons, Bill, Walter, and Richard, carried on the family tradition of service with distinction – Richard later serving as deputy attorney-general of British Columbia, and Bill Vogel serving as Chairman of the Board of Surrey Metro Savings Credit Union.

Sod-turning ceremonies for the new Rosedale-Agassiz bridge. Left to right: Phil Gaglardi, WAC Bennett, Ken Kiernan, Lyle Wicks. September 15, 1954.

The Fraser Valley portion of a 718-mile natural gas pipeline from Edmonton to Vancouver began to be constructed in 1953. Chilliwack and Surrey at first opposed the granting of natural gas distribution rights to the B.C. Electric Company, fearing its monopolistic strength; but Surrey Council was placated somewhat in 1955 when B.C. Electric built the largest gas turbine in the world at Port Mann to produce electricity from natural gas. In 1957, natural gas began to flow into thousands of valley homes.

The Fraser River was being viewed more and more as a barrier than a resource, and residents clamoured for new bridges all along its length. When the Mission Bridge collapsed in 1955, town residents panicked; aldermen phoned Gaglardi for assistance; the highways minister sent a ferry scow. Four months later, Mission reported its lifeblood ebbing. A sawmill and a cannery closed, retail stores suffered a slump, and even the Vancouver Symphony Orchestra cancelled a performance because most Mission audiences hailed from the Abbotsford-Matsqui side of the river.

On July 23, 1956, Gaglardi presided at the opening of a Mission Bridge that, although restored, was still an antiquated, one-lane structure shared with the railway. The highways minister felt constrained to make a promise: "As soon as it is economically feasible, you will have your new bridge; we don't need to be reminded because we are the most bridge-buildingest government since Confederation."

The year 1956 also witnessed the completion of the multi-million dollar Agassiz-Rosedale Bridge, replacing the archaic ferry system. In 1957, the new Pitt

River Bridge greatly improved traffic flow along the Lougheed Highway; and in the same year, more than one thousand Maple Ridge and Langley residents attended inaugural ceremonies for the first ferry service from McMillan Island to Albion. Another ferry service operated from Barnston Island to the Surrey mainland, running every two hours and shutting down at midnight. Barnston Islanders complained that they were the "only responsible people in the Valley to be locked up at night."

The completion of the Oak Street Bridge in June 1957 provided a quick, direct route between Vancouver and Richmond. The river delta region's most spectacular engineering feat, however, was the construction, under the South Arm of the Fraser of the Deas Island Tunnel, renamed in 1967 after George Massey, a local member of the Legislative Assembly, environmentalist, and long-time advocate of a tunnel link between Delta and Richmond.

Six 2,100-foot concrete sections were placed in the river bed to a depth of forty feet below sea level; the four-lane tunnel could accommodate seven thousand cars per hour. Queen Elizabeth presided at the opening on July 15, 1959. Tolls were collected on both the tunnel and the Oak Street Bridge until 1964. Inauguration of the Tsawwassen ferry terminal in 1960 rounded out a streamlined transportation network, which now connected the delta area as a unit to both the Vancouver metropolis and Vancouver Island.

Meanwhile, traffic congestion in the Fraser Valley had reached alarming proportions. The Old Yale Road, the Trans-Canada Highway, and the Pattullo Bridge could not handle the immense number of vehicles. The worst traffic jam in British Columbia's history occurred on the May 24 weekend in 1956, when thousands of motorists were held up for as long as nine hours. In August, the Abbotsford Board of Trade and other groups demanded that Gaglardi make good on a 1953 pledge of a valley freeway. Construction finally started in 1960.

On a fine June day in 1964, Premier Bennett officially opened the Port

The new freeway cut a divisive swath through the valley, heralding the age of the commuter.

Mann Bridge. Unique in North America, the bridge has a prefabricated orthotropic deck of very lightweight construction, stiffened with U-type steel stringers and bearing girders. It measures 1,200 feet from footing to footing and the northern approach is one mile in length.

The old Trans-Canada Highway was renamed in different areas: from Pattullo Bridge through Whalley it reverted to King George VI Highway; Whalley to Mount Lehman Road became Fraser Highway; and in Abbotsford and Chilliwack, it became South Fraser Way.

The new highway permitted thousands of Vancouver motorists to stream into the valley, and a speed limit of seventy miles per hour effectively halved the size of the valley. From Langley, in the valley's heart, to downtown Vancouver, travelling time was now less than an hour. New Westminster was bypassed by the new route, with the result that the Royal City lost its precedence over Vancouver and that city at last established its long sought hegemony over the region; valley residents now spoke of "hopping down to the Coast."

The Port Mann Bridge and the Highway 401 freeway had a marked impact on valley life. The age of commuting now truly dawned, allowing people to dwell virtually anywhere in the valley, even if they worked in the city.

The route of the freeway followed closely that of the old Telegraph Trail; but its construction was not without cost. A number of large working farms were destroyed. Each cloverleaf required 30 acres of farmland, and municipalities such as Surrey and Langley were left badly fragmented. Furious district councils demanded unsuccessfully that there be farm crossing overpasses for every mile of road. Church ministers argued that their congregations would suffer from being divided by a highway that could only be crossed by overpasses every five or ten miles.

Some farmers bitterly fought expropriation of their land for the new freeway. Charlie Perkins of Port Kells had built a small park on his property to honour his fallen air force buddies from World War I. A huge fir tree stood proudly in one corner of the park, over which Charlie stood guard. The stubborn farmer aroused such a protest in the community that the highways department built a curve to reroute the freeway past the old fir.

Alas, vandals set fire to the tree, and now only its high stump remains; but for years, motorists have observed little crosses placed amongst the ivy covering the blackened hulk, in tribute to Charlie Perkins's fallen comrades.

The flying of light aircraft became a popular pastime for many Lower Mainland residents during the fifties and sixties, and municipal airports mushroomed throughout the valley. At Pitt Meadows, the airport was built on traditional Katzie land, where huge potlatches were held in the old days, and the wild potato had grown in abundance.

Commercial flying with Trans-Canada Airlines was also thriving. The City of Vancouver operated Vancouver International Airport from 1948 to 1962, when the federal government assumed jurisdiction and built a new terminal building, designed to handle five million passengers a year. One Hatzic farmer revelled in annually flying a flat of fresh local strawberries to his prairie relatives.

On the evening of December 9, 1956, fierce winds and rain lashed the eastern end of the Fraser Valley. TCA Flight 810, a North Star aircraft with 59 passengers and 3 crew members, taxied down the runway at Vancouver Airport and headed east for Calgary. Captain Alan Clarke was an experienced pilot and had received a detailed weather briefing prior to departure. At 6:52 p.m., Clarke radioed Vancouver that he had a fire in his Number 2 engine and was turning back. The plane shuddered and banked, caught in one hundred mile an hour headwinds thirty-five miles southeast of Hope. Clarke desperately sought to maintain altitude.

At 7:10 p.m., a NORAD radar operator at Birch Bay noted Flight 810's blip at just 10,000 feet—only 2,000 feet above the icy mountain peaks. Then the blip disappeared from his screen.

Far up the jagged slope of Mount Slesse, the aircraft had slammed into eternity. The crash site wasn't located until May 14, 1957, when three mountaineers found a chunk of fuselage in the snow. Severe avalanche conditions prevented further searching near the summit. Paddy Sherman, later publisher of the Vancouver *Province*, combed the slopes in subsequent expeditions and reported much wreckage in small fragments, and bits of bodies.

Chief Coroner Glen McDonald landed on Mount Slesse by helicopter. His searchers found a foot enclosed in a shoe; a badly charred body in the nose cone of the fuselage; mail and money—which TCA officials collected in potato sacks; a saucer size skull, camera film; and bits and pieces of metal, including an 8 by 3 foot Merlin engine compacted to a 2 foot square hunk of twisted metal. Coroner McDonald decided it would be futile to attempt further searches for body fragments. He pulled out a Book of Common Prayer and adapted the Burial At Sea verses to "Burial On The Mountain," in what must surely be one of the strangest funeral services ever performed.

Bareheaded, in the presence of two Mounties and a few of the airline's searchers, high on an icy ledge, McDonald committed the victims of the crash to God. Even as he spoke, an avalanche started on another side of the mountain, its echo reverberating among the canyon walls below. Then the coroner erected a crude cross, tied together from bits of wood. McDonald and his companions left the site in silence, each person awed by the scene.

Later, McDonald recommended that the Mount Slesse peak area be declared a provincial cemetery in order to prevent the site's desecration by inquisitive treasure hunters, who might search for the body of Kwan Song, a Chinese passenger, rumoured to have carried on him eighty thousand dollars in cash. The suggestion was adopted by the provincial cabinet. On December 9, 1957, Trans-Canada Airlines unveiled a granite memorial to the victims on the forest road leading to Mount Slesse on the north bank of the Chilliwack River.

The pace of urbanization in the Fraser Valley accelerated with every improvement in transportation. Between 1951 and 1961, four acres of farmland were subdivided for every acre of undeveloped bush area. The incredible pressure on hitherto agricultural districts caused haphazard residential growth in cluster communities, without regard to fertility of the soil. Arable farmland was disappearing fast.

Farmers argued that they would only be able to resist the easy money of land developers if agricultural subsidies were increased, and large tax breaks

granted to them. Town councillors argued that their commercial cores must expand in order to service a growing area, and that this necessarily meant encroaching upon surrounding farmland. A typical problem area was Abbotsford, where the village population spilled over into two other municipalities, Sumas and Matsqui, creating "three-cornered" confusion.

A few districts groped their way toward some degree of control over the land. Delta, Surrey, Richmond, and Pitt Meadows all passed bylaws to protect the most fertile farmland by prohibiting subdivision of less than five acres within designated areas. But this did nothing to prevent the breakup of large productive farms. Reeve John Kirkland of Delta addressed the dilemma by simply stating that the farmer was entitled to his capital gain if offered an attractive price for his land.

Looking south on Garden City Road during flooding in Richmond, November 1954.

The Lower Mainland Regional Planning Board criticized the growing uncontrolled sprawl, and urged individual municipalities to control subdivisions better, citing inadequate sidewalks, shopping facilities, schools, and roads, and the absence of water and sewer systems as the consequence of haphazard planning. In Queensborough, brand-new homes were built in rows behind deep ditches containing slime, refuse, and excrement—and many rooming houses in the area were without lavatories.

Districts which tried to cope with these growth problems met with stiff opposition from landowners who resented any infringement on their right to use their land for any purpose they chose. In Langley, Chief Planner Ken Major began a career spanning more than twenty-five years, treading a delicate path among advisory planning committees, developers, and councillors, in an attempt to achieve balanced growth.

The principle of the non-conforming use was recognized as a result of a court challenge to Langley's Town Planning Commission, which had prohibited one Howard McLeod from selling food and other goods from his gas station, because he was outside a commercially zoned area. The Supreme Court affirmed the right of businesses to continue their activities on a site previously unrestricted in usage. Art Knapp closed his garden centre in Langley when his business signs were ordered removed by council as offending the municipal sign bylaw. Knapp raged, "Would you sooner have a thistle patch with an ugly shack and a dilapidated outhouse in the middle of this fair little city, or a colourful garden spot?"

By 1961, the population of the Fraser Valley exceeded three hundred thousand people. Residential growth in Richmond and Surrey was phenomenal; by 1957, only one in five Surrey residents had resided there for more than five years. That same year, Yorkshire Trust began construction of 1,100 homes on Mary Hill in Port Coquitlam, where three bedroom homes were offered for sale at $16,000, with $1,000 down payments and National Housing Act financing at 6.25 percent interest. Unfortunately, most banks discriminated against rural areas by refusing to finance homes in regions which lacked water and sewer systems, despite perfectly functioning wells and septic fields.

As planning gained influence during the sixties, tempers flared ever more frequently between landowners and local councils. Overlapping jurisdictions created confusion and slowed approval processes; by the mid-sixties, some four hundred boards, councils, commissions, and planning officers directed subdivision planning and land usage. Mobile homes disfigured the countryside, and residents complained of wrecked cars littering farms. Shopping centres such as Guildford Town Centre changed the spending habits of rural residents. Strip malls made their debut. Farmers staged mass protests over property assessments which reflected just a small percentage of the value of their large holdings.

White Rock seceded from Surrey in 1957, seeking autonomy for its goal of becoming a purely residential community catering to retirees. Rural post offices were closed, as the postal system was centralized; and the small country store died an ignominious death. In Surrey, all north-south roads were designated "streets", while east-west roads became "avenues," all bearing numbered names. Longtime valley residents complained bitterly of the loss of heritage road names, as Surrey's Tobacco Road became plain 111th Avenue, and Chickadee Lane became 101 Avenue.

It is common today to regard the fifties nostalgically, as a quiet time of law and order. It is certainly true that community standards tended to be conservative, as a generation that had grown up in the Depression and come of age during the World War II turned its energies towards building a stable society in which to raise its families.

However, that very conservatism, compounded with the new alienation of the sprawling suburbs, and the bleak future that Cold War politics seemed to bode for the world at large, was giving rise to an angry young generation. Juvenile delinquency, street gangs, and promiscuity provoked widespread concern. In Surrey, vandalism of homes began to be a serious problem, one that continues to the present day. Liquor offences among youth multiplied and judges often accused parents of contributing to their children's delinquency.

In New Westminster, a new practice of listless teenagers was to "just hang around." The *Columbian's* editor observed: "They mill and wander about like so many extras on a crowded movie set. Their meanderings are directionless, their interests vague. Like restless nomads they shift from café to café and laugh and smoke and drink coffee. Some are recruited into autos and roar away to adventures beyond the lights. Others just stand and practise nothingness."

Long hair and tight pants became fashionable with the Elvis Presley generation. Juvenile deliquency was blamed, variously, on booze, rock 'n roll, and crime comics. Red Robinson promoted rock concerts in the valley. At one dance in

Mission City in 1961, matters spun out of control when, while Buddy Knox entertained inside, hoodlums threw beer bottles at police outside, smashing parking meters, and throwing rocks. Outdoor rock concerts at Aldergrove Lake Park aroused an entire community in protest.

In 1955, when Mr. Justice Wood sentenced six valley youths to prison for a case of gang rape in Matsqui, and ordered six strokes of the paddle for each of them, he commented: "There seems to be a sort of epidemic of this type of thing." In 1957, fifty-two year old Gerald Eaton was hanged at Oakalla for the murder of eight year old Carolyn Moore of Langley.

Daring bank robberies by groups of well-armed men abounded, as did the inimitable poultry thieves. Farmer Rooke of Hammond petitioned for council to remove some brush from the road allowance by his farm, as it afforded thieves a cover for stealing his turkeys before Thanksgiving Day each year; his wire fence was cut repeatedly and birds removed to waiting cars.

Langley's elderly grandmother, Matilda Harjula, became so frustrated by repeated armed robberies of her Hilltop country store that she armed herself with a shotgun. On one September evening in 1964, she fired at an intruder in the dark, and then called police. A constable arrived to find a Haney Correctional Institute escapee wounded in her back yard. All next day, friends phoned Matilda to congratulate her, but she replied, "It doesn't seem right; it isn't at all lady-like for me to shoot a man."

By the sixties, most municipalities had signed contracts with the Royal Canadian Mounted Police for policing services. A few communities, such as New Westminster, Delta, and Matsqui today have their own police forces.

For the less jaded, there were of course events such as the Cloverdale Rodeo, May Day, and even a Surrey doll buggy parade. Girls were courted at drive-in theatres and seniors discovered curling. Exercising was in, and gymnasiums proliferated. Glen Valley residents held their sixtieth annual basket picnic in 1962; and Mrs. Shimek of Hatzic thought she would recreate some good old Depression atmosphere with a Hobo Tea, at which guests were served "pokes" of tasty morsels tied to wooden poles and eaten on tin pie plates.

People debated fiercely the scrapping of the school strap. Others howled about the Sunny Trails nudist colony, established in 1952 in a Surrey woodland area. Schoolchildren grimaced in 1955 when they were inoculated with the new anti-polio Salk vaccine. That same year, local councils divided on the issue of fluoridation; whether it reduced dental decay or not, many residents just didn't favour tampering with the water supply. Fur coats were in, and much of the fur came from muskrats which inhabited the deep ditches of Richmond and Delta. The *Columbian* described the muskrat as "an adorable creature, except for his tail."

The beaver returned as an unwelcome nuisance in 1962, when a family of the creatures built a dam in Washington State which caused flooding on a farmer's land in Langley. Repeated protests by G. Copeman and Langley Council failed to move Washington authorities to act. As a result, during clandestine night forays, the dam site was dynamited, but the canny beaver rebuilt even stronger dams within a few days. The local editor observed that the matter could well turn into an international incident if this one beaver family continued to "botch brotherhood." A few years later, environmentalists would worry about a much bigger dam threatening the Skagit Valley.

Motorists enjoyed weekend jaunts to old haunts including Mud Bay, White Rock, Garibaldi Park, and Harrison Hot Springs, the latter gaining fame as an international tourist resort. Car-train collisions occurred with worrying frequency. Radar traps imperilled the swift, and Vancouver motorists caught for speeding in the valley became furious when handed a court summons instead of a mere ticket by the Mounties.

Magistrate R. Payne lectured one city driver, who claimed that he should not have been dragged through the court system when a ticket would have sufficed. "It may happen that way in Vancouver," he said, "but it doesn't work that way out here." The magistrate then fined the defendant $15 plus $2 in court costs and warned that he had made the sentence light because "there probably was not much traffic at 5:00 A.M."

By the early sixties, television and radio were blamed for decreasing attendance at rural churches, now that services were broadcast live. Awe over Yuri Gagarin's space mission turned to fear that perhaps now the Russians were more powerful than ever. Two old Chevrolets were traded by one young man for a brand new geiger counter, while civil defence authorities in the valley taught courses on radiation.

Horseback riding became popular with women. Horse trailers rolled along valley roads and equestrian centres sponsored many riding events. The Glen Valley Fox Hunt amused men and dogs. After all of the foxes had been rooted out and killed, coyotes were hunted—until finally, by the seventies, horsemen were forced to satisfy their lust for the hunt by chasing the scent of a rag soaked in fox urine, dragged along a trail by a fellow huntsman.

Oil companies poked around the valley, digging test holes. Black gold was discovered at Matsqui and Langley, with a few wells eventually producing up to two hundred barrels a day.

The gold of Slumach's Lost Mine was also still pursued, though Vancouver City archivist Major J.S. Matthews heaped scorn on the old legend, calling it "pure rubbish." In protest of Major Matthews's utterance on the subject, a Vancouver *Province* news team reported that the chief of the Coquitlam Indian Reserve had guided them to a site high in the Pitt Lake mountains, where they had staked a claim covered by thirty feet of snow. If the glacier ever melted, they hoped to find gold there.

Not to be outdone, the New Westminster *Columbian* produced a feature story on a Haney trapper named Wally Lund, who became convinced that the mother lode lay in a crevice on Pitt Polder's Sheridan Hill. His son-in-law, Danny Scooch, later dug a deep shaft near the crevice. Neither man found gold, but Danny did find a large wooden bucket which was identified as a product of the old Fort Langley cooperage, dating from the 1850s.

Queen Victoria's proclamation which created the colony of British Columbia in 1858, was discovered in a long locked vault in the basement of an old London building in 1952, and the document was placed in the British Columbia Archives in Victoria in 1953.

The 1958 British Columbia Centennial celebrations inspired every Fraser Valley community to sponsor projects of lasting benefit. Port Coquitlam constructed a thirty-five thousand dollar public pool. Surrey and Chilliwack opened Centennial Museums. Princess Margaret arrived to participate, as did a contingent of Royal Engineers, whose bright scarlet uniforms contrasted with the khaki of Canadian Engineers from Camp Chilliwack, offspring of the English units.

Centennial celebration on Annacis Island, July 1, 1958.

The Vancouver *Sun* opined that Fort Langley would be the showcase for the 1958 events: "The restored fort should be the centre of the drama of history. It should be re-opened in a re-enactment of that significant birthday, with all the colorful saga of the gold rush...."

Thanks to the efforts through the years of Judge Howay, Willard Ireland, and the Native Sons and Daughters, the restoration of the fort became a reality. The Fort Restoration Society, under Alex Hope, built upon the work of its predecessors, raising funds and obtaining commitments from both the federal and provincial governments. The land was acquired as a National Site and the rebuilding of the Big House, one bastion, the palisade, and landscaping proceeded under the careful direction of J. Calder Peeps, University of British Columbia professor of architecture, who was determined to recreate an authentic version of the 1858 post.

On a hot, sultry July day, Princess Margaret reopened the old fort after a troop of the Chilliwack Engineers marched through the main gate and met the Princess's own Royal Engineers for a changing of the guard.

"Little did Queen Victoria realize," orated Alex Hope, "that 100 years after she proclaimed the colony of British Columbia, her great great granddaughter would visit the birthplace where her decree was read, in the far wilderness of Empire."

Pitt Meadows is a low-lying area some 10 miles long and 4 miles wide, which forms a marshy alluvial fan from the confluence of the Pitt and Fraser Rivers north to the lower end of Pitt Lake. Governor James Douglas was enchanted with the area and in 1860 he wrote: "The banks of the Pitt River are exceedingly beautiful. Extensive meadows sweep gracefully from the very edge of the river towards the distant line of forest and mountain. The rich alluvial soil produces a thick growth of grass and scattered groups of willows." Unfortunately, the rich lands were also subject to the whims of *ta coutchi* and, despite many attempts to drain and dyke

Princess Margaret and Premier Bennett tour the restored Hudson's Bay Company fort as part of the 1958 centennial celebrations, Fort Langley.

the area, it was not until 1950 that the land was finally claimed by man.

Dr. Jan Blom of the Netherlands was a far-sighted farm credit manager who stumbled upon Pitt Meadows in 1949. A gun club was anxious at the time to sell some 6,700 acres it owned, following the 1948 flood ravage.

Blom saw the potential for reclaiming thousands of acres of lowland and swamp for cultivation. He purchased the land for forty thousand dollars. He also formed Pitt Polder Limited ("polder," in Dutch, means reclaimed land), establishing a unique partnership among Dutch financiers and Canadian capitalists Leon Ladner and Walter Koerner, all of whom he convinced of the potential for his reclamation scheme.

The reclamation project proved to be an overwhelming success. Dr. Blom supervised the draining, dyking, and clearing of thousands of acres of reclaimed land. He then arranged for several dozen Dutch families to emigrate to the area, to whom the company sold and leased land which was ideally suited for dairy farming. Soon, prosperous farms dotted the landscape. By 1968, 44 percent of all milk producers on the polder were of Dutch origin, shipping through the Fraser Valley Milk Producers Association.

Dutch immigrants arrived in large numbers in the Matsqui, Sumas, and Chilliwack regions during the fifties and early sixties. Their timing was propitious. Large numbers of farm families in the Fraser Valley were losing their youth to urban employers; hence, many farms were available for purchase, as parents were unable to pass the land on to their children as an ongoing endeavour. Moreover, most of the immigrants were young couples, willing to work long hours in the fields to carve out a new life far away from the shambles of postwar Europe.

Finally, the passage of the Milk Industry Act in 1956 established a stable pricing and production system for the dairy industry, based upon the purchase of quota as a condition of operation. The Dutch settlers gravitated naturally to dairying as the key agricultural pursuit of the valley, and one with which many of them were familiar from an early age.

Traditional truck garden plots were efficient for vegetable growing, but agricultural activities like dairying, berry growing, and hops required large acreages. Some sixty-eight acres of pasture land were needed to support a herd of thirty-six milking cows.

Yet the pace of subdivision had eliminated thousands of large holdings by 1970, and the day of the small farmer had passed. Farming was now an industry. The tremendous success enjoyed by some farmers' cooperatives, such as the Surrey Co-operative Association, which boasted ten thousand members in 1967, reached a hiatus point and then began a steep decline in the early seventies. By 1977, the Surrey Co-op was in receivership.

Planners and politicians grappled with the threats to the Fraser Valley as bread basket of the province. In a lively town meeting held at Aldergrove in 1959, the Honourable Ken Kiernan contended, "We are living in a $1.50 per hour economy and up. Let's stop paying the farmer 50 cents." Eric Flowerdew stated that "the most valuable asset in Canada is the top six inches of soil." Mayor Doug Taylor of Matsqui stressed the importance of the family farm unit.

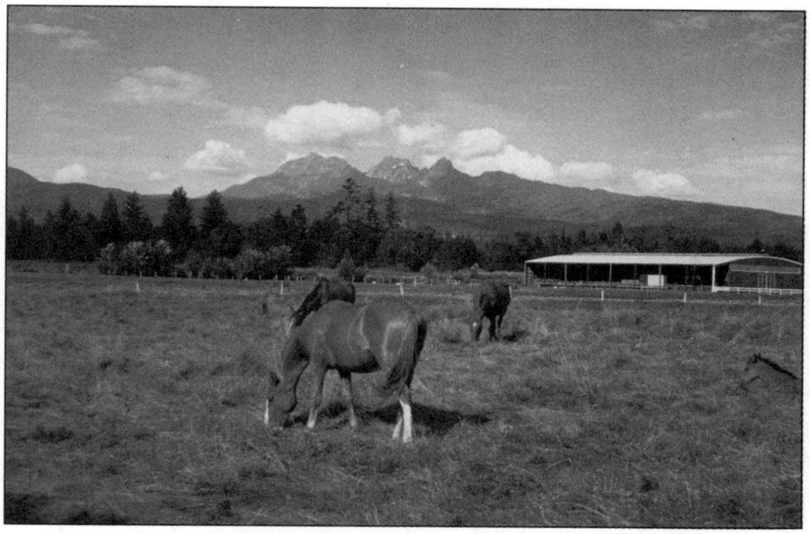

Horses graze peacefully on a Maple Ridge farm below the Golden Ears.

Taylor was a veteran mayor whose life was dedicated to the promotion of agricultural interests; one of his schemes involved a system of government purchase of development rights from farmers in order to preserve farm usage in perpetuity. Mayor Taylor also campaigned for the creation of green belts, a measure ultimately adopted by Victoria, and correctly predicted a new urban centre stretching from Abbotsford to Clearbrook.

Farming issues shook Fraser Valley communities. Independent farmers fought a losing battle against marketing regulations. There were anomalies; a Surrey farmer was fined ten dollars for selling milk to the public at a quality above the standard set by the B.C. Milk Board. A 1963 increase of one cent per quart for milk brought protests from Vancouver housewives, and angry retorts from dairy farmers.

Marauding dogs killed sheep and poultry, drawing threats from farmers to shoot every canine that entered upon private property. At the same time, bulls ran amok regularly in neighbours' gardens and on public roads, causing councils to consider calling in game wardens, since the police and pound keepers were incapable of rounding up the large, snorting creatures.

Yet there were many improvements to the farming life. The tractor did not grow impatient or tire like a horse; milking machines were efficient; and heat lamps kept piglets and chicks warm. 4-H clubs proliferated, encouraging boys and girls at an early age to nurture a steer and then show the animal at the Pacific National

Exhibition held in Vancouver. Fresh vegetable stands lined highways and byways in Lulu Island and Delta, while strawberries and raspberries were offered at the roadside by farmers' children in Langley and Mission.

Dr. R. Nicholson reminded dairy farmers one Thanksgiving of the many reasons why people carried on with farm life, and that, despite the elements, the heartaches of crop failures and stock losses, there were many incomparable moments of bliss and peace; but the ultimate reason for staying on the land was "because their homes, their farms, their herds are the creation of their own efforts and ingenuity; because these things have become a part of their very being."

As senior governments assumed greater responsibility for health, welfare, and care of the aged, municipalities closed boarding homes and old age facilities, such as Langley's Langholm. Others were discovering that the valley was an excellent environment for the dispossessed, indigent, and those requiring special rehabilitative care. The Salvation Army opened a large complex for boys in Langley

Berry pickers at McKim farm on Steveston Highway, ca. 1950.

in 1967 named the House of Concord, where instruction in farming and the trades was given. Another Salvation Army project was the establishment of a rural alcoholic treatment hostelry in Hatzic's Miracle Valley. Meanwhile, hundreds of children were placed in rural homes by the Vancouver and Catholic Children's Aid Societies. Most of these children were eventually adopted by their foster parents.

Essondale's population passed four thousand by 1968. The majority of inmates lived in open wards. In an effort to improve patients' self-esteem, appeals went out to the public for clothing donations. Winnifred Mather of the *Province* even recruited professional models from Vancouver and helped patients hold a fashion show.

Although improvements to facilities were ongoing, much trouble brewed over the living conditions at Essondale. The public, moreover, lived in constant fear of the all-too-frequent escapes of psychopathic patients. The government changed the name of the facility to Riverview in 1965 in a feeble attempt to alter its image.

It had become clear that the provincial government regarded mental health

as of only secondary importance to physical well-being. In 1967, mental patients were allotted only $6.25 per person for care, compared to $23.25 per person for the physically ill.

A reporter described her one day "detention" at Riverview's Crease Clinic in 1967:

> "I was assigned to a cell-like room with no curtains and the window itself black with dirt. The walls were painted a sickly green, although 'painted' was hardly the term for it—'daubed' would be nearer the truth... The floor was ringed with a black ring of dirt that could've been scraped with a knife. Apart from the bed, which no-one had bothered to wash before I was put in it, the only other furniture was a very dilapidated chest of drawers...The ordinary dormitories offered no privacy at all, not even curtains around the beds...One doesn't expect to find dirty nurses in dirty uniforms with dirty fingernails in a modern hospital."

The reporter concluded that many physicians who sent their patients to Riverview had never visited the premises themselves, and they should think twice before sentencing the mentally ill to such a miserable existence. A tour of Riverview by fifteen members of the Legislative Assembly in 1968 resulted in demands for more qualified staff and replacement of the fifty-five year old West Lawn unit, a four-storey structure sheltering some 750 "empty-eyed, slack-jawed men."

Trouble brewed at the British Columbia Penitentiary in the sixties. On April 20, 1963, a guard fired shots at three convicts escaping through a window; the prisoners responded by hurtling Molotov cocktails—gasoline-filled light bulbs—which missed the guard but exploded in flames. When the alarm sounded, the convicts took guard Pat Dennis hostage and trussed him up. They then demanded that radio personality Jack Webster be summoned to negotiate for them.

Webster arrived at the scene and promptly went into the barricaded washroom where the convicts and Dennis were huddled; his first sight was one convict, his face bloodied, hovering over the helpless guard with a knife. Webster shunted back and forth all night, listening to the convicts' demands, and pleading with them for the guard's release. Early next morning, other prisoners who had failed to return to their cells began smashing windows and setting fires.

Troops from Canadian Forces Base Chilliwack and the mounted police were called in. Tear gas bombs were fired and the rioters fled back to their cells. One of the three convicts with Webster feared a rush and told the broadcaster to telephone the warden that if they were attacked, both Dennis and Webster would be killed. Webster complied. The crisis was finally defused when the hostage-takers agreed to give up if authorities transferred them to eastern prisons. Their wish was granted; Webster personally accompanied two of the convicts to the airport.

The overcrowded conditions in the ancient penitentiary complex contributed to the ongoing unrest which now dominated prison life. In order to reduce the penitentiary's population, the government transferred some 250 convicts to a new drug detention centre in Matsqui in 1965. This left 550 inmates at the Pen itself. Then Agassiz Mountain Prison, heretofore a receptacle for convicted Sons of Freedom Doukhobours, altered its orientation to include some of the older

Westminster Abbey and Seminary at Mission. In addition to serving as a monastery and training ground for the priesthood, the complex caters to students from throughout BC for weekend retreats.

prisoners, who were not considered to be escape risks. New Westminster City Council demanded that the penitentiary be dismantled and prisoners farmed out to other institutions. The federal government promised to close the prison within ten years. Eventually, it was closed in 1980. Now, the archaic entrance façade at the Sapperton site is the last remnant of the troubled institution.

A welcome addition to the Fraser Valley landscape occurred in 1957, when the Benedictine monks opened their abbey and seminary above Mission City, the seminary being planned as a boarding school for students training for the priesthood. The beautiful 120-acre setting overlooking the broad sweep of the Fraser was chosen by monks in 1944 for its resemblance to St. Benedict's Monte Cassino location near Rome. As Abbott Eugene recalls, "We almost ran to the edge of the cliff, and then there was a moment of giddiness and astonishment to see the classic garden below."

The abbey cornerstone, laid in 1953, was from Monte Cassino; the tower's ten bells, the largest weighing 2,500 pounds, were cast at Whitechapel Bell Foundry in London.

As with the St. Mary's pioneers of nearly one hundred years before, the monks are largely self-supporting, cultivating the soil, and raising beef and dairy cattle. Tourists are welcome; while fields are used by community soccer teams, and groups of students from throughout the province spend weekend retreats at the monastery.

The monks rise each morning at 4:30 a.m. and devote four hours to study, five hours at manual labour, and then three hours in church services and prayer. A chief contributor to the monastery's growth was Father Bede Reynolds, a California millionaire who discarded his worldly goods and took the Benedictine vows of "poverty, chastity, obedience, and stability."

The first junior college in the Fraser Valley was founded on the site of the dilapidated Seal Kap dairy farm on the Salmon River, directly across from James McMillan's 1824 camp and two miles from Fort Langley. The property, formerly part of the old Hudson's Bay Farm, was purchased by the Evangelical Free Church of America, which opened Trinity Junior College with an inaugural class of seventeen students in 1962. Founding President Calvin Hanson, and his board intended the new institution as a two-year transfer college for students preparing for the ministry who wished to complete a full degree programme from a public university.

Without any government aid, Hanson gathered around him men and women committed to the development of a modern campus with high standards of excellence. Many top-ranking professors accepted lower salaries in order to become part of the Trinity experience. Books, material, and labour were donated by scores of supporters. By 1964, dormitories, classrooms, library, chapel, and a magnificent gymnasium were completed, and Education Minister Les Peterson broke sod for a science building.

"Virtue lies in the struggle, not in the prize," orated Peterson, who was somewhat awed with the progress made by the privately funded institution. Future Member of Parliament Benno Friesen served as Dean of Students, and Dr. Robert Thompson, former national Social Credit party leader, and educator, served on staff. When enrolment topped two hundred students, the College Board broadened its focus and developed a curriculum catering not only to students preparing for the ministry, but to all students wishing to obtain a liberal arts education with a Christian perspective.

Rural school education entered a turbulent era. Sex education films shocked parents, most of whom claimed that children were sufficiently exposed to farm life biology without graphic portrayals of human anatomy. Parents were also upset over the refusal of the provincial government to help finance school buses for students living within three miles of school. In Surrey alone, one thousand children walked more than 2 miles to school along narrow-shouldered roads.

Labour relations continued to deteriorate in the school system. A 1954 janitorial strike in Langley witnessed parents keeping nine schools open in defiance of "scab" taunts. Binding arbitration became the norm for teacher salaries. Possession of alcohol and cigarettes at school became commonplace, and the focus shifted to attacking drugs. In one celebrated case, a judge ordered the reinstatement of a student who had been expelled for taking one puff of a marijuana joint in a school washroom.

In 1961, a modernized St. Mary's School and dormitory opened at Mission, accommodating three hundred native students. But integration into the public school system was already under way, and several students simply boarded at St. Mary's and attended the local high school. By 1968, complete integration was achieved, although students from throughout the valley continued to board at the dormitories. Alas, the old mission buildings were demolished by bulldozer, the historic Oblate cemetary vandalized, and even the grotto was flattened. An old altar which had been hand-carved by Father Fouquet was rescued from the rubble.

The attrition of time served to eliminate many old historic buildings from the Fraser Valley scene. Fortunately, talented Langley artist Rudi Dangelmaier had been touring the province since 1937, painting prominent buildings in water colour, oils, and poliment, artist's materials consisting of naturally coloured clays mixed with binders and preservatives.

Dangelmaier's work centred on wooden structures of the Fraser Valley, which were depicted so vividly that every weathered board and crack became as lifelike as human flesh and veins. The British Columbia Provincial Museum exhibited 45 of his works on tour over a two-year period. The entire collection of 158 paintings was later acquired by the Fort Langley Legacy Foundation for permanent display.

Fraser Valley barn with silo, Delta, painted by Rudi Dangelmaier.

People were increasingly eager to preserve relics of their past. The B.C. Farm Machinery Museum was opened in Fort Langley in 1966. At Harrison Mills, Acton Kilby found that more people were coming into his store to look at his antique wares than were purchasing goods; so he decided to convert his establishment into a museum. Kilby hauled in his wife's Indian baskets, ancient muskets, a spinning loom, and hundreds of old knickknacks, and charged admission.

East of Fort Langley, the abandoned Morrison house, former home of Joe Morrison, who died in 1963 at the age of 102 years (at the time he was British Columbia's oldest native born white man), was cared for by J.J. McLellan. The old house was built in the 1870s and McLellan always left the door unlocked because visitors loved to walk in and spend idle hours reading newspapers from the 1880s which had been pasted to the walls. One day, someone tried to peel away a page from a wall and, unsuccessful, cut out an entire section of the wall and hauled it away. McLellan boarded the home up in disgust.

The transportation improvements which were in place by 1964 set the pattern of travel and commerce for the ensuing half century. Industrial plants emerged along the Highway 401 freeway. Regional shopping centres were strategically located in towns ripe for rapid growth. The noise of factories and pollution from lumber mills caused protest. Booming Chilliwack was even told by the Pollution Control Board in 1967 that it must cease its century-old practice of dumping raw, untreated sewage into the Fraser, and install a treatment plant.

Port Coquitlam Citizen of the Year Harold Routley campaigned vigorously against the contamination of his beloved Coquitlam River, and later led the drive to build the seventeen mile PoCo Trail around his town. Landowners also complained of erosion of their land by some four to eight cubic feet per year into the Fraser which, they claimed, was caused by the vibrations of fast moving Canadian National Railway trains.

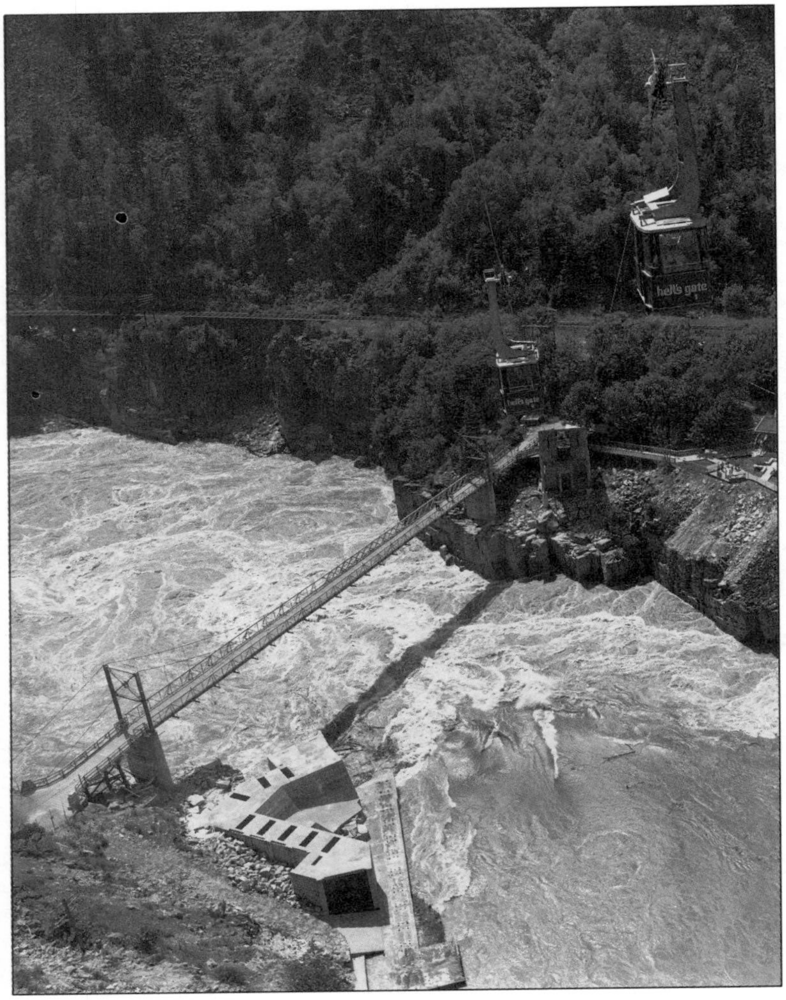

Aerial view of the fish ladders at Hell's Gate.

In 1968, Fort Langley, Surrey, and Delta protested unsuccessfully against the proposed routing of Roberts Bank-bound coal trains through settled areas. After the spur line was built, residents complained of coal dust which clouded and polluted the atmosphere emanating from speeding trains.

The fish ladders installed at Hell's Gate proved so effective that the 1958 sockeye run was one of the largest in history. The mysterious sturgeon was still snared, and in 1962 Gerry Miller caught a 824-pound monster that was shipped frozen to the Smithsonian Institution, where molds of the fish were cast for display.

Whonnock fisherman Floyd Sidwell lassoed a bear swimming in the Fraser one day and pulled the animal aboard. The bruin was not impressed, and began demolishing the fishboat, snarling, clawing and chewing at cabin walls, the net drum, and even a hot exhaust pipe. Floyd fled to the cabin and locked himself in, but the bear smashed a window. Floyd then swung at the bruin's protruding snout with his bare fist. That did it. The bear splashed over the side, made it to shore at Glen Valley, and was last seen by Mrs. J. Hassell ambling through her vegetable garden.

The extremes to which bureaucracy will sometimes go to perform a perceived duty defies the imagination. Eighteen-year-old John Watt shot and killed a 130-pound cougar which had stalked his mother and sister near the family's Langley farm in July 1967.

Instead of being given a medal, the lad was promptly charged with hunting without a licence by a wildlife conservation officer. Watt was convicted by the local magistrate, who praised his actions but advised that he was obligated to sentence him to thirty days in jail, suspended. Subsequent protests from the community resulted in a cabinet order-in-council quashing the conviction.

Sasquatch sightings continued to be made in the Harrison region. Mrs. George Chapman of Ruby Creek saw a huge hairy man step over her garden fence one day. She gathered her children and ran down to the Fraser, where she heard the creature utter an ear splitting roar.

Witnesses later viewed footprints which measured sixteen inches long, eight inches across the ball of the foot, and four inches across the heel; there were five toes imprinted and no claw marks.

Indian Mary Joe of Katz told the Harrison Centennnial Committee that "white men won't see Sasquatch, they don't smell good enough."

Albert Ostman of Fort Langley told of being held captive for several days by a Sasquatch family near Bella Coola. Two prospectors reported the sighting in 1957 of a huge man-like beast on Spuzzum Glacier, thirty-five miles from Harrison Hot Springs. Numerous affidavits have been sworn and other sightings made, but the best evidence of the existence of the legendary ape-like creature are the photographs taken and casts made of giant footprints. John Green, former editor of the Agassiz Advance, has studied the Sasquatch stories, hunted for clues, made casts, and published books on the subject.

In 1969, a sheriff's deputy at Gray's Harbor, Washington, told Green that he saw an animal which "was not a bear...it had a face on it and feet instead of paws...it had breasts." Footprints measured by Green at the scene were 18.5 inches long and the creature was estimated to stand 7.5 feet tall and weigh 350 pounds. Although there have been a number of hoaxes uncovered, the persistence in Indian lore, the credibility of witnesses, and the footprints found, all indicate the probability of there existing a rare species of ape-like being in the rugged wilderness of the Pacific northwest.

Minority groups of varying racial and cultural backgrounds were being met with a greater tolerance by the sixties. Hungarian refugees were embraced warmly and sheltered in Abbotsford and other communities in the wake of the 1956 Budapest uprising.

Yet living conditions for many minorities remained deplorable. Chinese and Sikh farm workers newly arrived in Canada were packed into windowless panel trucks and shunted to and from farms, where they often toiled twelve hours in the fields under primitive conditions. In the cranberry bogs of Richmond, female Chinese were offered as prostitutes by field masters to any passers-by. On Indian reserves, meanwhile, drunkenness exacted a terrible toll, and many families lived in filth and squalor.

As a 1958 centennial project, Fraser Valley natives initiated the Cultus Lake Indian Festival. The festival revived the art of canoe making, as tribes from the Lower Mainland competed in canoe races each year, although they had to battle the constant wash of reckless power-boaters, which often swamped the native craft. At New Westminster, civic officials staged a colourful Indian Days festival in 1967, which bore some resemblance to the Queen's birthday celebrations of the 1860s. Hundreds of Indians from ten tribes participated in war canoe races; bands played; and the Queen was still toasted.

Some native reserves were prospering economically. Virtually every valley band leased part of its holdings for agricultural, forestry, commercial, industrial, or residential use, thus obtaining much additional revenue. A few long-term leases were challenged by native leaders, who claimed that they or their fathers had been cheated. Thus, Chief Bernard Charles of the Semiahmoo Band protested in vain the leasing terms for White Rock's Semiahmoo Park, negotiated in 1942. Some reserve land was purchased outright, including the forty acres acquired by Surrey Council from the Royal Kwantlen No. 2 Reserve of the McMillan Island Band.

Indian Days canoe racing, New Westminster 1967.

The struggle to preserve vestiges of Stalo culture had its occasional victories. The potlatch ban was removed in 1951. In some families, the native tongue was spoken and passed on between the generations. A significant event occurred in 1963, when Mary Peters and Adeline Lorenzetto of the Seabird Island Reserve took up the ancient Salish loom and revived the art of weaving.

The Salish weaving revival was in large part attributable to Oliver Wells of Edenbank Farm, who steeped himself in Hill-Tout and native lore. He gently but persistently encouraged natives to regain pride and develop their potential by exploiting the richness of their heritage. Wool from Edenbank was delivered directly to Indian weavers.

By 1967, a number of native women had taken up the trade, and colourful blankets and tapestries were being displayed and enjoyed in eastern valley communities and at exhibitions. Both Peters and Lorenzetto have won first prizes throughout Canada for goat-wool blankets, cotton rugs, and baskets. In 1967, Mary Peters was commissioned to weave a 225-square foot tapestry for Montreal's Hotel Bonaventure. The two artisans also provided displays at Expo '67. International recognition of their work has ensued.

Oliver Wells represented the third generation of a family which had closely interacted with the Stalo natives for over a century. Allan Fotheringham, who grew up in Sardis, wrote a eulogy upon Wells's death in 1970, stating that Canada's 1967 Centennial was really all about men like Oliver of Edenbank:

> "...A man who loved the land and lived on it and nourished it in the tradition of his father and his father's father who founded Edenbank Farm in 1867; a man who worked quietly and raised a fine family and served his community and whose influence spread in ripples...He became a respected naturalist, anthropologist, artist, and writer... Decades before the word 'ecology' became fashionable, Oliver Wells was devoting a prime section of his land to his famous sanctuary as a refuge for birds. He knew instinctively

what the editorial writers and politicians have only now finally grasped: that a land that cannot support animals will not long support Man. He was a truly educated person who realized that Man must—first of all—be at peace with his surroundings...."

The struggle to reconcile man to his valley was destined to become the premier challenge for planners, politicians, and residents in the years ahead.

CHAPTER SEVENTEEN

WHITHER A VALLEY

On a cold clear Halloween night in 1978, a tired David Morgan drove his cattle truck the last few miles along the freeway, turning off at the 232nd Street Langley exit. It had been a long haul down the Fraser Canyon from Kamloops, and he was anxious to unload the seventy-seven feeder calves bawling behind him.

At about 10:30 P.M. Morgan approached the Deacon farm and slowed his vehicle. Then in the shadows he saw figures milling about.

An angry mob of ten men and women obstructed the Deacon driveway. There was some shouting, and several people gestured at Morgan to move his truck away. John Deacon stood with his hands on his hips, confronting the crowd. These were his neighbours. Unlike him, most of these men and women only hobby farmed and worked in the city. They objected to his feedlot operation, claiming it to be dirty, smelly, and noisy. Most of all, they objected to cattle trucks coming and going at all hours of the night along their quaint country road.

While the crowd argued with and shouted at John Deacon, Morgan sat in his truck at the roadside. Then the Royal Canadian Mounted Police arrived, as did the Langley bylaw enforcement officer.

After hearing the complaints of the neighbours, the police officer scratched his head and consulted with the bylaw officer, who finally "ruled" that Langley's noise bylaw was violated by the late night cattle truck activity. He ordered Morgan to drive away and return to the farm in the morning. Morgan duly drove off, sleepy-eyed while the crowd dispersed in joyous spirit. Deacon stood staring after they had all left, uncomprehending. The bylaw officer later wrote a report describing him as "an angry farmer."

Meanwhile, Morgan parked his truck for the night at an Abbotsford strip mall, and returned to the Deacon farm in the morning to off-load the calves. A few days later, Dr. Albert Anderson attended the calves and found sixty of them to be suffering from shipping fever. Nine calves died, and most of the remainder contracted pneumonia and were sold at a discount. Deacon sued the obstructing neighbours in Supreme Court and lost. His counsel, Donald Nundal, had difficulty making all of his submissions before an extremely hostile judge. The judge even took Nundal into his private chambers and told him he was not impressed with the case, and that the lawyer "had a monkey for a client." Deacon appealed.

The British Columbia Court of Appeal disagreed with the trial judge and allowed the farmer's appeal on the basis that the obstructing neighbours had unlawfully prevented the calves from being unloaded and further, that the bylaw officer possessed no authority to send away the truck. The noise bylaw, moreover, did not apply to bona fide farmers working in an agricultural zone. John Deacon was awarded damages from his neighbours.

The Deacon case illustrated the degree to which the Fraser Valley had changed from a rural bread basket to a suburban garden. In fact, the Agriculture Protection Act of 1989 provides a ninety-day notice period for any person seeking to sue a farmer in nuisance respecting his agricultural operation. The Act also affords the farmer a complete defence to such action if he is operating within the by-laws and in a manner "in accordance with generally accepted farming practice...."

Downtown Abbotsford, early 1980s, looking west. Clearbrook in Matsqui and Abbotsford have become one large commercial unit, despite being governed by separate municipal councils as of 1992.

The vast majority of valley residents had arrived since 1948, and few of them were farmers. Many of the newcomers objected to the multitude of barnyard aromas permeating the air, with pig farms becoming a prime target for attack. In Matsqui, urban dwellers in Clearbrook protested against the smell and dust emanating from new and larger poultry barns. But although the size of farm buildings was increasing, the size and number of working farms was shrinking.

Alarm bells were now ringing; politicians sensed a real threat to both agriculture and the rural fabric of the province. Green belts gained favour. Delta's member of the Legislature, Bob Wenman, unsuccessfully proposed a private member's bill in 1971 to dedicate belts of farmland in perpetuity. Then Dave Barrett and the New Democratic Party were elected in 1972. Bill 42 was quickly introduced to freeze all agricultural land so designated by the new B.C. Land Commission, the administrative body charged with the enforcement of the legislation.

The Fraser Valley exploded. Fiery meetings were held in every district. "Dictatorship" and "Communism" epithets were hurled from the lips of speculators and community leaders alike. Langley and other municipalities openly defied the government by ignoring its changed assessment orders, which entailed sharply increased taxes upon hobby farms and bushland, exclusive of a house and "garden lot." (Presumably the NDP believed that any spare acres not being intensively farmed represented a country estate owned by some wealthy landowner.)

Writer Paul St. Pierre agreed with the objectives of the Land Commission Act, but was concerned with the awesome powers of the commission, writing: "The bureaucracy, if firmly based, well financed, well entrenched, well-led and vigorous, will in time reach a position of independence from the democratic process which will enable it to win any challenge."

The Vancouver *Province* railed: "The government's farm plan reads like George Orwell's Animal Farm. As democracy, it's a scandal. It must be fought. By everyone. With all the strength society can muster."

Agriculture Minister Dave Stupich asserted that the Land Commission Act was the most far-reaching legislation in Canada with respect to the control and preservation of farmland. He explained that the government was becoming involved in the total land use planning of the province in part because of the lack of coordinated planning by municipal authorities.

Mass protest meetings continued to be held, however, and when government members did show up, they were frequently booed off the stage. Ironically, most municipal councils in tandem with regional districts were moving towards land freeze bylaws similar to the zones established by the Land Commission.

When Social Credit was returned to power in 1975, the new government failed to repeal the land legislation it had so caustically denounced. It did, however legislate amendments to the Act in order to render the Agricultural Land Reserve more palatable. The most important of these was the provision of an appeal mechanism to a committee of cabinet by the affected landowner. In time, sizable portions of land would be removed from the land reserve on the basis of marginal soil fertility classifications.

In 1971, George Spetifore declared that farming was finished in Delta, due to marketing problems and lack of public interest in agriculture. Spetifore was the largest grower in the valley, cultivating seven hundred acres of vegetables.

Another Delta resident was equally frustrated. Chung Chuck had worked hard over the years; now his potato patch was surrounded by subdivision development, and pressures mounted for him to sell out. Although Chung no longer challenged the Potato Marketing Board, he still spent money freely on law books and lawyers. He was estimated to have appeared in court some eight hundred times in his life, and was sent to jail on about forty occasions.

Chung Chuck drove trespassers off his land by rushing at them with a meat cleaver. On his front door he mounted a sign which read: "U MONKEE ME TOO MUCH, BAD LUCK + ACT CRIMINAL AGAIN FOR YOU." His last major battle came in 1977. Chung allowed thirteen houseboats to moor adjacent to a plot of waterfront land he owned on the Fraser, for which he charged rent. Delta Council regarded these floating homes as a slum. But what most perturbed aldermen was that Chung refused to sign a land use contract which would facilitate the exacting of taxes by Delta. So one day, Delta municipal engineers were dispatched to shut off the water supply to the houseboats.

Chung Chuck brooked no trespassers, official or otherwise; and he certainly was not going to allow a bunch of bureaucrats to interfere with his tenants' water supply. When the engineers arrived, he grabbed his shotgun and stood in his potato patch in his overalls and suspenders. The police soon appeared on the scene, then the media, to watch this white-haired old Chinese farmer fighting against officialdom, standing alone in his field under a hot summer sun. The impasse lasted until the arrival of Chung's lawyer, Allan Thackray. Chung finally put away his gun, and police, reporters, and engineers went home.

Chung was charged with "having a lethal weapon with intent to endanger the public peace." He appeared for the trial dressed in his finest, a creased suede jacket with red plaid shirt and tie. Some of his houseboat tenants showed up, too, wearing jeans with tee shirts embossed with "Chung Chuck, Potato Grower." (The judge ordered the shirts covered up.) The trial was before a jury and lasted twelve hours.

The prosecution suffered from the problem that police had been unable to find Chung's shotgun to tender in evidence. The jury deliberated over three hours and then returned a verdict of "not guilty." Chung shrugged, grinned, and sauntered out of the courtroom. Chung Chuck's life was recorded in a documentary filmed by the Canadian Broadcasting Corporation in 1985. He died in 1986 at the age of eighty-eight.

Defiance of marketing boards by stubborn farmers continues to this day. Most such rebels have been as unsuccessful as Chung Chuck. Cloverdale vegetable grower Jim Gardiner refused to raise his prices to the consumer as required by minimum price regulations of the B.C. Vegetable Marketing Commission. Grant Tocher of Glen Valley challenged the dairy quota system and lost his battle in all courts. Surrey chicken farmer Christine Delight defied the Egg Marketing Board by refusing to register and obtain a quota license for her 2,400 birds, since she could not afford the one hundred thousand-dollar price tag for such a purchase. Mrs. Delight acceded to the board's edicts in early 1990 by selling 2,100 of her chickens to her key urban customers - still keeping the birds in her own farm coops. The Egg Marketing Board decided that this was just a ploy and issued a seizure order against the birds. In 1992, the BC Court of Appeal ruled in Christine's favour and overruled the Board.

Sixty-three year old Arjen Pellikaan of Chilliwack has battled the milk board for nearly twenty years. Pellikaan produces ethnic products such as paneer, a soft cheese very popular in the East Indian community; but because he makes the food with unpasteurized milk, the dairy board obtained an injunction against him in 1990, even though supermarkets sell unpasteurized cheese made outside British Columbia. Pelikaan says the government's real motive in persecuting him is to protect the dairy cartel and the British Columbia oligopoly of Dairyland and other huge producers.

Vancouver grocer Ishwalal Patel is furious about the board's attack on Pelikaan, stating that the governments of Manitoba and Ontario have given grants to farmers to develop paneer and other ethnic products. "People like him," says Patel, "should get credit - instead they try to push him down."

The creation of the Agricultural Land Reserve failed to halt the surge of speculation in Fraser Valley real estate. Both legitimate developers and shady promoters rushed to buy and sell land which held potential for subdivision, based upon long-term regional plans which anticipated the controlled expansion of towns. Many prominent figures got into the development business, such as Delta's Tom Goode, only to face financial ruin when the market soured, or attempts to remove land from the land reserve failed.

In Aldergrove, high rolling financier Richard Cavolo blew onto the scene in the mid-seventies and set up a ranch, where he boarded horses for Hollywood movie stars. He also began investing heavily in British Columbia real estate. Cavolo was a former banker who produced a phoney balance sheet for his newfound Canadian bank, which supplied him with a large line of credit. He kited mortgages, borrowed money from elderly women on insufficient security, and even talked National Hockey League stars into investing in a Mount Baker condominium complex that never materialized. Such was Cavolo's magnetism and charm that on the day he was convicted of fraud, some of the very women whom he had bilked wept and clung to him as he was led away to jail.

The scruffier side of the land development business in the late seventies centred upon rapidly growing Surrey. Colourful Walter Link lived on a posh estate

Steveston, 1965.
Since this photo was taken the working riverfront has lost much of its character to urban sprawl.

overlooking the Hazelmere Valley. Link was a master at turning any land transaction into a confused labyrinth of options, mortgages, and side agreements. Eventually nailed for tax evasion and fraud, Link served fourteen months in prison and emerged wearing his black cowboy boots and dark shades, a chastened man who still pursued business deals zealously, albeit more discreetly.

Link possessed a certain amount of class that impressed even the police. At one of his last court appearances before parole, Link walked over to the investigator who had slaved for two years accumulating the evidence to convict him, and shook his hand heartily.

A reporter at the scene noted, "There goes Walter Link into the sunset," to which a police officer replied, "Yeah, but just look at that guy. After all he's been through, he's still got a lot of razzle dazzle left in him."

Ed McKitka was a brilliant, mercurial politician who became a folk hero in Surrey, where he served as mayor. His loquaciousness extended to feeding confidential information about land development to friends, such as Walter Link. Ever outspoken, McKitka was always surrounded by a swirl of controversy, as he shot from the hip on all issues, defending himself as "a man of the people" up against the Establishment. Wire-tapped conversations served, however, to convict him of several breach of trust charges.

Under the relentless cross-examination of able prosecutor John Hall, McKitka spluttered and stammered and rambled on nonsensically. Even as he was led off to jail, the former mayor protested that he had always acted in Surrey's best interests. Hundreds of Surrey voters wrote letters of support for McKitka, causing one former Surrey alderman to shrug and note: "Everyone loves a rogue."

By 1990, the population of the Fraser Valley exceeded 750,000 people. Municipalities struggled to balance the pressure for growth against agricultural and environmental concerns. A few municipalities joined the Greater Vancouver Regional District, which had been taking an increasing interest in the valley. The regional district's 1980 plan for the Lower Mainland called for "A metropolitan area and five Valley towns and other urban areas linked by efficient transportation

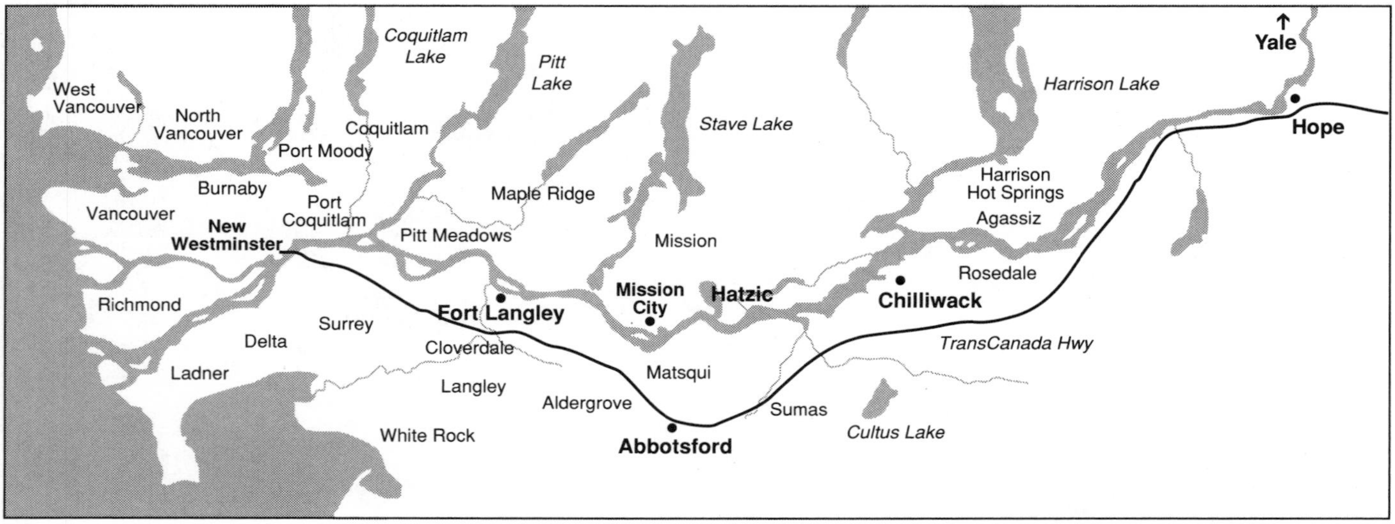

facilities and surrounded by productive farmland, stable rural areas, and protected environmentally sensitive and recreational areas."

The five key towns envisioned by the regional district were Langley, Haney, Mission, Abbotsford-Clearbrook, and Chilliwack. Surrey, Delta, and Richmond, all viewed as chiefly metropolitan areas. Eastern valley municipalities have resisted joining the regional district, however, fearing the loss of rural identity; and in 1991 Richmond Council declared that the district would henceforth be known as the "City of Richmond."

Municipalities have wrestled with escalating financial problems as they cope with residential housing and ancillary services. In the seventies, many councils levied impost fees upon developers to cover the cost of roads, water, sewer, parks, and schools required by subdivisions. One small developer, George Foster of Langley, challenged the council's right to extract the fees from his company. The British Columbia Court of Appeal determined that the Langley impost fee bylaw was *ultra vires*—beyond the scope of the municipality's authority—but refused to order the fees returned to Foster. The Municipal Act was amended a few years later to provide for a system of development cost charges based upon a more rational relationship between the type of subdivision created and the actual services necessitated, but it is still an imperfect system. As with farming, the business of land development has become primarily the business of large moneyed players.

The fears of Chung Chuck respecting property rights have largely been realized. One consequence of the Foster case was a reaffirmation of the fact that landowners possess no inherent right to subdivide their property. Property use, moreover, may be circumscribed by zoning bylaws. The tremendous powers granted to planning departments has made the chief planner in each district a czar within his or her domain. From golf courses to drag strips, when planners make their recommendations to council in regard to rezoning applications, they are free to exercise their personal opinions and tastes as to whether the enterprise will enhance the neighbourhood, or even private doubts about the economic viability of the proposed business.

Hatzic Lake, Coast Mountains in background.

Much controversy occurs over the issue of soil fertility, the classification of which affects the removal of land from the Agricultural Land Reserve. The most vivid example of this issue was the furor over the Gloucester Estates Industrial Park proposed for Langley, where 634 acres of land sat for ten years after the 1976 application of the owner for land reserve exclusion. Council, bureaucrats, residents and owner engaged in a vitriolic debate before the green light for the park was finally given. Gloucester soil is not the most fertile in the valley; yet the argument remains that one can always grow forage crops on any well-drained land.

Another burdensome issue is non-conforming land use in the valley.

Thousands of cottage industries, from machine shops to craft centres, are conducted illegally from homes and farms. There are so many of them, in fact, that bylaw enforcement officers usually only seek injunctions against such uses if neighbours complain. Such businesses are distinguished in law from those legally non-conforming uses which pre-dated the zoning bylaw and have been continued over the years without interruption.

The improved industrial and commercial tax base enjoyed by valley municipalities has provided funds for urban renewal in towns which were becoming downright shabby from decades of neglect. Attractive landscaping, new façades, awnings, and red paving stones have been added to most main streets. Downtown Ladner has been tastefully restored in heritage mode, as has Cloverdale.

Perhaps the greatest scale of downtown revitalization, however, has occurred in New Westminster, where the dirty waterfront has been transformed into a delightful 16.2 hectare mosaic of shops, condominiums, promenade, and modern public market with clock tower.

The Westminster Quay Public Market opened on July 19, 1986, to the strains of marching bands and the whistles of boats and trains, all reminiscent of a scene from the 1939 royal visit. The quay boasts seventy thousand square feet of space

Aerial view of modernized New Westminster Quay, with both Pattullo and Skytrain bridges beyond, 1991.

and portends a renaissance of the Royal City. An estimated $200 million of direct investment has been generated by the quay; from the promenade one can stroll along the Fraser's shore, visit the S.S. Sampson museum, and watch the boats go by, as the fishermen set their nets as they have done here for generations. Inside the market are numerous craft shops, restaurants, fashion boutiques, and fresh produce and fish stalls. There is a festival-like atmosphere which residents claim far outstrips Vancouver's Granville Island Market. (Yes, the old rivalry between the two cities continues.)

The excitement of the old interurban railway was revisited in 1986, when Skytrain established a terminal near Westminster Quay to connect the downtown cores of Vancouver and New Westminster. Vancouver residents have rediscovered the Royal City as a city of surprises, resembling San Francisco in many ways, with its steep hills, a beautiful setting, and a history steeped in tradition and colour. Gone are many of the slummy crumbling buildings which used to litter the waterfront; some older structures have been sandblasted and given a heritage veneer. "Columbia Street presents a schizophrenic array of stylish façades," states Vancouver *Sun* writer Robin Ward, "and none [sic] are the same. Individualism and Edwardian confidence are celebrated here." Skytrain now connects to Surrey and there is talk of New Westminster once again becoming the hub of the valley.

Much of the success in restoring the Royal City is attributable to former City Curator Archie Miller, who has worked indefatigably to preserve and enhance New Westminster as a heritage centre, as well as a modern city. In 1982, Miller assisted in the production of a television programme, setting forth the goals of city council: a new bridge to Annacis Island, a Skytrain terminus, a college, a new courthouse, and tasteful homes on the hillside where the British Columbia Penitentiary once stood. Many of these goals were realized within five years, and at this writing all of them, and more, are either accomplished or within grasp.

By the late seventies, both Vancouver and New Westminster required expanded courthouse facilities. When the old Vancouver courthouse closed in August 1979, some of its elegant Victorian furnishings were discarded as being unsuitable for the ultra modern concrete structure erected down the street.

County Court Judge Stewart McMorran of New Westminster astutely obtained permission from Chief Justice Nathan Nemetz to rescue "a few furnishings" for use in the new Royal City courthouse. Interpreting the Chief Justice's consent very broadly—and anxious to preserve the furnishings before they were purloined by some other party—in the dead of night, Judge McMorran and his raiding party pulled up in a large van to the back entrance of the Vancouver building, and proceeded to remove hand-carved oak tables, fine high-backed chairs, maroon drapes, and other items dating from the 1900s.

Thanks to the judge's rescue mission and his painstaking efforts in supervising construction of the new facility at Begbie Square, we are left with a tasteful heritage style courthouse which engenders respect and dignity for the judicial process. Mr. Justice McMorran now sits as a Supreme Court judge. His Lordship's efforts also extended to rescuing much of the ornate oak panelling from the old New Westminster courthouse, a building now itself restored.

The evolution of the Fraser Port authority has played an important role in the development and destiny of the Fraser Valley. Resisting attempts by successive governments to place New Westminster under the jurisdiction of the National Harbours Board, the New Westminster Harbours Commission demanded local control. By 1961, some 50 percent of the Fraser's trade was with Asian countries, and lumber exports remained an important factor in the local economy.

In order to broaden its base to achieve autonomy, Commission members met with representatives of lower Fraser Valley districts in 1965 and formed the Fraser River Harbours Commission, serving communities from Langley and Haney to the sea. The commission assumed jurisdiction over the river channel and foreshores in Maple Ridge, Pitt Meadows, part of Langley, Coquitlam, Fraser Mills, Port Coquitlam, Surrey, New Westminster, Delta, and Richmond.

The new Commission has played a vital role in ensuring that shipping, environmental, industrial, and recreational needs are kept in a careful balance. Commissioners have combatted silting, listened to Delta residents complaining of wash from freighters, and found ways to contain the smoke which sometimes belches from vessels in port. The port authority administers six hundred water lot leases and licences ranging from marina use to log boom storage. It even collects rent from fishermen's docks, which is often paid grudgingly. More than once, in fact, fishermen have paid by dumping sacks of fish at the commission's office.

A major function of the Harbours Commission is to control river pollution. Before 1970, the Fraser was clogged with wood waste and debris; offal from a meat-packing plant poured into the water via Brunette Creek; garbage was thrown into the Fraser by residents. At least cosmetically, the river clean-up since 1970 has been wondrous. Most of the dumping practices have been stopped, and by the close of the eighties, the Commission could boast of a 90 percent reduction in wood waste on the river, thanks in part to the new boom bundling policies of the forest industry.

The Commission attempts to deal with polluters using a low-key approach, a policy which occasionally boomerangs. When one woman was caught hurtling her garbage into the river one day at Langley, she interpreted the patrol boat captain's mild scolding as an offer to store her waste; she proceeded to bombard Commission headquarters with telephone messages advising that her garbage bags were ready for pick-up.

When the Roberts Bank superport was built in the early seventies, the Harbours Commission adapted to the changing needs of world trade and approved the development of Annacis Island as a port facility. Dune buggy enthusiasts lost their sea of sand, as part of the island was converted into shipping yards and holding areas. Japanese auto makers were interested in acquiring storage space at the new site, and by 1977, 120 acres of land were occupied by Annacis Auto Terminals. Soon enormous freighters were docking at Fraser Annacis. Similar deep-sea facilities were installed at the Fraser Surrey docks, managed by Johnston Terminals. Fraser Port facilities handle in excess of 5 million tons of cargo per year in the main arm of the Fraser, and a further 12 to 15 million tons of coastal shipping in the shallower North Arm, the latter chiefly wood products. More than 1,500 fishboats and 3,000 pleasure craft compete with log booms, tugs, barges, and scows for moorage on the river.

The Roberts Bank superport.

In 1977, the Fraser Port Authority encountered environmental trouble in Richmond. The Commission allowed a portion of three hundred acres it owned in the municipality to be used by Richmond as a landfill. But substances deleterious to fish were being dumped at the site, and Environment Canada ordered the landfill to be closed. Richmond desperately wrestled with the problem and even released a million worms to gorge on the garbage. Charges of damaging the Fraser fish habitat were laid, however, to which the Commission ultimately pleaded guilty.

But the problems of the landfill remain. Coyotes proliferate in pursuit of rats, and all manner of garbage continues to be dumped—one day, officials found ten thousand new Italian women's shoes for the left foot. (The corresponding ten thousand right foot shoes were discovered at another dump.)

One of the more unusual problems along the Fraser in the modern era has been the increasing number of floating homes. Many houseboat owners were former squatters who failed to obtain permission from the commission or private foreshore owners to moor their boats at river's edge. Local councils wrestle with complaints from nearby residents about sanitation, as sewage is frequently dumped directly into the Fraser.

At Grant's Landing, in Langley, home to twenty-six houseboats, council agreed in 1990 to allow expansion to forty homes, provided sewage was first treated before being dumped. Monty Grant, feisty owner of the foreshore rights, defends the collection of colourful boats with the comment: "One person's shanty is another man's palace."

Although river clean-up is visibly improving with respect to surface debris, the pollution of the Fraser's waters continues apace. The Fraser River Estuary Management Program, or FREMP, resulted from a 1981 estuary study which rang alarm bells of concern for the future of fish, waterfowl, and recreation. Bruce Hutchison noted with despair that in less than two centuries since Simon Fraser had made his famous journey, the white man's civilization "threatens to derange the river's infinitely complex life and a social organism far older than his own."

The Fraser River Coalition, a citizen's group, was formed as an umbrella organization for various environmental groups, and it induced the provincial government to create a Fraser River Task Force. As a result of the task force's investigation, some fifty-one pollution charges were laid against property users - more charges than in all of the previous decade. The task force reported that among the toxic substances being dumped into the river were creosote, glue, alcohol, iron, zinc, lead, copper, arsenic, and ammonia.

Less than 7,000 acres of an estimated 45,000 acres of marshy wetlands remain intact in the Fraser Valley. The key marshes are at Sturgeon Bank, Mud and Boundary Bays, the lowlands of the Nicomekl River, and the numerous islands located at the mouth of the Fraser. Rich nutrients form in the delta river area particularly, resulting from the ebb and flow of the ocean tide, the oxygen supply, and speedy photosynthesis. Crabs, herring, and eighty-six species of fish spend part of their lives in the estuary, and in spring, 300 million salmon fry travel downriver to feed in the shallow depths before migrating out to sea. Up to 10,000,000 of these fry return to the river to spawn.

As well, huge numbers of waterfowl—200,000 ducks and 20,000 snow geese alone—winter in the estuary; a million others visit while migrating; and thousands of other birds, including hawks, eagles, gulls, herons and sandhill cranes reside year-round in the valley's marshy havens.

Two key waterfowl refuges exist in the Fraser Valley: the Reifel Sanctuary, and the Pitt Polder Green Belt and Wildlife Management Area, located just south of Pitt Lake.

The Fraser estuary is threatened by a host of enemies: sewage treatment plants; accidental chemical spills; waste from over one hundred industries; overflowing storm sewers; and the dumping of dredged silt, mud, and waste onto wetlands. Over a billion litres of waste reaches the Fraser each day and fecal coliform counts render the estuary unfit for swimming. Shellfish contamination is common. Industrial expansion, such as at Roberts Bank and Vancouver International Airport, has contributed to the erosion of wetland areas.

The recent battle over the Terra Nova lands indicates an increased level of concern for wetlands encroachment on the part of valley residents. The site itself consists of 330 acres in Richmond's northwest corner, bounded by the Fraser River and Sturgeon Bank; 220 of these acres were rezoned in the 1980s for a 413-unit residential housing development.

What created a boil of controversy was the fact that the lands were not only a refuge for wildfowl, but formerly the site of farms which earned British Empire awards for the quality of their wheat and cattle. The owner, Milan Ilich, was brother-in-law of former Richmond Advisory Planning Commission Chair Olga Ilich, and had contributed to Premier Vander Zalm's leadership campaign. The Land Commission denied the Ilich application to remove the lands from the Agricultural

Land Reserve, but the Cabinet's Land Use Committee allowed the Ilich appeal. Richmond Council then voted for the development to proceed. Subsequent court challenges, based upon allegations of bias on the part of a councillor, were unsuccessful.

In Delta, a controversy similar to the Terra Nova dispute has brewed since 1981, involving 520 acres of the old Spetifore farm. These lands were removed from the land reserve, again by cabinet order, upon appeal of a refusal of the application by the Land Commission. Moreover, George Spetifore also happened to be a Social Credit fund raiser.

Whatever the merits of the lands for farming—and they would appear to be considerable - one cannot help but be cynical about a political process which overrides both the Land Commission and public hearings. As Alderman Steeves stated, "It's not just the leftover eco-freaks from the 1960s who are involved in this fight. You look at the people who are fighting Terra Nova and you see the middle-class is saying 'we need open space and farmland to make this the kind of community where we want to live.'"

A wide variety of community groups are rallying in the Fraser Valley to protect their quality of life. Pitt Polder and Langley residents fought Greater Vancouver Regional District plans to establish a huge garbage dump in one of the two regions —so Cache Creek became the ultimate recipient. B.C. Hydro has thus far been thwarted in its attempts to build another major transmission line corridor south of the Fraser.

Most recently, petroleum companies have been stalled in their plans to establish vast underground storage facilities for natural gas in the valley—although the David Anderson Commission of Inquiry recommended that drilling and well production proceed. Several Fort Langley residents even took to the streets in 1990 and formed a human barricade to block gravel trucks loaded with aggregate for nearby subdivisions from pounding incessantly through village streets.

Regional parks have fared well, although one cannot safely cycle or jog on valley roads other than a few dykes here and there—there are no really quiet rural roads anymore. Municipal councils seem unable to get together to create even one jogging and cycling trail that crosses district boundaries.

Major parks such as Cultus and Alouette Lakes are seriously overcrowded, and in the wonderful mountain region north of the Fraser, recreational activity is limited to skiing at Hemlock Valley, hiking, and boating on a few restricted lakes, some of them dangerously littered with deadheads. Most of this mountain region is the preserve of large forestry companies and the Crown; and one soon discovers that the Crown encourages people to poke around near their many prison camps in the area about as much as McMillan Bloedel welcomes tree-huggers.

Somehow the immense flushing capacity of the Fraser rids the river of enough pollutants to allow the fishery to survive. Hatcheries, such as Chehalis River, produce salmon and trout fingerlings to bolster Nature's supply and combat attrition. As they have since the 1870s, fishermen complain of closures, Yankee overfishing, and bureaucracy.

But traditions die hard. Every April, Mike Waska of Fort Langley still weighs anchor to fish for the oolichan. He states, "I've never known there not to be fish in this part of the river on April 28." Invariably, he and other fishermen of the Fraser scoop up bulging nets with thousands of squirming oolichan during the week of the 28th, selling much of the catch to customers locally.

The dismantling of the British Columbia Penitentiary was hastened by the terrible 1975 riot in which hostage Mary Steinhauser was killed. Although many prisoners were dispersed to points east of the province, maximum security institutions at Mission and Matsqui received a fair share of the transfer quota. At Matsqui Institution, an eighteen hour riot in 1981 left a pile of charred, smoking debris after inmates burned down several buildings.

Valley residents continue to be apprehensive over the proliferation of prisons around them, with neither provincial or federal officials responding to appeals for relocation of the institutions to remote areas. Meanwhile, prison authorities have found ways to turn the habitat to their advantage. A 1990 hunger strike at an Agassiz prison ended abruptly after guards opened cell windows, letting in swarms of ravenous mosquitoes.

Coquitlam politicians and residents remain concerned about escapees from Riverview's maximum security unit, although most who flee are from other holding areas, and are less a threat to society than to themselves. By 1988, the number of patients detained at Riverview had decreased to about one thousand, as the chronically ill were sent to other institutions.

In 1991, a new policy of dispersal of harmless mentally ill patients into the community was well under way. Dr. John Higenbottam, a Douglas College psychology instructor, who studied the community dispersal potential for Riverview, noted that "Studies have shown that the major reason why mental patients break down is because there's nothing for them to do...We will have to make people understand that they are not exposing themselves to danger if there's somebody mentally ill living near them."

Amidst the onslaught of urbanism, pollution, and dwindling green space, valley residents manage to carry on certain traditions and to retain identity. Characters still abound, many of them rugged individualists who do not hesitate to tackle powerful Establishment forces. When First City Capital Corporation evicted Denis Almas from his King Neptune Restaurant on the New Westminster waterfront, preparatory to demolishing the building, the stubborn Almas barged his restaurant downriver to a dock on the Fraser's North Arm—with the side of his barge sporting a "Going Fishing" sign. He later reopened near his old location.

The growth of private contracting businesses in British Columbia has been strongly influenced by the activities of the non-union Rempel and Kerkhoff company groups, based in Abbotsford and Chilliwack respectively. Founding contractors Ewald Rempel and the Kerkhoff brothers are castigated by union bosses and academics, but these men are colourful, controversial men of principle, who contribute generously to their communities.

Thousands of other smaller contractors live in the valley, and may be described as less anti-union than pro-independence—men and women who are equally suspicious of big government and unions. From their "Dallas"-like family compound in Langley, the flamboyant Vandekerkhove family plan the next stages of expansion of their Super-Save gas station chain, including the occasional price war to keep the big gas companies on their toes.

On Barnston Island, a character of a different kind made life hot over the years for the ferry operators who ply the monotonous route back and forth to the Surrey mainland all day. In 1969, an ornery island dairy farmer drove his truck over the ferry ramp so that the front wheels were on the ramp and the rear wheels were on the ferry; then he shut off his engine, locked his doors, and sat inside, glaring. All attempts to move him failed.

Schoolchildren had to be transported to their island homes by fishboat. Finally, near midnight, the farmer moved onto the ferry. When he repeated his actions on July 16, he was charged, convicted and fined for obstruction. It transpired that the farmer was angry because the ferry workers - who received no lunch break—took two twenty minute coffee breaks!

In 1981, ferry workers staged a one day strike following the shotgun threats of the same Barnston Island rogue who, they claimed, had harassed them and their predecessors for twenty years.

The "Bible Belt" tradition of the eastern Fraser Valley is reflected in social issues, such as the banning of striptease shows in Abbotsford, and opposition to Sunday shopping. When businessman Ralph Jacobson sought an FM radio licence from the Canadian Radio-television and Telecommunications Commission in 1982 for his "Christian Canadian Family Radio Station," he was enthusiastically supported by Conservative members of Parliament Bob Wenman and Benno Friesen.

Trinity Western University is a private institution with full degree granting status.

The Commission refused Jacobson's bid on the basis that his station would cater unduly to mainstream Christian denominations without sufficient regard for other religious traditions. Friesen was bitter, stating, "I think we should recognize as a fact of life that there is a bias against religious broadcasting."

The one issue which has galvanized many valley residents is abortion. Nowhere in the province is the "pro-life" movement stronger than in South Surrey, Langley, Matsqui, Abbotsford, and Chilliwack. Each year, mass hospital society meetings are held in these and, of course, other communities, where the two opposing forces on the abortion issue do battle. Thus far, the "pro-lifers" have dominated hospital boards.

Trinity Western University has evolved as a prominent, uniquely Fraser Valley educational institution which stresses leadership, excellence, and Christian ethics. In

1979, Trinity Western College was granted full four-year programme degree-granting powers, and in 1985, the legislature approved the official name change to "University." Unfairly accused of being merely a "bible college" by some, Trinity Western is, in fact, the only truly private university in British Columbia.

The quality of education in the Fraser Valley has improved steadily at post-secondary levels. Fraser Valley College boasts two major campuses—at Abbotsford and Chilliwack—and integrates hundreds of its courses with the community at large. Kwantlen College serves the central and western valley, and has recently opened a beautiful new Surrey campus.

Plans are afoot for another major university, and Asian interests have purchased a large parcel of land near Aldergrove for a university which would cater specifically to students from South Korea. Clogged freeways and high city rents encourage students to look closer to home for post-secondary education. Indeed, planners from the Greater Vancouver Regional District talk of the centre of the Vancouver metropolitan area moving outward to Surrey by the first decade of the twenty-first century.

The Abbotsford Air Show is an annual world class event.

The spectacular Abbotsford Air Show held every August has become an international event. In 1989, 123,500 people squeezed into the airport by 11:00 a.m. for the Saturday show, with some 60,000 people turned away. Growing participation in the show by Eastern Bloc nations has drawn spectators to view such exotica as Soviet MiG fighters and the world's largest aircraft, the AN 255 transport plane. Airshow Canada executives Patrick Reid, Ron Price, and Al Hurtubise have exerted stupendous efforts to ensure the continued success and reputation of the annual event as the finest of its kind in North America.

There persists an ongoing tradition of informality in valley life. At Chilliwack's Royal Hotel, a sign greeted guests for many years:

> "Boots and spurs must be removed at night before retiring. Every known fluid (except water) for sale at the bar. Towels changed weekly. Insect powder for sale at the desk. All guests are requested to rise at 6 a.m. The sheets are needed for tablecloths.
>
> The Management."

The spittoons are gone from the old country stores, but then again so are most of the stores themselves. But neighbours still lean over fences to chat; clients walk into lawyers' offices without appointments; sand castles are built at White Rock Beach; while Ken Passmore, the valley's premier auctioneer, still holds his antique auctions around and about, keeping the bidding going long and hard on both the $10 and the $1000 items.

Every Christmas, schoolchildren gather to sing carols inside the palisade at

The Abbotsford Air Show.

the old fort at Fort Langley; while at Hunter's Tree Farm in Mount Lehman, you can cut your own Christmas tree, sip hot chocolate with marshmallows, and walk on Winnie The Pooh story trails through the woods overlooking the Fraser.

Even the banks are decidedly informal. Pinstripe suits are rare; and once or twice a year you will find your banker dressed in jeans, cowboy boots, and sporting a Stetson in honour of the Cloverdale Rodeo or just good old "Country Days."

Credit Unions exemplify the valley spirit. Offering a wide range of services and a friendly atmosphere, credit unions have become major players on the financial scene. Surrey Metro Savings Credit Union boasts twelve branches in the valley and ranks as the second largest credit union in Canada. Van City Savings Credit Union ranks first in Canada, with Richmond Savings Credit Union third. A key element in the uniqueness of the credit union is the right of the members to cast their votes and elect a board of directors at the annual general meeting.

Approximately 3,500 Stalo Indians live in the Fraser Valley today. During the last ten years there has occurred a noticeable resurgence of pride within the native community. Indians successfully run many projects, such as the Coqualeetza Education Centre, schools on Seabird Island and Chehalis, and economic projects on reserves. At Kilgard, the local band operates Sumas Clay Products, a brick factory which it purchased in 1979. After initial reverses, the company is today showing a profit and selling its product throughout North America. Its bee-hived kilns even provided the paving tiles for many of the ALRT stations in the lower mainland.

In a large barn nestled beneath the southern slope of Sumas Mountain, the Kilgard band has also rediscovered some of its heritage. In 1980, the barn was converted to a long house and the 130 native villagers began performing the ancient spirit dance, partly in desperation over the terrible prevalence of alcoholism, crime, and drug abuse among them. Kilgard Elder Ray Silver attributes both the success of the brick company and the drastic decline in substance abuse to the "spiritual guidance of the long house."

The return of the spirit dance to the Fraser Valley has not been without controversy and cost. In 1978, Chief Coroner Glen McDonald investigated the death of Elliott Henry, a Chilliwack native, an alcoholic. Henry was seized by fellow natives one day and forced into long house initiation in the hope that his "soul would be purged."

Henry was blindfolded, fed only water and soup for several days, thrown naked into the icy Vedder River, and pummelled with rattles made of deer hooves. Unfortunately, Henry's body was too weakened by booze to survive these rites, and he died from dehydration. A coroner's jury of three whites and three natives was sensitive to remonstrances from the Indian community that spirit dancing not be condemned. The jury concluded that the death was due to misadventure and recommended a medical check-up for future initiates before the ceremony.

At Chehalis, as well, village elders attribute the decline of alcoholism—from 75 percent to 25 percent of the band population—to spirit dancing. The Chehalis Public School resembles an old cedar long house. Inside, displays of handwoven baskets, clothing made of bark, and deerskin drums greet the students in this all-native school. Over 130 students are taught both mainstream curriculum and traditional Stalo skills, such as weaving, dancing, singing, and the rudiments of the Halkomelem language.

Many Indian bands have obtained good leadership in managing reserves, a task which is no mean feat. "It's like a little municipality," noted Chief Carl Leon of the Katzie band, "You've got a lot of meetings to go to and negotiations to do."

Two of the earliest women chiefs to become active in the native rights movement were Genevieve Mussel, of the Chilliwack band, and Gertrude Guerin, of the Musqueam band. In recent years, in general, reserve society has fostered an increasing prominence of women in leadership roles.

The current nationwide agitation respecting Indian land claims has had little impact in the Fraser Valley. Young, educated Stalo natives have learned how Joseph Trutch and his cronies robbed valley reserves of the most fertile land after James Douglas retired; others protest Fraser fishery closures with vehemence.

But true to their ancestors, the Stalo have never been prone to resolving disputes in a warlike manner. Moreover, many bands have made prudent investments over the years and, if not in every case prospering, are becoming increasingly self-sufficient.

Greater pride and awareness on the part of the Stalo is reflected chiefly in all-Indian events. However, there is the odd cross-cultural bonding, such as the employment of Chief Joe Gabriel's nephew Milton as an historical interpreter at the Fort Langley National Historic Park. Milton says that his ancestors were "pretty crafty at trading; they had been trading among themselves for thousands of years before Europeans came here. They pretty much got what they wanted for the price they wanted...In the Hudson's Bay Journal they call us lazy, but they just didn't understand our way of life."

In 1984, St. Mary's Mission School and Residence closed its doors forever. In

1986, the provincial Crown granted title to the adjacent site of the old St. Mary's School to the Dewdney-Alouette Regional District for development of the Fraser River Heritage Park.

The park, when completed, will reflect the entire fabric of valley history and will consist of five heritage centres: an arts centre boasting a performing arts theatre, museum, and regional art gallery featuring artistic works of the early settlers; secondly, a Fraser River Study Centre, which will focus upon the life of the river, with replicas of river craft, salmon spawning channel, and dyking models, as well as a logger's museum; thirdly, a Stalo Cultural Centre, to be built on a terrace overlooking the Fraser, including a long house artifact display, pit-house replica, theatre, linguistic resource library, and native food garden; fourthly, early façades of Mission City buildings will be erected; and, finally, there will be an Oblate Interpretive Centre which will focus upon a full size reproduction of the famous grotto.

The discovery in 1991 of the Hatzic Rock, just a few miles to the east of Mission, has sparked a province wide interest in Stalo culture. Just as developer Harry Utzig prepared to bulldoze over his 2.8 hectare field for a housing development, local natives and archeologist Gordon Mohs discovered a huge Transformer rock on the site, around which they unearthed an ancient long house some five thousand years old, together with thousands of artifacts.

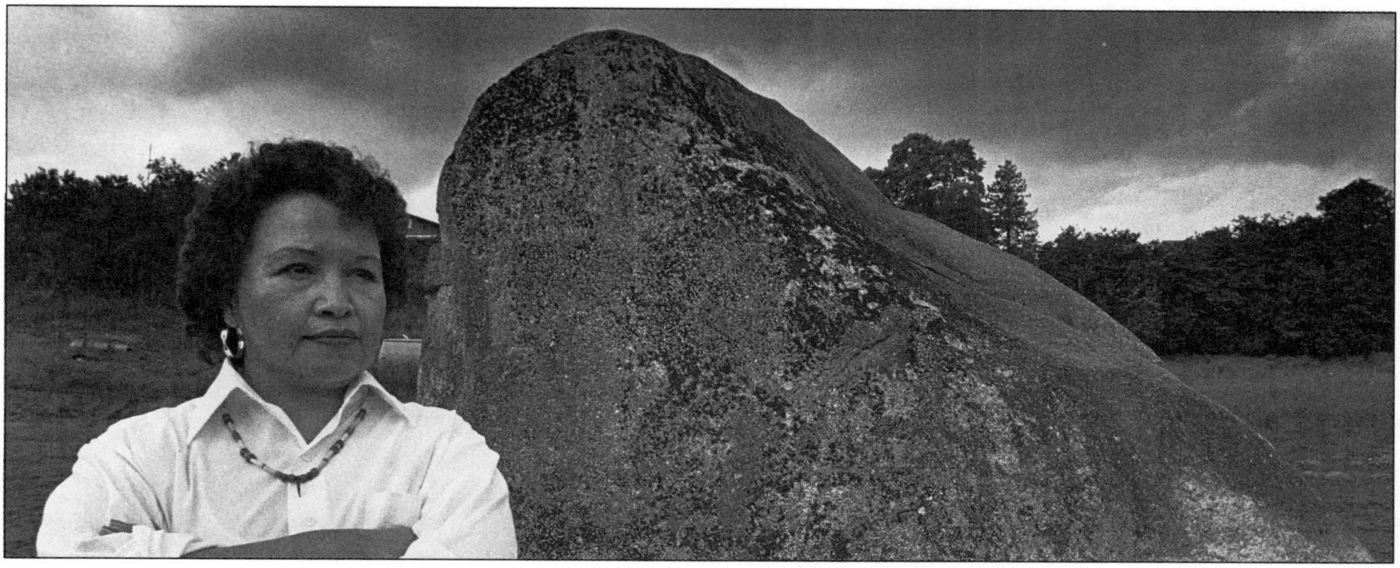

Linnea Battel poses beside the Hatzic Rock, site of one of the most important archaeological finds in North America. The battle to save the site still rages.

A second long house found at Hatzic Rock carbon dates back to 7000 B.C. The site is believed to be one of the oldest intact native villages representing long-term habitation to be unearthed in North America. As the news spread, thousands of curious visitors descended upon the Hatzic Rock, and it has had to be cordoned off to protect the excavations.

The Friends of the Hatzic Rock Society quickly formed, and thanks to intensive lobbying by numerous community groups, individuals, and Mission District, the provincial government designated Hatzic Rock as an historic site to temporarily stave off the bulldozers.

The tireless Linnea Battel has worked with Friends of the Fort, the Fraser River Heritage Park, and Hatzic Rock volunteers. She envisions a future tourist circuit which will introduce visitors to Indian culture at Hatzic Rock, followed by a boat trip down the Fraser to view Fort Langley and the impact of the fur trade on that culture.

Projects such as the Fraser River Heritage Park and the preservation of Hatzic Rock are the products of community efforts to portray the Fraser Valley's past in a colourful, vibrant, living demonstration of culture and history. Throughout the valley, dedicated volunteer groups are working toward similar goals.

Period-costumed dancers at the Fraser River Heritage Park in Mission.

The Fort Langley Legacy Foundation, chaired by the able David Radler, raises funds to assist with projects such as the acquisition of the Rudi Dangelmaier art collection, and reconstruction of buildings in the old fort. The Friends of the Fort functions as a volunteer association working to enhance the fort as a tourist destination, operating a gift shop on the park premises. In Steveston, the old Gulf Georgia Cannery is being restored by the federal government, again in cooperation with community volunteers. Similarly, the nearby Britannia Shipyard will eventually be displayed in circa-1900 working order for the public to enjoy.

The Heritage Conservation Act provides for the preservation of heritage sites and objects by cabinet order and municipal bylaw. Most preservation efforts have been spurred by private groups cajoling governments, and the struggle is difficult and exacting. Magnificent old trees are removed at the stroke of a planner's pen. Historic Edenbank Farm has disappeared beneath the concrete of a condominium housing development.

In 1990, Musqueam Indian leaders began a fight against a highrise on the site of an ancient Stalo village; the Marpole Midden, says anthropology professor Dr. Michael Kew, "is our only source of information about a significant period of our history. To destroy it would be a crime."

In Ladner, a group of residents unsuccessfully opposed the bulldozing of the historic William Ladner home—in a protest scene repeated constantly throughout the valley. Surrey District's mad rush toward urban sprawl has trampled under the remains of many ancient burial sites, and the historic Semiahmoo Trail has all but disappeared:

"Now the trail is lone and dreary,
Only ghosts of yore bewail
The passing of the Red Man
From the Semiahmoo Trail."
-Anon.

Another relic of the past disappeared when, on November 15, 1983, the *Columbian* rolled off the presses for the very last time. For months, the 123-year-old newspaper had struggled with dwindling circulation, until finally the owner was forced into bankruptcy, a victim of poor management and competition from both the Vancouver dailies and community weeklies.

Unlike in 1869, when John Robson laid the newspaper to rest, this time the *Columbian* did not die in peace. The creditors' claims amounted to $7.5 million. Even as the judge made the bankruptcy order, the *Columbian's* owner was in the company cafeteria pleading with thirty senior employees to raise $2 million in order to rescue the newspaper. The pleas failed. Bitterness permeated the disgruntled staff members, who blamed management for a tragedy which they said could have been averted. The editor, nevertheless, declared with pride in this last issue: "We've been around longer than the automobile, longer than manned flight, longer than Canada's been a country and B.C.'s been a province. It's been a proud legacy, rich in footnotes."

Few British Columbians boast deep roots in their Pacific province. We are the California of Canada, a Lotusland to which many people migrate in order to shed their past and begin a new life. But roots are compelling; we are the product of our past, personally and as a community and nation. The native peoples realize this; now even the social mainstream is stirring.

On September 29, 1985, a special passenger train departed from New Westminster Station and travelled through the valley in commemoration of the seventy-fifth anniversary of the opening of the B.C. Electric Railway service to Chilliwack. The following year, Expo '86 coaches ran from Abbotsford to New Westminster, giving passengers the thrill experienced by the pioneers of the old interurban.

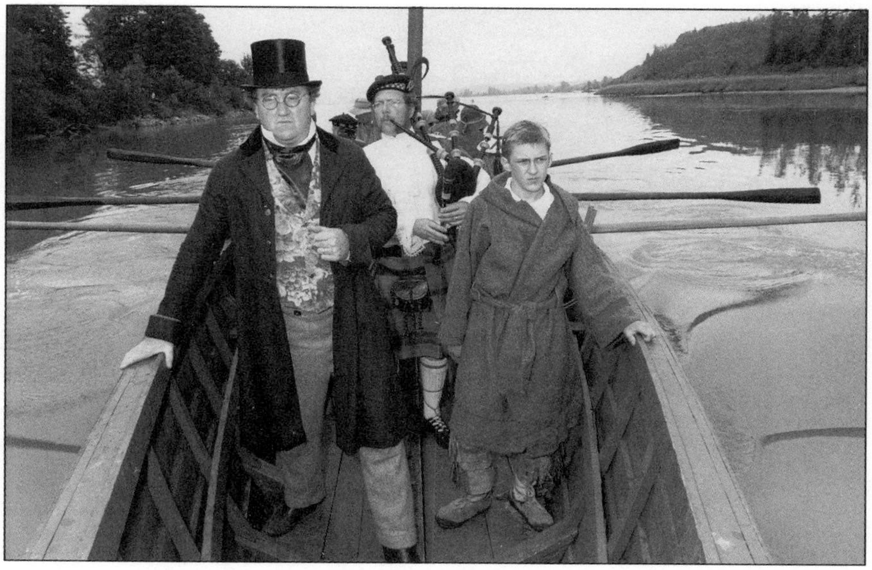

"Brigade Days" at Fort Langley, an annual re-enactment of fur traders arriving by bateaux from Interior posts.

Boat passengers may now enjoy a return sternwheeler cruise from New Westminster Quay to Fort Langley aboard the *Fraser River Connection*, complete with live commentary on the many historic sites along the way.

On the river delta, cyclists enjoy riding the dyke from Steveston, passing by ancient Stalo fishing sites, dilapidated river sheds, and abandoned cannery pilings. Steveston, like Ladner, is getting a face-lift, but renovations are taking the form of wooden sidewalks, traditional false-front façades, and a fisherman's wharf. Once again the waterfront is becoming accessible in this historic fishing village, where more than one thousand clustered seiners and gill-netters make Steveston, still, the fishing capital of Western Canada.

In August of every year, the recreated fur brigade of 1858 paddles a few kilometres down the Fraser to Fort Langley, to be greeted by a thousand well-wishers. From the wharf the traders, their shoulders laden with furs, are escorted to the fort, to be welcomed by "Chief Trader Yale" and regaled with spirits, while the red Hudson's Bay Company ensign flaps stiffly in the breeze. Meanwhile, costumed artisans entertain visitors by handcrafting barrels from staves and forging implements.

Every November 19, Queen Victoria's proclamation of British Columbia as a colony is read by a towering, bewhiskered Sir James Douglas, who is then duly sworn in as governor by a black-robed Judge Begbie. The provincial premier and his (or her) cabinet watch the proceedings impatiently, and the assembled schoolchildren stare up restlessly at the strangely costumed men standing on the porch of the Big House. Finally, the premier and the cabinet are ushered inside the Big House to warmth and refreshments.

Inside the Big House, the premier and the cabinet sit in a dimly lit room and hear a few petitions from community groups. The cabinet room is then cleared, a brief council held. Then the politicians shuffle out smiling, don coats, and sally forth to their homes and ridings.

The Big House falls silent. The scent of cedar fills the air; the floorboards creak. A few stray visitors linger behind to ramble a while; they gaze into the office of the chief trader, where a gargantuan desk sits littered with stacks of accounting

Rural scene below the Golden Ears, Maple Ridge.

journals. One can picture James Murray Yale scratching away there, sighing every now and then as he thinks of his nemesis, James Douglas, ensconced in luxury at Fort Victoria, and the hordes of Yankee gold miners foraging up the Fraser as so much rabble invading his peaceful territory.

Outside, the western clouds disperse and shimmers of pale sunlight dance across the tips of the Golden Ears. A flock of Canada Geese passes low overhead. The great gates of the fort creak shut for another day. A freight train rumbles in the distance. Fishboats bob gently at the deserted river wharf; across the narrow channel, native children on McMillan Island shout at play on their soccer field beside the little white church.

Dusk descends and the breeze rises. The sun's dying rays flicker for a few moments on the broad swath of the Fraser, then disappear, leaving behind the blackening current churning on its final odyssey to the sea. It is true that the river no longer has the first word in the course of the valley's history; but it will have the last. Bridged, dammed, polluted and exploited, the Fraser rolls on, timeless, a proud purveyor of Nature's bounty and fury. Let the modern settlers of the Fraser Valley ignore the river. No matter; their lives are the merest increments on the yardstick of history. Yet the record of Man will forever carry the muddy mark of the Fraser through the ages. And we shall be the richer for it.

CHAPTER NOTES

INTRODUCTION

P. 15. "How fast the time has gone!": Bruce Hutchison, *THE FRASER*, pp. 321-322.

CHAPTER ONE—THE RIVER PEOPLE

P. 22. Differences between Salish peoples: Wayne Suttles, *COAST SALISH ESSAYS*, p. 13.
PP. 19-21. Yuculta raid: Lerman, *THE LEGENDS OF THE RIVER PEOPLE*, p. 26.
P. 22. Sturgeon fishing techniques: *THE COLUMBIAN*, May 9, 1981.
P. 23-24. "concepts of ownership of resources" : Wilson Duff, *THE UPPER STALO INDIANS*, p. 77, 86.
P. 27. The blanket-beating wives: op. cit. Lerman.
P. 29. "Oh, the white man's dancing is worse": Thomas Crosby, *AMONG THE ANKOMENUMS*, p. 105.
P. 30. Slalakums: op. cit. Duff, pp. 117-18.
P. 30. Sasquatch capture: *VICTORIA COLONIST*, July 3, 1882, p. 1.
P. 30. Whattlekainum: *THE COLUMBIAN*, July 9, 1970.

CHAPTER TWO—THE ODYSSEY OF SIMON FRASER

P. 34. "inured to hardship; of unconquerable will": E.O.S. Scholefield, "Westward Ho! Magazine," 3 (1908).
P. 35. "We have every reason to be thankful" : Simon Fraser, *LETTERS AND JOURNAL*, 1806-1808, pp. 88, 91, 96.
P. 36. "They make rugs of dog's hair" : Ibid., pp. 100-101.
P. 36, "The Fraser does not flow at all" : Maclennan, *THE RIVERS OF CANADA*, p. 249.
P. 37. "Feast of fish, berries, and dried oysters" : op. cit. *LETTERS AND JOURNAL*, pp. 102-05.
P. 37. "I was there when Simon Fraser came" : Bruce McKelvie, *FORT LANGLEY: OUTPOST OF EMPIRE*, p. 4
P. 38. "The river is therefore not the Columbia" : op. cit. *LETTERS AND JOURNAL*, pp. 105-06, 109.

CHAPTER THREE—THE BIRTH OF FORT LANGLEY

P. 42. "batter the fort down with a four-pounder" : Akrigg, *BRITISH COLUMBIA CHRONICLE: 1778-1846*, pp. 159-60.
P. 43. "I am convinced they must be ruled with a rod of iron" : "Introduction To George Simpson," *JOURNAL OF OCCURRENCES*, p. lvi.
P. 45. "fine tall good looking man, but his people are of low stature" : *JOHN WORK JOURNAL*, Dec. 13.
P. 46. "I distributed a few presents among the natives" : James McMillan, *"Extracts From Mr. Chief Trader McMIllan's Report of His Voyage & Survey From The Columbia To The Frazer's River."* (Dec. 31, 1824)
P. 46. "important benefits would result" : *GEORGE SIMPSON'S JOURNAL*, pp. 76-77.
P. 47. "We wish Fraser's River to be established next season" : Ibid. pp. 115, 124, 248.
P. 47. McMillan's journey on *CADBORO* and Whattlekainum: Mary Cullen, p. 17.
P. 48. "The schooner was brought close to the shore" : *FORT LANGLEY JOURNAL* , JUNE 27, 1827 to JULY 30, 1830, pp. 7-11.
P. 48. "The picketing of the fort was now completed" : op. cit. pp. 9, 11, 12.
P. 50. Annance reference by Simpson: *BLACK BOOK*, quoted in Ramsey, *FIVE CORNERS: THE STORY OF CHILLIWACK*, p. 12.
P. 49. "Dull and monotonous—everything has taken on a winter appearance" : op. cit. *FORT LANGLEY JOURNAL*, pp. 39-41.
P. 50. First Fort Langley Christmas: ibid., pp. 41-42.

CHAPTER FOUR—LONELY OUTPOST OF EMPIRE

P. 54. "This warfare keeps the Indians of this vicinity" : ibid., pp. 47-52.
P. 54. "We hear from the Indians" : ibid., pp. 51, 59.
P. 55. "A dispute arose betwixt a Musqueam woman" : ibid. pp. 60-62.
P. 56. George Simpson's journey described: op. cit. Cullen, p. 20.
P. 57. "The banks now erected themselves" : "Part of A Dispatch, 1829." HBRS 10:37, p. 37.
P. 57. Fraser Canyon journey described: Jean Cole, *EXILE IN THE WILDERNESS: THE BIOGRAPHY OF CHIEF FACTOR ARCHIBALD MCDONALD*, p. 135.
P. 57. "Indians about us every hour of the day" : op. cit. *FORT LANGLEY JOURNAL*, p. 70.
P. 57. Simpson's impressions of Fort Langley: op. cit. Cullen, p.21.
P. 58. McDonald's policies: ibid. *JOURNAL*, p. 85; op. cit. Cole, p. 149; Jamie Morton, "Role of The Big House," unpublished Parks Canada manuscript, p. 14.
P. 59. Yale and Matrimony: J. A. Grant, "James Murray Yale," unpublished manuscript, Mss. 182, PABC, p. 51.
P. 59. "These, being the principal Indians of this neighbourhood": op. cit. *JOURNAL*, p. 89.
P. 61. Battle of Fort men and Yucultas: op. cit. Jean Cole, p. 149; McKelvie, p. 49.
P. 61. "All the Indians hereabouts collected into the Fort today": op. cit. *JOURNAL*, p. 112; Cole, pp. 149-50.
P. 62. Life and progress at the Fort: *WASHINGTON HISTORICAL QUARTERLY*, Vol. 1, No. 4, p. 265.
P. 62. "I have descended to oil and blubber too" : op. cit. Cole, p. 160.
P. 63. "In regard to Ft. Langley and Nisqually" : "Fort Langley Correspondence," Dr. McLoughlin to Simpson, Mar. 3, 1835.
P. 64. The *BEAVER* arrives: op. cit. Akrigg, pp. 294-95; and Derek Pethick, *"S.S. BEAVER: The Ship That Saved The West,"* (Van. 1970), p. 13.
P. 65. The Yuculta attack: op. cit. J.A. Grant, pp. 58-60.
P. 65. Yale and his new wife: ibid. pp. 59-60.
P. 66. Douglas comments re: Yale: "Fort Langley Correspondence: Chief Trader Douglas To Yale, Nov. 21, 1838."

CHAPTER FIVE—THE WORLD OF JAMES MURRAY YALE

P. 69. Stalo population and economy: op. cit. Wilson Duff; and Robin Fisher, *CONTACT AND CONFLICT: INDO-EUROPEAN RELATIONS IN B.C. 1774-1890*, pp. 46-47.
P. 70. "dunning them into something like exertion" : op. cit. "Fort Langley Correspondence, Oct. 14, 1839, Douglas to HBC, London, HBRS 6:216.
P. 70. "made us eat our cakes without butter" : "Letter, Yale to Simpson," Jan. 15, 1840. HBCA D.5/5 p. 239a-239b.
P. 71. Yale's report on fire and effects: op. cit. "Fort Langley Correspondence," J.M. Yale to Simpson, Feb. 10, 1841.
P. 71. Dr. McLoughlin orders re: cattle removal: "Letter, McLoughlin to Douglas," May 11, 1840, HBCA B. 223/6/27 pp. 10-11.
P. 72. "Cromarty would be at the big cauldron" : Jason Allard, "Hudson's Bay Rations," *VANCOUVER PROVINCE*, May 1, 1923.
P. 74. The Dance Ronde: Jamie Morton, "Fort Langley: An Overview of the Operations of a Diversified Fur Trade Post 1848 to 1858," unpublished manuscript, Environment Canada, pp. 232-33.
P. 74. "Many of them have a dignified look" : Charles Wilkes, "Narrative of United States Exploring Expedition During the Years 1838-1842, vol. 4, pp. 370-71.
P. 75. Stalo and Kanaka women fighting: Jason Allard, "Reminiscences," *VANCOUVER DAILY PROVINCE*, Oct. 25, 1924, p. 24.
P. 75. "The welcome that Mr. Yale extended me" : op. cit. McKelvie, p. 61.
P. 75. Reaction of natives to Father Demers: Jacq. Kennedy, "Roman Catholic Missionary Effort and Indian Acculturation In The Fraser Valley, 1860-1900," UBC, Apr. 1969, pp. 16, 22.
P. 76. "The place itself appears a perfect Eden" : James Douglas, "The Hargrave Correspondence, 1821-43," ed. G. Glazebrook, Champlain Society 24 (Toronto, 1938) pp. 420-21.

P. 78. "Before he reached the head of the falls" : "Yale Letter To Simpson, Dec. 28, 1847," HBCA D.5/20 pp. 697-700.
P. 79. "The preparations for opening the new road to the interior": "Letter, Douglas & Work To Governor & Committee," Dec. 5, 1848.
P. 80. Mrs. Allard & Ft. Yale incident: Jason Allard, *VANCOUVER PROVINCE*, May 1, 1923.
P. 81. Allard and Yale's dog: op. cit. J.A. Grant, p. 74.
P. 82. "The greatest evils here seem to spring" : "Letter, Yale to Simpson," Oct. 22, 1852, Add Mss 182, folio 6, No. 41, PABC.
P. 83. Brigade arrival and fur packing: op. cit. Jamie Morton, pp. 84, 97-98; and William Yates, "Reminiscences," E/E/Y2, PABC, p. 4.
P. 84. "I presume it was not intended that we should relinquish the salmon trade" : "Letter, Yale to Douglas," Nov. 13, 1855, AB40, Ya 2, PABC.
P. 84. "Pray, my friend, do not despair" : "Letter, Douglas to Yale," Oct. 23, 1856, B. 226/6/12, p. 120.
P. 85. "The price paid will come on average to about 15 shillings": "Fort Langley Correspondence," Douglas To Yale, May 7, 1850.

CHAPTER SIX—GOLD RUSH

P. 87. James Houston story: Don Waite, *THE LANGLEY STORY*, pp. 33-36.
P. 88. "I cannot help admiring the wisdom and foresight of the Indians" : "Letter, Douglas To Sir George Simpson," July 17, 1857, B. 226/b/13, HBCA.
P. 90. The story of Speel-set: Oliver Wells, *THE CHILLIWACKS AND THEIR NEIGHBOURS*, pp. 130-31; and Paul Murphy, *THE HISTORY OF FORT LANGLEY*, p. 99.
PP. 91-92. Dr. Friesach tour and quotes: Dr. C. Friesach, "An Excursion Through B.C. in the year 1858," reprinted in *B.C. HISTORICAL QUARTERLY*, Vol. V, No. 3, pp. 223-230.
P. 93. "Christian cities will dwell in the land" : Victor A.G. Bulwer-Lytton, *THE LIFE OF EDWARD, FIRST LORD LYTTON*, (London, 1913) II, p. 293.
P. 94. "Martha, how would you like to go to New Caledonia?" : Cruikshank, "The Maclure Story," A. Ms. 188, File 5, (1958), MSA Museum.
P. 94. "We were in a second Eden!" : John K. Lord, "At Home In The Wilderness: What To Do There and How To Do It. A Handbook for Travellers and Emigrants," 3rd. ed. (London, 1876), pp. 341-42, 347.
P. 95. "The arrival of so many strangers is unpleasant" : "Letter, Douglas to W.K. Smith," quoting from Yale letter, Apr. 19, 1858, B. 226/6/15, pp. 49-50, HBCA.
P. 95. "The door is scarcely opened when the small space allotted": *HARPER'S WEEKLY*, Oct. 9, 1858, p. 644.
P. 96. "The ball was conducted with the best possible decorum" : "Letter, C.C. Gardiner," November 17, 1858, reprinted in Robie Reid, ed. "To The Fraser Mines in 1858," *B.C. HISTORICAL QUARTERLY*, Vol. I, No. 4, (Oct. 1937), pp. 243-53.
P. 97. Crime at Ft. Langley: op. cit. Jamie Morton, pp. 138-39.
P. 98. Nov. 19, 1858 ceremonies: *VICTORIA GAZETTE*, Nov. 25, 1858, p. 1.

CHAPTER SEVEN—THE SAPPERS OF STUMP CITY

P. 101. The Derby site as new B.C. capital: op. cit. Jamie Morton, p. 192; and D.B. Smith, "The First Capital of B.C.: Ft. Langley or New Westminster?" *B.C. HISTORICAL QUARTERLY*, Vol. XXI, Nos. 1-4, pp. 17-23.
P. 102. Ned McGowan War: W.E. Ireland, ed., "First Impressions: Letter of Col. Richard C. Moody, R.E. to A. Blackwood," Feb. 1, 1859, *B.C. HISTORICAL QUARTERLY* 15 (1951), pp. 96-97 and 104-05.
P. 103. Moody and Sapperton site clearing: op. cit., D.B. Smith, p. 44.
P. 104. "Queensborough is not only genuine Anglo-Saxon" : *VICTORIA GAZETTE*, July 9, 1859, p. 1.
P. 104. "In the neighbourhood of the huts and stores" : Quoted in A. Woodland, *NEW WESTMINSTER: THE EARLY YEARS, 1858-1898*, p. 10.

P. 105. Rev. Ed. White experiences: "Rev. Ed. White Diary, Jan. 1, 1859-Dec. 31, 1866," E/B/W58, PABC, pp. 9-15.

P. 108. James Houston story: *THE COLUMBIAN*, May 15, 1958, p. 1. (May Day edition.)

P. 108. Pre-emption system and Trutch survey: W.N. Draper, "Pioneer Surveyors In The Fraser Valley," *B.C. HISTORICAL QUARTERLY*, Vol. V., No. 3, pp. 215-16.

PP. 109-110. Settlement statistics: A. Siemens, *THE LOWER FRASER VALLEY: EVOLUTION OF A CULTURAL LANDSCAPE*, Tantalus Research Ltd., Vancouver, 1966, p. 37; and Gibbard, J., pp. 189-91.

P. 110. "commerce on the lower Fraser was confined" : ibid. Gibbard, pp. 190-91.

P. 110. Population statistics: Angus Gunn, "Gold and The Early Settlement of B.C."

P. 110. Douglas' Indian policy: Paul Tennant, *ABORIGINAL PEOPLES AND POLITICS: THE INDIAN LAND QUESTION IN B.C. 1849-1989*, p. 29.

P. 111. "not being farmers, Indians did not ask for very much" : Wilson Duff, *THE INDIAN HISTORY OF BRITISH COLUMBIA*, p. 61.

P. 111. "at a future date with the progress of the white colonists": "Letter, Lord Lytton to Douglas," May 20, 1859.

P. 111. "interests of the Indian population are scrupulously" : "Letter, Moody to Douglas," Apr. 28, 1863.

P. 111. Douglas lectures Moody re: Indian rights: "Letter, Douglas to Moody," referred to in "Papers Connected With Indian Land," p. 27.

P. 113. "Keekwillie holes, a large, deep round hole" : Florence Goodfellow, *MEMORIES OF PIONEER LIFE IN BRITISH COLUMBIA*, Harrison Lk. Hist. Society, p. 13.

P. 113. Discovery of hot springs at Harrison Lk. : Belle Rendall, *THE LEGENDARY HARRISON HOT SPRINGS*, p. 196.

P. 113. Jonathan Reece and The Whatcom Trail : Imbert Orchard, *FLOODLAND AND FOREST: MEMORIES OF THE CHILLIWACK VALLEY*, pp. 9-10 and 13-15.

P. 114. "The Fort at Upper Langley is one of the most notable features" : *NEW WESTMINSTER TIMES*, Nov. 19, 1859, p. 1.

P. 115. Rev. Crickmer street preaching scene: op. cit. Don Waite, *THE LANGLEY STORY*, p. 48 and 50.

P. 116. Arrival of Ladner brothers: Ed. Terris, "Ladner: A Pioneer Study," pp. 50-52.

P. 117. Henry Bates petition: *THE BRITISH COLUMBIAN*, May 23, 1861.

P. 117. "In the evenings came reminiscences..." : op. cit. Mckelvie, p. 90.

P. 118. "Mr. Newton, the agent in charge" : *THE BRITISH COLUMBIAN*, Sept. 3, 1862.

P. 118. "Most of them had their pack of baggage" : Dorothy B. Smith, ed., "Lady Franklin Visits The Pacific Northwest," Memoir No. XI, Victoria, 1974, PABC, pp. 38-39.

PP. 118-119. Further Lady Franklin visit quotes: ibid., pp. 41, 52, 59, 46, and 58.

PP. 119-120. "The blankets were thrown down with 15 or 20 Indians" : *THE BRITISH COLUMBIAN*, Oct. 3, 1861.

CHAPTER EIGHT—TELEGRAPH TRAIL

P. 123. The slaying of Dr. Fifer: B.A. McKelvie, "The Slaying of Dr. Fifer," in *MAGIC, MURDER AND MYSTERY*, Cowichan Leader Ltd., 1966, pp. 91-93.

P. 124. "I cannot easily comb my hair" : D.W. Duthie, *A BISHOP IN THE ROUGH*, London, 1909, pp. 57-58.

P. 124. The broken stern wheel: *THE BRITISH COLUMBIAN*, Feb. 20, 1862, p. 1.

P. 125. Royal Engineers' achievements: Beth Hill, *SAPPERS: THE ROYAL ENGINEERS IN BRITISH COLUMBIA*, p. 90.

P. 125. Captain Gossett: R.L. Reid, "The Assay Office and The Proposed Mint At New Westminster," Victoria, 1926, PABC, pp. 22-24.

P. 125. "looking very old just now" : Mary Moody, "Correspondence Outward; Letters to her Mother and Sister, 1854 & 1858-63," PABC, quoted in *SAPPERS*, p. 119.

P. 126. "The concourse of people upon the wharf" : *THE BRITISH COLUMBIAN*, Nov. 14, 1863.

P. 126. "probably attracted the entire population of the lower mainland" : op. cit. *SAPPERS*, pp. 122, 143-44.

P. 127. "A pyramid of gold and gems would have been less acceptable" : "B.C. Papers," May 16, 1864.

P. 127. "An extensive suite of apartments has already been added": quoted in Alan Woodland, *NEW WESTMINSTER: THE EARLY YEARS 1858-1898*, p. 12.

P. 128. "I had not seen even in the West Indies" : "Letter, Seymour to Ed. Cardwell," in "Govs. Douglas and Seymour Despatches to London 1863-1867, March 21, 1865, PABC.

P. 128. Chilcotin War: op. cit. Akrigg, p. 305.

P. 129. "We proceeded with them to the vicinity of the altar" : *THE MAINLAND GUARDIAN*, quoted in J. Cherrington, *MISSION ON THE FRASER*, p. 5.

P. 130. "Wherever he saw evil he immediately attacked it" : Kay Cronin, *CROSS IN THE WILDERNESS*, p. 151.

PP. 130-31. Father Fouquet and Morality: J. Cherrington, "St. Mary's Mission, 1861-1910," unpub. UBC Thesis; and *O.M.I. MISSIONS*, 1863 p. 207; *O.M.I. MISSIONS*, 1864, pp. 264-65; and *THE BRITISH COLUMBIAN*, Mar. 17, 1862, May 23, 1863, and Dec. 2, 1863.

P. 132. "removed from the centres of white population" : Judge Begbie, "Report On B.C., 1872," Ottawa, I. B. Taylor, pp. 27-28.

P. 132. Thomas Crosby activities among natives: Thos. Crosby, *AMONG THE AN-KO-ME-NUMS*, p. 176.

P. 133. The Telegraph Trail: R.C. Harris, "The Route Adopted By The Government Between New Westminster and Yale, 1865," *B.C. HISTORICAL NEWS*, Winter, 1983; and op cit. Siemens p. 73.

P. 133. "The horse, instead of cantering along easily" : op. cit. Gibbard, p. 13.

P. 134. "The whole machine is in a strange incomprehensible muddle": "Letter, Douglas to A.G. Dallas," Nov. 8, 1867, in "Private Letter Book of Sir James Douglas," PABC.

P. 135. "A genial, pleasant gentleman, fond of good living" : Howay and Scholefield, *BRITISH COLUMBIA: FROM THE EARLIEST TIMES TO THE PRESENT*, Vol. II, pp. 288-89.

P. 135. "reduced to what is necessary" : "Journals of the Legislative Council," p. 16.

P. 135. "The Indians really have no right to the lands" : J. Trutch, "Report On The Lower Fraser Indian Reserves," Aug. 28, 1867, in "B.C. Papers Connected With The Indian Land Question," p. 42; and op. cit. Fisher, pp. 164-65.

P. 135. "A proper appreciation of the importance of settlement" : *THE BRITISH COLUMBIAN*, Oct. 14, 1868.

P. 135. "Some days ago came new men who told us" : "Petition From Lower Fraser Chiefs," in "Letters, Durieu to Seymour," Dec. 6, 1868, cc file 503, PABC.

P. 136. "in an unsuitable location with a bog on one side" : *THE BRITISH COLUMBIAN*, Oct. 8, 1864.

P. 136. "small, low room with a canvas ceiling" : *THE BRITISH COLUMBIAN*, Dec. 5, 1861.

P. 137. "Drunken squaws have for their own protection" : "B.C. Despatches, Seymour to Cardwell," May 1, 1865, p. 302.

P. 137. "a white and a Chinese lunatic, who are so violent" : *THE BRITISH COLUMBIAN*, Aug. 22, 1861.

PP. 137-38. Patient's chart: Doris Brownlee, "A Short History of the Royal Columbian Hospital and its Auxiliaries," Jan. 1973, New West. Public Library, p. 3. (unpub. paper.)

P. 137. Father Fouquet and the hospital: Helen Pullem, *NEW WESTMINSTER: THE REAL STORY OF HOW IT ALL BEGAN*, New Westminster, 1985, pp. 109-12.

P. 138. "In nine minutes from the time the leading ropes" : quoted in Mather, *NEW WESTMINSTER: THE ROYAL CITY*, p. 39.

P. 139. "It is well known that of all the foreigners" : *THE NORTH PACIFIC TIMES*, Feb. 22, 1863.

P. 141. "Although the time and place of disembarkation" : *THE BRITISH COLUMBIAN*, Sept. 24, 1862.

P. 143. "He was another Canadian" : "Reminiscences of William Yates," E/E/Y2, PABC, pp. 4-5.

P. 143. "The disasters were met with philosophy" : Norm Hacking, "Steamboating On The Fraser In The Sixties," p. 1.

P. 1143. "To me, a sternwheeler slapping" : Jan Nicol, "ingredients Of Our Community," unpub. Abbotsford School District Paper, p. 31.

PP. 144-45. "Struggling up the river against the stream" : R.C. Mayne, *FOUR YEARS IN BRITISH COLUMBIA AND VANCOUVER ISLAND*, quoted in Mather, pp. 66-68.

PP. 145-46. Mrs. Nahu and *Maria* disaster: Jason Allard, "reminiscences," *VANCOUVER PROVINCE*, May 1, 1923; and Ovid Allard's Notebook, SR 75, PABC.

P. 146. *Fort Yale* disaster: Roland Carey, "The Jamieson Brothers—Tragic Pioneers," in "Pioneer Days In British Columbia," ed. Art Downs, *B.C. OUTDOORS*, pp. 149-51.

PP. 147-48. The Great Fire of 1868: Thos. Perry, "Land Use of Matsqui Prairie Region of the Lower Fraser Valley, 1858-1892," unpub. West. Wash. Univ. Thesis, Dec., 1984, pp. 43-45.

P. 149. Judge Begbie: *THE MAINLAND GUARDIAN*, Mar. 16, 1870.

CHAPTER NINE—STRUGGLES OF THE SOIL

P. 151. Farm statistics: op. cit., Gibbard, pp. 218-19.

P. 151. "many of the settlers around me would have given much" : Rev. Alex. Dunn, *PRESBYTERIANISM IN B.C. AND EXPERIENCES IN LANGLEY AND MEMOIRS OF THE PROMINENT PIONEERS*, New Westminster, Jackson Printing Co., 1913, p. 5.

P. 152. The Crown Grant System: Robt. Cail, *LAND, MAN, AND THE LAW: THE DISPOSAL OF CROWN LANDS IN B.C. 1871-1913*, Vancouver, UBC Press, pp. 23-24.

P. 154. "We are not a lazy and roaming-about people" : "Petition of Chiefs of Lower Fraser," July 14, 1874, in "B.C. Papers Connected With The Indian Land Question," p. 137.

P. 154. "We must all admit that the condition of the Indian question" : Geo. Stewart, *CANADA UNDER THE ADMINISTRATION OF THE EARL OF DUFFERIN*, Toronto, Rose-Bedford, 1878, pp. 492-93.

P. 155. The Durieu System: E. Titley, *A NARROW VISION: D. CAMPBELL SCOTT AND THE ADMINISTRATION OF INDIAN AFFAIRS IN CANADA*, UBC Press, 1986, p. 13.

P. 156. "When all were seated" : op. cit. Alex. Dunn, pp. 6-7.

PP. 156-57. "What struck me very forcibly" : ibid. p. 4.

P. 157. "In those days you were never alone" : Beulah Probert, in *GROWING UP IN THE VALLEY*, ed. Imbert Orchard, PABC, 1983, p. 67.

P. 158. "Paid $10 for oxen at Langley" : "Alben Hawkins Diary, 1874-1880," PABC.

P. 158. "No school since last month" : "John Jessop's Diary of School Inspections, 1872-1877," PABC.

P. 159. "At the time of my visit there were 32 girls" : "Canada, DIA Report, 1875," pp. 54-55.

P. 160. "We used to have lots of fun" : op cit. *GROWING UP IN THE VALLEY*, p. 24. (Cornie Kelleher)

P. 160. "They were always degrading us" : Mary Englund, "Indian Memories of Mission School," *SOUND HERITAGE: VOICES FROM B.C.*, ed. Marg. Whitehead, PABC, Douglas & McIntyre Ltd., 1984, p. 38.

PP. 160-61. Billy Bristol: Hope & District Hist. Society, *FORGING A NEW HOPE 1848-1948*, 1984, p. 167.

P. 162. "A very slow and jolting ride" : "Violet Sillitoe Journal," quoted in B. Ramsey, *FIVE CORNERS: THE STORY OF CHILLIWACK.*

P. 164. Pioneering women: S. Nickols, *MAPLE RIDGE: A HISTORY OF SETTLEMENT*, p. 8.

P. 164. The Fraser Slide: op. cit. Gibbard, p. 280.

P. 165. Moving the Derby church: Waite, *THE LANGLEY STORY*, p. 103.

PP. 165-66. Julia Apnaut story: ibid., pp. 100-01.

P. 166. Dr. Tolmie at the Big House: op. cit. J. Allard, *REMINISCENCES*, pp. 1-2.

P. 166. Reeve Gibbs: op. cit. Waite, pp. 78-81.

P. 169. Surrey characters: F. Treleaven, *THE SURREY STORY*, Vol. II, 187-1879, pp. 23-24.

P. 171. "People from Ladner dressed up" : Les. Ross, *RICHMOND: CHILD OF THE FRASER*, pp. 51-52. (Ida Steves)

P. 173. "it was unwise to make the asylum too comfortable" : Val Adolph, *THE HISTORY OF WOODLANDS*, New Westminster, 1978, p. 9.

P. 174. Prison report: op. cit. Gibbard, pp. 306-07.

P. 177. "When the people of Langley could see" : op. cit. Dunn, p. 55.

CHAPTER TEN—RAILWAY BOOM

P. 181. "The tide of immigration is rolling in" : Helen Pullem, *QUEENSBOROUGH*, New West., 1975, p. 9.

P. 185. John Oliver: James Morton, *HONEST JOHN OLIVER: THE LIFE STORY OF THE HON. JOHN OLIVER*, p. 39.

P. 187. "We have no telegraphic" : *CHILLIWACK PROGRESS*, June 6, 1894.

P. 188. "The magnitude of the dyking task" : *THE DAILY COLUMBIAN*, May 28, 1894.

P. 189. "The streets were thronged with people" : Ibid. January, 1891, quoted in Mather, p. 103.

P. 190. "Told all the women on Ramage Street" : *THE BRITISH COLUMBIAN*, June 15 and 29, 1946.

P. 190. "A milk dealer's team took fright" : *THE DAILY COLUMBIAN*, Nov. 30, 1891.

P. 190. "an overflow from the WC in rear of the city hall" : *THE BRITISH COLUMBIAN*, June 15, 1946.

P. 190. "I spent the following night" : Frances McNab, *BRITISH COLUMBIA FOR SETTLERS*, London, Clapman & Hall, 1898, p. 215.

P. 191. Slumach story: Art Downs, ed. *SLUMACH'S GOLD: IN SEARCH OF A LEGEND*, Surrey, Heritage House Pub. Co., 1981.

PP. 191-92. Smuggling rings: *THE COLUMBIAN*, May 17, 1969.

PP. 192-93. Alex Houston escape: Judge Begbie, "Bench Books," Vol. XVII, June 7, 1893.

P. 194. "Our celestial friends from the Flowery Kingdom" : *THE CHILLIWACK PROGRESS*, Oct. 20, 1892.

P. 194. "Industry, economy, sobriety and law-abidingness" : *THE VICTORIA TIMES*, March 10, 1885. (Judge Begbie)

P. 195. "Yip is one of the ugliest looking specimens" : *THE VANCOUVER PROVINCE*, April, 1900.

P. 197. "Two sounds I have never forgotten" : T.E. Ladner, *ABOVE THE SANDHEADS*, p. 131.

P. 197. "My biggest set was 900 sockeye" : *THE VANCOUVER SUN*, Jan. 23, 1962. (Marco Vidulich)

P. 198. "Two small canoes lay moored" : op. cit. Frances McNab, pp. 213-14.

P. 199. Cannery practices: op. cit. Ed. Terris, *LADNER*, p. 116.

P. 200. "boys ran away from the fields" : J. Redford, "Attendance At Indian Residential Schools in B.C., 1890-1920," UBC Thesis, 1978, p. 52.

P. 201. The 1893 Christmas: Ed. Villiers, *MAPLE RIDGE NEWS*, Dec. 23, 1981, p. B5.

P. 203. "Our citizens can take steps" : *THE CHILLIWACK PROGRESS*, Feb. 25, 1892.

P. 203. Dead horse incident: op. cit. Waite, *LANGLEY*, p. 120.

P. 205. "In the sickly sight of Sunday's dawn" : *THE COLUMBIAN*, Sept. 9, 1899.

CHAPTER ELEVEN—THE GOLDEN YEARS

P. 209. Fish strikes and unions: op. cit. Les. Ross, *RICHMOND: CHILD OF THE FRASER*, p. 125.

P. 213. "Send up the gas boat, 25 cons have made" : *THE BRITISH COLUMBIAN*, Jun. 14, 1955, p. 15.

PP. 214-16. Bill Miner Story: Don Waite, *TALES OF THE GOLDEN EARS*, pp. 69-74; *THE COLUMBIAN*, May 9, 1980.

P. 216. "Well, doctor, I think I'll be goin'" : "Whatever The Weather: Red-Shirt Bill and The Royal Mail," in *SETTLING THE FRONTIER*, ed. I. Orchard, p. 103.

P. 218. The Harrison Hermit: op. cit. Belle Rendall, *HEALING WATERS*, pp. 13-16.

P. 219. Bergemeist: op. cit. *GROWING UP IN THE VALLEY*, pp. 35-36.

P. 220. "There are many in every community who continue to dope": *THE CHILLIWACK PROGRESS*, Feb. 21, 1906.

PP. 220-21. Dr. Ben Marr: op. cit. Waite, *LANGLEY* p. 211.

P. 222. Barroom drinks: *THE CHILLIWACK PROGRESS*, Nov. 25, 1908.

P. 225. "Our rural schools are largely in the charge" : "1907 Surrey School Board Report."

P. 226. Chief Sepass and Eloise Street: *LEGENDS OF LANGLEY*, p. 142.

P. 227. Passion Play: Father A. Fleury, "The Passion Play," *1941 ANNUAL: OBLATE MISSIONS*, PABC.

P. 229. Clayburn bricks: John Adams, "Bricks and Buildings," *B.C. HISTORICAL NEWS*, Fall 1982, pp. 6-9.

P. 230. "The trip is a most remarkable one" : *THE CHILLIWACK PROGRESS*, Nov. 2, 1910.
PP. 230-31. Inaugural B.C.E.R. journey: Brian Kelly, "Chilliwack By Tram," pp. 3-4.

CHAPTER TWELVE—FOR KING AND COUNTRY

P. 233. "I've toughed it out all my life" : C.V. Tench, "The Gold Mine Murders of Nine B.C. Women," in *ANNALS OF CANADIAN CRIME.*
P. 234. Steamboat Mtn. scam: op. cit. *FORGING A NEW HOPE*, pp. 100-01.
P. 234. "It was the neatest, cleanest" : *THE BRITISH COLUMBIAN*, Sept. 15, 1911.
PP. 235-36. Father Fouquet travels: op. cit. *GROWING UP IN THE VALLEY*, pp. 38-39.
P. 236. Indian population: op. cit. Wilson Duff, *THE UPPER STALO*, p. 28.
P. 236. "I presume that these Indian reserves" *THE CHILLIWACK PROGRESS*, July 10, 1919.
P. 237. Indian reserve size: op. cit. Tennant, p. 98; and Robert Exell, "History of Indian Land Claims In B.C., *THE ADVOCATE* , Vol. 48, Nov/90, p. 876.
P. 239. CNR workers and sanitation: *THE CHILLIWACK PROGRESS*, Feb. 28, 1912.
P. 239. William Brown and moving hotel: op. cit. Waite, *LANGLEY*, p. 205.
P. 239. St. Bernard dog and train: *COLUMBIAN SUNDAY MAGAZINE*, Nov. 10, 1973, p. 11.
P. 240. "the wind blew like blazes" : Daphne Sleigh, *DISCOVERING DEROCHE*, Abbotsford Printing, 1983. (Interview, M. Williams and M. Moore)
P. 240. "Preparations for this safari were thorough" : *THE ABBOTSFORD HILL-TOUTS* , 1976, p. 16. (No pub. ref.)
P. 242. "There are those who think with a cheery optimism" : *THE DAILY COLUMBIAN*, Aug. 15, 1914.
P. 242. Baron von Mackenson: *THE CHILLIWACK PROGRESS*, Jan. 21, 1915.
P. 242. Chinese forced to subscribe: J. Morton, *IN THE SEA OF STERILE MOUNTAINS*, p. 230.
P. 243. Sampola Farm: op. cit. *HISTORY OF MAPLE RIDGE*, pp. 84-93.
P. 244. The FVMPA: M. Maclachlan, "The Success of The FVMPA," *B.C. STUDIES*, No. 24, Winter 1974-75.
P. 247. "The old habit of using streets as stamping ground" : *THE CHILLIWACK PROGRESS*, Oct. 23, 1912 and April 9, 1914.
P. 249. "When I was a girl guide" : quoted in Jan Nicol, "Ingredients of Our Community," p. 67.
P. 250. "If there is one thing that Canadians" : *THE CHILLIWACK PROGRESS*, Apr. 25, 1973.
P. 250. The Spanish Flu: Marg. Andrews, "Epidemic and Public Health: Influenza in Vancouver, 1918-19," *B.C. STUDIES*, No. 34, Summer 1977; and *THE COLUMBIAN*, Oct. 30, 1918.

CHAPTER THIRTEEN—FLIVVERS, FLAPPERS, AND JITNEYS

P. 254. Soldier Settlement: *REPORT OF THE SOLDIER SETTLEMENT BOARD OF CANADA*, Ottawa, 1921, p. 134.
PP. 254-55. Peace Arch ceremonies: *THE COLUMBIAN*, Sept. 6 and 7, 1921.
PP. 255-56. Sumas Lake Reclamation: Thos. Perry, "Sumas Lake Reclamation," unpub. paper, School Dist. #34 (Abbotsford) Apr. 1984.
P. 257. "To the working man, beer is no more" : J. Cherrington, *MISSION ON THE FRASER*, p. 112.
P. 258. Tom Sheaves trial: *THE BRITISH COLUMBIAN*, Sept. 2, 1926.
P. 259. "You couldn't catch the farmers" : D. Duffy, "Imagine Please," *EARLY RADIO BROADCASTING IN BRITISH COLUMBIA*, PABC, 1983, p. 7.
P. 265. "What are they kicking about?" : *THE BRITISH COLUMBIAN*, May 8, 1923.
P. 267. "The throne of democracy is in the small town" : *THE VANCOUVER SUN*, quoted in *MISSION ON THE FRASER*, p. 123.
P. 268. Trapp Technical School: *THE COLUMBIAN*, May 21, 1955.
PP. 268-69. "This great family lives in the cheery red buildings" : *THE VANCOUVER PROVINCE*, Mar. 11, 1928.
P. 270. "The proportion of Orientals to whites" : Pat. Roy, The Oriental Menace In B.C.," in *HISTORICAL ESSAYS ON BRITISH COLUMBIA*, p. 244.
P. 270, "The Japanese did make competition very difficult" : op. cit. Treleaven, p. 49.

P. 272. Volcanic Brown: op. cit. Don Waite, *TALES OF THE GOLDEN EARS*, p. 64; and *THE BRITISH COLUMBIAN*, Oct. 22, 1926.

CHAPTER FOURTEEN—DEPRESSION

P. 277. "high tea with tinned sockeye" : Geo. Woodcock, *BRITISH COLUMBIA: A HISTORY OF THE PROVINCE*, p. 211.
P. 278. VD men march: *THE BRITISH COLUMBIAN*, Mar. 7, 1936.
P. 279. Fraser Mills violence: *THE BRITISH COLUMBIAN*, Oct. 15, 1931.
P. 280. Matsqui relief problems: Zeke Doerksen, "The Depression In Matsqui 1930-1937," *B.C. HISTORICAL NEWS*, Apr. 1979.
P. 282. "members of Council were doubtful" : *THE LANGLEY ADVANCE*, Oct. 12, 1933 and May 2, 1935.
P. 282. "We have had 3 feet of water" : *FRASER VALLEY RECORD*, quoted in *MISSION ON THE FRASER*, p. 137.
P. 285. Dr. Raley and Coqualeetza: Peter Pirie, *THE STUMP RANCH*, Victoria, Morriss Printing Co. Ltd., 1975.
P. 287. Archie Barker exploits: *THE CHILLIWACK PROGRESS*, Aug. 31, 1949.
P. 289. Whieldon incident: *MISSION ON THE FRASER*, pp. 147-48.
P. 289. Chung Chuck: *THE BRITISH COLUMBIAN*, Sept. 25,28, 1929.
P. 291. "They piled their families and a few cherished possessions": op. cit. Treleaven, p. 66.
P. 291. Hop's Store: Hutcherson, *LANDING AT LADNER*, p. 101.
P. 291. Chinese delivers baby: *THE BRITISH COLUMBIAN*, Dec. 3, 1932.
P. 291. Varied backgrounds of settlers: *THE BRITISH COLUMBIAN*, May 6, 1933.
PP. 292-93. Alan Morley quotes: *THE VANCOUVER SUN*, Mar. 13, 1937.
P. 294. Tarred and feathered auto: *THE LANGLEY ADVANCE*, Sept.17, 1936.
P. 294. "Since the days that Chilliwack Hospital" : *THE CHILLIWACK PROGRESS*, Aug. 30, 1939.
P. 295. "As I approached the doorway, I stumbled" : *THE LANGLEY ADVANCE*, Jan. 16, 1936.
P. 296. Green Timbers: op. cit. Treleaven, Vol. II, p. 63.
PP. 296-97. The Royal Visit: *THE BRITISH COLUMBIAN*, May 31, 1939 & June 1, 1939.

CHAPTER FIFTEEN—WAR AND FLOOD

PP. 301-02. Sale of Japanese fishboats: Barry Broadfoot, *YEARS OF SORROW, YEARS OF SHAME*, Toronto, Doubleday Canada Ltd., 1977, pp. 114-15.
P. 303. Chung Chuck and Maeda family: op. cit. Hutcherson, p. 186.
P. 303. "The Mennonites are a menace" : *THE LANGLEY ADVANCE*, Mar. 18 and Apr. 1, 1943.
P. 305. Major Mahoney: New Westminster Historical Society, *THE ROYAL WESTMINSTER REGIMENT 1863-1988* , p. 43.
P. 304. "The mother of the Soviet aviator" : *THE LANGLEY ADVANCE*, Jan. 14 and Feb. 4, 1943.
P. 304. Kluck and Hitler: *FRASER VALLEY RECORD*, 1941, quoted in *MISSION ON THE FRASER*, p. 248.
P. 306. Sunbury fisherwomen: *THE BRITISH COLUMBIAN*, July 15, 1944.
P. 307. "For the first time the strain" : *THE BRITISH COLUMBIAN*, Jan. 21, 1946.
P. 308. Return of Japanese to B.C.Coast: *WE ARE THEIR CHILDREN*, Commcept Publishing Ltd., Vancouver, 1977, p. 82; and W.J. Langlois, ed., "Aural History," *SOUND HERITAGE*, Vol. III, No. 3, PABC, Victoria, 1974.
P. 309. "When we first came back" : D. Marlatt, ed., *STEVESTON RECOLLECTED*, Victoria, 1975, p. 72.
P. 310. "delicate finger nail clipper" *THE BRITISH COLUMBIAN*, Feb. 14, 1948.
P. 310. "Today everyone has his favourite program" : *THE BRITISH COLUMBIAN*, Feb. 19, 1949. (Mag.)
P. 311. Trapp Tech. Etiquette: *THE BRITISH COLUMBIAN*, Apr. 20, 1946.
P. 312. "We've got roads out here in the spring" : Ibid. Apr. 16, 1949.
P. 312. Sasquatch Inn: Ibid. Sep. 14, 1948. (Mag.)

P. 313. "Miss F. Steele has added" : ibid. Jan. 24, 1942 and Nov. 8, 1947.
P. 314. Mission Gauge: Eric Sanderson, ed., *NATURE'S FURY*, Vancouver, 1948, pp. 17, 47.
P. 316. "Suddenly a faint tremor ran through the ground" : ibid. p. 29.
P. 316. "they just picked up their tents" : *THE LANGLEY ADVANCE*, June 3&10, 1948.
P. 316. Flood statistics: Thos. Perry, "The Lower Fraser Valley and the Flood of 1948," School Dist. #34 (Abbotsford) Paper, Ser. A, No. 2.
P. 317. "stoves rusted, kitchen cupboards warped and twisted" : op. cit. *NATURE'S FURY*, p. 14.
P. 317. "What desolation meets the eye" : *THE FRASER VALLEY RECORD* , July, 1948.
P. 318. "The nervous community" : *THE BRITISH COLUMBIAN*, July 17, 1947.
P. 318. Judge Howay: "Frederick W. Howay (1867-1943) : Scholar and Friend," *B.C. HISTORICAL QUARTERLY* , Vol. VIII, No. 1, p. 8.
P. 319. "People of Fort Langley and British Columbia" : *THE LANGLEY ADVANCE*, Nov. 24, 1949.

CHAPTER SIXTEEN—PLANNERS AND SASQUATCHES

P. 321. "For years the station" : *THE LANGLEY ADVANCE*, Jan. 25, 1951.
P. 322. "I was born on a stump ranch" : *THE FRASER VALLEY RECORD*, quoted in *MISSION ON THE FRASER*, p. 197.
P. 325. Charlie Perkins' tree: op. cit. Treleaven, p. 29.
PP. 325-26. Mt. Slesse crash: Glen McDonald, *HOW COME I'M DEAD?*, Hancock House Publishers Ltd., Surrey, 1985, pp. 37-44.
P. 327. "Would you sooner have a thistle patch" : *THE LANGLEY ADVANCE*, Nov. 12, 1959.
P. 328. "They mill and wander about" : *THE BRITISH COLUMBIAN*, Oct. 9, 1954.
P. 329. "There seems to be a sort of epidemic" : ibid. June 25, 1955.
P. 329. "It doesn't seem right" : *THE LANGLEY ADVANCE*, Sept. 3, 1964.
P. 329. Tea party attack: *THE LANGLEY ADVANCE*, June 10, 1954.
P. 330. "It may happen that way in Vancouver" : ibid. Jul. 16, 1953.
P. 331. "The restored fort should be the centre" : *THE VANCOUVER SUN*, July 6, 1956.
P. 331. "Little did Queen Victoria realize" : *THE LANGLEY ADVANCE*, July 24, 1958.
P. 331. "The banks of the Pitt River" : "Letter, Douglas to Newcastle," May 31, 1860, "Papers Relating to the Affairs of British Columbia," Part IV, London, HMSO, 1862, p. 8.
P. 332. Reclamation of Pitt Meadows: J. E. Collins, "The Reclamation of Pitt Meadows," unpub. SFU Thesis, 1975.
P. 333. Aldergrove Town Meeting remarks: *THE LANGLEY ADVANCE*, Aug. 27, 1959.
P. 334. "because their homes, their farms" : *THE BRITISH COLUMBIAN*, Apr. 1, 1950.
P. 336. "I was assigned to a cell-like room" : *THE VANCOUVER SUN*, Mar. 4, 1967.
P. 338. Founding of Trinity Western College: Calvin B. Hanson, *ON THE RAW EDGE OF FAITH*, Langley, 1977.
P. 341. Sasquatch sightings: op. cit. *HEALING WATERS*, p. 34.
P. 342. "A man who loved the land and lived on it" : Allan Fotheringham, "Tribute to Oliver Wells," *THE CHILLIWACK PROGRESS*, Nov. 10, 1970.

CHAPTER SEVENTEEN—WHITHER A VALLEY

PP. 345-36. John Deacon case: *John Deacon and Deacon Feedlot Ltd. v. Heichert et al*, (BCCA), unreported decision No. 910/80; Mar. 10, 1982.
P. 346. *AGRICULTURE PROTECTION ACT*, S.B.C. Ch. 19. Assented to June 28, 1989.
PP. 347-48. Chung Chuck: "Chung Chuck, Potato Grower," *WESTERN LIVING*, May, 1978.
P. 348. Defiant farmers: *B.C. REPORT*, Feb. 26, 1990, p. 28; and Sept. 24, 1990, p. 37.
P. 350. "There goes Walter Link" : *THE COLUMBIAN*, Oct. 1, 1980.
P. 350. McKitka: ibid. Mar. 8, 1980.
P. 350-51. GVRD plan: "Lower Mainland Development Strategy," *GVRD HANDBOOK*, p. 29.
P. 352. Revitalization of New Westminster: Marianne and Mark Hamilton, "New New Westminster," *BEAUTIFUL BRITISH COLUMBIA MAGAZINE*, pp. 5-15.
P. 353. Mr. Justice McMorran: Jim Fairley, *THE WAY WE WERE*, Burnaby, Hemlock Printers, 1986, pp. 45-46.

P. 354. Fraser Port: Jacq. Gresko and R. Howard, ed., *FRASER PORT,* Victoria, Sono Nis Press, 1986.
P. 355. Grant's Landing: *THE LANGLEY TIMES,* Sept. 29, 1990.
P. 356. "threatens to derange" : Bruce Hutchison, *THE VANCOUVER SUN,* May 22, 1976, p. 4.
P. 356. The Fraser Estuary: Des Kennedy, "The Fraser Delta In Jeopardy," *CANADIAN GEOGRAPHIC,* Aug/Sept. 1986, pp. 34-39.
P. 357. Terra Nova controversy: *B.C. REPORT,* Apr. 3, 1989, pp. 16-18.
P. 358. "I've never known there not to be fish" : Keith Keller, "Eulachon On The Fraser," *CANADIAN GEOGRAPHIC,* Feb/Mar. 1988.
P. 358. "Studies have shown" : *THE ROYAL CITY RECORD,* Feb. 13, 1988, p. 6.
P. 359. Barnston Island: *THE COLUMBIAN,* Jun. 13 & Dec. 4, 1969.
P. 359. Ralph Jacobson: *THE COLUMBIAN,* Feb. 2, 1982.
P. 360. "Boots and spurs must be removed" : *THE VANCOUVER PROVINCE,* Jul. 31, 1971.
P. 361. Kilgard native culture: Leo Shiell, "Native Renaissance,"*CANADIAN GEOGRAPHIC,* pp. 60.66.
P. 361. Kilgard Clay: *B.C. BUSINESS,* June/1985, pp. 13-18.
P. 362. Spirit dance enquiry: op. cit. HOW COME I'M DEAD?, pp. 94-98.
P. 362. "Its like a little municipality" : *THE COLUMBIAN,* Jun. 11, 1981.
P. 362. "pretty crafty at trading" : *THE LANGLEY ADVANCE,* Aug. 1, 1990.
P. 364. "is our only source of information" : *THE PROVINCE,* Nov. 28, 1990.
P. 364. "Now the trail is lone and dreary" : *THE COLUMBIAN,* July 21, 1980.
P. 365. "We've been around longer than the automobile" : *THE COLUMBIAN,* Nov. 12, 1983.

BIBLIOGRAPHY

The following books and articles represent a sampling of the materials consulted during the course of researching this book. I am indebted to Anne Knowlan's *The Fraser Valley: A Bibliography*, which work should be the starting point for any research into Valley lore and landscape.

Adams, John D. "Bricks And Buildings: Clayburn Company And Its Village." *BRITISH COLUMBIA HISTORICAL NEWS*, Fall 1982, pp. 6-13.

Akrigg, George. *BRITISH COLUMBIA CHRONICLE, 1778-1846: BY SEA AND LAND.* Vancouver, Discovery Press, 1975.

Akrigg, George. *BRITISH COLUMBIA CHRONICLE, 1847-1871: GOLD AND COLONISTS.* Vancouver, Discovery Press, 1977.

Anderson, Frank. *BILL MINER: STAGECOACH AND TRAIN ROBBER.* Surrey, Heritage House Publishing Co. Ltd., 1982.

Blunden, Roy. *HISTORICAL GEOLOGY OF THE LOWER FRASER RIVER VALLEY.* Vancouver, University of British Columbia, 1975.

Broadfoot, B. *YEARS OF SORROW, YEARS OF SHAME.* Toronto, Doubleday Canada Limited, 1977.

Chambers, Edith. *HISTORY OF PORT COQUITLAM.* Burnaby, B.A. Thompson, 1973.

Cherrington, J. *MISSION ON THE FRASER.* Vancouver, Mitchell Press, 1974.

Cullen, Mary. *THE HISTORY OF FORT LANGLEY, 1827-1896.* Ottawa, National Historic Sites Service, 1979.

Downs, Arthur. *PADDLE WHEELS ON THE FRONTIER: The Story of The British Columbia and The Yukon Steamers.* Surrey, B.C., Gray's Publishing Ltd., 1972.

Downs, Arthur. *SLUMACH'S GOLD: IN SEARCH OF A LEGEND.* Surrey, Heritage House Publishing Co. Ltd, 1981.

Duff, Wilson. *THE UPPER STALO OF THE FRASER VALLEY, BRITISH COLUMBIA.* Victoria, B.C. Provincial Museum, 1952.
Duff, Wilson. "The Impact of the White Man." *THE INDIAN HISTORY OF BRITISH COLUMBIA.* Victoria, Provincial Museum of Natural History And Anthropology, 1964.

Fisher, Robin. *CONTACT AND CONFLICT: INDIAN-EUROPEAN RELATIONS IN BRITISH COLUMBIA 1774-1890*. Vancouver, UBC Press, 1977.

Fraser, Simon. *LETTERS AND JOURNAL, 1806-1808.* Ed. S. Kaye Lamb. Toronto, Macmillan of Canada, 1960.

Gibbard, John. "Early History of the Fraser Valley 1808-1885." Vancouver, University of B.C., 1937. M.A. Thesis.

Green, John. *ON THE TRACK OF THE SASQUATCH.* Agassiz, Cheam Pub., 1968.

Gresko, Jacq. *FRASER PORT: FREIGHTWAY TO THE PACIFIC.* Ed. J. Gresko and R. Howard, Vancouver, Sono Nis Press, 1986.

Gunn, Angus. "Gold And The Early Settlement of B.C. 1858-1885." Vancouver, UBC, 1965. (M.A. Thesis - Geography.)

Hacking, Norm. "Steamboating On The Fraser In the Sixties." *BRITISH COLUMBIA HISTORICAL QUARTERLY*, vol. x (January 1946), 1-41.

Hill, Beth. *SAPPERS: THE ROYAL ENGINEERS IN BRITISH COLUMBIA.* Ganges, B.C., Horsdal & Schubart Pub. Ltd., 1987.

Hope & District *FORGING A NEW HOPE: STRUGGLES AND DREAMS*, 1848- 1948. Hope, Hope & District Hist. Society, 1984.

Howay, Fred. *BRITISH COLUMBIA, FROM THE EARLIEST TIMES TO THE PRESENT.* Vancouver, The S.J. Publishing Co., 1914.

Hutcherson, W. *LANDING AT LADNER.* New York, Carlton Press, Inc., 1982.

Hutchison, B. *THE FRASER.* Toronto, Clarke, Irwin & Co., 1950.

Jenness, D. "The Faith of a Coast Salish Indian." *ANTHROPOLOGY IN BRITISH COLUMBIA: MEMOIR NO. 2.* Victoria, B.C. Provincial Museum, 1955.

Kennedy, Jacq. "Roman Catholic Missionary Effort And Indian Acculturation In The Fraser Valley 1860-1900." University of B.C. Essay, April 1969.

Kidd, Thomas. *HISTORY OF LULU ISLAND AND OCCASIONAL POEMS.* Richmond, Wrigley Printing Company Ltd., 1927.

Ladner, T.E. *ABOVE THE SANDHEADS*, Burnaby, Edna G. Ladner, 1979.

Lerman, Norm. *LEGENDS OF THE RIVER PEOPLE.* ed. Betty Keller, Vancouver, November House, 1976.

Lyons, Cicely. *SALMON: OUR HERITAGE.* Vancouver, Mitchell Press, 1969.

McCombs, A. *THE FRASER VALLEY CHALLENGE, AN ILLUSTRATED ACCOUNT OF LOGGING AND SAWMILLING IN THE FRASER VALLEY.* A. McCombs and W. Chittenden. Harrison Hot Springs, Treeline Publishing, 1990.

McKelvie, B. *FORT LANGLEY: OUTPOST OF EMPIRE.* Toronto, Thos. Nelson & Sons (Canada) Ltd., 1957.

McKelvie, B. "Jason Allard: Fur Trader, Prince and Gentleman." *BRITISH COLUMBIA HISTORICAL QUARTERLY* ix (October 1945), pp. 243-257.

MacLachlan, M. "The Success of the Fraser Valley Milk Producers' Association." *B.C. STUDIES*, Winter 174/75, pp.52- 64.

MacMillan, J. "Fort Langley Journal." James MacMillan and Archibald McDonald. Public Archives of B.C. June 27, 1827 to July 30,1830.

Marlatt, *D. STEVESTON RECOLLECTED: A JAPANESE-CANADIAN HISTORY.* ed. Daphne Marlatt. Victoria, Provincial Archives of B.C., 1975.

Mather, Barry. *NEW WESTMINSTER: THE ROYAL CITY.* B. Mather and M. McDonald. Toronto, J.M. Dent & Sons (Canada) Limited & City of New Westminster, 1958.

Matthews, W.H. *THE FRASER'S HISTORY: FROM GLACIERS TO EARLY SETTLEMENTS.* Burnaby, Burnaby Historical Society, 1977.

Maud, Ralph. *THE SALISH PEOPLE - THE LOCAL CONTRIBUTION OF CHARLES HILL-TOUT.* Vancouver, Talonbooks, 1978.

Miller, Charles. *THE GOLDEN MOUNTAINS: CHRONICLES OF VALLEY AND COAST MINES.* Mission, B.C., Fraser Valley Record, 1973.

Miller, Charles. *VALLEY OF THE STAVE.* Surrey, B.C., Hancock House, 1981.

Morton, James. *HONEST JOHN OLIVER.* London, J.M. Dent And Sons Ltd.
Morton, James. *IN THE SEA OF STERILE MOUNTAINS: THE CHINESE IN BRITISH COLUMBIA.* Vancouver, J..J. Douglas, 1974.

Morton, Jamie. "Fort Langley: An Overview of the Operations of a Diversified Fur Trade Post 1848 to 1858." Unpublished Manuscript, Environment Canada, 1990.

Murphy, Paul. *THE HISTORY OF FORT LANGLEY.* Vancouver, University of British Columbia, 1929.

Nelson, Denys. *FORT LANGLEY 1827-1927: A CENTURY OF SETTLEMENT.* Vancouver, Art, Historical and Scientific Assoc. of Vancouver, 1927.

Nickols, S. *MAPLE RIDGE: A HISTORY OF SETTLEMENT.* Sheila Nickols and others. Maple Ridge, Canadian Federation of University Women, Maple Ridge Branch, 1972.

Orchard, I. *FLOODLAND AND FOREST: MEMORIES OF THE CHILLIWACK VALLEY.* Victoria, Sound & Moving Image Div., Provincial Archives, 1983.

Pennier, Henry. *CHIEFLY INDIAN: THE WARM AND WITTY STORY OF A BRITISH COLUMBIA HALF BREED LOGGER.* ed. H. L. McDonald. West Vancouver, Graydonald Graphics, 1972.

Perry, Thos. "The Flooding of the Lower Fraser Valley, May 1948." In "Lower Fraser Valley History: Series A." Abbotsford, School District #34 (Abbotsford),1984.
Perry, Thos. "The British Columbia Electric Railway And Its Impact On The Economy And Settlement of The Lower Fraser Valley." In "Lower Fraser Valley History: Series A." Abbotsford, School District No. 34 (Abbotsford), 1984.

Pirie, Peter. *THE STUMP RANCH.* 1970.

Ramsey, Bruce. *FIVE CORNERS: THE STORY OF CHILLIWACK.* Vancouver, Agency Press, 1975.

Reimer, David. *THE MENNONITES OF BRITISH COLUMBIA.* Vancouver, University of British Columbia, 1946.

Rendall, Belle. *HEALING WATERS: HISTORY OF HARRISON HOT SPRINGS AND PORT DOUGLAS AREA.* B. Rendall, 1974.

Ross, Leslie. *RICHMOND: CHILD OF THE FRASER.* Richmond, Historical Committee of the Richmond '79 Centennial Society, 1979.
Ross, Leslie. *COLUMBIA PENITENTIARY.* Retired Federal Prison Officers' Association of B.C., 1984.

Siemens, A.H. *LOWER FRASER VALLEY: EVOLUTION OF A CULTURAL LAND-SCAPE*
Siemens, A.H. "Mennonite Settlement In The Lower Fraser Valley." University of British Columbia Thesis, 196
Siemens, A.H. *JAMES DOUGLAS, FATHER OF BRITISH COLUMBIA.* Toronto, Oxford University Press, 1971.

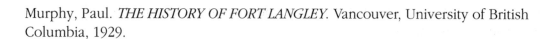

Suttles, Wayne. *COAST SALISH ESSAYS.* Vancouver/Seattle, Talonbooks and University of Washington Press, 1987.

Tennant, Paul. *ABORIGINAL PEOPLES AND POLITICS: THE INDIAN LAND QUESTION IN B.C. 1849-1989.* Vancouver, UBC Press, 1990.

Terris, Ed. "Ladner: A Pioneer Study." Western Washington State College Thesis, May 1973.

Treleaven, G.F. *THE SURREY STORY.* Surrey, B.C., Surrey Museum & Historical Society, 1970. vol.2

Waite, Donald. *THE LANGLEY STORY: AN EARLY HISTORY OF THE MUNICIPALITY OF LANGLEY.* Maple Ridge, Waite, 1977.
Waite, Donald. *TALES OF THE GOLDEN EARS.* Maple Ridge, Don Waite Publishing, 1975.

Wells, Oliver. *THE CHILLIWACKS AND THEIR NEIGHBOURS.* Vancouver, Talonbooks, 1987.

Williams, David *THE MAN FOR A NEW COUNTRY: SIR MATTHEW BAILLIE BEGBIE.* Sidney, Gray's Publishing Ltd., 1977.

Woodcock, Geo. *BRITISH COLUMBIA: A HISTORY OF THE PROVINCE.* Vancouver/Toronto, Douglas & McIntyre, 1990.

Woodland, Alan. *NEW WESTMINSTER: THE EARLY YEARS 1858-1898.* New Westminster, Nunaga Publishing Company, 1973.

Woods, J.J. *THE AGASSIZ-HARRISON VALLEY.* Chilliwack, McCott Publishing Ltd., Reprinted 1986.

INDEX

PHOTOGRAPH CREDITS

British Columbia Archive and Records Service: page 34 (catalogue no. PDP2258), 60 (HP11005), 70 (HP31404), 78, 81 (HP2656), 104 (HP9354), 117 (HP35410), 119 (PDP1891), 124 (HP763), 125 (HP41631), 127 lower (HP4347), 132 (76888), 158 (HP66486), 161 (HP10333), 162 (HP46127), 183 (74824), 186 (HP10337), 197 (77228), 198 (43095), 200 (HP63333), 201 (55567), 202 (HP45664), 205 (HP9367), 219 (HP77270), 222 (HP67097), 229 (74816-b), 241 lower (HP13108), 255 (HP66504), 257 (HP45688), 263 (HP45521), 273 (HP55295), 295 (HP32301), 296 (HP72611), 303 (HP54694-a).

John A. Cherrington: page 9, 10, 35, 333, 364.

CPR Archives: page 174.

Dairyland Foods: page 16, 157, 163, 188 upper, 225, 228, 230, 243, 244 upper, 249, 269.

Fort Langley National Historic Park: page 72, 73.

Fraser Valley Regional Library: page 285.

Glenbow Institute, Calgary Alberta: 227.

Langley Centennial Museum: page 20, 21, 23, 24, 25, 27, 36, 43, 56, 58, 59, 65, 93, 96, 106, 107, 109, 110, 130, 140, 141, 145, 146, 152, 179, 188 lower, 203, 204, 332.

Langley Times: page 365.

Matsqui/Sumas/Abbotsford Museum Society: page 175, 259, 281, 304, 346.

Native Sons of British Columbia: page 98.

New Westminster Public Library: page 13, 181, 190, 209, 224, 286, 342,

City of Richmond Archives: page 170, 239, 287 upper (photo by Ted Hinchcliffe), 288, 305, 306, 312, 313, 327, 334-5, 349.

City of Vancouver Archives: page 171 upper, 189.

Vancouver Public Library: page 64, 113, 142, 144, 187, 192, 194, 195, 196, 199, 210, 211, 212, 213 (photo by Philip Timms), 214, 217, 221 (Philip Timms), 223, 226, 231, 234, 237, 238, 240, 241 upper, 245, 260, 261, 262, 264, 267, 268 (photo by Leonard Frank), 270, 272, 275, 278, 287 lower, 290 (Leonard Frank), 292, 300, 302, 315.

Don Waite Collection: page 87, 114, 115, 156 (photo by W. J. Larmon).

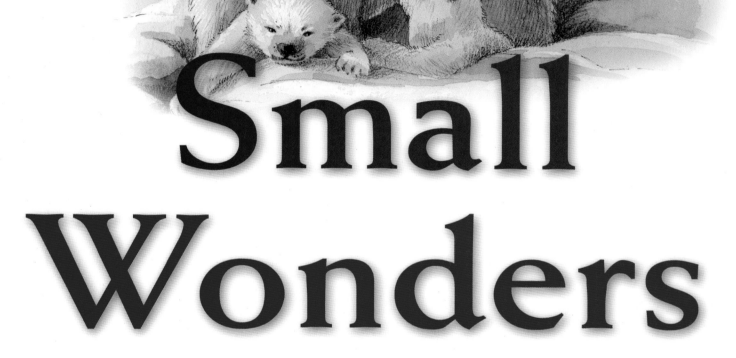

Small Wonders

Baby Animals in the Wild

Marilyn Baillie
Illustrated by Romi Caron

MAPLE TREE PRESS

Maple Tree Press Inc.
51 Front Street East, Suite 200, Toronto, Ontario M5E 1B3
www.mapletreepress.com

Distributed in Canada by Raincoast Books
9050 Shaughnessy Street, Vancouver, British Columbia V6P 6E5

Distributed in the United States by Publishers Group West
1700 Fourth Street, Berkeley, California 94710

Dedication

For Alexander, Caroline, Cici, and Cali, my small wonders

Acknowledgments
A warm thank-you to Publisher Sheba Meland, Executive Editor Anne Shone, and editor Kat Mototsune. A special thank-you to Romi Caron for her lively and engaging illustrations.

Cataloguing in Publication Data
Baillie, Marilyn
Small wonders : baby animals in the wild / Marilyn Baillie ; illustrated by Romi Caron.

ISBN 13: 978-1-897066-72-0 ISBN 10: 1-897066-72-4

1. Animals—Infancy—North America—Juvenile literature. 2. Animals—North America—Juvenile literature. I. Caron, Romi II. Title.

QL151.B33 2006 j591.3'9'097 C2006-900316-5

Design & art direction: Word & Image Design Studio
Illustrations: Romi Caron

We acknowledge the financial support of the Canada Council for the Arts, the Ontario Arts Council, the Government of Canada through the Book Publishing Industry Development Program (BPIDP), and the Government of Ontario through the Ontario Media Development Corporation's Book Initiative for our publishing activities.

Printed in China

A B C D E F

Exploring in the Wild

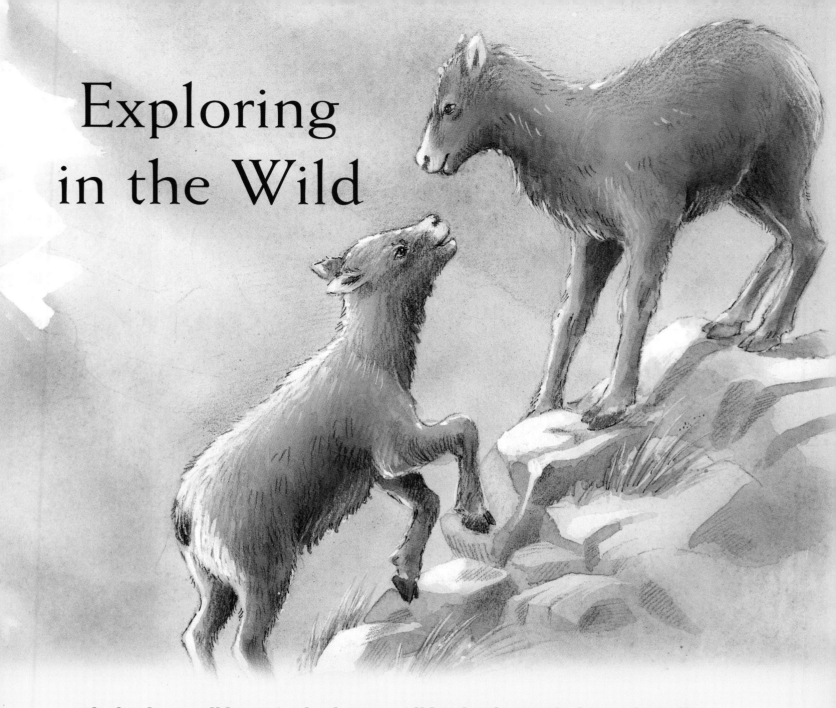

The land you call home is also home to all kinds of animals, big and small. Come and meet some of the youngest of them, the ones that are a lot like you.

While you might be learning to swim or ride a bike, these young animals are learning to get around, too. They have much to find out about life around them. Polar bear twins practice hunting for the day when they will be on their own. An orca calf learns to travel the ocean and find its own food. Lambs of mountain sheep tumble and stumble as their legs get used to hiking up high mountains.

All the amazing animals in this book share the land, the air, and the sea with us. Each one is ours to admire and protect.

Moose

Big animals are easy to spot, right? Well, if you go looking for a moose and her calf, you'll have a really hard time. They live deep in the northern woods. But on a sparkling summer day, you might see them in a quiet lake. They are keeping cool and searching for crunchy water lilies to eat.

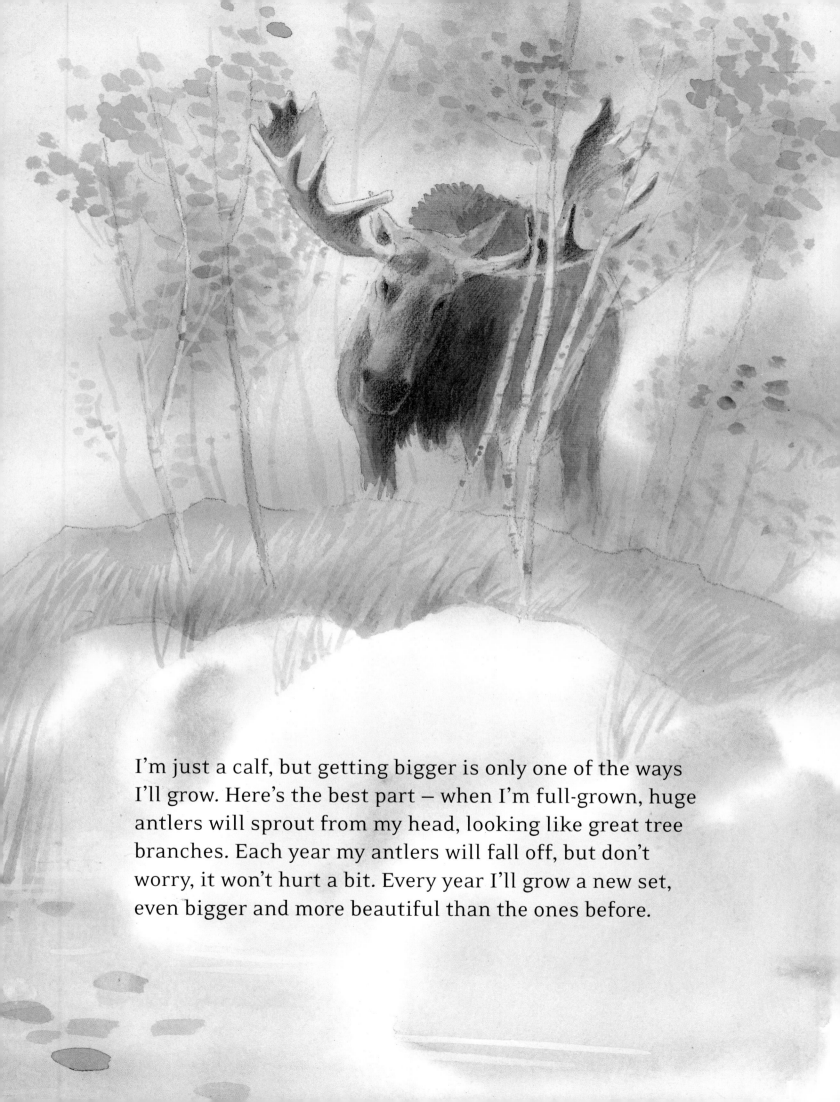

I'm just a calf, but getting bigger is only one of the ways I'll grow. Here's the best part – when I'm full-grown, huge antlers will sprout from my head, looking like great tree branches. Each year my antlers will fall off, but don't worry, it won't hurt a bit. Every year I'll grow a new set, even bigger and more beautiful than the ones before.

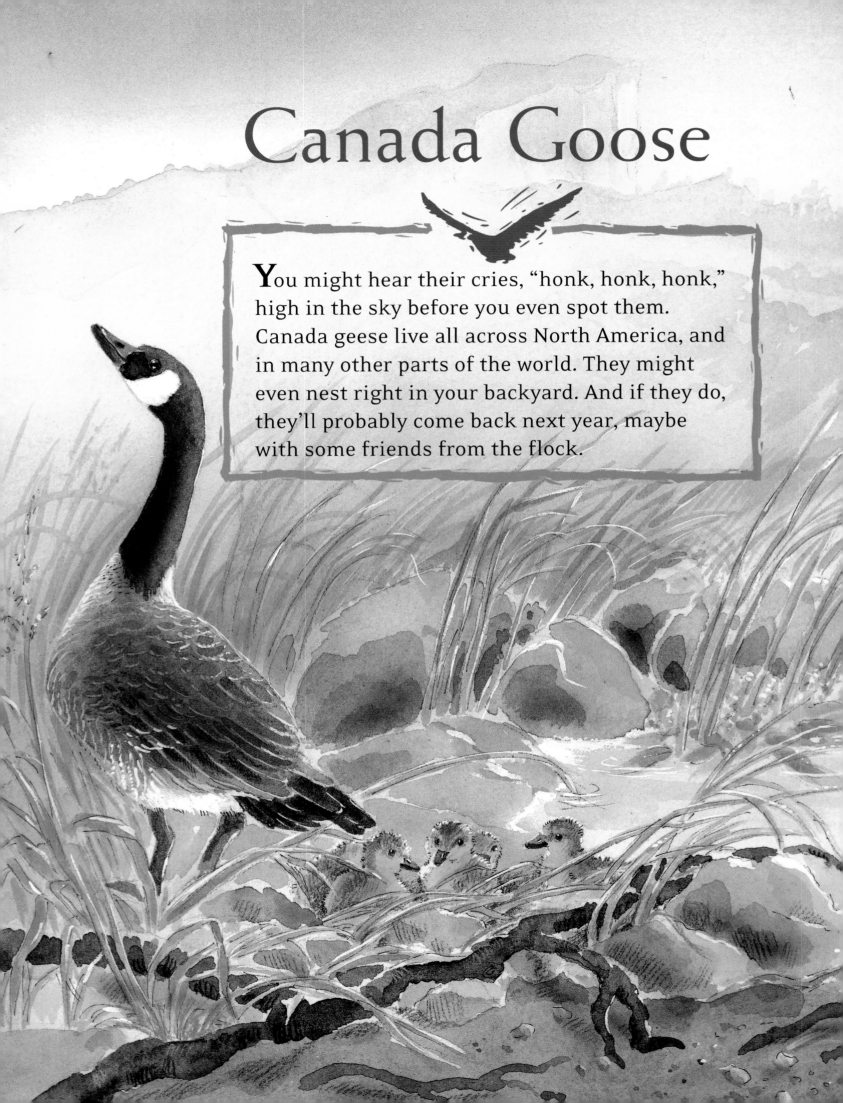

Canada Goose

You might hear their cries, "honk, honk, honk," high in the sky before you even spot them. Canada geese live all across North America, and in many other parts of the world. They might even nest right in your backyard. And if they do, they'll probably come back next year, maybe with some friends from the flock.

We might be cute, fluffy goslings now, but our mother and father are getting us ready to be great big birds. They keep very busy, working together to feed, clean, and care for us. And once we learn how to fly, you'll see us soaring through the air. We can hardly wait!

Polar Bear

Polar bears live so far north that snow blankets the land and huge chunks of ice dot the sea. The cubs' first home is a cozy den, dug into the snow by their mother. When they grow up, they will spend their time on the sea ice fishing and hunting for enough food to keep warm and active.

We're a cozy little family – my mother, my twin, and me. Mother feeds her rich milk to both of us so we'll grow big and strong. Soon we'll be tumbling over mounds of deep snow, following our mother to the icy water. There we'll learn to swim, and our mother will teach us how to hunt seals. Tumbling twin cubs now, and great hunters when we get big – that's a polar bear's life.

Wolf

You'll find wolves in all sorts of places, from shady forests to open farmland. They live in packs, or groups. Each wolf has a special place in the family pack, and they all follow and obey the strong leader. Wolf pups play all day long near their den, preparing for the day when they will hunt with the pack.

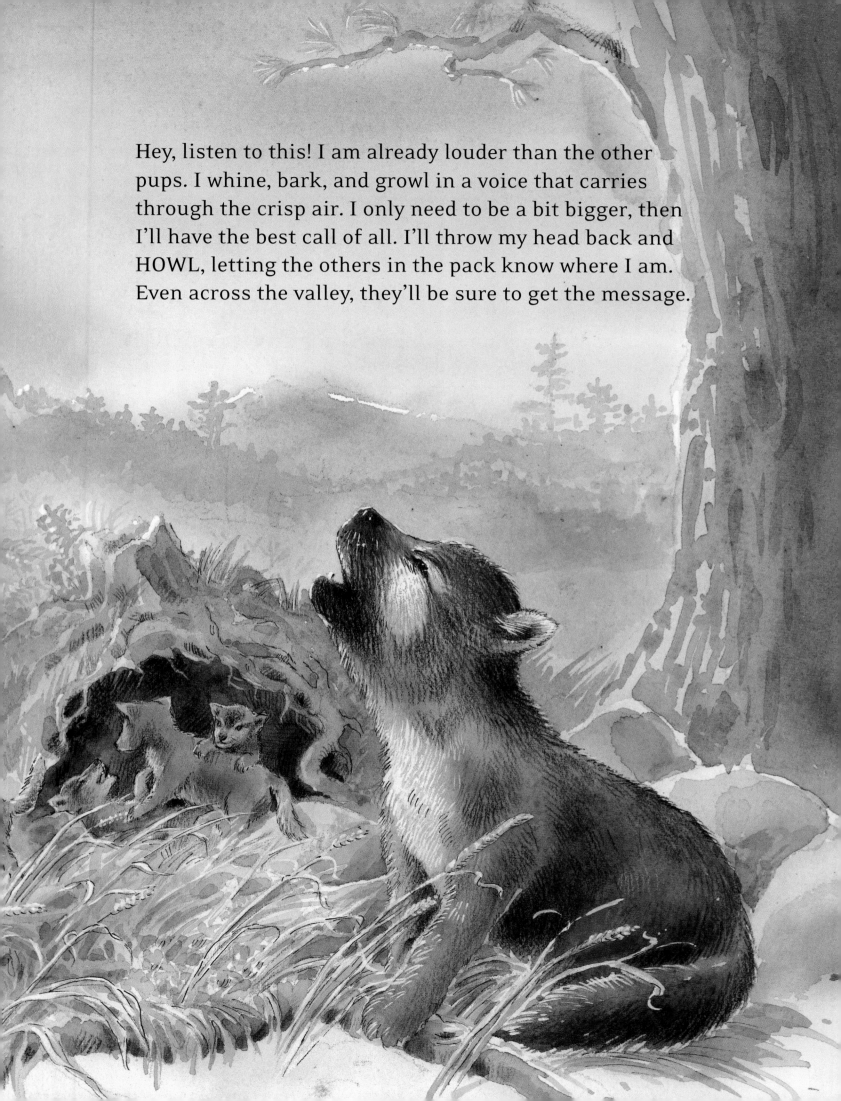

Hey, listen to this! I am already louder than the other pups. I whine, bark, and growl in a voice that carries through the crisp air. I only need to be a bit bigger, then I'll have the best call of all. I'll throw my head back and HOWL, letting the others in the pack know where I am. Even across the valley, they'll be sure to get the message.

Loon

When you tuck into bed by a lake, do you ever hear the strange, sad call of a loon? You might think that the crazy laughing sound is a little spooky, but it is how loons talk to each other. Loons are water birds that live on lakes. They build nests at the water's edge, but spend most of their time in the lake – fishing, swimming, even sleeping on the water.

Both our parents take care of us, but no one really has to teach us loon chicks how to swim. We had barely cracked out of our eggs and there we were, paddling around in the water. Soon we'll be able to dive after our own fish, cutting through the water, wings against our sides and webbed feet flapping. Now, if we get a little tired, we can still hitch a ride on the feathered backs of our parents.

Bison

You could never have counted all the bison that lived in North America long ago. Millions and millions grazed on the open grasslands of the plains. The First Nations people on the plains depended on the mighty bison for food, clothing, and more. Today, most bison live on ranches and in protected parks.

I'm one lucky calf. I romp and play with the other calves in our nursery group. All the mothers in the herd watch over us and keep us safe. They know right away if danger is coming, because they can smell things from far away. When I grow up, I'll be the biggest land animal in North America, and then I'll be able to take care of myself!

Raccoon

Raccoons aren't fussy about their food. They eat many different things, even garbage, that they find in forests, towns, and cities. Raccoons aren't too choosy about a home, either. They will live in barns, attics, chimneys, tree hollows, and caves. They need a den to keep warm and stay quiet through the winter. Once the winter turns to spring, it is in this den that their babies will be born.

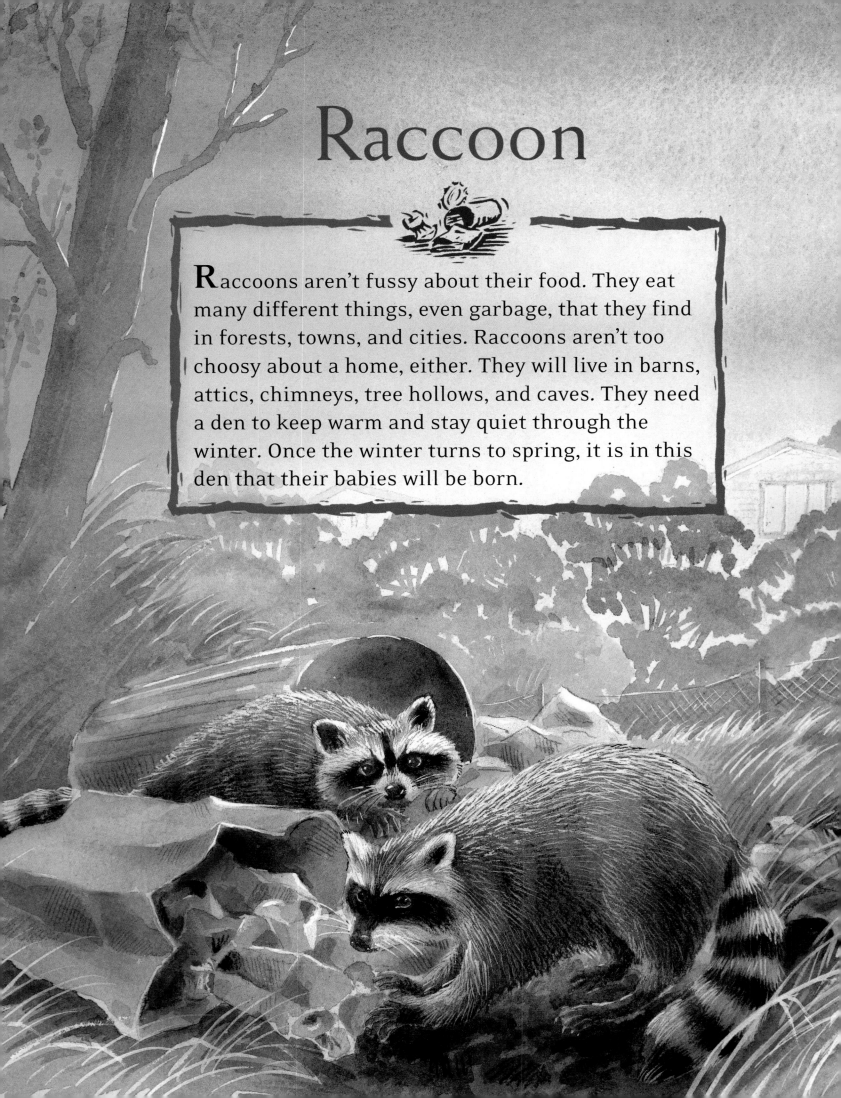

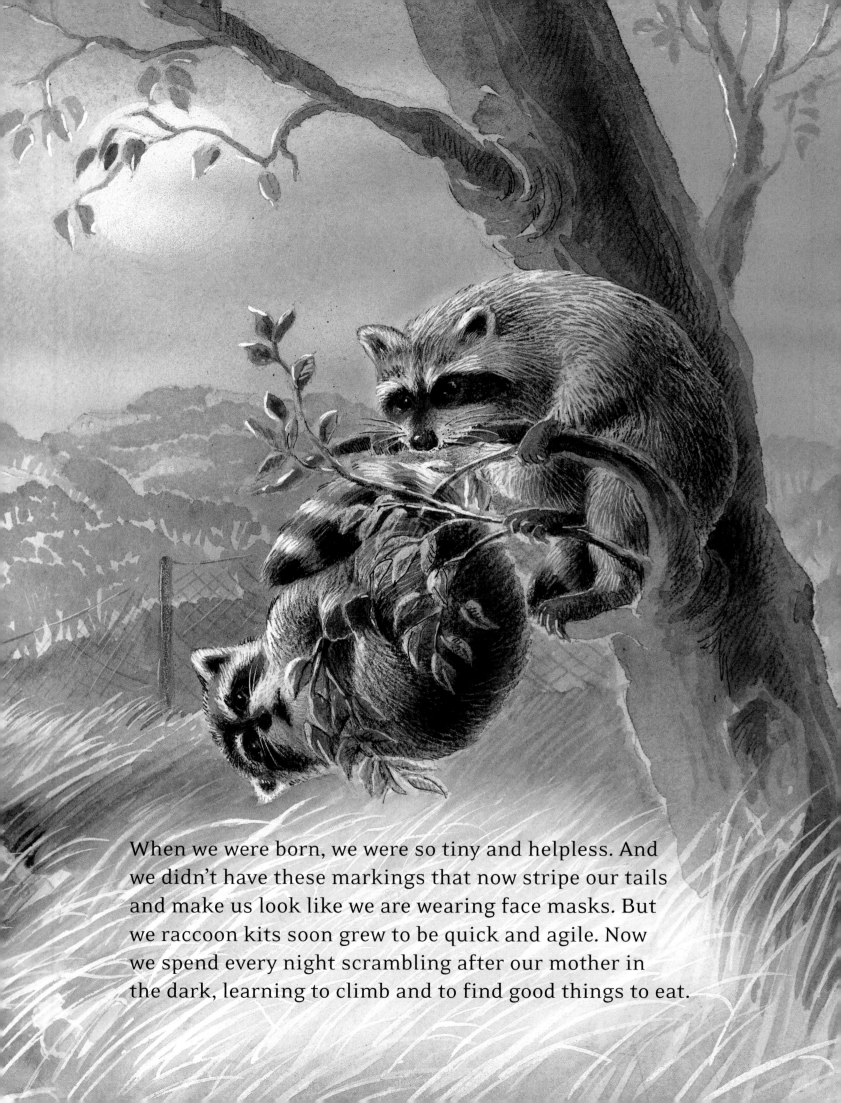

When we were born, we were so tiny and helpless. And we didn't have these markings that now stripe our tails and make us look like we are wearing face masks. But we raccoon kits soon grew to be quick and agile. Now we spend every night scrambling after our mother in the dark, learning to climb and to find good things to eat.

Cougar

Who has seen a cougar? Almost nobody! These big, beautiful cats hide out in the western mountains. But even if you don't see a cougar, stay alert when hiking through the foothills and mountains. This is the cougar's land. Each cougar has its own large space to protect, where it roams and hunts for food.

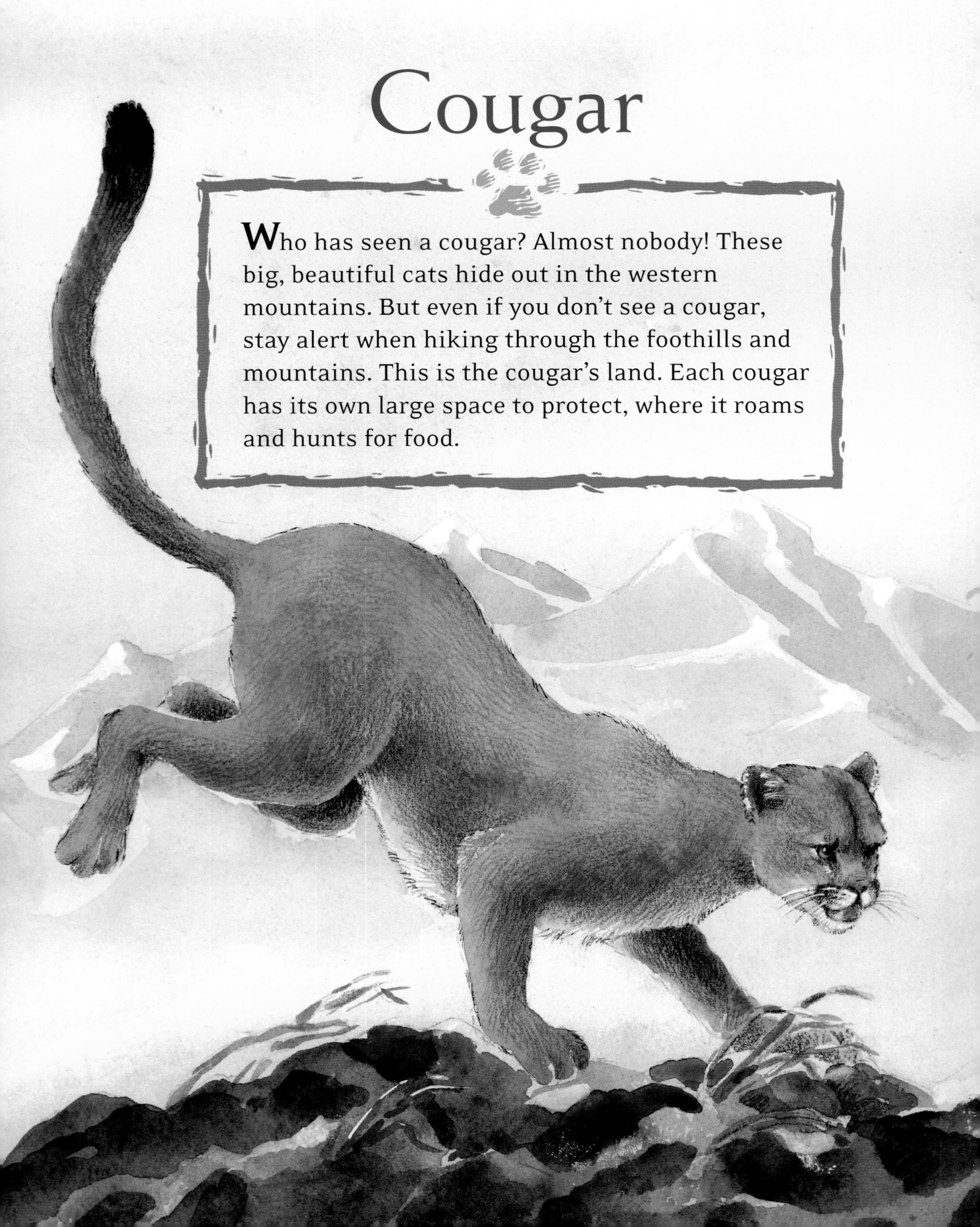

Do we look like cute pet kittens? Our mother cares for us just like a mother cat would. She licks our fur to clean us, feeds us her milk, and makes mewing sounds to keep us close to her and feeling safe. But we don't have kitten food to eat. We have to learn to catch our meals in the wild. We'll hunt quietly through the mountains with our mother until we can live on our own.

Beaver

What is your home like? A beaver's lodge has a feeding den, a resting den, and a strong, safe roof with a hole to let fresh air in. In case of danger, there are two escape tunnels. And to keep the house tidy, the food is piled outside and kept fresh in cool water. Look for these clever animals' homes in lakes and ponds.

Every beaver kit learns to be a builder, and I'm well on my way. My mother and father are always busy, building and teaching us to never be afraid of hard work. They're showing me how to cut down trees with my four front teeth. We'll use these trees to make dams to keep our home pond full of water. In the pond is a beautiful lodge made of wood – that's where we live.

Mountain Sheep

Who can climb the awesome heights of the Rocky Mountains? The mountain sheep can. Mountain sheep have hoofs that act like hiking boots, letting them cling to the rock. They nimbly climb up the mountainside to their summer pastures, or bound fearlessly down as winter forces them from the snowy peaks. They almost look as if they hang off the side of the steep cliffs.

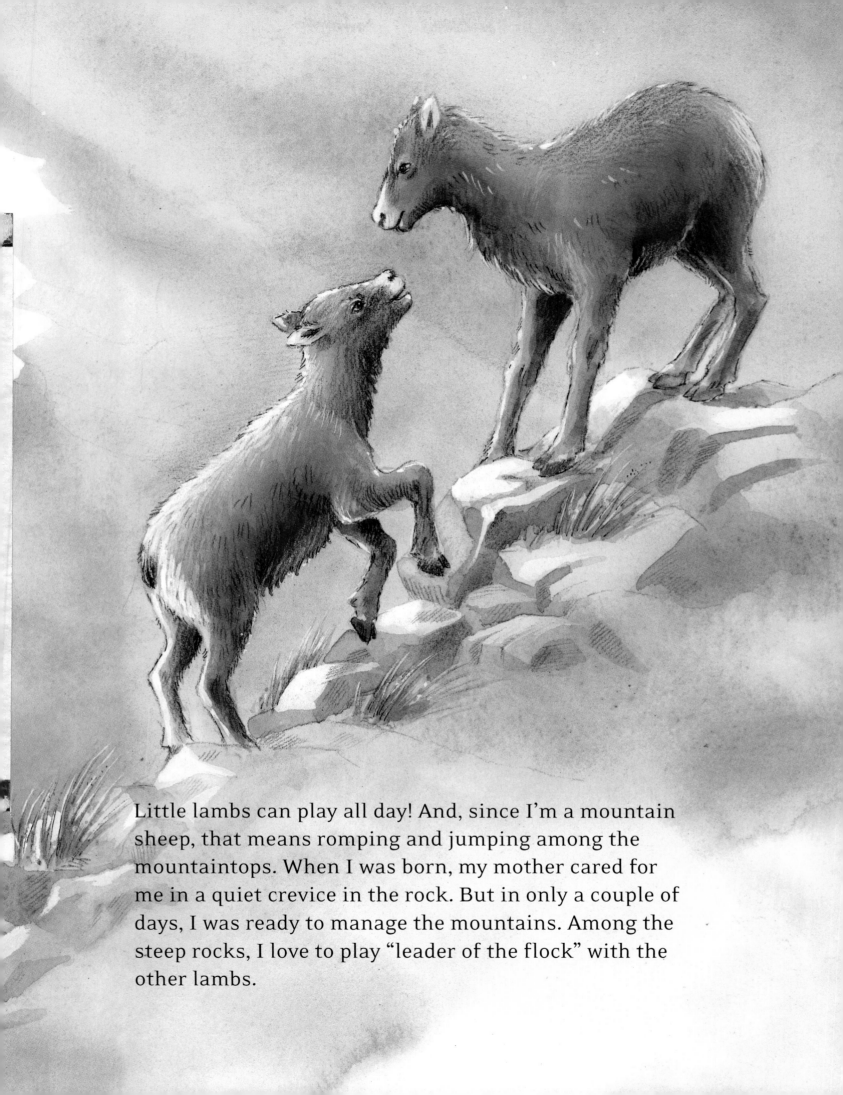

Little lambs can play all day! And, since I'm a mountain sheep, that means romping and jumping among the mountaintops. When I was born, my mother cared for me in a quiet crevice in the rock. But in only a couple of days, I was ready to manage the mountains. Among the steep rocks, I love to play "leader of the flock" with the other lambs.

Snowy Owl

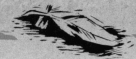

Have you ever seen a snowy owl fly by on its huge, soft wings? When it's time for these large, white owls to start their families, they fly up to the frozen Arctic tundra to nest. When the chicks are strong enough to fly, the snowy owls make their long journey south.

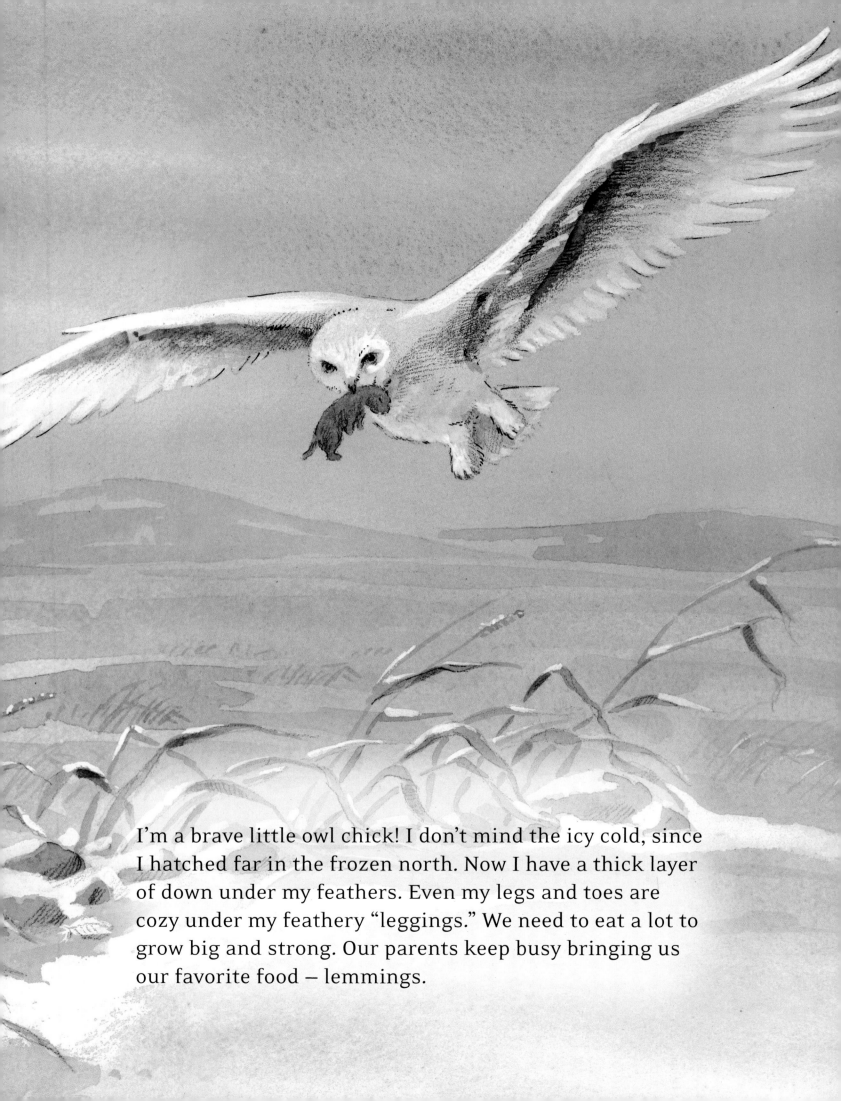

I'm a brave little owl chick! I don't mind the icy cold, since I hatched far in the frozen north. Now I have a thick layer of down under my feathers. Even my legs and toes are cozy under my feathery "leggings." We need to eat a lot to grow big and strong. Our parents keep busy bringing us our favorite food – lemmings.

Harp Seal

Harp seals spend their days swimming, diving, and fishing in the icy blue sea. They have to eat lots of fish to add to the thick layer of blubber that keeps them warm. When it's time to have their pups, harp seals swim down the east coast from the Arctic. The mothers haul their heavy bodies out of the water and up onto the ice to give birth to one pup each.

I am only one of the many fluffy, white seal pups born out here on the pack ice. It is safer and warmer for us to be in a group, but how can our mothers find us in this crowd? When I want a drink of my mother's warm, thick milk, all I have to do is call. She follows the sound of my voice and my own smell, and comes straight to me. Hurry, I'm hungry!

Caribou

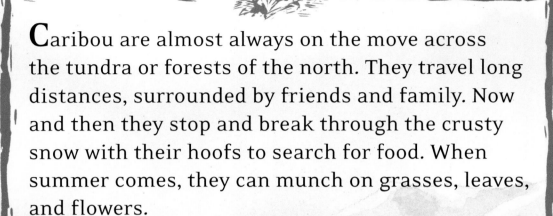

Caribou are almost always on the move across the tundra or forests of the north. They travel long distances, surrounded by friends and family. Now and then they stop and break through the crusty snow with their hoofs to search for food. When summer comes, they can munch on grasses, leaves, and flowers.

How long did it take you to learn to walk? I was able to get up and run the same day I was born! At first, my calf legs were a little wobbly, but now I can easily keep up with the herd. I can even follow when everyone jumps in to swim across a lake. The fur in my coat is made up of hollow hairs that help me float. It's a bit like wearing a life jacket all the time.

Orca

They soar out of the water, splash back, jump again, and slap their tails. These huge, black-and-white acrobats are orca whales. Every ocean is home to orcas. They live in the sea and are expert swimmers, but they are not fish. Orcas are mammals, and live in family groups, called pods.

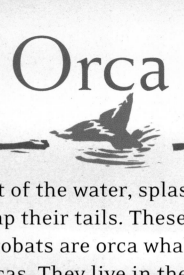

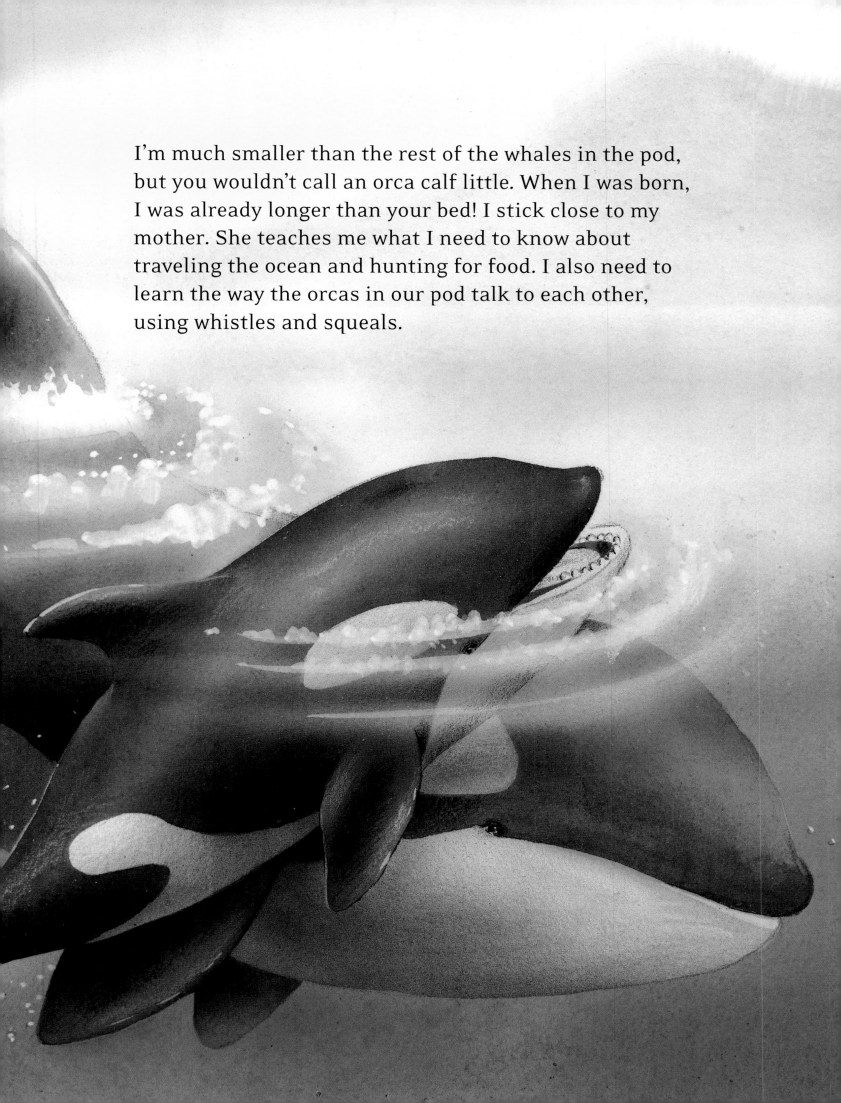

I'm much smaller than the rest of the whales in the pod, but you wouldn't call an orca calf little. When I was born, I was already longer than your bed! I stick close to my mother. She teaches me what I need to know about traveling the ocean and hunting for food. I also need to learn the way the orcas in our pod talk to each other, using whistles and squeals.

Have You Ever Wondered...

...how big MOOSE antlers can be?

Imagine being a large bull moose with spectacular antlers. Side by side, stretch out your arms with a friend. That would be the distance between the farthest tips on your antlers! And imagine: those antlers would drop off in the fall and then grow to be just as grand the following summer.

...about family life for the CANADA GOOSE?

Canada geese mate for life. When the mother is sitting on their nest the father, or gander, stands nearby on guard. After the goslings have hatched, the family struts away together, the mother leading the way, the father herding any stragglers. When the goslings learn to fly, the whole family takes to the air together.

...how POLAR BEARS stay warm?

The polar bear has the best fur coat, with two layers to keep the bear dry and warm. Long, oily hairs on top shed water just like a waterproof jacket. The dense, woolly underfur acts like a cozy sweater, keeping warm air inside. The polar bear's black skin absorbs heat, and a layer of fat under the skin adds insulation.

...how WOLF PUPS know who's the pack leader?

Wolf pups carefully watch the other wolves in their pack. Like us, they learn from their parents and other adults. A strong male leader holds his tail high and fluffs out his fur to display he is in command. A pack member shows respect by flattening its ears, tucking in its tail, whining, and licking the leader's muzzle.

...how LOONS talk to each other?

Besides the crazy laughing call you might hear, listen for a yodel sound. Only the male loon yodels to warn others that this is his territory and to stay away. A soft wail could be loon mates calling to each other, or loons simply greeting. And a short hoot sound is usually a loon family checking on family members.

...why the BISON (or buffalo) was so special to First Nations people?

The First Nations people who lived on the plains ate bison meat and made tipi covers and clothing from bison hide. They used every part of the bison for daily life: bison sinews for bowstrings and snowshoe webbing; bison bone for shovels, tools, pipes, and arrowheads. Even bison teeth, horns, and fat were used.

...how RACCOONS hold food in their paws?

If you look at raccoons' prints you will see that their paws are shaped somewhat like your hands. Their long front toes can spread out just like your fingers. This allows raccoons to grasp and handle their food, and even dunk it in water.

...why COUGARS are such good hunters?

Cougars are built to hunt. They have thick, strong necks, and powerful jaws with long canine teeth that clamp down, and other teeth that slice and cut. Like all cats, they hunt by sight and hearing more than scent. After silently stalking their prey, cougars attack in a flash with the full force of their muscular bodies.

...what a BEAVER lodge is made of?

After beavers cut down a tree, they help each other to strip off the branches. Then they drag or float the wood to the lodge building site. There, they weave the twigs and branches in and out and seal this with rocks, grass, moss, and mud. The dome-shaped lodge allows the main inside room to be above water level.

...why male MOUNTAIN SHEEP lock horns?

Two strong males, or rams, with great, large curling horns face each other. They race towards one another and crash head on. Then they step back and do it again. Each crash echoes through the mountains. Each crash shows who is the strongest. Finally, the winner gets to choose his mates first.

...what SNOWY OWLS eat?

Snowy owls prefer to hunt small mammals. In the Arctic, their favorite food is lemmings. If there are many of these mouse-like rodents, snowy owls have lots to eat and are able to lay up to 12 eggs. When the lemming numbers are down and food is scarce, the owls have much smaller families.

...how long HARP SEAL pups stay fluffy white?

Newborn seals are a yellowish color. Within three days, fluffy white fur covers them. At this time the pups grow rapidly on their mother's rich, fatty milk, and by their twelfth day they are three times their birth weight! It is now time to separate from their mothers. Their white coats shed to reveal a silvery coat with dark spots.

...how CARIBOU can travel such long distances?

Caribou have neat feet! Their large, cup-shaped hoofs have a split in the middle. On snow or tundra, the hoof spreads out, giving the caribou more spring and support. The sharp edges on the hoofs keep the caribou from slipping. The hoofs are also great paddles for the caribou when they swim across lakes.

...what an ORCA pod is like?

Orca whales live in family groups, or pods, of about five to 30 members. A pod is a group that swims and hunts together, and even has its own ways of talking to each other. The center of the pod is the mother-calf bond. Some babies stay with the mother even as adults and have their own babies.